EUGENE O'NEILL AT WORK

EUGENE O'NEILL
AT WORK

Newly Released Ideas for Plays

Edited and annotated by
Virginia Floyd

FREDERICK UNGAR PUBLISHING CO.
New York

To Donald Gallup
in appreciation—
days without end

Designed by Anita Duncan

Library of Congress Cataloging in Publication Data

O'Neill, Eugene, 1888–1953.
    Eugene O'Neill at work.

    Taken from the O'Neill notebooks for 1918 to 1943.
    Bibliography: p.
    Includes index.
    1. O'Neill, Eugene, 1888–1953—Technique.
I. Floyd, Virginia. II. Title.
PS3529.N5Z759   1981   812′.52   81-40460
ISBN 0-8044-2205-2   AACR2

Contents

1 · IDEAS: 1918–1920 NOTEBOOK

---

*O'Neill provides no titles for a number of ideas. Key words, taken from these ideas and summarizing their central focus, are used as working titles where so indicated by an asterisk.

Note: Titles listed here in roman type indicate an idea not developed or published. Titles in *italics* indicate that the idea was ultimately published.

2 · IDEAS: 1921–1931 NOTEBOOK

3 · IDEAS: 1931–1938 NOTEBOOKS

4 · THE LATE PLAYS—COMPLETED AND CONTEMPLATED: 1939–1943

APPENDICES

Illustrations

O'Neill's Drawings for Settings of Plays

Acknowledgments

For the realization of this book, I am grateful, first and foremost, to Donald Gallup, Curator, Collection of American Literature, Beinecke Rare Book and Manuscript Library, Yale University. To him, I owe a threefold debt: for his trust in asking me to edit, and giving me access to, hitherto unpublished material in the O'Neill Collection; for his direction in planning this book and his generous help and advice these last three years throughout the various stages of preparation; for his editorial comments and suggestions after reading the completed manuscript. I am indebted also to Anne Whelpley, Donald Gallup's assistant at Beinecke, for her assistance, suggestions, and many acts of kindness; to Stephen Jones, Karen Marinuzzi, and other members of the Beinecke Library staff; to Lisa Grinold, photographer at Yale Photo Services, for her efforts in reproducing O'Neill's faint pencil sketches of set designs; and to Yale University as legatee of the Eugene O'Neill Collection for permission to use quotations from the dramatist's unpublished notes and notebooks, his letters, and Work Diary—transcribed by Donald Gallup—and all other material in this book designated as part of the Yale O'Neill Collection.

Others who have provided assistance include John Hannon, Patrick Kelly, Constance Cameron, and Patricia McQueeney of Bryant Library; William O'Hara, president of Bryant College; my colleagues, Vera Krieger and Stanley Kozikowski; two O'Neill scholars, Tom Olsson of the Royal Dramatic Theatre in Stockholm and Peter Egri of the University of Budapest. For her sound editorial and critical judgment, her advice, and many beneficial suggestions regarding the preparation of this book, my thanks to Ruth Selden, my editor at Ungar. I am most grateful to my mother for sharing her "touch of the poet" and love of the theatre, for providing encouragement and inspiration, and to my family for support and understanding throughout the long journey to complete this work.

V.F.

Introduction

For twenty-five years, from 1918 to 1943, Eugene O'Neill chronicled his ideas for plays in a collection of notebooks intended for his own use, developing the more promising concepts into scenarios and drafts for dramas. Some of these he finished and published; others he worked on from time to time, but eventually decided he could never write; some he apparently never gave up hope of being able to complete. To read this long-withheld material is to witness the birth and development of a superb dramatist—America's only Nobel Prize playwright. For several reasons—the fragility of the manuscripts, their autobiographic revelations, the neglect of O'Neill in his own country in the two decades before he died—his widow issued instructions that this fascinating material be restricted to the public for twenty-five years after his death in 1953.

Finally, the long-awaited manuscripts are available now, in this book. O'Neill scholars will, obviously, want to explore in depth this collection of newly released ideas and notes; but those interested in American drama, and especially in the memorable plays of O'Neill, will also find in these pages much to intrigue them and to increase their understanding of the writer.

In their entirety, these manuscripts, mostly in notebooks, present a composite picture—O'Neill the playwright: his development from amateur to craftsman to creative artist, and the man: the intensely personal nature of his work. There are, in a number of extant dramas, obvious autobiographical elements; however, it is impossible to deduce their complete significance until they are properly placed in the context of O'Neill's total body of manuscripts and are studied in conjunction with the earliest notes and scenarios made for these works. No other dramatist of modern times has so exposed the secret recesses of his soul, and those of his parents and brother, as has O'Neill in the many ideas for plays recorded and, in some instances, developed in the 1918–1943 period.

The newly released writings in this volume are part of the Eugene O'Neill collection in the Collection of American Literature of the Beinecke Rare Book and Manuscript Library at Yale University. Some of the manuscripts in the O'Neill collection were given to Yale by the dramatist and his wife, beginning in the 1930s; others by Carlotta Monterey O'Neill after her husband's death, many with the stipulation that they be withheld until 1978. In March, 1978, I was given permission by the Beinecke Library to edit this material, excepting only notes and drafts relating to the Cycle "A Tale of Possessors Self-Dispossessed," which Mrs. O'Neill had herself authorized the curator of the collection, Donald Gallup, to prepare for publication. This book presents, generally in a chronological arrangement, the heretofore unavailable material.

Other reference sources from the Yale Collection include O'Neill's Work Diary, 1924–1943,* which provides valuable insights into the author's method of composition and accurate dates for some ideas, and several collections of correspondence—among them O'Neill's letters to his friends, Kenneth Macgowan and Dudley Nichols, and to Lawrence Langner, Theresa Helburn, and Robert Sisk of the Theatre Guild. Chapter 1 presents the undated ideas of the 1918–1920 period as they appear in the notebook. The dated ideas of the 1921–1938 notebooks are given chronologically in the second and third chapters. These four notebooks, 1918–1938, containing over one hundred ideas for plays, are published in their entirety. Chapter 4 contains concepts that were either completed or contemplated in O'Neill's final period, 1939–1943. As the secondary purpose of this study is to show what O'Neill did with his ideas for plays, commentaries follow the notebook entries for those he developed. While it is not obviously possible to publish here the hundreds of pages of notes, the complete scenarios, and drafts for all dramas, the representative material selected for inclusion in this volume demonstrates O'Neill's vision of, and plan for, unfinished works and the evolving process of composition for completed plays.

Here we find the dramatist adhering to the principles he learned in 1914 in George Pierce Baker's "47 Workshop" at Harvard: recording the original idea, writing a scenario, and, to add "meat," as he says, to this skeleton, setting down dialogue for a first draft. O'Neill states in one of the notebooks (1921–1931) that "the scenarios were written mainly to get the first idea for a play in some sort of form. I rarely referred to them when writing the plays"; however, entries in his Work Diary reveal that he did, at times, read over a scenario before beginning a first draft or when encountering a problem. While initial concepts about characters or themes often changed, the first draft evolves from its scenario. Modifications are usually the result of O'Neill's "reading"—particularly for historical dramas—between the completion of a scenario and the start of the first draft. In his early period, he often wrote, hastily, only one draft of a play. For example, he started the scenario for *Desire Under the Elms* on January 15, 1924, and worked on it until the 29th and for five days in February. On May 24 he took up the play again, completing it on June 16. The dramatist goes to the other extreme in the late 1920s and early 1930s during his middle period, spending

---

*At the time of this printing, the preliminary edition of the Work Diary has been published. O'Neill notes in the first volume: "1925 from memory & few records, diary of that year stolen & sold by former wife." The "Scribbling Diary" for 1925 appears as an appendix to the Work Diary in the second volume to facilitate comparison with the sketchy entries of 1925 found in the first volume.

over two years writing and constantly revising six drafts for *Mourning Becomes Electra* (1929–1931) and seven for *Days Without End* (1931–1933).

A comprehensive portrait of Eugene O'Neill at work, of his efforts to grow as a playwright, emerges from evidence in the notes and notebooks, in the Work Diary, and in letters. Theatrically and thematically, the material dating from 1918 to 1943 shows a cyclic movement. O'Neill began his career as dramatist in 1913, writing primarily one-act plays until 1918,* recording in that year ideas for similar shorts works in the first notebook. In 1918–1919 he started to think in terms of longer dramas and wrote *Beyond the Horizon, The Straw*, and "Chris Christopherson." Toward the end of the 1918–1920 notebook, the words "long play" frequently precede the idea he enters. The year 1920 is significant for two reasons: it heralds the era of multi-act plays and of experimental works such as *The Emperor Jones* and *The Hairy Ape*.

By the mid 1920s, having mastered the rudiments of dramatic technique, O'Neill, the craftsman, begins to experiment with theatrical devices—masks, choruses, soliloquies—and to revise and polish his work. While most plays in the early 1920s were written quickly, O'Neill, after completing *Desire Under the Elms*, starts "mapping out" sections in *Marco Millions* in July 1924 and "going over" them when he finished. The first acts of *Lazarus Laughed*, completed in 1925, "were destroyed and rewritten in toto." The author devotes two entire years, 1926 and 1927, to the four-act *Lazarus Laughed* and the nine-act *Strange Interlude*. In a letter to Macgowan dated August 7, 1927, O'Neill speaks of the latter:

> did most of a second scene two separate times and tore them up before I got started on the really *right* one! The point is my stuff is much deeper and more complicated now and I'm also not as easily satisfied with what I've dashed off as I used to be.

Encouraged by the success of *Strange Interlude* and determined to expand his creative powers, O'Neill contemplates a Grand Opus in 1927, "The Sea-Mother's Son," which he describes to Macgowan as "one of those timeless Big Things," having "ten or more *Interludes* in it" and to Russel Crouse years later as a "Nine play thing." He plans two trilogies in the later 1920s: "Myth Plays for the God-forsaken," composed of *Dynamo* and *Days Without End*, which he completed, and "It Cannot Be Mad?" which remains in scenario, and *Mourning Becomes Electra*, which he states "arouses my creative enthusiasm as the thing with the biggest scope to turn loose my intensest effort. . . . it will be the biggest thing I've yet attempted" (Letter to Macgowan, June 14, 1929).

---

*O'Neill's only long works before 1918 are *Bread and Butter* (four acts, 1914), "Belshazzar" (long play—six scenes, 1915), "The Personal Equation" (four acts, 1915), and *Now I Ask You* (three-act farce, 1916).

The year 1929 marks the end of a decade of experimentation for O'Neill: expressionism in *The Emperor Jones* and *The Hairy Ape*, masks in *The Great God Brown*, masks and choruses in *Lazarus Laughed*, soliloquies and asides in *Strange Interlude*, multiple settings depicting various nations and cultures in *Lazarus Laughed* and *Marco Millions*, an innovative scenic plan for an electrical generating plant in *Dynamo*. He utters a cry of emancipation "for good" from such techniques in 1929:

> No more sets or theatrical devices as anything but unimportant background. . . . To read "Dynamo" is to stumble continually over the sets. . . . Greater classical simplicity, austerity combined with the utmost freedom and flexibility, that's the stuff! (Letter to Macgowan, June 14, 1929).

He strives to bring this "classical simplicity" to his current work, *Mourning Becomes Electra*. When he sent Lawrence Langner the final typed script on April 7, 1931, he writes: " 'Interlude' soliloquies and asides only got in my way. . . . the mask idea has also gone by the board." Four months later he asks in one of his recorded ideas: is not "chief fault in plays" that up to now "they lack bone in comparison to their superabundant flesh and meat—that their rickety bones are too frequently braced by splints carpentered in the dramatic technique surgery?"

The inevitable challenge, the work of greatest magnitude, remained; on January 1, 1935, O'Neill enters the word "Cycle" in his Work Diary for the first time and an idea he has for an "Opus Magnus"—a series of plays that grew from four to six, seven, nine, and finally eleven dramas. After working three years on "A Tale of Possessors Self-Dispossessed," he states: "writing one of the units in this cycle is a much more complicated business than doing a single play, or half of 'Strange Interlude' or one of the 'Electra' trilogy" (Letter to Theresa Helburn, February 13, 1938).

By early June 1939, weary of the Cycle after having devoted four and a half years to it, O'Neill turns to two plays that had been on his mind "for quite some time": *The Iceman Cometh* and *Long Day's Journey into Night*. In 1931 he had recorded an idea for a "Symphony Form Play," using the "structure of symphony or sonata." He needed, he states, a

> fixed severe clearly apprehended form within which to create, now that I have finished breaking all realistic rules for modern drama—my adoption of archaic dramatic modes from Greek, Elizabethan—(or ultra-modern Expressionistic or Strindbergian modes)—not the answer because superficial, does not strike at main deep-rooted impulses of creative ego toward self-expression in musical structure rhythm.

He concludes the notation with a method to incorporate a musical structure: "a play in which each main character definitely represents a theme." Consciously or not, the dramatist uses the symphony form in *The Iceman Cometh*, saying of it:

"at the end you feel you know the souls of the seventeen men and women who appear—and the women who don't appear—as well as if you'd read a play about each of them" (Letter to Macgowan, December 30, 1940).

The Work Diary entry for February 19, 1940, reads: "Idea orchestral technique for a play—playwright as leader symphony, characters, chorus an orchestra (notes)." Three days later he takes up "The Long Day's Journey," for which he makes a list showing the characters' carefully orchestrated "shifting alliances in battle—(direct movements to correspond)." In the "Symphony Form" idea he contemplates "using rhythm of recurrent themes." He applies this concept to *Long Day's Journey into Night*, listing "recurrent items" to stress. On August 30 he interrupts work on the play to make his first notes for the Christ-Satan duality drama, "The Last Conquest." When he later writes its prologue, he has Satan describe himself as "director of the drama, ringmaster of the circus, leader of the orchestra."

In 1933 O'Neill made notes for a "Pyramid Form Play," which moves upward in "three stages—ascending from realism," to "poetry—symbolism—masks" to "music, pantomime—great marionettes—Fates" and then descends—"results in realism." The notes and scenarios for "The Last Conquest" indicate it would be a vast panoramic pageant, embracing the total scope of the Pyramid Form. It is set in "Jerusalem but also ancient Rome & capitals of today." In the early version only Christ and Satan are living; "crowds, minor speechless characters [are] all done with lifeless marionettes which are used by scenic designer as part of settings—background, dramatic & moving & changing." Satan is a ventriloquist; in the scene on Calvary, he is "dressed in old medieval black costume of executioner with a black mask covering upper part of face." The dialogue between the two protagonists, with its lyric Biblical quality, soars to new heights never realized previously by the author. He is not merely experimenting with theatrical devices here as in the 1920s; they are used purposefully as integral parts of a whole. Because of its creator's imagination and vision, "The Last Conquest," had it been completed, would have been his masterpiece.

The original idea for the "By Way of Obit" series (November 29, 1940) incorporates one of the theatrical devices used in "The Last Conquest"; each of the one-act monologue plays has "one character, one marionette (life-size) The Good Listener." Titles in the "Obit" series—"Pig of the Hell Hole play" and "Jimmy the Priest idea"—were listed two decades earlier in the 1918–1920 notebook. O'Neill comes full circle in the early 1940s, writing, as he did in 1918 and 1919, both one-act and multi-act plays. There is, obviously, one substantial difference between the end-products of the two periods. The early one-acters—with the exception of the sea plays—are clearly the work of an amateur. Understandably, the author tried to destroy the scripts for a number of them. The 1918–1919 long plays, "Chris Christopherson" and *The Straw*, are flawed—melodramatic and maudlin. In contrast, the sole extant "Obit" play of the late period, *Hughie*, is a classic in its genre, acclaimed, justifiably, as the best American one-acter, while

Long Day's Journey into Night is unquestionably the country's finest multi-act play. "The Last Conquest" would have been its equal in depth, intensity, universality. "Malatesta Seeks Surcease" would have become, in its final form, a tragi-comedy like *A Moon for the Misbegotten* and probably ranked with it. Of the three unfinished plays, the weakest in conception, because of its dual focus, is "Blind Alley Guy." Before the Walter White-Hitler connection is established, only the numerous autobiographical elements sustain the reader's interest. However, *Long Day's Journey into Night* in scenario, read without a total knowledge of all its autobiographical nuances, seems to have little potential for greatness.

Thematically, the ideas developed between 1918 and 1943 reveal a cyclic movement having two dominant motifs, which were introduced in early 1918–1919 efforts: 1) societal concerns—*The Dreamy Kid* and possibly "Honor Among the Bradleys"; 2) reminiscences: of friends—"Chris Christopherson" and the projected "Jimmy the Priest series"; of self—"Exorcism" and *The Straw*; of parents—"The Reckoning"; of a brother—the play of "Jim and self."

An analysis of the many ideas recorded in the notebooks and, in many instances, developed in scenarios and plays, refutes the charge that O'Neill did not address the social issues and problems of his day. Ever mindful of the prejudicial attitude of wealthy Yankee New Londoners toward his own Irish family, he planned to write a number of plays depicting discrimination, particularly against nonwhites. His first two plays with black protagonists, *The Dreamy Kid* (1918) and *The Emperor Jones* (1920), did not deal specifically with the black man's plight in white America, nor would his 1921 idea "Honest Honey Boy," the "tragi-comedy of Negro gambler" (based on the life of Joe Smith, whom O'Neill met at the Hell Hole in 1915 and cherished as a close friend for nearly two decades). The author made a second attempt in 1932 to continue the play about Joe Smith, who eventually emerges as Joe Mott in *The Iceman Cometh*. In 1923, in *All God's Chillun Got Wings*, he painted a grim picture of racial bigotry that destroys the self-esteem of an intelligent black man and reduces him to an inferior in the eyes of his white wife. From 1927 to 1934, O'Neill worked intermittently on a play, tentatively titled "Bantu Boy," depicting "the Negro's whole experience in modern times—especially with regard to America." In it, a noble African chief, who is drugged and transported to the United States as a slave, will not break before his cruel captors. His words voice the author's personal sentiments: "Freedom is God's white man." In 1935 O'Neill made a note for a "Runaway Slave play."

Two references indicate the author's plan to show oppression of Indians: the 1929 idea, "The House—"a play of ghosts from Indians down"—and the 1934 "Life of Sturgo Nacimbin"—a historical drama set in the early nineteenth century in Lower California, when "Indians by tens of thousands were perishing from hunger." "Uncharted Sea" (1929), like *All God's Chillun Got Wings*, depicts an interracial relationship, that of an American poet and a half-caste, who are viewed as pariahs by their fellow travelers on board the *Andre Lebon.*

O'Neill abhorred the exploitation—economic, social, and political—of his fellow man. In 1934, he outlines "The Germinating," based on Zola's novel, *Germinal*, intending to dramatize the tragic struggle of French miners to survive the brutality of their indifferent selfish bourgeois employers. Notes written four years later for a political-psychological play, "Robespierre," also set in France, focus on the public and private life of the foe of the aristocracy, who views himself as another Christ: "merciful friend and leader of poor & oppressed—the Son as Revolutionist who drove money changers from the Temple." As early as 1927 O'Neill had envisioned a drama on Robespierre; it was listed as the ninth work in a projected series of "plays about Atlantis (a history of Christianity)," focusing on the lives of religious and political oppressors of the Christian era. While O'Neill never completed the series, which concludes with a twelfth idea for a drama based on "Lenin" and a thirteenth on "The Second Coming," he did, shortly after the start of World War II, begin what may be considered an anti-totalitarian trilogy.

On January 4, 1940, the day after he completed *The Iceman Cometh*, O'Neill made his first notes for a comedy, with the tentative title "The Visit of Malatesta," whose hero, the legendary anarchist leader Cesare Malatesta, escapes from Italy in 1923 after Mussolini comes to power and seeks refuge with his former revolutionary friends, the Italian-American Daniellos. Like his historical counterpart, Enrico Malatesta, the protagonist has devoted his life to the anarchist ideals of social, economic, and political equality, ideals forgotten by his Americanized followers. Malatesta brandishes a two-edged sword: against the Fascist despotism of the old country and the enslaving tyranny of materialism in his adopted land. He sets out to reform not only Tony Daniello, who operates a speakeasy, his family, and Italian anarchist friends but also two corrupt Irishmen who frequent the "speak." The play, later entitled "Malatesta Seeks Surcease," contains many elements found in *The Iceman Cometh*: a barroom setting, the retreat to pipe dreams, political corruption and greed, and, primarily, a focus on anarchism.

For many years O'Neill viewed anarchism with its utopian goals as a preferable alternative to capitalism with its dehumanizing consequences: exploitation of the individual, the unequal distribution of wealth, and greed. The entry for 1907–1908 in "Cycles," O'Neill's division of his life and work, reads: "M. O. Grey —his studio—anarchism, Nietzsche." His good friends in later years at the Hell Hole, Terry Carlin and Hippolyte Havel, were anarchists. Saxe Commins, first a friend and subsequently his editor, was Emma Goldman's nephew. Self-portraits in a number of plays, Richard Miller in *Ah, Wilderness!* and Edmund Tyrone in *Long Day's Journey into Night*, voice "socialist anarchist sentiments." To Bennett Cerf in a 1939 letter, the dramatist expressed his fear that lack of "intelligence in our government" assured America's entering the war: "anyone who expects anything of governments these days except colossal suicidal stupidity seems to me a moron of optimism. Tell Saxe [Commins] I am rapidly becoming reconverted to a sterling Anarchism!" As late as 1946 at his last press conference during rehearsals for *The Iceman Cometh*, he described himself as a "philosophical anarchist."

Throughout the spring of 1940 O'Neill found himself unable to shake his "war obsession," writing in the Work Diary on June 25 that it "is becoming neurosis—can't save even myself by not working and despairing about the future of individual freedom." To show the consequences of the loss of freedom, he began "The Last Conquest," a "spiritual propaganda play," showing a futuristic world ruled by the forces of evil, personified by a Hitler-like "Divine Tyrant Redeemer," symbol of the "modern world spirit." The "propaganda" is obviously designed for Americans; for in O'Neill's totalitarian "brave new world" godlessness, indifference, and avarice cause the "death of democracy—men grew tired of the responsibility of living free with no higher law than the criminal code to define the use of freedom—their spirits corrupt and fat—the goddess of Liberty a fat woman in a circus—democracy with a paunch and bad heart and impotent." The play demonstrates the "duality of Man's psyche—opposites— with application [to] present world crisis: renunciation versus possession . . . the believer in the soul of man versus the condemned materialist." Engaged in the eternal struggle for man's soul are the two ancient foes: Christ and Satan, who, as the Minister of Spiritual Affairs, controls the dummy-dictator. There are several topical allusions to Hitler and his Nazi regime in the play: concentration camps, the crowd marching "goose-step up a mountain side," flags in the Amphitheatre of Games "with sickles, hammers, swastikas," the dictator's fear of being seen "consorting with a Jew," and his promise to Christ to manufacture a family tree showing Him to be "the son of an Aryan emigrant to Palestine."

To O'Neill, Hitler symbolized evil incarnate and represented the gravest threat to individual freedom in modern times. The specter of the Nazi dictator haunted his next project, "Blind Alley Guy," begun December 16, 1940. Initially, however, the work was another autobiographical memory play, depicting the complex relationship between the central character and his family. Emerging from another period of "war jitters" in July 1941, O'Neill made new notes about his gangster hero: "Tie-up through interpretation of his character with that of Hitler." Accordingly, he gives this character, Walter White, attributes found in Hitler: anti-Semitism, "inability to feel—hatred for Christ."

In the early notes, when the play was autobiographical and set in 1918, the parents, Ed and Tess White, were moral, selfless; in the revised outline they are selfish agnostics—"loss of all ethical and moral values"—and voice their support of the Nazi dictator. O'Neill changed the "date to year Hitler's seizing power— approval—what we need over here—purge, 1934." He describes the central motif of the play: "Recurrence argument of Ed and Tess about Hitler—opening Acts I, II, & IV—follow same pattern—each ends on note of affinity to Walt." O'Neill provides no explanation for the new characterizations of the Whites in late 1941 but emphasizes their loss of values, their bigotry, and their indifference to individual freedom. To the author, the family represents the microcosm that reflects the macrocosm. In "The Last Conquest," evil, personified by Satan and his Fascist dummy-dictator, wears a public face; in "Blind Alley Guy" evil is masked but nurtured in private by a family spawning a Hitler-like son. The author did not complete either play. The reason he gave Dudley Nichols on December 13, 1942, for putting aside "The Last Conquest" probably applies also to "Blind Alley Guy": his creative impulse is "blocked by the hopeless certainty that it could not be understood now, or its possibilities admitted—more than that, a feeling in myself that, until this war, which must be won, is won, people should concentrate on the grim surface and not admit the still grimmer, soul-disturbing depths."

By 1942 O'Neill had spent over two decades attempting to unveil "soul-disturbing depths" to his countrymen. In 1927 he made a notation for a "Modern Faust Play," which would have depicted the American character, as he perceived it, as having sold its life and soul for material things. The concept used in "The Last Conquest," "the duality of Man's psyche," reverberates throughout his work; two of the best examples are the ascetic artist Dion Anthony versus the materialist businessman William A. Brown in *The Great God Brown* and the ascetic poet John versus the Mephistophelian pragmatist Loving in *Days Without End*. *Beyond the Horizon* in the early period focuses on the plight of Robert Mayo, the doomed dreamer-poet. O'Neill planned a sequel, "a long play—taking up the 'Beyond the Horizon' situation where that play leaves off—'the play of Andrew.'" *Marco Millions* could be considered a continuation of the story of Andrew, the businessman who journeys to distant places to make his fortune. He would have become, in time, as spiritually deformed as Marco, given O'Neill's attitude to men who seek possessions. In *Marco Millions*, the Kaan says of the American-like Marco: "He has not even a mortal soul, he has only an acquisitive instinct."

O'Neill's heroines also possess this acquisitive instinct. Among the ideas for American historical plays is one called "Treason" (1924), which would dramatize the adult life of Margaret (Peggy) Shippen, Benedict Arnold's wife. The author states: "His treason greatly due to her influence, her love of good time & money." She seems to be an early precursor of Sara Melody, whose avarice and ambition also destroy her husband. The two men in Peggy Shippen's life—John Andre and Benedict Arnold—provide O'Neill with another opportunity to depict the idealist poet/materialist businessman conflict found in other plays. At the time he recorded this idea, the dramatist was outlining *The Great God Brown*, whose wife-mistress heroine—called both Margaret and Peggy—is desired by the artist Dion Anthony and the businessman William A. Brown. One message O'Neill obviously wanted to convey through "Treason" is that from this country's inception there would be men—and women—who, for money, betray its noble goals and ideals. Throughout the collection of ideas runs the betrayal motif. Judas is described in "The Last Conquest" as the "symbol of man's soul always for sale." Whereas

Judas "sold his spirit for the realistic value of 30 pieces of silver," Peter, who disavows Christ, denies the "spiritual self—the flesh denying the spirit." These two men who had professed to follow Christ become, by their denials, collaborators in His crucifixion. To the dramatist, they symbolize all those who through avarice or cowardice crucify anew Christ in their brothers. O'Neill's social message throughout his work and especially in "The Last Conquest" is "Love one another" and "All men are brothers."

O'Neill told Dudley Nichols on October 13, 1940, that *The Iceman Cometh* and *Long Day's Journey into Night* "have been on my mind for years"; he could have substituted the word "decades" for years. The first ideas for the two plays—both set in 1912 and classified in the second thematic category: autobiographical reminiscences—were recorded on the same day: June 6, 1939. While in the latter play, O'Neill tried to lay to rest the ghosts of his family, in the former he paid tribute to the close friends he had made at Jimmy the Priest's in 1911–1912 and the Hell Hole in 1915–1916. He had depicted his former drinking companions at Jimmy the Priest's twenty years earlier in two 1918–1919 plays: "Exorcism" and "Chris Christopherson." Major Andrews and Jimmy—roommates of Ned Malloy, a self-portrait—in "Exorcism" become in *The Iceman Cometh* the Major, later Captain Lewis, and James Cameron, "Jimmy Tomorrow." With the exception of the lovers, Linda-Anna and Paul Anderson, the characters in "Chris Christopherson" are based on actual people O'Neill knew at the waterfront saloon.

While the prototypes for the characters in the two 1918–1919 plays were habitués at Jimmy the Priest's, those for the majority of the outcasts in *The Iceman Cometh* were regulars at the Hell Hole. The author stated in 1940 that "the characters all derive from actual people I have known—more or less closely and remotely" (Letter to Macgowan, November 29, 1940). In his early character sketches, first set design, and notes, the playwright used the real names of these people. To the consternation of his wife Carlotta, O'Neill retained the friendship of many of these actual people—outcasts, alcoholics, losers all—throughout his life. Six months after his death, she wrote:

> I have been going over papers from 1920–1950—& my amazement at the stupidity of man grows & grows. A man's choice of companions & business associates is so important. They can make or break him. All through these papers runs lack of discipline—(not taught in youth!) ignorance—& the wrong kind of influences & relations! . . . Of course, the heart-breaking part of all this is—what tragic results came from the so-called "Bohemian" existence of those few early years. The parasites, the spongers, the hangers-on, dogged this poor man's steps until Death stepped in. He never had a day's respite from someone writing for money—it was hideous! (Letter to Dale Fern, May 7, 1954).

In the 1918–1920 notebook O'Neill made entries for a "Jimmy the Priest series" and a "Gunman Series," which would include a play entitled "The Pig of the Hell Hole." Two decades later on November 29, 1940 he began the "By Way of Obit" series, which included "Pig of the Hell Hole play" and "Jimmy the Priest idea of guy who recited Homer." He developed the former one-acter on February 3 and the latter three days later. Seven of the eight one-acters are obituaries for people O'Neill had known. In the eighth he planned to eulogize his deceased Dalmatian, Blemie.

The "Obit" series was started a month after O'Neill finished the second draft of *Long Day's Journey into Night*. On October 28, 1941, a week after making notes for an "Obit" play, " 'Rudie' (the chambermaid play)," he recorded his first idea for *A Moon for the Misbegotten*. One word, "autobiographic," aptly describes the works of the last period; but it also applies to the collective writings of the dramatist as the long-withheld material—notebooks, notes, scenarios—for 1918–1943 reveals. Even projected historical dramas, such as the "Career of Shih Huang Ti" and "Philip II-Don Juan of Austria," would serve as autobiographical vehicles.

Nearly all of the ideas in the 1918–1920 notebook are self-revelations. Two refer to specific incidents that occurred in 1912. In "Exorcism" he dramatized his attempt to commit suicide at Jimmy the Priest's. The one-acter concludes with Ned Malloy, a self-portrait, uttering an affirmative "Nay" to death, to his old way of life. O'Neill's second brush with death was depicted in *The Straw*. The central character, called Eugene Murray in the first notes, has contracted tuberculosis and is sent to a sanatorium. Although cured himself, he is given only a "hopeless hope" that Norah O'Brien (later Eileen Carmody), a fellow patient whom he loves, will live. A number of ideas in this notebook reveal his ambiguous feelings for his second wife Agnes Boulton: "Silence," "The Little Things," "Man and Wife." Others seem to have been inspired by the townspeople of West Point Pleasant, New Jersey, where the couple lived from November 1918 to May 1919: "Honor Among the Bradleys," "Play of a Small Town," and "Man of 45."

In 1918 O'Neill wrote an eighteen-page scenario for "The Reckoning," which he revised (possibly in collaboration with his wife Agnes) in 1924 and entitled "The Guilty One." In the former, a pregnant Bessie Small tricks her lover, Jack Gardner, into believing he has murdered her stepfather and tells him he must marry her. He asks: "How does he know it's his fault? [He] says stories about her before he met her." Reluctantly, he decides to make "reparation for his crime" but "not to renew a connection with her which he feels to be a guilty one." He will start anew, take the surname "of the people on the hill": Cockran. In Act Two the wife, now called Elizabeth, threatens to expose her husband, who has become a wealthy New England businessman, if he does not run for Congress. He acquiesces but stipulates their son must "be sent away from her to school to escape her influence." He views her as "a fiend of a woman who has ruined his life and whom he hates from the bottom of his soul." In Act Three, set in 1917 in Washington, the wife, whose description is similar to Mary Tyrone's—"her manner is furtive and timid"—again threatens to reveal her husband's "crime" if he refuses to oppose the declaration of war in Congress. His failure to do so would make him guilty of two murders: her stepfather's and their son's should he be killed in war. She is vicious in her attack: "His hate for her" has "taught her to hate, too." On being told the story, the son gets the "same idea that his father has always had—that she is a wicked woman, hard and cruel, who has caused his father untold misery by her inexcusable deceit. . . . It is too fiendish! Why, she must be mad to have done such things, to have lived the life she has!"

"The Reckoning" is obviously a veiled version of *Long Day's Journey into Night*, but its focal point is the sins of the parents against each other. Clearly, the cause of the family tragedy is the mother, who may have been promiscuous and is described as a "fiend of a woman" by her husband and "hard and cruel" by her son. In *Long Day's Journey into Night* Edmund tells his mother: "It's pretty hard to take at times having a dope fiend for a mother!" The flaw with past interpretations of Mary Tyrone/Ella O'Neill is that the major emphasis has been placed on the word "dope" rather than on "fiend." Her drug addiction is merely the consequence of her problem and not the cause of it. Ella O'Neill seems to have been, as notes for portraits of her in other works reveal, a selfish, sensuous, sexually frustrated woman, who may even have been unfaithful—if not physically, at least mentally—to her husband. In *Strange Interlude* the young Gordon says of his mother, the neurotic Nina-Ella, who must fight to "control her nerves" and who has been promiscuous both before and after marriage: "She makes me sick"; he smashes the present her lover Darrell gives him. When the couple kiss, Gordon stands hidden in the doorway "in a passion of jealousy and rage and grief, watching them." After Nina rejects the plan to go away with him, Darrell contemplates telling her husband the truth but thinks: "there are things one must not say . . . memory is too full of echoes . . . there are secrets one must not reveal—memory is lined with mirrors!"

To preserve some "secrets," O'Neill in *Long Day's Journey into Night* made his father the villain, blaming his miserliness for much of the family tragedy; on the surface the mother appears to be the victim, but a careful reading of the play and the early notes for it reveals her to be the victimizer. A hint of the author's true feelings for his father is found in the last act in a scene foreshadowed nearly two decades earlier in the 1924 "The Guilty One," the revision of "The Reckoning." The "perfect" son of the latter scenario, called Jud and a self-portrait, is depicted in "The Guilty One" as an irresponsible drunkard who has gotten the heroine, Mildred Lord, pregnant. He feels only scorn for his mother, who is an elusive specter in the household, but has deep love for, and an excellent relationship with, his father, Jim Smith, who is given the same physical traits as James Tyrone. In one scene he confesses the sorrows of the past to his son: "I've lived twenty-two years of hell, Jud. Because—of a mistake. Life was mine, then!"

The scenario of the 1918 "The Reckoning" and the extant fragment of the 1924 "The Guilty One" are discussed at length here because their autobiographical characters are presented in different guises in subsequent plays: the selfish

deceitful mother who destroys her husband and betrays her son by allowing him
to be sent away from her; the father who regrets the choices he had made—in
his profession and his marriage, which is a "mistake"—and who is made to feel
"guilty" by his wife; the rebellious, dissipated son who resents the mother's betrayal and cannot have a normal, loving relationship with a woman; she is often—
like Mildred here, Ada in *Dynamo*, and Dora in "Blind Alley Guy"—an object of
sexual desire and seduced.

After completing "The Guilty One," in which he depicted his parents, O'Neill
devoted his creative efforts to portraying his brother Jamie. The author had, because of his ambiguous feelings for his parents, turned, in life, to his brother for
companionship, affection, and guidance. One of the most significant autobiographical sections in the canon is Jamie's speech to Edmund in *Long Day's
Journey into Night*:

> And because I once wanted to write, I planted it in your mind that some-
> day you'd write! Hell, you're more than my brother. I made you! You're
> my Frankenstein! . . . I love you more than I hate you. . . . I'll do my
> damnedest to make you fail. . . . The man was dead and so he had to
> kill the thing he loved. . . . he doesn't want to be the only corpse around
> the house!

The 1918–1920 notebook contains an idea for a "long play—Jim & self— showing influence of elder on younger brother." O'Neill later tried to obliterate the
words "Jim & self," drawing many lines through them, and to eliminate or conceal the brother figure originally written into some works; but he wrote this
specific "long play" over and over.

In April 1924, five months after his brother's death, O'Neill resumed work
on *The Great God Brown*, developing an "idea for doing it with masks" and using
the Faust-Mephistopheles concept. In his "Memoranda on Masks," the dramatist
speaks of the successful production of *The Great God Brown* and then mentions
Goethe's *Faust*:

> In producing this play I would have Mephistopheles wearing the Mephi-
> stophelean mask of the face of Faust. For is not the whole of Goethe's
> truth *for our time* just that Mephistopheles and Faust are one and the same
> —are Faust?

One of O'Neill's dominant motifs is man's good-evil dichotomy. In some plays
the duality is represented by one figure; in others by two characters—opposites.
The Great God Brown is a strange combination of both. There is the "good"
William A. Brown and the "bad" Dion Anthony who is, however, split, wearing
Pan-Devil masks to conceal his ascetic face. In his notes for the play the author
stressed the bonds that unite these two men, who have been "close friends since
their school days. They have always been exact antitheses. They needed, completed each other while at the same time subtly hated each other for the need."
Dion, a would-be artist, is a failure; he becomes dissipated, drinking and fre-

quenting whorehouses, ignoring his wife, who is consoled by the "good" Brown. In the notes for the last scene of *Long Day's Journey into Night*, Jamie, returning from Mamie Burns' brothel, staggers into the Tyrone living room "drunk and nasty" and asks his brother: "Where'd you make off?—the good boy, eh?—come and stay home—the bum comes home late, drunk, fine!" In time, Brown begins to imitate Dion in an attempt to possess Dion's creative ability, his personality, and his wife. When Dion dies, his "Devil/Pan-Ascetic" mask is assumed by Brown. The agony of sharing the dead "brother's" burden proves to be too much for Brown; he dies but as "Dion Brown"—Man; Mephistopheles and Faust, Jamie and his brother, are one.

In the published version of *Days Without End*, O'Neill uses a split character, John Loving, to illustrate man's duality: the "good" John and the Mephistophelian Loving. In the early November 1931 notes, however, the author had contemplated using two distinct characters, as in *The Great God Brown*, to represent man's dichotomy. He planned to show John, a self-portrait, in the first scene

with friend, brother (?)—the Mephistophelian character—a man of the same age who has been his friend since boyhood—who is a living reminder and participator in all his past—in all his struggles, dissipations, despair, love affairs, former marriage—a former Catholic like himself—a sneering sceptic now about religion and everything else—a philosophical Nihilist—dissipated, Don Juan and a bachelor—but a torch song sentimentalist at heart—with great charm for women.

In his description of Jamie Tyrone in *A Moon for the Misbegotten*, O'Neill repeats the same words and phrases that are used for the friend-brother: "Mephistophelian quality," "sneering," "Sentimental," "charm" which has "kept him attractive to women." In *The Great God Brown*, Dion Anthony cynically calls himself a "Don Juan."

In the last scene of *Days Without End*, John gets the Mephistophelian "Loving outside of himself" and sees him as "Devil he sold soul to—but if he is Devil then his opposite, Christ, must be true." In an early concept of the scene, a contrite Loving kneels before a crucifix in a Catholic church, begging Christ to "forgive thy poor damned soul! Oh, Brother, forgive Thy poor damned fool!" Loving lies joyfully "on his back his arms outstretched in the form of a Cross"; John then "arises from his knees, his arms outstretched before the Cross," saying: "I believe again." The two figures become integrated in the one person, John Loving.

The scene with a damned, but repentant, soul before a Cross is repeated in "The Last Conquest," "laid in a secret place deep within the duality of man's soul." The good-evil conflict is waged here by the ancient foes, Christ and Satan. To rid man forever of the vaguest memory of Christ, Satan launches his last campaign, a mock reenactment of the Crucifixion. Before the scene on Calvary is played out, he "makes up the conventional Mephisto[phelian]. face." Over the years he has become a hopeless alcoholic and urges Christ to "give it up—let's get drunk—Baudelaire." After the Last Supper the previous night, dreading the coming Crucifixion, Satan had started drinking heavily, saying: "It is better to be drunk when meeting ghosts." In *The Great God Brown* Cybel tells Dion, who calls himself "The Prince of Darkness": "You were born with ghosts in your eyes."

On Calvary, Satan keeps a vigil beside the Cross: "You are a long time dying, Brother." He begins the parable of the "Siamese Twins—the duality of man." One twin, the Realist, comes to hate his sensitive ascetic twin—"denies brother-hood." Following a ceremony in which he is proclaimed Emperor of the World, the Realist strangles his twin. The next morning attendants think a terrible mir-acle occurred: "in the great royal bed there is only the one figure, that of the Great Emperor, who during the night had committed suicide." In spite of the fact that he is predestined to crucify Christ, Satan shows great love for Him, pleading: "Let me take your place—I can stand crucifixion." In one version, as Satan starts to leave Calvary, he hears the voice of Christ: "Someday thou shalt be at my right-hand in Paradise." Satan responds: "Brother, I will remember that promise—it shall be my blessed isle." In *The Great God Brown*, Dion, before his death, states: "Into thy hands, O Lord"; he speaks to his mask comfortingly: "Tomorrow we may be with Him in Paradise." When Dion mocks the "good Brown" to Cybel, she exclaims: "But you are like him, too! You're brothers." Dion replies: "Poor Billy! God forgive me the evil I've done him!"

The three characters—Dion in *The Great God Brown*, Loving in *Days With-out End*, and Satan in "The Last Conquest"—while depicted as symbols of evil—aspire after good, confess their sins, and are apparently forgiven. Each bears a strong resemblance to Jamie Tyrone, who in *A Moon for the Misbegotten* comes to Josie to confess and be forgiven. What links the latter play with the former three is Jamie's revelation of opposing dreams, which appears only in an early draft. When he tells Josie he doesn't dream, she argues: "That's a lie. Two dreams we all have. They're deadly enemies. It's a fight to the death to see which will own your life." He tells his first: "the cynic who believes in nothing—as he tells her grows full of disdainful pride." Josie calls it a "Lucifer dream" and urges him to confess the second. He replies: "Kid stuff—dates back to school—cate-chism—the man who loves God, who gives up self and the world to worship of

---

°O'Neill uses similar words to describe the emotional strain of writing these auto-biographical plays. He says on March 25, 1925, that he finished *The Great God Brown* "in tears. Couldn't control myself!" After completing *Days Without End*, he in-formed Russel Crouse: "all the time I was sweating blood getting this opus out of my system." *Long Day's Journey into Night* was, the dramatist remarked, "written in tears and blood."

God and devotes self to good works, service of others, celibacy." Josie comments: "Ah, that's the one you really love, isn't it. . . . Well I've been trying to seduce a Saint. Or to tempt a Lucifer." Because Josie is a woman, there may be a tendency to overlook the fact that she is O'Neill's alter ego in *A Moon for the Misbegotten*. In the scenario for Act Four, Josie states: "This is the night when the moon bore twins, me and my brother here." One of the early titles for the play is "The Moon Bore Twins." Satan in "The Last Conquest" narrates the parable of the Siamese Twins; Brown speaks of Dion, saying: "We're getting to be like twins." In view of the emphasis on the strong bond between "brother" characters in these plays, Jamie's words to Edmund in *Long Day's Journey into Night*—"You're more than my brother"—take on a new significance.

In *The Iceman Cometh* Hickey uses the word "brother" when he addresses Parritt who, in the notes, seems to be yet another thinly veiled portrait of Jamie O'Neill. Parritt has just traveled east from California where he had betrayed his mother, as had Jamie. Erie uses the word "brother" when addressing the Night Clerk in *Hughie*, which, like *A Moon for the Misbegotten*, is an obituary for Jamie O'Neill. Erie narrates the story of his wasted life to the Night Clerk in an effort to form a friendship with him. Erie's account of his gambling adventures captures the imagination of the clerk who, at the close of the one-acter, "resembles a holy saint, recently elected to Paradise." Erie produces a pair of dice for "a little crap," his soul "purged of grief."

In the scenario for *Long Day's Journey into Night*, completed just before O'Neill started the "Obit" series, Jamie informs his brother that bribery—"I'm laying 10 to 1"—is needed to get by St. Peter. In this play O'Neill calls himself Hugh in the first dramatis personae. He had used this name earlier for a self-portrait in his original scheme for *Mourning Becomes Electra*, planning to depict once again a brother versus brother conflict. Hugh Mannon would be his mother's "pet"; he is described as being "like" her: "gay, volatile, handsome." Orin's "intense love" for his mother would, "since boyhood," be "defeated by her indifference to him." Because of his jealousy "of her love for his brother Hugh" and "his resentment toward her," Orin has "instinctively taken the line of imitating his father in everything."

After having finished the fourth draft of *Mourning Becomes Electra* in October 1930, O'Neill visited the Escorial in Spain; the trip inspired him to develop a "Philip II-Don Juan of Austria" play. As he envisioned this drama, these half brothers are rivals not for the love of a mother but for the affections of their father, Charles V. The author obviously identified with the idealistic Juan, abandoned as a child by his mother, who "played and sang for Charles at Ratisbon" after the death of his wife and who is described as "pretty, heedless, no serious brains, but attracting opposite sex." As the title of the play implies, the focus would have been Juan's conflict with his older brother Philip, who, out of jealousy, destroys Juan. A similar conflict is found in an idea for the historical drama (previously cited) developed earlier in 1925, "Career of Shih Huang Ti." The first Emperor of a unified China was the son of a singing girl, who had been the concubine of Lu Pü-wei, a wealthy merchant, and I-jen of the house of Ch'in. Shih Huang Ti has incestuous feelings for his mother who, after her husband's death, defies Chinese customs and resumes her relationship with her former lover. His punishment foreshadows that of Adam Brant in the first version of *Mourning Becomes Electra*; Lu Pü-wei "poisoned himself knowing he will soon be murdered if he doesn't." The Emperor's real rival for his mother's affections is his brother, her favorite, who leads a rebellion against Shih Huang Ti and is ordered by him to commit suicide.

In the late 1920s O'Neill developed a number of ideas whose central figure is a self-portrait. Like the autobiographical Ned Malloy in the 1919 "Exorcism," some heroes attempt to commit suicide; all are placed in a life-death decision-making situation. On March 8, 1927, the author began " 'The Sea-Mother's Son' series of plays based on autobiographical material" (W.D.). In the 1929 scheme for the "opus," the "man (40) lies in the hospital at the point of death—he is at the crisis." In scenes from childhood and young manhood enacted before him, the "character of himself is taken by himself while a man wearing his mask takes his place in bed." At the end of the work, the man says "Yes to his life and gives up the comfort of return to Mother Death." In 1929 O'Neill states that the "opus" will have "ten or more *Interludes* in it"; "my sub-title is to be The Story of the Birth of a Soul—and it will be just that!" While O'Neill never "consciously" completed this multi-play "opus" as he specifically envisioned it, the "character of himself" is taken by numerous protagonists "at the crisis" in many ideas and dramas. In the 1929 "Scheme for a Life of Man play," he planned to use "life-sized puppets" to reenact the life of the hero: "his father or his mother for example—while in his memory they remain alive as they were." The memory of his father and mother—depicted "alive" *as they were*: in this statement lies the key to total understanding of the many autobiographical plays, haunted as they are by the ghost of James and Ella O'Neill.

On March 4, 1927, O'Neill began work on *Dynamo*, describing the "real plot" as the story of "Reuben's psychological mess over his father and mother's betrayal and how he at last deifies and finds her again." In the first 1927 scenario, the hero, James White, possesses the author's physical traits and a "duality in character": his boyish nature conflicts with a "demonic cruel spirit." His mother, forty-five, is assertive, a religious fanatic. She had been "indifferent" to her husband "until she found she could completely dominate him," and from that point on "she has felt for him a scornful affection." The father, fifty-five, a short fat man with a round face, bald head and pale blue eyes, is a "meek unassuming soul, dull but kindly." Their marriage has been a "loveless affair." In the 1928 scenario the mother has an "oval face, curly black hair, straight nose and good brow." Her figure, "still youthful," is "extremely feminine. She is all female." Her mouth reveals her inner discontent: "It is a strong small mouth, energetic and stubborn, full-lipped, sensual and selfish." Reverend Mr. White is now an over-assertive, overbearing stern Old Testament moralist with a "fanatical ideal of purity." When he met his wife—"gay, light-hearted & pleasure loving," the "flesh had conquered him," and for this he feels "hatred and guilt." The mother regrets her marriage as her other suitors "have since risen in the world and could have given her its delights which she remembers with regret."

The son is "by nature inclined toward his father, his natural sympathies are with him"; but he loves his "mother's femininity, her charms, although he feels like his father that she is a weakness, that he must struggle against her." The mother encourages her son to become a businessman, rather than a minister, and, like Mary Tyrone, tells him "sly tales of the real privations she has had to undergo." He, however, "has a secret love for poetry—erotic and sensual." After the mother betrays her son by revealing a confided secret to her husband, James leaves home, rejecting his parents' Old Testament God. When he returns two years later, his "demonic cruel spirit" completely dominates him. "It is as if he had grown a mask of sneering mocking indifference over his own face." After he discovers his mother has died, he feels "queerly drawn" to the massive earth mother, May Fife, who loves him "like a son." At the same time, he experiences a strong sexual attraction for Ada, her daughter, but views it as an impure weakness. He gets a job at the power plant and begins to worship the great Mother Dynamo; "God has become Mother who is Electricity—his search to know Her, love Her, adore Her." He considers his affair with Ada, who becomes pregnant, a sin "against his celibate priesthood," requiring "human sacrifice" in atonement. In the last scene of the play he builds an altar before the dynamo "in the temple," longing to become one with the Goddess Mother figure. He climbs to the core of the dynamo; "his arms are outspread to press it to his heart, it is as if he were crucified upon it. A terrific flash of light." When workmen enter, they see his shrivelled figure "hanging as if nailed to the face of the Dynamo."

Dynamo was intended to be the first work of a trilogy, "Myth Plays for the God-forsaken"; its second, *Days Without End*, would have been a Catholic version of *Dynamo*. The focal point of these plays and many of the ideas in the late 1920s is the hero's search for religious certitude, associated in some way with his mother. Reuben was to have become a Baptist minister, John a Catholic priest; shortly after they reject their faith, their mothers die, and both sons feel guilt and seek a mother substitute. John marries a woman who resembles his mother: Erda (Elsa), the "primitive poetic Mayan earth spirit," but betrays the wife-mother by having an affair. His guilt and her seemingly fatal illness fill him with despair, and he goes to a Catholic church with a gun, determined to sacrifice himself before the statue of Christ and the Virgin. O'Neill agonized over the end of this play. Should his hero be saved? He feared critics would regard this solution as a desire on his part to return to Catholicism. Because *Dynamo* had been a critical failure, it was foolhardy to follow it with another religiously oriented play. Nevertheless, O'Neill felt compelled to write *Days Without End*: "I felt a need to liberate myself from myself." *Days Without End* is the dramatist's account of his own spiritual odyssey; *Long Day's Journey into Night* focuses primarily on his parents, and *A Moon for the Misbegotten* on his brother.

O'Neill labels the original idea for *Days Without End*: "Play of Catholic Boyhood." He heads the first set of notes: "His dead selves—masked—7, 14, 21, 28, 35, 42—(he is 49)?" He then writes: "In his childhood his mother had played and sung sad, sentimental songs of lost love" and a most significant line: "Mother's torch song—as to lost sweetheart Death and the Father have stolen." O'Neill's mother played the piano, and she possibly sang sad, sentimental songs—but *had* she sung torch songs of lost love? The section devoted to John Loving's childhood contains autobiographical data: his father was not a "strict C[atholic]. like mother"; "Idealization of father as L. gradually grows to resent Mother's absorption in Catholicism—her death when L. is 14—agony of remorse for inner religious rebellion when she becomes seriously ill—frenzy of piety—prayers for her." While Ella O'Neill did not die physically when her son was fourteen, she died to him psychologically; for he was approximately this age when he discovered she was a drug addict, and he did pray that she would be cured. In a second version, the mother discovers her son has abandoned his faith and is "broken-hearted—dies soon after . . . at mercy of country quacks." Shortly "after his mother's death, he goes in for analysis—longing for priest hearing confession."

Days Without End is O'Neill's lament for his loss of Catholicism and his own struggle, using the guise of his hero, to return to it; for return he did, at least mentally. His entries for 1932 and 1933—when he was writing this play—in "Cycles," an account of his life and work, state: "return toward Cathol[icism]." In a letter to Dudley Nichols dated May 29, 1932, the dramatist said:

> Funny, your writing me at this particular time about affirmation. I am changing inside me, as I suppose one always does, or ought to do if there is growth, when one has passed forty, and even the most affirmative Nay! of my past work no longer satisfies me. So I am groping after a real, true Yea! in the play I'm now starting [*Days Without End*]—a very old Yea, it is true, in essence, but completely forgotten in all its inner truth that it might pass for brand new. Whether I will be able to carry the writing of it up to Yea! remains to be seen.

To affirm this "true Yea!" in *Days Without End*, O'Neill discarded the earlier ending in which John Loving shoots himself before the statue of Christ and the Virgin. On August 5, 1933, while working on the sixth draft of the play, O'Neill stated in his Work Diary: "Making change back to Catholicism—more direct." In the final text the hero is reconciled with Christ.

The fate of Orin Mannon, the self-portrait in *Mourning Becomes Electra*, is identical to the one originally devised for John Loving. Haunted by the loss of his mother and her betrayal, Orin shoots himself—not in a church but in the Mannon "Temple of Hate." The play was completed in 1931 before the "true Yea!" period. Orin's father feels "affection of a kind" for him but "forces him into West Point,

hoping the discipline will cure what he thinks is Orin's weakness of character."
Ezra Mannon's true reason, like the father's in the early 1918 "The Reckoning,"
is to protect his son from the mother's influence—possibly James O'Neill's real
motivation for sending the young Eugene to boarding school. Ezra is a "stern,
grimly-religious man" with "grey-blue eyes—big features and a tight-lipped
severe cold-blooded mouth." His wife Christine is a "tall full-bosomed, heavy-
limbed striking-looking woman with thick reddish-brown hair." Her mouth is
"large and sensual." Underneath her "coldly self-contained exterior she is a
creature of violent repressed passionate powerful will."

While "sought after by the young men of her own set," Christine was fascinated by the novelty of the handsome stern Mannon and "set out to make him
fall in love with her." Their marriage, however, "had been a romantic mistake."
Her "passionate, full-blooded femaleness has never found sex-satisfaction in his
repressed morally-constrained, disapproving sex-frigidity." The "small New England seaport town" where the Mannons go to live after their marriage is specifically identified in the scenario as New London. Christine "has always hated
the town of N. L. and felt a superior disdain for its inhabitants"; she lives "in a
superior isolation." Her habit of dressing extravagantly goes against her husband's "Puritan grain and seems to him as evidence of a sinful strain in her."
Like Mary Tyrone in the early notes for *Long Day's Journey into Night*, Christine, in the scenario, pays for her clothes "out of a generous yearly income left
by her father," who has spoiled her.

When her husband and son go to war, Christine falls in love with Gus-
tave/Adam Brant and "gives herself" to him without reserve; a "fierce tide of
long-repressed passions sweeps over her, overthrowing all the religious and social
taboos of her training." In the scenario the lover is given the physical attributes
of the dramatist. He is a Harvard graduate, a loafer, living on an allowance his
father provides. Christine loathes sleeping with her husband when he returns
from the war and contrasts her lover's caresses with the "coarse love of Mannon
whose loving has never in their married life aroused any satisfying response in
her." After Christine poisons her husband, Lavinia enters the bedroom to hear
her father gasp one word before he dies: "guilty."

The lovers are poisoned in the scenario rather than shot as in the final text.
Gustave has been invited to the Mannon home by Orin in a feigned gesture of
forgiveness and reconciliation. He "feels like a Judas" preparing the glasses of
wine: poison for Gustave, a sleeping draught, so identified by Lavinia, for the
mother. He expects to find only the dead lover the next morning in Ezra Mannon's bed but discovers his mother's dead body by the bedside. In a rage of
jealousy, he exclaims: "You came to your lover's bed. . . . What a terrible
woman—how corrupt—how cruel—how lascivious and foul—and I thought you
were sweet and fine and good—I loved you—I thought you loved me—and you
betrayed me!" Reminiscent of Larry Slade's penance to Parritt—that he commit
suicide—to atone for his psychological murder of his mother, Lavinia commands

Orin in the scenario: "And now go in and do your last duty as a Mannon." Orin responds: "Aye! I see! Well, there's no help for that now! And then maybe they'll let me alone." Guilt-ridden and longing to be free of his ghosts, he enters the Mannon house and shoots himself.

In July 1931, three months after having finished *Mourning Becomes Electra*, O'Neill recorded an idea for "House with the Masked Dead": "Man (& wife?) comes in house (Greek) auto broken down—masked family . . . gradually the tragedy that has happened in this house long ago." The Greek house in this idea is apparently modeled, as is the Greek-styled Mannon home, on the Chappell mansion located on Whale Oil Row on a hill overlooking the city of New London. The idea was probably inspired by a then recent trip O'Neill had made to New London; his Work Diary entry for July 1, 1931 reads: "revisit Pequot Ave. old time haunts." Two years earlier he recorded an idea for "The House," using a New England home as "a symbol" of man's life "and its intermingling with other lives—sprung up on its hill." In the New England play, "The Reckoning" (1918), after deciding to begin a new life, Jack Gardner (the Gardiners—spelled thus— like the Chappells, were socially prominent New Londoners) takes the surname "of the people on the hill": Cockran.

O'Neill returned to the New London house on Pequot Avenue, his family home, dramaturgically in 1940, using it for the setting of *Long Day's Journey into Night*. The play is at first set in 1907 on the Tyrones' thirtieth wedding anniversary. The Father has forgotten the occasion and "acts hurt & sentimental about it—she [the Mother] reminds him how often he has forgotten—or remembering, pretended to forget, hoping I had forgotten—so there need be no presents." The passage provides some indication of the couple's relationship—that the wife's antagonism for her husband is deep-rooted and has been festering for years. The Mother possesses the "duality of character" in this play. The dual aspects of her nature are noticeable particularly in Act Three of the scenario after she has made several trips upstairs for a morphine injection: "M. very hipped up now, her manner strange—at the moment a vain happy, chattering girlishness—then changing to a hard cynical sneering bitterness with a biting cruelty and with a coarse vulgarity in it—the last as if suddenly poisoned by an alive demon." This act is dominated by the Mother's "flood of reminiscences—life before her marriage an idyl." Of the years after her marriage, she says: "I don't want to remember—In fact I don't remember—as much of time since then like a dream." She urges the maid to "drink to anniversary" and says her husband "doesn't like anniversaries"; they "remind him [he is] getting old—14 y[ears]. older—was great mistake—more like father."

The dialogue of James and Edmund Tyrone in the last act resembles that of the father and son in the 1924 "The Guilty One." Jim Smith's statement "Life was mine" echoes words the elder Tyrone/O'Neill used onstage as Edmond Dantes in *Monte Cristo*. The son in the 1924 play says his mother "must be mad to have done such things, to have lived the life she has." James Tyrone despairs over his wife's condition: "When the poison is in her, she isn't responsible, like crazy woman . . . done all I can—all medicine can—suppose nothing to do now, no hope, be resigned to live with crazy woman." He reveals his deep affection for Edmund, telling him he doesn't have to go to the State Farm to be treated for tuberculosis: "go anywhere you like I don't care what it costs if it makes you well and you'll get hold of yourself & be a man. Don't you know you're my son and I love you?"

The main difference between the scenario's last act and the published text's is that in the former the mother converses rationally with her sons and husband, leveling bitter accusations at them throughout the scene. She is particularly vindictive to her husband. When he urges her to go to bed, she tells him: "I am sure I do not want to remember you." The sons and their problems are peripheral characters and concerns in the early notes; the major focus is the relationship of the parents (as the tentative title, "Anniversary," heading the scenario for the last act implies). Like Elizabeth in "The Guilty One," Mary Tyrone is described as a liar and fiend and is, like her, the "guilty" spouse. The one word the dying Ezra Mannon hurls at the wife who has betrayed and destroyed him is "Guilty!" In *Mourning Becomes Electra*, as in other plays, including *Long Day's Journey into Night*, the mother is trapped in a marriage she regards as a "mistake." The lover in *Mourning Becomes Electra* becomes the symbol of betrayal and escape for the wife from a loveless marriage; drug addiction serves the same purpose in *Long Day's Journey into Night*.

The last two autobiographical plays O'Neill worked on before he ceased writing in 1943 could be considered sequels to *Long Day's Journey into Night*. In the first idea recorded for *A Moon for the Misbegotten*, the author remarks that the work is "based on story" told by Edmund in the first act of *Long Day's Journey into Night* "except here Jamie principal character and story of play otherwise entirely imaginary except for J.'s revelation of self." Set in 1923, the year Jamie died, the drama would be a eulogy for him. The projected second play, "Blind Alley Guy," would be the dramatist's "revelation of self" and his complex relationship with his parents. It is set, in the first notes, in 1918, the year O'Neill wrote "The Reckoning." The hero is initially named "Ricky," a nickname for Richard, used for the self-portrait in *Ah, Wilderness!*. As a small boy, Ricky "is quiet, reserved, solitary, obedient and compliant on the surface because he is indifferent, but subject at times to fits of strange cold formidable fury." He "feels himself an alien" and becomes rebellious, frequently running away from home as a youth and hopping "freights—gets to know hoboes—feeling of kinship with them as outcasts who can't belong [to] social structure." He "hates the small town where everyone knows everyone" and the family's "lower middle class sufficiency which is neither poverty or wealth."

O'Neill began "Blind Alley Guy" on December 16, 1940, exactly two months after completing *Long Day's Journey into Night*, which depicted incidents that occurred in his life in 1912. He apparently had a twofold purpose in developing the first version of "Blind Alley Guy": to dramatize those early years of his life's cycle—7, 14, 21—he had intended to portray in *Days Without End* and to take his story beyond *Long Day's Journey* into the 1912–1918 period. An analogy can be made bewteen the fictitious "outcasts who can't belong to social structure" and the alcoholic misfits O'Neill befriended at the Hell Hole in his "Bohemian" years. While traits and attitudes of the dramatist are given to the central figure, those of Ella and James O'Neill are attributed to Ricky's parents, Ed and Tess White. The focal point of the early concept of the play is the love-hate family relationships.

In the January 1941 notes Ed White is "a good, simple, hard-working man, uncomplicated, sense of what is right & wrong, religious in a mild way, an affectionate family man" but "bewildered by any display of passion." His wife is described as having thick grey hair almost white, big eyes, heavy brows, wide full-lipped mouth. She has kept her figure and is "still an unusually good-looking woman for her age." Like Mary Tyrone, Tess has a "strange, withdrawn, ingrowing quality—dreamy & detached." Her personality is "a contrast—by turns complete relaxation into a vague, day-dreaming quietude" or alert and aggressive. Ed is ten years her senior. She seems to be a "congenial mate on the surface," but underneath she is disappointed in him; "she had dreamed of him as romantic, passionate lover—the reality had been too mild, too much." Tess "married him after her great romance—she had fallen passionately in love with roving ranch hand." Because of her strong religious beliefs, she "wouldn't let him seduce her"; but, like Nina Leeds, she "regrets" not having given herself to her lover. Tess is surprised when Ed proposes—"friend, never thought of him as lover—accepts on rebound after lover left—imagines it's no good in bed with her—only way to permit, react." Her first child is "a disappointment—next child dies—then at last a son—and she stops having children." Tess has "never been able to mend her way of unequal love"; she has "come to love her son more than her husband." Like Christine Mannon and Mary Tyrone, Tess has inherited money from her father; her house and property are a "remnant of big ranch" her father owned. And, like these two women, Tess assumes a "superior distinctive pose among townswomen."

In July 1941 O'Neill emerged from another period marked by "war jitters" and devoted to his antitotalitarian play, "The Last Conquest." At this time "Blind Alley Guy" changes from an autobiographical work to a propaganda play. The hero, now called Walter White and resembling Brecht's Arturo Ui, is a Hitler-like gangster. His parents and sister are given entirely new characterizations; they have lost "all ethical and moral values . . . no faith in old religion—government all grafting politicians—sex morality of no meaning, ancient bigotry." O'Neill changes the date of the setting to 1934—"year Hitler's seizing power"— and gives his hero the Nazi dictator's traits and background. The dramatist draws a parallel between Hitler, whose friends (Röhm and his followers) supposedly plan to "double-cross him" and Walter, whose wife betrays him.

"Blind Alley Guy" is a thematic coda to O'Neill's work—autobiographical
and societal/political. On the familial level, the author began in the late 1920s
a series of plays depicting himself and his relationship with his parents. He initially named the hero of the 1927 *Dynamo* James (his father's name) White and
the central character of the 1940–1943 "Blind Alley Guy," Walter White. Both
young men are rebels, leave home, and become fanatics; Reuben White worships
the god electricity, Walter White a Nazi dictator. Both have relationships with
women for purely sexual reasons. The two women betray, and are betrayed by,
these men and behave similarly when abandoned by them: Ada has defied her
parents and "taken to going out nights and joy-riding with boys, gets a bad reputation in the town and is reckless about it"; Dora "goes to pieces—gets reputation
as wild girl, parties, scrapes, booze, affairs which mean nothing." Both women
become pregnant but neither has the child; to please Walter, Dora has an abortion; to passify Reuben, Ada worships the god Electricity with him and is sacrificed. Perhaps the most striking similarity is the way the heroes die: the two men
are electrocuted. Reuben wants to become one through death with the Mother
Dynamo; at the end of "Blind Alley Guy," Walter is "in love with death now—
all he ever loved anyway." While Ada is actually electrocuted just before Reuben,
when the clock strikes the moment of death for Walter, Dora, who sits in a
"straight back armchair—rigid, clutching arms," feels "pain like electric shock."

The parents in *Dynamo* and "Blind Alley Guy" and their relationships are
similar. These likenesses extend also to the Mannons in *Mourning Becomes
Electra*. Many of the words used to describe Amelia White, Tess White, and
Christine Mannon are identical: they all have kept their "youthful" figures, have
"big dark eyes," and are "full-lipped," "sensual," "passionate." Amelia is "all
female"; Christine possesses "full-blooded femaleness." The former had been
"gay, light hearted, pleasure-loving" before marriage; the latter, a "thoughtless,
merry, pleasure-loving girl." Just as Tess "regrets" the loss of her lover, the other
two women remember fondly all the other suitors they could have married. Christine, like Amelia and Tess, "never found sex satisfaction" because of her husband's "constrained disapproving sex-frigidity." Christine's marriage had been
a "romantic mistake"; Amelia's, like Tess's, is a "loveless affair." Much of this
information about fictitious mothers corresponds to material in the notes about
the admittedly autobiographical Mary Tyrone, who in the scenario says that her
marriage was "a great mistake"—that her husband was "more like father." Mary
Tyrone has a "young, graceful figure"; "her mouth wide with full, sensitive lips";
her "dark brown eyes appear black. They are unusually large and beautiful, with
black brows and long curling lashes" (Tess has "long lashes, heavy brows"; Christine has "pronounced eyebrows almost meeting in a straight line above her nose").

What is written of Tess is true of all these wives: she had dreamed of her
husband as a "romantic passionate lover—the reality had been too mild, too
much—she had come to love her son more than her husband." Theirs was a
selfish love—that demanded much of the sons, gave little in return—and in the

case of Christine, a tenuous love. She betrays the son through her passionate affair with Adam Brant. Each of the other mothers betrays her son in some way and ultimately destroys him. Reuben, Orin, Walter die violently. Edmund could possibly die, but his mother, locked in her own self-centered world, ignores his pleas for help. Even the noble earth mothers, like Cybel and Josie, cannot save Dion Anthony and Jamie Tyrone (both haunted by Mary Tyrone-like mothers); they can only act as priestesses to comfort the dying.

It is particularly significant that O'Neill in "Blind Alley Guy" smashes the mother mystique, his previous sentimentalized view of the mother. Tess White in the last notes is totally amoral, selfish, aggressive—a snobbish bigot and supporter of Hitler and his Nazi regime. She is, in this propaganda play, the precursor of the "Divine Mother" of the World Savior in "The Last Conquest": the "Mother Goddess of Destruction and Death," "Our Gentle Lady of Cannibalism." Significantly, in view of the destroyed heroes of the canon, the Divine Mother is described as "a faithful image of man's permanent longing for the security of suicide." In her, the whore and mother figure become one. When Satan puts the Savior-dictator to sleep, he starts to place him in the Mother-statue's arms but sees she is embracing someone else; he calls her a "very unholy lady!"

Two dominant motifs of O'Neill's work merge in "Blind Alley Guy": autobiographical memories of the past and his social concerns for man's present and future well-being. Appropriately for our time, the latter takes precedence in this work. By changing the autobiographical characterizations of the Whites and portraying them as godless materialists who support the ruthless German dictator, O'Neill delineates the prototypes of the apathetic Americans who later inhabit the totalitarian World State of "The Last Conquest" and willingly submit to its tyrannical "Hitler-like leader." In his notes for this play, the author writes: "The spirit is intangible, unseen while greed and power are realistic facts" and "Imperialism has reached its final expression, men are spiritually dead." In his early 1918–1919 play *The Straw*, O'Neill offered man only a "hopeless hope." One of the titles he considered for "The Last Conquest" was "More Than Straw for the Drowning." O'Neill's primary purpose in writing the antitotalitarian trilogy in the early 1940s was to make modern man aware of the threat to individual freedom, that his own inner flawed nature posed the gravest danger to its preservation. The message he wished to impart is spoken by the formerly enslaved people of the World State: "It is good to be free—to have a soul again— to know there is good and evil in our hearts and we can choose."

It is unfortunate that the author never completed "The Last Conquest." He put it aside in December 1942 to finish *A Moon for the Misbegotten*. To read the entries of the Work Diary for the first four months of 1943 is a painful experience; the man, as dramatist, is dying. On January 31 he writes: "what I am up against now—fade out physically each day after about 3 hours—page a day because work slowly even when as eager about play as I am about this— Park[inson's]. main cause—constant strain to write." The March 10th entry reads: "eager but little done because nerves jumping out of hands, arms—can't control." As she had for years, Carlotta was typing the manuscript of *A Moon for the Misbegotten*. O'Neill notes on April 21: "bad bad night C. taking job in fine spirit & doing fine at it." She alone knew the effort involved in completing this play and stated later: "Moon I loathe that play—for personal reasons! . . . The whole thing was a ghastly business—it was at that time his real illness took hold of him! He was not at his writing best" (Letter to Dale Fern, August 15, 1953).

O'Neill's method of composition was unique. He could only create—in his final days as throughout his career—by *writing* his ideas himself in that peculiarly small scrawl of his. Dudley Nichols states that he had offered to write "The Last Conquest"

> out for him as he had told it to me and then keep rewriting successive drafts until it would be very near to what he imagined, but of course this was impossible. He could no more do this than he could dictate his work. His handwriting was a part of his mind, almost a part of his imagination, which is what makes his MSS so fascinating. His hand stopped, his work was stopped, and he knew it.

In 1944 Lawrence Langner sent the dramatist a Sound Scriber, hoping that he could dictate his plays. O'Neill experimented with the machine but was unable to compose in this manner. However, in a practice session, he read his "favorite bit"—Larry Slade's "let me live" third-act speech. He tells Langner:

> When I played the record back and listened to the voice that was my voice and yet not my voice saying: "I'm afraid to live, am I?—and even more afraid to die! So I sit here, my pride drowned on the bottom of a bottle, keeping drunk so I won't see myself shaking in my britches with fright, or hear myself whining and praying, O Blessed Christ, let me live a little longer *at any price*!" . . . well it sure did something to me. It wasn't Larry, it was my ghost talking to me, or I to my ghost.

O'Neill in his earliest efforts as an amateur playwright in 1918 tried to memorialize the friends he cherished and to exorcise the tragic familial memories of his youth. Friends and family members died—but not to him; they forever haunted him. His ideas and plays are dramaturgic and autobiographic milestones—reminiscences for his dead, the mainspring of his tragedy and his greatness—on his long day's journey through life. On June 18, 1937, O'Neill recorded one of the final ideas in his notebooks: "Day," depicting the "history of a day's life of man." The setting is "the family house he has inherited—the dead (his mother, father, his old nurse)" and in the next scene "his brother." The man confidently proclaims "a new life, freedom" will begin at high noon. At the stroke of noon his "confidence in himself fades . . . as they become strong, he shrinks back into their circle."

V.F.

A Note on Editorial Method

Eugene O'Neill's handwriting, minuscule at all times and nearly illegible in his last writing years 1939–1943, presents a number of problems. There is, however, a consistent pattern in his letter formation that, along with various mechanical aids, facilitates the work of transcription. Only a few words in the hundreds of manuscript pages remain undeciphered.

In the presentation of ideas from the notes and notebooks, I have not altered O'Neill's text substantively; the content is reproduced intact. Some types of grammatical errors have been rectified; misplaced apostrophes in the possessive form and misspellings have been silently corrected; initial or closing quotation marks and terminal punctuation, when omitted, have been supplied. Words that appear as later insertions have been incorporated without note in the text; an occasional omitted word has been supplied in square brackets.

Although I have not attempted to reproduce all of O'Neill's deletions, those canceled words or phrases that have some particular significance appear either within square brackets or are supplied in the notes. Occasionally, O'Neill cancels entire ideas, labeling them "no good." Such cancellations and comments are cited in the footnotes, all of which are the editor's.

The author's original titles are used to identify the ideas; the final titles he later gives those he develops into plays appear in square brackets. I have also supplied, within square brackets, titles for untitled ideas, using words from the entries that summarize the central focus. Dates that O'Neill assigns his ideas appear in parentheses under their titles. Dates that I have determined for these ideas are within brackets.

Title headings of major plays are in boldface type. Titles of published plays in the text are italicized; those assigned unpublished works and ideas are placed in quotation marks. The letters "W.D." after a passage in quotation marks indicate an entry from O'Neill's Work Diary.

V.F.

About the O'Neill text

All material quoted separately from the O'Neill notebooks and manuscripts is marked in the outside margin by a vertical rule. Where this material is quoted within the editor's own text, the source is clear from the context.

Excerpts of O'Neill material not marked by a rule are from sources other than the notebooks and are clearly identified within the text.

The symbol ° before a title heading indicates an undeveloped or unpublished idea.

1 • Ideas: 1918–1920 Notebook

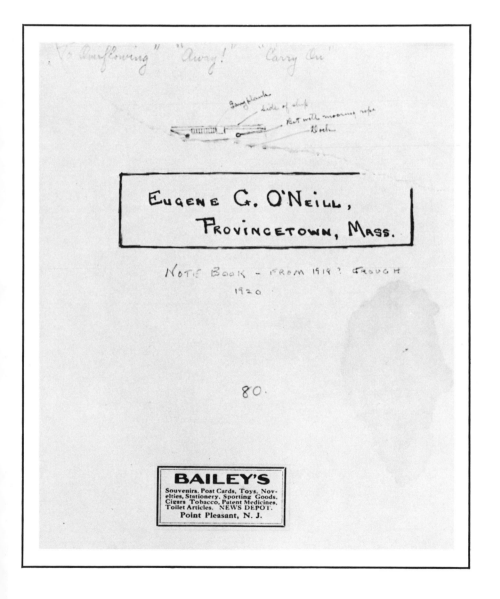

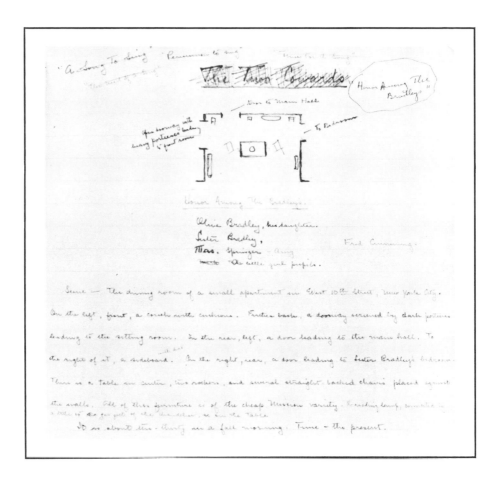

°HONOR AMONG THE BRADLEYS*
[1918]

Olive Bradley, his daughter
Lester Bradley
Mrs. Springer—Amy   Fred Cummings
A little girl pupil

Scene—The dining room of a small apartment in West 10th Street, New York City. On the left, front, a couch with cushions. Farther back, a doorway screened

---

*O'Neill lists five alternate titles for this idea: "The Two Cowards," "A Song to Sing," "The Need of a Song," "Permission to Sing," and "Time for a Song."

by dark portieres leading to the sitting room. In the rear, left, a door leading to the main hall. To the right of it, a sideboard with hat. On the right, rear, a door leading to Lester Bradley's bedroom. There is a table in center, two rockers, and several straight-backed chairs placed against the walls. All of this furniture is of the cheap Mission variety. A reading lamp, connected by a table to a gas jet of the chandelier, is on the table.

It is about ten-thirty in a fall morning. Time—the present.

Olive Bradley is a woman in her early twenties, tall, slender, her shoulders stooping a trifle. An abundance of pale blond hair frames a face [which must have once been almost beautiful]* with delicate, finely-drawn features. [Now, however, it suffers from her] Her expression is one of jaded joylessness hardened by an obstinate pride—[too defiant to acknowledge its own weariness even to itself.] Her blue eyes are large and intelligent, her mouth firm-lipped and resolute. She is dressed [somberly but] with a faultless taste which has the hint of having seen better days about it.

Lester Bradley is a man of fifty-five rather under the medium height, has figure inclined to a dignified portliness. His face, small-featured but handsome, has an expression of disdainful well-bred superiority. His hair is dark, greying at the temples. [His manner is either one of portentous disdain or of an outer indifference.] He speaks dictatorially as if every word he uttered was absolutely the last which could be said on a subject. Only his grey eyes play false to his carefully cultivated imperturbability—they shift, and hide, and are afraid. His mouth, too, in unguarded moments, droops into weakness. He is dressed immaculately in a dark business suit and patent-leather shoes.

---

* Material in brackets was deleted by the dramatist.

O'Neill's second wife Agnes states that her husband conceived the idea for "Honor Among the Bradleys" shortly after they moved to West Point Pleasant, New Jersey on November 21, 1918, following an encounter he had, while taking an exploratory walk, with a poor family, the "town outcasts." The father, a red-faced man who never worked yet had money to drink, "was stretched on a hammock, a woman was hanging quilts on the line. There were three young girls all blond and beautiful and all pregnant." They were just three of the seven "innocent looking" daughters who mysteriously became pregnant. Agnes writes that her husband completed, revised, and typed the play and "was going over his script" when he was summoned to New York for rehearsals of *The Moon of the Caribbees*, scheduled to open December 20, 1918 (Agnes Boulton, *Part of a Long Story*, New York, 1958, p. 261). In the "List of All Plays" (Appendix B), O'Neill identifies "Honor Among the Bradleys" as a "one-act play written at West Point Pleasant, New Jersey" in 1919. He destroyed the manuscript of this comedy, which was never produced.

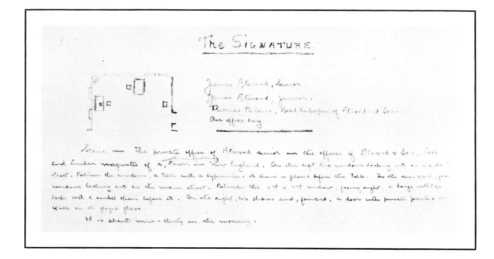

°THE SIGNATURE
[1918]*

James Atwood, Senior
James Atwood, Junior
Thomas Perkins, Head bookkeeper of Atwood and Son
An office boy

Scene—The private office of Atwood senior in the offices of Atwood & Son, Coal and Lumber magnates of a small manufacturing town in New England. On the left, two windows looking out on a side street. Between the windows, a table with a typewriter. A chair is placed before the table. In the rear wall, four windows looking out on the main street. Between the 2nd & 3rd window, facing right, a large rolltop desk with a swivel chair before it. On the right, two chairs and, forward, a door with private printed in black on its glazed glass.

It is about nine-thirty in the morning.

One-act play†

---

*O'Neill recorded this idea in late November or in December 1918. During this period he was experiencing financial problems and was disturbed by the notices, requesting payment for an old debt, that his wife Agnes received from Arthur Jones, who threatened to put the matter in the hands of a lawyer. There is no evidence to indicate the dramatist developed this idea.

†The paragraph that follows was entered later in the notebook after "The Little Things," a "play of a married couple's life together."

The Signature—poor simple clerk—old—remarkable penman—is given check to fill out—can't resist temptation—fills in own name—starts bank account at other bank—writes out all checks to firm—Is called in to explain—tells of life—no friends, relatives—no one to write to—never had chance to make his glorious signature stand for anything—etc.

°THE TRUMPET*
[1918–1919]†

Characters

The Deaf Librarian
The Dumb Towncrier—Hank
The Blind Beach-Cleaner—Gid—(Gideon)
Sammy—assistant to the D.T. & B.-C.
Two Ladies

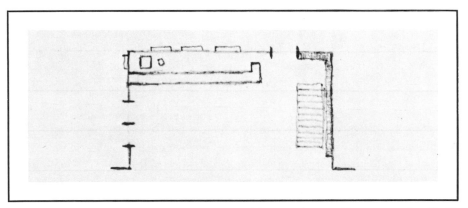

Scene—The office room in the public library of a small town on the N. E. sea-coast. On the left, forward, are the double doors, with storm doors outside

---

*O'Neill considered two other titles, which he subsequently discarded, for this idea: "Merry Christmas" and "The Deaf, the Dumb and the Blind."
†The play's first title, "Merry Christmas," and its December 26th setting suggest the possibility that O'Neill developed this idea in late 1918 or in early 1919 when he returned to West Point Pleasant after the opening of *The Moon of the Caribbees* in New York on December 20, 1918. Barrett Clark identifies "The Trumpet" as a one-act comedy written in 1919 (*Eugene O'Neill*, New York, 1926, p. 40). O'Neill, however, does not include this one-acter in his "list of all plays ever written by me." If the dramatist did complete "The Trumpet," he considered it such an inferior effort that he destroyed all notes and drafts of it.

them, of the main entrance. In the rear, exending two-thirds of the distance from left to right, is the librarian's counter. Behind it, her table desk with card indexes on it, and a chair. Four windows, one to the left, three in the rear of counter let in a flood of the early afternoon sunshine of a cold 26th of December. To the right of the counter, a doorway. The remaining space in the rear is occupied by book shelves, as is also the entire lower wall on the right. In front of these shelves, a staircase facing front leading to the reading room on the second floor.

In the rear, above the windows, a sign is hung giving notice in large letters that: "Talking in loud tones is forbidden."

The Librarian is a slight little woman about 38 with a small, homely face; dark brown hair faintly tinged with grey; a hesitating, wistful smile; eager hazel eyes, anxious to please but continually clouded with a dreaded perplexity, due to her self-consciousness about affliction. Her voice is soft and gentle. She wears a simple, dark dress.

The Town Crier is a tall stout man in the fifties with a fat, red face glowing with good health. His features are slovenly and ugly but redeemed by a pair of twinkling blue eyes, small and round, alive with a good-natured, if childish, humor. His hands are volubly conversational. The fact that no one understands this finger language does not disturb him in the least. A monologue satisfies him. He is dressed in a dark overcoat which age has faded to green, the collar turned up about his ears. A disreputable cap covers his bald spot and the fringe of grey hair which still survives. His trousers are spotted and baggy; his shoes patched and muddy.

The Beach-cleaner is a round-shouldered, scrawny individual about the same age as his friend. His face is thin with a lean hooked nose overleaning a thick-lipped mouth. His expression is sly and cunning and incorrigibly shiftless. Alone with his crony, he is full of malicious chuckles and crackling humor; but, feeling himself under observation, he assumes a hypocritical sadness, a dignified resignation such as he thinks befits his affliction. Dark spectacles cover his sightless eyes. He wears an old stained yellow hunting jacket, lined with fleece—evidently a gift of charity—dirty corduroy trousers, a peaked cap of the same material with earcaps, and goloshes.

Sammy is a boy of twelve, red cheeked and stout, primed with annoying activity. As assistant to the T[own]. C[rier]. and the B[each]. C[leaner]., he recognizes himself as a decided factor in the life of the community and his manner is correspondingly superior and assertive. When he forgets his station in life for a moment, he is just a rollicking, healthy boy with a nice, engaging smile.

The Two Ladies are just that. They are both middle-age. From style of their clothes it is evident they are not native daughters but have transplanted themselves hither from the city. There is enough unconventionality in their apparel to indicate the itch for art in some manifestation. They might be painters who look at pictures or writers who read books.

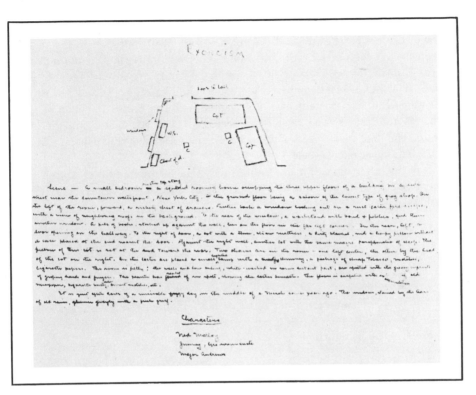

°EXORCISM
(1919)

Characters

Ned Malloy
Jimmy, his roommate
Major Andrews

Scene—A small bedroom on the top story [of] a squalid rooming house oc-
cupying the three upper floors of a building on a side street near the downtown
waterfront, New York City—the ground floor being a saloon of the lowest type
of grog shop. On the left of the room, forward, a rickety chest of drawers. Farther
back a window looking out on a rust-eaten fire escape, with a view of neighboring
roofs in the background. To the rear of the window, a washstand with bowl &
pitcher, and then another window. A pile of books, stacked up against the wall,
lies on the floor in the far left corner. In the rear, left, a door opening on the
hallway. To the right of door, a cot with a thin, straw mattress, a dirty blanket,
and a lumpy pillow without a case placed at the end nearest the door. Against

the right wall, another cot with the same meagre paraphernalia of sleep. The pillow of this cot is set at the end toward the rear. Two chairs are in the room— one left center, the other by the head of the cot on the right. On this latter are placed a small lighted lamp with a smudged chimney, a package of cheap tobacco, matches, cigarette papers. The room is filthy; the walls and low ceiling, white-washed in some distant past, are spotted with the greasy imprints of grop- ing hands and fingers. The plaster has scaled of[f] in spots, showing the lathes beneath. The floor is carpeted with an accumulation of old newspapers, cigarette butts, ashes, burnt matches, etc.

It is just after dark of a miserable foggy day in the middle of March some years ago. The windows, stained by the tears of old rains, glimmer grayly with a fresh grief.*

[THE STRAW]
(1918–1919)

The Matter of a Pound or the Laughing Sailor†

Scene—The Sanatorium

Characters

The Doctor
The Assistant

---

*The dramatist apparently conceived the idea for "Exorcism," an autobiographical account of his 1912 attempt to commit suicide at Jimmy the Priest's, in early 1919 when he resumed work on "Chris Christopherson," a play depicting his former drink- ing companions at this barroom. The author indicates in the "List of All Plays" that he wrote this one-act play in 1919 while living in a rented house in Provincetown and in the "Cycles" (Appendix A) that he completed it that year before his birthday, October 16. His wife Agnes states that her husband "was working out an idea for a play" prior to the couple's move on September 10, 1919 from their seaside home, Peaked Hill, to a rented cottage in Provincetown. The one-act comedy was produced at the Provincetown Playhouse in New York on March 27, 1920. It was never pub- lished as O'Neill ordered the destruction of all existing scripts. Alexander Woollcott's review of April 4, 1920 in the *New York Times* provides some information about the plot. The suicide attempt of Ned Malloy, a self-portrait, is thwarted when two drunken friends yank "him back from the brink of the grave." He has, in effect, killed his despairing self; for the "person revived is a new person, the life ahead is life in a new world."

†The author probably made this entry, which reflects his earliest concept of *The Straw*, in January 1919 when he was working on the first draft of the play. The idea

Characters (*continued*)

The Head Nurse
Visitor from the South of the County
Eugene Murray, a patient
Norah O'Brien, a patient

O'Neill erased all the notes he made for this play on two pages of the note-book. Only material that can be deciphered with certitude is included here. These are the earliest recorded notes for *The Straw*, an autobiographical play based on the dramatist's experiences at Gaylord Farm Sanatorium where he was treated for tuberculosis.* By calling the character who represents him "Eugene" in the notes, the author contradicts his statement that the autobiographical aspects of the play were unintentional. The prototype for Norah O'Brien, whose name is changed later to Eileen Carmody, is Kitty MacKay, a patient who fell in love with the young O'Neill. The name "Nora" is assigned to one of Eileen's sisters in the published text. Only six characters appear here in contrast to the twenty—plus other patients of the sanatorium—in the final version. In the published version the first scene is set in the Carmody home in late February while in the early notes it opens in "a room of the main building of a sanatorium for cure of tuberculosis on a sunlight morning on a day in Spring." As he does in other early ideas for plays, O'Neill lists the order in which his characters appear in this scene:

Sanatorium
      //   Patients
      //   //   Eugene & Norah
      //   Eugene & Norah

---

for this drama came to him, as Agnes Boulton recalls, in early summer 1918 while he was reminiscing about the period he spent at a sanatorium and "the girl there whom he had almost forgotten." The dramatist did not finish the first version of *The Straw* before leaving Provincetown in November 1918, as he indicates in the "List of All Plays," but in January 1919 after moving to West Point Pleasant. He then wrote "Chris Christopherson" before starting the revised version of *The Straw*, which he completed before he left New Jersey in May 1919.

*He read Strindberg and decided to become a playwright during this period of con-finement, seemingly ordained by fate. In a letter to Lee Simonson in early 1938, O'Neill states: "The Docs now tell me that X-rays show no evidence whatever of my ever having T.B.!"

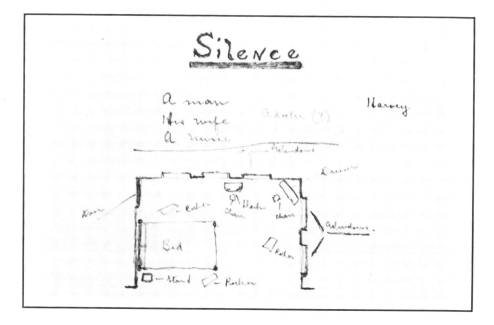

°SILENCE
[1919]

A man   Harvey
    A doctor (?)
His wife
A nurse

One-act play

Silence—Man who has gone from Scotland to Africa to make fortune for girl he loves—alone in silence of wilderness for five years—comes back comparatively rich—marries girl—buys house in town—but can't stand noise—practically gives away house to get away from city—buys house in country to get quiet—far away from everything—wears felt slippers, etc.—gradually comes to hate wife for noise she makes washing dishes, sweeping, etc. They have child—can't endure child's crying—goes to see Doc.—on verge of nervous breakdown—has fight with wife on account of some noise—tells her he is going back to wilderness—packs bag—she breaks down when she sees he is in earnest—implores him to stay—finally he gives in, his past love for her still strong. They kiss and are reconciled. He puts down bag. Then kid starts bawling in the next room. She hustles out to it and, forgetting, slams the door with a bang behind her. Husband shudders—looks after her with reawakened hate—picks up bag, tiptoes softly to outside door, opens it quietly and goes out shutting door silently behind him.*

SHELL SHOCK†
(1918)

Jack Arnold
Herb. Roylston
Bobby Wayne

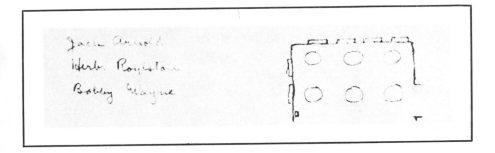

Scene—A corner in the grill of the New York club of a large Eastern University. Six tables with chairs placed about them are set at regular intervals in

---

*Two entries for "Silence" appear in the notebook. The first, encompassing the dramatis personae and set design, was probably made in early 1919. The stated idea for the one-act play, the second entry, which follows "The Little Things," a marital play, and "The Signature," was apparently written in spring 1919 when O'Neill discovered his wife was pregnant and feared a child would create additional confusion and tension in his household. "Silence" reflects the author's frustration as he attempts to cope with the noisy environment of his wife's West Point Pleasant house: the menagerie of cats and dogs, the stoves that had to be shaken down daily, the windmill that started with "a clank, a rattling groan, a whirring." Agnes describes a quarrel that erupted when her husband, who was unable to work at that time, suggested that she write. She responds: "I thought this whole plan, being alone here and everything else—your goddamn solitude—was so *you* could work!" After this outburst, O'Neill, like his hero in "Silence," walked to the front door and left the house (*Part of a Long Story*, p. 255). It is doubtful that O'Neill ever completed this play. No information—other than the material recorded in the notebook—exists.

†O'Neill lists two alternate, but canceled, titles: "Butts" and "A Smoke." This idea predates all previous entries in the notebook. *Shell Shock*—whose hero, Jack Arnold, a self-portrait, believes, mistakenly, that his "great chum" died in battle—was written after O'Neill moved from New York to Provincetown, following the tragic death of

two rows of three from left to right. In the left wall, three windows looking out
on a side street. In the rear, four windows opening on an avenue. On the right,
forward, the main entrance to the grill.

It is the middle of the afternoon of a hot day in September, 1918. Through
the open windows, the white curtains of which hang motionless, unstirred by the
faintest breeze, a sultry vapor of dust-clogged sunlight can be seen steaming over
the sticky asphalt. Here, in the grill, it is cool. The drowsy humming of an electric
fan on the left wall forms an audible background of silence. A bored, middle-
aged waiter stands leaning wearily against the wall, between the tables in the rear,
gaping and staring listlessly out at the avenue. Ever[y] now and then he casts an
indifferent glance at the only other occupant of the room, a young man of about
thirty dressed in the uniform of a Captain in the Red Cross* who is sitting at the
middle table, front, sipping a glass of iced coffee and reading a newspaper. The
Captain is under medium height, slight and wiry, with a thin, pale face, light
brown hair and mustache, and grey, eager eyes peering keenly through tortoise-
rimmed spectacles.

FF
°CHRIS CHRISTOPHERSEN

Characters

Chris. Christoffersen
Anna,† his daughter
Johnny the Priest
Larry, bartender
Martin O'Brien† ⎫
Captain Hall   ⎬ of
First mate   ⎪ the
Steward   ⎭ ship

Chris Christopherson.—bo'sun—captain of barge—
Linda, his daughter.
Danny Mahon, second mate of the Belfast tramp
    Londonderry.

---

his friend Louis Holladay on January 22, 1918. The "List of All Plays" indicates that
the author completed the one-acter before beginning *The Rope*, which bears the date
"3/1/18" on its final page. Apparently forgetting the original title assigned *Shell
Shock*, he calls it "At Jesus' Feet" in the list. A typescript of it, which O'Neill sent
to the Library of Congress, is extant. Its copyright date is May 5, 1918. *Shell Shock*
was never produced, nor was it published until its inclusion in the 1972 collection of
early plays, *Children of the Sea*, edited by Jennifer McCabe Atkinson.
*Bobby Wayne emerges in the finished draft as "Robert Wayne," an officer in the
Medical Corps." Arnold is a "Major of Infantry, U.S.A." and Roylston a "Lieutenant
of Infantry, U.S.A."
†The name "Anna" is written over "Linda" and "Martin O'Brien" over "Danny
Mahon."

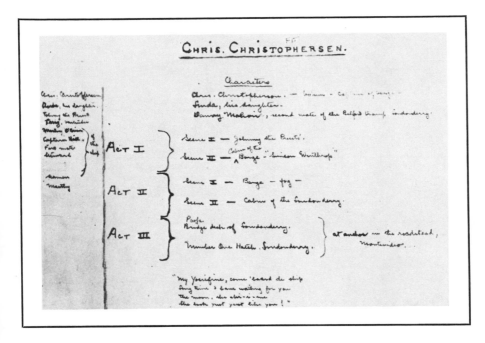

seamen
Marthy

ACT I
: Scene I—Johnny the Priest's.
: Scene II—Cabin of the Barge—"Simeon Winthrop"

ACT II
: Scene I—Barge—fog—
: Scene II—Cabin of the Londonderry

ACT III
: Poop
: Bridge deck of Londonderry
: Number One Hatch, Londonderry
: at anchor in the roadstead, Montevideo.

"My Yossifine, come 'board de ship
Long time I bane waiting for you
The Moon, she shi-i-ine
She look yust yust like you!"

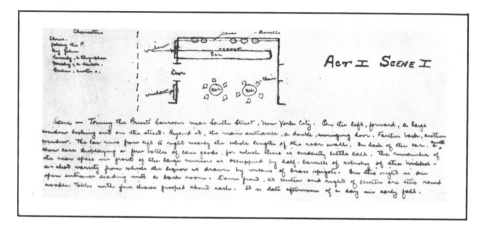

Characters

Chris.
Johnny the P.
Big John
Kennedy, a telegrapher
Mickey, a sailor.
Devlin, another s[ailor].

ACT I SCENE I

Scene—Tommy the Priest's barroom near South Street, New York City. On the left, forward, a large window looking out on the street. Beyond it, the main entrance, a double swinging door. Farther back, another window. The bar runs from left to right nearly the whole length of the rear wall. In back of the bar, a small show case displaying a few bottles of case goods, for which there is evidently little call. The remainder of the rear space in front of the large mirrors is occupied by half-barrels of whiskey of the nickel-a-shot variety from which the liquor is drawn by means of brass spigots. On the right is an open entrance leading into a back room. Down front, at center and right of center, are two round wooden tables with five chairs grouped about each. It is late afternoon of a day in early fall.

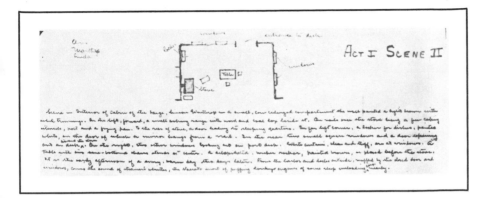

Chris
Marthy   ACT I SCENE II
Linda

Scene—Interior of cabin of the barge, Simeon Winthrop—a small, low-ceilinged compartment, the walls painted a light brown with white trimmings. On the left, forward, a small cooking range with wood and coal box beside it. On nails over the stove hang a few cooking utensils, pots and a frying pan. To the rear of stove, a door leading to sleeping quarters. In far left corner, a locker for dishes, painted white, on the door of which a mirror hangs from a nail. In the rear two small square windows and a door opening out on deck toward the stern. On the right, two other windows looking out on port deck. White curtains, clean and stiff, are at windows. A table with two cane-bottomed chairs stands at center. A dilapidated, wicker rocker, painted brown, is placed before the stove. It is the early afternoon of a sunny, warm day two days later. From the harbor and docks outside, muffled by the closed door and windows, comes the sound of steamers' whistles, the staccato snort of puffing donkey engines of some ship unloading cargo nearby.

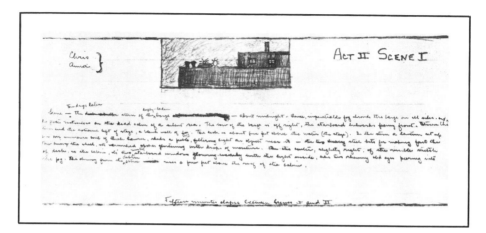

Chris   ACT II SCENE I
Anna

Scene—Ten days later—The stern of the deeply-laden barge—about midnight—Dense, impenetrable fog shrouds the barge on all sides and she floats motionless on the dead calm of a silent sea. The bow of the barge is off right, the starboard bulwarks facing front. Between the stern and the extreme left of stage, a blank wall of fog. The deck is about five feet above the water (the stage). In the stern a lantern set up on an immense coil of thick hawser, sheds a feeble, filtering light on objects near it—the two heavy steel bits for making fast the tow line—the wheel, its varnished spokes glistening with drops of moisture. In the center, slightly right, of the visible stretch of deck, is the cabin, its two misty starboard windows glowing with the light inside, like two rheumy old eyes peering into the fog. The chimney from the cabin stove rises a few feet above the roof of the cabin.

Fifteen minutes elapse between Scenes I and II

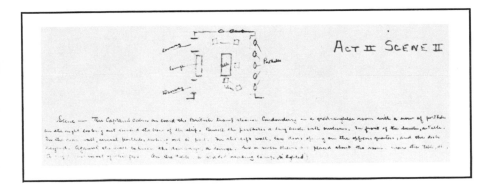

ACT II SCENE II

Scene—The Captain's cabin on board the British tramp steamer Londonderry—a quadrangular room with a row of portholes on the right looking out toward the bow of the ship. Beneath the portholes a long bench with cushions. In front of the bench, a table. In the rear wall, several portholes looking out to port. In the left wall, two doors opening on the officers' quarters, and the deck beyond. Against the wall between the doorways, a lounge. Six or seven chairs are placed about the room, near the table, etc. A rug covers most of the floor. On the table, a shaded reading lamp is lighted.

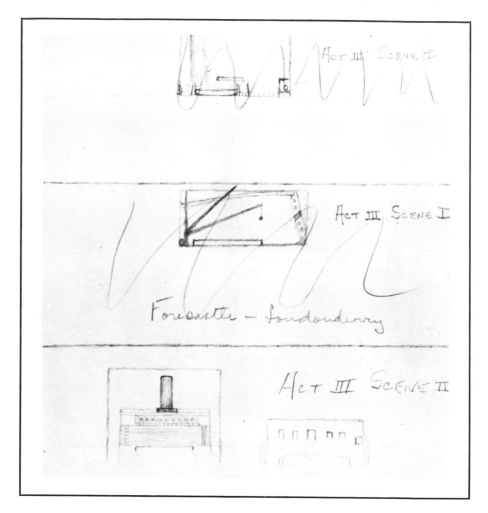

CHRIS CHRISTOPHERSON
(1918–1919) *

O'Neill began making notes and an outline for "Chris Christopherson" in summer 1918. Finding himself "stumped," he put aside the play and wrote *Where the Cross Is Made* and the first version of *The Straw*, which he finished in January 1919. He then took up "Chris Christopherson" again and completed the first draft in spring 1919. Even though he made extensive revisions that summer, as George Tyler, the producer, suggested, the play failed when it opened the following March in Atlantic City. The dramatist notes in the "List of All Plays" that he wrote a new four-act version of "Chris Christopherson" when he returned to Peaked Hill in summer in 1920, renaming it first "The Ole Davil" and then *Anna Christie* for the 1921 production.

The change of title—from "Chris Christopherson" to *Anna Christie*—seems to symbolize a dramatic shift in focus. Chris, the central figure in the early version, tries to prevent his demure, innocent daughter Linda, or Anna as she is later named, from marrying a man bound to the sea. The father-daughter clash is only a minor theme in *Anna Christie*. In this version Anna, depicted now as a prostitute, is the main character. Like Jim Tyrone in *A Moon for the Misbegotten*, she is an alcoholic, drinking to forget the gray dawns and dissipation of the past yet yearning to find moral regeneration and peace. Her major conflict is with herself when she falls in love but deems herself unworthy of her lover, Mat Burke, who in the first version is named Martin O'Brien, Danny Mahon, and, finally, Paul Anderson.

As depicted in "Chris Christopherson," the lovers are totally imaginary, lifeless figures, so weakly conceived that this production was doomed from the beginning. Even the mild-tempered, lovable Chris becomes a melodramatic caricature when he is abruptly transformed at the end of the play into an insanely jealous would-be murderer. The portrait of Chris in *Anna Christie* is credible and approximates the real-life figure O'Neill used as a model. The other characters in "Chris Christopherson" who reappear in *Anna Christie* are portrayed

---

*The set designs for "Chris Christopherson" follow the notebook entry for *Shell Shock*, which was written in early 1918. Information cited in this discussion of "Chris Christopherson" is taken from the original handwritten manuscript, dated "winter/ spring 1919," which is among the O'Neill holdings at Yale and totals ninety-four pages when transcribed and typed. O'Neill expressed a desire to write this play during the week he spent in New York after *The Rope* opened on April 26, 1918. He reminisced about his loyal friends, his drinking companions in that city, and told his wife Agnes that "he had an idea now for a new play." While in New York, he had a conversation with Joe Smith, whose story about a gangster inspired the dramatist to write *The Dreamy Kid* when he returned to Provincetown in May. After completing this one-acter, he outlined "Chris Christopherson."

exactly as the author originally conceives them. From the beginning, they were instilled with life, based as they were on actual people the author had known well—old friends from his 1911–1912 drinking days in New York. Agnes Boulton, O'Neill's wife at the time the play was written and revised, maintains that the atmosphere and the odd characters at Jimmy the Priest's were an obsession with him. She observes: "Old Chris—how real *he* was! It was Chris that Gene really knew and loved, and old Marthy too—and the bums and outcasts in the first act down at Johnny the Priest's saloon on South Street in lower New York; the longshoremen, even the mailman."[*]

The dramatist wrote three autobiographical works in 1919: *The Straw,* "Chris Christopherson," and "Exorcism." A number of characters in the latter plays reappear twenty years later in *The Iceman Cometh.* After this 1939 work he wrote a series of dramas that were, in essence, obituaries—for his parents and brother, for Hughie, and others who had died. Similarly, many of the early plays are tributes—epitaphs—to recently deceased friends he had known at Jimmy the Priest's: Driscoll and Jimmy Byth, who both committed suicide, and Chris Christopherson, who either drowned in, or died on the frozen ice of New York harbor as he was returning to his barge after a drunken spree on shore.

"Chris Christopherson" not only anticipates the atmosphere and characters of *The Iceman Cometh* but also re-creates some of the seamen from the Glencairn Cycle and a situation presented in one of these plays, *The Long Voyage Home.* In the first version of the opening scene of "Chris Christopherson," two sailors, Devlin and Mickey,[†] join those drinking at Johnny the Priest's. Mickey is described as "middle-aged, squat, and round-shouldered, monkey-like in the disproportionate length of arms and legs. His pock-marked face, weather-tanned, has a broken nose twisted askew which gives him the grotestque expression of a contortionist when he grins." His counterpart, Mike Driscoll in the Glencairn plays, is "a brawny Irishman with the battered features of a prizefighter"; depicted as Yank in *The Hairy Ape,* he is described as having a "gorilla face." Understandably, Mickey recognizes Chris in the barroom scene as an old sailing mate; the Swede is actually Ollie Olson of the Glencairn plays and portrayed in them as "a stocky middle-aged Swede with a drooping blond mustache and round, childish blue eyes." Here, as Chris, he is "a short, squat, broad-shouldered man of about fifty with a round, red face and a drooping yellow mustache, his mouth childishly self-willed." Both Olson and Chris express the same dislike for the sea and utter similar statements: the former says: "Yust work, work, work on ship"; one of Chris's last lines in the play is: "Yust work, work, work all time." When Mickey and Devlin discover Chris is the captain of a coal barge, they vehemently

---

[*]*Part of a Long Story,* p. 279.
[†]O'Neill probably intended to depict this character in another play in the Jimmy the Priest series: "The Ruin of Mickey."

urge him to sign up with them on "a beautiful hooker that'll take us flying south through the Trades," reminiscent of the attempt made by the sailors in the bar-room in *The Long Voyage Home* to get Olson to ship out with them again. It is not friendship that forces the two Swedish characters to return to sea but betrayal by a woman: Freda in *The Long Voyage Home* and Linda-Anna in "Chris Christopherson."

In the latter play's first draft, the captain of the Londonderry is named Jessup and his First Mate is called Hall. They, two other seamen—Jonesy and Edwards—who are added for the forecastle scene, and the steward Glass are characterized in terms similar to those used to describe the sailors of the Glencairn Cycle and *Ile*. The other characters, the regulars of the barroom, are depicted in the early notes and draft as they would be later in *Anna Christie*. In the first version, however, Chris's dialect is "a queer mixture of English with a Swedish accent, colored by expressions—and curses—picked up in years of intercourse with cosmopolitans before-the-mast patois of ships flying the flags of various nations"; and Marthy "speaks in a coarse, mannish voice. Her big mouth is thick-lipped and droops laxly. Some of her teeth are missing."

The names of two other habitués of the barroom, Big John and Kennedy, are changed in the first draft of the play to Jack Burns and Mr. Adams. While omitted from *Anna Christie*, they will reappear twenty years later in *The Iceman Cometh*. The middle-aged, bull-necked, squat, aggressive Jack Burns, who tries to bum drinks from others, is the counterpart of the bullet-headed, jowly Pat McGloin, a man in his fifties, who has what Harry Hope calls an "I'll-have-the-same" look on his map. Hope is named Tom in the early notes for *Iceman* just as Johnny the Priest is at times called Tommy-the-Priest in the first draft of "Chris Christopherson." Agnes Boulton is incorrect in her assumption that Adams, simply because he is a salesman, is an early glimpse of Hickey. The two men are totally unlike in physical appearance, mannerisms, and personality. The character *is* depicted in *Iceman* but as Willie Oban, who is again called Adams in the first notes and draft of the 1939 play and whose real-life prototype is the son[*] of "Al" Adams, the notorious "policy King" and "King of the Bucket Shops."

The age of Adams in 1919 approximates that of the 1912 Adams-Oban character seven years later. The Adams of "Chris Christopherson" is, in some ways, similar in appearance to Adams-Oban but is more dissipated—bloated and bleary-eyed—ill-kempt and grimy. When first seen in both plays, the Adams character is

---

[*]Adams is probably modeled on the second son of the "policy king," Louis, who was imprisoned on Blackwell's Island for attempting to shoot his father. A *New York Times* article ("Island for 'Al' Adams's Son," November 5, 1904, p. 7) states that as he boarded the police boat, Louis held a conversation with "the mate of the steamer, Michael J. Burke, a friend of many years." If Louis Adams was, as depicted, a regular at Jimmy the Priest's, it is highly possible that O'Neill knew him and Burke, whose name is used for the sailor-lover in *Anna Christie*.

sitting in the same position—asleep with his head resting on his arm. The 1919 Adams insists: "I'm a gentleman. Everyone knows." In his first speech, Adams-Oban boasts that his presence provides "the atmosphere of culture here." He relates the story of his father to illustrate the fact that he was "born in the purple" and concludes by saying: "Everyone in the world knows." Both characters are threatened with expulsion from the barroom for annoying customers: Tommy commands Adams to "go upstairs and do a flop" because he drinks and talks too much; Tom-Harry Hope tells Rocky to give Adams-Oban "the bum's rush upstairs" because he noisily sings an obscene sailor song. Both men resist eviction, promise to behave, and beg to be allowed to remain downstairs with their friends.

In his notes for "Chris Christopherson," O'Neill made few corrections in the descriptions of his former friends at Jimmy the Priest's; he had only to evoke his memories to characterize them. In contrast, the passage describing Chris's daughter is nearly indecipherable. Drawn totally from the author's imagination, Anna is a static and lifeless character, a golden-haired goddess of physical perfection but totally devoid of human emotions.

Anna is a tall, blond, fully developed girl of twenty, built on a statuesque, beautifully-moulded plan—a subject for a sculptor with the surprising size of her figure so merged into harmonious lines of graceful strength and youth as to pass unnoticed. There is something, too, of the statue in the profile of the perfect model of her face (with a dream of wistful, romantic desire, wholly unconscious of itself). But her expression is alert, mobile, intelligent. Her wide blue eyes betray anything of the dreamer. They shine with an eager, wistful light. Her smile is a trace of her father's good-nature, only in her detached, induced by a feeling of confident self-sufficiency. She has her father's strong jaw, also, but toned down from obstinacy to strength. She is dressed simply in a blue tailor-made suit. She speaks slowly with an English accent, her voice low, distinct and clear-toned. There is about her whole personality something inhuman and suggestive.

O'Neill had a clear concept of Anna's lover in the earliest notes only when he was depicted as being an Irishman:

Danny Mahon is a tall, broad-shouldered young officer of twenty-five, his strong, active figure lithe and graceful. His hair is black and curly; his face sun-bronzed; his eyes dark and handsome, merry with a reckless good-nature; the white teeth of his self-indulgent, sensual mouth flashing in a smile tantalizing in its self-assurance. His laugh is rollicking, devil-may-care and infectious. He is handsome, and the women of the kind he has met love him, and he knows these things and is full of self-confident pride thereat. He is second mate and well content with himself and the future. Life in general, and the life of the sea in particular, seems fine to him, and he is careless of what may happen, feeling that for him everything that comes must bring an adventure, as is his due. For the rest he is fearless, quick-witted and intelligent enough, uneducated since his fourteenth year save in the rough school of the Seven Seas.

No corrections are made in this description but a wavy line through the section indicates the dramatist discarded it. Possibly this virile character could have brought the cold Galatea and their relationship to life had O'Neill not changed him from an Irishman to a second generation American Swede from Minnesota and tried to impose some of his own biographical background on this new character. What emerged was a smug unfamiliar type who aroused neither the dramatist's nor the audience's understanding and sympathy. Contrary to this usual practice, O'Neill does not describe this revised character until he is actually introduced at exactly mid-point in the play:

Paul Anderson is a tall, broad-shouldered handsome blond young fellow of about twenty-five with a clear-cut, strong-featured face marred by a self-indulgent mouth continually set in a lax smile of lazy good humor. His blue eyes, large and intelligent, have an absent-minded expression as if his thoughts were constantly turned inward into some dream world of his own. His low deep voice drawls a little as he speaks. He is dressed in the simple blue uniform of a Second Mate.

While this character was once an ordinary sailor before his rise to Second Mate, and there is a seaman named Paul in three of the Glencairn plays, Anderson is not modeled on the cycle character, who is a stocky accordion player.

While the dramatist had considerable difficulties plotting the second half of the play—after the lovers meet—he had no problems with the first scene, which begins with a barroom dispute between Jack Burns and Mr. Adams. The dialogue, characters, and action of the first draft of this scene—from the entry of the two longshoremen to the entrance of Chris and departure of the proprietor—is transferred intact to *Anna Christie*. Neither Marthy nor Chris's daughter, however, appears in the scene. A letter from the latter, announcinng her arrival from England in two days time, starts old Chris off on a joyous binge, supposedly his last before sobering up permanently. Mickey and Devlin join him to celebrate their return from a long sea voyage. Another, more serious, argument then erupts between the sailors and Chris who, as a barge captain, is accused of betraying the sea. The old man defensively explains why he hates "dat old Davil" sea, how it brought such sorrow and death to his family. The sailors are touched by the man's sincerity and misfortunes and admit: "It's a dog's life anyway." The curtain closes with Chris buying drinks for everyone and happily singing "My Yosephine."

The second scene opens in the cabin of the barge with Chris nervously awaiting his daughter's arrival and trying to devise a scheme to get Marthy off the barge without hurting her feelings. Like the characters in the first scene, Marthy has a deep affection for Chris. Understanding his nature and "knowing the signs in a man," she had packed her "duds noon yesterday." By the time Chris explains the situation, Anna arrives and the quick-witted Marthy pretends to be a saleswoman to avoid scandalizing the prim daughter. Anna is shocked at the word "hell," drinks tea rather than whiskey, and comes from England equipped with an apron which she fastidiously dons before making lunch for her father. She informs him she was not a mere "nurse gel" but "really more of a governess," teaching the children and sharing the family's library. She was entrusted to cousins when her mother died; but they were "so religious and strict, prayers morning and evening" she leaves, gets a job as a typist, and is content for a time. "The thing which jerked me out of the rut was that my employer—the barrister—a man of forty with a wife and children, fancy!—suddenly took it into his head to make love to me."

Anna informs Chris she plans to get a job immediately to earn money for college: "I want to get away from being just a woman—to live a man's life. I won't grow stale—and womanly. I won't." Unfortunately, the character's desire is fulfilled. O'Neill's early concept of Anna, a flawless creature physically and morally, makes her a doll figure rather than a realistic flesh-and-blood woman. Agnes Boulton states that as her husband struggled throughout the winter and spring of 1919 trying to breathe life into his heroine

> Anna seemed very aloof from us . . . though Gene did his best to make her speeches sound convincing, as he read them aloud. I used to secretly wonder how old Chris had ever come to have such a daughter. She didn't like herself either, it seems, and even then was secretly rebelling and a year or so later became a prostitute*

Chris's attitude to his daughter is tender, loving, solicitous. He wants to provide for her and persuades her to postpone getting a job to make one trip to Boston on the barge. "It'll be a lark," she says as she sets out to give her father speech lessons to improve his English. Chris, ecstatic in his daughter's presence, views her efforts with amusement and responds with a happy rendition of "My Yosephine."

The major difference between the opening scenes of Act II in the first draft of "Chris Christopherson" and *Anna Christie* is that the barge is safely at anchor in the latter but is rounding Cape Cod and heading for Boston in dangerous fog in the former. In both versions, the fog is dense and threatening, but Anna gazes in wonder at it, having fallen completely under the spell of the sea. Chris tries in vain to warn her about "dat ole davil" and tells her of the many wrongs the sea has inflicted upon their family, emphasizing the suffering the women endured. In the early version, the sea does not cast forth her lover; rather Anna and her father become outcasts upon it after an accident. The tow line connecting the barge with another in the coal convoy breaks, setting them adrift in the track of a steamer. The warning horn is also broken, and no signal can be given to ward off impending disaster. Chris's only concern is the safety of his daughter. Just before the Londonderry hits the barge, father and daughter manage to escape in a small

---

*Part of a Long Story, p. 278.

rowboat and are rescued by the crew of the steamer and taken, in the second scene of Act II, to Captain Jessup's cabin, where Anna and the Second Mate, Paul Anderson, meet.

The barge is not the only casualty that evening; its captain becomes one, too. It is not the loss of the barge that shatters Chris but the thought that he might lose his daughter to the dashing Second Mate. It is at this point that the characterization of Chris falters. In the first half of the play Chris is presented as a warm, jolly, lovable person—perhaps a perfect re-creation of the drinking, singing companion O'Neill knew so well. This totally human, believable character disappears and is replaced in the second half of the play by a jealous, suspicious, irrational maniac capable of murder. During the inquiry to investigate the cause and consequences of the accident, the Captain informs Chris he must work as an ordinary sailor to pay for his and Anna's passage to Buenos Aires and be quartered with the other seamen in the forecastle. To maintain discipline, the Captain says he may have only a brief visit each evening with his daughter. The Second Mate offers to vacate his cabin for Anna, whom he obviously finds attractive. Looking as though he were being led to the guillotine, Chris is escorted from the Captain's cabin; he pauses for a last anxious glance at his daughter who, with great composure, regally sits sipping coffee Anderson has brought to her. She reprimands the Captain in her proper English accent for "coming so fast through the fog" and demonstrates she is not, as he first feared, a "drunken slut of a barge woman." He goes to the bridge to smoke a cigar, warning Anderson: "No monkey business." Anna is delighted at the prospect of spending a month at sea and tells Anderson she feels as though she has come "home—after being away for a long time—nothing could ever be the same again—nothing you'd been through before counted any more." Anderson says that now after three years at sea he has the same feeling, one of total freedom:

No ties, no responsibilities—no guilty feeling, like the sea—always moving, never staying, never held by anything—never giving a damn—making the world part of you, not being a grain of sand carried, buried and lost and held back by other grains. Not American, Swede—but citizen of the sea which belongs to no one. Not a wife, marriage, an anchor but women of all lands and races—Woman! You might convert me.

Just as Anderson takes a surprised Anna in his arms and kisses her, Chris enters and in a long speech warns his daughter about "dat old davil's tricks." No happy song concludes this scene—only an angry tirade; Chris shakes "his fist at the sea, saying with helpless rage, 'dirty ole davil!' "

A month elapses between the second and third act, and the Londonderry has just anchored in Buenos Aires. The third act opens in the seaman's forecastle. Two young sailors, Edwards and Jonesy, warn Chris he is likely to acquire a son-in-law the next day when they all go ashore. The malicious mess room steward, Glass, a lover of practical jokes, enters and says he wants to talk to the gullible

Chris "man to man" about what is doing on between Anna and Anderson, whom he describes as a gambler, drinker, and womanizer, a man who "leaves broken-hearted girls behind in every port." Saying he is glad he doesn't "have a decent daughter to worry about," Glass lies and tells Chris Anna has accepted Anderson's proposal; they will be married the next day. Goaded to murderous anger, Chris exclaims: "Ay swear Ay kill him first." The scene closes as Chris takes out his sheath knife to sharpen it, muttering that there is only one way to save Anna from "dat ole davil's grip."

As he would with *Anna Christie*, O'Neill found it difficult to devise a suitable last scene for the play and revised it numerous times. In the earliest version, Chris, clutching his knife, hides in the shadows on the bridge deck and is just about to step forward to kill Anderson, who stands at the rail looking out at the sea, when Anna appears. Chris hears his daughter lash out at him: "that same silly idea of his—about the sea—the old devil, he calls her—which will swallow me up." Anderson says that Chris has

got enough of the old sea superstitions in his blood to make him believe in his ghosts. It's fear that's the matter with him. He's swallowed the anchor, as the sailors say. It means to lose your grip, to whine and blame something outside of yourself for your misfortunes, to quit and refuse to fight back any more, to shrink from further things and be content to anchor fast on the thing you are. I swallowed the anchor the day I became Second Mate. You have swallowed the anchor, too.

Anna finally admits she loves him but does not want to be the forgotten wife living on land alone. Anderson tells her of his plan to work hard to become Captain, for then she will be able to live on board with him when he sails. Only when Anna expresses her great happiness does Chris drop his knife, step forward, and, in the reconciliation scene, declare:

Ay'm too ole fallar for keep—young girl. So—Anna—you marry him. It's all right. (To Anderson with resentment) Ay don't swallow anchor. Ay'm ole fallar, but Ay bet you Ay fight dat ole davil till last end come, py yimmy! (He shakes his hand defiantly at the sea).

Striving to suggest a happier future for Chris, O'Neill wrote a new ending on April 11, 1919. In it, Captain Jessup asks Chris if he wants the berth of the ailing bo'sun who is to be hospitalized the next morning. In response, Chris

(looks all around him wildly as if he wanted to run and hide—then in a panic-stricken tone) "Yes, sir. Ay take yob." After the captain bids him "goodnight, bo'sun," Chris's face softens and he shakes his fist at the sea and says, "No man dat live goin' beat you, py yingo!" Once again the strain of "My Yosephine" is heard and the curtain falls as he grumbles cheerfully. "It's hard yob, bo'sun on dis rusty tea-kettle—yust work, work, work all time. Ay better turn in for sleep, yes."

When the play's producer, George Tyler, expressed his dissatisfaction with this revised ending, a new one was written and sent to him on June 17, 1919. This version contains no substantive changes. Early in the final scene when Chris is about to stab Anderson, Anna "flings herself between the two men." She informs Anderson she can never marry him, and, when Chris furiously attacks the man verbally, she exclaims: "You go too far, Father! Haven't I told you I wouldn't—Isn't that enough for you? Do you want everything? Oh, go away from me! I almost—hate you—now!" Anderson again tries to persuade Anna to marry him, promising she would not "have to settle down in a landman's way. We'll not leave the sea—you and I. The sea shall be our mother and the mother of our children. No, you will be beside me, with me, a part of me—always!" Chris stretches out his arms to his daughter, but she ignores him for Anderson's embrace. Chris's "head is bowed, a great sob shakes his shoulders." Again Anna heartlessly disregards her father's grief, lost to all but her love: "I was so sad Paul—I wanted to be dead—and now I'm so, so happy." In utter despair, Chris exclaims, "Ay might yust as well be dead" and "raises the knife above his breast." Anderson forces the knife out of Chris's hand. The revision then follows the scheme of the first draft: the reconciliation and the captain's offer to Chris, with the final curtain falling to the strains of "My Yosephine."

This new scheme, like earlier drafts of the ending, is melodramatic and lifeless; the characters and situation lack credibility. O'Neill worked on the play again that summer and was still making cuts and revisions before the premiere the following March in Atlantic City. The reviews were unfavorable, and while the play was given a warmer reception in Philadelphia, "Chris Christopherson" never opened, as planned, in New York. The dramatist spent the next summer writing a new draft of the play, changing its basic concept and emphasizing Anna's inner conflict and the relationship of the lovers rather than that of the father and daughter. Although he was still not satisfied with this latest draft, he sent the play to the Theatre Guild in early 1921, stating that he was willing to make changes in it. He received no response. In his letter of February 9, 1921 to Lawrence Langner, he complains: "There I had been waiting for three weeks thinking about changes in a play they were not even considering." By mid-1921 the title was in a state of suspended limbo—its focus on neither Chris nor Anna but on the force that both united and separated them—the sea. Writing to Kenneth Macgowan on June 8, O'Neill says: "I'm full of future hopes. Hopkins has, I think, taken my 'The Ole Davil.' " The play, in its final revised four-act version, opened as *Anna Christie* on November 21, 1921.

O'Neill always spoke of *Anna Christie* with contempt, angry at himself for prostituting his artistic vision with a makeshift happy ending that haunted him for years. On May 8, 1932, he wrote to Langner, suggesting that the Theatre Guild revive *Anna Christie* with "the last act played as I obviously intended in the writing not the conventional happy ending as directed by Hoppy—I could heighten the sea-fog-future uncertainty atmosphere by slight cutting and rewriting."

Nearly ten years yater, when Ingrid Bergman starred in *Anna Christie* in San Francisco, O'Neill urged Langner* to see the production to evaluate its potential as a New York revival, adding: "I couldn't sit through it without getting the heebie-jeebies and wondering why the hell I ever wrote it—even if Joan of Arc came back to play 'Anna.'" A clue to the ultimate cause of the failure of "Chris Christopherson"-*Anna Christie* is provided in O'Neill's response to August 24, 1941 to Langner's suggestion for a road tour of the play:

> Re Anna-Bergman, the road idea seems good stuff. The fact is "Anna Christie" is the stalest of all my plays—stale from much use, and stale because it is the most conventional playwrighting of anything I've done, although its subject matter was damned unconventional in our theatre of 1921. You will notice I did not include it when picking representative plays for my Nine Plays book, despite its success. The chief value I set on it is the character of old Chris. It is a play written about characters and a situation —not about characters and life. "The Iceman" is worth a hundred "Anna Christies."

O'Neill connects these two plays in his mind yet was probably unaware why he did so. There are many similarities between the first act of "Chris Christopherson" and *The Iceman Cometh*: the atmosphere, action, dialogue, and—above all— characters. He succeeds in dramatizing these—and for the same reason: they are autobiographical in nature; O'Neill was able to bring life to the characters because they were men and women he knew. He had a natural aversion for the English; few prim and proper ladies with Anna's original moral perfection appeared on his early horizon. "Chris Christopherson" becomes a disaster the moment the English-reared Anna crosses Chris's threshold. In the early scenes of *Anna Christie*, the heroine, as prostitute, is credible. This late version flounders, however, as the first draft does, when the author tries to present a realistic man-woman love relationship.

O'Neill spent more time on "Chris Christopherson"-*Anna Christie*—from 1918 to 1921—than on any of his other early plays. He always considered the combined work a failure; however, it forms an important link, joining the characters of the early semi-autobiographical sea plays and those of the 1939 autobiographical *Iceman*, representatives from two groups he had known in his early life—those he had met at sea and those on land at Jimmy the Priest's waterfront saloon.

---

*Letter of July 29, 1941, to Theresa Helburn with a postscript to Langner.

[°PLAY OF A SMALL TOWN]*
[1919]

Play of a small Town—one hundred characters or more—the humanity of these people as individuals—their despicableness as mob—all of this shown by their reactions to a central idea, which, as individuals, they can accept liberally or at least tolerate—but as mob, as the town, they are intolerant, tyrannical—a plea for anarchistic theory as opposed to specialistic. The Town is the chief character.

°THE LITTLE THINGS
[1919]†

"The Little Things"—the play of a married couple's life together showing how in their first love the ideal persons which are the real souls of each shine out and are recognized as mates. But the little things, the annoyances, the deadly commonplaces of life build up gradually a mask for each of them. The old true idealism is overclouded. The little things form new personalities for both in each other's eyes. For years they live this way together, irritated, provoking each other, strangers yet still in love with the hidden true soul in each other although chaffing, wondering, bewildered, asking themselves what they can possibly see in the conglomeration of common, petty meannesses by which they recognize each other in their every day relationships. Finally the wife is dying—and the little things are rousted by this big fact—and they see each other again as in the first days—etc.

---

*A tragic incident that occurred in spring 1919 probably inspired the idea for the "Play of a small Town." One morning, while living in New Jersey, O'Neill discovered the body of his beloved dog, Brooklyn Boy, on his front lawn. Agnes Boulton states that the dog's "throat had been cut from ear to ear, and he was laid there so that his fatal wound could be plainly seen" (*Part of a Long Story*, p. 281). The couple believed this cruel act reflected the animosity detected on previous occasions in neighbors and some townspeople of West Point Pleasant, who had never accepted the "strange, silent man" living in their midst.

†"The Little Things" and many of the marital "problem plays" that follow it were apparently conceived in spring 1919; one concept links these ideas: the dramatist's ambivalent feelings for his wife Agnes. No attempt will be made to date the following ideas, which are presented here as they appear in the last section of the 1918–1920 notebook. Most of these entries were recorded in the one-year span—from spring 1919, after O'Neill completed the first draft of "Chris Christopherson," to spring 1920, before he began the second version of it. Only two plays—the one-act "Exorcism" and the four-act *Gold*—were written in this one-year transition period when O'Neill was searching for ideas that could be developed in multi-act works. The words "long play" precede several ideas in the last section of the notebook.

[°MAN OF 45]*

Long play—man of 45—most popular doctor in small town—a personage. His wife, 40, with a life of her own in social activities—a leader. They started out with romantic illusions—married when he had still been medical student, she a college girl. The little things of their small town life have erected a wall between them. They feel they have lost youth. It is the doctor's 45th birthday.

[°THE OLD GAME]

Long play—[word erased]—its rutty insignificance before war—his possibilities as officer—the war ends—he comes back to face the old game.

[°*BEYOND THE HORIZON* SEQUEL]

Long play—taking up the "Beyond The Horizon" situation where that play leaves off—The play of Andrew.

[°T.B. SAILOR]

Long play—abandonment of the T.B. sailor by whaling captain in Marquesas—his care by natives and restoration to comparative health while the Islanders are scourged by his disease—the coming of the Missionaries, etc.—His fight against them, preaching the real gospel of Christ—etc.

[°MAN AND WIFE]†

Play—Man & wife—when first married and he is struggling for success as writer she wants to have a child—He is strongly against it on account of their uncertain situation, for child's sake, etc.—their first serious quarrel takes place about this. As he forges on to success, too engrossed in his work to notice anything else, she draws away from him, developing an alien, independent life. Their family life ceases to exist. She becomes involved with the woman's movement, champions her own sex. She is at the height of her enthusiasm for this when success commences to fall on him. He becomes disillusioned with hope fulfilled, with

---

*O'Neill draws a line through this material and labels it N[o]. G[ood].
†The dramatist draws a line through this idea and labels it N[o]. G[ood].

himself as an end, and vainly seeks for something outside of himself on which to pin his life. The idea of the old home life, the desire for a child which will be him and yet not him, takes hold of him. He falls back on his wife only to stand aghast before the immeasurable gulf which now separates them. He tries to overcome this by entering into his wife's interests; but intellectually he is too remote from them. His endeavor to get closer to her only widens the gulf. She is aware of his disdain and hates him for it. Finally, as a last desperate resort, he proposes to her that they should have a child. She is amazed, disgusted, refuses. Tells him she cannot live with him any longer. He interferes with her work, her interests. They need not get a divorce. They will just live alone. He is left to himself and as the final happens he is talking with an interested calculating air to their young, healthy slavey.

[°MONOLOGUE]

A psychological monologue—telephone, etc.

[°NICKEL POOLROOM]

The nickel poolroom in New Orleans—

[°PLAY OF FAMILY]

Play of family—man & woman married 50 years—grandchildren, etc.—man Irish Fenian—hatred for England—woman of old German-American stock—Revolution, etc.—happy until split by war

°I SPY

"I Spy"—Comedy of Provincetown—

°CHRIS CHRISTOPHERSON*

Chris. Christopherson—captain of coal barge—long play with all action taking place on the barge

---

*The word "Done" is written across this idea.

[°THE OLD FISHERMAN]

One-act play—the old fisherman who, abused and ignored by his children, pretends to be mad so as to be sent to asylum.

[°REINCARNATION]*

Idea for long play—reincarnation—oldest civilization, China 1850 (?)—modern times during war—South Sea Island, 1975—Same crises offering a definite choice of either material (i.e. worldly) success or a step toward higher spiritual plane—Failure in choice entails immediate reincarnation and eternal repetition in life on this plane until spiritual choice is made.

[°JIM AND SELF]

Long play—Jim & self†—showing influence of elder on younger brother.

°FORTY YEARS**

"Forty Years"—Bachelor—40th birthday—Friends and relatives give surprise party—he is just going out to visit girl—thinks he is still young—the kindly attitude of his guests convinces him that youth is gone, etc.

°SAILOR'S SNUG HARBOR

"Sailor's Snug Harbor"—The old wind-jammer, tramp-steamer sailor—the incurable liar and romanticist—one leg gone—finger off—battered face—the victim of a thousand strokes of bad luck—no kith or kin—has all of his life

---

*O'Neill draws a line through this idea and writes: "Done by Algernon Blackwood." He is referring to a 1918 reincarnation play, *Karma*, by Blackwood and Violet Pearn. In the first act—set in ancient Egypt—a dancing girl persuades her lover to break his priestly vows. When reborn into later eras in subsequent acts, she continues to destroy her lover/husband. In the Epilogue she becomes aware of her past errors and atones for them.

†O'Neill made an effort to obliterate "Jim & self," drawing numerous lines through these words.

**A line is drawn through this idea, indicating O'Neill discarded it.

been living in the lies of imagination he has come to believe in himself—receives a letter from an old chum telling of his happy life in the bosom of family, etc.— for one moment he sees his life in its stark reality of unrewarded suffering—is stunned—but immediately is off again in a dream of what might have been if he had married the one girl he loved in his youth.

[°SERIES]

Stories—Jimmy the Priest series—"The Astronomer," "The Hairy Ape," "Fireworks," "The Ruin of Mickey," "This Way Out" ("Tomorrow") "The Lunger,"* "Chris."

Sanatorium Series—"Kitty,"

Gunman Series—"The Dreamy Kid," "The Dirty Half-Dozen," "The Pig of the Hell Hole," "Exit Baby Doll"

[°GERMAN SPY]

Story about German Spy who inoculates himself with T.B. in order to live unsuspected on Mexican border (Arizona) and direct German propaganda in Mexico.

[°HIS MASTER'S EYES]

Dream story—horror—about the dog who obeys his master's eyes—wife has lover, etc.

[°SPANISH SAILOR]

Story of Spanish sailor on board the "Antilles" when she was torpedoed— scoffer at home—forgets all scepticism when danger comes—kneels down to pray—prays too long—others skip over side—he is lost.

---

* Louis Sheaffer states that one of O'Neill's fellow lodgers at Jimmy the Priest's was "a broken-down telegrapher known as 'the Lunger,' who was prone to spells of violent coughing. . . . Since he daily consumed more than a quart of the five-cent whiskey, his coughing before long was permanently stilled" (*O'Neill Son and Playwright*, Boston, 1968, p. 201). In the earliest notes for "Chris Christopherson," one of the regulars at Tommy the Priest's is Kennedy, a telegrapher.

O'Neill enters the titles for three plays but provides no information about them: "The Pier-head Jump," "Millions of Bubbles," and "The Last Sailing Ship." Under the word "Discarded," the author lists the following titles: "Again," "The Knock on the Door,"* "The Answer," "Quinine—Scoffin's," "The Thumb-Nail," and "The Mermaid Wife."

THE FIRST MAN†
[1920–1921]

I have finished the first draft of my new long play, "The First Man," and am now going to set it aside to smoulder for a while in the subconscious and perhaps gather to itself a little more flame therefrom. It looks so good now, I'm afraid of it. At this stage of the development, they all look fine, I've found.

(*Letter to Kenneth Macgowan, March 18, 1921*)

O'Neill's earliest titles for *The First Man*—"Expeditions" and "The Oldest Man"—support Sheaffer's theory that the dramatist had "lifted his story idea from ancient literature—the legend of Jason and his quest of the Golden Fleece. Paralleling the early fable, Curtis Jayson is about to embark on an imporant expedition to a remote land; and just as the old hero used and finally sacrificed Medea to his advancement, the scientist has exploited his wife in his career."**

---

*"The Knock on the Door," like several other entries, was conceived before O'Neill started to record his ideas in the 1918–1920 notebook. He identifies this work in his "List of All Plays" as a one-acter he wrote in 1915. It is uncertain when he destroyed this play and other early failures, written while he was at Harvard. Apparently he decided in late 1918 to rewrite "The Knock on the Door" as the title appears at the top of the page following the entry for "Honor Among the Bradleys." The title, on this otherwise blank page, was subsequently erased.

On the back of the front cover of the 1918–1920 notebook, O'Neill records an idea for a World War I sea play conceived before he purchased this book.

(America gets into war—news after he is on board)
(Friend, sailor, who is exempt and is going to work in munitions gives him book—looks like him—so he is able to ship—)
(He's short a couple of hands. He'll sign you on and be glad to do it a couple of days out)
(Friend stole book from American sailor)

†To maintain chronological order, discussion of the play appears here although the first idea for it is not included in any of the notebooks.

**Louis Sheaffer, *O'Neill Son and Artist*, New York, 1973, p. 47.

The First Man is the second of the domestic dramas O'Neill wrote in the early 1920s: *Diff'rent* (1920), *Welded* (1922), and *All God's Chillun Got Wings* (1923). It is, like *Welded*, another autobiographic expression of what he desired, indeed expected, in his marital relationship with Agnes Boulton: the complete submergence of a woman's individuality to the dominant male. The author was distressed when his wife became pregnant, as is Curtis Jayson, a self-portrait, regarding a child as a wedge that would weaken the marital bond, a threat to a quiet, harmonious atmosphere in which to work. O'Neill apparently conceived the idea for *The First Man* soon after the birth, in 1919, of his son whom he nicknamed "Shane the Loud." It bears some similarity to an earlier idea for a play entitled "Silence," whose hero—while not an anthropologist—travels "from Scotland to Africa to make fortune for girl he loves." He marries her but in time "comes to hate wife for noise she makes. . . . They have child—can't endure child's crying." There is something prophetic about the ending of "Silence" as the hero, like the author, eventually walks away from a troubled marriage. Later, in a letter to Macgowan dated August 7, 1926, O'Neill states that he was never cut out to be a father and that children—even his own—tend to "get my goat."

The dramatis personae of the earliest notes for *The First Man* lists a character later omitted in the published text: Curtis and Martha Jayson's five-year-old son, Jack. The inclusion of this child must have presented the dramatist with a number of problems. In the published text the childless Martha is motivated to form a friendship with Edward Bigelow, a widower, by her motherly interest in his children, a concern that blinds her husband to the possibilities of scandalous rumors about his wife and best friend. The existence of this child would also eliminate the sentiments voiced by John Jayson for a grandson and the spiteful, envious manner of Curtis's sister Esther and his sister-in-law Emily, who have produced only daughters, toward Martha. The most profound consequence of the existence of a child would be to lessen the dramatic effect of Curtis's discovery of his wife's pregnancy—his fear that they could no longer "go on living the old, free life together," that their relationship and his wife's total dedication to him would be destroyed.

While the setting of all the acts is the same in both the early and late drafts, the time differs in the fourth act: six years—rather than three days—have elapsed in the early version since Martha's death. The longer lapse was devised apparently to allow Curtis to complete his five-year expedition to Asia and return to keep the promise he had made to his infant son: "When he's old enough, I'll teach him to know and love a big, free life."

The early notes contain the scenario for only the first act, which opens on "Saturday p.m. in summer." Curtis is preoccupied with a scientific paper and impatiently retreats to his study when Bigelow begins a discourse "to Martha on his children." Curtis's younger sister Lily enters and shows her "displeasure and suspicion at seeing the two of them together." When Bigelow leaves, she warns Martha about the ugly rumors circulating in the town. Lily advises Martha to have a child; it would "keep Curtis from further roving, etc. Martha embarrassed—finally confesses she is pregnant—afraid to tell Curtis— Lily suspicious of this."

All the other members of Curtis's family arrive. When Curtis asks Martha to come into the study to take some notes, "Lily bursts forth with her news— tells of M.'s defiant attitude when she spoke of Bigelow—of her fear of Curtis in regard to secret, etc. They all gabble—all their suspicions are aroused." Martha senses their hostility when she returns; she "is made defiant by their very politeness—welcomes the news that Bigelow has come in car—goes. The gabble breaks out again indignantly at her rudeness, etc."

As in the earlier *Bread and Butter*, which is also set in Bridgetown, Connecticut, O'Neill presents not only the problems confronted by a couple within the framework of marriage but the assaults of philistine small town inhabitants that come from without, and, primarily, how these inner and outer pressures affect the artist, the man of dedication as he strives to reach a goal. At the end of *The First Man*, Curtis, having resolved his inner conflict by asserting his determination to continue his work, turns on his hypocritical sister Esther and sister-in-law Emily who—with their husbands—form a kind of chorus of townspeople, like the one used later in *Mourning Becomes Electra*: "What do you know of love— women like you! You call your little rabbit-hutch emotions love—your bread-and-butter passions." While *The First Man* is merely a continuation of previously explored themes and techniques rather than a dramatic leap forward, O'Neill was able, through his autobiographical hero, to express the inner tensions he experienced as he attempted to play the two roles demanded of him at a specific time in his life—one as artist, the other as husband and father.

2 • Ideas: 1921-1931 Notebook

WHITE
°HONEST HONEY BOY
(1921)

"Joe"—the tragi-comedy of negro gambler (Joe Smith) *—8 scenes—4 in N.Y. of his heyday—4 in present N. Y. of Prohib[ition]. times, his decline.

°THE HOMO SAPIENS†
(1922)

Characters

Zoroaster Brown, a college professor
President of the University
       tress (?)
Proprietor of an animal store
The Great God Pan—or Dionysus (?)
Priests, Ministers, etc.
Scientists
Republicans, Anarchists, etc. / the happy medium—
               (benevolent capitalism)
Factory girls
People
Organ grinder & monkey
Policemen
Lunatics
A poet
A sculptor
A painter
Nymphs

---

*The author makes several attempts to dramatize the life of this friend he made in 1915 when both frequented the Hell Hole. An entry in the Work Diary, dated May 25, 1932 states: "notes & outline Old Joe Smith idea play." Joe Smith emerges finally in 1939 as the black gambler, Joe Mott, in *The Iceman Cometh*.

†O'Neill draws diagonal lines through the entire idea and writes "Discarded." In a letter to Macgowan in summer 1923, he explains why he discards this idea: "As for actual writing, there is the 'Homo Sapiens' Express[ionistic]. effort which I may do if I ever feel that way again. Not very definite that, but with a mind full of 'Polo' I'm sort of 'off' everything else original at the moment."

Scenes

Scene I   —Office of the president of University—Tar & feathers
Scene II   —An animal store—chicken hawk & a stuffed snake
Scene III   —A hermit's cave in the Berkshires—a year later
Scene IV   —A cathedral in N. Y.—statues of Buddha, Christ, Vishnu,
                 Mohammed
Scene V   —A laboratory "   "
Scene VI   —A newspaper plant "
Scene VII   —A factory—song of the shirt
Scene VIII   —A market place—organ grinder & monkey—statue of Mob
                 & Capitol)
Scene IX   —Brooklyn Bridge—a man should know when to die (Zara-
                 thustra)
Scene X   —A station House   mysticism
Scene XI   —A lunatic asylum—poet—("He is sane") contempt
Scene XII   —A hilltop in a forest

Scene VIII
Tomorrow you shall be King

                                    Tell us the truth—You want to live.
When Burnham wood shall move   I want to die
  to Dunsinane to die.
                                           Judge enters
transplant—transfigure   I want to live.
                                    Then you are insane to want to die.
The snobbery of the saneless   Pan (4th scene)—They have forgotten me.
                               They live outside life, etc.—for a reason
He sees by electric light   Scene II
What does he see?   Our eagle flew away—but I can sell you
                                 a chicken hawk (buzzard turkey)
                              Our National emblem—token of Thanksgiving
                                 —but this is an age of substitutions
                              I wish a serpent.
                              St. Volstead* preserve us! We have only
                                 one preserved in alcohol.
                              Even in death he is defiant.

     Scene I—Office of the University president—a huge mahogany desk with
a radiophone instalment on it—exaggerated Oxford architecture. Entire arched

---

*O'Neill probably refers here to the Volstead Act passed by Congress in 1919, which
provided for Federal enforcement of prohibition.

doors and tall arched windows in rear. The President is seated before the desk—
a well-fed elderly man in scholastic cap and gown but with the face and manner
of Warren Harding or a movie banker. There is the clatter of a typewriter from
the next room. The President is listening eagerly at the horn of the radiophone.
By the side of the desk is a blackboard on which is chalked a sort of score card
for a football game with the four quarters divided off. The names of the colleges—
Yarvard & Hanton—stand out prominently. The whole right wall of the room is
an enormous college banner of red and white horizontal strips with Yarvard in
blue letters across it.

The radiophone is calling out the score at the end of the third quarter—
Hanton 10, Yarvard. . . . Then it stops. The President sweats and fumes. He has
been called back from the game and does not know what happened in the third
quarter. Then the machine announces the decision of the Board of Trustees:
Mr. Brown must be fired. The President is glad. He will vent his resentment at
missing the game on him. He summons Brown. Brown appears. At the same moment the Radiophone begins the report of the fourth quarter.

Brown is a stiff, angular man of 32, prematurely aged and stooped, dressed
in an old suit threadbare and covered with patches but painfully neat. He is a
strange contrast. His body is meek, servile, diffident in all its poses and gestures,
his face a mask of horned-glasses and studious respectability. But behind the
mask an unleashed, bewildered spirit is writhing in freedom, and his eyes glare
boldly and resentfully through the glasses.

The President begins to state the case against Brown in stilted blank verse.
His manner is that of a businessman reproving a subordinate for inefficiency. He
is constantly interrupting himself with comments on the progress of the game in
the excited slang of a fan.

THE GREAT GOD BROWN*
(1922)

Play of masks—removable—the man who really is and the mask he wears before the world—also abstract idea behind play the spirit of Pan that Christianity corrupts into evil—pagan flesh becomes evil—Architect—a failure—drink—married to good unimaginative girl—children—his friend and rival, unimaginative—success—creative spirit in former has no outlet—becomes destructive—Cybel—earth mother corrupted into prostitute symbol—Series of brief scenes in each act—sets very simple.

Develop

O'Neill began *The Great God Brown* on April 23, 1924 and made an outline on the 29th, developing an "idea for doing it with masks." After finishing *Desire Under the Elms* on June 16, he took up *The Great God Brown* again, devoting four days to the outline, set it aside, and resumed work that summer and fall on *Marco Millions*. In the early scheme for *The Great God Brown*, the naked face and the masked face depict "the conflict between inner character and the distortions which outer life thrusts upon it"; only later is the mask used "as a means of dramatizing a transfer of personality from one man to another."†

The doomed artist-idealist with a split personality depicted in this work appears in two earlier plays in which the heroes are given similar names: John Brown in the 1914 *Bread and Butter* and Zoroaster Brown in the 1922 idea, "Homo Sapiens." The surname is used again in *The Great God Brown* but for a character that is their antithesis: the unimaginative, materialistic businessman William A. Brown. As the original idea for the play suggests, he is not yet in conflict with himself but with the artist-dreamer Stanley/Wint Keith. However, from the very start, O'Neill conceives them as complementary parts of a whole. "They have always been exact antithesis. They needed, completed each other while at the same time subtly hated each other for the need. Both had just enough of each other in them to idealize and be jealous of the rest." O'Neill provides additional external motivation to exacerbate the insidious, personal rivalry between the two young men: a family feud originating in the animosity of the two fathers, who contribute different qualities—as their sons would later—to their contracting firm: the elder "Keith had furnished the stolid, self-satisfied business ability and Brown the aspiration and 'pep'—always wanted to be an architect, swore his son should be and Keith, in turn, subtly resentful at the other's superiority, swore his son must be too."

---

*O'Neill draws diagonal lines through this idea and writes: "Great God Brown 1925."
†Kenneth Macgowan explains O'Neill's purpose in using masks for the play in a program note for the "Greenwich Village Playbill."

The main purpose of the first two scenes of the early prologue, which has four scenes and three settings, is to depict the jealousy and bitterness of the two fathers; each will sacrifice the future happiness of his son to defeat a hated rival. The curtain rises to reveal the Browns' living room; its furniture—"pretentiously in the bad taste of the successful small town bourgeoisie"—resembles in its arrangement the courtroom setting of the Casino in the later prologue. Mrs. Brown sits "in the attitude of a judge." Her husband "stands and harangues after the manner of a lawyer pleading—or prosecuting—a case." The question before the court is whether their son Billy, who has just passed his entrance exam at Yale,

shall study to be an architect, as his father wants, or a lawyer as mother's snobbishness craves. Billy dutifully is silent. He is a fine, healthy, likable well dressed good-looking American boy, his face intelligent and sensitive for its class but with no trace of genuine creative ability about it. The Father wins his case by appealing to Mother's vanity and snobbishness, superiority over Keith.

Scene Two of the prologue is set in the Keiths' living room, which—while it also looks like a courtroom—contains old-fashioned horsehair furniture. Mrs. Keith is urging her husband to send their son to Yale to study architecture.

Old Keith, a tall, lean man with a stubborn, set face sits in the rocking chair of judgment. Mrs. Keith, thin, frail, faded but still sweet, is pleading anxiously. Wint stands behind the sofa, nervous and fitful, a slender, vital figure. He is masked. His parents are not. His mother finally wins her case by appealing to K[eith's]. jealousy of partner.

While the Pier of the Casino is not specifically mentioned, moonlight dominates the prologue's third scene; the sound of waves on the beach and dance music in the distance can be heard. Billy enters with "Ellen,* masked," who is described as "pretty, intelligent, full of joy and vitality but at the same time a romantic dreamer." She rejects Billy's offer of marriage, saying she loves Keith. The fourth scene, a continuation of the third, reverses the action of the final draft's prologue. In the first outline, Keith, alone and unmasked, "questions himself unhappily" before his romantic encounter with Ellen/Margaret. The prologue closes with Brown, the "good loser—very moved"—congratulating his friend—"Keith embarrassed."

Most events which transpire in the time lapse between the prologue and Act I are the same in the final version and early outline which states: Keith is "half-through his course of architecture in Yale" when his father dies, leaving him a petty fortune. He marries and "goes to Paris to study art after having sold out his interest in business to old Brown." After five years of the good life abroad, he is forced for financial reasons to return to the United States. The plot takes a

---

*The word "Ellen" is crossed out, and "Margaret" is written above it.

different turn here, for Keith then goes with his wife and children to live with her mother and father, who "started as house painter with ghost of artistic aspiration—enough for him to sympathize with K[eith].'s ambitions—and failure. For K. has failed, is really heart-broken, realizes he isn't a painter, hasn't the stuff."

During these same years, William, though hurt by losing the woman he loves, "goes on his steady, successful way." When he finishes college, he joins his father at Brown & Son. One significant event, later eliminated, occurs in Brown's life: he marries a girl from the best family shortly after graduation. Their marriage, like so many others in O'Neill's plays, is disastrous; it is based solely on friendship and not on love.

She has a child which is born dead, nearly dies herself, becomes model social wife, model home, entertainments, etc., maintains her position and raises him socially. They never quarrel. They live in unthinking resignation—except in flashes. W. remembers K. and his lost love.

At the outset of the 1924 notes, Brown appears to be the central figure. The first scene in the four parts—each of which represents a season—is set in "the draughting department of Brown's office"; the second takes place in the "library of Brown's home." In the early version Brown receives no request from Ellen/ Margaret to give her husband a job but magnanimously offers his rival a partnership after discovering his financial plight. Keith refuses but accepts a position as draughtsman and proves to be a superior architect. Though jealous, Brown sees that Keith is invaluable and responsible for the firm's rating as the best in the state. Fifteen years go by. Keith grows to hate what he is doing; his drinking

has become the town scandal. He reforms now and this for wife's and daughter's sake. But she understands, never blames, teaches daughter to shield him. He grows estranged, hates her & daughter for the pity he feels in them, gradually come to blame them for his situation, etc. His health begins to fail, his heart to go back on him.

By the time O'Neill concludes his outline, Keith's role in the play is as significant as Brown's. Yet initially, he is obviously a minor figure, a foil. At the beginning of the outline, Keith is described in a very short passage as representing the "immoral, non-responsible life—life intensely living, regardlessly continuing, requiring perfect freedom in which to develop naturally. In the condition of society, such natures become warped, tend to devour themselves, to destroy."

In contrast, the dramatist devotes two long paragraphs to characterizing Brown. The main action of the play occurs in the "fifteen years later" period; for O'Neill describes Brown at the age he would be at that time. He is portrayed, as he would be later in the first scene of Act Two of the published text, as "the successful provincial American of forty." The early notes provide greater insight into his character; he is the personification of the American ideal, a well-rounded realization of success: "complete attainment of an assured position—a self-made edifice made of the solid bricks of negative value. Abstractly, he is the idol in which we glorify our denial of all the spiritual values which make life live. He is life regulated by a formula of fear into a machine-made compendium of axioms." There are traces of the later Brown of Act Two, Scene Three in a passage in which he is individualized: "Personally, he is in no way detestable; rather he is in every way, likable. His appearance is impressing. He looks rather like the statue of one of the many Roman Consuls. There is an incongruous distinction about him. One feels imposed upon by this objectless and reasonless quality, for his life is without true distinction whatsoever."

O'Neill completed the first outline for the play in early 1925 in Bermuda. After condensing the two-play version of *Marco Millions*, he turned to *The Great God Brown* on January 25 and worked on it continuously until the end of March. The Work Diary entries for 1925 are sketchy; for, as the dramatist explains, they are written "from memory and few records, diary of that year having been stolen and sold by former wife." On February 2 the author remarks that he thought he had the play "doped out" but that it was "coming out all different." By this time he had written a new outline, adding a scene in "the best parlor of a brothel" in the first act. In contrast to the final version, there is no second brothel scene in the notes. Although a prostitute is mentioned in the original idea recorded in 1922, she is omitted in the earliest scheme. Her role now in Keith's life resembles that of the prostitute in Michael Cape's in *Welded*. Keith retains his original name; there is no suggestion yet of his Dionysian-Christian dichotomy, nor does his wife Ellen, now called Estelle, represent a Faustian Marguerite. The fact that the sitting room in the last scene of the third act is specifically designated as Keith's indicates that this character does not die in Act Two as he will in the final draft. The "Sitting room, Estelle's cottage" is specifically cited as the setting for the first scene in Act Two and the third scene in Act Four.

A diagram in the second set of notes, undated but probably devised in early February 1925, reveals precisely how the play is now "different" and how close O'Neill is to his final dual conception of the characters. The diagram contains more Faustian connotations than are found in either the first or final version of the play; the Marguerite figure passes through the normal woman cycle but degenerates into a mistress symbol while the Devil emerges triumphant in the Keith-Brown conflict.

In his diagram O'Neill traces the evolving stages of the mask-person duality of his two central characters. As in so many of the other plays, their fate—the courses that will tragically converge—has been irrevocably sealed by the past. As a child, Brown destroyed the picture drawn by the four-year-old Dion Anthony (as Keith is now called), who, to protect himself from injustice and cruelty, assumed the mask of the Bad Boy Pan. The original Dionysian unity shatters after this incident and produces good Brown and bad Dion, whom Margaret loves but

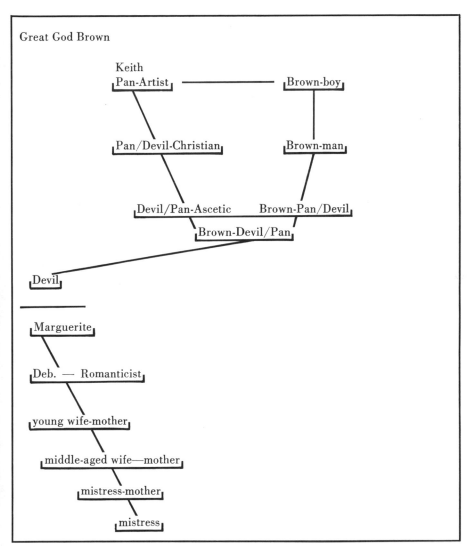

Great God Brown

spurns when he reveals himself unmasked as the ascetic Anthony. As the creative Dion, he is a successful architect; as a man, he laments the rejection of his true self and becomes Mephistophelian. In the published text only Cybel, the earth mother-prostitute, accepts, understands, and loves the unmasked ascetic Anthony. When Dion dies, Brown, longing to possess Margaret and his rival's creative power, assumes Dion's mask. At mid-point, the diagram shows the merger of Brown and Keith-Dion's "Devil-Pan" nature. What is transferred to Brown is Dion's demonic agony and tormented soul. He becomes, in effect, Dion Brown. Both Dion Anthony, who calls himself Man, and Dion Brown, whom Cybel calls Man, die regenerated in the final draft—their unmasked faces resembling Christian ascetics, their lips forming a half-forgotten prayer, the "Our Father." The Dionysian unity, the behind-life force in the play, is restored. The mistress-prostitute emerges as the earth-mother comforter, assuring them of rebirth and regeneration after death.

O'Neill devised now a new outline for Act Four. The first scene was to have closed with "Dion and Brown and millionaire," but this line is canceled. At the bottom of this page, the author makes a notation for a closing to replace the one discarded: "Dion and Brown and masks of Dion and his own." Dion's name appears twice in Act Four but only in the first scene, in which he apparently dies. It is possible that Brown, who is alone in the second scene, assumes the mask of the dead Dion at this time. The third and final scene of the play is divided into three sections: Margaret and sons; Margaret and sons and Brown; Margaret and Brown.

This version of the play, closing with a scene between Margaret and Brown, suggests two possibilities: that O'Neill planned a semi-happy ending for the couple similar to that devised for the lovers of *Anna Christie* and/or that Margaret assumes the role of Earth Mother to a dying Dion Brown. Cybel is not even mentioned in any of the play's early outlines, the last of which is so similar in structure and character identification to the final version. In a letter to Kenneth Macgowan O'Neill states that he is "so chuck full of 'Brown'" and that "the first half of 'Brown'—first draft—is just about finished" (March 1, 1925). His next letter on March 14 reveals that he plans to include the Cybel character: "The two women's parts in 'Brown' will take some playing. Clare [Eames] would be wonderful for one if it turns out as difficult and important as so far—but the man? The Man?" The last words of this statement indicate that O'Neill knew how he would end the play, focusing on the regenerated figure of Dion Brown as Man, and that he envisioned the two characters this term represents as one entity, symbolizing Dionysian wholeness. To make an audience aware of this concept, the dramatist wanted one actor to play both Anthony and Brown.*

O'Neill was motivated by personal as well as artistic considerations in his attempt to establish the love-hate relationship, the interdependence, and the self- and other-destroying natures of these two characters. In *The Great God Brown* the dramatist developed not only the 1922 "Play of Masks" idea but also an idea recorded earlier in the 1918–1920 notebook: "Long Play—Jim and self—showing influence of elder on younger brother." The last act of the autobiographical *Long Day's Journey into Night* certainly reveals Jamie's destructive influence on

---

*O'Neill sent a telegram to John Barrymore, asking him to play both roles: "Am taking liberty send you my latest play The Great God Brown thinking may interest you as vehicle. Dion in first half and Brown in rest of play should be played by same actor but you alone could do this." (Draft of telegram is in the Landauer Collection, Dartmouth College Library.)

his brother. This work, however, is not a long play devoted solely to the two brothers but to the entire Tyrone-O'Neill family. As the early notes and, to some extent, the published text reveal, *The Great God Brown* is an attempt to write a long play on "Jim and self." The word "brother" appears a number of times in the play. For example, in Act Two "Brown reaches out for the mask of Dion like a dope fiend after a drug" and says: "Hurry, Brother! It's time we were home." There is a dual autobiographical statement here: a reminder of Ella O'Neill's use of drugs to escape reality now linked with a similar attempt by her author-son to seek release from his own tortured inner self by identifying with his brother.

In the original scheme for the play O'Neill uses the naked face and the masked face to depict the conflict between inner character—as, for example, Dion Anthony—and the "distortions which outer life thrusts upon it." In February 1925 the author found that his original plan was "coming out all different." As he works out the complex relationship between Dion Anthony and Brown, he discovers a second use for the mask: as a means to show the "transfer of personality from one man to another." He states that the two characters "have been born, brought up, in the same town, on the same street." Both go off to college with Brown finishing and becoming a success and Dion dropping out and becoming a wastrel. In time, Brown begins to imitate Dion's actions—drinking and frequenting brothels—and gradually assumes his personality. He tries to possess exclusively the two women in Dion's life* and, finally, his very being by wearing his mask. Like Jamie in *Long Day's Journey into Night,* Dion can say to Brown: "Hell, you're more than my brother.† I made you! You're my Frankenstein!" There are indications in the early notes for *The Great God Brown* that the original theme of the play would be the Faustian fall of Brown through his contact with the Mephistophelian Keith/Dion (read influence of elder on younger brother). In two later portraits of his brother, O'Neill describes his face as having "a certain Mephistophelian quality" in *A Moon for the Misbegotten* and a "Mephistophelian cast" in *Long Day's Journey into Night.*

In *The Great God Brown* Dion explains why he assumed the Pan-Mephisto-

---

*Dennis Murphy, a retired police officer who worked on New London's Barbary Coast—the Bradley Street area—and a former friend of Jamie O'Neill, informed me in an interview in 1969 that at one time the O'Neill brothers "liked the same girl." He was on duty as a security officer at the Montauk Inn the night the two engaged in a verbal and physical fight over this girl. Murphy states: "Gene and Jamie were steady customers at the gin mills and bawdy houses."

†Speaking to Margaret in the first scene of Act Four, Brown describes his relationship to Dion and says: "We're getting to be twins." The concept is repeated in later plays. In "The Last Conquest," Satan, who calls Christ "Brother," tells the parable of the Siamese Twins. O'Neill's early title for *A Moon for the Misbegotten* is "The Moon Bore Twins."

phelian masks. When his friend, Billy Brown, destroyed the picture in the sand and then laughed, Dion felt betrayed by a person he had loved and trusted.* To avenge himself, Dion, the frustrated, failed artist, becomes the dissolute architect. In the notes, Brown is motivated to study architecture simply to compete with his rival. Jamie O'Neill was a frustrated writer turned bum. In *Long Day's Journey into Night* Jamie says to his brother: "Because I once wanted to write I planted it in your mind that someday you'd write." O'Neill, in his earliest description of Keith/Dion, states that if creative natures are not allowed to develop naturally, they "become warped, tend to devour themselves, to destroy." Keith/Dion, the would-be artist, like Jamie O'Neill, the would-be writer, willfully destroys himself.

There are many echoes of the exchange between Dion Anthony and Brown in the third scene of Act Two of *The Great God Brown* in the last-act conversation of the brothers in *Long Day's Journey into Night*. Brown urges Dion not to drink: "It's your funeral." Dion says: "When I die he goes to hell. . . . I'll make him look in my mirror yet and drown in it!" Brown then taunts him: "Go easy. I don't want your corpse on my hands." Using similar statements, Jamie tells Edmund: "The man was dead and so he had to kill the thing he loved. . . . The dead part of me hopes you won't get well. . . . He wants company, he doesn't want to be the only corpse around the house!" O'Neill says on March 25, 1925 that he finished *The Great God Brown* "in tears! Couldn't control myself!" There is one other recorded instance of a play being "written in tears"—the autobiographical *Long Day's Journey into Night*.

There are also definite similarities between Mary and James Tyrone in this play and the masked parents of Brown and the unmasked parents of Keith/Anthony in the first outline of the prologue for *The Great God Brown*. In using the masked face and naked face, O'Neill, again unconsciously, reveals the dual nature of his parents. Masked, Mrs. Brown is aggressive, snobbish, overdressed, clearly superior to her "always smiling" husband who has an inferiority complex. She, like Mary Tyrone, claims to have had musical ability as a girl; he, like James Tyrone in the first scene of *Long Day's Journey into Night*, is still in love with his wife and "puts his arm around her affectionately." Unmasked, Mrs. Keith is extremely vulnerable, nervous, sweet, and obviously dominated by her stubborn, insensitive, volatile husband. In the final draft, she remembers other nights in June when the moonlight was warm: "I remember the June I was carrying you,

---

*Dion Anthony is four years old when this traumatic event, which shaped his whole life, occurs. When Jamie O'Neill was six, he contracted measles. He is accused by his mother in *Long Day's Journey into Night* of disobeying her and going into his younger brother's room. As one passage in the play demonstrates, his mother never forgave Jamie when the baby contracted measles and died. Perhaps this incident led Jamie, like Dion, to become "the Bad Boy Pan," to rebel against God and protect himself "from His cruelty."

Dion—three months before you were born."* Her husband's tirade against his wastrel son, threatening to turn him out in the gutter, will be repeated almost word-for word later by James Tyrone to Jamie: "Colleges turn out lazy loafers to sponge on their poor old fathers! Let him slave like I had to! That'll teach him the value of a dollar! Let him make a man out of himself like I made myself."

The first idea for yet another late play appears in *The Great God Brown*; the strange relationship of Josie Hogan and Jim Tyrone in *A Moon for the Misbegotten* is similar in many aspects to that of Cybel and Dion. The notes for the latter play contain a section where Josie and Jim describe their opposing dreams, revealing dual natures identical to those of the split characters in *The Great God Brown*: the whorish/virtuous Cybel and the Mephistophelian/ascetic Dion Anthony. Josie dreams of herself as both "the triumphant beautiful ruthless harlot" and the "virtuous married women whose joy is to be slave to husband, children and home." Jim's first is "a Lucifer dream: the cynic who believes in nothing"; in the second, he is "the man who loves God, who gives up self and the world to worship of God and devotes self to good works, service of others, celibacy." Josie tells him: "Well I've been trying to seduce a Saint. Or to tempt a Lucifer." O'Neill first described the focus of *A Moon for the Misbegotten* as "Jamie's revelation of self." If this character's confession to Josie is indeed a revelation of an actual dual nature, then the similarly split Dion/Anthony is O'Neill's early Lucifer/Saint portrait of his brother.

Jamie O'Neill died November 8, 1923; five months later the dramatist started *The Great God Brown*, a play in which one character, Dion, dies, leaving a "brother" who thereafter expresses a strong death wish. The structure and focus of the play develop in response to the growing emphasis, the evolving characterization of Keith/Dion. One of the most significant changes in the first outline, which stresses the Keith-Brown relationship, is the addition in the second of a scene in a bawdy house. Like Jamie—who quotes "The Harlot's House" and frequents Mamie Burns's establishment in *Long Day's Journey into Night*, Keith visits a brothel for a "heart-to-heart talk concerning the infinite sorrows of life." In a later version, a second similar scene is added and the character of Cybel created; she, in turn, becomes the precursor of Josie Hogan.

The two women are described physically in similar terms: strong, healthy, full-breasted, wide-hipped, animalistic. Both are Earth Mothers who are inwardly virtuous but wear the outer mask of whore to the world. Cybel says: "I gave them a Tart. They understand her." Yet she is still able to retain her "real virtue." Only before the Dion-Jamie character do they unmask; only in the pres-

---

*Perhaps another unconscious autobiographical reference connects Dion and Jamie O'Neill. Ella O'Neill would have been six months pregnant in the month of June. She married James O'Neill on June 14, 1877; Jamie was born on September 10, 1878. The most autobiographical reference in *Great God Brown* occurs in Act I, Scene 3 when Dion reveals his hatred for his father and his great love for his mother.

ence of these two women do the men remove the mask of the cynic and reveal their true natures and vulnerability. Cybel addresses Dion as "Kid Lucifer"; Josie calls Jim "Lucifer." Like Josie, Cybel rescues Dion from the gutter and takes him in for a night to sleep; like Tyrone, Dion has a death wish: "To fall asleep . . . and never be called to get on the job of existence again." The women express similar romantic sentiments: Cybel: "I do love you. It takes all kinds of love to make a world"; Josie: "I have all kinds of love for you." Yet they also have maternal feelings for the lover as son; Cybel states: "What's the good of bearing children. What's the use of giving birth to death." Josie calls herself "a virgin who bears a dead child in the night." The parting scenes in both plays are almost identical; both Cybel and Josie sense instinctively—and correctly—that they will never again see the two men—that they leave to keep a rendezvous with death.

In his unconscious attempt to re-create his brother's life, degeneration, and death, O'Neill conceives Cybel: woman as prostitute. An even more important figure in Jamie's life, however, was woman as mother. Margaret is only a vague peripheral shadow in O'Neill's first outline; however, as the Keith/Dion/Jamie character developed, her role became more sharply defined. In the diagram of the second outline, she emerges from innocent girlhood to enter three successive stages of motherhood. Just as Cybel can be viewed as the prototype for Josie Hogan, Margaret is an early view of Mary Tyrone. Margaret is uprooted from her home and family immediately after marriage, accompanying her husband for five years on his travels while he pursues his artistic career. In the early notes, they are not able to afford a home when they return and are forced to live with her parents.

In the first outline Margaret has a son and daughter, but in the final draft she has three sons as does Mary Tyrone/Ella O'Neill. The most striking similarity between the two women, of course, is their inability to face reality. Mary Tyrone refuses to accept the fact that her son is suffering and may die; Margaret cannot bear to look upon Dion unmasked and see his real agonized face. The rejection by the mother-figure leads ultimately to despair and the psychological or actual death of the men. The situation of both women in the final scene of the two plays is identical. Mary Tyrone drifts in a drug-induced fog, failing to recognize her husband and sons, while Jamie bitterly quotes Swinburne's "A Leave-taking": "She would not know." Unaware of all around her, Margaret kneels before the mask of Dion; yet ironically she never truly knew either of the two men she had lived with. To emphasize Margaret's "leave-taking," O'Neill adds an epilogue* to the final draft which is not in any of the earlier outlines. Mar-

---

*In a letter in 1935 to Leon Mirlas, an Argentinean critic who had informed the dramatist of the successful production of the play in Buenos Aires and sent his critique of it, O'Neill writes:

As for the epilogue to "Brown," perhaps you are right from a historical standpoint. Perhaps, if I could be properly objective about that play, I

garet bids her three sons good-by "with strange finality" and surrenders herself to the memories of the past—to a time before her marriage, the night Dion first proposed to her. Similarly, Mary Tyrone regresses completely into the past to her early days preceding her marriage when "in the spring something happened to me. Yes, I remember. I fell in love with James Tyrone and was so happy for a time."

Significantly, *The Great God Brown* originated as an idea for a "Play of masks." While the masks are used consciously to achieve artistic and thematic goals, they also become metaphorically a device to conceal O'Neill's personal, but perhaps unconscious, purposes. Only after reading the notes for *A Moon for the Misbegotten*—particularly the revealing passages on Jamie Tyrone/O'Neill—is it possible to grasp the significance of the characterization of Keith, his gradual development in the outlines, and eventual emergence as Dion/Jamie. Once the Dion/Jamie relationship is understood, so, too, is the significance of *The Great God Brown*, a "long play of Jim and self," and its obvious parallels with the late autobiographical dramas, *Long Day's Journey into Night* and *A Moon for the Misbegotten*.

In a foreword, which, unfortunately, has never preceded any published edition of *The Great God Brown*, O'Neill sounds his revolt against the realistic theatre, claiming that it is unable to probe "the unknown within and behind ourselves." This short essay is a preamble for a longer one, "Memoranda On Masks," written in 1932, which states that the dramatist must find a method to present the inner drama—the "profound hidden conflicts of the mind . . . or confess himself incapable of portraying one of the most characteristic preoccupations and uniquely significant, spiritual impulses of his time."* O'Neill recommends the use of masks to depict the new "drama of souls." He cites the success of *The Great God Brown*—a mask drama, "the main values of which are psychological, mystical, and abstract"—as proof of the "deeply responsive possibilities in our public."*

In urging a return to the spirit of Greek grandeur, the author is championing an imaginative theatre, one which would spring, "by virtue of man's imaginative interpretation of life, out of his worship of Dionysus . . . a theatre returned to its highest and sole significant function as a Temple where the religion of a poetical interpretation and symbolical celebration of life is communicated to human beings."†

---

might agree. But I love that epilogue. For me it rounds out the whole play as inevitable poetic experience in life. It moves me deeply. And there you are. It's a case of love, you understand, so it's no good your asking me to be critical about it! I simply refuse to be!

*"Memoranda on Masks," *The American Spectator*, November 1932.
†"A Dramatist's Notebook," *The American Spectator*, January 1933.

THE GREAT GOD BROWN
*Author's Foreword**

This play is not merely naturalistic or realistic. It is also an attempt to express the vast inarticulate before which these issues are, of necessity, dumb. [It is written from a conviction that what one may see or hear or guess through a peephole—even in the most interesting of houses—is sometimes not enough.]† We have had quite enough of life invading the theatre. It is time the theatre invaded life. [Life in terms of life cannot reveal more to us than our own bewilderment. Life in terms of the theatre, as an art separate and distinct from the simulacra of what we term reality, may find expression for the great forces of which that reality is but a doughy symbol. Naturalism and realism, even at their deepest are so circumscribed by their limits that their articulateness is bound to be spiritually inarticulate. This play is inarticulate from a desire to] Holding the mirror of a soul up to Nature is one thing. Holding the kodak of a mind is quite another—an infinitesimally lesser. It is time we returned to the former if only to prove that the theatre still has a soul unsullied by contact with appearances. The theatre should be a refuge from the facts of life which we all feel, if we do not think, have nothing to do with truth. Not refuge in the sense of a narcotic, a forgetting, but in the sense of an inspiration that lifts us to a plane beyond ourselves as we know them (realism), drives us deep into the unknown within and behind ourselves. [to a plane transcending. The theatre should reveal to us what we are.] The theatre should stand as apart from existence as the church did in the days when it was the church. It should give us what the church no longer gives us—a meaning. In brief, it should return to the spirit of its Greek grandeur. And if we have no gods, or heroes to portray we have the subconscious the mother of all Gods and heroes. But for this realism is insufficient.

---

*Undated but included in the second collection of notes, labeled "The Great God Brown—incidental stuff on," written between January 25 and March 28, 1925.
†O'Neill cancels the material within brackets in this section.

[ALL GOD'S CHILLUN GOT WINGS]*
(1922)

Play of Johnny T.—negro who married white woman—base play on his experience as I have seen it intimately—but no reproduction, see it only as man's.

[DESIRE UNDER THE ELMS]
Under the Elms†
(1923)

Play of New England—locate on farm in 1850, time of California gold rush—make N. E. farmhouse and elm trees almost characters in play—elms overhanging house—father, hard iron type, killed off wives (2) with work, 3 sons—all hate him—his possessive pride in farm—loves earth to be as hard—in old age in a moment of unusual weakness & longing marries young woman, brings her back to farm, her arrival brings on drama, youngest son falls for her

Brothers to Cal (?)

It is unfortunate that the first recorded idea for *Desire Under the Elms*—of all the entries in the notebooks—is not more specifically dated. There are some similarities between this play and Sidney Howard's comedy *They Knew What They Wanted*, completed in November 1923, whose elderly hero, an Italian farmer, marries a young woman who is seduced by one of her husband's workers and becomes pregnant. Sheaffer states that in early 1924 O'Neill explained an idea that he had for a play to Kenneth Macgowan. Because the story contained some elements found in Howard's play, which "he had lent Eugene a short time before," Macgowan thought it a case of "unconscious plagiarism."** Had Macgowan voiced his suspicions, the dramatist could have proved his innocence in this matter by producing his 1921–1931 notebook; the 1923 entry for "Under the Elms" is immediately preceded by two ideas recorded in 1922 for *The Great God Brown* and *All God's Chillun Got Wings*. The first entry in O'Neill's Work Diary, "got idea for 'Desire Under the Elms,' " dated January 1, 1924, is obviously a carry-over from 1923, an idea conceived and developed before he began keeping his work record.

---

*O'Neill writes: "All God's Chillun Got Wings 1923" over this idea.
†The author was not satisfied with this title. The statement, "title not good try again," appears in the left margin. After completing the play, he writes: "Desire Under the Elms 1924" over this idea.
**Sheaffer, *O'Neill Son and Artist*, p. 126.

O'Neill was not motivated to develop his early concept for "Under the Elms" by Howard's play but by his brother Jamie's tragic death on November 8, 1923. He was so distraught that he went on a protracted drunken spree, attending neither the wake nor the funeral service. During this period, as the last surviving O'Neill, he obviously thought of his dead, of the accusations of his mother that her husband was responsible for causing her so much suffering, of the ensuing discord between the father and his sons. O'Neill needed no external source to provide inspiration for the conflict between the "father, hard iron type, killed off wives" and the three sons who "all hate him"—the focal point of the original idea; he had only to look within his own family to discover a similar struggle. The two lazy elder sons in the play, a composite picture of Jamie—who harbored feelings of unnatural love for his mother and of hatred for her drug addiction—are strongly attracted to their father's new wife but were callously indifferent to the sufferings of the former wife. The father's two wives, the feisty, materialistic Abbie who desires a home and the long-suffering second wife who is "killed" by her husband, represent the two natures of Ella O'Neill. Like *Long Day's Journey into Night*, *Desire Under the Elms* is an autobiographical memory play.

The dramatist began the scenario for "Under the Elms" on January 15, 1924. The next day he gave the play its present title. Working daily, he had by January 29 completed the scenario for Parts One and Two and started the dialogue for Act One. He devoted another brief period—from February 4 to 11—to the play and then left Ridgefield, Connecticut, to attend rehearsals for *The Emperor Jones*, *All God's Chillun Got Wings*, *Welded*, and his adaptation of *The Ancient Mariner*. The author did not take up *Desire Under the Elms* again until May 24. He completed the first draft on June 8 and "finished going over" the play from June 9 to 16 and July 1 and 2.

The few pages of early notes for *Desire Under the Elms* in the O'Neill collection at Beinecke provide details in the description of the Cabot home that are later eliminated: the elms develop their appalling humanness

When the wind does not keep them busy minding their routine properties as trees as usually from sunset to dawn.

(The wall of the house should come far front, as near to the proscenium line as possible. The front wall of each of the four rooms must be in a separate removable section so that the interior may be shown separately or in any desired combination.)

The early setting for the play's numerous scenes differs from that of the final draft in only three instances. The exterior of the farmhouse is the setting for the entire fourth scene of the first part. Scene One of Part Three opens nearly a year later, revealing the kitchen and only Eben's bedroom rather than both bedrooms. Scene Four of Part Three shows just the kitchen and not Cabot's bedroom. As first conceived, Ephraim Cabot is seventy rather than seventy-five; his son Eben is twenty-eight and not twenty-five.

While literary sources (the Greek legends: Oedipus, Medea, Phaedra) provided the inspiration for some elements of *Desire Under the Elms* (incest, infanticide, the revengeful, rejected stepmother) autobiographical aspects—the author's family—dominate the work: the miserly, exploitative father; the twofold portrait of his mother; the brother, a combination of the vulgar older brothers, aged thirty-nine and thirty-seven (the median represents the ten-year difference between Jamie and the dramatist who, as Eben, is first depicted as twenty-eight; Jamie is also the sole beneficiary of property in California where Peter and Simeon go to find gold); the author, as Eben, a self-portrait, in conflict with his father.

In an interview in 1924 when he was attending rehearsals for *Desire Under the Elms*, O'Neill denied the accusation that the play was autobiographical:

> When all is said and done, the result of this first part is legend. It isn't really true. It isn't I. And the truth would make a much more interesting and incredible legend. I see no hope for this except some day to shame the devil and myself if I can ever muster the requisite interest and nerve simultaneously.*

Not until 1940 did O'Neill acquire the nerve to "face his dead," to complete the incredible legend, repeating consciously in *Long Day's Journey into Night* themes and characterizations he had used, possibly unconsciously, in *Desire Under the Elms*.

°SILENCE IS WISDOM
(1923)

Comedy of "Silence is Wisdom"—the man, impressive looking but inwardly empty, who never says anything because he has nothing to say—some incident of his boyhood has engraved this on his mind—He gains bourgeois success, social standing, etc. all by being a solid man whose silence eternally gives consent—He gains a great rep[utation]. for shrewdness (wisdom)—It is only at last when he suddenly becomes convinced of his own wisdom that he decides to talk—gives himself away by relating the ridiculous incident of his boyhood as foundation stone of his wisdom.

---

*Quoted by Philip Weissman in "Conscious and Unconscious Autobiographical Dramas of Eugene O'Neill," *Journal of the American Psychoanalytic Association*, 5 (1957), pp. 432–460.

[°BALAAM'S ASS]
(1923)

Balaam's Ass—a satire—the ass to be the hero—with spiritual insight—
Balaam the materialist

MARCO MILLIONS
(1923)

O'Neill made an entry in his notebooks of the first idea for every major play he wrote from the early 1920s until 1935 with one exception: *Marco Millions*.* The Work Diary provides no information about the date the dramatist conceived the original idea† as the outline for the play was completed before he began to keep this written record. A letter to Kenneth Macgowan dated Friday, Summer 1923 indicates the author had only recently started *Marco Millions*:

> Am reading and taking millions of notes, etc. A lot of what the actual writing must be is now clear—and a lot isn't but will, God willing! I'll soon start a lengthy scenario of the whole to find out just how and where I stand—then get right after the reading, I hope. There's a lot of reading still to be done. I feel satisfied with the development—elated, even! The child will be either a surpassing satiric Beauty—or a most Gawdawful monster. Beauty, I fondly opine. Satiric or not remains to be seen—but Beauty must be the word!

The fruits of O'Neill's efforts that summer have survived: a lengthy scenario and a large collection of the "millions of notes," excerpts from *The Travels of Marco Polo*, the historical hero's actual account of his journey to the East and stay at the court of the Great Kaan. These notes read like a travelogue; but the focal point of the scenario, as of the completed play, is the traveler, the heralded ideal specimen of western civilization, a youth of average intelligence, with little worldly experience but possessing a secret touch of the poet, whose journey is not a pilgrim's progress—even though he is the pope's ambassador—to convert idolators and to discover the spiritual treasures of the East but an extensive business trip to exploit its material wealth. In both the early and final drafts Marco's poetic aspirations are mocked by his father and uncle, two avaricious merchants, whose tutelage on the journey to the east arouses the latent acquisitive instincts of the impressionable youth. At the Great Kaan's court, Marco becomes rich and powerful and rejects the ruler's spiritual counsels and his granddaughter's love. When Marco fails the Kaan's test and reveals he is flawed

---

*He may not have felt the need to record an entry for this drama, identifying it with an earlier idea in the 1918–1920 notebook: "The Play of Andrew," which was originally to have been a sequel to *Beyond the Horizon*.

†Sheaffer asserts that while researching *The Fountain*, written in 1921–1922, the dramatist "ran across references to Marco Polo that aroused his interest," adding that as "O'Neill's image of Polo came into focus, it owed less to the telescope of history than to the satiric eyes of Sinclair Lewis, the Lewis who immortalized the prototypal go-getting American businessman as 'Babbitt' " (*O'Neill Son and Artist*, p. 111).

emotionally and enamored only of money, the Princess dies of a broken heart. The published play concludes with Marco's gaudy display of his wealth when he returns in the last act to Venice and his childhood sweetheart Donata. The early draft's final scene shows him incarcerated in a Genoese prison dictating his memoirs.

Two late entries in the 1918–1920 notebook suggest the earliest indication of the theme not only of *Marco Millions* but also of other plays contemplated and written in the mid 1920s:

the idea for a drama of reincarnation contrasting the oldest civilization of China and that of modern times—same crises offering definite choice of either material (i.e. worldly) success or a step toward higher spiritual plane; long play taking up the "Beyond the Horizon" situation where that play leaves off—the play of Andrew.

As the businessman-merchant who had "been almost a millionaire—on paper" in *Beyond the Horizon*, Andrew is possibly a prototype for the characterization of Marco Polo, one of the many heroes O'Neill uses to demonstrate the consequences of man's dual conflicting materialistic and spiritual longings. In "Homo Sapiens," the idea he was developing in 1922 just before he began *Marco Millions*, the businessman-poet dichotomy is suggested by two contrasting characters: the success-obsessed president of an eastern ivy league university and the idealistic faculty member, Zoroaster Brown, who is about to be fired. Buddha, Christ, Vishnu, and Mohammed—statues found in a New York cathedral in one scene—and Zoroaster assume more specific roles and universal dimensions when O'Neill abandons this expressionistic 1922 play and infuses the religious concepts they represent into *Marco Millions*, a play that also incorporates the two previously mentioned ideas: a mercenary merchant who develops and displays, when opportunities arise, the greedy acquisitive nature of the Western world, stifling within him any higher inclinations that could be realized fully in the spiritually superior Eastern civilization he encounters.

After O'Neill outlined *Marco Millions* in Summer 1923, he set aside this play to write *Desire Under the Elms*. The greed of the New England Puritan Cabots is as destructive to the human spirit as that of the Italian Catholic Polos; the hypocritical Ephraim Cabot sets out to learn God's message in the same manner Marco sets out—with the pope's advice, which, as O'Neill notes, is similar to that given by Polonius—to bring the message of Christianity to the East. The cries for "gold" of Cabot and sons echo the exclamations for "millions" of Polo Brothers and Son. On July 17, 1924, the day after he finished the Puritan play, O'Neill resumed work on *Marco Millions*. On completing it, he immediately started *The Great God Brown*, whose hero—William A. Brown—is a materialistic businessman, the antithesis of the earlier Zoroaster Brown whose counterpart now is the idealistic but doomed poet Dion Anthony. The pattern that emerges from the plays of this period, particularly *Marco Millions*, is a systematic attack on

American greed and acquisitiveness. O'Neill did not envision his hero as an Italian adventurer but as a typical example of one of his mercantile countrymen, as his letter to Macgowan in Summer 1923 demonstrates:

> Am working hard as hell on Marco. It's going to be humorous as the devil if the way it makes me guffaw as I write is any criterion—and not bitter humor either although it's all satirical. I actually grow to love my American pillars of society. Polo Brothers & Son. It's going to be very long in first draft, I imagine, but I'm letting the sky be the limit and putting every fancy in.

As the lengthy 1923 scenario and the copious notes indicate, the author made no attempt in his initial efforts to curb his desire to research his material thoroughly or to restrain his imagination, which conjured such a vast vision of the play. The 1923 scenario had six parts:

MARCO MILLIONS
(Peaked Hill—Summer 1923)

Part One

Scene One   (forestage) The Grand Throne Room in the palace of Kublai Kaan, Cambaluc

Scene Two   (forestage) Marco Polo's cell in the fortress of the Malapaga, Genoa (1298 (45 yrs old)—four years after return to Venice)

Part Two

Scene One   (forestage) Exterior of a window of Donata's home on a canal, Venice (1271)

Scene Two   The Journey to the East

	Stage One	—Christ (Jerusalem) (1271, Nov.)
3	Stage Two	—Mahomet (Persia)
years	Stage Three	—Buddha (India—Tibet)
elapse	Stage Four	—Primitive Shamanisese (Mongolia—The Great Wall)
	Stage Five	—Lao-Tze (China) Cambaluc

Two years elapse

Part Three

Scene One   (forestage & int.) The Little Throne Room, summer palace of the Kaan at Xanadu, "the City of Peace"

Scene Two   The Mission of Discovery—First
                                              Second
                          15 yrs.   Third

Part Four

Scene One   Same as Scene One, Part Three

Scene Two   The Return of the Tourist—On board the Royal Junk of the
                              Princess Kokachin* (1292–1294)

Part Five

Scene One   Same as Scene One, Part One. Grand Throne Rome of the
                                        Kaan's palace at Cambaluc
                          (The letter)

                          (One year later)
Scene Two   The Homecoming. First at the house of the Polos, Venice
                          (1295)

Part Six

Scene One   Same as Scene One, Part Five

                          (One year later)
Scene Two   Marco's cell in the prison at Genoa

Originally, the dramatist intended to use a flashback technique with an incarcerated Marco, who had been captured in the war between Genoa and Venice, dictating his memoirs to Rusticiano of Pisa, a writer of travels. In addition to this fellow prisoner, other characters in the scenario that would later be eliminated include Marco's oldest daughter, Fantina; his brother Maffeo; the son of Kublai, Prince Mangalai, who died in 1280; the Kaan's Four Empresses including "Jamui—favorite wife—the 'Great Consort' "; the Privy Council; and the Priest of the Dead. The two Dominicans who are appointed by the pope to accompany the Polos to the East but who lose heart and turn back at the first stop are given names: Friar Nicholas and Friar William.

O'Neill always read a considerable amount of material for the historical plays he either completed or contemplated; however, extant notes—which he labels "preliminary work"—indicate none was so thoroughly researched as *Marco Millions*. The heading "Section Two of Part Two" is followed by numerous pages providing a detailed description of the "Natural resources, Industry, Sport &

---

*Spelled Kukachin in the published text.

women & warfare" found at each of the five stages of Marco's journey. The dramatist carefully organizes the information provided in *The Travels of Marco Polo* about each region, emphasizing, in particular, the different religious practices, customs, and prevailing attitudes but, above all, the existing or potential wealth. At least one page is devoted to each of the following:

Dates —whole career of Marco Polo
Possibilities for the Missions
Data —Marco's Missions
Places & dates (China)
Astrological and religious beliefs and customs
Data —Kublai
Data —Elder Polos association with Kublai
Data —Voyage home
Data —Return to Venice, battle with Genoa, Marco's capture
Data —Rusticiano of Pisa

The most important section of the notes, labeled "Data—M. P. personally," contains information the playwright uses to characterize Marco and a reference indicating he possesses American traits:

Called "Il Milione"—no transcendent superiority of character or capacity—no comparison to Columbus—shadowy image of man in book: practical, brave, shrewd, prudent, keen in affairs, and never losing his interest in mercantile details—sparing of speech (The American Ideal!)—contempt for those whose consciences would not run in customary grooves, and on his own part a keen appreciation of the World's pomps & vanities—of humor there are hardly any signs in his book—gravity never disturbed—M's book so defective in regard to Chinese manners and peculiarities—remarkable arts and customs are never alluded to. Was Polo's book materially affected by the scribe Rusticiano? Impossible to conceive of sober and reticent M. P. pacing the floor of his Genoese dungeon and seven times over rolling out magniloquent bombast.

The long list of proverbs that is inserted in the notes seems strangely out of place, but most of them reflect the Kaan's attitude to Marco after long observation of his guest: "An avaricious heart is like a snake trying to swallow an elephant (or a discontented mind)"; "The man with money speaks the truth"; "If you have money, the devil will grind for you." The proverb the Kaan tries in vain to teach Marco is "Man is a small heaven." The Kaan makes a more strenuous effort in the scenario than in the published text to bring moral and spiritual awareness to the callow youth who comes to his court. What O'Neill does here and in his next plays such as *The Great God Brown* and *Dynamo* and what he strives to do in the unfinished "Robespierre" and "Blind Alley Guy" is to present a young man in an early scene and show him at one or more later stages in his life after external forces have interacted, usually fatally, with the character's inner flawed condition.

The scene depicting the funeral service for Kokachin is placed first in the scenario but is later transposed intact to the end of the play. In the early outline, the drama opens and closes with the scene in Marco's prison cell, with the intervening material becoming a type of play-within-a-play. Marco's only purpose in dictating his memoirs to Rusticiano is to promote business for the house of Polo. His own inner corruption leads him to believe he can obtain his release from prison by offering bribes to jailers and government officials. His "spiritual hump" has become even more pronounced than it was in the Kaan's court; exposure to the great man's wisdom and goodness has had no effect on him. In contrast, the Kaan's contact with this living symbol of Western Christianity and civilization proves to be a painful learning experience, disillusioning him and shattering his hope for religious reassurance. O'Neill's notes stress a significant historical fact: that the Kaan's request to the pope for a hundred wise men is based on his personal desire to become a Christian. Ideally, these witnesses of Christianity would justify the Kaan's conversion. He is quoted in *The Travels of Marco Polo* as saying:

> "Following my example, all my nobility will then in like manner receive baptism, and this will be imitated by my subjects in general; so that the Christians of these parts will exceed in number those who inhabit your own country." From this discourse it must be evident that if the Pope had sent out persons duly qualified to preach the gospel, the grand khan would have embraced Christianity, for which, it is certainly known, he had a strong predilection.*

The Kaan scorned the Nestorian Christians under his domain. In the scenario, a priest of this Eastern church accompanies Kokachin's bier into the court, but a Confucian priest is substituted in the final text. The Kaan's grief at the end of the play is the result of his granddaughter's death; his utter despair can only be explained by his awareness that Christianity is even more ineffectual than the religions of the East to correct man's moral deformity.

O'Neill's vision of his characters and the manner in which they embodied his theme were so clear and certain in the summer of 1923 that the scenario he wrote at that time becomes in essence, with only a few minor changes, the basis for the finished play. The author devoted sixty-seven days in 1924—from July to October—to "Mister Mark Millions," as the play was then entitled, writing the dialogue and transforming the original six-part scenario into a massive four-part first draft. On October 10, the work is described in the Work Diary as "two full long plays." Not until mid-October did he confront the problem of the play's length.

The Travels of Marco Polo (The Orion Press, New York), p. 117.

The first draft "Marco" play is now finished. It has been an interesting job but a long one. I should say the play is two good long plays of $2\frac{1}{2}$ hours each—at least! So you see it's really two plays I've done. Luckily, without premeditation, the piece falls into two very distinct—and exactly equal in length—halves. Which may prove a la Peer Gynt that "God is a Father to me after all even if He isn't economical."

(Letter to Macgowan, October 12, 1924)

In January 1925 when O'Neill condensed the two "good long plays" into the drama's final form, the present three-act work, he eliminated the two prison scenes and Part Three of the 1923 scenario. He retained not only the sequence of all the other sections but also their content. Parts Two and Four become the first two acts of the play; Parts Five and Six and the transposed funeral scene of Part One are combined to form the third act.

The playwright uses an approach in this early work that will be repeated in one of his last creative efforts: he takes an actual historical figure, an idealistic admired leader of men, and makes him an instrument to promote the moral and spiritual regeneration of his fellow men. In *Marco Millions* a philosophical potentate of the East, the Kaan, tries to convert an American-type Italian; in the late unfinished play, "The Visit of Malatesta" ("Malatesta Seeks Surcease"), the noble anarchist hero—an accurate portrait of Enrico Malatesta—attempts to reform his former countrymen, the Italian American Daniellos. Like the Kaan's, Malatesta's efforts fail.

Unfortunately, O'Neill omits the two scenes in Part Three of the scenario depicting the Kaan-Marco relationship, which is one of his best examples of the many manifestations of the materialist-businessman/idealist-poet conflict. In some plays the struggle is centralized within one person; in *Marco Millions* the battle is waged between two opposing characters. The scenario's Part Three opens in the Kaan's summer palace two years after the Polos' arrival. During these years the Kaan, aided by his wise men, philosophers, poets, and scientists, has made a futile attempt to educate Marco. All his teachers conclude that Marco "is a clod, fit only to be a practical man, a merchant or a politician—or both." In handwriting that is exceptionally large for him, indicating information to be stressed, O'Neill notes:

They all agree on his three faults and his three virtues: bigotry, his gross materialism, his servile acceptance and fear of authority; his virtues—he is fearless, he is capable and energetic, he is a child in development, fidelity to himself, his duty. Has he a soul? No. (Kublai thinks the Pope must be a philosopher like himself, that Marco is his cynical assertion of the impossibility of wisdom.) Then what is within him, what faith makes him live? He has no faith but only three unthinking beliefs—in the divine right of money, in the divine right of property—things as they are (business as usual), in the divine right of himself as the ruler and possessor of both.

In the next paragraph, and in his usual handwriting, O'Neill presents the reflections of the Kaan who emerges from the 1923 scenario as one of the dramatist's noblest and wisest creations. When the two elder Polo brothers returned home after their first visit, the Kaan began studying the teachings of Buddha and of Christ. While "impressed with the essential identity of their truth," he is distressed by the hopeless materialism of the Polos and "amazed by the contradictory manner in which truth becomes distorted in human life, the dogma of religion." To the Kaan the West epitomizes the unspiritual.

Marco seems to him the perfect type of the man who, East as well as West, is destined to survive and create civilization according to his desire, the God who becomes lost in Man, the flesh-God—a second childhood of the race. He sees the East as partially redeemed from this by its hard-won culture but the West seems to have no culture—or to have destroyed it. The Pope has lamented his lack of wise men—which Kublai takes as a confession on his part of the sorry state of things—and has sent him Marco as an example of that hopelessness—youth, the past and the future. And Kublai resolves he will send him back to the Pope with a soul as a symbol of the peaceful conquering of the West by East, as a symbol of what the union might produce in Man—the union of absolute materialism with abstract thought. God has manifested himself again and again vainly to Man. Now He is without hope until Man manifests himself to Him.

In the finished play fifteen years elapse between the last scene of Act One, when Marco first arrives at the Kaan's court, and the first scene of Act Two, in which he returns from a mission, having become a full-fledged despotic Mayor. In the scenario, however, Marco's transformation—his growing materialism and spiritual paucity—is a gradual process as depicted in the second scene of the omitted Part Three: "The Mission of Discovery." O'Neill describes the consequences of Marco's three missions:

Discovery One   —With the Spirit of Commerce—Finance. Marco invents
                   paper money through which Man loses all contact with
                   the worth—and exchange—of the goods he produces.

Discovery Two   —With the Spirit of Earth (Agriculture)—Marco invents
                   Landlordism as the national reincarnation of Feudalism.
                   Man loses all creative contact with the fruits of the earth.

Discovery Three —The soul of man is a citadel which the Gods may lay
                   waste but not conquer.

The Kaan sends Marco, as a lieutenant, on the third mission to observe the Tartars' attempt to conquer a city defended by a leader who fearlessly faces certain slaughter yet resists surrender. On his return, Marco demonstrates the siege gun he has invented to the Kaan "who foresees that such inventions will make war heroically meaningless and constantly more horrible. 'I am sick of governing men. They will only their own destruction.'"

In addition to deleting passages that reveal the Kaan's despair, the dramatist also omits some humorous scenes such as the one in which Marco returns at the end of his fifteen years of duty and announces that he is now qualified to be a governor of a whole province instead of a mere city. The Kaan agrees and describes the one he has in mind: "It is a very unruly aboriginal province. They have boiled and eaten their last few governors." Marco boasts that the first thing he will do is to make a law prohibiting cannibalism, asserting proudly that his subjects "will find him a tough proposition if they become subversive." The elder Polos are suspicious of the Kaan's offer and warn Marco privately that some jealous person in power "wants to get him out of the way, to do the dirty jobs. Now, if they could manage it, would be the time to go home taking their wealth with them."

In the early, as in the late, version, Kokachin's love for Marco is not returned; but in the scenario it is the Kaan rather than his astrologer, Chu-Yin, who urges the captain of the junk that will transport the Princess to Persia to look into her eyes each day. The farewells are said at court in the 1923 version rather than at the royal wharf at the seaport of Zayton, the only new scene O'Neill devises for the final draft of the play. The final scene at the Kaan's court a year later and the Polos' homecoming remain as originally conceived. There is substantial evidence that the author planned to retain the prison scenes up to the time he was forced to condense the "two full long plays" into one in January 1925. Displaying his usual thrift, he uses the reverse side of two typed pages of dialogue from the second prison scene to write the first outline for *The Great God Brown*, which he began on January 27, four days after he completed condensing *Marco Millions*.

These two typed pages of dialogue, numbered 8–4 and 8–6, represent an advanced stage of composition and development and are excerpts from the first draft of the play which O'Neill completed in fall 1924. On page 8–4 Marco's wife Donata complains bitterly about one line in his book:

> Donata: It's where you say that that pretty pagan Princess cried when you left her. (Following her own thoughts—jealously) I suppose it's regret for that heathen hussy that makes you so grouchy at times?
>
> Marco: Don't talk silly. Can't a man be miserable.

This exchange raises the possibility that the source of Marco's misery could be the remembrance of what he saw in Kokachin's eyes—the purity of genuine love untainted by any self-centered motive. The slight chance that there is hope for change in him fades as he talks disgustedly of the corruption in the prison. On page 8-6 he tries to get his wife to bribe the jailer:

> Marco: But you might try—perhaps a woman—but don't pay too great a price—

Donata: (Suddenly with full dignity of virtuous womanhood) No! Not
            that! Not even for you!

Marco: (Stares at her blankly—irritably) I don't know what you're
            talking about. I was saying don't offer more than a thousand.

Donata: (Let down) Oh, all right.

Giovanni: (Appears at door again) Shake a leg, lady. You can't stay all
            night. All lights out in a minute—and I wouldn't trust Mister
            Millions alone with you in the dark. This is a respectable house.

Donata: (About to burst) YOU—!

Marco: Ssshh! (He kisses her—in a whisper) Keep your temper. Try
            a thousand.

As O'Neill's later plays—especially the nine-act *Strange Interlude*—attest,
mere length would not compel O'Neill to eliminate the two prison scenes. Nor
was he motivated by theatrical considerations. Even in his bleakest early plays
like "The Personal Equation" and *The Straw*, the dramatist leaves man with some
faint glimmer of a hopeless hope that change is possible. As a last scene, however,
the prison walls—like the four walls later in the Tyrone household—seemingly
trap a character who has already become a captive of the past and doomed in the
hopelessness of the present. The epilogue that is substituted for the second prison
scene is ambiguous, an open-end finale. In it, Marco, whose dress—that of a Vene-
tian merchant of the late Thirteenth Century—links him irrevocably to the past,
rises from his aisle seat in the first row after the curtain closes and leaves the
theatre to enter the present world of reality. He shows greater awareness of his
affinity with the stage character in the scenario than in the final version. In the
former, he "banishes the momentarily disturbing—yet, of course, incredible—
suspicion of any identity between the hero of the drama and himself." Curiously,
it appears O'Neill is trying to incorporate in the epilogue an idea he had approximately three years earlier: contrasting the oldest civilization of China and modern times and offering man again "a definite choice of either material success or
a step toward a higher spiritual plane." The final line of this idea suggests a
possible purpose for the epilogue: "Failure in choice entails immediate reincarnation and eternal repetition in life on this plane until spiritual choice is made."
The point O'Neill makes in both the form and content of the epilogue is that
modern existential man still has, and must make, a choice.

The dramatist calls Marco an "American pillar of society" and depicts
him as a self-made millionaire who uses Chamber of Commerce rhetoric. Marco
is described in the scenario's epilogue as "a trifle irritated and puzzled, and not a
little bored as his thoughts, in spite of himself, dwell for some passing moments
upon the play." Vaguely he remembers, like the typical American businessman
today, what the word "Christ" in the Christianity he professes actually means.

The presence of others in the audience should serve to remind him of the brotherhood of man. However, in the published text, his glance at others is "impersonally speculative, his bearing stolid with the dignity of one who is sure of his place in the world." His luxurious limousine arrives; and Marco—in typical American bourgeois fashion—"With a satisfied sigh at the sheer comfort of it all, resumes his life." In contrast, Marco in the early epilogue "walks with the crowd as one of them" in leaving the theatre and goes to "the nearest subway entrance and disappears." While he, too, is disturbed when his thoughts dwell on the play, he recovers quickly and "begins to whistle untroubledly, to hum with self-appreciation, to think of his homey apartment with its awaiting him there sandwich and cold bottle of beer."

Both versions of the epilogue—the early one depicting Marco as the proletarian representative, the later as the bourgeois capitalist—contain the possibility, slight though it may be, for change, for inner renewal, that the reenactment of man's ever ancient, ever new dilemma will finally inspire a spiritual rather than material choice. Were this miracle to occur, millions of reincarnated Marcos would find themselves repeating the Kaan's message to the Pope, which appears at the bottom of the scenario's final page: "I wish to know of the old God men murdered in their image. He must be true God." In O'Neill's next statement looms the suggestion that modern man's life is an eternal force that compels even the Gods to laugh:

We are all made of the nature of the Everlasting Dramatist. Our lives are theatre—in the worst sense—the history of Man the forced posturing of an actor to empty benches. The Gods laughed once—then grew ashamed and went away.

O'Neill has a definite purpose in mind when he adds the epilogue. By depicting his hero as a contemporary countryman, the dramatist reminds audiences and readers that they, like Marco, are given a choice: either to reject the mirrored materialistic self playing to an empty house or to accept the fact that man, having the "nature of the Everlasting Dramatist," can make his life theatre—in the best sense.

[STRANGE INTERLUDE]
Godfather*
(1923)

Play of the woman whose husband (married just before he left—affair) is killed in war—aviator—falls in final practice—in flames. Shock of news.† She becomes ultra-neurotic, hysterical, desperate, goes in for many love affairs—finally at 20, disgusted with herself and broken down, longing for normality and health and, most of all, motherhood as a final peace, she marries a naive, young man just out of college. Her affection for him is maternal—but mostly as the healthy father of her child. Then she discovers on visiting his home—his own people—that insanity runs in his family. Causes a hatred in her for very thought of having child by him—dislike for him, feels he has cheated her. She meets classmate of his who has become doctor. (And also boy husband begins to doubt himself because no child, to grow more incapable and childish) She finally goes to him as patient—he is a neurologist—and confesses everything. He takes a daring stand. For both sakes. She bears son—falls in love with doc & he with her—Husband becomes very proud, capable, confident, successful. She has more children by the doctor. These children grow up instinctively hating the Doc, loving their mother and husband. Especially the latter, who clings to them as his backbone. They copy him, admire him, even look like him. The Doc fades into a small town practitioner. Finally in a fit of guilty desperation, the wife, seeing children more & more estranged, tells husband everything—except about insanity—but he cannot believe, thinks only jealousy and neuroticism—even consults Doc about her—Doc denies—After many years, husband dies—65 or so. They, very old, marry. This finishes estrangement of the children, grandchildren. Very old, they wait for death to let them speak the truth.

The source of the original idea for *Strange Interlude* was to become a subject of controversy that was resolved only after a court decision in 1931. A Georges Lewys, the pen name of Gladys Lewis, brought suit, which she eventually lost, accusing O'Neill of plagiarizing her book *The Temple of Pallas-Athenae*. The notebook containing the 1923 idea and a collection of scenarios, including *Strange Interlude*, became Exhibit 2 in the March 13, 1931 trial. A statement on the inside cover of the notebook reads: "Legal stuff in first two pages is there because this book was a part of evidence in ridiculous 'Strange Interlude' plagiarism suit." At the time of the trial, O'Neill was in France. His deposition states he had made his first notes for the play in 1923 after a former aviator of the Lafayette Escadrille told him the story that was to become the basis for the plot—

---

*O'Neill draws slanted lines through this idea and writes: "Strange Interlude 1926–1927."
†The author deletes a statement after "news": "her child is born dead."

of a girl whose aviator fiancé had been killed in World War I. In the 1923 idea O'Neill depicts his heroine as the flier's widow; he later reverts to the true story in the 1925 scenario but embellishes the many real-life details. His heroine, Nina, accuses her father of preventing her marriage to the deceased lover; seeking revenge, she gives herself promiscuously to wounded servicemen. As in the original idea, Nina marries a man (Sam Evans) whose family is afflicted by a hereditary strain of insanity. She has an affair with her husband's best friend (Ned Darrell) but has only one child by him—Gordon, whom she names for, and identifies with, the dead lover. Ultimately, the play becomes a study of a neurotic woman whose selfishness destroys the lives of the three men she needs to fulfill herself.

The first of the two scenarios, with its heading "Nantucket—Summer 1925," was written in a ten-day period, from the fifth to the fourteenth of September. Four tentative titles appear at the beginning of the scenario: "Down In Flames," "Brought Down in Flames," "This Strange Interlude," and "The Haunted & Hunted." The list of characters and their ages "at first appearance" follow. Only the last two names in the middle column remain the same throughout the many versions.

EARLIEST ERASED FORM	CORRECTED 1925 LIST	FINAL FORM
Nina Bayne	Nina Lee—19	Nina Leeds
Art Truesdale	Phìl Adams—25	Harry—then Sam Evans
Ned Marsh	Ned Darrell—25	surname Steele, then Darrell
Doctor Amos Aimsworth	Doctor Amos Mott—56	eliminated
Professor Henry Bayne	Professor Henry Lee, Nina's father—55	Professor Henry Leeds
Gordon Truesdale	Gordon Adams (21 when he died) *	Gordon Evans
	Gordon Shaw	Gordon Shaw
	Charles Marsden, a novelist—30	Charles Marsden

While the doctor is eliminated, his first name is used to identify one of the two characters O'Neill adds to his dramatis personae: Mrs. Amos Evans and Madeline Arnold.

As originally conceived, the play had six acts, the first three containing two scenes. O'Neill later changes the form to nine scenes and finally on August 23, 1926 to nine acts. The following section illustrates the early stages of structural development:

---

*This statement describes Gordon Shaw, Nina's lover, and not her son.

	Scene One	—Professor Bayne's home in a small college town in New England—December 1918.
Act One	Scene Two	—Hospital for crippled soldiers—Two years later.
	Three	
	Scene One	—the Truesdale family house in northern New York— two years later.
Act Two	Four	
	Scene Two	—Arthur Truesdale's rented commutor's house on Long Island—eight months later.
	Five	
	Scene One	—Same as last—four months later.
Act Three	Six	
	Scene Two	—Same as last—one year later.
	Seven	
Act Four	Scene	—Their apartment in N.Y.—Eleven years later.
	Eight	
Act Five	Scene	—Their estate on Long Island—Ten years later.
	Nine	
Act Six	Scene	—The same—Ten years later.

The descriptions of the characters in the 1925 scenario differ substantially—and often dramatically—from those in the final draft of the play.

Nina:

Her eyes are beautiful—a grey blue, looking at you seriously, steadily, friendly but unmoved, deeply indifferent to everything but their own visions, a dreamer's eyes strangely out of place and made more startlingly fascinating by this contrast. This is how Nina had been before the news of Gordon Shaw's death crash. Her nervous breakdown has not changed her appearance at all but has stolen all the quality of integrity, the directness, the steadfast purposefulness of her character from her. She seems now more vital than ever but it is nervous, overcharged, hectic, at loose ends. Her eyes seem continually shuddering before some terrible enigma, puzzled, bewildered, wounded to their depths and made defiant and resentful by their pain.

Her father:

Gentle, mild, cynical and liberal professor of psychology. Still preserving his good looks, his pose of cultured gentleman among barbarians, there is yet a worn-out, resigned quality to him, a sense that he feels himself finished and is not proud of what he has made of life. Unable to face himself, he has been proud since the death of his wife five years before (a "lady," a mistress of the home, maternal & well-contentedly mediocre—ideal mate for him) of Nina's brilliant and scholarly accomplishments, of her marriage to the noted athlete then of rich family! Now he is broken, a bit pitiful in his attempt to regain his poise-defense, confused and frightened.

Doctor Aimsworth:

Neurologist, old friend of Bayne—the attraction of opposites—has made a pose of natural rude, direct, crushing bluntness—to the point of vulgarity at times.

Adams:

Figure inclined to softness and flesh, his face full without a line, characterless in the sense of undeveloped—great timidity, the lost quality of one who has not found himself either with women or among men and begins to be consciously inferior about it. Yet there is underlying strength in his face, an obstinate will, and one believes there is something in him, not of a high order of intelligence surely, which might be released for and constructive efficiency under the proper guidance and stimulus. At present he is a wandering aimless lost pet animal whom everyone half-way adopts but never seriously. The result is to make him more inferior. He laughs a bit but has no sense of humor. The world is too much for him.

Marsden:

Has written civilized books about the Americans of his boyhood and college days—colorless people moving against a background of colorless prosperity. His style is modelled after James—his work is passe, gutless. Within, his soul seethes with bitterness although outwardly he is urbane, ironical, cynical and of irreproachable poise. Deeply sensitive beneath, he has the reputation of being a worldly disillusioned cynic. He is bisexual. Men treat him as they would a woman to a degree. They can do this because there is nothing effeminate in either his appearance or manner. They love to confide in him—feel a real affection for him. Women likewise treat him as one of themselves; they can be half-dressed before him, he is a good gentle tolerant listener to their interminable revelations about their inner, misunderstood lives. What his mind sees can never come out in his work.

Ned Darrell:

His speech blunt and incisive, his black eyes keen and disturbing—has a sharp, ironic humor—is eminently self-confident and sure—feels he has his own life and others' lives & all desires, motives, etc. pinned to a card and indexed—has had many affairs—the gratification he gets is a vanity-satisfaction, a sense-of-power satisfaction. He has created this for himself into a belittling of love, of superiority as a scientist.

The following synopsis of the nine scenes of the 1925 scenario contains only information that differs substantially from that found in the finished play.

| *Scene One*:   Sitting room of Professor Bayne's home—evening in winter of 1917.

Professor Bayne has asked Doctor Aimsworth to examine his grief-stricken daughter who enters wearing "hat, rouged and powdered, carries travelling bag but is in bare feet & nightdress. She is walking in her sleep," planning to join Gordon who "is going up up—up. 'I must go with him before he comes down in flames.' " When awakened, she announces her decision to become a nurse. She has not spoken to her father since Gordon's death but now says: "I've forgiven you. Now I'll get to forget you." When she leaves, her father falls to his knees, but there is no admission of guilt nor any hint that his opposition to the marriage is motivated by selfishness or incestuous feelings. Although listed in the dramatis personae, Marsden does not appear in this or any scene of the first scenario.

| *Scene Two*:   Dispensary at the sanatarium for disabled soldiers—years later

A "Scene with Father first" is indicated; yet only Nina, Marsh (Darrell), and Truesdale (Evans) appear here. Marsh is disturbed by Nina's promiscuity and asks her "what it was in her that made her give herself to Seaton, Morehead, Lane and a dozen others since she has been there. It's all masochistic—a mother's instinct gone wrong—delight in debasing herself. What she needs is to get married." Truesdale—his choice of a husband for her—enters and "has queer love scene with Nina."

| *Scene Three*:   The Truesdale home in northern N.Y. state years later.

Truesdale, who is a proofreader for a publisher, reluctantly takes Nina to see his mother. The pregnant Nina is told that her husband's "father died insane and his brother is in asylum now." When Mrs. Truesdale proposes a substitute father for her child, "Nina is amazed but mother says she has suffered too much to be bothered by moral right or wrong."

| *Scene Four*:   Their half, two-family house on L[ong]. I[sland]. near city.

Nina confuses her aborted child with Gordon: "it is her destiny to kill G. over and over again."* Truesdale has lost his job, blames himself for his wife's sickness, and appeals to Marsh to see her. The doctor gives Nina an ultimatum: adultery or an asylum for Truesdale. "No time for morals—his heredity will get him. The case fascinates him by its perversity. She surrenders with strange intentness. He must remember she still loves Gordon."

---

*Orin Mannon uses nearly identical words in *Mourning Becomes Electra* to describe his feelings after he kills Adam Brant.

Scene Five: Same as last—some months later. Scene between Marsh & Nina. |

Ignoring the doctor's warning that "it means the madhouse for T.," Nina plans to divorce her husband and to marry Marsh. He argues that the proposal is dishonorable, a betrayal of friendship; he finally admits his fear of responsibility; "he will not marry her, cannot be bothered with a mistress, hates children." He leaves for Europe. The abandoned Nina, after confirming her husband's suspicion that she is pregnant, "with bitterness suddenly bursts out will call him Gordon!"

Scene Six: The same—about a year later. |

Pride in his son inspires Truesdale to become a hard-working journalist. Nina is now in second place. When Marsh returns from Europe, "her attitude is one of bewilderment, fear, resentful longing, but her love comes back—but not the same love now. Her passion burnt out, it is now love of a mother for him. There is nothing to do but—wait."

Scene Seven: The Truesdales' home 11 years later—a very costly Park Avenue apartment. |

Truesdale "has become a very high-salaried general manager, a successful American type." No birthday motivates Marsh, as in the final draft, to bring a gift to his son Gordon who, with "his back to T[ruesdale]. but facing M[arsh]. & Mother, deliberately breaks it. His hate wounds M. who has lost ambition, is still in same position at hospital, depends more and more on Nina." Marsh asks bitterly: "What are we waiting for?"

Scene Eight: The Truesdales' country home on L.I.—ten years later. |

Truesdale is now "vice president of the company, making large money. Gordon, after a famous career in both studies and athletics, has graduated from Yale." This scene, like the second, differs completely—not only in setting but also in characterization and action—from its later counterpart. Marsh "has become physically prematurely old," is ironically humorous and philosophical about his loss of ambition, and loves Nina more and more. In an outburst of hatred for husband and lover, Nina, who has aged "but is still beautiful," tells Truesdale the whole truth. He does not believe her: "It would be complete suicide. It is her condition." Marsh is now "heartbroken at the revelation that she hates him. She suddenly knows that neither Truesdale nor Marsh is the father. Gordon then is the real father. Immaculate conception, Marsh says with a bitter laugh—and now what am I? Friend."

Scene Nine: The same—ten years later, the day of Truesdale's funeral. |

Gordon has "gone into Wall Street—is junior partner in daring new firm there." He tells his mother and Marsh he is going to be married and "forces himself to say without bitterness: 'and I suppose you'll be getting married, too?' They are surprised, confused as two young people." After wishing them happiness, he says he cannot see them for a long time because of his father and leaves. Nina and Marsh are alone in the garden,

huddling each other for warmth and comfort. "There are only the two of us alive, might as well get married—for comfort sake." Nina tells her dream of the previous night—that Gordon Shaw had come out of the sky and carried her up to heaven with him. Marsh says that in his dream he had made some great discovery—the secret of life to heal mankind of all fleshly ills. She pats his hand. Perhaps those dreams will begin to come true—soon. Perhaps nothing has really happened to us after all. Marsh—Interlude.

There is no hint in the September 1925 scenario that O'Neill planned to use stream-of-consciousness asides. He had read Freud earlier that year, as he indicates in Work Diary entries: *Beyond the Pleasure Principle* (1/21/25) and *Group Psychology and the Analysis of the Ego* (3/10/25). His statement of March 13, 1926, when he was writing *Lazarus Laughed*, may reflect an inspiration to incorporate soliloquies: "New ideas on everything crowding up—think I've got hold of right method for doing Strange Interlude when I come to it." To the 1925 notes for *Strange Interlude*, O'Neill adds a section headed "Method—1926":

Method—Start with soliloquy—perhaps have the whole play nothing but a thinking aloud (or this entrance for other play—anyway the thinking aloud being more important than the actual talking—speech breaking through thought as a random process of concealment, speech inconsequential or imperfectly expressing the thought behind—all done with the most drastic logic and economy and simplicity of words (Thought perhaps, always naturally expressing itself to us—thinking itself—or being thought by us—always in terms of an adolescent level of vocabulary, as if we thereby eternally tried to educate to mature self-understanding, the child in us.)

Carrying the method to an extreme—one sees their lips move as they talk to one another but there is no sound—only their thinking is aloud.

On September 28, 1925, O'Neill informs Macgowan that both Lazarus and his women play are "elaborately scenariod—wonderfully I believe." He decided to write *Lazarus Laughed* first, and did not begin "scheming out" *Strange Interlude* until May 16, 1926. He devoted twelve days that month to making notes and writing the second scenario for the play. The section that follows provides a detailed analysis of this 1926 scenario; it also incorporates information from the Work Diary, showing the relationship between this second outline and the first draft and establishing the dates of composition for the nine scenes of this draft.

The only section in the second scenario that is specifically dated—May 23, 1926—is one entitled "New novelist character"; it is a "scheme for use of Marsden's character" in each of the nine scenes. The section reveals the role that other characters, as well as Marsden, play in these scenes. The following outline, while using only O'Neill's words, is a condensation of the section:

Begins Scene One and is on until the end (as already written).

Scene Two: Hospital scene—Nina and father and Marsden. (He comes back, sent by father to smooth things over.)

Scene Three: Evans homestead—Nina and Sam and mother.

Scene Four: Sam and Nina's ½, two-family house, L.I.—Marsden—Her father has died. They talk about last days—resentment against marriage to Sam. Nina and Steele* and Marsden and Sam— (Something Sam does to irritate her beyond bearance makes her say Yes at end of scene.)

Scene Five: Same—Marsden and Nina—(he is full of death of mother, she of birth of son)—Sam and Nina and Marsden.

Scene Six: Nina and Marsden (still thinking about mother's death—not been able to work until just lately)—She guesses his love for first time—Steele shows his passion to Marsden—Marsden, in pique and jealousy, tries obliquely to reveal secret to Sam. Steele tries to tell Sam.

Scene Seven: Marsden and Gordon (aged 12). (Novel—only one with guts —which took him up to the age of adolescence—Nina little girl—Gordon asks story—M's bitterness comes out in veiled story of years between he tells). A revealing in past of queer bond of sympathy and hatred that unites Marsden and Steele. Their periodic efforts to break away. M's futile trip to Europe, Steele's equally futile efforts to do research work, to fall in love, marries, is divorced, etc.

Scene Eight: In the garden on L.I.—Marsden has married in the interval (?). Steele bitter—son's graduation—festivities—sees him coming with Mrs. M[arsden]., ideal mother—wants nothing, gives—Gordon's admiration for her.

Scene Nine: Same—Marsden and Steele and Nina—Marsden very old, spiteful at end when he thinks they're going to get married.

(These last two scenes should have a sort of hazy quality of flowing memory —of passage of time with the events and people past, the leading characters who stand still, growing old.)

Scene One is the longest and most detailed section in the scenario, reflecting the many new concepts O'Neill had developed for characterization and action. As in the first scenario, the Professor's friend—now called Doctor Mott—has come

---

*Marsh, Nina's lover, is called Steele here but Darrell in Scene Two.

"surreptitiously to observe and diagnose" Nina's case. When Marsden enters, O'Neill experiments for the first time with his new thought method:

> Marsden's mind absorbs the scene, describing his appreciation, criticism of it, and from the room to the Professor and the Professor to his dead wife, to Nina, to wonderings about his own feeling for Nina, his craving for love blocked by his memory of his mother and his first experience in sex in dollar hooker shop.

Professor Lee's name has not yet been changed to its final form, but he is described as in the published text as being snobbish, selfish, jealous. Marsden maliciously assaults the guilt-ridden man verbally with a word picture of an encounter he had with Nina and Gordon one spring day on campus: "Gordon so like a Greek God. He was a bit coarse-grained for a god—only flaw in Gordon too fleshy." In an aside, Lee thinks: "Too fleshy to him. Marsden is positively womanish in gushing about men."

Nina enters with Mott, whom O'Neill—in an inserted passage—describes as "a man with the aggressive vitality of a frankly sensual nature, of an overgrown boy curious about sex and not afraid to be Rabelasian." Mott analyzes Marsden mentally: "Half and half—bisexual—good for her friendship but tantalizing, not enough, no solution there as he had hoped—Marsden to him would be ruin. If father had only let them marry—either satisfaction or disillusion then—now had only dream, ideal hard for man to compete with." Marsden and Mott support Nina's plan to go in training to be a nurse. Nina resents the doctor, thinking he must have sexual theories about her: "needs man—not sex, love! Why didn't Gordon take her, rape her—furious at him, then conscious-stricken; I should have given." The scene ends with the reflections of Lee: She thinks "of her tawdry men instead of him" and of Marsden: "all emotion however genuine—always ugly—repellent."

O'Neill started the first draft of Scene One on June 1, 1926, finished it on the eighth, and then made three futile attempts to write the second scene. On July 27 he decides "to go back to old idea for scene"—to the sanatarium setting of the 1925 scenario, expanding his earlier treatment. The sanatarium is the setting for Scene Two of the second scenario. Darrell, one of the doctors there, is worried about Nina but "tries to throw it off—'What is Hecuba to him?'" Nina enters and tells Darrell she has been fired—"seems Crosby 'kissed and told.'" The doctor attacks her: "They all did—should think the memory of Gordon would have stopped her." The action in the rest of the scene is the same as in the first scenario. As long as O'Neill retained the sanatarium setting, he has serious problems developing this scene. Possibly he wanted to draw from his own life experience and depict an atmosphere familiar to him. Apparently he made the decision early in August to set Scene Two in the library, the choice for the final draft, as his letter to Macgowan on the seventh implies:

> I did most of a second scene two separate times and tore them up before I got started on the really right one! . . . The point is my stuff is much deeper

and more complicated now and I'm not so easily satisfied with what I've dashed off as I used to be. Naturally, until I hit my stride—or rather found *the one* action & place for the second scene I felt rather sour on life generally.

On August 22, 1926, O'Neill "finished damned 2nd scene" and started the draft for the third scene. Only one line—and this is crossed out—appears for this section in the second scenario: "Nina—(writing letter to Marsden)." He omits entirely a synopsis in the second scenario for the fourth scene, which he began writing on September 1. He did not need to make a second detailed outline for these sections as Acts Three and Four in the final text merely re-create and develop the third and fourth scenes in the first 1925 scenario.

O'Neill revised the first three acts of *Strange Interlude* from the first to the tenth of October and then went to New York where he spent a considerable amount of time that month and the next with Carlotta Monterey. As the purpose of this work is to present the sources and influences that contribute to the formation of the dramatist's ideas, one point should be made here. While O'Neill's contact with this woman, who was to become his third wife, did not alter the firmly fixed basic concept of the Nina Lee of the 1925 scenario, this character's new emotional intensity in the second outline probably reflects Carlotta's at this particular time.

The first days of December 1926 were spent revising *Marco Millions* for publication. Then, as he writes Macgowan on the seventh, he intended to go "on to Strange Interlude. With all that's inside me now I ought to be able to explode in that play in a regular blood-letting by the time I get to it." After going over the first four acts in early January, O'Neill began the fifth act, in which Nina displays a new abandonment, the desire to give herself passionately to her lover.

In the second scenario for Act Five, as in its first draft which O'Neill started on January 11, 1927, Nina's pregnancy gives

her feelings of oneness—life—God—beyond—her unscrupulousness—Sam is nothing—let him go crazy—Gordon forgotten as individual—has become life within her—remembrance of her giving herself to Darrell—feeling immediately she had become pregnant—his guilt—she has wanted to give herself many times since but he has refused—plans how to divorce, marry D.

The only significant difference in the sequence of events between this outline and the final version is that Sam surmises Nina is pregnant before Darrell's appearance. Sam's pride infuriates her: "He is not the father—what right has he—outrage—her decency affronted—she turns on him harshly 'Nothing!' "

O'Neill omits several ideas found in the 1926 scenario for Act Six from the first draft, begun on January 18. Marsden's jealousy of Darrell is "now turned toward Sam who seems so undeservedly happy in contrast to his own misery—M.'s affection for baby—his dream, if only Sam would die, has money could take care of Nina and baby—would be his baby—he would love wife and child—

dreams—ashamed of himself." He tells Nina that Darrell has a mistress in Europe and, when he sees her reaction, all his suspicions are "aroused about child— says meaningly he will have to have a good look at baby someday—Nina afraid—his jealousy reminds her of father's—she proves this, kisses him, leaves M. in a turmoil." Nina's love is reawakened during the unexpected visit of Darrell who "wants to see child—at first she denies this—he must go away." After the words "Knock wood," written in parentheses at the end of the section, O'Neill adds that Nina "begins to laugh and knock wood—wilder." When Sam asks her: "What's matter," she repeats the word "nothing" over and over. She faints and the three men "carry her upstairs." Nina's dramatic speech—"You are my three men"—is missing here and probably was not written until the following July; an entry for the fifteenth of that month states: "going over sixth act—wrote new ending."

On January 28, 1927, O'Neill starts the first draft of Act Seven. The notes in the 1926 scenario for this act provide insights into the various characters and their relationships:

Nina versus Darrell—last few years she has only held on to him out of a remorseful pity—she feels that Darrell by the way he has let his career go is himself the cause of Gordon's hate. Twice he has gone to the length of getting himself engaged—clings to him out of revenge or love—has gradually become with Sam an accepted wife figure in the background of his business ambitions for himself and his son. In spite of herself, she wishes his death.

Darrell versus Nina—has alternated between periods of wild love for her and contented submission to her will as her lover—hatred of Sam, longs for Sam's death in spite of himself, and a threat to tell him everything and ruin him, hatred of his son for his love for Sam, grown to dislike son, seeing him always now as the real rival who lost Nina for him, even dreams of his death—two expeditions represent his real attempts to break with Nina. His other attempts— debauches, women, aimless wandering in Europe—are only the result of quarrels, rage & pique.

Nina versus Marsden—she has come more and more to make him a sort of father-mother substitute. He encourages Sam's growing superior contempt for Darrell—he delights in Gordon's dislike for Darrell—he has accepted Darrell as Nina's lover because he is sure the love is on his part, that on hers it is entirely physical.

Sam—Nina an abstract figure whom as by a law of nature, he loves, respects, desires at intervals. He adores his son—the proof of his manhood. His friendship for Darrell is the same but tinged with a superior contempt. Marsden he regards with increased affection and respect.

Act Seven is one of the most developed sections of the scenario; it concludes with a long passage of dialogue, most of which appears later in the final draft of the play. The heading states: "End of Scene VII—between Darrell and Gordon—

breaks his present with Sam's appearance at very end." There are two differences between the early and late versions: in the former, Darrell very nearly tells Gordon that he is his father; after Darrell's "men of honor" speech, Gordon in an aside thinks: "I love him—like I do my father."

The setting for Act Eight in the 1925 scenario—the Truesdales' country home—is changed to a yacht anchored along the route of a college regatta in the second scenario and the first draft of the scene, started on February 8, 1927. In June 1926 O'Neill attended Boat Day in New London, an annual contest between Yale and Harvard and includes a similar sporting event in the play. However, the contest in the scenario is lifeless; the scene lacks excitement as O'Neill has not, as yet, included Gordon's fiancée Madeline Arnold, whose presence arouses Nina's neurotic feelings of jealousy and hatred. Because of the recent death of Sam's aunt, Nina has sent for his mother "on the plea of her being all alone, but really because she has become so jealous of Gordon's increasing reserve with her, of Sam's control and influence over him." Darrell is also on the yacht "because Nina has said he ought to come. In spite of himself he is proud of Gordon, and he is inquisitive. The news that Sam's mother is to be there intrigues him; he wants to study her."

Nina "feels cut off from everyone, bitterly lonely, and in a queer narcotic state again." Her isolated condition parallels that of Sam's mother, who is described as "lost." Her son is indifferent and impatient with her. "She feels queerly jealous and resentful of Nina and blames her for her treachery to Sam now; she prides herself she was never unfaithful to father." It is she and not Nina who tells Marsden about the insanity in the Evans family.

Then Marsden guesses the rest. He feels again a keen jealousy of Darrell as Nina's lover, father of her child—but overcomes this because he knows Darrell's pulling away from her. He is cruelly satisfied at her punishment, gloats, then suddenly overcome by a complete understanding and a great wave of pity for her.

O'Neill begins the first draft of Act Nine on February 19, 1927. The two extant fragments of this act in the 1926 scenario show O'Neill contemplated two different endings for the play. The first appears early in the notes and seems almost a continuation and conclusion of Scene Nine in the 1925 scenario. It begins: "Last Scene—Who can know the beginning of an act of where it goes?" A exchange between Nina and Darrell follows in which they try to find the words they will use to tell Gordon the truth about the past:

Nina   This is our truth. We love. This is our son—and wait by the gate until he comes—We are your truth. You are ours. You are our son, and Harry is our friend and yours.

Ned   And until then? (kisses her hand)

Nina   (With a wan but tender smile) Here in the garden—You can sit very still and smell the flowers—and taste the air from the sea—and listen for the twinge of twilight in the heart—and watch the sun descend into a dark black hill—and feel my hand (She bends over and they kiss).

Ned   (Tenderly) Well, after all, God—(He looks up quizzically) Truth is a secret. Sometimes by a miracle of grace, two people learn the one secret together—and keep it!

Nina   Yes? And keep it!

Ned   So, after all, we—

Nina   Yes, after all, we—

C[urtain].

The second fragment is closer to the ending of the final version; for Nina is consoled not by her lover, Ned Darrell, but by the father-figure, Marsden. They praise Sam and discuss his will and their work on the biography of Gordon Shaw. The play closes with the following speeches:

Nina   (As Gordon flies off—a last bitter protest) God the Father—the Sons of God the Father have all failed—it is time a Daughter of God the Mother came on earth to try to save us. I will be happy!

M.   You've got to relax—you've got to obey life.

O'Neill worked on the play, "going over" it until February 28, 1927 and, in a letter written to Macgowan that day, announced: " 'Strange Interlude' is finished. It's the biggest ever! It's a 'work.' I'm tremendously pleased with the deep scope of it. Nothing like it has been done before. After which, I'll sign myself up as my best press agent, what?" He continued, however, to make revisions and wrote Macgowan again on March 24, stating that although the play is finished, "I won't regard as absolutely ready for production until I've let it rest and gone over it again some months hence." The dramatist put aside the play for a two-month period but spent much of May, June, and July going over it. His July 25th Work Diary entry states: "Finished going over Act Nine—will call this play finally finished now!"

°TREASON
(1924)

American historical play of Margaret (Peggy) Shippen, darling debutante of Philadelphian society, who married Benedict Arnold. His treason greatly due to her influence, her love of good time & money, on his unstable nature. Her letters to British in N. Y. to buy stuff for baby shows she knew about plan. Perhaps Andre was her lover. His death and Arnold's disgrace & poverty might have explained her wonderful fidelity to Arnold in his misfortunes—a sense of retribution—finally real love for man who comes to live entirely in her.

O'Neill's heroine in *Strange Interlude* is doomed because of her inability to adjust to loss in the tragic aftermath of World War I. Shortly after making the first notes for this work, the dramatist records an idea for a play based on a historical figure whose destiny is determined not only by her flawed character but also by the actual events of war. Like Nina Leeds, Peggy Shippen is a mercurial neurotic who, as O'Neill's early notes indicate, plays a major role in the destruction and downfall of the men in her life. Many brief ideas are merely recorded in the notebooks and subsequently forgotten. "Treason" is an exception as O'Neill makes three later attempts in the 1930s to complete it—researching material and writing a plot outline and scenario. From the start he senses the dramaturgic potential of his complex heroine. The story of her tragic life contains several themes that appear in other plays of the 1920s and in the Cycle plays of the 1930s.

Like Sara Melody, Peggy Shippen is ambitious, avaricious, and determined to possess a more stately mansion. During the British occupation of Philadelphia, she meets and captivates Captain John Andre, a sensitive, impressionable young man with a touch of the poet, a dramatist and actor. Whether she merely uses him as an escape from boredom or actually feels genuine love for him is uncertain. Soon after the British evacuation she quickly makes another conquest: the heart of General Benedict Arnold, commander of the American forces in Philadelphia, a prosperous New England merchant who continues to amass wealth—by fair means or foul—throughout his years in the army. What obviously intrigues O'Neill is the contrasting natures of these two men, the opportunity to depict the poet/idealist-businessman/materialist conflict found in so many of the plays.

For a dramatist obsessed by the Faustian legend, the "Arnold plot," as he calls it, offers unlimited possibilities—a hero who sells not only his soul but his country for money. Margaret (Peggy) Shippen is no Marguerite; she is the cause of man's damnation rather than salvation. Strangely enough, O'Neill records the first idea for "Treason" during the period he is working on his original outline for *The Great God Brown*, whose wife-mistress heroine—called both Margaret and Peggy—is desired by the artist Dion Anthony and the businessman William A. Brown. The early notes, however, show that "Treason," like *Strange Interlude*, is primarily another "woman play."

81

One aspect of "Treason" merits consideration here. While researching the life and character of his historical heroine, was O'Neill conscious of the many similarities between her and his mother? Like Ella O'Neill, Peggy Shippen was brought up in a comfortable, respectable household and idolized by a protective father. At the age of eighteen she defied her family and on April 8, 1779 married the even-then notorious General Arnold, a man twenty years her senior, who was embroiled in a legal dispute with the civil authorities of Philadelphia over his questionable financial schemes. Peggy Shippen Arnold had a deceptive dual nature. Demure and innocent before marriage, she displayed a sensuality after it that surprised and delighted her jaded, experienced husband. She used her fascinating chameleonic qualities—innocence and sexuality—to get whatever she wanted from men: luxuries and favors from Andre and American officers prior to the act of treason, the personal protection of General Washington and his sympathetic subordinates after Arnold's betrayal and flight to the British. At times she was sweet, light-hearted, gay; occasionally, her other side emerged— morbid, moody, prone to self-induced hysteria. Shortly after the birth of her first son, Edward, on March 19, 1780, her husband became commander of West Point. In late August she left family and friends to join him. The discovery of the treason plot the following month made her a perpetual outcast, homeless for the rest of her life. Her husband, during the years of exile in England, turned to privateering on the high seas and to what she called "unfortunate speculation" in land. After Arnold's death in 1801, his wife, like Ella O'Neill, became deeply involved in settling her husband's financial affairs and died two years later of cancer.

As O'Neill's notes suggest, Peggy's "wonderful fidelity to Arnold in his misfortunes" is the result of her guilt feelings; her own sense of retribution, like Lavinia Mannon's, demands self-imposed bondage to the visible symbol of her crime. Letters prove that as early as the month after her marriage to Arnold, Peggy is fully cognizant of her husband's plan to betray his country. As a member of a Loyalist family, she has no qualms during the early stages of the treason plot. In contrast, Arnold struggles with his conscience. He had fought courageously against the British in the Quebec Campaign; a leg wound, leaving him permanently crippled, serves as a painful physical reminder of his former loyalty to the American cause. In 1777 he bravely defended his native state of Connecticut; four years later he would lead British troops in a savage raid against New London. The specific request that O'Neill refers to in the notes is contained in a letter Peggy Arnold sent Andre in July 1779; she asks for material for gowns and shoes, "one piece of diaper for napkins," and "one piece of clouting diaper." Andre's response, dated August 16, 1779 and found after the plot fails, is used by officials in Philadelphia to expel Peggy Arnold from that city after she sought refuge there.

If Andre was her lover, the affair pre-dates her marriage; the two correspond but never meet again after his transfer to New York. Undoubtedly, the tragic events of September 1780 filled her with a double sense of guilt. After his fatal meeting with Arnold, Andre was captured by American forces on the 23rd; the incriminating evidence on West Point defenses led to his trial and hanging. Just before the discovery of his part in the treason plot, Arnold managed to escape by barge to the British ship *Vulture*. Although she later confessed to a friend that she had directly influenced her husband to surrender West Point, Peggy played the role of the innocent, abandoned, hysterical wife, deceiving General Washington and other gullible American officers before whom she appeared in her dressing gown—disheveled, detached, seemingly unconscious of the real world around her. While her mental state is similar to Mary Tyrone's at the end of *Long Day's Journey into Night*, her physical appearance following these traumatic events resembles Con Melody's after he has killed the mare: her eyes are vacant, lifeless; her inner spirit crushed.

A pattern emerges in the notebooks and Work Diary; as he regresses step by step into American history, O'Neill shows the effects of this country's three major wars on women. He finished *Strange Interlude* in July 1927, read the galley proofs in November, and attended rehearsals in December. The following October he got what he called the "Electra idea," although he did not actually begin his Civil War trilogy until the next spring. On November 11, 1931, he completed the "last job" on *Mourning Becomes Electra*. Less than three weeks later, on December 1 and 2, he is reading and talking notes for the "Arnold plot idea." His Work Diary entry for December 6 states: "tentative sketch acts, scene plans." In 1932 he spent eleven days in January and the first week of February writing a plot outline and scenario for the "Arnold idea." On February 7 he notes that while the scenario is finished he is "very dissatisfied with conception as whole— no integrity to it yet." Two days later he is "reconsidering" his work on the play and on the 12th writing a "new end." He takes up the work again on May 13: "Treason play idea (notes—have new conceptions about this—think I will let 'W[ithout]. E[nding]. O[f]. D[ays].' rest a couple of days)." His statement the following day—"Treason play idea & Cal. Clipper Idea (notes new conceptions these two projected plays)"—is most significant and provides a possible explanation for the discarding of the "Arnold plot idea."

The California Clipper Idea becomes "The Calms of Capricorn" the next year, one of the Cycle plays. While researching "Treason," O'Neill seems to have found material that led not only to new conceptions of this play but provided the inspiration for another Cycle play. While General Washington, Alexander Hamilton, and Lafayette were convinced of Peggy Arnold's innocence, Aaron Burr, who had been raised by her father's uncle, knew of her guilt. A closer bond existed between Burr and a woman who was even more fascinating and dangerous than Peggy Arnold—Mme. Stephen Jumel, to whom he was married, from whom divorced, and over whom he apparently fought a duel with Alexander Hamilton. Mme. Jumel, née Bessie Bowen, was possibly the illegitimate daughter of George Washington and a Rhode Island prostitute. Three months after the last reference to the "Treason" play in May 1932, O'Neill makes preliminary notes for "The Life of Bessie Bowen."* There is a definite link between this play and the "Arnold idea," as the May 14, 1932 note suggests. O'Neill worked alternately throughout December 1934 on the "Career of Bessie Bowlan" and "The Calms of Capricorn." There is additional evidence that ties Burr to the Cycle plays. Included in a collection of notes O'Neill made while researching material for the plays is a page citing significant dates in Burr's life. A list of quotations from Byron to be used in *A Touch of the Poet*, including one directed "to Norah ironically," appears on one of the following pages in the folder.

Although O'Neill discards "Treason," elements of it surface in the two extant Cycle plays: *A Touch of the Poet* and *More Stately Mansions*. Like the young Peggy Shippen, Sara Melody defies her father and marries a man whom she ruins through her avarice. Peggy Arnold, the coquette, emerges as Deborah Harford, a neurotic prone to hallucinations, who makes an unfortunate marriage to a New England merchant. Nora Melody personifies the other side of Peggy Arnold—the sweet and patient wife who displays wonderful fidelity to her husband in his misfortunes. There are definite traces of Benedict Arnold in Con Melody—an Irishman who must have wrestled hard and long with his conscience before donning a British uniform, who becomes an outcast after his disgrace in a foreign land where he is mocked and scorned by its inhabitants as was the American traitor, Benedict Arnold, in England.

°GOD GOES GAGA
(1924)

(Scheme)

Get every a.m. newspaper in U. S. Clip out and classify into typical examples of Americans completely (suddenly, incongruously, abysmally) breaking loose and throwing over all inhibitions in one crazy lustful gesture.

°THE GUILTY ONE
(1924)

While living in Provincetown in 1918, O'Neill wrote, and subsequently discarded, an eighteen-page scenario entitled "The Reckoning."† From this scenario, revised and expanded in 1924, a four-act play, "The Guilty One," emerged. Only a fragment of this completed play exists: the first eight pages of Act Three and one page, the last of the work and numbered eighteen, from Act Four. The fol-

---

*See 1927 idea for "It Cannot Be Mad?" for discussion of the evolution of this play.
†Typescript is in the Theatre Collection of the Houghton Library, Harvard University.

lowing statement appears on a small card inserted in the folder before this fragment:

> 7 Pages of The Guilty One.
> cuts and writing by Gene.
> This was a collaboration and then Gene turned the play over to Agnes.
> Have completed script, 4 Acts.
>   Statement by Agnes Boulton or Max Kaufman   J[ohn]. VanE.K.

The important phrase in this notation is "writing by Gene." It is significant that O'Neill's agent, Richard Madden, initially corresponded with the dramatist directly while negotiating the play's production with William A. Brady. A telegram dated September 5, 1924* indicates that the play had been completed and was then in the hands of the producer; in it Madden asks O'Neill to wire him "at least five tentative titles for Brady to choose in substitution Guilty One." After reading the play, Brady apparently requested certain revisions. As O'Neill was writing *Marco Millions* and attending rehearsals for the New York première of *Desire Under the Elms* in the fall of 1924, Agnes revised "The Guilty One." She seems to have encountered problems, as her husband notes on January 10, 1925: "Tried to work on A[gnes]'s 'Guilty One' today—read three acts but no interest. Last 2 acts very bad—need reconstruction" (W.D.). On February 7, 1925, Madden sent a cable* to O'Neill, who was then in Bermuda: "Brady will start rehearsal Guilty One immediately he receives revised script." A week later, on February 14, 1925, O'Neill states: "I went over last 2 rewritten acts of A[gnes]'s and my 'Guilty One' which she is rushing on to get off to Brady" (W.D.). Madden's six letters, written between February 17 and May 12, 1925, are addressed to her although he continued to send O'Neill cables discussing production plans for "The Guilty One."

It is difficult to determine precisely how much Agnes actually contributed to "The Guilty One."† She could have taken the easy route for a fledgling play-

---

*The folder for "The Guilty One" at Yale contains Madden's wire and cable to O'Neill and six letters to Agnes. The dates of Madden's correspondence to the couple suggest O'Neill asked Agnes in February, when he was working on *The Great God Brown*, to continue negotiations for the play's production with Madden. Internal evidence indicates that O'Neill wrote much of the dialogue in the nine-page fragment. Agnes probably wrote the description of the setting for Act Three and its opening dialogue between Mildred and the maid.

†Agnes had shown a lack of enthusiasm in the past about reworking her husband's castoffs. In the summer of 1918, when she was experiencing creative difficulties on her current project, "The Captain's Walk," he gave her a copy of *Now I Ask You*, a three-act farce-comedy written two years earlier, and suggested she adapt it as a novel or revise it as a play. Although rejected, the offer was his attempt to appease her for taking "The Captain's Walk" and transforming it into a one-act play, *Where the Cross Is Made* (*Part of a Long Story*, p. 192).

wright and simply retained the types of conflicts and people that are characteristic of her husband's work; however, much of the dialogue of this play, which
was not part of the 1918 scenario, is clearly O'Neill's. The action of the extant
third act of "The Guilty One" indicates that the story line of its missing opening
acts would follow that of the first two acts of "The Reckoning." The setting of the
latter is a blacksmith shop in the village of Hillvale, Ohio in spring 1890. In the
first act Bessie Small, stepdaughter of the shop's owner, Stephen Donohue, tells
her lover, Jack Gardner, she is pregnant. He callously informs her that he "isn't
the marrying kind. She can't tie him down to a wife and brats. . . . how does
he know it's his fault? says stories about her before he met her." He goes out
for a drink just before Donohue, half drunk, enters and tells his stepdaughter
"he'd damn soon make Jack marry her" if she shames him. If humor had been
injected into this scene, the dialogue and confrontation of Donohue and Bessie
would resemble that of Phil and Josie Hogan in *A Moon for the Misbegotten*.
When Jack returns, he shows the extra drinks have had an "appreciable effect"
on him. The two men argue: Donohue grabs a hammer and Jack, "in his fit of
drunken anger hits Donohue on the head with it." Seeing that Jack believes he
had killed her stepfather, Bessie urges him to leave town immediately and go to
Chicago where she will join him later. After he leaves, Bessie gets some water and
throws it on Donohue, who groans and comes to. In the second scene Bessie confronts Jack and threatens to have him convicted if he does not marry her, insisting he is her child's father. She suggests they go to a New England foundry town
to live. Jack agrees, saying he will "make a model life a partial reparation for his
crime." He wants her to know, however, that while he will marry her he does
not love her and will not live with her as man and wife. "He is determined not
to renew a connection with her which he will always feel to be a guilty one, and
which he blames for all his misfortunes."

Act Two is set in the living room of the Cockran home in a large manufacturing town in New England ten years later. The reformed Jack, now John
Cockran, has risen from his job as common mill-hand to partner of the company.
Because he is popular with his employees and represents the "monied mill-
owners," he has been asked by Jim O'Brien, the Democratic boss of the district,
to run for Congress. In a second scene a maid informs Bessie, now Elizabeth
Cockran, that a half-witted man wants to see her. The visitor is her stepfather,
who has come to beg financial assistance. When Donohue enters, some fleeting
sense of recognition comes to him; he "lifts his hand in a rage as if to strike
her." He tells her his life story—that he had lost his shop, turned to drink, and
cannot work anymore. He shows her a knife and says he wants to kill the man who
wronged him even if he has to hang. All he wants is to go back to Ireland and
"end his days in peace." She informs him he will find a ticket to Queenstown at
the Aid Society the next day. "It opens up a way for her to get rid of this living
evidence of the lie on which she has built her life."

Cockran ponders O'Brien's proposal that he be a candidate but is "afraid his past life will be uncovered." His wife is "on the point of confessing her lie, of setting him free" but feels "he hates her and would cast her off." She begs him to accept the nomination and, when he refuses, threatens once again to reveal his past. "His idea of her has never changed since she forced him to marry her. He believes her to be absolutely unscrupulous and cruel. He accepts for son's sake— But he will never speak to her again except when people are by. In future she is dead to him—a fiend of a woman who has ruined his life and whom he hates from the bottom of his soul." He stipulates one condition: that she leave their son's future to him. "He must be sent away from her to school to escape her influence."

The setting of the third act is the library of the Cockran's home in Washington, D. C. in early April 1917. Several new characters are introduced: young Jack Cockran, now twenty-six; his fiancée, Harriet Lathrop; and John Cockran's secretary, Albert Simms. The father, now an influential senator, plans to deliver a speech favoring America's entry into the war; in a patriotic gesture, the son intends to enlist "in the aviation service" that day. John has tried to protect Jack by sending him "away to school when he was so young. In spite of the great love he has for her, he really knows very little about his mother." Her hatred and jealousy of the rival for her son, Harriet, is similar to that of the mothers in later plays: Nina in *Strange Interlude*, Christine in *Mourning Becomes Electra*, Deborah in *More Stately Mansions*. But it is Mary Tyrone whom Elizabeth (Bessie) resembles most; in that act she "has aged greatly, even her hair is now white. Her manner is furtive and timid. She seems to be always attempting to shrink into a corner, to avoid being seen or talked to." The son, "her only reason for living," knows only this wary side of his mother. When she discovers the nature of the speech her husband is to make that day, her other side, which is similar to Mary's, emerges; it is the "signal for a wild burst of hysterical fury for him. She becomes strong, dominant." If her husband refuses to urge Congress not to declare war, "she will smash him utterly. She will tell the world what he really is—a murderer hiding behind a mask of success and respectability." John "crumbles" before her attack. "His hate for her, his years of obliviousness to her existence, his constant attempts to estrange J. from her have taught her to hate, too. . . . He must fight to save his son or he would be guilty of a double murder—the death of her stepfather and her son would both be on his conscience."

The title of the original 1918 version of "The Guilty One" is appropriate; there is indeed a "reckoning"; the couple eventually comes to terms with the past, with each other—but only after each, like many central characters in later plays, has made a confession. When the mother makes a "clean breast" to her son, he begins to get the "same idea that his father has always had—that she is a wicked woman, hard and cruel, who has caused his father untold misery by her inexcusable deceit. . . . It is too fiendish! Why she must be mad to have done such things, to have lived the life she has!" When John hears of the "trick played upon him all his life, he is dumbfounded. . . . He also confesses that, looking back on it now, he finds himself guilty of having done his best to stifle her life and made her miserable, to separate her from Jack." Told he must judge his parents, the son says that "if he is to forgive, then they must forgive—each other."

The word "guilty" is used frequently in "The Reckoning" to describe John Cockran, but it applies primarily to his wife, whose whole life is based on a lie. She is responsible for her husband's suffering, self-recrimination, and unhappiness and her son's abnormal upbringing, leading to his sense of loss and alienation. This short play is an immature effort to depict a veiled version of the autobiographical conflicts of *Long Day's Journey into Night*; its focus, however, is the sins of the parents against each other and their son, who is described as being "so perfect." O'Neill seems unwilling in 1918 either to face or to admit his own contribution to his family's tragedy.

In contrast, in the 1924 script the son, Jud, is portrayed as a "guilty one," repeating his father's early mistakes: excessive drinking and callously using women. Like many of O'Neill's characters, his physical attributes reveal a dual nature. "His face shows little sign of dissipation*—he is still too young—but it is revealed in his manner and in his voice. He has really great sweetness and charm—but it is obviously being ruined." His mother is named Cora; his father Jim or, more formally, J. J. Smith. The setting of the extant fragment's Act III is a drawing room in the home of the millionaire president of "the Pasterson Tin-Plate Products, at Pasterson, N. J.," the state in which Agnes had lived, rather than a New England town, her husband's favorite locale; the time is 1924, reflecting the reckless postwar era in America, rather than the tense 1917 period.

The roles played by the son's fiancée, Harriet Lathrop, and the father's secretary, Albert Simms, in "The Reckoning" are now combined in the personage of Mildred Lord, the nineteen-year-old private secretary of the millionaire. She resembles in appearance and attitude the lifeless and prim Linda/Anna of "Chris Christopherson" and is described as "very pretty—very well-bred. Her dress is dark & plain—but against it her vivid beauty flares up all the more brilliantly." In an action that is similar to his father's years earlier, the spoiled, self-centered son has seduced Mildred, who is obviously in love with him and is apparently pregnant. The discovery that the affair has been another one of Jud's careless flings prompts Mildred to submit a letter of resignation effective the following Tuesday.

The third act opens with Mildred taking an inventory of the furnishings of the drawing room and the garrulous maid lamenting the condition of the dining room, scene of one of Jud's wild drunken orgies the previous evening and now littered with broken bottles. The maid praises Mildred for what she has accomplished in that unhappy household: "It's a queer house, Miss—not like other

---

*The word is spelled "disappation" in the typescript; the correction is in O'Neill's handwriting.

people's houses—and I'll say that you've done something to make it more human. And as for Mr. Judson—why for a while there you had more influence—although it seems now that he's gone back—worse than ever."

Jud enters displaying the "monotonous talkativeness of the morning after" to which Mildred—or Milly, as he calls her—fails to respond. O'Neill's usual father-son conflict is missing from this play. Jud does call his father the "old man" but also a "good sport" who, though awakened at 5:00 A.M. that morning by the noise in the dining room, merely asks his son if he is having a good time. Jud adds: "He's got a joy complex which he transfers to his son." Mildred responds: "Your ventures into the idiom of psychoanalysis are inaccurate—to say the least!" It is the mother against whom the son vents his anger. When he discovers she has asked for an inventory, he exclaims: "It seems as though she even wanted to keep tabs on the furniture—know just what everything costs—where everything is—just as she has with everybody in the house. Tagged and labelled. And what good does it all do her? I never saw a more miserable person than mother."

The dialogue of the young couple recalls that of Anna and Paul Anderson in the early version of "Chris Christopherson." When Jud tries to persuade her not to go away, Mildred displays a restlessness like Anna's: "I—want to see something more of life." He argues: "You are certainly the only life in *this* house." She chides him: "Except what you bring in—late at night." Jud warns Mildred she should remain in the house for her protection and security: "Here, you're really a member of the family." She responds bitterly "(with meaning—and a high color) 'Decidedly!' "

The father-son relationship in the next section is similar to the one that is finally established between James and Edmund Tyrone in the last act of *Long Day's Journey into Night*. Jim Smith bears a strong resemblance to the elder Tyrone, who is described as "still remarkably good looking" at the beginning of the play and as "a sad, defeated old man, possessed by hopeless resignation" at the end:

His shoulders sag slightly, and he has grown decidedly larger around the waist. His hair is white. He is still handsome. He is also well dressed, and has become a man of the world, with the manner of one used to authority. But when he is not speaking—in repose—his face shows lines of care—a worn, harassed look.

Like Edmund, Jud seeks the solace of the bottle after a drunken binge: "I was just going to get a drink Dad—you know—'a hair of the dog that bit you!' I feel nervous." Smith hesitates: "Well, I guess it won't hurt you." When Jud expresses a desire to discuss private matters, the father remarks that the issue would not be money: "I've kept you pretty well supplied, eh, Jud? (harshly) But you enjoy it. That's more than can be said of any other member of the family." The son entreats his father to go in for yachting or racing: "It'd get you out of yourself. As it is—as it's been ever since *I* can remember—it's been nothing but business—or home here alone. Up in your room by yourself. (awkwardly) And it isn't as if you and mother were—well, you know what I mean—pals. And, Dad, I notice it's been getting worse lately—for you."

The father explains his one purpose for making money: "I want *you* to enjoy it, Jud!—in *your* way! I want you to be free—to keep away from all the cursed, grinding monotony of this damned life! Power! Position! Money! Look at it! (with a violent gesture) See what it means to me!" The son remarks sadly: "You and Mother sure do lead the worst known lives, Dad.—No friends—no amusements—nothing! And you could have everything." The father responds: "No. *She* doesn't enjoy it much, either. Doesn't all this—what you see of your mother and me—this home—turn you against marriage? Don't let life get you. Live yourself. Be what you are. I've lived twenty-two years of hell, Jud. Because—of a mistake." Smith's next line—"Life was mine, then!"—has echoes of both James Tyrone's "late day for regrets" passage and Edmond Dantès's "The world is mine!" speech in *Monte Cristo*. Smith lowers his voice and says: "I should have gone one—my own way—the way I wanted—but I was weak!" This section ends with the son asking what had happened in the past and the father's refusal to tell him.

The last page, numbered eighteen, of "The Guilty One" probably corresponds to the final page of O'Neill's early eighteen-page scenario. The son in the former seems to have made a double discovery: the truth about Mildred's reason for leaving and his parents' past—that their marriage was loveless from the start, that his conception was the catalyst for the family tragedy. His parents and Mildred watch him "with consternation" as he prepares to depart from the house forever. He suddenly turns and begs Mildred to go with him. She "draws back growing crimson" and asks: "Are you crazy?" Jud's admission that he has been fighting against loving and needing Mildred is followed by a line that is crossed out: "Then when Dad told me—why you were going—I tried to get drunk—and forget." He then exclaims passionately: "I didn't know I loved you. . . . We'll be married—right away—and go somewhere." Mildred reaches out and touches him; "a sudden illumination comes over her face." Jud informs his parents: "We've got to do this!" There is no response. "Smith and Cora are silent—they cannot forget their tragedy. They both seem completely broken." This section concludes with Mildred asking Jud: "But—they? (there is compassion in her voice) What will—they do? (To Cora) Won't you—come with us?"

The extant nine pages of "The Guilty One" contain much from the original script and represent, for the most part, the work O'Neill did on the play before he turned it over to Agnes, who apparently wrote a second draft when Brady requested revisions. Madden's first letter (February 17, 1925) to Agnes indicates that Brady had received the proposed changes in the manuscript and was "all aquiver waiting for the script." In subsequent letters Madden states: Brady "does not think the revised version as good as the original draft but there are many things in it he would want to use. He feels he would like to produce the play as originally written" (March 17, 1925); "Your letter of the 19th states that if Brady does not want to hold on to "The Guilty One" you would like to get it away and have it worked over again" (March 30, 1925); "I included in my cable to Gene yesterday the query about "The Guilty One" as I did not feel that in your letter of the 27th you have fully answered my question about carrying on with Brady" (March 31, 1925); "I am certain a little later on when you feel quite right and Gene has the time that 'The Guilty One' can be materially improved. I am sure you can cover the suggestions I made" (May 12, 1925).

There are several reasons why "The Guilty One" was never produced. Two days after Madden's letter of May 12, Agnes gave birth to a daughter, Oona, and probably lost interest in the play. O'Neill was working on *Marco Millions* throughout the summer of 1925 and was, in addition, displeased by Brady's attitude to him. Brady attacked *Desire Under the Elms*, which was proclaimed "guiltless" in a censorship drive, when his own play, *A Good Bad Woman*, had been closed for immorality. Sheaffer maintains that O'Neill,

> recalling Brady's equivocal role in the censorship drive and his slur at *Desire*, intervened when the producer wanted to renew his option on Agnes's "The Guilty One"; at Eugene's urging (he also was motivated by the feeling that the play, on which he had done some work, was not good), Agnes withdraw her script.*

While it is impossible to ascertain precisely how much O'Neill contributed to "The Guilty One," the extant fragment clearly demonstrates an important fact: that as early as the mid-1920s he collaborated on a play which revealed his still-concealed feelings at that time in his life: animosity for his mother, sympathy for his father, guilt for bringing them, through his birth, to the abyss of suffering. The autobiographical glimpse of O'Neill's parents in "The Reckoning" and of them and himself in "The Guilty One" provides a type of prelude for the full-scale symphony of portraits in *Long Day's Journey into Night*.

O'Neill Son and Artist, p. 166.

[LAZARUS LAUGHED]

Play of Lazarus*
(1924)

Play of Lazarus—the man who had been dead for three days and returned to life, knowing the secret.

Play of Caligula
(1924)

Play of Caligula—not mad but a truth-seer and driven mad by that—the great satirist who made his horse a consul and wished the world had but one neck—who transferred his love from other, to wife, to males, to a horse.

Lives of Caesars
(1925)

"Lives of Caesars"—series of scenes each about the Emperor showing the gradual degeneration, as the Caesars became gods, of power. Julius & Augustus to Domitian & Heliogabalus.

Prior to the mid-1920s, no concept for a play changes more—theatrically and thematically—during the process of composition than the original one for "The Laughter of Lazarus." The first scenario, written in a ten-day period, from September 1 to 10, 1925, incorporates two early 1924 ideas: "Play of Lazarus" and "Play of Caligula." In the scenario, Caligula, after his entrance in the third scene, assumes a role that is as significant as that of Lazarus. O'Neill scales down the 1925 idea "Lives of Caesars"; only the reigning Tiberius appears. Using this extant scenario, the dramatist worked from October 12 to November 20, 1925, on a first draft, completing the dialogue for five of the eight scenes.

1925 Scenario

While music, dancing, and a moderate amount of laughter are included in the 1925 scenario, the most complex and innovative experimental devices found

---

* O'Neill draws slanted lines through the three ideas that follow, writing "Lazarus Laughed 1926–27" across the first and "L L" across the other two. He links the three ideas with a brace in the right margin and scrawls the word "combine."

in the completed play—the masks and choruses—are omitted. In contrast to the later 1926 scenario, which incorporates these devices, the first stark outline focuses solely on the battle waged between the forces of good—symbolized by the man who has seen what lies beyond the grave—and evil—represented by the two Roman Caesars who view Lazarus as a threat to their power. While all the characters but Lazarus wear masks in later versions, in the early draft everyone is unmasked except Lazarus, who wears a black kerchief over his eyes as the light hurts them and prevents him from seeing. Without the masks and choruses, representing the people of various nations, the 1925 outline lacks a universal tragic dimension and becomes the story of one man rather than Man.

Compared to the published text with its massive choruses, the first scenario has a small cast of characters: Lazarus, his wife Miriam, his parents and sisters; three groups of Jews; Cotta, a centurion; legionnaires; Greeks of both sexes; Roman senators, patricians, and soldiers; galley slaves; Tiberius Caesar; Gaius Caesar Caligula; Marcellus, a Tribune; and three—rather than one—courtesans: Claudilla, Junia, and Pompeia. No exterior view of Lazarus' home is visible in the early first scene; the setting of the fifth scene is a Roman galley rather than the garden of Tiberius' palace; the play ends at sunrise and not dawn.

O'Neill describes Lazarus in two ways: physically, he "is a dark, olive-complected man of forty-five or so, with a mass of grizzled black hair and a heavy beard. His face is gaunt, furrowed deep with lines of suffering and death, his forehead broad and wrinkled by thought, his black eyes deep-set." Spiritually, he is "illumined by a light from within—a soft phosphorescent radiance which illumines his face as if tiny invisible flames were caressing his flesh and cleansing it of sorrow and death." His eyes stare "straight before him with an uncanny concentration in a vision. There is something rapt and devout about his motionless attitude—a quality of Eastern prayer." Some of these attributes will later be eliminated as are those used to describe the unmasked characters: Miriam has a "pale, beautiful, sorrowful face"; Martha is a "buxom Jewish housfrau"; Mary has a "trace of sly humor and healthy coquettry about her smiling lips and dreamy eyes"; their parents are an "aged white-haired couple, gentle and bewildered."

Scene One—Room in the home of Lazarus at Bethany—Twilight (L. 45)

Family and friends gather for a feast to celebrate the recent miracle; yet Lazarus remains strangely silent—as he has been since his return from the dead. The guests mention many misfortunes that led him in the past to long for death: the loss of his five children—here all sons; his wife's chronic illness; his poverty. The story of the miracle is not told—as it will be later by the Seven Guests and a Chorus—but by one man, Jacob, who "does so according to St. John" and concludes by saying: "Then Lazarus laughed and Jesus blessed him and departed. Such a laugh; do you suppose he will ever laugh again?" In a loud voice Lazarus says: "Yes," adding: "My spirit answered yes as he desired me; and his spirit blessed mine, and all darkness became light and I blessed God and laughed with new life." His laughter is "so full of acceptance and joy, so devoid of fear or malice, that it is like a bird's song in spring, but powerful, hypnotizing, casting a compelling spell." Although the room is dark, Lazarus professes to see "everything—behind and beyond to any length of time—every end a beginning, every beginning an end, and all without beginning or end." When lights are brought in, "Lazarus shields his eyes with a cry of pain. They start to take them away but he says no—lights, feast, dancing & music—he will bind a kerchief over his eyes—black. He goes gaily from one to one greeting them. He sees clearly now." When the guests want to know what is beyond, Lazarus replies: "There were laughing stars and suns that sang and dancing motes of dust. And there was no fear of Death. The fear of Death is Death! Laugh with me." At the end of the scene he begins to laugh; all join him except Miriam, who says she cannot because "your laughter has come in unto me. It is the laughter of the son I have never borne you."

Scene Two—Some years later—Exterior of the House of Laughter which was
          Lazarus' home—eight o'clock of a luminous night blazing with
          stars (L[azarus]. 35)

From within the house "comes the sound of cymbals and semi-barbaric dance music"; without, groups of Orthodox Jews and Jesus' followers taunt each other and, wearying, join in a general condemnation of Lazarus. He appears on the roof and "stands like an idol among them. He takes the black bandage from his eyes and lovingly addresses the stars as his brothers in God." The two groups below demand that he "put a stop to his heathen idolatry" and his attempt to "revive Pan—or Dionysus." In this first version, Lazarus' sisters, Mary and Martha, do not confront their parents prior to the announcement of Christ's death; but all four die when the Roman soldiers come to take Lazarus prisoner. Even with the dead bodies of his family before him, Lazarus stands unmoved, joyously exclaiming: "But there is no death!" Noticeably missing here is the lament of the followers of Lazarus, expressing their fear of death as the Roman soldiers lead him away.

Scene Three—Some months later—A street in Athens—ten o'clock of a bright
          moonlight night (L. 30)

As Lazarus enters in a car-chariot, a crowd gathers before the pillars of a temple in a square in Athens, repeating the wild rumors that are circulating: that he is really "a Greek—a God risen from the dead—Dionysus or Pan perhaps who has come back to free Greece. He has promised that no one who believes in him can ever die." This entire scene is devoted to the exchange between Lazarus and Caligula, who commands the squad of Roman legionnaires, "a youth of 21—tall, pale, thin, his pale eyes sunk in his head, his temple hollow, his forehead bulging and somber, his body heavy and shaggy—troubled with insomnia (3 hours sleep a night)—and nightmares." When Caligula begins a grotesque dance, yelling coarsely, there is shocked silence, disgust, and fear. Furious at the people's rejection, Caligula orders his soldiers to "hack their bodies apart. Rape and enslave and kill!" Lazarus laughs and asks the tyrant: "Why kill, O future Caesar, except for joy in murder? And how can murder give joy when there is no fear of death?" When Caligula throws down his sword and cries hysterically, Lazarus says gently: "You must laugh, not weep; for you are destined by God to reveal that when Man creates a God in his own image, he adores a clown." Caligula begs to be told why he dreads dying.

Lazarus pats his head: "Caesars die. Caligulas die. Man's body dies but his life lives on. Each one must feel this in his heart and kill his death with laughter. Caligula stares at the crowd. "I think I can learn to laugh at Man—and at myself perhaps—if you will love me, Lazarus." "I love all who loving can laugh with joy at life!"

The section concludes with Lazarus leading his followers in a procession to the fields for a Dionysian celebration of nature, which is symbolically repudiated by Caligula, who savagely lops off flowers from their stems and "breaks out into a sort of hysterical, insane giggle."

Scene Four—Month later—Just inside the walls of Rome—midnight—thunder
    and lightning (L. 25)

The senators—their faces tired, cynical, dejected—denounce Tiberius, who has fled the city in fear after commanding they meet. In their midst Lazarus stands "like the statue of a detached, contemplative God. The aura of light surrounds him." Caligula "squats like a monkey" beside Lazarus and says: "Kill Tiberius. I shall be Caesar! The Empire shall be one fierce laughing face bright with the blood of Death. I have learned to laugh." Lazarus responds: "Fool! You are laughing with hate of life—you drink blood to drown your fear of death. You must learn to laugh with love." The Roman soldiers return after slaughtering the followers of Lazarus and reject Caligula, who mistakenly thinks their salute is directed to him. "Not you old Hobnails! We cry hail to Laughter, the God, the conqueror of Death. We'll make you a God, Lazarus." He refuses, laughing.

Scene Five—Some days later—the poop deck of a Roman galley—two in the
    morning—moonlight (L. 20)

This scene, set at the wharf at Capri rather than at Tiberius' villa-palace as in subsequent drafts, reflects O'Neill's love of the sea. Lazarus "stands by himself in the darkness at the end of the poop, lighted only by his own luminous aura which appears brighter than ever now. He also appears much younger. He stares out over the sea." In this first scenario Caligula demonstrates great affection for Miriam; he asks her a series of questions:

Why has Lazarus refused to be Caesar—or God? Why does he grow younger all the time? Why does Lazarus bring death wherever he goes? And why does he Caligula love him so when he ought to hate—to kill him for that would assure Tiberius' favor? And why can't you laugh, Jewess—why do you always smile at him so sadly?

Miriam responds only to the last inquiry and provides an explanation, not found elsewhere, for her inability to laugh: "To me he is always dead—a spirit reborn into flesh who may not be touched by human love or tears, who lives in a beyond, who is the Son I have never had born in a life where I am not yet born." Before they leave for the palace, Caligula warns Miriam to watch over Lazarus as Tiberius "will surely attempt his life."

Scene Six—Banquet hall in the palace of Tiberius at Capri—four in the morning (L. 20)

The scene is one of utter dissipation. Almost naked slaves wait upon the table. "Courtesans, male and female, and nobles, prematurely aged by debauchery, loll about the table on couches. Tiberius sits at the head, right on a raised throne. Sitting at his feet are the three favorite courtesans, Pompeia, Junia, and Claudilla." Tiberius' big face is "blotched by dissipation, his eyes small and protuberant, his expression cruel and grim, his speech slow and drawling. Timorous in his old age and superstitious." Everyone is drunk except Tiberius, who wants his head clear when Lazarus arrives. Caligula enters and informs Tiberius that Lazarus is the "son of a Roman God by a Jewess." Wearing a bandage over his eyes, Lazarus is led in by Miriam. At Tiberius' command the bandage is removed. The courtesans clap their hands in admiration of his beauty; the guests gasp: "It is a God."

Tiberius boasts of his cruelties and sins; Caligula moodily gulps wine, "drinking as if to drown his thoughts." Having fallen in love with Lazarus, the courtesans conspire to kill Miriam. Junia receives Tiberius' permission to offer poisoned fruit to Miriam, who is encouraged by Lazarus to eat. Caligula screams: "Do not, Jewess! Live. Marry me. I shall need your care when I become a God." In this scenario Miriam is portrayed as an attractive woman; she does not grow older as Lazarus grows younger—a phenomenon of later drafts, establishing a mother-son relationship. Miriam appears to die; then her "lips move and she laughs gaily from far away." Tiberius is "overcome by superstitious terror" and orders Junia to be taken away and strangled. Lazarus is led away; the court flees in fright. The attitude of the seventy-six-year-old Tiberius, alone now with the "very drunk" Caligula, resembles James Tyrone's to Jamie in the last act of *Long Day's Journey into Night*. Caligula sings a low camp song, and Tiberius "looks at him grimly: 'Another Phaethon!'" Caligula boasts that he has learned to laugh without fear, without guilt. For a moment his laugh

is strangely clear and inspired, then it suddenly breaks into coarse foulness. "You see! That is where I remember lust and blood and hate and fear—murder and death and corruption. Lo, I must drink! Hail, my good grandfather. I drink to your long life. Live forever and cheat me."

He falls into a drunken stupor; Tiberius motions his guards: "Take this carrion away!"

Scene Seven—A room in the palace of Tiberius at Capri—dawn

This scene differs substantially from its counterpart in later versions as it is set in another room of the palace and does not continue the action of the previous one. To pass the time until Lazarus returns from burying Miriam, Caligula —a dominant figure in this scene—taunts Pompeia; yet he wishes her success in seducing the object of her passion. "If he could once see Lazarus suffer as a human being, then he would know pity and be able to finish his laughter." When Lazarus returns, Caligula expresses his love for him and his desire to change:

I am sick, Lazarus. I would be clean—or else I must revenge my soiled hands upon a filthy mankind. If I could only believe—believe!—that one man in the world, without thought of favor, saw and loved the real Caligula under my flesh and skin—then I might laugh!

On hearing Lazarus proclaim his love for him, Caligula, overcome with happiness, begins to laugh clearly and exclaims exultantly: "I will go down and swim, dance on the sand, sing with the sun."

Pompeia, alone with Lazarus, "tries all her seductive tricks but to no avail." She says that for love of him she has killed Claudilla and has begun to poison Tiberius. Lazarus will be Caesar, and she his empress. Lazarus rejects her offer; she attempts, but fails, to stab him and in a rage summons Tiberius. The emperor only cackles at Pompeia's accusation that Lazarus tried to seduce her. Frustrated, she warns that Lazarus will become Caesar; he must be tortured and put to death. Tiberius, shuddering in fear, reluctantly orders his soldiers to summon the people to a special show at dawn: "If I could only silence his laugh, I might feel myself Caesar again."

Scene Eight—Caesar's throne in the amphitheatre—sunrise

From his throne, with Pompeia at his side, Tiberius watches his soldiers torture Lazarus. In the first scenario Lazarus is not gagged and only laughs in answer to Tiberius' many questions: why he laughs; what he found beyond the gates of death; by what power he was restored to life. Lazarus tells Tiberius that in the grave he had "found the true love of life which was and is and always will, without beginning or end—God" and that he had seen among the "Gods and rulers of Egypt, Greece and Rome two brother specks there—two Caesars— Julius and Augustus—and soon there will be three." Tiberius cries out in terrified rage: "Kill him!" Caligula rushes in with a cohort of soldiers but arrives too late to save Lazarus. Tiberius laughs "a horrible grating mocking croak at which Caligula turns on him furiously," strangling him. The new Caesar in this version does not take a spear to inflict the final death blow on Lazarus, but, in the closing monologue—the longest speech written for the play—he addresses the crowd, describing the horrors he will inflict on his subjects. He provides a demonstration, ordering a centurion to stab Pompeia, who has thrown herself at his feet begging for mercy. Caligula warns the multitude: "Behold, O sacrificial cattle, the first sacrifice to my divinity! Behold and beware! For Lazarus the Laughter is dead and Death is Caesar!" The curtain closes as the crowd races panicky after the departing Caligula, shouting: "Hail, Caesar! There is Death!"

1926 Scenario

On March 3, 1926, O'Neill began "reading for Lazarus" and making new notes: quotations and paraphrased passages from Aristotle and Nietzsche; selections from historical works on Tiberius, Roman history, and books on mythology. He made copious notes on Dionysus,* "whose mother died in bearing him," calling him twice the "Son of Semele"† and, as such, possibly identifying with him. The author states on March 6, 1926: "Started actual work on Lazarus—went over first scene—don't like as is!" (W.D.). He spent the next two days on a second scenario for "The Laughter of Lazarus." In the new first scene, the "Feast of Thanksgiving for his return from the dead," the Biblical (St. John) encounter between Lazarus and Jesus is described. Then Lazarus "seemed to see his family and friends about him for the first time and looked from one to one and began to laugh."

Lazarus' home in Scene Two is described as "the house of pagan laughter; a sort of Pan-cult is growing up around him." The Jews and Nazarenes display greater animosity for Lazarus here; "they surround house and are about to fire it and massacre inhabitants when soldiers arrive to take Lazarus to Tiberius who

---

*Because of the many references to Dionysus in O'Neill's plays, a significant passage from the notes is included here:

The religion of D. was, for those who lived in it, a complete sacred representation and interpretation of the whole of life—fills for them place of Demeter, is the life of the earth through the grape as she through grain—so also he fills place of Apollo as music—is the inherent cause of music and poetry—he inspires—explains phenomena of enthusiasm, the secret of possession—by a higher and more energetic spirit than one's own, the gift of self-revelation, of pouring out of oneself through words, tones, gestures! D. is the Deliverer "Eleutherios"—and of such enthusiasm and ecstasy and, in a certain sense, an older patron than Apollo himself.

†Her lover Zeus, who had come to her as a man, complied with her request to appear in his divine form. The fire of his thunderbolts killed her; from her ashes, he rescued his unborn son, Dionysus, who later delivered Semele from Hades.

has heard rumors of him and his laughter." The action of this scene and the three that follow is the same as that in the first scenario. In the sixth scene more emphasis is given here to Tiberius than in the earlier outline. He is desperately lonely and grief-stricken because he was "forced to give up wife he loved (Agrippina) and marry Julia, daughter of Augustus, whom he later had to divorce for adultery and 'dreaming nature'—a drunkard from start." Junia, now called Valeria, is "disgusted with her old master and weary of corrupt Roman lovers, has fallen in love with this laughter." In the seventh scene Pompeia makes no charge of attempted seduction but insinuates that Lazarus is poisoning Tiberius. Instinctively, he knows that she has been rejected and says: "So he refused to lie with you? If I could silence his laugh, I would feel myself Caesar again."

In the last scene the dying Lazarus describes the life that awaits him: "the light of the million dancing suns tuned to the pulsing throbbing heart of space, the musical rise and fall of eternal laughter." When Caligula enters the amphitheatre and discovers that Lazarus is dead, he angrily smothers a struggling Tiberius and addresses the crowd, saying that now "Lazarus, the great laughter, is dead" evil has triumphed over good. Caligula's lengthy speech, part of which is quoted here, is one of O'Neill's strongest indictments of mankind's evil:

I'll rule an Absolute God of Madness! You'll see in me a deity in your own image! You'll adore yourself! I'll make your pettiness collossal—a brutish drunken Titan stamping in the gutted entrails of the world! Senselessly I'll build mountains where plains have been and level mountains to plains to exemplify to you the essence of your wisdom! . . . I'll make my dullest horse a consul and senators shall kneel and kiss his tail to prove the Olympic dignity of government! . . . Oh, I'll be your perfect prototype, good folk of Rome, Your synthesis! I'll interpret you in such great characters that even the farthest stars will see and wonder!

As though it were responding in a solemn prayer service, the crowd shouts "in servile admiration: 'Ave Caesar! Ave Caligula!' "

On March 9, after completing two scenarios and a draft of the first five scenes for the play, O'Neill was still "doping out new scheme for it—not satisfied with old method used so far" (W.D.). Obviously influenced by the currently successful run of *The Great God Brown*, in which the major characters wore masks, he devised a new plan for *Lazarus Laughed*. Recording his progress, he states: "Lazarus—mask-chorus conception shapes up wonderfully" (W.D., March 10); "Much reconstruction needed and sloppy writing in first draft to be pruned—written in too much of a hurry last fall—mind too distracted" (W.D., March 12).

Included in the second 1926 collection of notes is the complex system O'Neill worked out at this time for the use of masks in the play. The section provides a complete, specific description of the seven types and ages. (*See next page.*)

The masks in the first two scenes are "naturally Semitic in racial character—in Scene Three Eastern & Greek—in the remainder of the scenes Roman." While

Lazarus Laughed
Masks

The masks to be worn by the various crowds are type-masks arranged in series of seven according to the following formulas of age & type

	(1) Kind & Content / Truthful / Simple / Humility / Sensuous	(2) Happy / laughing / Loving & lovable	(3) Unhappy / Jealous / & Tortured / Grief-tears	(4) Strong / Proud / rebellious / & defiant	(5) Senile / envious / &cringing / &hypocritical	(6) Cruelty / Hatred / &fanaticism / &revenge	(7) Weak / Sorrowful / Sensitive / Self-conscious
1) Youth 14–21	1–1	2–1	3–1	4–1	5–1	6–1	7–1
2) Young Manhood 21–28	1–2	2–2	3–2	4–2	5–2	6–2	7–2
3) Manhood 28–35	1–3	2–3	3–3	4–3	5–3	6–3	7–3
4) Manhood 35–42	1–4	2–4	3–4	4–4	5–4	6–4	7–4
5) Middle age 42–49	1–5	2–5	3–5	4–5	5–5	6–5	7–5
6) Maturity 49–63	1–6	2–6	3–6	4–6	5–6	6–6	7–6
7) Age 63 on	1–7	2–7	3–7	4–7	5–7	6–7	7–7

O'Neill planned to have a special chorus of seven (Old Women rather than Old Men in the first two scenes), he had not, as yet, conceived the idea to use masks double the size of the others for it. The masks of the Seven Speaking Guests in the first scene are to be "more recognizably individual personalities than the crowd masks—that is they partake of the crowd but are foreground individuals." This concept would also apply to minor speaking characters in the rest of the play. "The masks of Martha, Mary, Father & Mother are individualized reproductions of their own faces, with however a distinct trace of the type background in each. Thus Martha is type 1-3 as a recognizable foundation for her own character. Mary is 2-2—Mother & Father are 1-7."

While Miriam's face with its half-mask is described here as it is in the final version of the play, the incongruous mask-mouth contrast* of Caligula and Tiberius, reflecting their dual natures and desires, does not appear in the 1926 notes. Caligula's half-mask is bright crimson; his large light bright blue eyes "stare out, feverish and wild." His nose is Puck-like rather than sensual; his mouth is childish, self-indulgent "with its cruel soft sensual lips a vivid scarlet." He appears to be nothing more than a naughty, malicious sprite. In contrast, Tiberius' mouth, as well as his half-mask—"of a pale heliotrope color, blotched with purple"—is totally evil: "gross, revolting, with loose thin pale lips of a livid purple color." In later versions his mouth will lose this "gruesome purplish tinge" which will then be attributed to Caligula's mask.

Scattered passages throughout the second set of notes show the evolution of the two Roman Caesars and reveal O'Neill's ambivalent attitude toward them. The notes reflect his dilemma; he veers in two directions, torn between the historical attempt to portray Caligula and Tiberius as evil monsters and his own inclination to depict them as vulnerable human beings—victims caught in a web of tragic circumstances that force them to stifle their natural goodness. The dramatist ultimately shows—as the mask-mouth dichotomy suggests—that it is impossible to draw a clear-cut battleline between good and evil as, for example, between two opposing forces—the virtuous Lazarus and the wicked Roman tyrants. The terms "good" and "evil" are not mutually exclusive as they apply to O'Neill's characters. In an important passage not included in the final version of the play, Tiberius—speaking not only of man but of himself—states:

He dies a guilty infant—protecting his innocence, denouncing the filth of others from his cradle as from a rostrum—this morbid baby with a long hand! this foul prattler of three score & ten! O anomaly of Man who loves to prove life guilty, whose life is a long dying! If you could only interpret that first cry of man fresh from the inertia of the womb as a cry of joy, of thanksgiving, of vic-

---

*The mask represents what the character appears to be or what he wants to be; the mouth reveals what he really is or could be if his true nature were allowed to assert itself.

tory, of knowledge, of God-like laughter. Laughter of one who can then know in his heart—now am I conscious of my aspirations. It is now my privilege as God to become man. Now let it be my accepted obligation and—as man I must raise— the God in me!

In the 1926 outline for the sixth scene, Tiberius overcomes his fear and makes Lazarus sit beside him; "he becomes friendly, tells his own story, pleads for youth again." He maintains that he "wants youth back not for leachery as everyone thinks but to regain the purity and decency of his old love." Near the end of the scene, he says he will put Lazarus to death if he does not tell him the secret of youth, of death. Tiberius believes Lazarus "has cure to regenerate, etc. Then he stops, strangely moved, 'I do not want to kill you, Lazarus. I feel a strange love for you, etc.' " The emperor expresses a desire to confess: "One gets old, one gets talkative, one wishes to confess, to say this thing one always has kept hidden, one's innermost secret—and one is alone!" The scene concludes with Tiberius becoming once again the tyrant; he boasts of "his cruelties and his perverted lusts." Life has tortured him, he argues, and now he will torture life; he will appoint Caligula his heir. The concept from Aristotle contained in the final line of his philosophic discussion of this life and the one beyond—"A. re- turn to the heroic, rebirth of the hero in Man which made him a demi-God"—is developed for Lazarus' "gift of life" speech at the end of the fourth scene but is later excised:

Dying as man, Man the demi-God, laughs with laughter of the Infinite. As laugh- ter I disappear, fuse into space, melt into suns, dissolve into the eternal tides that is the blood of God to [word erased] again as laughter of creative change welling from God's deep heart! In this faith must man grow into Man, the hero.

Paradoxically, Lazarus' aspiration—to attain the highest good, to become Man the demi-God—produces a fatal flaw in his character *as man*: his inability to experience human love. It is Pompeia who detects his weakness. For all her promiscuity, she craves a pure but complete love that embraces both the physical and the spiritual. She displays great sympathy for Miriam and asks Caligula: "Did Lazarus love his wife?" Caligula replies: "He loves everything but no one thing, everyone but no one man or woman." As man—husband, son, friend— Lazarus is an anomaly as perverse for his species, in his own way, as Caligula. Although thoroughly depraved and a slave to base desires of the flesh, Caligula, like Pompeia, longs to spiritualize the physical as his near-protestation of love for Miriam indicates. Lazarus represents something dormant in him—his only hope to laugh with purity, without "coarse foulness—the inspiration needed to become a whole man." When Lazarus dies, so, too, does Caligula's hope: "Be- hold, bear witness to a tear—the tear of Caesar—the first and last my eyes shall ever know—shed for the death of laughter!"

In the 1926 notes, O'Neill assigns the last speech of the play not to Caligula— as in the final version—but to Lazarus, who seems to realize at last the good-evil dichotomy within himself as well as his fellow man; he explains how he lost the God in himself:

The tragedy is that Man forgets! . . . As the day of his birth recedes he forgets the God in him. . . . He grows alien and afraid and an outcast from the spirit of life. Sin is born—guilt & conscience—as he becomes aware of his meanness as man and blames it on devils & evil. He thinks of himself as a hero fighting the dragons of evil. Alas, this dragon is a grave worm born in himself and he is a feeble actor making brave faces into a mirror and saying "I am a warrior!" If he could see what applause his audience would give to his last gesture how happily would he die, acting the hero! . . . And if one should speak to him of God he says resentfully I am an unhealthy animal—therefore there is no God in me—therefore there is no God. Such logic comforts his dying. He invents original sin to explain his craven forgetting of his original virtue, his laughing innocence. "I was born soiled." This craven lie—never "I have soiled myself." Or if he even admits weakness in himself, he weeps at the same time with pity for that weakness. When he does not deny, he pities. Thus he always spoils and coddles himself. He remains his own mother.

Following this section is one labeled "For last words of play?":

Father I am thy son!
Thou canst not forsake me! (laughs)

or   Father, what was all this question of forsaking?

or   Father, shall I tell you how Lazarus whose name I bear lost the God
     in myself (spoiled child, etc.)

Lazarus   (who finds that his followers soon forget his laughter) The tragedy
          is that Man forgets!

While some of this material is omitted in the final version of *Lazarus Laughed*, much of it re-emerges in one of his last works. The concept "that Man forgets" becomes the theme of "The Last Conquest." The two central characters of this play repeat Lazarus' exact statements: Christ says, "Father, I am thy Son! Thou canst not forsake me!"; the Devil asks, "Shall I tell you how Lucifer whose name I bear lost the God in myself?"

The many similarities between *Lazarus Laughed* and "The Last Conquest" suggest O'Neill may have used discarded notes from the former when writing the latter. The same divine/profane trinity of characters appears in both plays:

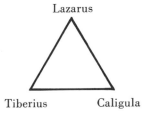

In the early work, Lazarus—a Christ figure—confronts a tyrant, Tiberius, and is both feared and loved by the killer of men's bodies, Caligula. In "The Last Conquest," Christ is brought before another despot, the World Dictator, and is alternately hated and loved by the killer of men's souls, the Devil.

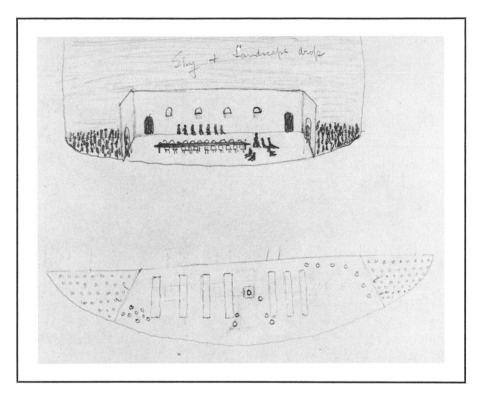

Act I, Scene 1, Lazarus' home in Bethany:
top, discarded sketch; bottom, scenic plan used

O'Neill discards the top drawing with its single table. The stage directions of the final draft indicate he uses the bottom scenic plan. Several long tables are "placed lengthwise to the width of the room. . . . On the left, a doorway opening on a road where a crowd of men has gathered. On the right, another doorway leading to the yard where there is a crowd of women. Inside the house, on the men's side, seven Male Guests are grouped by the door. . . . The Chorus of Old Men, seven in number, is drawn up in a crescent in the far corner, right, facing Lazarus. . . . On a raised platform at the middle of the one table placed lengthwise at center sits Lazarus."

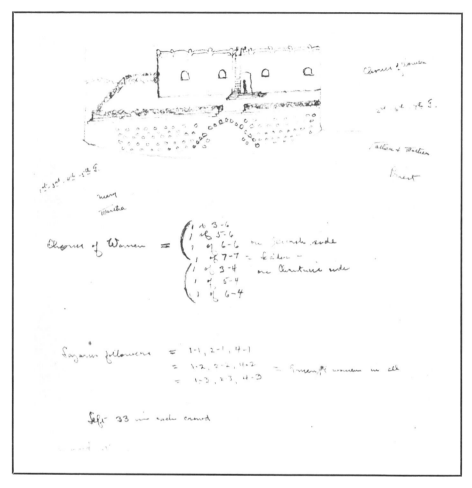

Act I, Scene 2, Outside the House of Laughter

O'Neill depicts in this drawing the setting described in the final draft of this scene: "On the road in the foreground, at left and right, two separate groups of Jews are gathered. . . . The adherents of Jesus, the Nazarenes, among whom may be noted MARTHA and MARY, are on the left; the Orthodox, among whom are Lazarus' FATHER and MOTHER and a PRIEST, are at right. Between the two hostile groups in the same CHORUS OF OLD MEN in the formation like a spearhead, whose point is placed at the foot of the steps leading to the terrace."

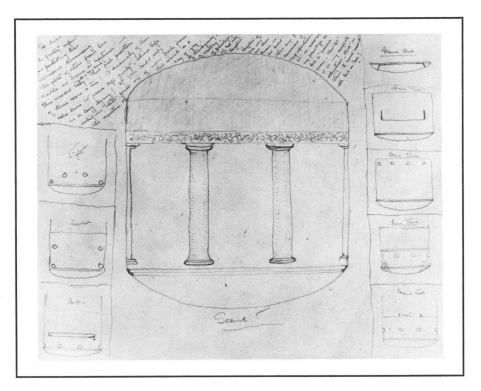

General schemes for the eight scenes
(O'Neill erased the word "Four" on the center scene.)

Scene One   (Act I, Scene 1) : Exterior and interior of Lazarus' home.

Scene Two   (Act I, Scene 2) : Exterior of Lazarus' home.

Scene Three   (Act II, Scene 1) : A square in Athens.

Scene Four   (Act II, Scene 2) : Inside the walls of Rome. In the foreground, a portico of a temple with massive columns.

Scene Five   (Act III, Scene 1) : Exterior of Tiberius' villa-palace at Capri. Triumphal arch in rear foreground with massive columns leading up to it.

Scene Six   (Act III, Scene 2) : The banquet hall in the palace of Tiberius. In the center of the room, a table in front of Caesar's chair.

Scene Seven   (Act IV, Scene 1) : The banquet hall in Tiberius' palace. Lazarus sits at the right; Tiberius sits on the other side of the table.

Scene Eight   (Act IV, Scene 2) : Arena of an amphitheatre. Tiberius sits on the throne on the left at the extreme front. Off right, Lazarus is being burnt alive.

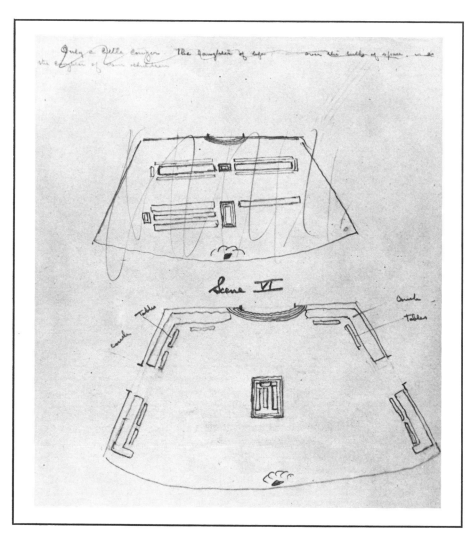

Scene 6 (Act III, Scene 2), The banquet hall in the palace of
Tiberius: top, discarded sketch; bottom, scenic plan used

Top, Act III, Scene 2, Tiberius' throne; bottom,
Act IV, Scene 2, Crucifixion of Lazarus

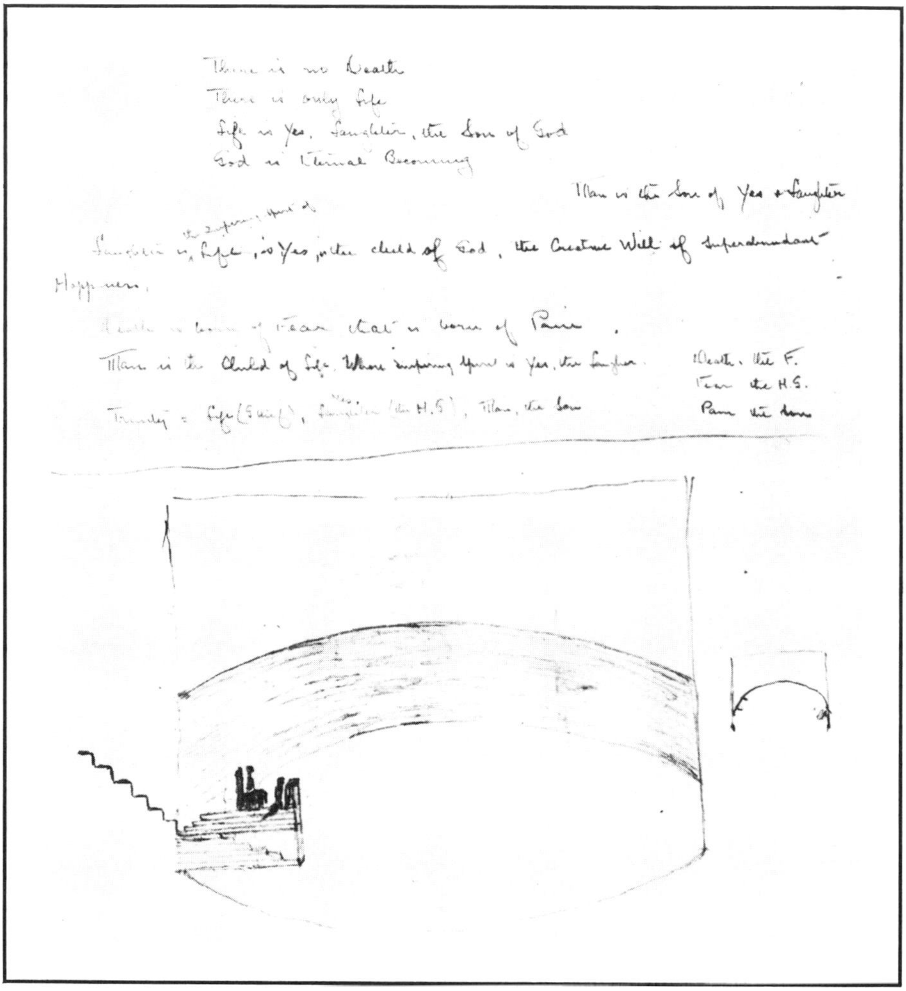
There is no Death
There is only Life
Life is Yes, Laughter, the Son of God
God is Eternal Becoming
Man is the Son of Yes & Laughter
Laughter is Life, is Yes, the child of God, the Creative Will of Superabundant Happiness.
Death is born of Fear that is born of Pain.
Man is the Child of Life, whose inspiring spirit is Yes, the Laughter.
Death, the F.
Fear the H.S.
Pain the Son

Act IV, Scene 2, Arena of the Roman amphitheatre

On May 11, 1926, the day he finished the draft of *Lazarus Laughed*, O'Neill drew the settings of the eight scenes as he envisioned them. Some set designs for "The Last Conquest" seem to be duplicates of these early drawings: Christ standing before the World Dictator and Lazarus before Tiberius; the Amphitheatre of Games where Christ is mocked and the one where Lazarus is reviled; Christ's cross dominating the Hill of Execution and the one on which Lazarus is crucified. The message—brought by two characters who have been resurrected after death and, therefore, no longer fear it—is the same in both plays: Man must neither fear human tyrants nor forget his God or his own demi-God nature, that only the fear of death threatens his freedom in this world and stifles his "yes" to both worldly and eternal life.

To convey his message, O'Neill constructs the two plays as religious pageants, using the devices of Greek theatre. The set designs suggest the scenes should be staged to provide a tableaux-like effect. Two short statements in the 1926 notes explain O'Neill's goal: to recapture, through a type of mystery play, the spirit of Chartres for unbelieving modern man by plunging him into an era when faith permeated life:

There are plenty of Christian myths. There is no reason why we shouldn't use them—interpret them—à la Greeks—thus reverse true spirit of religion was the theatre—
What did the Greeks have that we haven't got? First, faith in their own lives as symbols of life! Hence, faith in their own courage. Hence faith in their own nobility. Hence, faith in the nobility of Fate. Hence, in a word—True Faith!

The decision on March 10 to use masks and choruses in *Lazarus Laughed* had theatrical, as well as thematic, consequences as O'Neill discovered. The unmasked Lazarus, completely surrounded by masked characters, becomes the focal point of the play; his words, repeated now in the refrains of a chorus, stress the message of the drama. In a letter to Macgowan, O'Neill explains his purpose in showing Lazarus unmasked in the first scene: "The dramatic effect of this scene ought to be an arrowhead of concentration directed at the one man who is real and live in the midst of false, dead people" (January 12, 1927). The new concept also had a profound psychological effect on the author, providing the incentive and inspiration for a creative burst of energy; he completed the play's first draft in two months. On May 14, 1926, he writes Macgowan:

Lazarus Laughed is finished—first draft—the 11th, but there will be lots to do on it once Budgie gets it all typed. . . . It is so near to me yet that I feel as if it were pressed against my eyes and I couldn't see it. I wish you were around to "take a look" before I go over it. Certainly it contains the highest writing I have done. Certainly it *composes* on the theatre more than anything else I have done, even "Marco."

O'Neill revised *Lazarus Laughed* until June 10 when he states: "will call that play done now—think it fine stuff but know no one will ever produce it" (W.D.). Still not satisfied with the work, he was "going over" it again from December 17 until December 29 when he declares: "Lazarus finished—is immensely improved" (W.D.). The author's letter to Macgowan the following day discusses the changes he made:

> I have been laboring for the past two weeks like hell on "Lazarus" and I have made what are very grave alterations and cuts—especially in the first scene which I have taken out of the Bible—all the Saint John Gospel stuff out, etc.—and most of Lazarus talk, relying on a few sentences of his and his laughter. The scene has now, I think, real mystery and power—is much shorter, of course. It was always, to my mind, the weakest in the play. There was too much in it that reminded one of a regular Biblical play—a bad start for Lazarus. I have also paid particular attention throughout to getting the chants of the Chorus and Crowd into a more definite sound pattern. And I have cleared up Caligula at the end and trimmed all the loose ends throughout. It is now, I think, a much better play.

O'Neill spent nearly a year and a half in the early 1940s on "The Last Conquest," which depicts despots of some future age who are even more ruthless than the Roman Caesars. Perhaps his preoccupation with this play led him to consider a revival of *Lazarus Laughed*. In his letter of December 31, 1943 to Lawrence Langner, he comments on the timeliness and timelessness of the play:

> Now give heed to this and reread it carefully in the light of what that play has to say today. "Die exultantly that life may live" etc. "There is no death." (spiritually) etc. Also think of the light thrown on different facets of the psychology of dictators in Tiberius and Caligula. Hitler doing his little dance of triumph after the fall of France is very like my Caligula.

The two religious pageants, *Lazarus Laughed* and "The Last Conquest," should be viewed as O'Neill's attempt to instill in his countrymen what the Greeks had "that we haven't got"—what he calls "True Faith." By this phrase he is not suggesting the modern equivalent of a grandiose other-worldly scaling of Mount Olympus. O'Neill is much more interested in the quality of life on the plain below: men possessing "faith in their own lives as symbols of life"—faith in their own nobility and courage. Few contemporary artists have felt the utter anguish and despair O'Neill experienced when Hitler's totalitarian might swept through Europe, threatening the freedom of all men and nations. What the dramatist knew historically from World War II he incorporates in "The Last Conquest." What he envisioned prophetically a quarter of a century earlier he depicts in *Lazarus Laughed*. The message that links these plays is that there are values a man must be willing to die for rather than cringe in fear before tyrants, that life without freedom is but a death-in-life condition. Lazarus, who has no fear of the Roman tyrants, is described as "real and live in the midst of false dead people." O'Neill's comment on the timeliness and timelessness of *Lazarus Laughed* is as true today as when he made it forty years ago. If modern man fails to heed the message of that play, he may be entering upon the totalitarian era of world dictatorship predicted in "The Last Conquest."

°CAREER OF SHIH HUANG TI
(1925)

Career of Shih Huang Ti, Emperor of China, whose rule ended in 209 B.C. He destroyed all books etc. before his time so that history should begin with his reign. The theme of a great man who tries to throw off the destructive load of the past and start a new generation on a fresh beginning—his battles with the past.

In 1925 O'Neill records two ideas for plays that would depict the public and private lives of pre-Christian despotic rulers: the "Lives of Caesars" and the "Career of Shih Huang Ti." From his reading he discovered a direct connection between these ideas; his notes for the latter play contain quotations from *The Decline of the West* by Oswald Spengler, who considers "Shih Huang Ti as 'contemporary' with Augustus. Shih Huang Ti intended a position for himself and successors akin to that of 'Divus' in Rome."[*] Two years later in 1927 O'Neill conceived a number of ideas for plays on religious and political oppressors of the Christian era in his projected series of thirteen "plays about Atlantis (a history of Christianity)." Only two of these ideas were developed: the ninth on Robespierre and the thirteenth for "the second coming," which inspired "The Last Conquest" in the early 1940s. These and the other attempts of nearly two decades to depict history's infamous tyrants and oppressors of the human spirit reveal a major concern of the author: man's struggle to preserve individual freedom and to attain economic, political, and social justice and equality.

As his Work Diary indicates, O'Neill worked sporadically for nine years after first recording his original ideas in 1925 for the "Career of Shih Huang Ti":

5/3/29	Worked on Shih Huang Ti play idea (reading)
5/4–5/29	Shih Huang Ti idea (notes)
7/17–18/29	Shih Huang Ti idea (notes)
7/12/32	Shih Huang Ti idea (reading)
11/5/34	Shih Huang Ti play (ideas)
11/8/34	Shih Huang Ti (reading old notes)

The dramatist's notes of 1929 are based on material found in A. E. Grantham's *Hills of Blue* and Oswald Spengler's *The Decline of the West*, Volume I. While the author apparently never wrote a scenario for the play, his notes indicate the important aspects of the Emperor's "career" which he planned to include.

What was possibly his first total exposure to Taoism had a profound—and lasting—effect on him. Years later in 1937 he would name his home in California Tao House—the right way of life. O'Neill devotes a lengthy section to Taoism's condemnation of greed and materialism, noting statements by K'ung Fu Tzu (551–479), thinker and statesman, that emphasize the ethical aspects of the Tao:

---

[*]Oswald Spengler, *The Decline of the West*, Volume I (New York, 1926), p. 112.

"Without goodness no one can long withstand either misery or opulence"; and "the noble concentrates on righteousness, the mean on acquisition."[*] The dramatist was fascinated by the symbolism associated with the contrasting yet complementary female/male forces. Yin is identified as

> the dark fluid, passive, brooding female, Yang the light, strong, active, generating male principle, the triumphant and heroic splendidly ideographed by banners catching the first radiance of the sun, while the Yin principle of death was pictured as the dark womb that absorbs light, not to destroy it, but to let it rest and recuperate. . . . Even more, in a way it made civilization, for the Yin and the Yang were only modulations of an ultimate oneness, which, though undefinable by words, was spoken of as the Tao (p. 24).

Artistic inspiration and nature are linked in Taoism. According to Grantham, Chinese culture was born "among the stars and begotten by the wonder their splendour and marvellously regulated movements awoke in the soul of the first dreamer." Observing the sun and the moon instills in him "the vision of the sacredness of life, of the Divine without and within him, which made his conscience hear and answer the call for restraint and reverence" (p. 25).

O'Neill intended to depict not only the public life of Shih Huang Ti but also his personal familial conflicts—"his identity of the past with his mother." The dramatist establishes the following chronology in his notes. In 253 B.C. Chao Hsiang, the destroyer of the Chous, arrogated to his successors the "Son of Heaven's prerogative of sacrificing to the Lord on high, definitely setting up his house as the one round which all champions of the idea of unification should rally." He sent his young grandson I-jen as a hostage to the court in Han Tan, the capital of Chao. There I-jen fell in love with a singing girl, the beautiful concubine of Lü Pu-wei, at that time one of the "wealthy merchants interested in politics and backing centralization as conducive to improved trade." Lü Pu-wei correctly predicted the house of Ch'in[†] would emerge the winner among the contending states and, to promote his own interests, he financed I-jen and gave him his concubine for a wife. I-jen returned to Ch'in with her and eight months later Chêng (Shih Huang Ti) was born. This future conqueror of all China was probably the son of Lü Pu-wei rather than I-jen and not the legitimate heir of the house of Ch'in. In barely more than a decade King Chao Hsiang, his son Hsiao Wen, and grandson I-jen died, leaving the thirteen-year-old Chêng to govern. His mother and Lü Pu-wei exercised a kind of regency. "What Chêng owed his father was the support of Lü Pu-wei, without whose shrewd counsels and wide-

---

[*]A. E. Grantham, *Hills of Blue* (London, 1927), p. 21. Page references to this book, for passages cited in O'Neill's notes, appear in parentheses in the text.

[†]A similarity of names in this historical material can be confusing. Shih Huang Ti of the Ch'in dynasty conquered Ch'i, an independent state, in 221 B.C.

spread influence Ch'in's military victories would have lacked the requisite permanence and cohesion."

Chêng, when he set out to unify China at the age of twenty-nine, is described as "a man with a prominent nose, large eyes, the breast of a bird of prey, the voice of a jackel, the heart of a tiger, the benevolence of a wolf, one who while in difficulties would flatter men, but devour them the moment he had reached his goal" (p. 42). In a nine-year period he conquers the six states: Han in 230 B.C., Chao in 228 B.C., Wei in 225 B.C., Ch'u in 224 B.C., Yen in 222 B.C., and Ch'i in 221 B.C. He is thirty-nine when he made Chien of Ch'i, "the last ruler who attempted to maintain independence, perish of hunger among the pines and yew-trees of a graveyard" (p. 41). O'Neill indicates that the play is to open with this scene between the unfortunate Chien and the conqueror Chêng in the graveyard. After subduing Ch'i in 221 B.C., Chêng assumes the title Shih Huang Ti—"First Sovereign Lord." Translated literally, "shih" means "first" and "huang" signifies "emperor" or "august ruler." To the Chinese, the word "ruler" denotes a father, rather than a military, image.

Family love, as Grantham points out, is the "cornerstone of China's social structure" (p. 21). Yet Shih Huang Ti is as cruel and ruthless with members of his family as with his enemies. He has heard rumors about his possible illegitimacy. Since the death of his father, his mother has flaunted Chinese customs by maintaining a close relationship with Lü Pu-wei. To silence the gossip, Shih Huang Ti disguises a handsome youth, Lao Ai, as a eunuch and sends him to his mother's palace. In time Lao Ai becomes ambitious and acquires power, rank, and wealth. When an investigation seems imminent, he organizes a rebellion. "It failed completely. Lao Ai beheaded by the enraged King—head paraded with those of his following—body torn to bits by chariots" (p. 43). Shih Huang Ti angrily banishes his mother to the distant palace of Fuyang at Yong but soon discovers he is not yet powerful enough to defy the tradition of filial piety and is forced by indignant public opinion to take her back to the palace in the capital, Hsien Yang. Shih Huang Ti has incestuous feelings for his mother and views his younger brother, Chêng Kiao, who is her favorite, as a rival. Chêng Kiao stirs up the troops he commands. When the rebellion fails, Shih Huang Ti orders his brother to commit suicide. Lü Pu-wei also becomes a victim of the Emperor's wrath and is ordered to leave the court and return to his own estate. Even there Shih Huang Ti persecutes him, demanding to know his precise relationship with the house of Ch'in. Finally, when condemned to exile in Ssüchuan, Lü Pu-wei "poisoned himself knowing he will soon be murdered if he doesn't."

As his councilor, the Emperor selects one of Lü Pu-wei's clients, Li Ssü, an ambitious climber with a tendency to despotic radicalism who has a

> passion for root and branch reforms—violent break with the past—but of destruction, contempt of the old, craze for change, boundlessness of schemes, brutality in execution, reckless territorial rearrangements, wiping out of inherited wealth and power, the theoretical enfrancisement and

practical exploitation of masses, substitution of arbitrary violence for quiet rule by law and precedent, shattering through fear of any stir of opposition, the least freedom of speech, thought or action—all these characteristics of revolution (pp. 43–44).

After his triumphant consolidation of China, Shih Huang Ti has to decide how the newly conquered territories are to be ruled: by the party of violence and maximum centralization led by Li Ssǔ or the "party of conciliation, slow change, and minimum centralization led by Wang Kuan and the majority of scholars, clearly representing the wishes of the conquered as well as the most practical possibilities of the situation" (p. 44). Wang Kuan advises the Emperor to "delegate his authority over distant provinces to trusty relations to make sure of support in case of trouble and to overcome difficulties of governing vast Empire from one center" (p. 44). Li Ssǔ maintains that the pitiful weakness of the Chous was the result of such delegation. Because the conquered Chous ruled by virtue of fire, the Ch'ins "must from mystic necessity rule by virtue of water, the element that destroys fire" (p. 46). The Emperor cuts up his empire into thirty-six shires; six becomes his fate number. "Water belongs to the Yin principle of the universe and this governs the even, divisible numbers like six, and black is its typical color. Therefore, black was used for court robes, banners, the people were called the Black Heads, six became the leading number for all measuring" (p. 46). Shih Huang Ti transforms his people, passive by nature, into alert bodies of submissive officials and well-disciplined armies to secure or enlarge frontiers. Masses of chained convicts are used to construct roads, bridges, and gigantic buildings. Herds of peasants are "torn from homes and transplanted to fresh lands—the rich and noble were removed from one section of the Empire to another to deprive local patriotism of leaders."

Once again O'Neill would have the opportunity to present in this play the theme of good versus evil. On the one hand, the ruthless Emperor is vehemently opposed by scholars who follow the standard of right conduct taught by the sages of old and handed down in ancient writings. They believe "in the innate goodness of the human heart. Let rulers endeavor to be like Yao 'grave, enlightened & profound' or like Shun 'wise, mild, reverend & sincere, governing the people with benevolent solicitude, with justice ever tempered by mercy' " (p. 47). On the other hand, Shih Huang Ti is encouraged to reject these doctrines by Li Ssǔ, who maintains that "man's nature is evil and needs external discipline by instruction and above all a lively fear of punishment not only to keep it good but to make it good, goodness being a wholly artificial product" (pp. 47–48). O'Neill depicted the thirteenth century Polo Brothers and Son in *Marco Millions* as "American pillars of society"; he may have considered making an analogy here between the avaricious leaders of ancient China and their modern counterparts. His notes include a comparison Grantham makes between the politicians of China who used Li Ssǔ's theory to justify "their cruel methods of enforcing obedience to their innovations much as modern captains of industry coined the theory of backward races and low standards of living to trick out their voracious colonial expansions and commercial exploitations with philanthropy."

In 213 B.C., Li Ssŭ shows the Emperor how he could at a single blow "lay the shades of the past, silence the scholars and cripple patriotism" by destroying all books and official records except those of Ch'in. The punishments for non-compliance were severe:

> Let those who appeal to antiquity in order to abuse the present be slain with their entire kindred. Let those who fail to get their proscribed books burnt within thirty-one days of the proclaiming of this edict be branded and transported with shaven heads, an iron ring round their neck to the frontier to labour for 4 years on the building of the Great Wall (p. 49).

O'Neill points out that these threats did not deter all scholars for when Kasti, the first Han, reinstated books

> from the sides of caves, the roofs of houses, banks of rivers, volumes were produced by those who had risked their lives for their preservation— history states that from the lips of old men were taken down ancient texts which had everywhere perished except in the retentive memories of veteran scholars.*

Once all books advocating the Emperor practice frugality and austerity are supposedly destroyed, Shih Huang Ti indulges in his favorite labor—building. He has 270 palaces—exact replicas of those of every ruler he defeated—built on the northern bank of Wei above Hsien Yang and 400 in the rest of the empire. In 212 B.C. he sets 700,000 castrated convicts to work on a new palace near the capital. This is also to be his mausoleum, and an entire mountain has been tunneled and excavated to complete it. He fears assassination and has palaces within a radius of seventy miles linked up by walls and secret passages—"all fully furnished with women, etc.—move into any one at minute's notice—no one could tell where he would spend night" (p. 50). This labyrinthian structure is recommended by the magician Lu Shêng "to ward off evil spirits and facilitate the search for the fungus of immortality Shih Huang Ti desires." Like the Roman tyrant Tiberius, who beseeches Lazarus to tell him the secret of youth, of death, the Chinese Emperor—because of his heinous crimes—is afraid to die. Years earlier the magician advised Shih Huang Ti to send an expedition of 3,000 young boys and girls in search of the drug of immortality on the "mystic island of P'êng lai." A large collection of precious gifts was sent to the Immortals who inhabited the enchanted isles of the Eastern Sea to entice them to send the Emperor the precious plant. No one ever returned. Lu Shêng and another magician, Hin of Han, secretly flee because they consider that Shih Huang Ti—with "his violent, cruel and despotic nature, his delight in tortures and executions, his mania

---

*O'Neill identifies the source of this information only as "China" by Douglas.

for authority"—did not deserve immortal life. The Emperor blames scholars in the capital for turning the magicians against him and has 460 executed, buried alive, and sends the rest to work on the Great Wall.

Two omens warn the Emperor of impending disaster. First, a meteorite falls in Honan and someone writes these words on it: "On Shih Huang Ti's death Empire shall be divided" (p. 53). He retaliates by having everyone in the neighborhood slain and burnt to cinders. Second, "one of his messengers walking on the road at night was stopped by a stranger who offered him a ring of jade and said 'Within the year the Dragon Ancestor will die. Take him this ring' " (p. 53). Shih Huang Ti recognizes the ring at once as the one he had thrown into the Yangtze-kiang in 219 B.C. He fears death is imminent, consults the trigrams, and is told journeys would bring good fortune. In November 211 B.C. he sets forth down the Yangtze and lingers at his beloved Lang Ya, drinks "in its mountain-air and its sea-air and revelled in its views over the Ocean, which with the perpetual unrest of its multitudinous waves, the limitless stretches of its wind-swept skies seemed the image of his own soul" (p. 54). Again he asks the magicians "about the wonder-island* on the edge of the world where the plant of immortality grew" (p. 54). He turns back to the West and feels ill and dies near the Ford of P'ing yuen on July 22, 210 B.C.

While O'Neill derived historical data on the life of Shih Huang Ti from Grantham's book, he read Spengler to discover the philisophical and political climate of pre-Christian China. Spengler speaks of a Second Religiousness, which consists of a deep piety that fills the waking consciousness and "appears in all Civilizations as soon as they have fully formed themselves as such and are beginning to pass, slowly and imperceptibly, into the non-historical state in which time-periods cease to mean anything." He sees this Second Religiousness as a necessary counterpart of Caesarism, "which is the final political constitution of Late Civilizations; it becomes visible, therefore, in the Augustan Age of the classical and about the time of Shih Huang Ti in China. In both phenomena the creative young strength of the Early Culture is lacking. But both have their greatness nevertheless."†

Spengler maintains that what the Stoics were in Rome, the Confucians were in China—a "handful of narrow ideologues who concealed dissatisfaction under philosophy and thenceforward sought to advance their ideals by conspiracy." Shih Huang Ti has always been presented as a villain by Confucian historians

---

*At the same time O'Neill was making extensive notes for the "Career of Shih Huang Ti" in May and July 1929, he was also working on *Mourning Becomes Electra*. Grantham's references to the "mystic island of P'êng lai" and the "wonder-islands" may have inspired O'Neill's description of the "blessed isles"—the elusive, desired refuge of all the Mannons in the New England trilogy.

†Spengler, II (1928), p. 310.

because he suppressed the various schools of philosophy and burned books. Spengler views the great Burning of the Books as "nothing but the destruction of one part of the politico-philosophical literature and the abolition of propaganda and secret organization . . . Taoism, on the other hand, was supported as preaching the entire renunciation of Politics."*

The last page of O'Neill's notes describes some of the Emperor's personal conflicts, which would be included in the work.

°PLAY OF SHIH HUANG TI†

The final identify of the Past with his mother—then with Death—his last defiance the defiance of Death—he will live forever—search for the herb of immortality—

The fear of death the fear of incest (?)

The final yielding

[°LOVE AND WOMEN]
(1925)

A symbolical play about love and Woman taking material from de Gourmont's "Physiology of Love"—ironically humorous—or perhaps tragic and sinister—taking the spider, the praying mantis, etc.—stories of their deep savage life compulsions as insects working out in human forms—i.e. the reverse of the usual process (as per Čapek's "Insect Comedy") of using insect forms in thinly veiled symbolism of humans.

The Spider as the absolute arch-Type of most naked feminine instinct.

°LIFE OF SAINT PAUL
(1925)

[O'Neill never developed this title.]

---

*Ibid., p. 434.

†*Editor's note*: Because of the recent discovery of the treasures at Xian, China, the play would be particularly relevant today. Archaeologists have partially uncovered a pit near the tomb of the Chinese emperor and have found 6,000 life-size clay figures of soldiers strategically placed to guard Shih Huang Ti's burial place.

(

[°PRESTER JOHN]
(1926)

Historical material—interpretative

Play of Prester John or of Sir John Mandeville done in the old English prose of his book—story of the dragon-maiden main theme—a play for children and all of us.

°SQUAREHEAD SAGA*
(1926)

The Saga of Ollie—"Squarehead Saga"—Romantic Tale of a little, gentle, poetic-minded youth on a North Dakota farm who loves nature, is content to realize the heroic ideal of his lady, a great hunk of a girl who dreams sentimentally of the old Viking heroes of her race, of Eric who discovered America, who contrasts Ollie with another suitor, a big hunk like herself who has been in the Navy 3 years and now owns a Ford with a body like a torpedo and is a heavyweight wrestler of sorts when not laboring on the farm. He and Ollie are good friends, he wants Ollie to get the girl but he feels, quite simply, that she will marry him because she wants to. Ollie resolves to become another Eric the Red or the bard of same, he tries to get into the Navy but can't pass, he gets a try-out on a square-rigger but the height makes him sick when he's sent up to paint the skyrail yard and [he] drops the brush & paint but finally gets a job on a private yacht, owned by a Danish-American who has made millions in wood pulp. The daughter of this man, of the same name and nature as his old sweetheart, has turned in a navy hard-driving, hard-drinking but athletic in school & college, but now cynical & disgusted with money and everything. One night in the moonlight she hears Ollie playing & singing & she & he talk. He tells her his romantic dreams, and of the Princess he must save whose name must be _____. She is intrigued, all her latent romantic tenderness aroused. In like manner, the old man comes up to hear Ollie talk and play, and he tells of his knightly, ruthless deeds in tearing down forests and making them into pulp. Then they see daughter walking on edge, screams, falls off. Ollie jumps after her although he can't swim. The old man says Ollie can't. Millionaire asks, can you? Yes but too damned cold, etc. Scene ends with their being pulled aboard, daughter tells father she couldn't be saved, had to save him.

Wherever he goes, to his music, men talk of their loves and heroic deeds.

---

*O'Neill draws slanted lines through this idea and writes in the left margin: "Made into fantastic movie scenario 1927."

In an undated letter in summer 1923 to Macgowan, O'Neill discusses many new ideas for plays, including "one of the Norse sagas (of Eric the Red, for example), if I remember their quality aright. These in addition to what you mention as possibilities in new treatment." Three years later on August 22, 1926, he got what he called an "idea for fantastic whimsical play 'Squarehead Saga'" (W.D.). The next day he wrote the first outline for the scenario, which contains a reference to Eric the Red. Nothing survives of the work he did on this play in 1926 except the original idea recorded in the notebook. As his comment in the margin indicates, he did make an attempt the following year to write a "fantastic movie scenario—Ole Olsson's Saga"—using this idea. A subsequent letter to Macgowan explains his motive: "I'm also trying to write the original story, around my idea for 'The Squarehead Saga' for the films. Needs must when the devil drives. I also have financial worries at present. The Tiffany people are still very hot after me but, so far, their proposition isn't good enough" (March 24, 1927).

Work Diary entries describe his progress with the movie scenario of which two pages are extant.

10/22/27   Started making "Squarehead Saga" into scenario for pic-
            ture treatment—fantastic whimsical comedy—would be in-
            teresting if can get anyone to do it.
10/23–28/27 Worked on scenario for Squarehead Saga
10/29/27   Squarehead Saga (typing & revising)
10/30/27   Finished Squarehead Saga

It is highly possible that O'Neill was inspired to write "Squarehead Saga" after hearing accounts of the Norse legends ("if I remember their quality aright") from his former drinking companion at Jimmy the Priest's in 1912, the old Swedish sailor Chris Christopherson. A definite relationship is established through the use of names. Chris Christopherson makes his first appearance as Ollie Olson in three of the *S.S. Glencairn* plays. The hero is named Ollie in the 1926 idea and Ole Olsson in the 1927 movie scenario. The brother of the latter character is given the same background as Ollie Olson's in *The Long Voyage Home*, having worked on the farm until he was eighteen and then going to sea. He eventually enlisted in the United States Navy, served six years as a gob, and has just returned to the farm when the story opens. "He is the largest and most powerful of the family, and is the proud possessor of a white skin, tattooed from neck to waist with all sorts of gorgeous and patriotic designs as a result of his career as a sailor." Like Ollie's rival in the original 1926 idea, he is a wrestler and takes an immense childlike pride in his picturesque torso. He uses any "excuse to exhibit himself and as the wrestling matches which feature his father's entertainments offer the finest opportunity for this, he is taking up heavyweight wrestling quite seriously as a sideline to farming."

Ole Olsson, the hero of the 1927 saga, appears to be another self-portrait;

"he is slight and small and dark with his preoccupied dreamer's eyes, absolutely unlike his brothers or parents except that his disposition is as naive and kind and childlike as theirs." He is useless at the hard labor on the farm, yet he "loves the earth of the fields and all the plants and animals with a poet's passion." He compensates for his inefficiency in practical matters by developing his artistic talents. He plays the accordion and is the musician at all the dances. Above all, he is a great storyteller and entertains all the neighbors at the rough dinners his father gives on festive occasions with accounts of the heroic Scandinavian sagas he has studied. Accompanying himself on the accordion, he recites whole sagas for their entertainment.

These recitations have an extraordinary effect on his hearers. They become so fascinated and moved that they seem to see the whole history of ancient sea-raids and savage fights and discovery of strange lands unfold before their eyes in the big barn of this Dakota farm. They see themselves as characters in the tale as Ole unfolds it. And Ole, of course, being very romantic, always sees himself as the hero of the saga. On these nights, Ole is as favored a character as in the legendary times of his tales, the skald (poet) at the court of the Viking chief would have been. He is admired and respected and held in awe.

However, in the light of day the spell is broken, and Ole is viewed once again as an ineffectual lovable young man, "who isn't much use and is undoubtedly a bit queer in the head." His family coddles and spoils him and laughs "with good-humored fondness at his well-meant but bungling attempts to work beside them. He is the butt of the coarse but good-natured jokes of his huge brothers who adore him in spite of their teasing. While Ole laughs cheerfully with them at his blunders, secretly he is sad. He considers himself a misfit, a failure." He begins to wander more and more frequently out to the hills where he plays his accordion and transports himself "in another world of his imagination, the ancient legendary world of the Sagas, where he sees himself as a daring Viking prince, sailing the sea which he (Ole) has never seen." At times he visits the farm animals and plays to them and tells them his dreams. He is particularly fond of a donkey he has had for many years and which he rides wherever he wishes to go. His father has given each of his brothers an automobile on their twenty-first birthday, but because of fear, Ole has never ridden in one. While Ollie's rival in the 1926 idea "owns a Ford with a body like a torpedo," Ole's youngest brother, Sven, has a "rakish Ford roadster fitted with a torpedo body."

The fragment concludes with a note that Ole is "deeply in love with Astrid Helstrom, the daughter of a neighboring farmer, "a tall powerful blond girl of eighteen who is so strong that she is able to do a man's work on the farm." If the 1927 movie scenario followed the original 1926 plot, Ole will leave Astrid— who seems to be the precursor of Josie Hogan—and the farm, go to sea, and meet and love the princess daughter of a capitalist king, thus fulfilling his romantic dream.

If O'Neill's art imitates his life in the picture he paints of the misfits at Harry Hope's saloon in *The Iceman Cometh*, endlessly recollecting their pasts, it is possible that "Squarehead Saga" is based on some story related to the dramatist by the real-life Chris Christopherson or on actual aspects of the old sailor's early life, heightened by the author's imagination. There is a double irony in O'Neill's attempt to write this saga: during the many years they honored the American playwright, the people of Sweden were totally unaware of his efforts in the mid-1920s to portray one of their own and Scandinavian mythology; the dramatist could not have known at the time he was planning his saga that during the years when he would later be rejected by his own countrymen, Stockholm's Royal Dramatic Theatre would give birth to and sustain the O'Neill tradition.

[DYNAMO]*
(1926)

Dynamo stops—interlude, pipes of Pan—Dynamo begins again—Water-fall—Neanderthal man

"Mother Dynamo"

"He who sees Pan, dies!" [words erased: Background human]
Man becomes giant, dynamo woman

Play of Dynamos—the despairing philosopher—poet who falls in love with balance equilibrium of energy—his personification of it—his final marriage with it—the consummation ending with his destruction.

$$G[od] : M[other] = M[other] : Machine$$

In the late 1920s O'Neill began a trilogy, "Myth Plays for the God-forsaken," envisioning it—as he later notes—as "3 plays to be in one book—'Dynamo' (rewritten), 'Without Ending Of Days' & 'On To Hercules'" (W.D., 7/19/32). In a letter to Joseph Wood Krutch dated June 11, 1929, he explains that he uses "the word trilogy in the very loosest sense, three plays, entirely independent of each other but all written around the general spiritual futility of the substitute-God search." The reviews for *Dynamo*, when it premiered in New York on February 11, 1929, castigated both the work and its author, who had, unfortunately, identified it in a program note as the first play of a trilogy. Exactly a month later he comments to Robert Sisk: "it was a great mistake for me to have said anything in advance about a trilogy or even to hint that it had anything to do with what was wrong with us, or to mention Gods, dead or alive, in any connection."

News of the unfavorable reviews—reaching the author in France immediately after *Dynamo* opened—did not deter him from his plans to continue the trilogy. He worked fourteen days in February and seventeen days in March 1929—and intermittently in the following years until 1937—on the third play, "It Cannot Be Mad?," subsequently given a number of other titles: "On To Betelgeuse," "On To Hercules," "The Life of Bessie Bowen," and "Career of Bessie Bowlan." While this play was never completed, "Without Ending of Days," the second play of the trilogy, emerged—after many title changes—as *Days Without End*, which had, like *Dynamo*, a religious theme and was a critical failure when produced in 1934.

Years later O'Neill concedes *Dynamo* may have stepped "on its own feet dramaturgically speaking"; he then adds: "I'm not sure it does, at that, because 1929 criticism is no test. Any play which mentioned God, either favorably or unfavorably, unless as a childish, humorous, ignorant negro myth, in that year

---

*O'Neill cancels this idea and writes "Dynamo—1928" across it.

of disgrace was automatically a poor play in any critic's book" (Letter to Lawrence Langner, August 24, 1941).

The dramatist knew he had made two fatal errors that were, in part, responsible for the misconception of *Dynamo*'s central theme. He believed he let the play out of his hands too soon after completing it. When revising the play for publication, he attempted, as he told Langner, to point "up the human story of Reuben's psychological mess over his father and his mother's betrayal and how he at last deifies and finds her again (the real plot of the play which no one seems to have seen in any of its implications but which I thought was obvious)" (Letter of March 25, 1929). Part of the dramatist's creative process was to "nurse" a play through the rehearsal period. Unable to attend rehearsals for *Dynamo*, he apologizes to Langner, saying: "I might have been of help in clearing it up in spots." He then vents his anger on the critics, who failed to perceive the themes he had woven into the fabric of the play:

> no one seems to have gotten the real human relationship story, what his mother does to the boy and what that leads to in his sacrifice of the girl to a maternal deity in the end—the girl his mother hated and was jealous of —that all that was the boy's real God struggle, or prompted it. This all fits in with the general theme of American life in back of the play, America being the land of the mother complex. . . . not a damn one mentions it. They were so damned hot on the general religious theme that they couldn't see the human psychological struggle without which (I agree with them here) the play is fairly lifeless comment on an old hat question.
>
> (Letter of March 11, 1929)

The key to understanding the statement O'Neill makes in *Dynamo* is the simple equation found in his first 1926 idea for the play—G : M = M : Machine. The substitute-God search leads the young hero to equate his mother with God. Betrayed by her but still obsessed by the mother complex, he finds a substitute in the maternal-looking, life-sustaining machine—the dynamo—which he "deifies and finds her again." He achieves a mystical union with her—a "consummation ending with his destruction." The term "Neanderthal man" in the original idea seems an echo from *The Hairy Ape*, a play which O'Neill mentions frequently in his letters* when discussing *Dynamo*. Yank's substitute God search leads to a

---

* "The first part derives from the method of simultaneous exterior and interior I used with such revealing effect in *Desire*. The second part derives its method (use of sounds) remotely from *The Hairy Ape*. I use sounds very pronouncedly throughout the play as a definite dramatic motive."

(Letter to Theresa Helburn, February 25, 1928)

"In structure and method of staging it will be an onward development deriving from the *Ape* and *Desire*. The dialogue will be à la *Interlude* but, as it deals with more simple people psychologically, it will have more of soliloquy and less of the quick aside thought."

(Letter to Kenneth Macgowan, April 27, 1928)

reverse of *Dynamo*'s equation—Machine : G = G : gorilla. At the outset of the play Yank equates the machine with a God-force; his substitute-God search leads to his destruction at the end by a gorilla's embrace. Yank is the apotheosis of Neanderthal man physically and psychologically as he attempts to scale the modern evolutionary ladder from machine to animal to human. In contrast, the hero of *Dynamo* is a Neanderthal spiritually. He rejects the modern-day Christian God—identified in his mind with his tyrannical father—and regresses to the most primitive religious rites, believing the Mother God is personified in the machine idol and demands human sacrifice. The concept of primitive worship is reinforced by another line in the initial idea: "He who sees Pan, dies." This line can be interpreted in two ways. According to legend, the cry was heard when the veil of the Temple was rent at the time of the Crucifixion. After this lament, the oracles were forever silent. The central character in *Dynamo* views himself as a savior. When he is crucified in the Temple—the generator room, the message of the Dynamo Mother God is heard no more. In the notes for *Lazarus Laughed*, written just before *Dynamo*, O'Neill identifies Pan as the companion of Dionysus, who was viewed by the Greeks as

not merely the soul (spiritual form) of the vine but of all that live in flowing things of which the vine is the most emphatic example. . . . Pan has almost no story—but a presence—spiritual force of Arcadia & its ways of human life. Breathing of remote nature—things which the religion of D. loves—Pan joins the company of the Satyrs of spirits of wild vegetation, the reed-music.

In one of the early drawings for the 1928 play, O'Neill depicts the *flowing* waterfall beside the power plant. The spirit of Pan breathes in the "dynamo woman" who, after manifesting herself to her son, kills him.

The information in the preceding section provides a retrospective view of O'Neill's total vision of *Dynamo*, of its major theme: the hero's substitute-God search, which is equated with his perception and pursuit of the constantly evolving mother figure; his own mother merges with Mrs. Fife, who is identified with the Mother Dynamo. O'Neill actually conceived the first idea for *Dynamo* two years after his own mother's death and two years before he records the original concept in 1926 in the notebooks. In discussing his progress on *Marco Millions* with Macgowan, he writes: "Also I have new ideas—one for a play to be called *Dynamo*, queer and intriguing" (August 19, 1924). Developing the American-type materialist millionaire with his spiritual hump possibly inspired the author to plan a play demonstrating the religious vacuity—as he perceived it—in this country.

O'Neill wrote two scenarios for *Dynamo*—one in 1927, the other in 1928. While the first is dated "Summer 1927—Spithead," Work Diary entries reveal that most of it was written in the spring of that year. The author worked on the "idea for *Dynamo*," developing the characters, on March 4, 22, and 23 and from April 5 to 8, and writing a scenario from April 10 to 13.

Characters

Benjamin*
   James White, law student
       Jonathan*
   Reverend Thomas White, his father
   Elizabeth White, his mother
   Bill Mallory, an electrical engineer
   Dorothy, his daughter
   Mary, his wife
   Ernest Hardy

Although only a few lines are used to describe the characters in the published text—and, presumably, the production script of the play—they are clearly and comprehensively delineated in the first scenario.

James White, the twenty-two-year-old hero, possesses contrasting dual characteristics and some of the author's physical attributes; his

face large and striking-looking, the nose prominent and acquiline, the wide mouth thick-lipped and sensual, the jaw heavy and obstinate—small pale-blue eyes keep his dark face from repelling one with its self-assertive harshness and hardness—eyes boyish and appealing, of a nature naturally strong that has been made weak and self-doubting by being under the domination of a stronger will since early childhood—voice too reflects the duality in his character—diffident and pleasing and musical but when emotionally aroused it changes to a high-pitched, grating discordant tone that is like a demonic cruel spirit possessing him.

James's mother, who is given a strange mystic other-world quality, is "very like him in appearance except her eyes are black and concentrated, the eyes of a fanatic." Her marriage to the Reverend Thomas has been a loveless affair, arranged by her father, also a minister. "Her strength and dark good looks completely dominate" her husband. She is forty-five, tall, thin, wiry and energetic. Her voice is "assertive, discordant but resonant, the voice of a natural exhorter—the wife of a minister of the Lord, not of the man, White, and her son, on whom all her jealous love has been concentrated, is her son by one of the Lord's annointed—a grandson of God, as she is the daughter-in-law of God."

Reverend Thomas White is a "square set, short and rather fat man of fifty-five" with a small mouth and round pale blue eyes. His outer manner is "complacent, sanctimonius, holier-than-thou superiority due to his position as a Baptist minister and pastor of a flock of sinners." He is a pious man "whose Bible has always been the inspired word." In contrast to later versions, he is depicted

---

*O'Neill inserts these after changing the son's name to Benjamin and the father's to Jonathan.

here as a "meek, unassuming soul, dull but kindly, preferring to be lowly and unnoticed but forced to live in prominence to carry out his duty."

Bill Mallory is a "small, wiry man of fifty with a sharp little face, bristly ginger-colored hair and mustache, grey eyes keen, cunning rather than intelligent, thin mouth bitter and scornful." His cruel remarks make him unpopular and prevent him from getting positions for which he is qualified. He is a "bitter, loud-spoken atheist—manner nervous and high-strung—continually irritable and nagging." His relentless persecution prompts three sons to leave home. His love is "concentrated on daughter, coddled and spoiled—for wife feels the affection a marksman feels for a target."

Mary Mallory not only endures her husband but incredibly adores him. She is "large, fat, abysmally nerveless and good-natured, with the huge blank soft beautiful eyes of a cow—instead of cud ruminates over days full of a routine of household duties—mentally about two years old."

Dorothy has a strange complex nature that is a "combination of the good traits of these two." She has a "pretty, round graceful figure, beautiful eyes and light hair—character cheerful and maternal while at the same time quick and energetic." She also has her father's "spiteful temper deep in her but disapproves of it and keeps it firmly under control."

Ernest Hardy is a "big, hulking young fellow, average in looks and intelligence and every other way—strangely under the influence of Mallory but is superstitiously afraid of his atheism—in love with Dorothy."

1927 Scenario

April 10, 1927—"Scenario first three scenes of Part I" (W.D.)

Scene One—The parsonage—the mother uses the meek father to oppose Jim's marriage.
        (Reverend White, Mrs. & James—Reverend & Mrs.)

The emphasis in this and other scenes in the first half of the play is on the "human relationship story." Much of the scene presents the filtered thoughts of the characters. James thinks of his love for Dorothy and feels guilt for concealing it. His mother watches him, "guessing what is on his mind, jealous and planning how to get him away from D." Her husband, completely oblivious to the tension between them, worries about his duties and next Sunday's sermon. When James goes for a walk, she voices her fear that he is "smitten with Dorothy" and that her father is getting the best of White, who angrily says he will forbid James to see her again.

Scene Two—The Mallory home—The father, sceptic, arranges a test—He wants her to marry young electrical engineer.
        (Mallory, Mrs. & D.—D. goes to primp up—Mallory & Mrs.—
        Mallory—Mallory & D.—Mallory & James)

Discovering Dorothy's love for James, Mallory, seething with fury and jealousy, plans a test for the "numbskull," who—he claims derisively—"will make a hell of a lawyer." Mallory wants to "hit him below the Bible belt." When Mrs. Mallory—who has great affection for James—cries, her husband sends her from the room and forces Dorothy to eavesdrop. To James he narrates a sordid story he had read in the newspaper; he pretends to confess he has killed a man in self-defense and escaped from jail. The struggle begins in James; it is his duty to denounce Mallory or become an accomplice in the sin. Dorothy now seems a child of sin to him. He runs from the house, seeking his mother's counsel. Dorothy denounces her father and then becomes bitter because James hesitated and went off without seeing her.

Scene Three—Garden of the Parsonage—The mother uses the father to summon
the Old Testament God of Vengeance
(James—James & mother—James & mother & father)

James longs to tell his mother what has happened but believes it is dishonorable to do so. Desperately, he cries: "Mother!" Mrs. White is overjoyed by the story, pretends to understand his love for Dorothy, and encourages him to denounce Mallory to the police. She appeals to God—the God up in the heavens, everywhere, and calls her husband from the house to lead them in prayers. He obeys meekly, mildly. "She takes up his prayer fiercely, exhaustingly, summoning the God of the Old Testament as if he were her father—The summoned God speaks the words she desires out of the night to the receptive, nerve-shattered, hysterical James. To him this is a miracle. God has spoken; God will enter the heart of Dorothy and her father." After her son goes to the police station, Mrs. White tells her husband Mallory's "secret." The first sound of thunder is heard. In the first scenario, she is extremely frightened of lightning. Although used briefly here, the ominous thunder-lightning symbolism anticipates the re-emergence of the dead mother as the "Mother Dynamo."

April 11, 1927—"idea 4th and 5th scenes" (W.D.)

Scene Four—Garden of the Mallory home
(James & father & policeman—James, father, Mallory & D.
& wife—Mallory & D. & wife)

Mallory watches the lightning "with a technical aesthetic pleasure—his old god, Electricity." He laughs and calls Dorothy from the house when he sees White, James, and two policemen approaching; he sneers when arrested and says he "wants White and his family to be laughed out of town. . . . Lightning is going to get his church someday on top of that hell without lightning protection." Discovering the hoax, James is "overwhelmed with shame and grief" and denounces his complacent father and "his God who he feels has played a trick on him—a stupid God. He runs off leaving his father speechless."

Scene Five—The Garden of Parsonage—Thunder storm—the church is struck
        (James & father—James & father & mother)

Terrified by the storm, Mrs. White is praying—"strange exultance that this storm is a symbol of the wrath of God smiting the Mallorys." Her son enters like a frightened child and finds comfort in her arms. He is not motivated, as in later versions, by the awareness of her betrayal—her revelation of the "secret" to his father—when he turns on her and God, saying: "There is only the bitter mocking God of the Mallorys, the god of Electricity. . . . She is a symbol of his father's God—his father's wife, not his mother. She has deliberately offered him up, a human sacrifice to this God She tells him to beware of the vengeance of God." When the church is struck by lightning, James rocks with wild laughter. "There is no God except Mallory's—the devil—the devil of Electricity—he cheers on the flames—his father comes—asks stupidly where he's going—James, wildly mocking, says he wants to know God—he's going out into the world to study Electricity."

Part Two

April 12, 1927—"Sketch first three scenes of Part Two" (W.D.)

Scene One—Sitting room of the parsonage—one year later
        (James & father)

James returns home to discover his "mother has died of cancer after ineffectual radium treatment which has not helped her but hastened the end—Her body is laid out in the next room." He has completely changed and looks and acts like a mechanic. He is "absolutely indifferent to his mother's death, his father's grief." James explains why he left home; he felt it "his mission, a vision (like St. Paul) the voice of the storm & the burning church calling him to his vocation—[has] gotten a job as electrician's helper." Now he hopes Mallory, whom he considers a priest, will give him a job in the power plant. To him all women "have become unimportant personifications of the Great Female Principle of the Universe—God has become Mother who is Electricity—his search to know Her, Love Her, adore Her." He tries to convert his father, who exclaims: "Monster. Leave this house!" James strikes a final blow, arguing that "a radium treatment would act adversely on his mother who was an unbeliever, an atheist where the God Electricity was concerned."

Scene Two—The Power House—The Dynamo assumes female form
        [idea presented here but discarded: "Hardy super., Dorothy now his wife"]
        (James & dynamo—James & D.)

Considering it the "final touch to crown his joke," Mallory gives James a job as an oiler at the power house. Alone with the dynamo, he experiences "queer emotional reactions as to a female thing. He polishes and caresses his God, like a priest an idol—he is the elected one." When Dorothy enters, he becomes aroused and "desires her body—that was all his love had ever amounted to—sex—she is intrigued by the change in him—feels guilty toward him." During the past year, she has defied her parents and "taken to going out nights and joy-riding with boys, gets a bad reputation in the town and is reckless about it." She realizes she still loves him and wants to marry him. "They make a date to meet—he is left with dynamo (the first faint suggestion of the sacrifice comes to him here)."

Scene Three—The Dawn—The stars, space, the water, the earth, energy, etc.— Seduction of Dorothy—and sacrifice
(James—James & D.—James)

James has been working out his theories of the new God. "He loves this Dynamo-Mother-God who is very real and living to him now with a terrible incestuous love—some bar which must be broken down before he can achieve union with God and Supreme Enlightenment—some sacrifice he must make to atone for his former heresies—the answer comes to him—it is his love for Dorothy." Believing he has sinned against his celibate priesthood and insulted the Mother Deity, he decides Dorothy must become a "human sacrifice—she will enter the Deity." Dorothy's entreaty to marry her "seems to him a final temptation of the Evil One. She sees his eyes, guesses, terrified she sinks helpless to her knees— She moans with terror, saying only his name. He kneels besides her and invokes his Great Mother Goddess, Electricity."

April 13, 1927—"Sketch last scene Part Two" (W.D.)

Scene Four—The Power House—The rite of sacrifice to the Mother Deity—His death causes lights to go out all over Town.
(James & dynamo)

Deeming himself "worthy to celebrate the final mystery with her" in the temple, James "makes a crude altar before the Dynamo—holds a service—improvises ecstatically a crazy invocation of the Goddess—desires union with her." He opens his arms "as if to embrace the Goddess. If she will bless him, a mortal, with her love, he will become immortal, a God, a possessor of cosmic energy— eternal atom incarnate." He imagines he hears Her consent to this final mystery and says: "You have called me and I come. Come, Mother." He climbs to the core of the Dynamo; "his arms are outspread to press it to his heart, it is as if he were crucified upon it. A terrific flash of light—men outside—burst open the door— from the darkness come a strange voice, as if the Dynamo were speaking: 'He who looks upon Pan must die!' " The flashes of the men pick "out a little shrivelled figure, like that of a monkey, hanging as if nailed to the face of the Dynamo.

They shut the Dynamo off. The figure sags, then falls in a crumpled heap to the floor." The line—"And perhaps the Hairy Ape at last belongs"—would have been appropriate here if it had not been used to conclude the earlier 1921 play. The first scenario ends with Mallory looking at the form in frightened awe and saying: "The damned lunatic! What did he think he was getting away with, I wonder?"

O'Neill made three attempts to continue work on *Dynamo* in 1927—on May 28, June 4, and June 5 when he decided "stuff done so far on it is no good" (W.D.). On September 30 he drove from New York to Stephenson, Connecticut with Carlotta Monterey to "look at Hydro-Electric Power Station for *Dynamo*" (W.D.). The fall of 1927 was a time of personal conflict and decision, preceding, as it did, O'Neill's flight with Carlotta to Europe the following February. Although the dramatist resumed his regular work routine after establishing residence in France, he did not begin making explanatory comments in the Work Diary for some time. The first entry occurs on March 13, 1928, presumably the day he wrote new descriptions for the characters of *Dynamo*. An introductory comment states: "Play method (?)—Pick out one or two or three characteristic sentences and thoughts expressing the unique relationship between the characters and life, itself, to God." He incorporates this scheme into a general discussion and rough outline of the first two scenes.

1928 Preliminary Notes

Characters

Some of the characteristics of the parents have been interchanged. The formerly meek, complacent, unassuming Baptist minister is now a "booming-voiced, over-assertive personality, autocratic and overbearing, a stern Old Testament moralist who always manages quite simply to identify his own will with the will of God." His formerly assertive, love-starved fanatical wife is a "mild-looking silent woman," whose persistent iron will is carefully hidden "beneath her meek, submissive exterior."

O'Neill said that *Dynamo* marked a "move back" but its husband-wife relationship anticipates that found in two later plays. Foreshadowing that other New England Puritan, Ezra Mannon, the husband has an "old fanatical ideal of purity"; as a youth he had "sworn to himself an oath of celibacy." However, after meeting his future wife Elizabeth, Christine Mannon's precursor, he was "overcome by her prettiness, the flesh had conquered him. She was gay, light-hearted and pleasure-loving." He has always regarded his marriage "as a weak compromise of his spirit with the world and at the same time [has] been proportionately intense in the passion her flesh arouses in him, a hold that has never weakened with the years, continually stimulated as it is by the reverse hatred and guilt he feels for his conquering love." While in the 1927 scenario theirs had been an arranged marriage, it now resembles James and Mary Tyrone's. "Although bound to each other by a tie of deep love and passion, there also exists a strong tie of hatred between these two. She has always hated her love for him as a weakness that made her prefer him to many suitors more suitable from a practical standpoint who have since risen in the world and could have given her its delights which she remembers with regret." She bitterly resents his profession, his devotion to the "Old Testament deity who has deprived her of the world and its sensuous social graces and power." Most of their conflict centers "around the person of their youngest child—he has four sisters who have been married off after mother's guile has triumphed and influenced their affections toward men of the world." The son feels, like his father, that his mother is weakness, "that he must struggle against her." While his father wants him to be a minister, his mother encourages him to go into business to make money; "she appeals to him with sly tales of the real privations she has had to undergo." The mother triumphs again, for he chooses "the law as a substitute for The Law—his father in his mother's medium." The section ends with the following line: "The tragic struggle of the individual of the Soul of Man against the race of men."

Part I, Scene One

In the preliminary notes for the first scene, the names of the father and son have been changed to Jonathan and Benjamin Light. The husband and wife— seemingly reincarnations of Strindberg's Captain and Laura—engage in a "bitter struggle with each seeking to influence Benjamin." A decision must be made about their son's future and they "have been collecting their forces for the battle they know must come between them." The mother thinks of her prosperous daughters and is jealous because "they have gotten what she once desired and missed" by marrying Jonathan "against her better judgment, compelled by his masculinity—he, in his turn, blames her sex for triumphing—her feminine body betraying his will as it had when he first fell in love with her." The minister feels that he is a failure. "It is the lust of the flesh—his wife—that he blames for this. Her body has remained in full control over his will. It is in bed that she gets his consent to Benjamin going to college."

Once in college, Benjamin, embittered and lonely, "falls in love with the classics. To him they bring a sensuous delight he hasn't known before. He has a secret love for poetry—erotic and sensual—which he feels is a sin against the God he fears." An implied belief in the Old Testament God and His morality is deeply rooted "in the background of these three people's minds & feelings." Benjamin never rebels against his parents or his father's Old Testament God "until shortly before the play opens when he falls in love, as desperately and wholly as only a person of his character could," with Dorothy Mallory, a fellow student majoring in science, the daughter of his father's bitter enemy, an atheist. Benjamin's "impractical idea is that he will get Dorothy to elope with him and then, confronting his parents with the accomplished fact, will obtain their forgiveness. His ambition is to become a professor in the classics—the college as a sanctuary where he can be safe." Discovering her son's love for Dorothy, Mrs. Light plans to use the information as a weapon, knowing her husband would "seize on any opportunity to get him out of Mallory's clutches" and consent to a business career.

Part I, Scene Two

The name Mallory has now been changed to Fife, and new information is provided about the family's background. The father, born in the United States of poor Scottish immigrant parents, is forced to go to work after grammar school. He rebels against his father, a religious tyrant, and becomes an atheist. He studies electricity at night school and gets a job in a power house. Electricity becomes his God. Resenting life and his own inability to qualify as an engineer, he "becomes darkly and vaguely radical, a devourer of Carlyle's *French Revolution*, [takes] pride in calling himself a Jacobin, he talks ominously of the guillotine— but religiously refuses to associate himself with any modern radical movement (this is partly his Scotch caution, partly his scorn for all his fellows—they have no guts)." He loves his dynamo—Electricity, his wife, and his daughter "because she has a tongue that can be as scathing as his own and a strong will of her own he cannot bully." There are traits in Fife—especially his "biting sardonic humor"— which will later be found in Larry Slade in *The Iceman Cometh*.

The mother is described in terms that will later be used to portray Rosa Daniello in "The Visit of Malatesta" and is called May, the name assigned to Rosa's daughter. May Fife "is a simple soul, good-hearted, a bit of a sloven, taking everything with a maddening unawareness dreaming heavily and emptily, her stout body bovinely at peace in life. Lazy, sentimental and inefficient," she views her husband as a "romantic figure in her dull stupid life." Like Rosa Daniello and Nora Melody, the sensual, maternal May "had been an easy victim" and became pregnant. Fife's "grudging contemptuous offer to marry her had been for her the noble gesture of a noble soul and she has unfailingly adored him and his daughter ever since. She is one of those women who likes their men to torture them a little." In this ideal mother figure, there is "something sweet about her unselfish love for husband and daughter, something strong in her animal closeness to Nature."

The daughter, now called Ada, "combines her mother's physical appearance with her father's character." She resembles other O'Neill women—Abbie, Sara, Josie; "her body has soft, rounded feminine contours, full-breasted and broad-hipped. Her round face with its big dark eyes and dark skin and hair and soft mouth is exceeding attractive." Like Sara Melody, "she bullies both of her parents, sees through her father, loves her mother deeply and feels immensely close to

her—and takes up her defense whenever her father picks on her." When her
mother "in a silly moment of crazy confidence" tells her she had been born out
of wedlock, Ada has felt like an outcast. She takes on "her father's scornful attitude in regard to morals."

1928 Scenario

O'Neill begins the second scenario with another—and in some instances
new—interpretation of the characters. There is "an atmosphere of poverty" about
the Light parsonage, "a little old New England white frame cottage." The prints
of scenes from the Bible hanging on the walls of the sitting room are identified
as "the Return of the Prodigal and Jacob and Isaac." The reference to Jacob is
particularly appropriate as is the change of the young hero's name from Benjamin
to Reuben. The Biblical Benjamin ("son of the right hand") was his father
Jacob's favorite, most beloved son. In contrast, Jacob is harsh with Reuben ("behold, a son"), warning him: "Unstable as water, thou shalt not excel." In the
new scenario, the son, as Reuben, has lost the romantic poet-dreamer quality he
had as Benjamin, as well as his desire to imitate his father and become a minister. As Benjamin, he is "by nature inclined toward his father, his natural sympathies are with him." Yet he also feels strangely drawn to his mother. Along with
the name Benjamin, O'Neill seems to have discarded sensitive autobiographical
details of the family's complex relationships. Just as Benjamin's mother Rachel
died in childbirth, so, too, did Ella O'Neill, psychologically, because of Eugene's
birth. Significantly, as she lay dying, Rachel named her son Ben-Oni, "son of my
suffering."

Unlike his Biblical counterpart, Jacob, who wrestled with an angel, Reverend
Light struggles with his private devil—the temptation of sensuality, "betrayed by
a large sensual mouth, the full lips tending to droop at the corners, to part and
pout with carnal desires when his will relaxes its vigilant exorcising." Inwardly
he "has suffered and still suffers from a sense of a sin of weakness that he has
never been weak enough to allow himself or his God to forget or forgive him."
Outwardly before the world, his "personality is that of a rigid Old Testament
moralist." He wears a mask of "superior complacent white-robed shepherd among
black sheep, a sad and a bitter man at times bearing many bitter grudges against
his life."

His wife, now called Amelia, is depicted here as extremely sensual—unlike
descriptions of her in the earlier drafts. She has a "still youthful and active body.
Her figure is extremely feminine, she is all female, her breasts are noticeably
large and firm, her waist slender, her hips and thighs broad and round. She must
have been exceptionally pretty as a girl." She has an "oval face, curly black hair,
straight nose and good brow." Like her husband, she wears an appropriate mask
—of "passive, calm and capable resignation to the duties of her life as an ill-paid

minister's wife." Her mouth, however, reveals her inner discontent. "It is a strong small mouth, energetic and stubborn, full-lipped, sensual and selfish, pulled in and down at the corners into lines of resentful self-denial."

Reuben, at twenty-two, resembles both of his parents—"their physical characteristics being in him accentuated." His mouth is his father's but "exaggerated to a degree in its drooping-lipped sensuality and weakness, but with a pleasing boyish smile to redeem it." Like his father, he has fair skin, big feet, heavy hands. "His finely modelled nose and brow are his mother's." His eyes are a "queer combination of both parents', large and wide apart and deep set like his mother's but at the same grey-blue color as his father's." The general impression that Reuben gives is "of a dark deeply troubled animality beneath his surface— that positive bullish masculinity of his father curiously intensified in him by the influence of his mother's positive femininity. Yet at the same time warring with it, repeating the struggle and compelling attraction—the struggle between his parents.

Part One

The four scenes of Part One in the second scenario differ only slightly from those in the 1927 outline. The first two scenes are relatively the same. In the third, "a scene of recrimination" between Reverend and Mrs. Light is followed by one in which Reuben repeats Fife's story to his mother. The element of betrayal—by the mother—is added here. She relates the "secret" to her husband, who rushes to the police. Reuben turns on his mother for betraying his confidence and on his father who, having discovered the truth, returns, angrily denounces his son for making him appear ridiculous, and orders him from the house. When Reuben goes upstairs to pack, Mrs. Light follows him. "In the face of the lightning, he denies his mother." The scene ends with Reuben challenging "God to strike them all dead" and rushing out into the storm. The fourth scene opens with the conscience-stricken Ada bitterly accusing her father of unfair tactics. She is horrified when informed of her illegitimacy by her mother, who "remarks placidly in love everything all right." When the distraught Reuben passes, crying out: "There is no God, there is no love," Ada calls out beseechingly in vain, her words unheard in the storm.

Part Two

Two titles—possibly alternatives to the one given to this play—appear beside the heading for Part Two: "Modern Stations of the Cross" and "Colossal Moonbeam." Fewer notes exist for this section than for the first and third parts, and no attempt is made to divide the action into scenes. Ada and Reverend Light are described in the second scenario as they will be later in the published text. O'Neill makes his hero younger ("nearly twenty") in this version. In the two years since he has left home, Reuben has changed completely; his face is older than it should be.

His manner is now callous, sneering and hard-boiled. It is as if he had grown a mask of sneering, mocking indifference over his own face—a mask that is handsome in its way, compels attention but repels while it attracts. His eyes are either mocking and malicious, or dreamy with a strange, obsessed fanatical quality.

He has succeeded in wiping out "the sensitive boy in him."

Fife does not appear in Part Two in the published text but does in the scenario. "His manner is more caustically irritable than ever, all good nature has gone out of it, he seems to bear a grudge against the world for some guilt he feels and is too stubborn to acknowledge to himself." Strangely, few references are made to Mrs. Fife throughout the entire collection of notes until now. Part Two opens with a scene between her and Reuben that provides the first indication of the prominent role she will eventually play. When Reuben enters, "she speaks of Ada—he is interested—flesh—feels queerly drawn to Mrs. Fife—asks her queerly if she can persuade Fife to give him job in plant." Fife sees the request "as a way to make up with Ada."

Reuben, the Prodigal Son, goes home and confronts his father, who is grieving over his wife's death two weeks earlier. Reuben grieves not; he believes "it is all for the best—his mother would have weakened him—she was the last one binding him to the old—why he had sent her the notes—necessary to convert her—her last words assure him she was converted." He tells his father of the books he has been reading and his conclusions—"that there is only Evil left in world—Evil the vamp that fascinates him—meaningless energy that has killed God and made life meaningless, killed man's soul—he is going to fight Evil at power house—but his father sees the truth that he has fallen in love with this female evil—has become a priest of Satan." The scene ends with each trying to convert the other and the father ordering him from the house. Unlike the published text, this scenario shows Light, rather than Reuben, leaving to visit Mrs. Light's grave.

Reuben again meets Mrs. Fife; he is "strangely drawn to her—she tells him Fife will give him job." At the very end of Part Two Reuben sees Ada and confidently "talks to her of his newfound faith in the beauty and power—the Evil—of life, his sense of the unity in Evil—the God in it electrocuted." He makes a date to meet her at the power house, saying he "is never going to leave plant—sleep there, if they'll let him."

Part Three

While there are more notes for this section in the 1928 scenario than for the other two, they merely serve to reflect O'Neill's uncertainty about the ultimate fate of his characters. The lengthy outline for Part Three includes a number of plot developments which do not appear in either the 1927 scenario or the published text: the reconciliation of Light and Fife; Reuben's proposal of marriage to Mrs. Fife, for whom he feels an incestuous attraction; Light's visit to the power house and his attempt to convert Reuben.

Scene One—Three months after—night late evening (last of sunset)—shows the exterior of the power house.

The scene opens with Fife accusing his wife of being in love with Reuben. Defensively, she says she loves him as a son. Fife suspects Ada is having an affair with Reuben and begins "to hate and fear his dynamos." Fife and the minister have reconciled—"feels drawn to him and L[ight]. to him. Memories of his early Calvinism move deeply in him—belief in a spirit of evil reborn." Light enters followed by Reuben, who is in a state of exultation. Fife fears that a great crisis is approaching, but Light is "excited by it, he will then face the devil and wrestle his son's soul back—L. thinks he is converting F. but must come back."

Scene Two—Shows interior dynamo room

Mrs. Fife contemplates the dynamo, imagining she has taken over her husband's job and that Ada and Reuben are her assistants. Mrs. Fife "knows that the generator is happy—the reason for its new song—is because Ada is pregnant—has become a generator of life too—and she loves Reuben because he has fulfilled his mission in life (and the men are so worried about her song)." When Reuben enters, he questions the dynamo: "What is wrong—doesn't she love him— he finally appeals to Mrs. F. as 'mother' to tell him—she comforts him, tells him the generator loves him—she knows it—the generator has told her." Reuben's love for Ada restrains him from making the "final experiment"—the sacrifice of human life to the dynamo. He also feels a "duty to life—dynamo—not to leave life without leaving life behind." He has "fasted, scourged himself, stayed away from Ada" in an attempt to purify himself and be worthy of the dynamo. A "strange scene" follows between Reuben, Mrs. Fife and the dynamo. He says "queerly I wish you weren't married. I'd like to marry you. You'd help me, etc. She tells him strangely Well, if I weren't a wife and mother I would marry you. You need someone to look after you."

Scene Three—Wall of generator room restored—interior of switchboard room and 66,000 volt switch gallery.

Reuben enters and tries to calm the fears of the nervous staff gathered in the switchboard room. He goes up to the high tension switch gallery and "genuflects" before the switches, addressing them "in an invoking chant"; he indentifies himself with them; "they are the male, the means by which the female passion principle makes itself manifest—they must conquer her, enter into her and become one with her, absorb and be absorbed—then the Force behind Life—God—will become equally male and female and life will achieve new unity." Ada enters and exults with him, feeling the life in her. They stand in the same attitude as the switches; he asks her "to kneel before him and acknowledge as a representative of femininity his identity and leadership." She is frightened but does so. He then leads her up to the roof; "the whole idea of the cosmos will be changed after he becomes the Savior—comes back out of the D[ynamo]. imbued with the passion principle."

The last two scenes of Part Three are not fully developed in this first version of the 1928 scenario; they are presented as they appear in the notes:

Scene Four—Shows the exterior, all interior being now cut off. Reuben and Ada appear on roof of the generator room.

Scene Five

Starts queer marriage with Mrs. Fife as priestess in front of dynamo—then suddenly realizes D[ynamo]. should be real bride—cry of ecstasy sinking down, dying out, then rising again like a new born child. You have a child —I have fulfilled my purpose. Cut me off and be done.

A long section, "State of Mind of Reuben," which follows the outline, reveals that the dynamo has become for him the personification of the mother figure. He identifies Mrs. Fife with the dynamo, but the incestuous union he desires with this earth mother is denied him. Now he longs only to become one with the God mother figure "but feels there is still something the Dynamo demands of him before she will let him possess her, feels keenly that somehow he is still impure, unworthy of the miracle of the promised union and revelation." He attributes his defilement to his relationship with Ada and thinks: "If she were only dead—Then he suddenly feels with terror that that is the answer—that the Dynamo demands that final sacrifice of him—he must kill the flesh he loves to be purified and make himself worthy of her spiritual love." He goes to the generator room; "he must ask the Mother herself." He sees Mrs. Fife there, addresses "her as mother," and asks: "What is she saying?" Mrs. Fife assures him that the "generator loves him" and wants to tell him: "I love you, Reuben. You're my son. I always wanted to have a son." Everything seems clear to Reuben now; "one human life is of no importance beside the good of the race—the need of the birth of a Savior who will know God and be able to bring salvation to men from suffering and unhappiness—Ada loves him and surely he can make her see this and be a willing sacrifice." Reuben is seized with an ecstasy of love for the Dynamo, kisses it." He goes to the roof to meet Ada and explains the

whole unity of life in Electricity, as symbolized in the plant to her—in the Dynamo is the king man has found between essence Electricity & man—through it the electricity which is his life unites with Electricity which is all life to produce electricity which he can control and guide—the Dynamo is an inspired creation of man's—it is the new idol given to men by God—that in it they may meet again.

Three new outlines for Part Three follow the section on Reuben's "State of Mind"; two are incomplete, but the third, containing six scenes, suggests that Reuben sacrifices only himself—and not Ada as well.

On August 18, 1928, O'Neill announces he has "Finished Dynamo" (W.D.). He spent the next three days and the first week of September "going over the typed script" and mailed it on the 10th to the Theatre Guild. Unable to attend rehearsals, he sent a five-part "dissertation" dated September 9, 1928:

I—Stage Effects

O'Neill stresses the importance of starting early in rehearsals to get the stage effects exactly right:

the thunder and lightning and sound of the water flowing over the nearby dam and the hum of the generator. . . . If these sounds are dismissed until the last dress rehearsals—the usual procedure in my experience—then the result must inevitably be an old melodrama thunderstorm and a generator sounding obviously like a vacuum cleaner, and not only will the true values of these effects be lost but they will make the play look foolish.

He laments he never got the sound his scripts specified because he "was never able to overcome the slipshod old-fashioned disregard of our modern theatre for what ought to be one of its superior opportunities for expressing the essential rhythm of our lives today." He urges that someone with the "right mechanical flair be sicked on this aspect of *Dynamo*" and be sent to look around and listen in the General Electric plant at Stephenson, Connecticut. "My scene scheme is a concentration of the features of this plant."

II—The Sets

O'Neill gives specific instructions for the set designs and states: "I am enclosing with the script my own plans by way of suggesting what I want. I am also enclosing a map of the [Stephenson] plant I happened to run across in a book of Hydro-Electric engineering." He requests that the outside walls in the first two parts be angled "so that everything would always be visible. I wouldn't feel any compulsion to stick to any strict realism in these sets." He concludes this section, saying: "Let me wind up with an emphatic yawl that there be no lights up between the different sections of Parts One and Three which I call scenes only by courtesy."

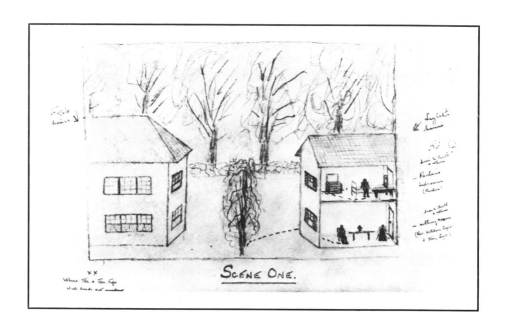

SCENE ONE.

SCENE TWO

142

SCENE THREE

III—Casting

The Theatre Guild did cast the actors O'Neill suggests for three major roles: Glenn Anders as Reuben, Dudley Diggs as Fife, and Helen Westley as Mrs. Light. The author expresses his doubts about finding the right person to play Mrs. Fife.

Ah, here's the rub—the fattest (in more ways than one!!) part in the play and the hardest to cast. I have no suggestions—only a warning, that if whoever plays it is ever conscious of being funny for a moment, or rides her lines for laughs, I will swim back all the way from China with a kriss between by murderously-gritted teeth and slay that actorine!

IV—Cutting

"Parts One & Two—I've been over twice. Part Three I've been over once. It seems pretty tight now but I'm too close to judge without hearing rehearsals."

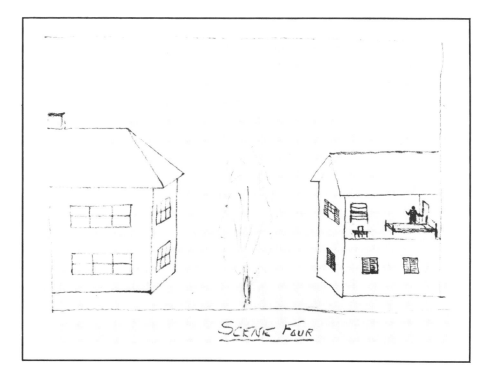

SCENE FOUR

V—Conclusion

O'Neill ends his "dissertation" by saying he doesn't "think *Dynamo* is a repertory play. If ever a play was for its own theatre to stand on its own feet this is. It ought to create as much argument and discussion in its way as *Interlude* did."

The dramatist's drawings for the set designs, sent with the script, were, for some years, presumed lost. They were found by Saxe Commins, the author's editor, who wrote to Carlotta O'Neill on March 18, 1932, saying: "The accompanying drawings were listed among the missing for a long time. Of course, they were in the safest place all the time—tucked away in the corner of the vault." An examination of the drawings reveals the differences between the production script and the published text. The set designs for the first four scenes of Act One and the first and third scenes of Act Two correspond to the descriptions of these sections in the published text. No drawing is specifically labeled for the second scene of Act Two, but the setting is identical to that of the last scene in Act One.

On March 18, 1929, O'Neill received the proofs for *Dynamo* and spent the rest of the month cutting and revising it. On April 2 he decided to "rewrite part of it entirely and introduce new scenes end Act Two." He finished this work on

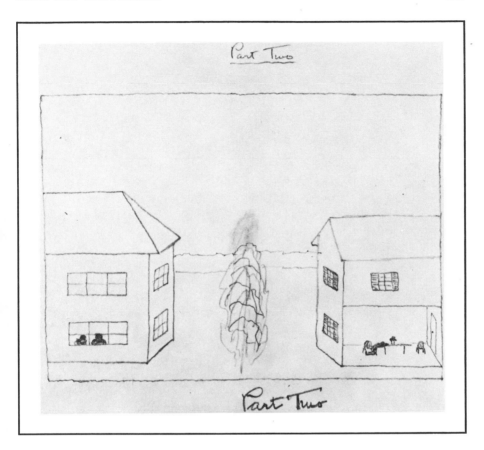

April 6 and "started new opening for Act Three." He revised much of the third act, as he states on April 12: "finish the job of cutting, revising and rewriting" (W.D.). His letter of June 14, 1929, to Macgowan reveals just how extensive the revisions were:

> I've been working like hell for the past week on *Dynamo*—second set of proofs which I've again done a drastic job on—cut the minister entirely out of the last part, etc. etc. It will be a much better play when you read it in the book. The new scenes, one entirely of thought soliloquy, help a lot in clearing up and emphasizing.

He also acknowledges here that the play's elaborate sets and theatrical devices are distracting: "To read *Dynamo* is to stumble continually over the sets. They're always in my way, writing and reading—and they are in the way of the dramatic action."

Some years after *Dynamo* was proclaimed a "flop" by the critics, O'Neill

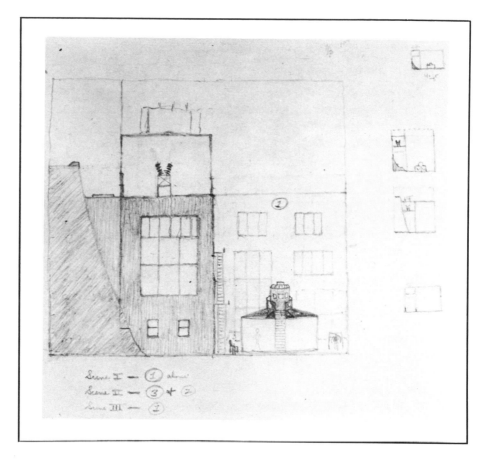

was still optimistic about it. In 1935, shortly after *Days Without End*—the second of the "Myth Plays for the God-forsaken"—was, like the trilogy's first work, pronounced a critical failure, O'Neill informs Leon Mirlas, the Argentine critic who had translated *The Great God Brown*: "*Dynamo* I intend to rewrite some day. It has the makings of a fine play but I am by no means satisfied with it as it is." O'Neill *did* write different versions of it in the following years. Even though *Dynamo* was vehemently attacked, he believed in the play—in the "human story" it told of the psychological effects on his hero of his father and mother's betrayal and the aftereffects: rejection of the parents' religion, the subsequent sense of loss, and the substitute-God search. He would continue this theme in *Days Without End*—the "Play of Catholic boyhood"—and return to it a decade later, presenting the purest and most autobiographical expression of it in *Long Day's Journey into Night*.

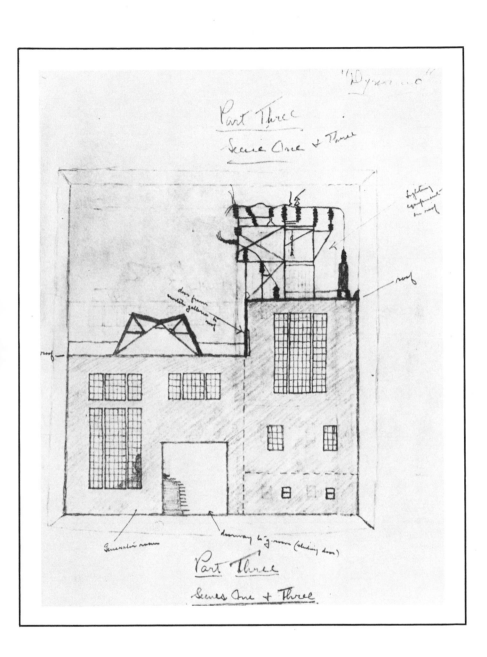

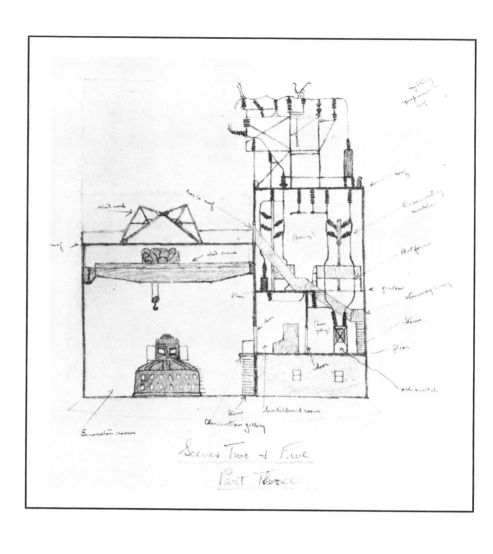

Scenes Two & Five
Part Three

[DAYS WITHOUT END]
Play of Catholic Boyhood*
(1927)

Play of Catholic boyhood—revolt—free-thinking scientist whose pride in man becomes the human reason—the rational world of fact—but always fighting against his deeply religious pull—his deadly fear that he will, as age enfeebles his reason or when the death of loved ones, etc. overcomes him emotionally with sorrow & despair, return to Church—this becomes his obsession—his wife whom he has taken for granted and to whom he has been unfaithful, rationalizing this to be nothing, died—the past, all his sins against her of omission & commission come back on him—letters of hers, a diary, show him a her he could now understand, who would have fulfilled him, if it had not been for his rational, analytical explaining away of her emotions & his own and his scorn for the irrational working of her mind. He feels he must confess, that he has sinned, that he must be forgiven. He wanders at night about New York, hounded & haunted by the past, regret, remorse—he longs to believe again in immortality, to meet his wife to tell her. He cannot bear his scientific concept of the individual's annihilation, of the unimportance of the human, of his own suffering. He insists on the importance of his own suffering, looking beseechingly and defiantly at the sky, in a canyon of skyscrapers, alone in the night—comes to a Catholic church, perpetual adoration, nuns before altar—he kneels down—his intellect and emotions fight—He asks the figure on the Cross "What is truth? Science is truth!" with a sneer and it seems to him the figure answers "What is Life?" and he cannot answer—and his emotions overcome him—he sees in the statue of the Virgin his own wife and child—he finally goes to one of the kneeling nuns—"I must confess!" She sees his despair and gets a priest. His intellect fights. He grows horribly humiliated one minute cursing himself for a renegade, the next minute he feels relieved and comforted—he prays to Jesus whose suffering he identifies as his own—prays to his wife, the Virgin—the priest comes—kind & understanding—Catholic?—"I am—was—am—was." Priest beckons toward confessional—he staggers up, starts to follow—but this move takes him away from Christ & Virgin, he sees only priest & the confession box of wood and even as he steps toward it automatically he takes a revolver out and shoots himself. The priest comes to him, [in] time to give him last sacrament as he dies. "Do you believe?" Desperately joyful, longingly he gasps joyfully "Yes, I believe" and his mind remembers part of his Apostle's Creed and he repeats it automatically. The priest gives him absolution. But as he dies his pride of Man says with a last sardonic defiance: "All the same, I don't believe."

---

*O'Neill cancels this idea and writes "Days Without End—1933" across it.

149

While O'Neill labeled the first scenario for *Dynamo* "no good" on June 5, 1927, he was still making plans that summer for his trilogy, "Myth Plays for the God-forsaken." The Work Diary entry for August 12, 1927, states: "wrote brief sketch in notebook for ideas for the plays 'Without Endings of Days'—'It Cannot be Mad?' ". The following year he worked on an outline for the former play on October 7 and 8 and on one for the latter from October 9 to 14, 1928. The dramatist made no other attempt in the 1920s to develop "Without Endings of Days," telling Macgowan on June 14, 1929, that he was off "the trilogy for a year or so" and citing several reasons:

> ... my messiness & bad judgment about *Dynamo* and its resulting sacrifice has had its reaction in making me temporarily cold toward the two ideas connected in my mind with "D." ... I wouldn't want to write the Catholic "Without Ending of Days" now anyway because of the queer coincidence that its story, although I had it written out long before I thought of breaking with A[gnes]., would be sure to be misinterpreted (especially by you psycho-sharks!) as thinly-veiled autobiography where the wife and two children of the play are concerned. And I wouldn't want that for the sake of anyone involved.

By the time O'Neill began the first of the three sets of notes for "Without Ending of Days"—written in 1931, 1932, and 1933—he had eliminated the "two young children"; nevertheless, the work is clearly discernible—rather than "thinly-veiled"—autobiography. The year 1927 was one of the most crucial in the dramatist's life; he experienced a great inner personal struggle, trying to play the ardent lover of Carlotta Monterey and the dutiful husband and father to Agnes and their two children. It was a period of tremendous introspection as the autobiographical ideas and scenarios in the notebooks reveal: *Dynamo* (3/4/27); "scheme for opus founded on autobiographical material"—"The Sea-Mother's Son" (3/8/27); "Play of Catholic boyhood"—"Without Ending of Days" (8/12/27); "Play of the Man-philosopher" (11/11/27). These ideas have one common denominator: the central character in each one is modeled on the dramatist himself.

While no physical description of the "good" John appears in the notes for "Without Ending of Days," the qualities attributed to him in the final version, *Days Without End*—the square jaw, blue eyes, feminine sensitiveness—are also found in Reuben, a self-portrait, who throughout the notes for *Dynamo* is described as having a "duality in his character." In Part One, while a "demonic cruel spirit" seems to possess Reuben at times, his boyish, appealing nature keeps it in check. In Part Two, when he returns home, "his manner is now callous, sneering and hard boiled. It is as if he had grown a mask of sneering mocking indifference over his own face." In the second set of notes for "Without Ending of Days," O'Neill shows the dual nature of the hero by depicting him as a character in a Lucifer mask, "the scoffing unbelieving devil-self—mask one's own face but twisted into an eternal ironical leer."

The main focus of these and other ideas in the late 1920s is the split hero's search for religious certitude, associated in some way with his mother. Like *Dy-*

namo, the first play of the trilogy, "Without Ending of Days" is "written around the spiritual futility of the substitute-God search"; in both works the object of the search becomes intrinsically and intricately identified with a constantly evolving mother figure. There are so many similarities in the notes that "Without Ending of Days" could be considered a Catholic version of *Dynamo*. The names of the heroes are significant: the old Testament's Benjamin and Reuben in the latter; the New Testament's evangelists, Matthew and John, in the former. Reuben's mother "summons the God of the Old Testament as if he were her father"; John Loving resents his mother's total "absorption in Catholicism." Her loving, forgiving Christ replaces Mrs. Light's harsh eye-for-an-eye Old Testament God.

Reuben is supposedly destined to become a Baptist minister and John a Catholic priest. Shortly after the two reject their faith, their mothers die, leaving the sons with a deep sense of guilt and the desire for an incestuous spiritual union through a substitute mother figure. Reuben's search for his mother leads to a longing to marry the maternal Mrs. Fife, who merges with the Mother Goddess—the Dynamo—whom he "deifies and finds . . . again." Having sinned against the celibate priesthood, Reuben builds an altar in the "Temple" and immolates himself as a sacrifice to his idol. John marries a woman who resembles his own mother—Erda (Elsa), the "primitive poetic Mayan earth spirit." Having broken his marriage vows, John goes to a Catholic church and kneels before the altar of the Virgin and Child—"identification of mother and Elsa with Her, himself with child, longing for reunion with them through Mother Goddess that really lures him to point of suicide before statue of Virgin." He takes out a gun and puts it to his temple exclaiming: "Father! Why hast thou forsaken me?" At that moment a "shaft of colossal light" falls on the cross, and he hears an inner voice commanding him to "let this chalice pass." Two alternative titles appear at the beginning of Part Two in *Dynamo*: "Colossal Moonbeam" and "Modern Stations of the Cross." In a note for "Without Ending of Days," O'Neill writes: "Follow out outlines of Stations of the Cross in Second Part (?)." The search for the substitute-God forces the heroes of the two plays to make their lives a veritable "Way of the Cross" in which they will inevitably fall, encounter a Virgin Mother figure, and, ultimately, be crucified and placed in the Pieta embrace of the mother.

O'Neill identifies the first of the three sets of notes for "Without Ending of Days," saying:

These are the first notes made after the writing of scenario in notebook four years previously (1927)—the original title, "Without Ending Of Days" was a quote from some book, which had remained in my memory, although I was never able to remember what book it came from, or the author, or anything about it.*

---

*Louis Sheaffer states the phrase "world without end" appears in a letter Robert Edmond Jones wrote O'Neill, who later tried "unsuccessfully to track down the source of the title" (*O'Neill Son and Artist*, p. 402).

First Set of Notes
July 1931

Written at Beacon Farm in Northport, Long Island, the notes elaborate on the original idea for the play. O'Neill shows his hero wandering about New York at "night below dead line—skyscrapers." His search for the dead mother leads to an encounter with "his dead selves—masked—7, 14, 21, 28, 35, 42—(he is 49)?." He recalls that "in his childhood his mother had played and sung sad, sentimental songs of lost love—genesis of that in the man's life that finds itself grotesquely expressed (to his intelligent nature, while he laughs) in the singing waiter songs of his early manhood—later in torch songs."* The songs of the mother, of a lost innocence, of illusion—symbolized by the "man's longing for projection of his dreams toward sky"—are drowned out by the city skyscraper's "torch song" of experience, of reality, with the "man and his masked past selves cursing their God—Coward! Liar! Murderer!—Echoes, gigantic, resound back from skyscraper cañon walls (loud speakers)."

November 26, 1931
Sea Island Beach, Georgia

The play is now called "Ending of Days" as the former title, "Without Ending of Days" becomes the name of the book the novelist hero, Matthew Russel, is writing. In these early notes, his wife Elsa, described as "mother—wife—mistress—managing secretary" with a "protecting love for him," has a child for her husband's sake in a futile effort to make him happy. Resembling O'Neill's second wife, Agnes, she cannot "awaken him to her" and must resign herself to "his absorption in his work, his dissatisfaction with the expression of his dreams, his restlessness and melancholia." She resents the close relationship he has established with a Mephistophelian character—"a man of the same age who has been his friend since boyhood—(who is a living reminder and participator in all his past—in all his struggles, dissipations, despair, love affairs, former marriage—a former Catholic like himself—a sneering sceptic now about religion and every-

---

*These torch songs—listed in the notes—include: "Oh, Give Me Something to Remember You By," "I Am Through with Love," "Body and Soul." O'Neill liked similar songs as the titles on the rolls purchased for his player piano, Rosie, reveal: "All Alone," "Can't Make My Eyes Behave," "Lesson in the Garden of Love." Perhaps Ella O'Neill, like the hero's mother, sang, as well as played, similar "sad, sentimental songs." As notes for plays which were never completed demonstrate, the dramatist seems strangely drawn to tragic historical figures who had mothers with musical ability. Barbara, mistress of Charles V and mother of the illegitimate Don John of Austria, as well as the beautiful concubine-mother of Shih Huang Ti, was a "singing girl."

thing else—a philosophical Nihilist).'' O'Neill considers the idea of making this man the hero's brother but discards this concept possibly because the character is too autobiographical, resembling his own brother Jamie (who is described as Mephistophelian in *Long Day's Journey into Night* and *A Moon for the Misbegotten*). In later notes this character becomes Arnold Post; Elsa's father, Hardy, a sceptic; and, eventually, the masked demonic side of the hero. A fourth character is introduced: a former classmate of the other two men—a Catholic convert—who is "always hoping to bring R. back to faith." He becomes in subsequent versions Loving, the convert; Ernest Boyd, a surgeon; and finally the hero's uncle, a priest.

In the first act Russell tells his two friends the plot of his new book "which is the plot of the play except with the end in which the hero shoots himself outside the confessional." He vehemently denies their accusation that the book is autobiographical, saying: "nothing like his wife or in their relationship—she doesn't mother him, etc." However, in the following scene with his wife, Russel reveals that the marriage in his plot is an "exact replica of his own." At the end of this first outline Russel is about to shoot himself outside the confessional when he "suddenly realizes the meaning of Christ on the Cross—and becomes Man to redeem men—eternal symbol of man crucified on the cross or mortal life—his identity and brotherhood with him—and is saved by this."

November 29, 1931

O'Neill returns to his former title "Without Ending of Days." His desire at this point is to "make (if possible) religion less definitely Catholic—more general—Christian religion." Yet the scene outside the confessional is retained and a final speech is added in which he addresses the "statue of Mary and the Child (becomes his real wife—mother and protector, Elsa—and the Child, his dead baby)." Elsa emerges here as the typical Strindbergian woman; because her husband has failed to provide her with "a meaning for love based on a belief in an end for life, as mistress and wife she no longer loves him but he holds her all the more strongly as pitying mother of a lost, despairing little boy." Her nature "demands that man give her a faith, a goal"; she turns to a person who can fulfill her desires: her husband's friend, Loving, an ardent Catholic. This name will later be given to the figure representing the hero's diabolic side.

December 6, 1931

Russel's first name is now Martin and his two friends are called Roger Cave and George Wayne. O'Neill begins his "plot sketching." The first two acts have one scene set in the Russels' New York apartment; the third has seven scenes, depicting the central character as he was envisioned in the first July notes: Scene One—Broadway—Loud speaking torch songs; Scene Two—Below the Dead Line

(Skyscraper cañon) ; Scene Three—Battery Park; Scene Four—Waterfront saloon; Scenes Five and Seven—Outside the church; Scene Six—Inside the church.

February 10, 1932
First Scenario

The central character is now named John, his Mephistophelian friend Post, the convert Boyd. In Act One Elsa discovers her husband's infidelity with her friend Lucy and in the second act confronts him, demanding an explanation, before leaving the apartment in a distraught condition to visit her mother. No information is given about Elsa's death at the end of this act; John merely receives a telephone call. The first scene in Act Three shows John and his two friends returning from the funeral and setting out for Broadway, where they meet a prostitute; the night of dissipation ends at the Church of Perpetual Adoration.

February 29, 1932
New Scenario

The central character, now Dr. John Loving, is still a unified person, although his later dichotomy is foreshadowed in a statement made about his two friends: "Boyd says Post a good influence—John reacts against his scepticism— or: Boyd is bad influence—John reacts against his faith—its the Mask in him." All that survives of this scenario is one page describing a scene in the first act between John and Elsa. He tries to hide his depression by discussing his playwriting efforts but finally reveals their desperate financial situation: "Stocks he had bought down to nothing, no dividends—felt he could retire from practice for few years, write scientific books he wants to write—if she only knew how tired he gets of the eternal procession of patients." She urges him to give up his general practice and go in for psychotherapy: "all the nervous misfit ladies and gentlemen confessing their domestic unhappiness" could cure him. He must not worry; "he has her, hasn't he—etc.—love scene between them." He feels he must continue with his play—that he will "probably make a botch of it but at least it will do him good mentally, he feels—get a load off his memories."

Second Set of Notes
May 7, 1932

The second set of notes introduces the "unbelieving devil self—the character in mask" who goes "with the character through all the scenes after the wife's death (or mistress—he is about to marry her (?) looking forward to consummation—their marriage to be a beautiful dream." This character keeps reminding him ironically, "once a Catholic always a Catholic. You will end up in the bosom of the church." The dramatist states that the character also represents

the hopeless nostalgia for the past—sentimentally and sadly plays different instruments in different scenes out of the past—the Man is never sure whether he means this or is laughing at him—Torch songs—
     Character—John Doe (John Johndel)
     Finale—Character (Grown large—Lucifer)—to crucifix—you always crucify yourself, Coward, and escape me.

May 9, 1932

"On To Hercules"
or
"Without Ending of Days"
(Notes)

For the first time, the hero is called "Loving." He is now a brilliant doctor who has gone in for psychoanalysis—"caused by religious promptings and desire to understand self (unconsciously)." Facts about his "Catholic boyhood" are presented. He was seven when his idealized father, a doctor—who was "not strict Catholic like mother"—died and fourteen when his mother became seriously ill. His remorse for an inner religious rebellion leads to a "frenzy of piety—prayers for her—prayer to Lucifer—L's guilt about mother's death, his superstitions that *if* he had prayed she might have been saved."*

May 12, 1932

In this section of the notes, O'Neill envisions the last scene and states: "think I can raise it up at end enough to realize the new assertion of life." The passage labeled "end of play" reveals the hero has not been able to free himself from guilt and maternal domination: "Mother worship, repressed and turned morbid, ends by becoming Death love and longing." His search for the mother brings him to the altar of the Virgin; his longing for reunion "lures him to point of suicide." At the same time it is "his old resentments against mother, against Elsa

---

*There are many autobiographical references in this section describing John Loving's early years. In the diagram that he made, the dramatist reveals the ambiguous feelings he had for his parents. Until he was seven and sent to boarding school by his father, Eugene views him as an "indefinite hero." At that time, the image of the "idealized father" died in him. Written beside "Adolescence" are the words: "Discovery of Mother's inadequacy," which can be translated as discovery of her drug addiction. Like his hero, he prayed that she might be cured and experienced a similar sense of guilt, believing that his birth had caused her addiction.

as mother substitute (infidelity) that keeps him from giving in to Catholicism—longing (confession)." The voice of Christ speaks to him just as he is about to shoot himself; and he expresses his "new awareness of Christ's Life of Sorrow and sacrifice of love for man: 'You are the Eternal Symbol of the Unknown God in us in which we all in our secret hearts believe—in which we must believe or the Spirit in Man shall die and his hope perish!' He offers this noblest Son of Man his love, puts his revolver at the base of the crucifix and makes the sign of the cross." The two characters representing Loving's dual nature react to the conversion. His kneeling uncle exclaims: "Oh God, I thank Thee! He is saved." The atheistic Hardy, with a strange envious resentment, calls him "Zarathustra's shadow gone finally weak" and then angrily denounces him: "Coward! Traitor!" Loving responds: "Old man, blinded by staring at outer space in the endeavor to escape seeing the space within yourself . . . Why not turn your telescope in the infinite space within man for a change? I think you find His spirit at its heart!" He then looks at Hardy affectionately and says: "Old foolish child, scared of an empty house you have made empty."

Possible changes theme (W.E. of D.)
Changes character to the Man, etc.

Dissatisfied with his bland sanctimonious hero, O'Neill gives him now a diabolical side, attributing the change to the role his mother played in his life. Loving's jealousy of his mother's dedication to the church leads him in revenge to identify himself with Lucifer and of him "with knowledge, science—rebellion—break with church which he hides for mother's sake—but secretly gloats 'if she only knew!'—only open rebellion refusal to be priest under excuse he feels no motive—compromise with suppressed religious feeling, choosing to become doctor." He takes a "secret evil pride" in his "treacherous scheming," realizing his mother's purchase of a medical practice for him has bought "his freedom from her—scientific freedom from church." As in *Dynamo*, the mother is responsible for the son's substitution of science for religious belief.

Loving falls in love with Elsa, the daughter of an astronomer. She is "willing to live with him, marriage nothing to her but he wants a sacrament." His mother disinherits him and dies soon afterward from a broken heart, leaving him to wonder if he would have abjured his scepticism had she requested him to do so before she died. His wife now views their marriage as a sacrament. He is unfaithful to her with a patient and "immediately feels horribly guilty and never can banish the feeling of sin, of having violated a sacrament." His guilt haunts him and "poisons his happiness—he feels an uncontrollable impulse to confess and be forgiven—wants to believe in her feelings of immortality but cannot—and represses a wish that he had remained a Catholic." He remembers Nietzsche's warning about "crisis seeking weak consolation" and swears to himself that he will never abjure his scientific faith. He decides to write an autobiographical novel (concealed) to cure himself and "get all this off his chest—and put all his fears into words and thus be able to exorcise them."

Another Scheme

In an attempt to make Loving's infidelity and guilt more explicit, O'Neill includes a scene in which Elsa tells Lucy she knows of her affair with John, that he had confessed to her. Elsa admits she was "mortally hurt, went out in park— sick—that was what started—she is about to confess her mortal illness but stops herself." Lucy claims she had merely wanted to spite her own husband but admits she is envious of Elsa's perfect marriage. Lucy absolves John: "He loves you, Elsa, more than I ever thought a man could love anyone." Later John asks Elsa if she has forgiven him. She says she has but adds that he has not forgiven himself; she "shows him where his guilty conscience comes from—old Catholic bringing up—sense of sin—he must get rid of it." He wonders if his infidelity wasn't a "strange impulse to be revenged on her, to desecrate the sacrament he has taught her to feel."

First Draft
Without Ending of Days

On May 15, 1932, O'Neill began the first draft of the play, trying to consolidate his previous schemes. The author provides no date of composition either in his notes or Work Diary for the extant scenario which he used for the first draft. While the following material is taken from this scenario, the dates that precede the scenes are those O'Neill assigns them in the Work Diary.

May 15, 1932—Start Act I

The play opens in the Lovings' living room with a "scene between Elsa and Lucy as before—except using 'interlude' technique bringing out John's infidelity with Lucy—and implanting of doubt in Elsa's mind—also Elsa's sacramental attitude toward her marriage." The act concludes with John's entrance, his expression of guilt, and admission of financial problems. Elsa is "suspicious and apprehensive at end."

June 1, 1932—Start Act II

In the first scene Hardy apologizes to his daughter Elsa for being away from home on scientific excursions throughout her childhood and adolescence; he is a stranger to her. His lecture at Columbia and not his daughter motivates his present visit to New York. He finally confesses he should never have married, that he has been lonely throughout his life, that he has his doubts "about worth of work for which he has sacrificed love and all human warmth." He claims that for most marriage is nothing more than a "legalized sex union," that people must do what she and John have done—"find real love first, test it by living together, then build an ideal around it, make it significant by sacrifice, make it holy." When Elsa uses the phrase "sacrament of God," her father wonders where she got religion. She responds by reminding him that his previous statement reveals "a religious attitude toward love and mating." In the second scene John tells Boyd, his uncle, the plot of his play; he "lapses into 'I'—then catches himself—only autobiographical in a way (has taken infidelity incident from playwright's life— classmate—reunion) most of scene as before." John's confession of infidelity to Elsa in the third scene resembles that in earlier versions, but the Strindbergian element taints their relationship. She forgives him, adding: "You will always be my husband—little boy—but never again my own lover—never my own any more—she must go out—walk alone—go to park."

June 15, 1932—Notes for revision: Acts I and II

Elsa-Boyd scene—cut "money security" speeches from Boyd, whole of "depression" in John
—tone down comedy element in Boyd—more dignified
—too much Irish in speech?
—Mother wanted John to be priest
—Boyd notices Elsa's resemblance to John's mother

—Instead of many experiences with women, Loving a virgin before marriage—
has hated idea—
—Cut John's story throughout—about his father—unnecessary after Boyd's
story?—etc.—description of crowd at party after Loving's story,
etc.—
—Toward end of story in one of his pauses—(it has grown dark)—John says
better—turn on lights—but Elsa immediately says no—face
averted—lights not turned on until after her exit
—Transfer most of "Endings of Days" stuff at end to Act 3, Scene 2
—"Endings of Days"—quote Bible chapter and verse

June 15, 1932—Act III, Scene I

Only a fragment of the first scene is included in the notes. John explains the dilemma of his novel's unfaithful hero to Elsa and asks her jokingly if she could forgive him in such a situation. The scene ends with Elsa in despair rushing from the house—"to death then end as before."

June 21, 1932—Act III, Scene II

O'Neill wrote three versions of the second scene, working on this particularly difficult section until July 17. He had a problem trying to decide precisely how Elsa was to die. In the extant version, she crosses the street, after wandering in the park; she sees a "car coming & seemed as if she couldn't get out of the way—sudden impulsion to stay—like hero in story—man driving swirved but car skidded, hit her, driving slow—knocked down, hit head on curb—silly affair." The good friend, Boyd—who is a physician in this outline—examines her and says she is in no danger from the head wound "but he doesn't like fever, [her] expression—if pneumonia ever sets in—."

In the next section John is shown holding a revolver in his hand and contemplating suicide. Life has no meaning without his wife, yet he feels "something must live on—love must be eternal—'gates of Death shall not prevail against it.' " He remembers her "goodness and unselfishness and protection of him—her perfect trust in him which he had betrayed—his agony of guilt for his sin—his feeling that he was responsible for her death—he murdered her—perhaps, even now, if he prayed he might get in touch with her spirit!—he might find her again." He kneels and tries to pray but realizes the hopelessness of his action without faith. "If he could go to confession and get rid of his sin, God would give him back his faith, he would know He had really forgiven him, too, he would know she was waiting for him, he could go on having feeling she was always by his side and his own death would mean reunion with her, he would find peace in his sorrow." He despairs completely and sees suicide "as the only way out for him." He is just about to kill himself when there is a knock on the door. He puts the revolver away, merely postponing the act, as his two friends, Hardy and Boyd, enter. They finally convince him to go out with them for a walk.

July 20–August 31, 1932

O'Neill made futile efforts to continue "Without Ending of Days." He makes notes reconstructing it "along lines new conception," states on seven occasions that he is working on a new outline or scheme, and indicates several times that he is doing "outside reading." Finally, on August 30, he began writing the dialogue for a new opening scene but notes the next day: "battle with it again—no flow—sunk!"

September 1, 1932

Work on "Without Ending of Days" was interrupted on September 1 when, as the dramatist states, he "awoke with idea" for "Nostalgic Comedy"—*Ah, Wilderness!*—and "worked out tentative outline—seems fully formed & ready to write." The reason why *Ah, Wilderness!*—with its autobiographical hero Richard Miller—was so "fully formed" in the dramatist's mind is obvious. The idea was no sudden inspiration; he had become introspective the previous year while working on the family background for the hero of the "Play of Catholic boyhood." Much of the material found in the notes for "Without Ending of Days"— the examination of his hero's life at ages "7—14—21"—lead him perhaps to do some wishful thinking and to conceive Richard Miller. O'Neill called *Ah, Wilderness!* "done for present" on October 3 and started a new mask scheme for "Without Ending of Days." He decided against this scheme and reverted "to original plan," completing the outline of the last act of the first draft on October 8.

The author wrote six drafts of "Without Ending of Days" in the next year. Significant information, recorded in the Work Diary—about these drafts—is presented here:

Second Draft:
(*1932*)

October   9—Start new additional Act One—old Act One being now Act Two
       24—Finished rewriting first part Act One
       25—Start rewriting old Act Two into new Act Three
November   5—Started Act Four—Scene One—rewriting old corresponding Act Three—Scene One
       12—Started Act Four—Scene Two—discarding entirely old corresponding Act Three—Scene Two
       20—Started Act Five—Scene One (this new—not rewriting)

Third Draft: *
(*1932*)

November 27—Notes by Scenes for revision
       28—Outline new 5–1, cut out old entirely (?)
       29—outline & notes—to clarify underlying psycho-mystical theme
December 22—call 3rd Draft finished
       28—thinking over—disgusted—feel strongly something fundamentally wrong with it as whole in spite of fine parts but can't get hold of right way to solve.

---

*The first longhand script, the dramatist's gift to his wife Carlotta in January 1934, indicates that O'Neill used the title "Ending Of Days" for the third draft and "Without End Of Days" for the fourth draft. The first pages of the longhand scripts and typed copies of drafts are reproduced in *Inscriptions: Eugene O'Neill to Carlotta Monterey O'Neill*, edited by Donald Gallup (New Haven, 1960).

Fourth Draft:
(*1933*)

February   8—Acts I & II—decide try this again—read over—encouraged
—decide cut out Elsa's Catholicism

            26—thinking over advisability mask scheme for whole play again
—with new slant

            27—decide go on to end now as is

March   2—Finish Act Five—Scene One but not satisfied—again reach
same old impasse—play always goes dead on me here where
it needs ɩo be most alive—or I go dead on it—something
fundamentally wrong

            3—Outline mask version—decide to give up trying finish this
Fourth Draft—fed up with it—decide to start all over and
use mask scheme which has been trying to force itself on
me for long—seems to offer solution

Fifth Draft:
(*1933*)

March   4—Started Mask Version and feel renewed life in play and enthusiasm in myself at possibilities—will rewrite every word
this time

            7—Decide to eliminate the character of "Hardy"—gives wrong
emphasis on theme

          14—redefinition "John" & "Loving"

          31—Finished Mask Version

April   2—Revising—Change title to "The End of Days"

            4—Decide on title "An End of Days"

          12—Send off to be typed—all I can do on it now

          13—Notes—queries for next going over

May   30—"Days Without End" find at last this obviously satisfactory
title in mentioning play to Cerf!

Sixth Draft:
(*1933*)

June   16—Started—revising Act I

          23—Finished new last Act

July   5—Finished! Send script to Saxe to retype

August   5—making change back to Catholicism—more direct

Seventh Draft:
(*1933*)

October   24—I—1—cuts & revisions

November 1—rewriting new opening scene

           2—I-1 new intermediary L & J scene

         12—Finish (send off to Saxe)

The most decisive draft is the fifth version of March 4, in which O'Neill decides to use the "Mask Scheme." In the earliest notes for the play, the hero does not experience any inner good-evil conflict; the two forces are externalized and appear in his friends: Post, the Catholic convert, and Boyd, the sneering Mephistophelian cynic. The hero merely reacts alternately to the good and bad influences they exert over him. The Faust idea is introduced at the beginning of the second set of notes in May 1932, describing the hero as a "character in mask—the unbelieving scoffing devil self." A year later O'Neill devises a plan to use two actors to depict his hero's dual nature—"John," representing his nobler side, and "Loving," wearing the "death mask of a John who has died with a sneer of scornful mockery on his lips."

The dramatist remarks that what he says about Faust in an article he wrote "has the germ of the treatment I've used in the new opus"*—*Days Without End*:

> Consider Goethe's *Faust*, which, psychologically speaking, should be the closest to us of all the Classics. In producing the play I would have Mephistopheles wearing the Mephisthophelean mask of the face of Faust. For is not the whole of Goethe's truth *for our time* just that Mephistopheles and Faust are one and the same—*are* Faust?†

In this statement O'Neill verbalizes for the first time a concept he had visualized through his use of masks in previous plays: that good and evil do not exist in isolation—are not mutually exclusive—when applied to man. Caligula and Tiberius in *Lazarus Laughed* illustrate this point. Their half masks are caricatures of all that is evil and base in them and in man; their mouths, however, reveal an inclination, a longing to manifest their suppressed nobler side. Amid the vast crowds of masked characters—displaying varying degrees of good and evil— Lazarus alone is unmasked and uncontaminated. As a Christ figure, he is a whole entity and, therefore, exempt from an inner good-evil split. The Dion-masked Brown of the second part of *The Great God Brown* is an early variant of the John-masked Loving. Like Hawthorne, O'Neill uses a visible symbol—the Mephisthophelean mask of the face of Faust, of the face of John—to remind man of the vestiges of original sin, the potential for evil within him.

What is new in *Days Without End* is that O'Neill chooses Catholicism rather than another more acceptable Christian denomination to depict the good-evil dichotomy of his hero. He explains why he made this decision in a letter written in 1935 to Leon Mirlas. The following is a passage from the rough draft of this letter; the sections he later deleted are in brackets:

> I chose Catholicism because it is the only Western religion which has the

---

*Letter of May 15, 1933 to Lawrence Langner.
†*American Spectator*, November 1932.

stature of a real Faith, because it *is* the religion of the old miracle plays
and the Faustian legend which were the sources of my theme—and last and
[blood]
most simply because it happens to be the religion of my [Irish background,
tradition and] early training and therefore the one I know most about. As
for propaganda, I need not tell you that [even if I were a believing Catholic
(which, of course, I am not at all, I would] my plays never have been, and
never will be, interested in converting anyone to anything except the possibility of the drama as an art.

The dramatist had tried, as he stated on November 29, 1931, to make the
religion of the play "less definitely Catholic—more general—Christian religion."
As a consequence, he was unable to develop his initial idea—"Play of Catholic
boyhood"—as he truly envisioned it. He made more drafts and revisions for this
drama than for any other and was only able to complete it after he returned to
his original idea. In discussing the work with Langner, he states: "I've made the
change back to Catholicism and the priest uncle in *Days Without End*—and it
sure is more definitely alive that way" (Letter of August 7, 1933).

Third Set of Notes
1933

Days Without End
(Later notes, drawings, etc.)

While O'Neill does not date his third set of notes, they were made after he
had made the "change back to Catholicism" on August 5, 1933, but before he completed the last, seventh draft on November 12, 1933. The dialogue has not yet been
sharpened to its final form; the uncle-priest's name is still Boyd and not Baird.
The notes contain two fragments from the last act. One, a passage from the act's
first scene which does not appear in the published text, reveals John's thoughts
about his masked self: "Loving was what inspired him with fear—he is getting
Loving outside of himself—can almost see him—murderer of Elsa—and sees
through his longing for union in Nothingness—skull—begins to see him as Devil
he sold soul to." Later John returns to Elsa's bedroom where the "struggle inside
him begins again—longing to believe—I would pray—if I only could believe
again." Loving commands him: "Don't go to Church. I will curse Him again—
defy Him." To John's "Ah! Then you do believe!," Loving responds: "No. There
is nothing. I hate seeing you go back."
The second fragment, written for Scene Two of Act Four, is apparently an
early attempt, after O'Neill conceives the masked Loving, to write the final lines
of the play. The passage contains a startling revelation: that the author originally
intended that Loving, as well as John, be reconciled with Christ at the end. Boyd
tells the kneeling John that Elsa will live.

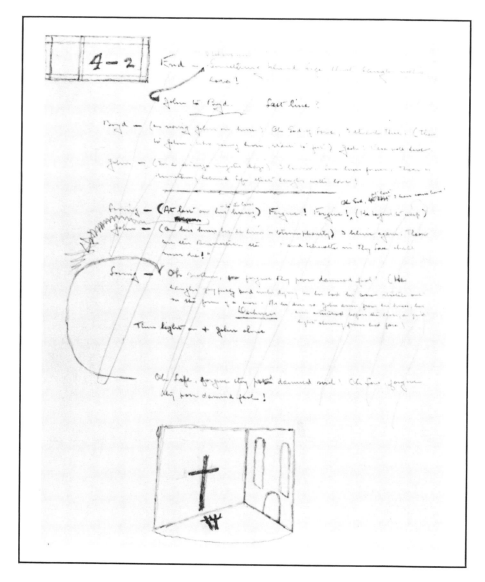

John: (In a strange mystic daze) I know. Love lives forever. There is
         something behind life that laughs with Love!

Loving: (At last on his knees—to the Cross) Forgive! Forgive! Oh, God,
         at last I have come home! (He begins to weep).

When John is redeemed, Loving does not "die" bitterly in this version; "he
laughs joyfully lying on his back his arms stretched out in the form of a cross."

John knows Loving is "Devil he sold soul to—but if he is Devil then his opposite, Christ, must be true—he can believe again." The last view of Loving as the Devil in this version—begging the crucified Christ for forgiveness—and as Lucifer in the published text—addressing the Cross: "Thou has conquered, Lord. Thou art—the End"—foreshadows the Devil in "The Last Conquest" and his love-hate relationship for Christ. In this last play, the Devil and his ancient adversary engage once more in a battle for the soul of man—and Christ again triumphs.

A set of drawings, labeled "Mask V," completes the third set of notes. One is a study-bedroom design for the first scene of Act Four; the other three are for the second scene of that act. The first of them, showing merely a crucifix and no human figure, is crossed out. The second reveals only one figure lying prostrate below the Cross. In the third John stands before the crucifix, his arms outstretched, while his dead self—Loving—lies beneath it, arms extended. O'Neill was very specific about the effect he wanted to create in this scene; in discussing Lee Simonson's sets, he states that all sets except the last church scene must have "the quality of being merely background for the psychological-religious drama in John Loving's soul." He acknowledges that it will be difficult to find

> the exactly right crucifix for the end. I want none of your sadistic Spanish Christs who give you the horrors, but a Resurrection Christ who will express "the Resurrection & the Life" John Loving finds in Him at the end—a spiritual exaltation transcending human suffering—an idealized exultant human God" (Letter to Langner, October 29, 1933).

O'Neill conceived the first idea for *Days Without End* on August 12, 1927, yet he did not complete the play until six years later on November 12, 1933. In view of the many problems he encountered, why did he cling so tenaciously to the desire to create this "Play of Catholic boyhood"? The reason is obvious: the drama contains a personal statement he wished to make during that particular period in his life. The notes for this play have more autobiographical references and revelations than are found in any other—with the exception of *Long Day's Journey into Night*. This 1940 work focuses primarily on O'Neill's parents; *A Moon for the Misbegotten* is his brother Jamie's play; *Day's Without End* is the dramatist's account of his own spiritual odyssey. In discussing this play, he tells Macgowan: "I felt a need to liberate myself from myself" and to express the "life preserving forces" (letter of October 25, 1933). He describes the feelings he experienced while writing the play to Russel Crouse: "I was sweating blood getting this opus out of my system" (letter of February 27, 1934). The words echo those used by O'Neill when discussing the composition of *Long Day's Journey into Night* and *The Great God Brown*, whose notes are more autobiographical than the published play. O'Neill restricted *Long Day's Journey into Night* from publication and production for twenty-five years after his death because it reveals the conflicts and dark secrets of his family. The notes for *Days Without End*, in their totality, reflect the personal inner struggle the dramatist waged on the battleground of his own soul. Despite his denials, and those of his wife Carlotta, he *was* expressing his own dilemma through his hero and seeking a similar return to his faith. There is specific proof of this in a personal and artistic record he kept—a journal listing significant events in his life, arranged in a seven-year cycle. This concept is reminiscent of the outline found in "The Sea-Mother's Son" and the very first line in the earliest notes for *Days Without End*: "His dead selves—masked—7, 14, 21, 28, 35, 42,—." For the year 1932–33, O'Neill writes:

> "Ah, W" (Writing D.W.E.) (return toward Cathol[icism]. away from tragic sense of life

The entry for 1933–34 states:

> Days W.E. (Finish D.W.E.) (return toward Cathol.)

Ah, Wilderness!—which has always been considered so atypical of O'Neill—should be viewed as a derivation from the autobiographical material the dramatist had accumulated—both mentally and artistically—for *Days Without End*. His words attest to this statement: "I'm so close to both these plays." He cites *Days Without End* as an example of a new trend in his work:

> For, after all, this play, like "Ah, Wilderness!" but in a much deeper sense, is the pay of an old debt on my part—a gesture toward more comprehensive, unembittered understanding and inner freedom—the breaking away from an old formula that I had enslaved myself with, and the appreciation that there is their own truth in other formulas, too, and that any life-giving formula is as fit a subject for drama as any other
>
> (Letter to Langner, October 29, 1933).

While he is announcing his movement away from his former tragic sense of life, he also seems to imply that he has come to a more "unembittered understanding" of himself, his family, and his past and has reached a stage of "inner freedom." *Ah, Wilderness!* is not only the precurser but also the prerequisite for writing *Long Day's Journey into Night*.

For good reason O'Neill hesitates to depict the central character of *Days Without End* as a lapsed Catholic—especially one who returns to his faith—fearing the gesture would be taken as having autobiographical significance. He cautions Macgowan that the ending will "trouble you a bit, coming from me. It was an end I resisted (on personal ground) but which finally forced itself on me as the inevitable one" (letter of October 25, 1933). Explaining why *Days Without End* was a "flat failure" in New York, the dramatist writes: "A play that even mentions any religion these days is doomed in advance—especially doomed if the religion happens to be Catholicism. They took the easy line of attack that I must have gone back to Catholicism" (letter of 1935 to Leon Mirlas).

If O'Neill had any intention of making a formal public "return toward

Catholicism" in 1932–34, the critical reception of the play and the antireligious attitudes in the country at the time may have made him reconsider. The phrase that is used repeatedly throughout the notes in reference to the hero of *Days Without End*—"once a Catholic always a Catholic"—seems to apply to the playwright, if only in the deep secret recesses of his heart. One thing is certain: he never lost his faith, his belief in God. Inserted in a first edition copy of *Days Without End* is a letter O'Neill wrote to its original owner in gratitude for that person's "sensitive appreciation in view of the narrow-minded hostility and antireligious prejudice which recently greeted this play."* He remarks:

> I do believe absolutely that Faith must come to us if we are ever again to have an End for our days and know that our lives have meaning. All of my plays, even when most materialistic, are—at any rate, for me—in their spiritual implications a search and a cry in the Wilderness protesting against the fate of their own faithlessness.

---

*Ten days before *Days Without End* closed, O'Neill told Macgowan: "I've had more letters from people about this play than any play I've ever written—which must prove something." He is dismayed that no one—except a few psychologists—saw the play "as a psychological study. No one grasped its Faustian undertheme, none saw what I intended in labelling it 'A Modern Miracle Play.' No one saw its larger—and obvious —aspect as a play which beyond its particular Catholic foreground is a drama of spiritual faith and love in general. . . . it holds audiences tensely and silently all thro' to six to ten curtain calls nightly. . . . And yet the critical jackasses have the nerve to say the technique doesn't come off! If we could get people in the theater, I really believe now this play could be a success—but the reviewers keep too many away, that's the trouble. It's alive for those who go" (letter of February 14, 1934).

°BILLIONAIRE
(1927)

Billionaire—vast symbolic play of the effect upon man's soul of industrial-ism—a man rises from a mechanic, becomes a billionaire—from a man with simple ambitions for success for the sake of wife and family & his standing in community, after his lucky investment with fellow mechanic, money suddenly pours in and bewildered, swamps & corrupts him & his family. It fascinates him by its power. He soon discovers that money is really beyond good and evil, that it can do no wrong. He experiments—even crime can be bought off—the laws whether of man or of God through his ministers are for sale. Money is really God—a billionaire is really God's envoy on earth, to a billionaire all would be possible—he directs his ambitions to become a billionaire—he buys many banks —he concentrates on making money with cash—his final ideal is to possess a billion in gold which will give him control of credit, etc. etc.—in the meantime, this wealth has corrupted his six children, each in a different way they become haunted, neurotic—He has thrown over his first wife, it pleases him to flout the laws, he lives with a harem of kept women, he gives each as an annual present the cost of the exact weight in gold her body represents—he wants their bodies to be gold to him—he is pleased with the illusion that everything he touches turns into gold, that he has the gift of Midas—and in the rear of his immense house he builds a temple, the exact replica of the Taj Mahal, a photo of which he has seen, and in it he puts an enormous solid gold figure of (God who gave Midas gift). He finally comes to the erratic point where everything he owns that can be made into gold, he has it done—But he finds it necessary to send for his old wife from time to time to tell her about his achievements. She insists on living still in their old cottage. She saves money as she used, in spite of the enormous income he allows her. She is a simple placid soul who thinks everything he does is right, even casting her off. She lives in the faith he will sometime come to visit her and settle down. He is obscurely irritated that he can never make her suffer, he finally dresses her in heavy cloth of gold, he loads her with gold jewelry and a massive crown, her heart gives out and she dies. His illusion is shattered, his is the tragedy of Midas, he sees himself and his children, he sees the gold as some-thing that possesses him, he makes up his mind to get rid of it, in a panic he starts to throw it away, give it away, it is hard even to throw away his income. He becomes like Jones in the forest, his accumulating gold possessing him, he throws it away on everything, he goes in for mad schemes, he gets the idea that to revenge himself on money, to insult it and kill it, he must spend it in absolute stupidity, do nothing useful. He has a mountain removed and builds it up again. His children take alarm—a lunacy commission is appointed. The father with a mad sagacity sets up the defense that a billion in gold cannot be mad, that if he is mad so is all industrial money—the decision becomes a symbol to the world—

airplanes wait to take verdict to all countries—masked multitudes before gates shouting "Billion in gold cannot be mad." And this is finally the doctors verdict and the world rejoices—and the man going into his temple and addressing the statue "You win," and shoots himself.

°IT CANNOT BE MAD?
(1927)

(Spithead—summer 1927—& on
voyage to Far East, fall 1928)

Characters of Part One

Ed Wilks
Mame, his sister
Mrs. Slade, a neighbor of the Wilks
Mr. McGee, superintendent of the orphan asylum
Bessie Wilks
Mrs. Tooker
Henry Tooker, her husband
Cecil Oldham
Howard Camp
Tom Braddock, representative of the Burns Automobile Co.

Scenes

Part One
Act One—Scene One   — Farm house in Indiana   1894   (12)
        —Scene Two   — The superintendent's office at
                        the orphan asylum   1900   (18)
      —Scene Three — Sitting room Mrs. Tooker's
                        home—Indianapolis   1903   (21)
       —Scene Four — Office of the garage   1905   (24)   C–19
                        (6 years elapse)
       —Scene Five — Sitting room of the Camp's
                        home   1911—B 30   C 25   — c 5 4 3 2°

4 years
Act Two—Scene One   — Sitting room their new home
                        1915—B 34   C 29   — c 9 8 7 6

°Figures represent the ages of Bessie and Howard Camp's four children.

—Scene Two — Braddock's
—Scene Three — Camp's workshop

Part Two
Act One—Scene One — Camps laboratory with rocket outside
—Scene Two   — Bessie's office, Camp Motor
                Inc. N.Y.   B 47   C 42   — c 22 21 20 19
—Scene Three — Motordrome | Paris studio | Cult colony, Cal | Saigon

Act Two—Scene One — Braddock's room in the temple of Midas in Detroit
—Scene Two   — Int. temple of Midas—the trial
—Scene Three — Ext.—the children are killed
—Scene Four — Int.—the children dragged in

"It Cannot Be Mad?" was originally conceived as the third work of the
trilogy, "Myth Plays for the God-forsaken"—"all written around the general
spiritual futility of the substitute-God search." In *Dynamo*, the first play of the
triology, Reuben Light's substitution of science—the worship of the "Mother
Dynamo"—leads to his rejection of his mother's Old Testament God; in *Day's
Without End* John Loving's "identification of himself with Lucifer" and "of
Lucifer with knowledge and science" inspires his rebellion against his mother's
Catholicism. In the trilogy's last play the substitute-God is money rather than
science for the main characters, who seem to foreshadow Sara Melody and Simon
Harford in *More Stately Mansions*. Part One of "It Cannot Be Mad?" traces the
meteoric rise to wealth and power of an impoverished orphan, Bessie Wilks;
Part Two shows the fall of an automobile industrialist, who retreats to—and
possibly commits suicide in—his Temple of Midas, a haven similar to Simon's
desired refuge—the Temple of Liberty, the summer house in the Harford garden.

The play opens in 1894; Ed Wilks and his sister Mame are making arrangements to send the rebellious twelve-year-old Bessie Wilks—possibly the daughter
of a deceased brother—to an orphan asylum where she remains until she is
eighteen. Bessie is later sent to work for a Mrs. Tooker but becomes dissatisfied
and leaves. She finds a position in a garage where she meets and marries Howard
Camp. In the six years that elapse between the fourth and fifth scenes, the couple,
like Sara and Simon Harford, have four children. "Their new home" is probably
a replica of Sara's more stately mansion. Like Sara, Bessie assumes a major role
in running the family business—Camp Motor.

One of the conflicts in "It Cannot Be Mad?" appears to be the rivalry between two automobile firms. Tom Braddock, who is introduced at the end of
Part One, represents the Burns Automobile Company at the outset of the play.
The concept for this character seems to derive from O'Neill's Billionaire in an
earlier idea in 1927—a man who "rises from a mechanic" and after his "lucky
investment with fellow mechanic [Howard Camp?] money suddenly pours in."
He has the Midas touch and builds a temple and "in it he puts an enormous statue

Scene One

Ed & Mame
> Living & dining room of the farmhouse—forenoon—Ed & Mame enter from kitchen slamming door behind them to prevent Bessie following—their conversation as in scenario—orphan asylum—

Mrs. Slade
> Bessie's protest—Mrs. Slade enters—Mame goes in to Bessie—Mrs. S. talks to Ed—

Mame
⤢ Mame comes back crying with hand bitten—Ed gets up furiously to go in and beat her—

Mrs. S.
⤢ Mrs. S. intervenes pityingly—she goes in—Ed & Mame's resentful talk—Mrs. S. comes back hurriedly—"I ain't ugly! It's you! It's you!"

Scene Two

McGee
The orphan asylum—office of McGee, the superintendent—p.m. six years later—

Bessie
⤤ McGee is discovered—Bessie announced—his thoughts—Bessie enters—his talk with her as in scenario—Mrs. T.

McGee
announced—he goes out to talk to her—B. alone—her bitter thoughts—

McG & Mrs. T.
> McG and Mrs. T. enter—scene of three—B. is engaged.

Scene Three

Tooker
Five years later—sitting room of Mrs. T.'s house—Bessie discovered looking for book—her thoughts as outlined in the scenario—scene before the mirror—her man's costume—

Mrs. T. & O.
> Tooker enters—scene with him as in scenario—Mrs. Tooker returns with her Englishman—

Bessie
⤤ Bessie goes upstairs—scene between three—Oldham takes his leave—scene between Tooker & his wife—Tooker

Oldham
< leaves—Mrs. T. calls Bessie—she comes down again—scene between them—Bessie gives notice she is leaving.

Scene Four

Editor's Note: Arrows indicate entrances and exits of characters.

of (God [Dionysus] who gave Midas gift)." When the Billionaire tries to give away his wealth, his children become alarmed. There is a trial and the cry is heard: "Billion in gold cannot be mad." Was this to be the fate of Tom Braddock in "It Cannot Be Mad?"? Scene One of Part Two is set in "Braddock's room in the temple of Midas in Detroit." In subsequent scenes there is a trial; children are killed and dragged into the temple. A repetition of the scene in which the Billionaire goes into his temple and shoots himself before the statue he erected would be an appropriate conclusion for "It Cannot Be Mad?". In the trilogy's first play Reuben immolates himself in "the temple" as a sacrifice to his goddess, the "Mother Dynamo." In the early versions of *Days Without End*, John Loving "takes a revolver out and shoots himself" before a statue of Christ and the Virgin in a Catholic church. The three trilogy dramas, as O'Neill envisions them, are Faustian modern miracle plays, demonstrating the futility of the search for a worldly substitute—science, knowledge, wealth—for the spiritual. Like the poet Francis Thompson in "The Hound of Heaven," which O'Neill often quoted, the heroes in the "Myth Plays for the God-forsaken" in their substitute-God search "fled Him down the nights and down the days." Their odyssey ends in a place of worship and the discovery of Him whom they sought.

Like *Dynamo*, the first outline for "It Cannot Be Mad?" was written at Spithead in summer 1927. The earliest reference to it in the Work Diary on August 12, 1927 links it to the second trilogy work, *Days Without End*: "Wrote brief sketch in note book for the plays 'Without Ending Of Days'—'It Cannot Be Mad?' " While O'Neill worked intermittently for six years on *Days Without End*, he did finally complete it. In contrast, he spent sixteen years trying to complete "It Cannot Be Mad?"—later giving it various titles—yet he failed to finish it. He started a scenario in October 1928 and worked on it twelve days that month and fourteen days in February 1929. In early March he started the dialogue, changed the title to "On To Betelgeuse" and finished Act One on the 15th, and began Act Two on the 18th. On May 2, he decided to put the play aside for the "time being and start on something else." On July 5, 1931 he made new notes for it but did nothing more until September 30, 1932, when he went over all his previous work on the play and gave it a new title—"The Life of Bessie Bowen." On November 28, 1934 the title was changed to "Career of Bessie Bowlan." He made a new outline and notes, remarking "fresh slant on this—new title—throw out combination Talkie scheme—can do without." The entire month of December was devoted to a new outline, notes, reading, set designs, character descriptions, and dialogue for Act One. O'Neill worked seven days on the play in January 1935, noting on the 20th: "(dialogue again—Act I) (this damned play won't come right—not big enough opportunity to interest me—should be part of something, not itself)." The next day he enthusiastically discusses the "Calms of Capricorn" Cycle and says: "grand new ideas for 1st two plays—will chuck 'B[essie]. B[owlan].' out of further present consideration" (W.D.).

"The Life of Bessie Bowen" reemerges as the seventh play of O'Neill's

Cycle with a new title: "Twilight of Possessors Self-Dispossessed." The dramatist made notes for it on August 29 and 30 and September 1, 1935, when the Cycle was entitled "A Touch of the Poet." The Work Diary entry for September 2 states: "'Twilight of Possessors Self-Dispossessed' (As this 7th Play follows in main plot-outline the old 'Bessie Bowen' theme, nothing further needed on its outline now beyond the revision notes I've done in past week)." According to the dramatist's new scheme, Bessie is the daughter of Honey Harford, the youngest of Sara and Simon's four sons. After a new first play, "The Greed of the Meek," is added to the Cycle on September 7, "Twilight of Possessors Self-Dispossessed" is renamed "Hair of the Dog." It becomes the ninth play when the Cycle is expanded again on June 7, 1936 to include "And Give Me Death." O'Neill contemplates abandoning "Hair of the Dog" as "part of Cycle" but resumes this work a year later on July 26, 1937, writing: "9th play—will require extra generation in new scheme—'Honey' to live till end?"

O'Neill labeled the Bessie Bowen drama "no good" and destroyed part of Act One, which he had completed, on February 21, 1943, stating at that time "and this play is basis for last play of Cycle now (with many changes)." "It Cannot Be Mad?"/"Life of Bessie Bowen"/"Hair of the Dog": whatever its form, this work was not destined to survive—either as a Cycle play or as part of the trilogy "Myth Plays for the God-forsaken." In his letter to Leon Mirlas in 1935, O'Neill writes:

> Yes, it is true that, as originally planned years ago, "Dynamo" & "Days Without End" were to be the first two plays of a trilogy and "It Cannot Be Mad" was to be the third. But the idea for the last play was always nebulous —and as, to date, it remains still vague and unformed in my mind, there is little prospect of its coming to life for a long time to come.

While O'Neill never completed the trilogy of the late 1920s, the demands it made upon his creative imagination encouraged him to conceive future multi-play works: the three-part *Mourning Becomes Electra* and his great Cycle of the 1930s.

[°FATHER AND SON]
(1927)

Father and son—do not know each other—in love with same woman.

°ATLANTIS SERIES
(1927) *

A series of plays about Atlantis (a history of Christianity). Take it into myth-folklore.

1ˢᵗ — Jesus ending with the Crucifixion (the journey up Calvary symbolical). The Old Gods—the Past of Man—crucifies Him.

2ⁿᵈ — St. Paul

3ʳᵈ — Constantine

4ᵗʰ — [erased]

5ᵗʰ — Middle Ages—St. Louis (?) or Geoffrey [Godfrey] de Bouillon

6ᵗʰ — The Renaissance—[erased: Borgias (?)]

7ᵗʰ — Luther

8ᵗʰ — Cromwell

9ᵗʰ — Robespierre—(Goddess of Reason)

10ᵗʰ — Napoleon (complete sceptic)

11ᵗʰ — Jefferson

12ᵗʰ — Lenin

13ᵗʰ — The Second Coming

°THE GUILTY ARE GUILTY
(One of Three Plays for Good Men and True)
(1927) †

Play of Mob—a satire in which a mob is shown forming (perhaps first formed of men in every uniform of every Order in U. S. (?)), in which the

---

*The Work Diary provides a date for this concept: March 7, 1927—"Idea for satirical Atlantis series of plays (history of Christianity beginning with Crucifixion)." A later entry on April 26, 1927 states: "Worked on Atlantis series plays notion." O'Neill develops only two ideas in this series: the "Thomas Jefferson Play" in 1932 and "Robespierre" in 1938.

†A specific date is established through the Work Diary entry for July 13, 1927: "Idea

mob mind is shown gradually taking hold, forcing the most hysterical into leadership, until they all gradually revert to the level of beasts as blood lust is aroused. In the meantime, their fleeing victim is rendered by fear into a like state until we have finally a howling mob of men with the faces of hideous apes haunting to death a man with the face of an ape horrible with terror and pain— or better still, not apes, but Solomon Islanders or Bushmen at a cannibal feast. It is the murder and lust of the crime, told and retold each time embroidered on, that rouses the desire to commit a like crime—the Idea—in the name of moral justice. This would be a play with the mask technique.

(Technique—1st Scene realistic)

°BANTU BOY
(1927)

Negro play of the Negro's whole experience in modern times, especially with regard to America—Bantu chief and his kraal—tricked, his honor played upon, drugged and he and wives captured—slave ship—America, sold into slavery— proud, sure of his integrity, he baffles his different owners who chain and beat him—finally property of exceptional planter who appreciates his quality—offers to free him—"Freedom is God's, white man. You cannot set me free. I am free." They try to convert him to Christianity but he cannot accept an all-white Christ the Christians have made him—let them give some evidence that his teachings live in white men's hearts—the Civil War—he is converted—he believes in the North's ideal freedom for slaves, he escapes—fights in Negro regiment—soon sees his regiment is patronized, looked down upon by whites—at the close of war he sees the joker in the freedom of slaves—freed to be slaves—in N. Y. he

---

Mob play—'The Guilty Are Guilty.' " The dramatist initially conceived this idea the previous year as his letter of May 14, 1926 to Macgowan indicates:

> I have many new ideas—for a play similar in technique & length to "Emperor Jones" with Mob as the hero—or villain rather!—done with masks entirely—showing the formation of a lynching mob from more or less harmless, human units—(a white man is victim of this lynching)—its gradual development as Mob & disintegration as Man until the end is a crowd of men with the masks of brutes dancing about the captive they are hanging who has reverted (as Jones but *white*) to a gibbering beast through fear. That is, it is the same lust and fear that made him commit his crime that takes possession of them and makes them kill him in the same spirit—of enjoyment, of gratified desire. (This is a botched explanation—but you get me. Not a pretty theme—but very true! I have a fine ironic title for it, "The Guilty Are Guilty.") The Masks could be equally well used in a vice-versa scheme to this.

is requested to leave a Church—he rebels against Christ—longs again for Africa—makes his way there as sailor—to his old kraal—just in time for first Zulu war—he sees the inevitable end, the industrial slavery that will be forced on his people in Africa, their own land, too—now an old man with a last despairing gesture he leads his tribe against the Boers—they are shot down—he is mortally wounded —he dies in the wilds, alone, but out of his despair comes a vision of prophecy, he feels the spirit of Africa proud of its black God telling him that that continent is his, his people's, that the whites' attempt to own it is illusion, that they are aliens, the land hates them, it waits, preying upon them, distintegrating them, their own lusts corrupting them, their yellow bastards a sign of their eventual ruin.

O'Neill's numerous attempts in the 1920s and 1930s to depict the plight of blacks in America reveal his deep concern and compassion for those victimized by society and their fellow man. Personal and social motives merge in his creative efforts to show racial injustice. The rejection of his Irish family by Yankee New Londoners forever sears his memory. The close association with Joe Smith, the black gambler with whom he roomed at the Hell Hole, reinforces his determination to combat racial discrimination. The dramatist's italicized words in the first recorded idea in 1922 for *All God's Chillun Got Wings* emphasize the close ties he formed with the black community while living in Greenwich Village: "Play of Johnny T.—base play on his experience *as I have seen it intimately.*"

Joe Smith's story of a black gangster he had known inspired O'Neill to write *The Dreamy Kid* in 1918. This play is followed by *The Emperor Jones* in 1920 and an idea the next year for "Honest Honey Boy," whose hero is " 'Joe'—tragicomedy of Negro Gambler (Joe Smith)—his decline." While the author makes notes and an outline for his "Old Joc Smith idea" eleven years later on May 20, 1932, his friend does not appear until 1939, when he emerges as Joe Mott, the black gambler in *The Iceman Cometh*. Throughout the 1920s O'Neill retains a genuine affection for Joe Smith, providing financial help and corresponding with him even after the flight to France in 1928.* On February 22 of that year the

---

*In one letter, undated but headed "touring in France now," O'Neill tries to provide his friend with moral, as well as financial, support:

I was damn glad to hear from you again! But damned sorry to learn the breaks are not coming your way. I sure hope the luck will soon change for you and you'll get on your feet again. You know you've always got my best wishes and that I am your friend and will always do anything I can to help you. I haven't forgotten the old days and your loyal friendship for me. I'm enclosing a check to give you a boost over this rough spot you've run into. . . . Buck up, Joe! You're not going to confess the game has licked you, are you? That isn't like you! Get a new grip on yourself and you can knock it dead yet! Write me a long letter soon and tell me all your news.

author lists the places he wants to visit while abroad in a letter to Macgowan: "There's Greece & Egypt and the East—and South Africa where I've always wanted to go and where I need to go for the new Negro play I've doped out and will write in the next few years." The play he mentions is "Bantu Boy," which, as Work Diary entries show, he works on intermittently from 1927 to 1934:

8/12/27   Wrote brief sketch in note book for ideas for the new Negro play I have had in mind. [The work is called "Bantu play" in his end-of-the-month entry.]
7/15–16/29 Negro play idea (notes)
12/3/31   Negro play (sketch outline acts—scenes—tentative)
12/26/31   Ideas Negro play—notes
12/28/31   Negro play (reading & notes)
12/31/31   Negro play (reading)
1/4/32   Negro play idea (new angles on plots)
8/25/34   "Bantu Boy" (notes)

These numerous entries lead to the expectation of finding an abundance of material showing how O'Neill develops this idea; however, only two sets of notes are extant. The first set represents the work done on December 3, 1931: "sketch outline acts—scenes."

Negro Play*

Scene One   — Bantu village—treachery of the white trader he trusts— the raid—capture—(Beginning of scene his marriage— great love for wife).

Scene Two   — The hold of a slaver—All except chief packed lying flat. He, for rebellion, is chained to butt of mainmast, kneeling, his arms outstretched chained to beam.

Scene Three — The slave market—auction—separation from wife—she cries, he tells her not to show grief before whites—curses whites when he is put up for auction.

Scene Four   — Ferocious resistance—escape—followed by a proud (and effective) non-resistance—he is bought by Carter White.

Scene Five   — His lonely heart-breaking grief for his lost wife—only show of weakness—chained to tree (or stake in clearing)

---

*There are several similarities between O'Neill's hero and Alex Haley's Kunta Kinte in *Roots*. After their torturous voyage from Africa to the United States on slave ships, both men retain their pride and black identity, bravely resisting the attempts of white men to enslave them. The trip to Africa of Haley, a descendant of Kunta Kinte, to discover his original "roots" parallels the return of O'Neill's central character to reclaim his heritage.

—moonlight—he calls to her, to the night, to the Black Gods of Africa to restore her to him—"You can't set me free, White Man. I am free."—then reunion with wife—weakness through gratitude and acceptance of lot.

Scene Six   — Finds wife Christian—asked by preacher she tries to convert him—he is fascinated by Christ figure but resists—loyalty to black gods—then news of war by white men to free slaves—his conversion by this—his escape to join Northern army—his duty as warrior king.

Scene Seven   — War—the black regiment—his disillusion.

Scene Eight   — Reconstruction—put out of church—back to Africa drive now—his wife refuses—Christian—final disillusionment—leaves her and children forever.

Scene Nine   — Africa—his native village—tales of the Boer's advance—hopelessness—spears against guns—he rouses them—the war dance.

Scene Ten   — The battlefield at end of battle—Boer's shooting, wounded —his death scene—hillside in back—gully—hyena laughter and gleaming eyes—he gets up a last effort, disperses them, silence, the roar of a lion a prophecy—death as red dawn comes over the black mountains.

The second set of notes, undated but—with their "new angles in plots"—probably written on January 4, 1932, define the three women in the play:

Negro Play

His old mother goes through the play with him—at the end she is 90 or 100—it is she who finally finds him on the battlefield in Africa and comforts him with her dark, triumphant prophecies of a black Africa as she dies—for her America has always been sensed as a white land, its climate, etc. white in feeling to her, alien—slavery there she has accepted as an inexorable fate, in the nature of things—she has always remembered her black gods of Africa, she has never been tempted by the sophistry of an all-color Christ of racial brotherhood—Christ is white—it is her struggle to keep her son true to his faith—struggle with the wife whose emotional nature reaches out for Christ, who fervently embraces Christianity as a comfort to make her resigned to slavery, reward of freedom in another world.

The wife* goes through the play—he has forced her to let two of his chil-

---

*A canceled section suggests a wife-mother conflict that is reminiscent of the Sara Melody-Deborah Harford struggle for the husband-son in More Stately Mansions.

dren be killed by poison his mother prepares soon after birth so they will not be born slaves—it is her guilt for these deaths that sinks her more deeply in Christianity—he is weakening toward Christianity himself when the next child is born—she dies from the childbirth imploring him to embrace Christianity and let the child live—at the same time his mother calls on the old Gods and speaking for them demands the child's death—he drives his mother from him.

It is this child that, just matured, an Americanized Christian, a pretty, cocky servant-maid lipping the white airs, ashamed of her father, has an affair with the master of the house and bears a yellow child—He kills her and the child, feeling his line polluted.

With his mother goes back to Africa.

[°PLAY OF ASTRONOMER]
(1927) °

Play of astronomer whose scientific convictions of the unity of creation, rhythm and beauty of all leads him into astrology.

°MODERN FAUST PLAY
(1927) †

Play of the man-philosopher, scientist or poet—who, at the age of 45, finding himself about to die, when doctors have given up hope, but full of a tremendous desire to live not for egotistic reasons—rather he is full of a desire and love of the peace of death—but because his work is not done and he feels it is of value to the human spirit—petitions God (Eternal Life) for time enough to finish even at the cost of the most horrible pain. And he is able to make this bar-

---

O'Neill's initial plan here shows that the husband in "Bantu Boy" murders his wife "at his mother's instigation" or—in an alternate scheme—"allows his mother to kill her." The relationship of the warrior king and his ambitious daughter, ashamed of her father, also foreshadows that of Con and Sara Melody. Like each of the Cycle plays, "Bantu Boy" depicts a period in American history—from the 1840s to the post Civil-War years.

°A Work Diary entry establishes a definite date: November 10, 1927—"Idea for astronomer-astrologer play." O'Neill returns to this "Play Idea—Astronomer" again on December 21, 1938.

†The Work Diary entry for November 11, 1927 states: "Idea modern Faust play— the selling of one's life (instead of one's soul) etc. Worked out tentatively in notebook."

gain with the Spirit of God within him that he must sell everything but his soul to God as the price of continued life, that he will have taken from him every-thing that makes him one with human life—wife, children, fame, money, etc.—that he must live alone in his own life, dead to life but at the same time alive—a pariah, an Ishmael. He accepts this bargain. He wills to live on. The rest in the play is his tortured struggle through the sorrow of solitude, of desertion, priva-tion and misunderstanding to complete his task—and as he comes near to finish-ing it he looks forward now and more eagerly to Death for he begins to doubt the value of his work, he hates it for the price he has had to pay. And finally when he finishes, it is with agonized relief that he calls upon God: "Now! I am finished."

Combine with Modern Faust play—(not the Faust of Goethe but similar spiritual tragedy of a Faustian character).

°THE SEA-MOTHER'S SON
(1928)

Scheme for doing the opus founded on autobiographical material—the man (40) lies in the hospital at the point of death—he is at the crisis—unable to speak, in a sort of coma, yet he hears and thinks clearly—the doctors are wor-ried—his wife and children are brought in to rouse him—they appeal to him—he hears them with detached affection but somehow he cannot get back to the plane where wife and children have any meaning for him or for the question that confronts him—he hears the doctor say it all depends now on whether he wants to live or not—only his own will for life or death can decide the issue—he must decide in solitude with his own life—and he questions his life, what has it been, has it any meaning that he should wish to continue it—peace is at hand, why shouldn't he accept it—there is a strong death wish in him which instinc-tively he fights against—he feels a pride in considering the issue, in knowing that this time if he is to be born into life again it must be by his own wish—voluntary life—and he begins to examine his old life from the beginnings of his childhood—he lies back and its important episodes, the influences that moulded him, are enacted before him—he is participator and spectator—interpreter.

(Method—after childhood and young manhood scenes, the character of himself is taken by himself while a man wearing his mask takes his place in bed.)

The end of play is where, accepting all the suffering he has been through, he is able to say yes to his life, to come back to the plane of wife and children, to conquer his death wish, give up the comfort of the return to Mother Death.

The probable date of this idea—based on Work Diary entries—is Novem-ber 6, 1928. Two events precede it: O'Neill's fortieth birthday on October 16 and his departure from Saigon on November 2 for Shanghai. He had "sailed sick" and did not fully recover from the flu until he had spent a week in late November in Shanghai's County Hospital. The voyage across the China Sea provides an appropriate setting for resuming work on the autobiographical "The Sea-Mother's Son." Like his forty-year-old hospitalized hero, the ailing dramatist is examining his old life at this time and making crucial decisions. He is also experiencing great remorse for abandoning his wife Agnes and their children and a sense of frustration about his deteriorating relationship with Carlotta. In Saigon the couple had had a serious argument, which would be continued in Shanghai and be followed by a bitter separation.

While the only extant scheme for "The Sea-Mother's Son" is dated 1928 in the notebook, the first idea for it appears a year earlier in the Work Diary:

3/8/27   Worked doping out preliminary outline for "The Sea-Mother's Son"— series of plays based on autobiographical material.
10/6/28   (Mediterranean Sea) worked on idea "The Sea-Mother's Son."
11/6/28   Worked a bit on "Sea-Mother's Son."
7/21/31   "The Sea-Mother's Son" (notes—"Nostalgia" (?)).
7/23/31   "Sea-Mother's Son" ("Nostalgia" notes).

Significantly, O'Neill's correspondence reflects his preoccupation with "The Sea-Mother's Son" while he is writing *Dynamo*, whose semi-autobiographic hero similarly seeks "the comfort of the return to Mother Death" (the Sea-Mother and Mother Death are synonymous). The letter of April 27, 1928, to Macgowan states:

> I've had lots of new creative notions—the old bean is in the pink that way. The grand opus of my life—the autobiographical "Sea-Mother's Son" —has been much in my dreams of late. If I can write that up to what the dreams call for it will make a work that I flatter myself will be one of those timeless Big Things. It has got me all "het up." It should be a piece of writing not like any that has ever been done before the way I plan it. My sub-title is to be "The Story of the Birth of a Soul"—and it will be just that!

On September 12, 1928—two days after sending the script for *Dynamo* to the Theater Guild—the author informs Benjamin De Casseres that "The Sea-Mother's Son" will have "ten or more *Interludes* in it, each deeper and more powerful than 'S.I.,' and yet will all be a unit. Believe me, Ben, I'm going to bull's-eye a star with that job or go mad in the attempt." Here O'Neill implies "The Sea-Mother's Son" series will contain ten plays; however, in a letter to Russel Crouse in 1935 he calls the work a "Nine play thing" and "a notion I had years ago for a combination autobiographical novel in play form for publication in book, not production on stage."

The last entry in the Work Diary for "The Sea-Mother's Son" is dated July 23, 1931. During this same month O'Neill starts the first set of notes for *Days Without End*, which—with its autobiographical plan and purpose—replaces

"The Sea-Mother's Son." The hero in the July notes for *Days Without End* encounters "his dead selves—masked—7, 14, 21, 28, 35, 42"; in the 1928 notation for "The Sea-Mother's Son," after witnessing scenes from his childhood and youth, "the character of himself is taken by himself while a man wearing his mask takes his place in bed." At the end of the play "he is able to say yes to his life." On May 29, 1932, while working on the second set of notes for *Days Without End*, the dramatist in a letter to Dudley Nichols states:

> Funny, your writing me at this particular time about affirmation. I am changing inside me, as I suppose one always does, or ought to do if there is growth, when one has passed forty, and even the most positive affirmative Nay! of my past work no longer satisfies me. So I am groping after a real, true Yea! in the play I'm now starting—a very old Yea, it is true, in essence, but so completely forgotten in all its inner truth that it might pass for brand new. Whether I will be able to carry the writing of it up to Yea! remains to be seen. This play is, incidentally—and most confidentially!—a development from my old idea for the second play of the "Dynamo" trilogy.

It is possible that O'Neill, like the heroes of "The Sea-Mother's Son" and *Days Without End*, is experiencing a desire at this time "to be born into life again"— which for John Loving included a return to Catholicism. The author states in his 1932 letter: "I am changing inside me." In the entries for this year and the one that follows in the seven-year biographical Cycle of significant events, he writes: "return toward Catholicism—away from the tragic sense of life."

[°LIFE OF MAN PLAY]
(1928)

Scheme for a Life of Man play—modern American man—the Stations of the Cross* sequence followed out in modern life—a scene in play corresponding to each Station—birth in humble surroundings, etc.—the lay characters in the play arc all life-sized puppets—some characters, at first alive, afterwards become

---

*The concept of the Stations of the Cross seems to have had autobiographical connotations for O'Neill. He gave Agnes Boulton a copy of *Thirst*, a collection of his first five plays. Sheaffer notes that the dramatist describes these as the "first five Stations of the Cross in my plod up Parnassus" in the inscription dated December 28, 1918 (*O'Neill Son and Playwright*, p. 273). The phrase appears in the notes for two plays. One of the two alternate titles, which appear at the beginning of Part Two of the 1928 second scenario for *Dynamo*, is "Modern Stations of the Cross." In a notation for *Days Without End*, O'Neill writes: "Follow out outlines of Stations of the Cross in Second Part (?)."

dead puppets to the man, his father or his mother for example—while in his memory they remain alive as they were—

(or perhaps this play should be confined to childhood and adolescence)

Develop

[°PLAY OF LOVE AND PASSION]
(1928)

Play of love and passion laid in Renaissance times or before—the idea that when the punishment for infidelity was torture and death in this life, adultery a mortal sin punished by an eternity of torture in the hereafter, that illicit lovers reached heights of ecstasy of self-sacrifice and elation on giving their bodies and souls that is unknown today—that raised love to a higher spiritual and physical plane by the value they set upon it and the price they gladly paid for it.

[°PLAY OF DIVORCED WIFE]*
(1928)

Play of wife who at divorce bargains with her husband and wills her children outright to him—she is never to see them again—the effect on her as her life goes on, and on the children as they grow up—a boy and girl—father has told them what mother has done.

[°PLAY ON DRAFT RIOTS]
(1928)

A play laid during the Draft Riots in New York in Civil War.

[°PARABLES OF CHRIST]
(1928)

Ideas for series of plays taking the different parables of Christ for subjects.

---

*The author reverses his own marital position in this idea. After leaving his wife Agnes and their two children, Shane and Oona, he sailed for Europe on the *S.S. Berengaria* with Carlotta Monterey on February 10, 1928. For nearly a year Agnes refused to file for the divorce, which was granted on July 2, 1929.

[°FALSTAFF-PRINCE HAL]
(1928) †

Play of modern character like Falstaff or Panurge—satire—character of the noble upright hero like Prince Henry as antithesis.

---

† A Work Diary entry shows that O'Neill tried to develop this concept five years later: April 16, 1933—"Notes Falstaff-Prince Hal idea."

[MOURNING BECOMES ELECTRA]
(1928)

Use the plots from Greek tragedy in modern surroundings—the New England
play of Agamemnon, Clytemnestra, Electra & Orestes—Oedipus.

While the first idea for *Mourning Becomes Electra* appears in the notebook
in 1928, O'Neill's statements indicate that his decision to write the "Greek tragedy" dates to spring 1926 after he had read Arthur Symons's translation of Hugo
von Hofmannstahl's *Electra*. In his letter of April 4 to Macgowan, he calls the
play a "beautifully written thing" and asks: "Why has no one ever done it?"
The Work Diary entry for April 26, 1926, reads: "Germ idea use Greek Tragedy
plot in modern setting." The work record for October 1928, shows that he had
decided to use the plot of the *Oresteia*, narrowing the focus to the "Electra idea."
Like Hofmannstahl, he turns to Sophocles, rather than Aeschylus, for his interpretation of Electra, portraying her sympathetically and depicting her crime of
matricide as an act of just vengeance. Wondering why Electra escapes punishment, he asks: "Why did the chain of fated crime and retribution ignore her
mother's murderess?—a weakness in what remains to us of Greek tragedy that
there is no play about Electra's life after murder of Clytemnestra."* As the title
chosen for the trilogy implies, his primary purpose is to present in this work
imaginative—but logically envisioned—events that follow the murder, showing
the avenger as unable to escape the tragic web of family fate. Throughout the
years of work on the trilogy, the dramatist remains completely under the spell of
his heroine; he says: "Electra is to me the most interesting of all women in
drama."†
Three years elapse between O'Neill's conception of his "germ idea" for
Mourning Becomes Electra in 1926 and the start of the scenario: May 19, 1929.
The long scenario for the first two plays of the trilogy contained in one of the
three extant notebooks in the Yale O'Neill Collection is used here to show how
the dramatist develops this idea. Previously published material—the "Working
Notes and Extracts from a Fragmentary Diary,"** dating from spring 1926 to
September 1931—is specifically identified to distinguish it from the Yale note-

---

*Fragmentary Diary, November 1928.
†Letter to Robert Sisk, August 28, 1930.
**Excerpts of the "Working Notes and Extracts from a Fragmentary Diary" presented
here are from Yale's photostatic copies of the eleven-page originals in the possession
of the American Academy of Arts and Letters.

books. Part of the entry from the Fragmentary Diary for April 1929—which precedes the scenario—is cited here as O'Neill discusses his deliberate departures from the Greek story:

> Electra loves Aegisthus—always fated to be mother's rival in love, always defeated—first for father's love, then for brother's, finally for Aegisthus'— reason for Clytemnestra's hatred for Agememnon sexual frustration by his Puritan sense of guilt turning love to lust . . . Clytemnestra persuades Aegisthus against his will to help her murder Agamemnon—method of murder, poison (woman's weapon)—Aegisthus bears strong facial resemblance to Agamemnon and Orestes.

Work Diary entries are included to show the problems O'Neill encountered while creating this massive three-part work.

Before beginning the scenario, the dramatist makes general notes on the plot from May 6 to 11 and more specific ones on the characters from May 12 to 18, 1929. Their descriptions are longer and more detailed than those provided for any other characters in the canon. He changes—in some instances several times—the names of the characters and the early concept he has of them in the scenario. Also undetermined at the outset are the titles for the three plays:

Electra Trilogy
Possible Titles for Three Plays & For While
Whole Work—Mourning Becomes Electra†
1st play—(Clemence)
2nd play—(Orin)
3rd play—(Elena)

Characters

Ezra Mannon, Brigadier-General in the Union Armies (56)
Clemence, his wife (41)
Elena, their daughter (24)
Orin, their son (22)
Adrien Labord (35)
Peter Oldham, friend of Orin (23)
Hester Sand (19)
Seth, the Mannons' old man of all work
Eva, his Portugese wife

Three points should be made about O'Neill's earliest conception of the characters. Hester/Hazel is not as yet Peter's sister. Seth's wife Eva will later be

---

†On May 18, 1929 O'Neill decides to keep this title (W.D.).

replaced by Hannah, the cook, who is eliminated during the fourth week of rehearsals; O'Neill states: "All right when she ran through all plays in first version—but not appearing only in last play." Finally, although he decides—as he writes in the Fragmentary Diary in April 1929—to omit Electra's sisters, Iphegenia and Chrysothemis, he includes descriptions and details about them in the May outline and calls them Effie and Crystal. The following is a brief summary of the descriptions of the characters.

May 12–18, 1929   Outline of Characters

Brigadier-General Mannon has a "mass of grey hair, almost white, with bushy black eyebrows over small, penetrating grey-blue eyes—big features and a tight-lipped severe cold-blooded mouth. His full beard is a shade darker grey than his hair." His old New England family has a tradition of service in the army and the church. While stationed at Governor's Island, he falls in love with and marries a New York girl, Clementina, of a rich merchant family. For her sake he leaves the army and becomes a lawyer. In time, he regrets his decision to resign from the service and blames his having done so on his wife. Unlike the published text in which marriage immediately turns "romance into disgust" for Clementina, "all real love between them" does not cease until their second child is born.

He is a stern, grimly-religious man, silent and inarticulate—for his first two children he felt little affection because they have little of his nature in them. He forces them (as sacrifices to his guilty conscience for having foresworn his career) against his wife's desires, into loveless marriages with rising young minister and an army officer, both men of his own type. For Orin he feels an affection of a kind as his only son, but he has no regard for him as an individual —for Elena, his baby, he feels an overwhelming love. He early sees that she is like him in nature and he makes her his friend and only confidant.

Clementina comes from old New York French Huguenot stock. Some physical attributes given to her apply to Carlotta O'Neill and are later altered. She is a full-bosomed, heavy-limbed striking-looking woman with thick reddish-brown hair and fair skin. Her eyes are beautiful, large and dark. Her nose is short and a bit gross with wide, flaring nostrils; there is something majestic and impressive about her, one feels that underneath her calm, coldly self-contained almost stolid exterior she is a creature of violent repressed passions and a powerful will. She speaks indolently in a rich contralto voice. She is dressed extravagantly but with perfect taste.

This habit of dressing extravagantly goes against her husband's "Puritan grain and seems to him as evidence of a sinful strain in her, an inclination toward vanity and worldly pomp." However, like Mary Tyrone in the early notes for *Long Day's Journey into Night*, she pays for her clothes "out of a generous yearly income left her by her father." Her husband, resembling James Tyrone, secretly "resents this income of hers which makes her so independent of his commands. He thinks it selfish that she spends all this money on herself—her clothes and her fine horses and carriages, expensive table linen, etc. instead of putting it at his disposal to further his career." Clementina's father had spoiled her; "she had had everything she desired and it seems to her quite as a matter of course that she should continue to indulge herself."

While the setting of the play in the published text is "one of the smaller New England seaport towns," O'Neill specifically identifies it in the scenario as his hometown New London. After he has changed Clementina's name to its final form, he says: "Christine has always hated the town of N. L. and felt a superior disdain for its inhabitants." Speaking of New London in *Long Day's Journey into Night*, Mary Tyrone remarks bitterly: "I've always hated this town and everyone in it." If the words "Huguenot Calvinism" are replaced by "Irish Catholicism" and "hero" is changed to "actor," the description of the Mannons' courtship—and possibly their marriage—applies to Mary and James Tyrone and—by autobiographical implication—to Ella and James O'Neill.

Clementina, "a thoughtless, pleasure-loving girl," had been "fascinated by the novelty" of this handsome

hero back from the war in full uniform. His seeming coldness had piqued her interest. She set out to make him fall in love with her and succeeded at the cost of losing her own head; but her passionate, full-blooded femaleness had never found sex-satisfaction in his repressed morally-constrained, disapproving sex-frigidity. Then, as a girl brought up in the strictest of Huguenot Calvinist social ethic, she had turned to motherhood as her only outlet.

Her feelings for her oldest daughters and her son are similar to Ella O'Neill's for her three sons; her first two children she loved to a degree. "Orin she had adored from the first." She had not wanted Elena and her dislike for her daughter "ripened into a concealed positive hate as the little girl grows up more and more strangely like her and yet alien to her through a strange admixture of her father's nature. For C. Elena is the living symbol of her marriage." Jealously Clementina resents her husband's "marked affection for Elena." The war breaks out, and she is glad when her husband goes back into the army. In the third year of the war, on a visit to New York, she meets Gustave and immediately falls in love with him. "A fierce tide of long-repressed passions sweeps over her, overthrowing all the religious and social taboos of her training." She gives herself to Gustave "without reserve, with the desperate boldness and masochistic pride in complete self-surrender of a woman of forty."

Gustave de Bouville, called Adrien Labord earlier in the dramatis personae and Armand de Bouville and Andre de Cairgnac later in the scenario, is totally unlike—physically—the Adam Brant of the published text. He is small and has the lithe physique of a fencer. His face is handsome with delicate, finely-chiseled features. His small mouth is sensual and self-indulgent, easily breaking into a disarming amiable smile, or a sneer of arrogant, supercilious disdain. His blue eyes are large and amorous. He has light-brown wavy hair, a small brown mustache, and the delicate hands and feet of a woman. He speaks in a carefully modulated, musical, insinuating voice. He is dressed as a true Beau Brummell of the period would dress.

The dramatist has not, as yet, worked out the intricate connection between Adam's parents and the Mannons. Here Adam is portrayed as the youngest son of a French colonel of noble blood in the Grand Armée who, after Waterloo, had, "out of his devotion to the fallen Emperor, refused to serve under the Bourbons, and had emigrated to America and married into a New York family of the same set to which Clementina's people belong and accumulated a small fortune." A Harvard graduate, Gustave has become a gentleman of leisure, "an exquisite man-about-town dabbling in the arts, his principal occupation that of a lover of women." Finally, he settles down at the age of thirty and buys a partnership in a brokerage business. At this time he meets Clementina, "whom, as a boy, he had adored from afar." He looks upon Ezra Mannon disdainfully as a "glum stick of a man" and—once the Civil War starts and Mannon is promoted to Brigadier-General—as a "grotesque joke, a stuffed shirt in an ugly, drab uniform." Gustave refuses to take the Civil War seriously and feels himself "French and aloof from this sordid fratricidal strife." He falls deeply in love with Clementina. "Up to that time he has simply played at love as sensual pleasure." Like Clementina, he longs for Mannon's death and vows this "despicable Yankee clod shall not take his woman from him."

The description of Elena contains phrases that apply more to Edmund Tyrone, a self portrait, in *Long Day's Journey into Night* than to the Lavinia Mannon of the final text. She is

extremely thin—arms and legs are long with long tapering hands and feet. Her face is striking-looking. She has great black eyes like her mother's. Her mouth is also a sensually-accentuated replica of her mother's, even to the trace of moustache on the short upper lip. Her cheekbones are high and broad, with hollows in the flesh beneath. Her forehead is low and broad, framed by a heavy mass of straight black hair.

Although she resembles her father in her manner, movements, and voice, there is always the "sense that this is all a discipline imposed on an impulse toward the free, self-possessed, animal grace of her mother's body." She returns her mother's dislike and feels only a tolerant indifference for her sisters, scorning them for letting themselves be "married off like sheep." Her feelings for Orin are strangely contradictory.

Her love for him has a good deal of the maternal in it. She realizes her mother's great love for Orin, and his for her, and [has] been jealous of this—tried to revenge herself on her mother by winning Orin from her—but without much success for the mother coddles and spoils him and Orin is very like her in character and hungry for a warm open love that Elena's repressed impulses are unable to give him. For her father Elena feels a love that amounts to adoration —sensed her mother does not love him, tries to give him her love as a substitute.

Elena hates Gustave—primarily because "he appeals to her sensual mother's nature in her that she feels is her weakness and shame." Discovering Clementina's infidelity, she feels a "fierce joy" and plans to "use this weapon to drive her mother forever out of her father's life." Yet, she is jealous of the "passionate love her mother is capable of feeling and inspiring" and is filled with "envious rage because she has had no male admirers. She treats males of her age with a timid protective mask of severe frigidity."

The section devoted to Orin contains few details about his physical appearance but much information about his relationship to other members of the family. The most startling revelation is O'Neill's reference to a second Mannon son— Hugh—who is Orin's preferred rival for the affections of the mother, foreshadowing once again the Jamie-Edmund relationship in *Long Day's Journey into Night*. Because no other reference is made to Hugh—who has no counterpart in the Greek story—except in the passage describing Orin, this section is quoted in its entirety—as is the material on the two older sisters who are eliminated in later drafts.

Orin—for a year lieutenant, then captain—of medium height—slightly built— vain of his good looks—strong mixture of feminine qualities. Since boyhood, finding his intense love for his mother defeated by her indifference to him and jealous of her love for his brother Hugh, his resentment toward her has instinctively taken the line of imitating his father in everything. But his affections find no satisfying object in his father's cold unemotional attitude. Balked in both parents, hating his brother, he has concentrated his love on Elena and they have become natural allies of their father against their mother and Hugh. It is their taunts of cowardice, added to the father's outraged insistence, that have driven Hugh into the war in spite of his mother's entreaties. Her pleading that the gay, volatile, handsome Hugh (as charming, polished, popular with girls, French and irreligious, so like her) is delicate, too rare a soul for war, has completed Orin's resentful estrangement from her, and she has let him go to the front with no more than a perfunctory concern. He is deeply imbued with the Mannon tradition of grim, unthinking patriotism and military service. He likes to dress in uniform. Secretly, unconsciously, he longs for a reconciliation with his mother, he still adores her. The news of Hugh's death fills him with joy and hope that now he will take his rightful place in her affections.

Effie—eldest daughter—married to a minister when she was still in her teens— borne two children by him—blond, blue-eyed, slender—appearance is vaguely reminiscent of both father and mother—neither pretty nor plain; she would pass as nice-looking. Her consciousness of what is constantly expected of her as a minister's wife has given her a self-conscious air of suspicious moral rectitude— at heart a gentle soul, easily moved to sentimental tears and pity. She does not love her husband—turns all her affection on her children and spoils them. She loves her mother and Orin, fears her father, and is in secret fear and awe of Elena—regards her with moral disapproval as headstrong and proud and un-Christian.

Crystal—a pretty young woman with a plump attractive figure, blue eyes and red-brown hair like her mother's but devoid of her mother's impressive character-istics—strength of will in her mother's character is lacking in her—has a selfish love for her mother and has always openly taken her side against her father whom she dislikes and fears—likes Orin, likes but feels superior to Effie who amuses her, but is frankly antagonistic to Elena whom she dislikes because she feels she is the stronger—a suspicious enigma she cannot understand. She has married, without much desire except that the rising young lawyer is good match —has had one child but the duties of motherhood bore her and she wastes little time on her offspring—is frankly pleasure-loving, socially-ambitious, considered a great asset to her husband in his career.

The physical description of Hester Sand, daughter of the town's leading banker, differs from the later portrait of her as Hazel Niles; their other attributes are, however, similar. Hester has a round full face, blue eyes, and a mass of curly straw-blond hair. Her nature is "open-hearted, charitable and free from all malice or pettiness, innocent and trustful, genuinely good." In her manner she is "frank, straightforward and resolute"; she has "an intelligent, if strictly limited, mind." Hester loves Orin, respects his father, and is perplexed by his mother, antago-nistic to Elena, and fond of Peter.

Peter* Oldham, the son of an "obscure doctor of straightened means but good family," is described as a "hearty, lovable, honest fellow, bluff and awk-ward and blundering in manner." He has a good-natured face and a clumsy but powerful body. When Orin graduates from West Point and, in the third year of the war, joins the army, Peter's affection for his friend and his desire to be near him prompt him to leave medical school and volunteer. He has no "easy intelli-gence, things come hard to him, but what few give him credit for, he possesses a strength of character, a stubborn perseverance toward his objectives that always gains them for him in the end." He is hopelessly in love with Elena, who "likes him as she would a big dog but at the same time his uncouth admiration annoys

---

*The name "Paul" has been erased here and "Peter" substituted. The dramatist must have changed this name after completing the scenario as this character is called Paul in it.

her for he constantly reminds her that he is about the only sort of suitor she can attract—orders him about as if he were her slave and he delights in obeying her." Peter and the General like each other, but Mannon "frowns upon his sloppiness in dress and bearing and continually reprimands him as if he were a buck private. Clementina tolerates him, but is bored by him—as far as he can dislike anyone, dislikes her."

More information about Seth, the Mannons' gardener—and his ties to the family—is provided in the early notes than in the final text. While he still has a grim forbidding face, "his blue eyes have a sardonic twinkle in them and at the rare moments when he allows himself to smile his face suddenly takes on a kindly gentle expression." He had been Ezra's orderly in the Mexican War and his father's orderly in the War of 1812, marrying the daughter of a Portuguese fisherman right after his return. "They have had children, all of whom have married and left them alone."

Omitted in the published text, Seth's wife Eva, who is Elena's assistant housekeeper, is nearly seventy; she has a swarthy complexion and brooding passionate black eyes.

Her relationship with her husband has been one long drawn-out battle of conflicting temperaments. They are one of those couples who one would predict couldn't live with each other for a year without murder being done, but who possess a deep primitive attraction for each other that survives all quarrels, that, incongruously enough, seems to be strengthened by continual strife as if strife were a fundamental tie between them—superstitious to a degree and is reputed to possess powers as a seeress, being frequently consulted by her compatriots. She reads cards, tea leaves, and has trances.

Scenario*

May 19, 1929, Story of the First Play—First Act

Before beginning the scenario, O'Neill states his intention is to keep the exact family relationship between Aegisthus and his first cousin Agamemnon and the rivalry between their fathers.† However, there is no suggestion in the extant sce-

---

*O'Neill's dedicatory passage, dated January 16, 1930, appears on the first page of the notebook: "To Carlotta—my wife—these first fruits (very unripe!) of my work in Our New Year—with all my deepest love and gratitude for all you have meant to me!—and all your help!—Gene."
†Fragmentary Diary, April 1929.

nario for the first two plays that the Aegisthus-Gustave character is related to the Mannons. The author's stay in France and his exposure to its inhabitants while writing the play probably motivate him to depict this character as a sensuous, self-indulgent womanizing Frenchman. In the scene that opens the play, Gustave tells Clementina that his father—"as a soldier of Napoleon"—is disgusted with him for "seducing the wife of a soldier absent at the front. The sin in his mother's eyes is his disgracing the family by involving it in a sordid scandal." The only way he can placate his parents is to swear that he is interested in Elena and not her mother. When Clementina becomes jealous, asking why he had to mention Elena, he passifies her by saying he "would as soon fall in love with a stone." Fearing the loss of her beauty and her lover to a younger woman, Clementina wants only to go "where they would be alone, where they weren't known, elope to France. He reminds her they would both be cast off. She would lose her allowance from her father, they would starve."

A passionate love scene follows, in which they forget all caution and go over the memories of their romance. Gustave is "driven mad" by the thought that her husband will return and "come to her bed," recalling that the last time the General was on leave "he had forced his cold, methodical lust on her in spite of all her evasions, sternly reminding her of her duty as wife." They realize they will not be able to keep her husband from discovering their love as they have been careless; it is a "matter of common gossip in their set in New York and especially in the small town of N[ew]. L[ondon]. where Clementina has become so well hated for her arrogance and exclusiveness and open disdain for its society." Motivated solely by jealousy and not, as in the final version, by revenge, Gustave contemplates killing the General. The scene ends with the entrance of Elena, who tells them the war is over. Stunned by her mother's indifference, Elena remarks: "If I had a husband, I would have thanked my God for his life." Her mother responds, cuttingly: "Wait till you have one before you bore us with your sentiments. It is time you had a husband." Elena replies: "I have my father—and my duty to him." She adds, ominously, that she must have a long talk with her mother and then leaves the room.

Story of the First Play—Second Act

There is no time lapse between the first and second act, which again opens with a scene between Clementina and Gustave, who are determined not to "give each other up for Elena or the General or anyone." They clutch "at their one remaining hope—the General's weak heart—husband's death as the one way out." The following scene, in which Elena accuses her mother of adultery, is similar to its counterpart in the published text. The one difference is the way Elena detects her mother's affair; she has had a key made to unlock the drawer where Gustave's revealing love letters are hidden. "These give away all their secret meetings in N[ew]. Y[ork]. in the room he had rented for that purpose. Elena says that she has stolen the letters knowing her father would be coming home soon." She is motivated by jealousy, as well as revenge, in the bargain she makes with her mother: give up the lover and she will keep, but not show, the letters to her father. She hates her mother "for the mental picture of her sexual abandon and ecstasy she has gotten from the details in the letters, for the passionate love of her lover, for her fulfillment in it—for this joy she has never known and feels she never will know. It seems to her to be horrible and evil, her mother the scarlet woman." Clementina says that if their positions were reversed Elena would want to marry the man she loves—"if the possibility of such great love were in you—but you are like your father." Elena replies strangely: "And I am like you, too, although I have always hidden it. So take care." The act ends with Clementina plotting her husband's death with Gustave—not by poison, as later, but by a "mistaken" overdose of his heart medicine.

Story of the First Play—Act Three

According to O'Neill's original scheme, Ezra Mannon's role in the play was to have been larger than it now is in the published text. He has already returned home at the beginning of Act Three, which is more than twice the length of the other acts in the first play of the scenario. Except for Orin—who is in an army hospital recuperating from a shoulder wound—the entire family is assembled in the drawing room: the General, his wife and Elena, Effie and Crystal and their husbands. It is evening after dinner. Two rooms are visible: the drawing room on the right and Mannon's study on the left, to which he now retires to read his mail. De Bouville writes that his son Gustave wants to marry Elena and urges the General "in the name of their old friendship, that G's suit should be favorably considered." Mannon's twinge of jealousy quickly changes to a passion of rage when he then reads "an anonymous, poison-pen letter, marked from the town, that warns him tauntingly of the relations between his wife and Gustave. The spasm of pain around his heart comes—he takes his medicine and pulls himself together." He asks a servant to summon Elena.

The scene shifts to the drawing room where Paul, Hester, the minister Alcott, and the lawyer Hull have joined the family. In a speech that would have become a long soliloquy, Clementina—sitting in the midst of chattering people—thinks only of "her own maddening situation," of the dreaded night ahead. "She must sleep with the General and allow him to possess her, even pretend to reciprocate his cold lust." Her husband's claim that his heart condition has improved convinces her that she will have to use the poison Gustave brought; "there is no hope along these lines." Ironically, Mannon has lied to his wife so that she will not worry about him; "he knows that his trouble is very serious, liable to be fatal at any time."

After Paul finishes telling the group of Orin's bravery in the war, Elena says her brother "is a true Mannon, his father's son, alive to his responsibility in preserving the honor and tradition of the family." Her mother remarks caustically: "Do not be so solemn, Elena. Haven't you any sense of humor about yourself? I am afraid that part of the Mannon tradition that concerned burning witches must be reincarnated in you." Elena replies aridly that "there are witches even now and . . . they will suffer flames of one kind or another." The family treats Elena as an "embarrassing alien in spirit. Only Paul stands by her." Elena goes to the study; and the group begins to criticize her, resenting her influence over her father. Paul says he "would esteem it an honor" if Elena would marry him. His words inspire Clementina to hope that "perhaps this limpkin will give her the chance to get Elena out of the house."

In the next scene in the study Mannon rebukes Elena for not telling him she has fallen in love in his absence. She admits that Paul has written her; but surely her father doesn't think she could love Paul. "She likes him on Orin's account, she will never forget how he saved Orin from drowning as a boy." Mannon hands her the letter from Gustave's father. "For a second a wild joy comes to her. Supposing, after all, it is she he loves. Then at once she remembers the letters to her mother. He is her lover." He then shows her the anonymous letter. Elena knows she must defend her hated mother to protect her father. His suspicions are partly allayed, yet his curiosity is aroused by her protestation of hatred for Gustave. Her father encourages her to reconsider; it would be a good match. Even though Elena voices her objections: she hardly knows Gustave and is repelled by his lack of ambition, "a strange conflict is going on within her, she cannot help being fascinated by the idea of being his wife, in bed with him, although she loathes herself, and G. and her mother, all the same because of this."

On her way to tell her mother that she is wanted in the study, Elena meets Paul. A sudden awareness of his love and desire to marry her gives Elena "a feeling of warmth, of security—at worst, he will always be a final means of escape from old maidhood." Alone with her mother, Elena informs her of the two letters, gloating over the one from Gustave's father and her intimation to her father that "she is not averse to the suit." She assures the outraged Clementina that she acted only to "sidetrack his suspicions, she would rather marry a leper than that cur!" Clementina enters the study, filled with murderous hatred for her husband and disgust that she must lie. He shows her the anonymous letter. Being forewarned, she has ready excuses: "all he is after is a convenient marriage—she couldn't approve since his reputation as a rake is too well known." Mannon is reassured but still jealous; "if he ever thought for one moment that she had been unfaithful to him, he would drive her out, publicly disgrace her, hound her until she was a pariah for all decent people." She soothes him, tries to use all "her physical blandishments to seduce him, make him feel she loves him physically in spite of her disgust." She pretends she has missed him during their two years of separation and that she wants his homecoming to mark "a new beginning of the close intimacy of their first days." She promises to sleep with him in his room rather than forcing him to come to hers. He tries to be tender but only succeeds "in being coarse. When he suggests their going to bed, she assents with well-feigned coy eagerness." The secret desires and fears of both are revealed: "her heart cries out: 'O God, let him die!' He is thinking of the Doctor's warning about no sex for a while—dismissing it contemptuously."

Story of the First Play—Act Four

O'Neill's original plan in the scenario calls for a multiple interior-exterior setting like the one he conceived for *Desire Under the Elms*. The last act of the First Play "shows the General's bedroom on the second floor, at left above his study, and C.'s bedroom on the right of the second floor, above the drawing room." There is an interior-exterior view of the characters in this first scene: Clementina, her face distorted in loathing, sitting upright beside the sleeping General; Elena in nightclothes, pacing before the portico pillars below. This is the shortest act in the scenario and the one most similar to its counterpart in the published text. Half of the material is devoted to the two women's inner state of mind—reflections intended for the "thought technique" later. Clementina "thinks with loathing of her physical humiliation," contrasting Gustave's caresses with "the coarse lust of Mannon whose loving has never in their married life aroused any satisfying response in her. And yet she is his wife, his property, she has borne four children by him. She bitterly questions all religion and morality where sex is concerned. Where her love is pure, she is impure; where she is impure, she is accounted pure."

Below, Elena, filled with disgust, bitterness, and strange jealousy, "guesses her mother has used her physical attraction. She goes without a qualm from lover's arms to husband's." Her mind dwells on phrases from Gustave's lascivious letters. "What filth physical passion is—and yet how it attracts her! She hates herself." Yet she wishes those phrases had been addressed to her. Then she would "take advantage of the situation and force Gustave to marry her. She would make him forget her mother in her arms! She feels she is really her mother's daughter, not her father's. She even helped to betray him to her mother that night."

In the scenario Clementina does not have to provoke her husband to bring on his heart attack; he wakes groaning in pain. As in the published text, she substitutes poison for his medicine, and Elena arrives just in time to see her father rise in bed and gasp one word before he dies: "guilty." She turns on Clementina and cries: "Whore!" While she wonders why her mother went to her own room, Elena does not find the poison box—the evidence used in the final draft to convince her of her mother's guilt.

| *June 21, 1929*   *Studying Greek Plays*

After finishing the First Play on June 20, O'Neill spent the next six days "studying Greek plays" before continuing the scenario. The words that are particularly significant in the original idea for the trilogy recorded in the 1928 note-book are "plots from Greek tragedy" and "Oedipus." O'Neill's intention from the start—and this is reinforced by the six-day reading period—is to combine the Greek sense of family fate in a modern approximation of the *Oresteia* and the theme of incest in *Oedipus Rex*. The two Greek works converge in the relationship of the Clytemnestra-Iocastê-Mannon mother and her Orestes-Oedipus son. What O'Neill emphasizes in the scenario for the second play of his trilogy—and what emerges as a dominant theme in the notes and final draft—is mother betrayal of the son; his attempt to avenge infidelity necessarily—to conform to the Greek models—leads to her physical death. Undoubtedly, the person who exerts the greatest influence on O'Neill—personally adverse but creatively beneficial—is his mother. His subconscious cry of rage against her—the alternating currents of attraction and revulsion—echoes throughout the canon.

June 27, 1929   Story of the Second Play—Act One |

A month, rather than two days, has elapsed since the General's death. Clem-entina waits in the study for her lover to come in disguise, having seen him only once, briefly, when she went to visit Orin in the hospital. Guiltily, fearfully, she connects the mysterious disappearance of Elena and the poison bottle she had carelessly thrown under an evergreen tree the morning after the murder. "There has been ugly gossip about the General's timely death, both in N[ew]. L[ondon]. and N[ew]. Y[ork]. but no real suspicion of them." The lover, now called Ar-mand, arrives, cowardly blaming her for their present situation. "He feels their love has been poisoned—their crime has changed everything—to be frank with himself he no longer loves her as he did, except when he is with her and forgets everything in her physical attraction—when he is away he catches himself long-ing for freedom from her, yet he knows now their crime has bound them in-dissolubly for life." Seeing his distraught state, Clementina tells him that there is no danger from the law but only Elena. Armand asks, smilingly: "Do you think she will kill us?" He then grows somber: "That is the trouble with vile crimes. They distort the mind. They punish themselves." Clementina assures him that she has convinced Orin that Elena has become unbalanced with grief. They need not fear. "He is her son. He adores her." As soon as Orin comes home, they will marry—"be free and in Europe will have only their love to think of."

In the next scene—outside the house—Elena tells Orin, who has just come home, the details of their father's death. Orin ignores his mother's possible role and is only repulsed by the fact that she had "taken to sleeping with his father." He warns his sister that what she is saying condemns her mother to death—"their mother!" Elena produces the poison bottle; "Orin, as the head of the family, now will act as a Mannon should to avenge his father when his eyes are opened to the truth!" Orin is indifferent until Elena explains her mother's motive: "lover—Armand de—Does he know him—the philanderer—the handsome darling of the ladies—the darling of their mother when her husband and son were risking their lives at the front!" In jealous fury, Orin exclaims: "I will kill him!" When reminded that his mother is more guilty than her lover, Orin denounces his sister, saying that he loves his mother and that they should go in; he wants to see her. A very significant—and autobiographical—development occurs here in the scenario that is later omitted. Elena says that she "is never going in the house again until it is cleansed of guilt and father's sentence carried out." She adds that her father made the will before he knew; "the money is her mother's, the food is her mother's—she does not like it flavored with blood." She has made arrangements "to stay with the Chappells* and tutor their daughter." Elena finally realizes that only their mother's infidelity enrages Orin; "he loves her, he is jealous." She will have to convince him of her guilt, for Elena is determined now "that their mother must die—and has purposely left the house so that she will never be suspected."

The time spent reading the Greek plays seems to have reminded O'Neill that the Mannon men should resemble each other. In the next scene—in the study— Clementina "shrieks with terror: and faints at the sight of Orin. Roused, she says that "she had thought it was his father." Elena's words return to "Orin's mind to rankle—he asks, looking at her somberly—why should she be afraid his father's spirit haunts the house?" Clementina responds to Elena's accusations, explaining the return to her room, the poison bottle, the word "guilty." Orin then makes the final charge: "harshly and sneeringly says I hear we are to have a stepfather. C. forces a scornful laugh, feels caught in a trap." Orin cites the details of the affair. His mother protests: "Lies! A madwoman's vicious lies." Desperately, she produces the two letters Mannon had received. The plan was Armand's father's; "it was all innocent enough. Orin reads and is convinced but he shows jealousy of A. even where E. is concerned—denounces him for a Don Juan—he forbids him to set foot in house again." Finally, Orin angrily asks her why she "had taken to sleeping" with his father again. Clementina, "sensing his jealousy, says it was his wish—his first night home she could not well refuse—

---

*The dramatist depicts them as the Chatfields in *Long Day's Journey into Night*— calling them "Big frogs in a small puddle"—and, most probably, as the Mannons in the trilogy. Ezra Chappell, like Ezra Mannon's father, made a fortune in trade. In 1830 Chappell purchased land on Huntington Street in New London and built four identical Greek-structured houses, which apparently inspired the author's concept of the Mannon home. The dramatist states in the Fragmentary Diary in April 1930: "This home of New England—House of Atreus—was built in 1830, say, by Atreus character, Agamemnon's father—grotesque perversion of everything Greek temple expressed of meaning of life." The four Chappell houses are in excellent condition today. "There is no such important row of Greek revival houses left standing in the United States" ("Chappell file" in the archives of the New London Chamber of Commerce, located in one of these historic buildings).

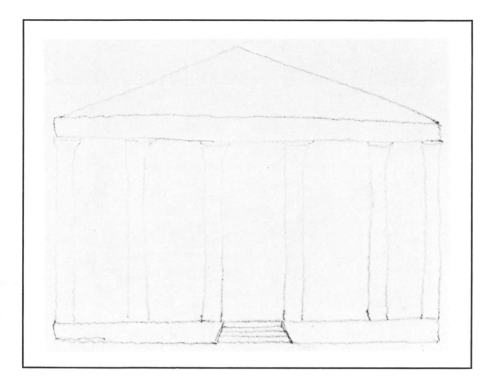

he knows his father—how domineering and autocratic." She tries to placate Orin; she "will be a real mother to him in the future—she will make up for all the past to him if he will let her. She draws him to her and kisses him. Orin melts and is transported with happiness—forgets his suspicions." He nestles against her and says that "he will devote his life to love for her, to protecting her, there will be just the two of them and they will be happy together!"

Story of the Second Play—Act Two

Orin sits at his father's desk in the study. He "has fallen completely under his mother's influence" and refuses to see Elena when she comes to visit him. "The week alone with his mother has been, in a sense, one of singular happiness for him"; yet fleetingly Elena's charges "return to torment him and poison his happiest moments. He can't believe his mother could be such a liar and hypocrite." Although she insists he see Hester every day, he "feels a morbid urge to give up Hester so he can be more completely his mother's."

Clementina enters and is alarmed to see him in the study; she has kept it and the father's bedroom locked since the funeral. Saying that he wants to take the curse of gloom off such a nice room, Orin "takes her in his arms—his attitude is like a lover's—and tells her how much he loves her, how much the past week has meant to him, there is sunshine in his heart always now. He kisses her lips." Orin expresses his regrets about his engagement to Hester. His mother "is angry but conceals it. He must marry her and set her free to escape and marry A. His jealous attitude is strange, more like a lover's than a son. Elena's influence over him is gone, and it only remains to get him off her hands." When Hester arrives, Clementina decides to go to mail a letter in which she tells Armand "suspicion or no suspicion they must fly to Europe at once and get married."

Paul enters, scolds Orin for his treatment of Elena, and gives him her message: "in the name of their love to read her letter and accept the packet." Orin reads two of Armand's letters and "can no longer doubt his mother's guilt. Phrases from the letter of desire, of remembrances of physical passion, of his mother's caresses, of her 'white body in his arms,' keep whirling in his mind, driving him mad. His one thought is of revenge, of killing A.—he suddenly begins to identify himself with his father, to feel as if it was to him his mother had been unfaithful." He longs to denounce her before Paul and Hester "as a murderess—and a whore" but discovers his mother has left the house. He sends Paul to summon Elena and urges Hester to go home and "forget him completely."

Elena arrives. Orin begs her forgiveness and says he will go to New York and shoot Armand "like a dog!" She sees "in a flash that his revenge must always be directed at A. alone, that he will never consider her mother's death, that will have to be something that she must contrive herself, without his knowledge." Elena unfolds her plan to Orin: he must write to Armand and tell him if he is a man of honor he will come to the Mannon house next Friday at nine. He will come if only to convince Orin of his mother's innocence. Elena reveals no more of the plan but promises their mother will not suffer. Before leaving, in an unexpected encounter with her mother, Elena exclaims: "You have won! You have made a fool and a weakling of my brother." Clementina smiles triumphantly: "I don't know what you are talking about. You are mad, Elena."

Story of the Second Play—Act Three

The third act opens in the study on a night several days later. "All four of the rooms are revealed. Mannon's bedroom above the study is in darkness." Unlike the published text in which Clementina commits suicide, the scenario follows the plot of the *Oresteia*; a daughter—willingly—and a son—unknowingly— avenge the father through the act of matricide. Clementina is shown in her room packing a traveling bag to go to New York the next day, determined to find out if Armand still loves her. She had planned to leave that day; but Orin asked her to stay to meet a friend of his, insisting his father's room be aired and prepared for this guest. Orin paces up and down in the study. Elena enters to give him moral support—"not where A. is concerned but in giving his mother the sleeping draught—she has told him it is a sleeping draught although it is a stronger dose of morphine than the one for A." She plans to hide in the study until the deed is done.

Orin sadly protests that "he feels like a Judas"; he would rather kill Armand outright and accept his punishment. Elena "insists on justice. They are executioners of the family's honor, not passionate killers." Orin assures her he has memorized the note the lover is to write "to make it look as if he had committed suicide." He has not, as yet, prepared the wine but was "nerving himself for the ordeal of the poison." Elena rushes him to the drawing room and pours out three glasses of port. The glass on the left is his mother's; the one on the right her lover's. Into the latter, Orin—"his face pale, his hand trembling"—puts the dose he had hidden in his pocket. "And now for the mother's. He hesitates, his lips moving without voice, his eyes pitifully questioning her." She kisses him pityingly: "Come to think of it—and of you—and her—I'd rather do it." They return to the study where she "speaks to her father's presence in the room, a prayer for him to give Orin strength. The whole success depends on his ability to convince his mother of his sacrificing love that made him summon A. to her to give them his blessing." He must then drink their health with them, escort Armand to her father's bedroom, persuade him to write the note, inform him that his death will settle the account in full—no harm will come to their mother.

Clementina's lover—now called Andre de Cairgnac—arrives, sensing danger yet seeking a way to atone for his crime. He longs for death and has even contemplated suicide. "He knows his love for C. is dying, only pity and loyalty remain of it, he does not want to fly to Europe with her—feels doom waiting for him and accepts it gladly, provided he can by a sacrifice of himself protect C. from sharing it." He feels an enormous sense of guilt as he had made her love him—"at first only through a curiosity, a vanity, a dislike for her husband, had ruined her life before he had come himself really to love her."

Clementina stops packing when she hears the ring of the front door and, coming to the stairs, asks Orin if it is his friend. She is overcome with emotion when she sees Andre. The lovers turn to Orin for an explanation. He says that he knew his mother never loved his father, that she deserved happiness and had asked Andre here "to discover your love beyond doubt of your further denial of it, to confront it and accept it myself, to tell you I regret my selfishness." His mother accepts this statement joyously, but Andre wonders half-believing, half-sceptical: "Is he lying—badly—too honorable for a liar—but why would he lie—some plan? whose plan?—he is too naive for plotting—his sister—yes, that's it." They drink their toasts. Orin takes Andre upstairs to show him his room, knocking briefly at the study door to signal Elena that the poison had been administered. She turns to the room triumphantly: "It is done! My dear father! You are avenged and it is I, your daughter, who have done this! Orin would never have dared!"

Once in his father's bedroom, Orin discards all pretense: "The play-acting is over." When Andre boldly tries to deny all accusations, Orin tells him he "has already been condemned and judgment has already been executed upon him. The wine he drank was poisoned. He is to die here where his father died, as his father died—only in his case death will be more merciful as it is morphia he has taken." Andre tries to escape, but Orin takes out a pistol and explains that no harm will come to his mother if a suicide letter is written. A great weariness steals over Andre; "he has wanted to commit suicide. This saves him the trouble, he will sleep and never wake up." Orin dictates the letter: "I choose death rather than life without the love of the woman I love. I have poisoned the wine. Death is the one way out for us both." Andre states he will surrender the letter only if he is given a few minutes alone with Clementina: "I only want to say farewell. My love—and her love—give me that right!"

Andre goes down to the study; Clementina embraces and kisses him. "She is in a transport of relief and happiness! Orin, dear Orin! She is full of dreams of their future." Andre listens in silence and caresses her tenderly. He says carelessly that he is tired and wants to retire. "They both yawn and she laughs. The poison is just beginning to take effect. They kiss—It is his farewell." Orin sees them embrace but controls his jealous passion. He enters the drawing room and suggests they all retire. The couple ascends the stairs. Orin "thinks revengefully of waking up his mother in the morning to see her lover's body. At the same time he dreams of the happy future alone with her now that A. will die. She will forget A., she will only have O. to cling to."

Feeling the effects of the poison, Andre makes his way to Mannon's bed and lies down. He addresses the spirit of the General: "It is just—here in his bed— she has imagination, that Elena—an eye for an eye—so be it!" The scene shifts to show Clementina coming out of her dressing room,

alarmed at the stupor that is making her limbs like lead. She grows suspicious— how strange Orin's action has been—too good to be true—not like him—why has he put A. in the General's room—why this deadly stupor—she fights against it—feels her sense leaving her—they have been poisoned!—A.!—she must warn him! She forces herself to stand, sways and almost falls, takes the candle from beside the bed, staggers to the door and across the hall and opens his door and, mechanically shutting it behind her, takes some steps toward his bed, calling drowsily Andre. Then her legs give way, she crumples to her hands and knees and drags herself, and candle still in one hand, to his bedside. She calls my lover, my dear lover and collapses finally by his bedside into insensibility.

Story of the Second Play—Act Four

The setting of Act Four is described as "the same except that now only the interiors of the two bedrooms are revealed. In Mannon's room the two bodies are in the same position we had last seen them. It is seven o'clock the next morning." Orin comes out to the portico, filled with superstitious dread because a dog had been lurking about the house all night; "it means death somewhere." He has mixed emotions about Andre's death; remorse and guilt are mitigated by joy. He thinks, gloatingly, of his mother's despair when he tells her of the suicide. Then fear grips him; "perhaps the dose of morphia given him might not have been strong enough." Hastening upstairs, he sees his mother's body beside the bed, "gasps with horror and runs forward and bends beside her—sees in a flash that she is dead." He rushes to the hall and sends Frank, the old butler, for his sister.

The next scene—showing the grief-stricken son beside the body of his mother—is later omitted; in the final draft of the play Orin is offstage when he hears "the sharp report of a pistol." Still offstage, he discovers his mother has committed suicide and rushes from the house to seek the consolation of his sister. The scene of discovery in the scenario has its counterpart in Sophocles' *Oedipus Rex*, one of the Greek plays O'Neill apparently studied before beginning the second part of the trilogy. Like Oedipus, Orin is filled with grief, guilt, and remorse and "sobs heart-brokenly:* 'Mother! Mother! Tell me it isn't true! Tell me!' " He kisses her cold lips and caresses her hair. "He is wild with love and anguish. She mustn't die, he has planned all their future together, nothing stands between them now, and A. is dead and she'll soon forget him, he was never worthy of her love. He, Orin, won't remember her part in his father's death, he is really glad his father is out of the way so they can be alone." After making this "terrible, broken confession to his mother's corpse," he suddenly realizes the meaning of her being by that bed. His sorrow changes to rage and jealous hatred: "What were you doing here? What did you come for? You came to your lover's bed— my father's bed—in which you murdered him. You came, knowing I was under the same roof, believing you were asleep. What a terrible woman—how corrupt—how cruel—how lascivious and foul—and I thought you were sweet and fine and good—I loved you—I thought you loved me—I would have done anything for you—and you betrayed me!"

When she enters the bedroom, Elena tries to quiet her brother: "Does he want them both to hang? Certainly, it was only a sleeping dose—it must have been shock that killed her—when she found him dead—or she had some of the poison that had killed her father and had taken that." Then, seeing her mother's body in the room, she is "taken aback," but her tone is triumphant: "The adultress and her love! Her father is avenged and the stain on the family honor is wiped out! She stands beside the corpses, glorying fiercely in her crime, cold and implacable."

Elena's thoughts turn from the crime to the possible punishment—"a rope

---

*When Oedipus discovers the body of his mother after she had hung herself, "a great sob broke from him, heartbreaking to hear."—*Oedipus Rex*, Dudley Fitts and Robert Fitzgerald translation in *Drama*, ed. Otto Reinert (Boston, 1966), p. 51.

around your neck—and mine"—if she and Orin do not prepare a plausible story for the police. She tells Orin they must pretend their mother had been disturbed by Andre's attentions, had tried to discourage him, and—acting with Orin—had invited him here. Andre had come and "promised he would give up his importuning. But you remember now he acted suspicious, he had handled the wine, you and mother were out of the room for a minute—when you came back he urged you to drink—and this morning you found them both dead—and his note on the table." As dazed as he is, Orin sees something incongruous: "You are making her out innocent." Elena replies that she does so for the sake of the family name, her father's memory; "she would like her mother to stand dishonored for all time." She forces Orin to take their mother's body back to her room. He lays it on the bed, pulls the sheet over her face, falls on his knees, and cries despairingly: "Mother! Mother! Why weren't you innocent?"

Meanwhile, Elena stands beside Andre's body, staring into his face. "She addresses it with a sort of stern tenderness. 'Rest in peace. You have paid. I loved you once. I forgive you—and I know now that you are there and I am here you know which one loved you the better, I or she, and that you forgive me.'" She feels, at last, that the spirit of her father, which once dominated the house "demanding the debt be paid," is at peace. In the last speech of the act, Elena looks to the future with hope: "I am free of two old loves that gnawed at my rest. I think I shall fall in love with Paul—and have children—and live 16 hours a day and sleep [with] P. But Orin must forget first. He will be a danger and a duty. He is weak for a soldier who has killed men. I will marry him to Hester and he will lose his guilt in her white innocence." She then goes out of the room to tell the butler to call the police.

The last line O'Neill records in the notebook containing the scenario for the first two parts of *Mourning Becomes Electra* is: "Electra Trilogy—Story of the Third Play—Act One." Nowhere does he explain why he did not write the scenario for this third play in the notebook. On July 15, 1929—four days after he finished the scenario for the second play—he states: "feel off of Electra for the moment" (W.D.). Having been granted a divorce from his second wife, he was making plans at that time to marry Carlotta on July 22. Three days after the ceremony he began the scenario for the third play and finished it on August 4. The dramatist must have, inadvertently, destroyed the earliest notes made for this play. In the only entry for August 1929 in the Fragmentary Diary, he notes: "have given Yankee Electra tragic end worthy of her—and Orestes, too."

Pertinent Work Diary entries are included here to provide a detailed account of O'Neill's subsequent progress on *Mourning Becomes Electra*.

Preliminary Work

8/15/29	MBE—studying for right dialogue style for it—rhythm derived from Biblical prose (?)
8/26/29	MBE—playing around with mask-technique notion
9/6/29	MBE—scenes—idea two-walled interiors, columns always in background
9/25/29	MBE—get brilliant notion introduction Cassandra—no N[ew]. E[ngland].—straight Greek characters—work enthusiastically on scenario along these lines
9/27/29	MBE—Cassandra scenario—get disgusted with it and abandon idea
9/29/29	MBE—start dialogue (naturalistic) on old scenario scheme
10/4/29	MBE—another false start—tear up all I've done
11/8/29	MBE—reading scenario over
11/11/29	MBE—start dialogue again—this time feel all set for it

First Draft

11/12/29	1st draft ["Homecoming"]
12/24/29	Start "The Hunted" (1st d[raft])
1/19/30	Start Third Play, "The Haunted"
2/21/30	MBE—Finished First Draft*

Second Draft

3/31/30	MBE—start writing second draft
7/11/30	MBE—finished Second Draft
7/20/30	MBE—decide try stylized soliloquies—rewrite all soliloquies

---

*Commenting on this first draft in the Fragmentary Diary on March 27, 1930, O'Neill states: "More of my idea was left out of play than there is in it! In next version I must correct this at all costs." He calls the draft "scrawny stuff—parts damned thrilling but lots more lousy—not enough meat—don't like Aegisthus character—hackneyed and thin—must find new one—not enough of sense of fate hovering over characters, fate of family—living in the house built by Atreus' hatred." In his letter the next day to Macgowan, O'Neill says that in comparison to the "Dynamo" trilogy, *Mourning Becomes Electra* "is a real trilogy carrying on the same characters, etc.— not just a general theme resemblance between plays. I've finished the first draft of all three. It was some job! But I'm pleased—in fact, enthusiastic. Of course, there's a hell of a lot still to be done. I intend to write it over twice more in longhand, with spells of letting it rest up in between."

Third Draft

> 7/25/30   MBE—no asides, stylized soliloquies°
> 9/16/30   MBE—finish Third Draft
> 9/20/30   MBE—read all over and am convinced stylized soliloquies
>   won't do†—that this 3rd draft is mistake except in its elimina-
>   tion of asides—convinced, too, that half-masks must be elimi-
>   nated

Second Set of Notes

A second collection of notes, dated August 27, 1930, contains revisions of the dialogue for the third draft. Most of this material is retained through the next drafts, but there are some significant differences between these notes and the final text. Act Two of *The Homecoming* has two scenes. In the first scene Lavinia is even more vindictive when she forbids her mother to see her lover; Christine's hatred for her daughter is more intense. In the second scene the lovers plot Ezra Mannon's death. After Christine administers the fatal dose to her husband in Act Four of *The Homecoming*, she goes to her room immediately and thrusts "the poison into the first hiding place." Asked by her daughter why she left her dying husband, Christine "stammers stupidly, 'To get my slippers.'" Later—when she faints—Lavinia "stares before her the look of horrified suspicion growing in her eyes. Then she suddenly turns and rushes into her mother's room. There is a pause. Then she returns with the little box of poison in her hands. She holds it in the light of the candle and stares at it with horrified dread."

°In his letter of August 28, 1930, O'Neill writes: "As for technique, it is modified [Strange] 'Interlude' with thought in a new sort of obsessed, driving, monotonous rhythm—but no short asides as in 'I.' And for all the principle characters, I use half-masks, not as I've used them before although the idea is suggested in 'Lazarus.' This is a Greek touch, if you will, although the masks themselves and the reason for their use is entirely un-Greek. My reasons for their use—they are many—are too long to go into here." (Letter to Robert Sisk)

†An entry in the Fragmentary Diary for September 21, 1930 reads: "stylized concep-tion—not time wasted—learned a lot—stylized soliloquies uncovered new insights into characters and recurrent themes—job now is to get all this in naturally in straight dialogue—as simple and direct and dynamic as possible—stop doing things to these characters—let them reveal themselves—in spite of (or because of!) their long locked-up passions. Keep mask conception—but as Mannon *background*, not foreground!—what I want from this mask concept is a dramatic, arresting, visual symbol of the separateness, the fated isolation of this family, the mark of their fate which makes them dramatically distinct from rest of world."

There is one curious statement in the notes for *The Hunted*, the second play of the trilogy. After murdering his mother's lover on this man's ship, Orin starts smashing the sideboard in the cabin. Lavinia then "goes to the table and picks up Payrus's things." It is possible that O'Neill is thinking, at this time, of Pyrrhus who, after his return from the Trojan War, is murdered by Orestes. Pyrrhus was the husband of Hermione, daughter of Menelaus and Helen, Clytemnestra's sister, and—because of this intricate family relationship—could be considered Orestes' cousin by marriage. Although the dialogue in the opening scene of Act Four of *The Haunted* reappears in the final draft, there is no indication in the notes that Lavinia has undergone a "remarkable change" by reverting to her earlier prim appearance.

Fourth Draft

9/22/30	MBE—start fourth draft
10/15/30	MBE—finished 4th Draft
11/19/30	MBE—Read 4th draft—fairly well satisfied—but decide [to] go ahead and rewrite on line of new ideas for changes in working out of plot—may give added values.

Fifth Draft

11/20/30	MBE—5th d[raft]
2/2/31	MBE—Typing & 5th draft finished
2/7/31	MBE—notes on cutting and revision—don't like most of new stuff in 5th draft—will delete and revert in general to 4th draft plot development
2/20/31	MBE—Revised Typed Fifth Draft Finished
3/8/31	MBE—Read over Fifth Draft—notes and scheme for revision, cutting, rewriting

Sixth Draft

3/9/31	MBE—Start Sixth Draft
3/27/31	MBE—finished Sixth (Final) Draft!

Third Set of Notes

A third source provides additional revisions for the dialogue—a small red book inscribed: "To Carlotta—As a memento of Our Happiness in France— these 'Mourning Becomes Electra' notes in this book I used to keep in the Renault on our travels to catch those so infrequent brilliant hunches!" This material was probably written on March 8, 1931—while the couple was vacation-

ing at Las Palmas, Canary Islands—just before O'Neill started the sixth draft
of the play. One passage, later deleted, occurs at the end of Act Four of *The
Hunted* and reveals what is only implied in the published text—that Lavinia
loves her mother's lover. Lavinia tells Christine, who is despondent after Adam's
death, that she can live.

> Christine: I will not live to remember your words. Wasn't it because you
> loved Adam?
> Lavinia: No.
> Christine: I am your mother and I am going to die. I loved him too. (As
> V[innie]. hesitates) I am a woman.
> Lavinia: (Forces out) Yes.
> Christine: Then I understand and I forgive you. Do you understand and
> forgive me?
> Lavinia: Yes.
> Christine: (Indicates the portraits) But they won't forgive either of us.
> You will be punished too. You should have given me and him to
> the law. It was your love for Adam that made you take the law
> into your own hands. You wanted to deal with your discovery—
> me—yourself.
> Lavinia: No! It was my respect for father.
> Christine: It was your hate for me!
> Lavinia: Have it your own way then. Why shouldn't I hate you? Father
> loved you better than me. Orin does, so did Adam—and you
> have always loved yourself better than me, that is the worst.
> Christine: Then you are me—
> Lavinia: Yes! You fool! Yes! I am you! Now go and die.*

On April 7, 1931, O'Neill sent Lawrence Langner the sixth draft† of the

---

*Unlike the published play in which she merely states Orin would kill himself if he
weren't a coward, Lavinia pronounces a similar death sentence on her brother in this
collection of notes: "And now go in and do your last duty as a Mannon." Orin replies: "Aye! I see! Well there's no help for that now! And then maybe they'll let me
alone."

†Enclosed with this draft was a letter in which the author states: "As you will see,
no departures in technique are involved. 'Interlude' soliloquies and asides only got in
my way in these plays of intense passions and little cerebration. The mask idea has
also gone by the board. It simply refused to justify itself in the final accounting. It
confused and obscured instead of intensifying. All that is left of it is the masklike
quality of the Mannon faces in repose, an effect that can be gained by acting &
make-up. The dialogue is colloquial of today. The house, the period costumes, the
Civil War surface stuff, these are the masks for what is really a modern psychological
drama with no true connection with that period at all. I think I have caught enough
Greek sense of fate—a modern approximation to it, I mean—out of the Mannons
themselves to do without any Greek theatrical effects."

play for the Theater Guild production; and in August 1931—after returning to the United States from France—he corrected the two sets of galleys. Rehearsals began on September 7, 1931. The third set of notes contains a unique section written in September and October: O'Neill's reflections during the rehearsals for *Mourning Becomes Electra*:

A general pruning for the acting version is indicated after hearing plays—all that meets the eye as O.K. does not hit the ear so well—and my pet nightmare of having too little always leads me into having too much!—but cutting is always easy FOR ME—I even like to do it!

(New York—rehearsals 2nd week) Went over Bobby Jones' designs for sets with him—marvelous stuff, as all his work is, BEST DESIGNER finest in world today, beyond question—no one in Europe to touch him—and above all, one of the few truly imaginative, creative, poetic IDEALISTS of artists in the modern theatre.

(New York—rehearsals 2nd week) Moeller starts "walking" plays—he is right—too much minor movement in my stage directions for new concentrated schemes of BOBBY'S settings—keep more static—Phil M[oeller]. has keen eye for right stage movement—fine sensitive feeling for rhythm of action—accord with mood of scene—splendid director to work with—so damned glad I held out for him as director.

(New York—rehearsals 3rd week) Have rearranged Act Two of "Haunted"—no new stuff except what I have put back from first typed script—simply a re-shuffling—but gains tremendously in cumulative drive.

[°GIRL FROM VIRGINIA]
(1929)

A girl is born in Virginia of Dutch parentage 1835 (?)—falls in love with romantic young boy of French parentage—marries him against parents' wishes—he's rolling stone, ne'er-do-well—they elope—join pioneers—go to California—hard struggle—she has child after child.

°UNCHARTED SEA
(1929)

"A[ndré]. Lebon"*—whole action on a ship—the half-caste and the American Poet, the drunkard who flies from reality to the negative acceptance of the East—the struggle in the half-caste's soul between East and West that makes her seek escape in opium and hates herself for doing it—these two are pariahs on the ship, among the various nationalities of bourgeoisie who in spite of their difference in speech think so much alike—they exchange glances, the man and woman—gradually come to stare into each other's eyes—a strange intimacy springs up—they have their deck chairs moved nearer—finally they sit side by side—neither understands the other's language so they cannot speak—the corrupt in crowd solidifies into a moral mob against them—finally one night he goes, when drunk, after bawling out the bourgeois mob in the smoking room, to her cabin—the love scene between them in which not a word is spoken—in which they become spiritually and physically husband and wife.

The conflict of races on board, the trend of the races of the world struggle today, the essential characteristics, the awakening of the East to the West, the growing dominance of the American idea exemplified even in the playing of the children (Adele, etc.).

The wreck of the ship from hitting a reef—the panic on board bringing out the common fear of death—the man laughs at this—he and the woman are left behind—the extra boat—the island—regeneration and happiness—the ships go by and they never signal.

---

*On October 5, 1928 O'Neill and Carlotta Monterey sailed "from Marseilles for Hong Kong China" (W.D.) on the *S.S. André Lebon*. The couple returned to France the following January. The dramatist worked on the "André Lebon ship idea" on February 15, 16, and 17 but discarded it at this time, saying he was "discouraged" by his inability to develop the idea.

°THE HOUSE
(1929)

"The House"*—a play in which a home (N[ew]. E[ngland].) is principal— show all the rooms—the house the symbol of the past, of hereditary influences— but in a larger way the symbol of man's life, of the home he tries to make his own out of a strange alien solitude of Time and Space and Nature—that becomes a symbol of his life and its intermingling with other lives—sprung up on its hill— to youth, manhood, decline, slow death, decay, passing back into nature—also in a particular way, a symbol of America, of the fineness of its ideals manifested and choked by the saneless growth of its prosperity—a play of ghosts from Indians down with present owner only living character.

°LIFE OF AESCHYLUS
(1929)

Life of Aeschylus—creator of God whom the Gods slay because he is a man becoming a God—the Demeter family theme—his drunkenness.

O'Neill made notes for his "Life of Aeschylus idea" on May 7 and 8, 1929, inspired perhaps by the work he had done on May 6 on his "Greek Tragedy plot idea," which later emerges as *Mourning Becomes Electra*, based loosely on the Greek dramatist's *Oresteia*. Although O'Neill did not complete a scenario, his two sections on Aeschylus—Outline of Life and Notes on His Work—show how he planned to develop this play and the themes he intended to include.

O'Neill begins by noting that Aeschylus was born in 525 B.C. in Attica. "His father, Euphorion, was probably connected with the worship of Demeter—(a priest?—what was his mother?)—Aeschylus himself was, according to some authorities, initiated in the mysteries of this goddess." Demeter would, it appears, become a mother figure, replacing the unknown maternal personage. A line in

---

*The "house" described here is probably the same as the Greek "House with the masked dead" in the July 1931 idea and modeled on Ezra Chappell's Greek-styled mansions (see discussion in *Mourning Becomes Electra*), located on Huntington Street—on a hill—in New London. The life of the hero—who lives in a New England town—in the 1929 idea intermingles "with other lives—sprung up on its hills." In his letter to Lee Simonson—undated but written shortly after the dramatist had moved into Tao House in December 1937—O'Neill states: "Thanks for the New London items! What a town! Like Saturn and Revolution, it sure devours its own children." In spite of the rancor he felt about his family's rejection by snobbish New Londoners, the dramatist returns again and again to his native town, using it for the setting of his completed dramas and ideas for plays.

the notes indicates that O'Neill would use here, as in other plays, the theme of the son's betrayal of the mother figure: Aeschylus went to Sicily and into veritable exile "because (when drunk?) he divulged the mysteries of Demeter," the earth goddess of agriculture, fertility, and marriage. The earth mothers in many of O'Neill's plays—from Cybel in *The Great God Brown* to Josie in *A Moon for the Misbegotten*—attempt to share these ancient mystery rites of purification with the son figure, who is haunted with guilt for some kind of betrayal of his mother.

In his idea for the "Play of Aeschylus," O'Neill notes that he plans to use the incestuous "Demeter family theme." Demeter is the daughter of Cronos—known as Saturn to the Romans—who devours all of his sons except Zeus to retain his position as Supreme God but later vomits them out. According to legend, Persephone, daughter of Zeus and his sister Demeter, is abducted by her father's brother, Hades, and made goddess of his underworld kingdom. During the mother's search for the daughter, the earth becomes barren and desolate. Demeter's travels to Eleusis lead her followers to honor her through the Eleusinian mysteries. Persephone is eventually allowed to go back to earth for four months each year, thus perpetuating the annual vegetation cycle. Demeter's Roman counterpart is Ceres, who is associated with rites for the dead as well as fertility. O'Neill uses the cyclical theme of death and resurrection of Demeter's male counterpart—Dionysus—in *The Great God Brown*. In view of his reference to Aeschylus as a "man becoming a god," O'Neill would undoubtedly have incorporated this myth in his play on the Greek dramatist who, after being slain by jealous gods, achieves a kind of immortality.

O'Neill lists all the significant events in the life of Aeschylus in the outline: the many times he appeared "as a competitor for the prize of tragedy," including his defeat in 468 B.C. when Sophocles won with the *Triptolemus* and his victory in 458 B.C. with the *Oresteia*; his rivalry with the avaricious Simonides; his return to Sicily, supposedly because of his "mortification at a defeat by Sophocles." O'Neill rejects this explanation and states Aeschylus left Athens the second time "because the alarm caused to women and children by the chorus of Furies had raised bad feeling against him." The American dramatist adds: "he was disheartened by the failure of his attempt to support the power of the Areopagus by his 'Eumenides' and uneasy at the growing power of the democracy, whose leaders must have regarded him with ill will." The last section of the outline describes the death of Aeschylus at Gela in Sicily at the age of sixty-nine: "Legend of his death that an eagle, mistaking the poet's bald head for a stone, dropped a tortoise on it to break the shell—the bird of Jove—it was held to fulfill an oracle by [which] he was to die by a blow from heaven."

The Greek playwright's many contributions to drama are discussed in the section labeled "Notes on His Work": introducing a second character and, possibly, "painted scenes in a rude form"; making dialogue more important than the chorus; improving masks and costumes generally—"it is said that he in some degree imitated the splendid dress of the hierophant in the Eleusinian mysteries." The following significant passages in the notes are quoted in their entirety:

* * *

Characteristics of Aeschylus' plays sublimity and grandeur of feeling and expression with less of the pathos we find in Sophocles and Euripides. "Prometheus" is his most pathetic play but we are made to feel Prometheus is a deity and removed above human pity. He brings before us more forcibly and more terribly than the other tragedians the unseen powers working out the doctrines of retributive justice and the mysteries of laws which control even the gods themselves. Not only are his heroes no men of common life but behind all their actions and sufferings we are made to feel the supernatural powers working out the punishment of presumption.

He so changed the system of the tragic stage that he has more claim than anyone else to be regarded as the founder (Father) of Tragedy.

Diction united to subject—Aeschylus is above all poets magniloquent, sometimes to a degree that in a lesser man would be turgid, abounding in sonorous words and daring metaphors.

It has been suggested, not without reason, that the apparent influence of the philosophy of Pythagoras may have been due to the poet's prolonged stay in Sicily.

O'Neill started a third section of notes for this idea, but only two lines appear on an otherwise blank piece of paper: "Play about Aeschylus" and "Philosophy of Pythagoras (influence)."*

[°TRAGEDY OF MAN]
(1930)

Farce—tragedy of man (or woman) whose life is made ridiculous and miserable by his obsession with little fears, worries, calamity—complex while when it comes to the real big fears he remains indifferent, cool and nerveless.

---

*O'Neill himself was influenced by one Pythagorean doctrine: the theory that numbers constituted the essence of life, that all relationships could be expressed numerically. Using *The Kabala of Numbers—A Handbook of Interpretation* by Sepharial, he found the phonetic value of the letters of his name to be "3," which, as he notes, signifies "Jupiter—expansion, increase, riches, success." (He did not have to determine the unit value of his middle name, Gladstone; William Ewart Gladstone's name is given as an example in the book.) One notation indicates that the dramatist was born before noon on October 16. The true solar date is twelve hours behind the secular date, and he uses October 15 to work out various systems in one chapter, "The Kabalism of Cycles."

[°THE MOTHER GOD DEATH]
(1930)

The hymn of Life, the hymn of Death—the Mother God Death—in dithy-
rambic style—a religious play with chants of the Oneness of Life and Death—of
Death the real and life the changing incarnation—of the longing for peace of
Man—of the psychic loss of love and woman worship—ending with a tremendous
ceremonial scene of the adoration of Death by vast crowds—a play of masks.

[°CHILDREN'S PLAY]
(1930)

Children's play (child contrasted with adult—leading adult)
The sensation we so often experience in our dealings with children, the feeling that they know something we do not know or no longer know, some magic
or divine marvel wherein perhaps may lie the key to our whole existence—children see the most discrepant things as most credible—the most impossible as
most certain—more faith in fairy tale than in sober narrative—regard all phenomena that break away from the course of natural causality as higher and
more real—miracle is reality—natural phenomena but reflection of higher, clearer
world—isn't he led by deeper, of more obscure, knowledge—does not come nearer
to the root of the mystery than we?

[°PLAY OF PSYCHO-THERAPEUTIST]
(1930)

Play of the psycho-therapeutist to whom a creative artist—genius or of great
talent—man or woman comes in torture and half-pleads, half-challenges to have
his devils cast out—the haunting ghosts of his past. He is about to give up, about
to commit suicide. The play is of how the doctor fights with his demons and him
until finally the artist transfers them one by one to him, as he is freed he enslaves
the doctor with his horrible bitterness, his blasphemies against life, his sins of
lust and cruelty. It breaks the doctor. And the final scene is where the artist has
mercy on the doctor and kills him to free him (as he had wished to do with himself) and all his ghosts come back, the ghost of the doctor added. And the artist
goes to give himself up for murder, to let the State cure him of his life and his
ghosts.

[°OLD MOTHER AND SON]
(1931)

Play of old mother and son and fair Swede companion (Amer[ican]. Hosp[ital].)—change to wife—the slow killing by suggestion (unconscious)—the irony of his self-righteous, naive innocence and real grief after the murder is done.

Perhaps a duality play with life-size marionette for subconscious self.*

°THE CALMS OF CAPRICORN
(1931)

Play whole action of which takes place on clipper ship bound round the horn and winds up in Shanghai Brown's boarding house in Frisco—what year best (?)—look up data on Shanghai Brown, if any.

O'Neill records the first idea for a clipper ship play on June 20, 1931, in the Work Diary.† In 1932—on March 20, May 14, and October 6 and 13—he interrupts work on *Days Without End* to make notes for this sea play, finding the "right title" for it, "The Calms of Capricorn," on March 8, 1933. He spends the month of December 1934 working alternately on the "Calms of Capricorn series 4 or 5 plays" and the "Career of Bessie Bolan." The word "cycle" first occurs on January 1, 1935: "Calms of Capricorn cycle (notes) (grand idea for this Opus Magnus if can ever do it—wonderful characters!)."

As originally conceived, the Cycle comprises four plays, depicting the interconnected—but separate—adult lives and careers of four brothers. The author makes a momentous decision on January 27, 1935, to assign a more prominent role to the brothers' parents: "story of Harford and Sara before 1st play opens—this may develop into additional 1st play, making five in all." The next day he outlines the "spiritual under-theme of Cycle" and spends January 30 "reading—drawing plans for scenes of the 1st—clipper ship—play." The Opus Magnus is given its first name on February 3: " 'A Touch of the Poet' Cycle (get this title for Cycle & like it—'Calms of Capricorn' having always been title for particular 1st play—clipper ship. Also decide new first play of Sara-Harford—marriage—parents, etc." At one stroke O'Neill has both the title and the germ of the

---

*Two titles, dated 1931, follow this idea but are not developed: "Dream hunch—Piers the Ploughman" and "Song of Roland."

†All quotations—unless indicated otherwise—in this discussion of the development of O'Neill's Cycle, "A Tale of Possessors, Self-Dispossessed," are from the Work Diary.

story for the only surviving Cycle play that he labels "finished"—*A Touch of the Poet*, which at this time is named "The Hair of the Dog." On February 25 he makes an outline and notes for its sequel, "Oh, Sour-apple Tree," later entitled *More Stately Mansions*. While writing the scenario for this sequel on March 9, O'Neill notes: "seems to be working out as built around Abigail [Deborah Harford, Sara's mother-in-law], new conception of her character." A new tentative title is given to the Cycle on April 25—"Threnody For Possessors Dispossessed," and notes are made on May 3 for the scenario for "The Calms of Capricorn," now the third play—"measurements, etc., plans for ship scenes." He uses two books to determine the exact measurements of the clippers for his settings: *Some Famous Sailing Ships and Their Builder Donald McKay* and *The Clipper Ship Era*. One page of his computations contains three sets of initials: "F.C.," "L.," and "J.B."—with numbers, such as "235 o.all," after them. The initials refer to famous ships built in Boston by McKay. His *Flying Cloud*, launched on April 15, 1851, set a new record—89 days—in a trip around Cape Horn to California. The dimensions of this ship correspond to the numbers written after the "F.C." notation: "Her length on the keel is 208 feet, on deck, 225, and over all from the knight heads to the taffrail, 235."* The other two ships cited in the notes are the *Lightning*, launched on January 3, 1854, and the *James Baines*, launched on July 25, 1854; both were purchased by James Baines and Company of Liverpool. *The Clipper Ship Era* contains valuable information about the types of men who formed the crews of these ships—splendid Scandinavian sailormen who could do any kind of work at sea "and took pride in doing it well" and " 'Liverpool Irishmen'—a species of wild men, strong, coarse-built, thick set . . . wallowing in the slush of depravity."†

Realizing the need for continuity in the Cycle plays, O'Neill inserts a passage in *More Stately Mansions*, in which Simon Harford envisions the future of his four young sons: "We want them trained to live with reality so when the time comes they will be capable of serving our Company—Ethan as manager of our marine division, Wolfe to direct the banking branch which we will own before long, Jonathan as our railroad executive, and Honey our representative in poli-

---

*Richard McKay, *Some Famous Sailing Ships and Their Builder Donald McKay* (New York, 1931), p. 142. O'Neill probably conceived his clipper ship idea while writing *Mourning Becomes Electra* after he had changed the setting for Act Four of *The Hunted* to Adam Brant's ship, the "Flying Trades," owned by Clark and Dawson. Among the popular chanties McKay lists is "Shenandoah," which is sung not only by Seth but also by the chanteyman just before Brant is murdered on his ship moored in East Boston. O'Neill finished *Mourning Becomes Electra* on March 27, 1931, and records the "clipper ship idea" three months later.

†Arthur H. Clark, *The Clipper Ship Era* (Riverside, Connecticut, 1910), pp. 120–121.

tics." "The Calms of Capricorn," which—according to the original idea—takes place on a clipper ship and in San Francisco, opens in 1857 and shows Sara Harford and her four sons leaving the farm she had salvaged when the family business went bankrupt.* Ethan, born in 1828 and the eldest son of Sara and Simon Harford, is the central character in this original third Cycle play. O'Neill devotes the entire month of May 1935 to it, making notes on the "voyages, record, etc." and writing a scenario for Act One and the two scenes of Act Two and an outline of the three scenes in Act Three and four scenes of Act Four. Of "The Earth Is the Limit," the fourth play—set in the 1860s and started on June 16, he remarks on June 30: "Finish Outline—decide not to write scenario of this one in book now but take up Outlines of remaining plays." In this work Wolfe, born in 1829, the aristocratic second Harford son, becomes a successful banker. Honey, who is three and a half years younger than Wolfe, is the main character in the fifth play, "Nothing Is Lost But Honor," which O'Neill outlines from July 2 to 28. Three days later he makes notes for the sixth play, "The Man on Iron Horseback," completing the outline on August 27. Notes suggest that O'Neill got the title for this play and the model—railroad magnate Jay Gould—for its hero, Jonathan, the third Harford son, born in 1831, from *The Robber Barons*,† on of the many books he used to research nineteenth century American history.

---

*Sara takes her sons and husband, who has amnesia, to the log cabin where the couple had first met. This "ten feet by fifteen" cabin, with its "garden near it—beans, potatoes, corn, peas & turnips," is an exact replica of Thoreau's hut at Walden, described in *The Flowering of New England 1815–1865* by Van Wyck Brooks (New York, 1936): "ten by fifteen . . . a door facing the cove . . . a bean-field close by, with a patch of potatoes, corn, peas, and turnips" (p. 359). O'Neill's notes from this book includes a reference to a "China summer house," p. 21, which is used later to depict Deborah Harford's summer house "with arched door, painted a Chinese lacquer red." Another passage seems to apply to Deborah. Brooks compares the women who "peered from behind the curtains" to "pixilated creatures . . . half dead and buried in their houses, or buried in the morbid family pride that flourishes where life runs low." Sara and Simon's early home in *More Stately Mansions* is in "a textile-mill town about forty miles from the city" [of Boston]. The references to Lowell, Massachusetts in O'Neill's notes suggest it is the site of Simon's five mills. He discusses his research for the Cycle in a 1935 letter to Leon Mirlas: "As you can imagine it involves a tremendous amount of reading and note-taking—for even if I find it beside my point to use much historical fact background, still I wish to live in the time of each play when writing it."

†Matthew Josephson, *The Robber Barons—The Great American Capitalists 1861–1901* (New York, 1934). Josephson discusses what "the coming of the Iron Horse meant" to those living in California (p. 81). O'Neill apparently got the first title for *More Stately Mansions*—"Oh, Sour-apple Tree"—from this book. In 1884 Gould, who had gained control of telegraph lines, was accused of holding back the presidential election returns which passed over his New York wires. A mad crowd "surged

One page of O'Neill's notes, taken directly from various sections of *The Robber Barons*, contains biographical data on Gould, whose father—like Jonathan's—came from old "Yankee stock." Gould is described as "undersized," a term O'Neill applies to Jonathan. Included in the notes is the information that Gould, as a schoolboy, wrote a composition, "Honesty Is the Best Policy"; yet he later cheated his backers in an attempt to corner the leather market. At the age of twenty-five, he "evolved a technique as a railroad operator, a technique of seizure and 'conversion' which was as magical as that of the alchemist who turned dross into gold" (p. 64). Determined to acquire a transcontinental line, this "Mephistopheles of Wall Street" began buying and consolidating railroads, including the unfinished Texas & Pacific line, which was to have a right of way to the sea. He found his way barred by Collis Huntington, leader of a ring known as the Pacific Associates, which controlled 85 per cent of California's railroads and the only two passes across the Colorado River canyon. A quotation O'Neill takes from *The Robber Barons* suggests Huntington and his partners were destined to play a role in "The Man on Iron Horseback": "As early as '65, with their main line almost completed, the group secretly acquired the charter of the Southern Pacific—books old holding company burned '68—offices moved [from] S[an]. Fran[cisco]. to Sacramento—new holding company set up to conduct business territory—*main interests are transferred to new company*" (p. 218).

O'Neill's original plan was to begin the action of "The Man on Iron Horseback" in 1876 in New York City in the midst of this 1874–1878 railroad war and close it in 1893, just before the three-year depression in which 156 lines collapsed. One man who profited from the ensuing panic was Pierpont Morgan, who had invited leading railroad barons—including Gould—to a conference in 1889—ostensibly to force them to comply with the Interstate Commerce Act. "The representatives of capital intended to show the railroad men the whip. They intended to convey to them . . . that further misbehavior would be punished by cutting off supplies" (p. 309). Within the next decade, Morgan, the autocratic banker and flamboyant sportsman and womanizer, would gain control "in 12 systems—some 55,555 miles of track, over 3,000,000,000 in capital" (p. 313). Wolfe Harford, the banker and central character of "The Earth Is the Limit," is probably based—in part—on Morgan who, like Deborah Harford, "remains a Bourbon to the end" (p. 451).

According to O'Neill's plan for the Cycle, Wolfe—and the other two Harford brothers—would reappear in "The Man on Iron Horseback." The author describes the Cycle of seven plays as

> portraying the history of the interrelationships of a family over a period of approximately a century. The first play begins in 1829, the last ends in

---

before the massive Western Union Building, singing 'Hang Jay Gould to a sour-apple tree!'" (p. 212). All further references to this book are from this edition and are followed by an arabic numeral to indicate the page.

1932. Five generations of this family appear in the cycle. . . . Each play will be, as far as it is possible, complete in itself while at the same time an indispensable link in the whole. . . . Each play will be concentrated around the final fate of one member of the family but will also carry on the story of the family as a whole.*

Honey Harford, the politician—who as a boy had been his bullying brother Jonathan's "admiring satellite"—would probably be used by this Gould-like character to obtain railroad subsidies in Washington. Huntington's letter of December 17, 1877 states:

"Jay Gould went to Washington about two weeks since, and I know, saw Mitchell, Senator from Oregon. Since which time money has been used very freely in Washington. . . . Gould has large amounts of cash and he pays it without stint to carry his points."

A few months later, May 3, 1878, Huntington writes privately that the Gould faction "offered one member of Congress $1,000 cash down, $5,000 when the bill was passed, and $10,000 of the bonds." . . . This curious conflict . . . was soon amicably settled between the two masterful financiers who had so many points in common, and who were subject to common dangers from without. . . . While pretending before Congress and all the world to be hurling defiance at each other forever, the two were agreeing that Huntington's Southern Pacific system should become Gould's railroad link with the sea.†

O'Neill starts the Cycle's final drama, "Twilight of Possessors Self-Dispossessed"—later called "Hair of the Dog"—on August 29, 1935 and writes on September 2: "As this 7th play follows in main plot-outline the old 'Bessie Bowen' theme, nothing further needed on its outline now beyond the revision notes I've done in past week." Bessie Bowen is called Bessie Wilks in the 1927 outline for "It Cannot Be Mad?," which is set—in its opening scene—in Indiana in 1894. At the beginning of the play, the twelve-year-old Bessie is sent to an orphan asylum by Ed Wilkes and his sister Mame, whose brother is apparently the child's father. After she leaves the asylum, Bessie marries Howard Camp and has four children and becomes an executive at Camp Motor. Places listed for the scenes of the play include: a Motordrome, the temple of Midas in Detroit, a Paris studio, a cult colony in California, and Saigon. When O'Neill revised this work for the Cycle—which depicts "five generations of a family" at this time—he makes Bessie the daughter of Honey Harford.

On September 7, 1935 O'Neill expands the original design of the Cycle to include an eighth work: "Playing around with idea new first play to precede 'Hair

---

*Letter to Robert Sisk, July 3, 1935.
†Josephson, p. 204.

Of The Dog' [later *A Touch of the Poet*], to go back to 1806 and show Abigail [Deborah Harford] as girl—marriage to Henry H.—and their house & parents— Henry's father [Evan] big character—title, 'Greed Of The Meek.' " Although the author says on September 16 that he is trying to put this play, which starts "at Revolution" out of his mind—"God knows don't want extra play tacked on to this damned trilogy unless it absolutely must be written"—he spends the remainder of the month making notes, an outline, and set drawings for it. He devotes the rest of the year and the first three months of 1936 to the play he finally entitles *A Touch of the Poet* on April 10, changing at that time the name of the eighth work to "Hair Of The Dog" and that of the Cycle to "A Legend Of Possessors Self-Dispossessed." He then continues the four-act "Greed Of The Meek," writing "a new outline of play with 3 Sister emphasis," but finds he cannot "solve problem of solution Abi[gail].-Andrew." On June 7 he "decides a 9th play may be necessary, preceeding 'Of the Meek' Greed—story on Andrew, Sisters, Kate from farm to French Revolution—write a plan of this." The following day he entitles this first work of what now becomes a nine play Cycle "Give Me Death" and completes the four-act outline that month. He then works alternately on *A Touch of the Poet* and "Greed Of The Meek," stating of the latter on September 17, 1936: "notes, last of IV & play—feel very depressed don't like end & this 1st draft is as long as 'Strange I[nterlude].' " The next day he decides to "throw away this damned play for time being & call it finished, pending revision and condensation."

Feeling ill and depressed, O'Neill left his home at Sea Island, Georgia, in October and went with his wife to California, where they would remain until October 1945. On December 29 he underwent surgery for appendicitis at Merritt Hospital in Oakland, California. His health problems were more serious than he had thought, and he remained hospitalized until the end of February 1937 and was ordered to take a long rest. He returns to the Cycle on June 20, working on the first four plays until July 25, when he made "notes for 5th, 6th, 7th, 8th plays." Of the ninth work, he says the next day: "will require extra generation in new scheme—'Honey' to live till end?" Unless the author changed this character's age, Honey Harford would be nearly a hundred in 1932 at the end of the Cycle.

On August 9, 1937, O'Neill writes: "definitely decide change title 'Greed Of The Meek' to new 1st play [formerly "Give Me Death"]—'Touch Of The Poet' to 3rd play—'Hair Of The Dog' to last (9th) play—'Lament for Possessors Self-Dispossessed' to whole Cycle." He spends the remaining months of 1937 working on "Greed Of The Meek," noting on November 29: "am stuck—don't like scenes 2 & 3 [Act Three] on ship" and on December 23: "Look over first draft, 1st Play —is longer than 'Strange I[nterlude].'—don't want this—but don't see how it can be drastically cut without ruining it—trouble is want to get too much in these plays for single length."

The dramatist sets aside the Cycle in early 1938 to develop the "Robespierre play" idea; during this period the "neuritis" in his arm makes writing "too painful." On March 25 he turns once again to "Greed of the Meek," finding it still too long—"and too psychologically involved in spots—feel I had better postpone rewriting 1st 2 plays until I've finished all others easier do then because of repeated themes first plays and last which complete circle." The following day he takes up *More Stately Mansions*, working on it continuously until January 20, 1939. The next two days he writes general notes "on all 9 plays, interrelationship." On January 23 he returns to *A Touch of the Poet* and—except for one day, January 29, when he checks on "dates, ages of characters, etc." for all of the plays—works on it until a third draft is completed on May 19. He concludes this particular period devoted to the Cycle as he began it—with "The Calms of Capricorn," now its fifth play, writing its prologue from May 23 to June 3. Still dissatisfied with it, he says on June 5: "Decide what I've done on 5th play is n[o]. g[ood]., so tear it up. Feel fed up and stale on Cycle after 4½ years of not thinking of any other work—will do me good lay on shelf and forget it for a while—do a play which has nothing to do with it."

On June 6, 1939 O'Neill records the first ideas for *The Iceman Cometh* and *Long Day's Journey into Night*; he takes up the Cycle briefly after completing the former on January 3, 1940, but does not continue working on it until he completes the second draft of the latter autobiographical drama on October 16. On October 20 he is convinced that the first two Cycle plays are "too complicated—tried to get too much into them, too many interwoven themes & motives, psychological & spiritual." The next day he asks himself if he should abandon these plays and "go back old 7 play Cycle, starting with what is now 3rd play—material too valuable for that." His entry the following day reads: "Having slept on it, awake with idea for four plays to take place of 1st & 2nd, expanding Cycle to eleven!—1st to go back to 1755 when the Three Sisters were young girls." On October 23 he decides to "go ahead & make notes & outlines for the four plays of new idea which would replace 1st & 2nd plays—very interested, as it is worth the time & trouble." During the next month he makes notes for these four "new" plays and for rewriting *A Touch of the Poet* and *More Stately Mansions* "into new scheme by carrying on the Three Sisters into these plays."

The dramatist indicates he worked only thirteen days in 1941 on Cycle plays: "The Calms of Capricorn," *More Stately Mansions*, and *A Touch of the Poet*. Taking up the latter on February 16, 1942, he remarks: "think may rewrite this to get at least one play of Cycle definitely & finally finished." He works on this play for 112 days in the next months and says on November 15, 1942: "Finish new version 'A Touch of the Poet' (5th play in 11 Cycle)—have made it much better play, both as itself & as part of Cycle—a triumph, I feel, considering sickness & war strain—still has minor faults—needs some cutting and condensing, but that can wait a while." His last comment on the Cycle, dated February 21, 1943, reads: "tore up the part of Act One, 'The Life Of Bessie Bowen,' I had written—n[o]. g[ood].—and this play is basis for last play of Cycle now (with many changes)." On this day he also destroyed the completed first longhand drafts of the Cycle's first two plays: "The Greed of the Meek" and "And Give Me Death." Sixteen years had elapsed between the time he recorded his first idea in 1927 for the Bessie Bowen play, "It Cannot Be Mad?," and this date of destruction; twelve years since he entered his initial idea in the notebook for "The Calms of Capricorn" in 1931. O'Neill's despair, the result of many factors—the war, ill health, the materialism of his fellow man, is reflected in his letter of July 17, 1940, to Langner: "The Cycle is on the shelf, and God knows if I can ever take it up again because I cannot foresee any future in this country or anywhere else to which it could spiritually belong."

On two occasions—in 1943 and in 1953—O'Neill destroyed unfinished Cycle plays*; only *A Touch of the Poet* and a typescript of *More Stately Mansions* were spared. In the prefatory note for the published version of the latter play, Donald Gallup, curator of the O'Neill Collection at Yale's Beinecke Library, writes:

> O'Neill was sufficiently satisfied with the play for the typescript to escape destruction when both longhand drafts were burned along with the first two Cycle plays in February 1943. He did, however, take the precaution of writing on a leaf laid into the typescript: "Unfinished Work. This script to be destroyed in case of my death! Eugene O'Neill."†

He concludes his preface by stating: "*More Stately Mansions* provides, even in its incompletely revised state, a better indication than does *A Touch of the Poet* of what he had intended in the Cycle."

---

*In a letter to Dale Fern dated March 4, 1954, written when the dramatist's widow was still living at the Hotel Shelton in Boston, Carlotta O'Neill states: "One of the most ghastly half-hours in my life was when (about a year ago, in this very room) I helped the Master destroy 4 plays out of the 'Cycle'—I thought I would die—& he looked as if he had!"

†*More Stately Mansions*, edited by Donald Gallup (New Haven, 1964), p. vii. The typescript was "inadvertently included" in material O'Neill and his wife sent to Yale in 1951. After her husband's death, Carlotta O'Neill gave Yale University permission to publish a revised version of *More Stately Mansions*.

3 • Ideas: 1931-1938 Notebooks

°RABELAIS PLAY
[1931]°

Gargantuan pantomime prologue with gigantic marionettes (?)

Main body of play the adventures of Panurge and his quest about marriage—

Use rum idea here—Rabelais announcer in promptor's box—mingles with audience too (?) King in stage box—play starts with Rabelais' dedication to him—

Introduce Dance of Death (?)

Rabelais in jester's costume under monk's robes—prologue outside of striped tents (French village fete music—R[abelais]. as barker introduces and describes characters (Grandgousier & wife, Gargantua, etc.) of pantomime who then pass behind tent (masked marionettes).

Then scene shifts to interior tent where pantomime is done (G's life)— pantomime brings action up to Panurge's day, real life contemporary with Rabelais, in which he partakes as the ego of Panurge.

°*LAZARUS*-COMBINATION TALKY
[1931]†

Scheme—Production of Lazarus as combination talky

Cut out double-sized mask chorus—incorporate material in chant of crowd.

Crowd masks with mouths that can open—fixed on flats painted with bodies (?)—or on dressed up wooden dummies fixed to platform, removable in sections.

Crowd chants to be done by trained choral singers in talky studio (hidden behind dummies) and sound recorded in talky, taking exactly same part as if visible, but sound seeming to proceed from mask mouths.

All roles except Laz[arus]. to be in talky—unreal real screen figures—Lazarus remains outside talky—(speaks lines outside on cue & gives cue—or speeches are recorded and then cut? Question of talky mechanics here).

Screen always ends at center. Lazarus to right of it.

°Idea is undated in the notebook but is entered in the Work Diary on July 6, 1931: "Dramatization of Rabelais (notes)." As the dates in the two notebooks of ideas for 1931–1938 overlap, material contained in them is combined and presented chronologically. The chronological order imposed here for ideas that are not dated in the notebooks nor cited in the Work Diary is reasonably accurate as O'Neill seems to have recorded them in a systematic way—unlike entries in the two early notebooks.

†Idea is undated but appears in the notebook immediately after "Rabelais play."

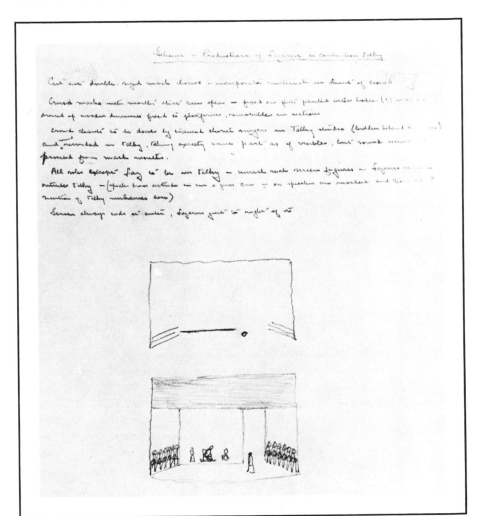

°HOUSE WITH THE MASKED DEAD
(July 1931) *

Man (& wife ?) comes in house (Greek)—auto broken down—masked family—silence—man & wife only speaking parts—gradually the tragedy that has happened in this house long ago—a tragedy of the old people which is causing a tragedy among the young is revealed (Pantomime—music?). The man & his wife take sides and become involved.

Two very old people (80 to 90) still alive in house—husband & wife or mistress—wanting to die before criminal secret in past is revealed—eternal conflict and mental plottings and torturings between them in which the masked dead take part—climax reacting of the different scenes the old drama might have taken "if"—always ending in impasse.

[°MAN AND HIS SOUL]
[1931]†

Man and his Soul—Soul, masked, feminine, beautiful—his life-long struggle is to possess her.

She is spiritual aspiration, pride, love in spiritual sense—at the same time she is humility, self-sacrifice, tender humanity and pity, goodness—the ideal.

He is mind, ambition, egotism, arrogance, worldly desire for self-eminence, craving for possession material, determination to succeed, iron will—at same time he is weakness, weariness, a turning back, a longing to fly from reality, a great fear of life and death, a fear of love which causes defiant reaction, a continual craving for possession [of] women in flesh, power over them, a false desperate lust for bodies.

---

*This idea is dated July 17, 1931, in the Work Diary: "Idea play—house-with-the-masked-dead and two living intruding strangers—notes." The Greek house mentioned here—like that in the 1929 idea, "The House"—would probably be a replica of Ezra Chappell's Greek-styled mansions on Huntington Street in New London. It is possible that this work would be a thinly veiled version of the autobiographical *Long Day's Journey into Night*; in 1931 James Tyrone would have been eighty-four; his wife seventy-three. A Work Diary entry for July 1, 1931, reveals that O'Neill was in New London shortly before he recorded this idea: "revisit Pequot Ave. [where the O'Neill family home is located] old time haunts." The true cause of the Tyrone-O'Neills' tragedy would apparently be disguised here as a "criminal secret in past" as it was in the semi-autobiographical "The Guilty One" in 1924.
†Undated but perhaps written at the same time O'Neill conceived his introspective "House-with-the-masked-dead" idea.

He scorns love, notorious for many affairs but has never married—pretends [to] scorn marriage—his one love is for Soul.

Noted as bachelor, he lives with Soul, whom no one sees—lives in continual strife, love and hatred—always his Soul loves him but refuses [to] give herself to him until he becomes worthy—until he purifies himself—always she goads him on toward the heights.

It is only at the moment of death that he finally possesses her.

She always demands that he give up the world for her—that he ruin (save) himself as the price of her love.

°ROMANTICIST
[1931]*

An exulting play of the man, romantic even to the point of mystic dreaming, a charming poseur with a flair for the romantic dramatic moment—always demanding and achieving from life more than itself—turning all commonplaceness into verve and color—all cynicism into belief.

A modern Pier Piper whom everyone follows—

A man who insists always on the beauty of things, the significance of the poetic interpretation of the thing, who makes sorrow beautiful so that the grieving enjoy their grief.

°GNOSTICISM   (Notes)
[1931]†

"Gnosis"—among majority of followers was understood not as meaning knowledge or understanding in our sense of the word but as "revelation"—secret and mysterious knowledge, not accessible to the uninitiate, not to be proved or propagated, to be believed in and guarded as secret, laid down in wonderful mystic writings.

Ultimate object individual salvation, assurance of fortunate destiny for the soul after death.

Central object of worship redeemer—deity who has already trodden the difficult way the faithful have to follow.

Holy rites and formulas—initiation, consecration—sacraments—baptism by water, by fire, by the spirit, for protection against demons, anointing with oil,

---

*This undated idea appears immediately after "Man and His Soul" in the notebook.
†The notes for "gnosticism" are undated but immediately precede the "Symphony Form" idea.

sealing and stigmatizing, piercing the ears, leading into the bridal chamber, partaking of holy food and drink.

Soul, on leaving body, finds path to highest heaven opposed by deities and demons of lower realms of heaven—only when in possession of names of these demons and can repeat right formula, or is prepared with right symbol, can find way unhindered to heavenly home.

Later, simplified, supreme secret taught in single name or formula—(name "Caulacan" among Basilideans).

Even redeemer-god when he descended to earth, to rise from it again, availed himself of these on descent and ascent.

Basis Gnostic religion Oriental dualism—two worlds in sharp contrast, good and evil, divine world and material, light and darkness.

Gnostic system makes great use of idea of fall of the Deity himself into world of matter—by this matter, previously inscrutable, is assimilated into life and activity and then arise the powers, both partly and wholly hostile who hold sway over this world.

Such figures of fallen divinity are those of Sophia (i.e. Ahamoth) and the Primal Man.

°SYMPHONY FORM PLAY
(August 1931) *

A play form—return of my old idea of using structure of symphony or sonata—justification [of] my unconscious use of musical structure in nearly all of my plays—impulsion and chief interest always an attempt to do what music does (to express an essentially poetic viewpoint of life) using rhythm of recurrent themes—is my, at times, blunderingly vague groping and missing caused by just the very fact that my use of musical structure *is* unconscious and ignorant of its own laws?—feeling of great need now for fixed severe clearly apprehended form within which to create, now that I have finished breaking all realistic rules for modern drama—my adoption of archaic dramatic modes from Greek, Elizabethan—(or ultra-modern Expressionistic or Strindbergian modes)—not the

---

*O'Neill makes no entry for this idea in the Work Diary in August 1931. He does, however, refer to it on other dates:

7/18/31 Symphony Form idea (notes)

11/28–29/31 Symphony structure for plays idea (reading)

2/19/40 Idea orchestral technique for a play—playwright as leader symphony, characters, chorus an orchestra (notes)

2/21/40 Orchestral technique for a play (notes—interesting, if think of play to fit but will do no more about it now).

answer because superficial does not strike at main deep-rooted impulse of creative ego toward self-expression in musical structure rhythm—when I attain clear knowledge and consciousness of such a structure as skeleton for all work will not my plays have real bone to them as well as flesh—up to now is not chief fault in plays that they lack bone in comparison to their superabundant flesh and meat— that their rickety bones are too frequently braced by splints carpentered in the dramatic technique surgery?

(Study authoritative books on structure of symphony, sonata, etc. and let's see!)

A play in which each main character definitely represents a theme—main exponent of—(?)

°PHILIP II-DON JUAN OF AUSTRIA PLAY*
(1931)

In his letter of January 8, 1931, to Lawrence Langner, O'Neill describes a motor trip taken the previous November, remarking: "I liked Spain immensely— by far the most interesting country in Europe I have seen." He was particularly impressed when, on November 13, he visited Escorial, where the mutilated body of Don Juan of Austria had been interred on May 24, 1579—by order of his brother King Philip II of Spain—in a sepulchral chamber adjacent to that of their father Charles V. On October 30, 1931, O'Neill began an outline for a historical drama based on these personages: "Idea for Philip II-Don Juan of Austria play—last scene clear" (W.D.). The following January he spent eight days reading and taking notes from Sir William Stirling-Maxwell's *Don John of Austria or Passages from the History of the Sixteenth Century 1547–1578*. George W. Cox states in his preface for this book that Stirling-Maxwell was perhaps inspired while writing *The Cloister Life of Charles V* to tell "the story of the high-spirited and shortlived Prince whose brief career is associated with the first serious check given to the power of the Ottoman Turk and with events which mark the turning point in the history of the Reformation throughout northern Europe." Although he cites numerous passages from Stirling-Maxwell's two-volume work describing Juan's naval exploits, O'Neill stresses a familial—rather than a military—conflict in his notes. The early titles for this play—"Philip-Juan" and "Juan and Philip" suggest its dual emphasis on Charles V's ill-fated illegitimate son and his older brother, the Prince Regent.

The play opens "just before Charles' retirement—preliminary scene making this clear (between monks (?) courtiers (?)—then Charles and Philip—Charles'

---

*To maintain chronological order, discussion of the projected play appears here although the first idea for it is not included in any of the notebooks.

grave admonitions about governing the world gravely received." Philip complains bitterly about "his half-brother's amorous antics—but lets envy show through—Charles notices this—Philip indignantly denies." In order to heighten the dramatic conflict between the brothers, O'Neill portrays Juan as being older than he actually is; he is only twelve (Philip is thirty-two) in 1557, the year Charles retired to the monastery at Yuste. He goes there to atone for his past sins—primarily his affair with Barbara Blomberg, Juan's mother. Of a noble family, she had "played and sung for Charles at Ratisbon to divert melancholy he felt after death of his Empress Isabella." Having received a generous allowance, the young mother was persuaded to abandon her son, who was then entrusted to a prudent curate. Philip and his sister, the Infanta Juana, knew nothing about their half-brother until Charles made his confession at Yuste. At the age of six, Juan is "sent to Leganes in Spain (near Madrid) where he lives several years under care of Massi (retired musician) and wife—education neglected—dressed as peasant." In 1554 Charles' Chamberlain, Luis Quixada, takes him to his home in Villagarcia and treats him like his own son. Shortly before the emperor's death, Quixada brings Juan to a house near Yuste. "Charles saw Juan frequently in last weeks of [his] life."

At the close of the first scene, the conversation between Charles and Philip is "interrupted by laughter off. Juan and lady-in-waiting he is making love to—C[harles]. outraged has him summoned—Juan comes—stonily lectured but unabashed." O'Neill later changes this section: "Juan's entrance with lady-in-waiting instead of alone—they burst in on interview—lady afterwards becomes Juan's mistress and Philip takes her from him (by royal command), only to find out Juan is tired of her and glad of the chance to be relieved." The rivalry between the brothers is established here in the very first scene; they vie not only for women but also for the attention and affection of their father.

Philip always envies the self-confidence, physical attractiveness and physical courage of Juan—his effortless success with women—his careless confidence that even God will forgive him all his sins—while Philip beneath his cold mask is timid, uncertain of himself, laborious, guilty, unable to give way to genuine emotion.

Juan envies (but good-naturedly) Philip's legitimate birth, his kingship—he always wants to be a king (for which he is unfitted, as Philip knows)—he gets angry at Philip for thwarting this ambition—thinks complacently that Philip is jealous of his powers in this direction.

O'Neill sketches two versions of the second scene. In the first, Juan is alone with Charles, who "notes his resemblance to his mother—pretty, heedless, no serious brains, but attracting opposite sex—love child as opposed to P[hilip]. who was conceived in gloomy purposive dynastic raptures—C. falls into sentimental rumination—the night J. was conceived—then catching J.

listening eagerly, stops abruptly—coldly irritated at himself—also guilty conscience—regretting son just as he is retiring from the world." Charles asks Juan what he wants to be. The son replies: "A soldier!" Charles "looks him over with a grim smile. 'Yes, you will make a good soldier!'" He then dismisses his son and "sends for confessor." In the second version, Philip is present during the meeting between his father and brother. "It is he who interrupts his father's sentimental ruminations sternly with a reminder of his coming retirement from world—J. angry—'I wanted to hear' (first time he ever felt like a son to C.)—'for a moment I was his son.'" At the end of this scene Juan and Philip are alone. "Juan's genuine but scornful affection for P. brought out, and P's repressed attraction for him—P's curiosity about J's technique with women, etc.—Juan says to come with him and talk with ladies-in-waiting—Vesper bell rings—Philip sternly says must go to prayers."

O'Neill apparently planned to include a death-bed scene, for he states: "Juan one of group of attendants, nobles & ecclesiastics who stood at midnight (Sept. 21) by bedside of dying Emperor—acknowledged by father shortly before he expired." After Charles's death, Philip's jealousy becomes more pronounced, his attitude more destructive. His love-hate feelings for his brother resemble Jamie Tyrone's in *Long Day's Journey into Night*. The dramatist certainly must have noticed the similarities between Juan's family and early life and his own: the musically inclined mother who betrays her son at his birth by abandoning him and who remains a vague shadowy presence in his life; the domineering father who separates mother and son—sending the young boy away to be cared for by others—who is estranged from his son but reconciled with him before dying; the father-son conflict depicted in the relationship between Philip and his sickly son, Don Carlos; the incestuous love of Don Carlos for his father's beautiful young third wife, Elizabeth of Valois.

According to O'Neill's notes, he intended to dramatize the tragic love of these two young people—and their deaths, which bear some resemblance to Adam Brant's and Christine Mannon's in *Mourning Becomes Electra*, the play O'Neill completed before he developed the "Philip-Juan" idea. Don Carlos opposed his father's brutal measures—butchery and burning—to maintain his control of the Netherlands. After the young prince's aborted attempt to flee the country, Philip—convinced that his son was engaged in political intrigues with his enemies in the north—entered his son's chambers with armed guards and placed him under arrest. Provided with details and reports by those close to the king, historians concur that Don Carlos—after months of incarceration—died by unnatural means—either by poison or strangulation—as decreed by Philip. Two months later the grieving young queen, who had been denied permission to visit her imprisoned stepson, died in premature childbirth. A fate similar to that of Don Carlos awaited Juan.

In 1567 Philip appointed Juan Admiral of the Fleet; three years later he was made Commander-in-Chief of the Holy League forces against the Turks. After his victory at the Battle of Lepanto, "Juan first desires to become a king." In his efforts to marry Mary Stuart and obtain a kingship in his own right, the young prince sought the aid of Gregory XIII, who had proclaimed Juan "a new Moses, a new Gideon, a new Samson, a new Saul, a new David without any of the faults of these famous men; and I hope in God to live long enough to reward him with a royal crown." Juan received but faint praise from Philip, who—when he discovered his brother's ambitious dream—used it to stimulate his zeal in the service of the king.

Lepanto seemed to mark a turning point in Don Juan's fortunes. Financial and moral support from Philip for new military ventures came grudgingly and usually too late to be effective. Tunis was taken from the Turks but later recaptured by them with disastrous consequences and great loss of life to the Spanish. Finally, the death of the Governor of the Netherlands irrevocably sealed the fate of Juan, who was told to proceed to this unhappy land as the king's viceroy and was forbidden by Philip to return to Spain. O'Neill's notes reveal his intention to depict the dramatic confrontation, the last meeting of the two brothers in 1576:

Juan disobeys Philip's orders & returns to Spain—Escorial—appointed Governor of Netherlands—dreams of marrying Mary Stuart & becoming King of England—end Sept. disguised as Moorish slave sets forth on journey northwards.

Immediately after this passage, O'Neill mentions the name of Juan's mistress —a lady of a noble family in Madrid, Spain—Maria de Mendoza "by whom he had daughter Anna." Love for this woman and a desire to provide for their daughter probably motivated Juan's return to Spain. At the age of seven, Anna —who apparently was conceived in 1570 when Juan was in Madrid—was entrusted, like her father, to the care of Quixada's wife, Dona Magdalena de Ulloa. Later Philip ordered her to enter the royal Benedictine convent of Las Huelgas, where she became perpetual Abbess.

In spite of his soothing expressions of assurance—that he wished to confide the government of the Netherlands to a prince of his own blood—Philip knew the dangers awaiting his brother. Charles V had been born in Flanders and loved it above all his other dominions; but Philip's harsh edicts against heresy— enforced by the Inquisitors—led to open rebellion against the Spanish in fifteen of the seventeen provinces. William of Orange, who had been brought up in the household of Charles V and had converted to Catholicism at that time, became a ruthless leader of the rebels. He opposed every overture made by the newly arrived viceroy, who—in a vain effort to win the people—was trying to learn their language and follow their customs. When the two leaders finally took up arms, Juan, aided by his cousin the Duke of Parma, won victory after victory.

Meanwhile, an even more decisive battle, which was ultimately to defeat Juan, was being waged in Philip's court. The young prince had sent his trusted secretary, Escovedo, to petition the king for money and men. Juan did not know that his trusted confidant in the king's court, the perfidious Antonio Perez, motivated by jealousy, had secretly vowed to destroy him. As O'Neill's notes indicate, Philip's mistress, the Princess of Eboli, was Perez's mistress, too. The unfortunate Escovedo learned of the affair, but before he could inform the king, Perez had obtained Philip's permission to murder the secretary. Three attempts to poison the victim failed; he was finally attacked and mortally stabbed by paid assassins.

The news of Escovedo's murder reached Juan at a time when he himself was gravely ill. He felt betrayed by his brother; and—in his last letter to him—he expresses his sorrow at being disgraced and abandoned by the king. Realizing he was dying, Juan made two requests: to receive the sacraments and to be buried in Escorial near his father. Throughout his life and especially at the time of death, Juan—like O'Neill—felt homeless and remarked: "Is it not just that I, who have not a hand's breadth of earth that I can call my own in this world should desire to be at large in heaven."*

The French historian, Brantôme, attributes the young prince's death "to poison administered by order of the King."† When Juan's body was opened for embalmment, the state of the intestines "exhibited appearances which some of the attendants supposed, and the camp rumour asserted, to be the effects of poison. The contents of the stomach were dry; and one side of the heart was yellow and black as if burnt, and crumbled at the touch. It was whispered in the army that Doctor Ramierez had put some deadly drug into the broth given to the patient, and that the deed had been done by the orders of the King."** Philip commanded that the body be brought back to Spain secretly. To avoid detection by the enemy, it was cut in pieces at the joints, placed in leather bags and carried on the pack-saddle of a horse. In the monastery of Parrazes, "the severed portions of the body were then put together, laid on a fitting bier and conducted with great pomp to the Escorial" where it was placed in the sepulchral chamber "adjacent to that reserved for the remains of the sovereign of

---

*Sir William Stirling-Maxwell, *Don John of Austria or Passages from the History of the Sixteenth Century 1547–1578* (London, 1883), II, p. 334.

†Ibid., p. 336. Quotation from *Œuvres complètes de Pierre de Bourdeille*, abbé séculier de Brantôme (Paris, 1822). Brantôme visited Madrid in 1564 and saw Philip II, Queen Isabella, Don Carlos, Don John, and the other personages of the Court. It is possible that O'Neill decided to call Adam Brant's mother Marie Brantôme after seeing the name Brantôme, which appears frequently, in Stirling-Maxwell's two-volume study.

**Ibid.

the Spains and Indies, to which, four years before, the bones of Charles the Fifth had been brought from the convent chapel of Yuste."＊

Although the play was to close with Philip's death in 1598, no specific events in the monarch's late reign and life are cited in O'Neill's notes. Except for the crushing defeat of Spain's Invincible Armada by the English in 1588, the twenty years that remained to Philip following his brother's death were relatively uneventful. The revolt in Aragon in 1591 over the affair of Antonio Perez would seem to be the only link O'Neill could use to continue the Philip-Juan connection. Philip spent most of his time in the years preceding his death in near isolation in his strange court at Escorial, shutting out reality and living with the past, haunted by the ghosts of those he had most wronged: Don Carlos his son, Don Juan his brother. Perhaps the king's self-entombment—so similar to Lavinia Mannon's in *Mourning Becomes Electra*—led O'Neill to state when recording his first idea for the Philip-Juan play: "last scene clear." The dramatist finished the fourth draft of *Mourning Becomes Electra* just before his trip to Escorial; two days after his return from Spain he was rereading it and deciding to "rewrite on line of new ideas for changes in working out of plot—may give added values" (W.D.).

°TESTAMENT FOR TOMORROW†
(1932)

5/23/32	Notes [for] new big idea "Testament," tentative title, Second Coming philosophical play
5/26/32	"Testament" (notes working out prologue)
7/20/32	Notes "On to Hercules" & "Testament"
11/9/34	"Testament for Tomorrow" (old "Testament" idea—fresh slant on this—start tentative outline & notes)
11/10–21/34	"Testament"—outline, notes, reading
11/22/34	"Testament for Tomorrow" (this idea [has] great possibilities but seems to have run away—too psychic on me—beyond theatre—will put aside for a time)

＊Ibid., p. 339.

†O'Neill provides little information about this idea other than these Work Diary entries. There is no record of it in either his notes or notebooks. In a letter to Dudley Nichols dated May 29, 1932, the dramatist says: "Some days before your letter arrived, I was making first notes on an idea that had suddenly come to me—a really tremendous affirmative conception for an opus magnus! But it must wait until I feel grown up enough to write it—if ever. I'm certainly not fool enough to think I'm capable of it yet—but I'll keep hoping!"

1/28/43   Work on files—destroy old notes for ideas of seven plays I
know I will never write now—"Testament for Tomorrow,"
etc.—dating back to Sea Island or to France

°ON TO BETELGEUSE
[1932]*

Do "On To Betelgeuse" super-expressionistically—verse form—

°THOMAS JEFFERSON PLAY
[1932]†

Induction—Political speech of Pres[ident]. of Today [on the] 4th of July
—evasive, opportunist, cowardly—Chorus of Crowd—(masked (?))—cynical,
spiritless, apathetic—speaker takes name of Jefferson in vain—
Play—Life of Jefferson, ending with his speech as President on ? about ?
Masked Crowd—interested, excited, enthusiastic or condemning, really feeling
their rights and responsibilities as voters.
End of Induction—End of President's speech—same spirit—again taking
name of Jefferson in vain—

°ROLLING RIVER
[1933]**

Idea

Three (or four ?) generations—eldest Grandfather, Grandmother, Friend who
had once been Grandmother's lover—all over
eighty—of Jeffersonian D[emocracy]., Emer-
sonian transcendentalist

---

*Idea is dated September 30, 1932, in the Work Diary: "Going over all I did in 1928
and 1929 on 'On To Betelgeuse'—new title 'The Life of Bessie Bowen'—thought may
take that up now but inspiration lacking today for any urge toward it." (See original 1927 idea, "It Cannot Be Mad?.")
†No date is provided in the notebook for this idea; it is entered in the Work Diary
on October 6, 1932: "Idea Jefferson Play."
**Idea is undated in the notebook but is entered in the Work Diary on January 11,
1933: " 'Rolling River' (idea—play of generations)."

—next, son & wife & son's Mistress (wife's friend)
—next   g[reat] grandson's name
                    same as g[reat] grandfather
—next   son's name same as
                              grandson's

Little old g. grandmother (84)—Dutch—across plains in covered wagon—team-
                    ster—Senator—
Little old g. grandfather (88)—Jeffersonian d[emocrat].—deist—Dec[laration].
                    of Indep[endence]. idealist about America—
                    N[ew]. E[ngland].(?)
Friend, French Huguenot, Corsican (85)
                    married when she is 17, he 21
                    across plain 1865

grandfather—R[ail]. R[oad]. builders—(66)
grandmother—Scotch-Irish—(63)
3 brothers to grandfather (?)—(64, 62, 61)

father—45
mother—45
mistress—

son—(21)
daughter—(19)

°LOVE PLAY*
(January 13, 1933)

Man & Wife—change of life period for both—man 50 or 55, woman 45 or
50—at the crisis when both have to bury youth forever, face that & the fact of
age & death—with only their love as faith—both disillusioned with all else—
An analysis of their love showing how their past selves, even of time before
they had met, longed for and dreamed of each other and found all substitutes

---

*A number of titles appear beside this tentative one: "Once, Long Ago," "Happily
Ever After," "A Kingdom, Long Ago," "The Far Off Kingdom," "Promised Land,"
"There Is Love," and "The Tapestry of Dreams." O'Neill lists the seven-year cycle
ages—7, 14, 21, 28, 35, 42, 49—on this page but cancels this section. Additional in-
formation is provided in the Work Diary entry for January 13, 1933: "Idea Love
Play (the different egos in people that in perfect love are mated)."

unsatisfying—how all their pasts are in their love—as if fate had woven of all strands of past a beautiful tapestry—

These pasts live with them in their life like ghosts in a haunted house—

Masks of Selves—little girl and boy of seven or eight

          —adolescence (girl 13, boy 14)

          —youth (girl 18—boy 19)

          —manhood & womanhood (he is 33, she is 28)

The main plot is the death of their respective youths & the reactions to that —or the departure for the unknown—(?)

Motive—that at the turning point, they both turn back to what they were fundamentally as children—turn back to solve their adolescent problem in each other's love—that this gives their love the courage and peace to face old age and death—another way of saying again "unless ye become as the little children ye shall not enter the kingdom"—that is, unless we have the key of that love which alone can enable us at this crisis in our lives to reconcile the future with childhood dreams, to see in its fulfillment an acceptance of that past, we can never find peace but must go on to death still seeking for a goal still unknown— it is by being able spiritually to become again these children we were, to re-absorb them into ourselves, that in spite of age and death, we can feel we complete the circle, are not cut off in the midst of a journey but have come home—the childhood problem of accepting life is become again their problem—

Scene One—sort of prologue scene—just the mere incident of a casual introduction—"I want you to meet—"

1—Boyhood—Girlhood—9–7

2—Youth—18–16

3—Young Manhood-Womanhood—27–25

    Previous marriages—man 1, woman 2.

    Two years difference in ages

    Meet when man is 36—woman 34

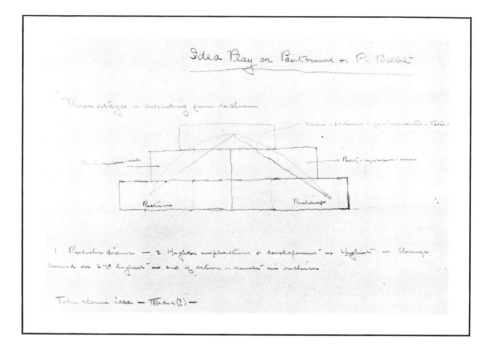

°PYRAMID FORM PLAY
[1933]°

Idea Play or Pantomime or P[antomime]. Ballet
Three stages—ascending from realism

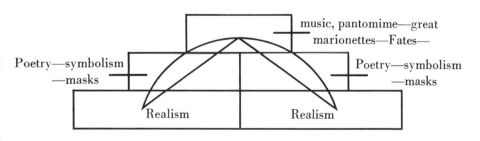

1 Realistic drama—2 Higher implications & development—Highest—
Change caused in 2nd highest—and of action—results in realism

Take classic idea—Medea (?) †

°The idea is undated in the notebook but recorded in the Work Diary on March 14,
1933: "Idea pyramid form play (or ballet)."
†O'Neill made previous attempts to write a play based on this Greek drama:

°THE REWARD OF DREAM
[1933]*

Marvelous love of the old man & woman—secret of long life, always said yes to life—always loved life—acceptance not submission—willing to sacrifice to live—

Old man—daily expectance of death—is it today?—his vision of death—as after love, the feeling of self dissolving—calm, peace, fulfillment—after the fulfillment of union with life—the drifting off—the sound in one's ears—rustling of a leaf, bird, noise of sea—the littlest things that make up happiness—drifting off to sleep—dying, the doze—death as reward for loving acceptance of life— into thy hands, O Life—as he has always felt—no rebellion against life, hence no rebellion against death—life blesses him with the reward of dream—he will go on following the dream, on & on—

His nickname for the woman he loves "Life"—

°REVERSE "INTERLUDE"
(MAN AND HIS FOUR WOMEN)
[1933]†

Man—Interlude technique throughout (& others also (?))
His mother—his wife—his mistress—his daughter (who are symbolically

---

11/27/31   "Medea" plot idea (notes)
 12/4/31   "Medea" plot idea (tentative outline acts, scenes)
12/29/31   Medea plot idea (reading)
12/30/31   Read description Lenormand's Medea play plot in Paris Herald
           clipping—great similarity to way I'd worked it out in my tenta-
           tive outline—so guess I must abandon idea—too bad!

Editor's note: An idea O'Neill enters in the Work Diary on April 24, 1933, should be inserted here to maintain chronological order: "Idea M   —harlot play (dream)"
*Idea is undated in the notebook but appears in the Work Diary on May 10 and 12, 1933: "Idea 'The Reward of Dream' (love play)."
†This undated notebook idea is recorded in the Work Diary on May 23, 1933: "Idea —3 women, 1 man—reverse [*Strange*] *Interlude* theme."
one and the same person).**
**This idea reflects O'Neill's attitude to his wife Carlotta. In a letter to her dated May 25, 1932, he writes "Mistress, I desire you . . . Wife, you are my love . . .

Alliance mother and wife against mistress and daughter—
Mother 68—wife 45—mistress 45—daughter 18—Man 50

Main theme—Man at his change of life period—a success, due to Mother
and wife influence, carrying out their ideal (materialistic)—comes to doubt all
his gods, to turn back to youthful ideals—reckless, irresponsible, spiritual, rebellious—passion and the flesh, illegal—at same time innocence, modesty of
youth, dreams, idealism—

Suddenly sells out his business—(gets brick house way up Maine, moved in
all winter)—(or house in South where there are no distinct seasons—doesn't
want to be reminded of seasons)—because death has suddenly become alive to
him, a question mark, and made of his life a question for him—

To this house he brings the four women—the mother disapproving, com-
plaining, but afraid to refuse to come, afraid of losing hold on him—the wife
frightened, bewildered but dutiful—the mistress, intoxicated with passion grab-
bing at youth through love again—the daughter, glad to dream with nature—

As play goes on, four women gradually approach each other so at end he is
with four figures exactly the same—the figure of wife.

Last scene when

He tries to become the son of his daughter, the father of his mother, the
husband of his mistress (wants to marry her)—the lover of his wife (who will
not commit adultery with him).

°SEQUEL TO *AH, WILDERNESS!*
(September 1934)

On September 1, 1932, O'Neill records his first idea for *Ah, Wilderness!*:
"Awoke with idea for this 'Nostalgic Comedy' and worked out tentative outline
—seems fully formed & ready to write" (W.D.). He puts aside his current work,
Days Without End, and devotes the next weeks to the new project, completing
the first draft on September 27. Two years later on September 13, 1934—in
response to Leon Mirlas's letter informing him of the success of *The Great God
Brown* in Buenos Aires—O'Neill writes: "I am sending you under separate cover
copies of *Ah, Wilderness!* and *Days Without End.* The first is a simple comedy
—nostalgic, sentimental recollection of the days of my youth, of the typical

Mother, you are my lost way refound . . . Daughter, you are my secret, shy, shrinking
one." Quotation from *Inscriptions: Eugene O'Neill to Carlotta Monterey O'Neill,*
edited by Donald Gallup (New Haven, 1960).
Editor's note: Two ideas that O'Neill worked on after "Reverse 'Interlude'" are recorded only in the Work Diary: "Spectator Sketches" (July 7 and 10, 1933) and
"Tides of Sargasso" (August 15, 17, and 27 and November 6 and 7, 1934).

family life of that time in the typical town of our states—of the customs and morals of these days as contrasted with what exists today." Ostensibly, the dramatist was vacationing at the time at Big Wolf Lake in Maine, but he spent most of August and the first week of September developing new ideas for plays.

On September 5 and 6, 1934, O'Neill made notes for a sequel to *Ah, Wilderness!*, which would have presented a tragic view of family life in the post-World War I period—life as it "exists today"—in contrast to the earlier sentimental picture of the Millers at the turn of the century. Lacking the joyous enthusiasm he felt for the original "Nostalgic Comedy," he decides on September 7 to "give up idea working up here—no impulse" (W.D.). He takes up the story of the Miller family—interrupting his work on the Cycle play, *A Touch of the Poet*—on January 9, 1936: " 'Ah, Wilderness!' sequel (for a change—notes—but don't make much of it" (W.D.). Only one page of these notes is extant:

Sequel to *Ah, Wilderness!*

1920
1921 (?)—15 years after "Ah, W[ilderness!]."—or 1919?

Miller	— 70?	
Essie	— 65?	
Sid	— 55?	
Lily	— 55?	Middletown
Arthur	— 34	
Richard	— 31	
Mildred	— 30	
Tommy	— 25	

Sid has become reformed drunk—doctor told him he would die—combination of puritanical disapproval of drink & complacent self-righteousness—but underneath attacks of unregenerate longings for good old days—still "star" reporter—

Essie is dead—died in '19—worry over sons in war brought on illness—cancer—and never got over shock of Arthur's death in '18—he was captain—

Lily manages house since Essie's death—

Mildred is getting divorce—lover—feels no responsibility toward two children—

Tommy has been U.S. aviation*

---

*O'Neill indicates here in a canceled passage that Tommy was killed in 1919. He is described as "typical, restless, hard-drinking wild disintegrated 'lost' generation."

Richard grad[uate]. Yale, 1911—goes into newspaper game with father—makes good—city editor—then war and he goes (27)—engaged before he goes—but on return breaks engagement—maimed, embittered, idealism murdered—lost leg?

Arthur has developed into smug, social-climbing, country club, golfing success—made "good" marriage to merchant's daughter (coal & wood business—or mill?) in 1911—is now assist[ant]. manager—(or owns chain filling stations, garage, is agent for car)—three children—but is loose on side—affair—

Miller—prostrated by death of wife—lost, bewildered in changed times—waiting for death—feels children alien, can't understand their view—same about everything—

°LIFE OF STURGO NACIMBIN
(SUGGESTED BY STORY IN BLANCO'S *JOURNEY OF THE FLAME*)
(September, 1934) *

The complete title of the source for O'Neill's idea, "Life of Sturgo Nacimbin" is:

The Journey Of The Flame
Being an Account of One Year in the Life
of
Señor Don Juan Obrigón
Known During Past Years in the Three Californias
as
Juan Colorado
and to the Indians of the Same
as
THE FLAME
Born at San José del Arroyo, Lower California, Mexico
in 1798
and, having seen Three Centuries change Customs and Manners, died alone
in 1902
at the Great Cardon, near Rosario, Mexico, with His Face Turned Toward
the South
Written down by
Antonio de Fierro Blanco
(pseudonym of Walter Nordhoff)

The Journey of the Flame purports to be a factual account of Juan Obrigón's muleback trip in 1810 from the south of Lower California to San Fran-

---

*The idea is dated September 1934 in the notebook and September 7, 1934, in the Work Diary: "Snake."

cisco Bay. Don Firmín Sanhudo, the king of Spain's Inspector-General of Colonies, made the journey to determine the strength of the Spanish in the Three Californias after the successful revolution in Mexico. The novel opens as guests gather to celebrate Juan's hundredth birthday. He is actually 104 years old, but custom decrees that a man tell the story of his life when he reaches a hundred years of age.

O'Neill, who boasted about his royal Irish ancestors, must have read with great enjoyment Juan's description of his father, an "Irish king," who, when his ship anchored in the harbor, jumped overboard and swam to land. Singing in Irish "like a mating nightingale," he persuaded Juan's mother, the best-born and most beautiful girl in the village of San José del Arroyo, to leave her father's house and to live with him. She told the young boy that his father, when drunk, had been taken away by sailors and that he had returned to his kingdom, a "great city called Ireland." The father's name, "O'Brien," was deemed too crude and unmusical for Spanish ears and was changed to "Obrigón."

The notes O'Neill makes for his play are from Blanco's Chapter XIII: "The Rock Aljibe of 'Hell Awaits Thee'—I See the Skeleton of Don Sturgo Nacimbin." When the travelers stop to rest near the water tank of *El Diablo Te Espera* where Nacimbin died, Juan asks for permission to visit the site. He has never forgotten the encounter he had when he was six with Nacimbin. Don Firmín recalls his meeting with Nacimbin and General Viconte's warning: "Beware of him. Should he become fanatic, there will be no place in New Spain for us, who now rule." O'Neill divides the story that Juan tells his guests—"The Life of Sturgo Nacimbin"—into three parts:

First part—Son of rich man—dissipated—married, two sons—adored by wife & old father who is fine character—irreligious. Fanatic monk comes to town —preaches—N[acimbin]. impressed—monk says [he] got it from New T[estament].—N[acimbin]. takes Bible from him—learns to read—takes Christ literally—death of father—his attitude—the funeral—gets rep[utation]. for being crazy—leaves wife & children to go into wilderness.

Juan's full account of this section provides additional details. While Nacimbin, as a youth, was squandering his father's wealth on women, gambling, and liquor, Indians by tens of thousands were perishing from hunger. They were neglected by the Spanish Governor, Luis Lopez; their Missions were plundered by Franciscans. After his marriage and conversion by the monk "whose eyes were fire and his tongue a scourge,"* Nacimbin changed not only his own way of life but that of nearly everyone he met. The Indians, who normally thought of

---

*The Journey of the Flame, Antonio de Fierro Blanco (Boston, 1933), p. 183. All further references to this book are from this edition; page references are in parentheses.

nothing but food, "ceased to eat when he came and went about in thought, wondering and troubled." While the Church hated him, "lonely priests welcomed him secretly." The Governor, on meeting him, remarked: "Ojala! But I must be elsewhere when it happens. For such as we Governors are, there is no place in this new order" (p. 184).

Nacimbin spent months learning the alphabet and how to read, refusing all offers of help: "This affair is between God and myself: He who gave the soul, and he who has it" (p. 184). When his wife, called La Paloma because of her purity and beauty, urged him to see his dying father, Nacimbin replied: "My Father is in Heaven." The old man, hearing this and similar Biblical quotations, "turned his face toward the adobe wall and died" (p. 184). The day of his father's funeral Nacimbin sat by an open door, reading the Bible. "A coffin-bearer touched him with one corner of the wooden box, thinking to rouse him, but Don Sturgo Nacimbin only drew his dagger, and, placing it across the Bible, dropped his head. They buried the old man, his father, without him" (p. 185). La Paloma's brothers, who took charge of Nacimbin's cattle, called him "loco." After announcing: "I must now go into the wilderness, and live alone, until I know what work God prepares for me," Nacimbin left his weeping wife.

Second part—N[acimbin].'s holiness—gives all to poor—tremendous influence on Indians—naked except breechcloth—S[ebastiani]. falls in love [with] N[acimbin].'s wife—but she won't give herself until N[acimbin]. casts her off—S[ebastiani].'s search for N[acimbin].—takes him back to wife—"obey thy conscience, woman"—spits.

Nacimbin visited Mission stations in the wilderness; and although he never broke his vow of silence, he brought comfort to isolated priests. Accounts explaining how he managed to obtain sufficient food in the desert vary: the heathen Indians went hungry themselves to provide food; birds brought seed to him; *Nopales*—edible cacti—bent themselves toward him. He ministered to all in need and had no desire to return home but was forced to do so by Sotelo Sebastiani, an ex-Admiral of Pearl-Divers and a strong, fearless man "without morals or breeding," who wanted Nacimbin's wife. She, hoping to be reunited with her husband, had sent Sebastiani to bring him back. When the two men stood before La Paloma, Sebastiani demanded: "Give her to me!" She asked her husband: "What shall I do, Sturgo?" When her husband replied: "Obey thy conscience, woman," she spat at him "and lived with Sotelo Sebastiani" (p. 187).

Third part—N[acimbin].'s horror of snakes—symbol of all evil—if he can conquer the serpent, he defeats Devil and the Era of Good comes—S[ebastiani]. now wants to marry N[acimbin].'s wife to get N[acimbin].'s property—no divorce—seeks N[acimbin]. in desert, far from water—N[acimbin].'s water in deer's bladder—S[ebastiani]. slashes it—N[acimbin].'s temptation to kill—throws knife away—goes to water tank—rattler—afraid—then goes in—is bitten—dies.

Discovering Nacimbin's great fear of snakes, Mexicans deduced that "the Devil had again taken a snake's form to defeat Nacimbin, and that, when without thought or fear he could lift a serpent from the ground, the New Era had come. People, watching anxiously, therefore laid harmless snakes in his path, with high hopes; but always they were disappointed" (p. 187). Because divorce was prohibited in Mexico, Sebastiani—wanting Nacimbin's property as well as his wife—stalked him in the desert, determined to kill him.

When Nacimbin was more than a day's journey from any water except the tank of *El Diablo Te Espera*, Sebastiani approached him, asking for a drink. After puncturing the water bag, Sebastiani rode "off without looking back." For one moment Nacimbin lost faith in God; "his hand hovered about his knife-hilt. Then he threw the knife from him as a temptation of Satan. Casting himself upon the broiling sand, Don Sturgo Nacimbin cried out in anguish to the Lord of Hosts" (p. 188). He forced himself to go to the water tank, which was a rounded cleft in high granite walls. The only approach to the pool of clear water was covered with squirming serpents. "He is brave who, passing among unnumbered waiting fangs, reaches this tank's polished rock sides to look into the hell of snakes below. But he who imagines it possible to pick his way across sand littered with deadly snakes stretched at length, or coiled, or in squirming masses, and drink, is no longer sane" (p. 189). Nacimbin waited until it was dark and then went in to drink and to die. "Half trust is lack of faith, and God deserted him. Had he boldly gone in by day!" If he had survived the ordeal, "he could never more have feared. Certain of his calling, he would have led the way, and all New Spain would have followed" (p. 189).

In the last section of his notes, O'Neill describes the fate of La Paloma and her two sons after Nacimbin's death:

His wife has become drunkard—sees vision of him—dies when he does.

His two sons hanged by governor (S[ebastiani].'s tool)—falsely accused of rape—they refuse [to] raise [a] revolt to save themselves—Indians try [to] raise their spirits or N[acimbin].'s from the dead—afterwards give up hope forever.

When she was drunk, Nacimbin's wife, now called Doña Pepa, sat looking at the road her husband had taken when he left her. On the day of Nacimbin's death, however, she remained sober. At dusk, she shrieked wildly: "Sturgo Nacimbin! Save yourself, loved one!" and died (p. 190). Sebastiani found willing accomplices to help him carry out his plan to dispose of Nacimbin's sons. "Both Government and Church feared all the Nacimbins, whispering among themselves: 'Who can tell what fool may give these boys a Bible?'" (p. 190). Officials had every reason to fear them, for Indians from all the Missions on the Coast gathered in Loreto; "it was said these two boys had but to raise a hand and every official and priest in the Californias would have died by Indian hands. To all such offers the boys merely replied, 'When the whole tree is rotten, what good would it be to lop off a few decayed limbs?'" (p. 190).

Juan concludes his story by describing what he saw when he finally reached the water tank of *El Diablo Te Espera*. Wrapping his legs in buckskin, he made his way to the slippery cliff where he stood looking down upon Nacimbin's skeleton "stretched upon the sand, but not near water. 'He died without drinking.'" As Juan spoke these words, Nacimbin's head turned its eye sockets toward him and "an arm bone twitched as a serpent crawled over it." While Juan attempts to rationalize the phenomenon—attributing the movement to "playful snakelets" inside Nacimbin's skull—he is deeply moved by this mystical experience. In the preface for his story, he told his guests he had to exercise great prudence before the powerful Spaniard, Don Firmín, when he expressed his desire to make a pilgrimage to *El Diablo Te Espera* as the Spanish still feared Nacimbin's influence over the oppressed poor.

> I went to see the bones of Don Sturgo Nacimbin, and I knew waves of emotion would surge over me; and being governed by feeling, not by reason, I might do or say that which would not fit with life as I must lead it. I will tell you about him, for at one time all the Californias waited breathlessly for his Revelation; and had he raised a finger, who can tell what might have happened? No one knew exactly what he hoped, nor why Nacimbin seemed to be our only escape from utter despondency. (p. 182)

O'Neill began "The Life of Sturgo Nacimbin" just after he had completed *Days Without End*, whose redeemed hero stands before a crucifix in the last scene, "his arms outflung so that his body forms another cross"; his dead self lies beneath it, arms extended. Describing the crucifix needed for this scene, the dramatist states: "I want none of your sadistic Spanish Christs who give you the horrors, but a Resurrection Christ who will express 'the Resurrection & the Life' John Loving finds in Him at end—a spiritual exaltation transcending human suffering" (Letter to Langner, October 29, 1933). Undoubtedly, O'Neill envisions a similar final scene for Sturgo Nacimbin—"stretched upon the sand," his body forming a cross; for he regards this Savior of New Spain as a Christ figure. Like Christ at Gethsemane, Nacimbin had cast himself to the ground, begging God to take the chalice of suffering from him. O'Neill describes Nacimbin's "temptation" in the desert: "power if he only says word."

On the day following the hanging of the Nacimbin brothers, when Sebastiani met the guilt-ridden Governor, he said to him jovially: "Wash thy hands, Pilate!" (p. 191). If he viewed the Governor as another Pilate, Sebastiani must certainly have realized that he had played the role of Judas in the Nacimbin family tragedy. While O'Neill never completed "The Life of Sturgo Nacimbin," he gained new insights working out this idea. There would be other corrupt officials and oppressed peoples—other Christ figures—in the plays he started, but never completed, in the early 1940s.

°ROMANCE OF AGED PLAY
(1934) *

The two old people who fall in love, much to scandal of children and grandchildren—persecution and opposition—

Romeo and Juliet both over 70—families enemies—Montague-Capulet situation—

Reaction toward nature youthful—recapture poetic spirit of youth with no desire to go back to the rest of it—run away to nature to escape families—who think it is second-childishness—and it is through this a chance meeting brings them together—

°THE GERMINATING°
[1934]†

Act One

Scene One—Pit head of the Voreux coal mine—(March—before dawn—4 when shifts go down—Étienne applies for work—meeting with old Vincent

---

°This is the second of the "two new ideas" O'Neill records in his Work Diary on September 7, 1934: "Snake and old courtship hints."

°Beside this title, O'Neill writes the words: " 'Germinal' dramat[ization]." This is O'Neill's only attempt to adapt a novel for the stage. The inclusion of Zola's novels in the collection of Edmund Tyrone, a self-portrait, reveals that his admiration for the French novelist dates back to 1912, the year of *Long Day's Journey into Night*'s setting. In a statement prepared on November 5, 1959, for the collection of letters he had received from O'Neill, Dudley Nichols recalls a meeting he had with the dramatist in 1927:

> I asked Gene what he was then working on and he replied that he was trying to do the life of a woman "without the padding of a novel." This was, of course, *Strange Interlude*, which I later reviewed so fortuitously. I always remember his ironic smile when he added "without the padding of a novel." He was a profound admirer of Zola and Zola's thorough penetration of his characters, but as a dramatist, with a passion for "leanness" and intensity in his probings of character, he felt every novel had too much excess writing. The instinctive dramatist must feel that way.

†The Work Diary provides specific dates:

11/23/34 "Germinal" (as an in-between work sometime, consider plan dramatizing Zola's novel—modern setting strike play always arouses partisan reaction—this story removed in time & place—(audience can see!)—and significant in light of what has happened since)

11/24/34 "Germinal" idea (outline & notes)

11/27/34 "Germinal" (finish tentative scene scheme—all for present on this)

Maheu—then meeting with the Maheus—mistakes Catherine for boy—(Toussaint Maheu, Zacharie & Chaval & Levaque (?))—Étienne gets job—(Jeanlin Maheu & Lydie—Mouquette)

Scene Two—Down in the mines p.m. just before quitting—the Maheus cutting in the seam—Chaval (25) waiting—meeting with him—Catherine already Chaval's mistress—she explains to Étienne—asks Étienne to be boarder (?) —visit of Dansaert & Négrel—outbreak of discontent—(Étienne speaks—already in International (?)—men come up from all around)

Scene Three—A l'Avantage Inn—meeting with Rasseneur & Souvarine—
Scene Four—Maheus' home
Scene Five—Grégoires' house—Maheude's visit with two children [Lénore and Henri] (& old Maheu (?))
Maigrat's store (?)
Maheus' home—visit of Madame Hennebeau—man & wife from Paris visitors—stockholders—gossip after they leave—
Étienne reading & studying (?)

Act Two

Scene One—The Bon-Joyeux—The dance followed by meeting (?)—the Provident Fund (?)—the International or Scene One, the Maheus'—Étienne reading & studying—
Scene Three*—The Mine—notice of the new scale
Scene Four—The Hennebeaus'—dinner—the committee of protest

Act Three

Scene One—Maheus' home—starvation—visit of G[régoire].
Scene Two—The Forest
Scene Three—Attack on the mine—troops—shooting

Act Four

Scene One—Maheus'—the strike is crushed—Étienne is repudiated—guilt, illusion lost—Catherine comforts him—love—resignation—finale, old man & Souvarine alone—Souvarine's resolve—
Scene Two—Mine shaft—Souvarine's work—as he works his exultant hymn of hate
Scene Three—Top of mine—S[ouvarine]. lets É[tienne]. and C[atherine]. go down

---

*O'Neill omits information for Scene Two.

Scene Four—Down in the mine—the flood and flight

Scene Five—C[atherine]., Étienne and Cha[val].—Cha[val]. and É[tienne]. fight—Cha[val]. stabs C[atherine]. for cheating,* he has knife—É[tienne]. kills Cha[val].—C[atherine]. dies

Act Five

Scene One—Maheus'—the strike is crushed—Étienne is repudiated—guilt, to old man [Vincent Maheu (Bonnemort)]—all over—the Grégoires come to make visit—he [Grégoire] goes—girl [Cécile Grégoire] left with old man—he strangles her and dies*

Scene Two—Étienne drowned in the mine*—dies with the vision of the future or is crushed by slide—slow crushing in of the walls—voice gets weaker & weaker

General Notes

Develop throughout the struggle in the old man—make it overtone of whole play—on the outside his acceptance of the mine as inevitable fate—his body blackened in and out by coal after 50 years—and the obscure awakening rebellion caused by seeing whiteness, health, food of bourgeois daughter [Cécile Grégoire].

°RUNAWAY SLAVE PLAY
(May 1935)

Germ for this idea in Thoreau's Journal ("Heart of Thoreau's Journal," p. 91).

> Just put a fugitive slave, who has taken the name of Henry Williams, into the cars for Canada. He escaped from Stafford County, Virginia, to Boston last October; has been in Shadrach's place at the Cornhill Coffee-

---

*O'Neill changes some incidents in *Germinal*. In the novel Chaval does not stab Catherine. When the Voreux mine collapses, Étienne and Catherine are trapped in the pit. The bank of the canal gives way, and—as the water rises—they climb to an upper passage where they meet Chaval. When Chaval humiliates Catherine, bartering food for sex, Étienne, in a rage of jealousy, kills him. Catherine dies of starvation two days before the workmen, in a rescue attempt, penetrate the rock. Étienne survives the ordeal and sets out for Paris at the end of the novel. Old Bonnemort does not die after strangling Cécile; Maheude, his daughter-in-law, intervenes when officials try to send him to the insane asylum and assumes responsibility for him.

House; had been corresponding through an agent with his master, who is his father, about buying himself, his master asking $600, but he having been able to raise only $500. Heard that there were writs out for two Williamses, fugitives, and was informed by his fellow-servants and employer that Augerhole Burns and others of the police had called for him when he was out. Accordingly fled to Concord last night on foot, bringing a letter to our family from Mr. Lovejoy of Cambridge and another which Garrison had formerly given him on another occasion. He lodged with us, and waited in the house till funds were collected with which to forward him. Intended to dispatch him at noon through to Burlington, but when I went to buy his ticket, saw one at the depot who looked and behaved so much like a Boston policeman that I did not venture that time. An intelligent and very well-behaved man, a mulatto.*

°DAY†

(June 18, 1937)

Seven Scenes—history of a day's life of a man—in terms Shakespeare's seven ages of man—day symbolical of whole life

The man's age is 45—mental and spiritual menopause—time of decisive new valuations—beginning of sin's declension in his life

Morning is memory—stroke of now, moment of present, when for 12 seconds life stands still in time—his boast and hope, moment of release, freedom from past

Afternoon is the attempt [to] go on free of past—but the tragic irony is that in spite of all brave boasts and self-delusions, it is a repetition backwards of morning to noon (awakening (birth) to middle age)—to night, sleep, death—from sleep to sleep—identity of pre-birth and death (man always feels strange nostalgia for a lost Land of Heart's Desire—pre-birth, a past life of which he has intuitive memories—every change in life he asks, "Is This The Land"—)

Uncompromising spirit—refusal take up hobbies as new interests—confusion of [roles], evasion, cowardice—cheating oneself in order to be comfortable—

End is his going to bed—saying goodnight to his ghosts—mother and

---

*Henry Thoreau, *The Heart of Thoreau's Journals* (Boston, 1927), p. 91.

†O'Neill writes an alternate title, "Home Circle," beside "Day." The Work Diary indicates he spent two days developing "Day":

6/18/37   New Idea for Play—1 day—symbolical idea—work on notes for it—grand to feel creative mind alive again

6/19/37   Notes New Play idea

wives, mistresses—the dead, the still living but dead to him—who, at the end, become as one person, speaking as one—

Combine with "Merry Wives of W[indsor]." idea

High noon (4th scene)—same sort of scenes as end—chorus of the past listening as he defies with confident bravado—proclaims new life, freedom, new ideals, new success of spirit—they listen with loving, tolerant, superior smiles—agree flatteringly—it is to begin at stroke of noon—slow noon strokes—silence—pantomime—his confident bravado changes to uncertainty, confidence in himself fades, loneliness, fear of future—as they become strong, confident—he shrinks back into their circle—then he forces courage back—blames them—defies them—says goodbye—they smile—he leaves—in chorus they call after him "don't go too far, don't come home too late, etc." (Before, they have admired his expressions of independence.)

Scene I —The family house he has inherited—the dead (his mother,
(boyhood—birth   father, his old nurse) *
etc., in expo-
sition)
Scene II —The house (his brother (dead), his sister (alive but mar-
(adolescence)   ried, away, dead to him), his 1st real love (alive, married,
                   away, dead to him)
Scene III—This house (
Scene IV—

°ROBESPIERRE†
(1938)

On January 13, 1938, O'Neill interrupts work on the Cycle drama, "The Greed of the Meek," to record his first idea for a "Robespierre play—notes" (W.D.). During a five-day working period in February, while "reading** for

---

*O'Neill is obviously attempting to write an autobiographical play. "Day" combines concepts found in two earlier ideas: "House with the Masked Dead" (July 1931) and "Reverse 'Interlude'—Man and His Four Women" (1933).

†To maintain chronological order, discussion of the work appears here although the first idea for it is not included in any of the notebooks.

**The previous year O'Neill asked his editor, Bennett Cerf, to send him books on Robespierre and the French Revolution. In a letter, dated 1937, the dramatist thanks Cerf for a particular book—probably Friedrich Sieburg's biography of Robespierre, which was translated and published in the United States in 1937.

Robespierre play," he compiles an all-inclusive list of significant "French Revolution Dates," starting with the "Oath of the Tennis Court" on June 20, 1789,
and concluding with the dissolution of the National Convention on October 26,
1795. Heading the second collection of notes for Robespierre—labeled "A Fantasy" and "Phantasy"—is the statement: "March 9, 1938 1st day of 7 to *see*." The
dramatist outlines nine scenes for the play:

> I—Arras—Father—daydream of the Incorruptible Judge—charity from the
> Church—identity Father and the King—
>
> II—Paris—the College—denial as revenge for humiliations—God the Father
> —identification of self with Son—merciful friend and leader of poor and
> oppressed—the Son as Revolutionist who drove money changers from
> Temple—who will come again to judge living and *dead*—who takes up
> Man's cause against Father—who renounces title of Son of God for son of
> Man—
>
> III—Arras—victory of being selected State General—
>
> IV—The Assembly—hooted down—martyr and persecution C[omplex].—im-
> pulsion Tancred crucifixion—
>
> V—Convention—growing contempt for actual proletariat as mob—deification
> of abstraction The People as Man and himself as Son of the People—
>
> VI—Dialogue with Goddess of Reason—altar, Notre Dame
>
> VII—Feast of Supreme Being
>
> VIII—Jacobin Club—suicide—
>
> IX—Guillotine—complete success, actual people and The People—and people
> contemplate treacherous man, betrayed him, should be kindred—they
> don't know who he is—his revenge to die, more speeches, leaves them but
> to pride—
>
> The head speaks—I am the Son, the arm of the People, the Son of God—
> I am God!

It's good so far except the author will break out into a writer's rash at
times and gets in between you and Robespierre when he attempts to prove
that he's an author writing literature—and German high-powered sentimental literature at that!

If you want to be amused sometime, read all the best known books on
Robespierre and the famous histories of the Revolution. If ever there was
a man who has never been seen except through the eyes of this or that
political or religious prejudice, he is it. They are given a man to understand and they end up stuck with a Charley McCarthy on their soapbox
laps.

The second collection of notes contains biographical information for Scene One and possibly the "daydream" sequence of Scene Two. The father, a lawyer, had seduced the daughter of a brewer and married her when she became pregnant with Robespierre. Unstable and emotional, the father was "unreliable about money—borrowed from sisters—drew so heavily on mother's resources that in 1768 when she died he renounced, for himself and children, his succession, having already received more than expectations." He abandoned their four children and his wife before her death in 1764, at age 29, and went to Germany, where he opened a school. In 1771 he came home and "may have seen children —pleaded cases bar at Arras from October 1771 to June 1772—then disappears —reported to have visited England and to have ended days in Channel Isles or America."

From the age of seven to fourteen Robespierre was "dependent on relatives —no family environment—After mother's death, he and brother went to live with grandparents at brewery." His sisters were sent to a home school for poor girls. Robespierre lived with his grandfather, a well-to-do tradesman, for five years—"passion for birds, kept pigeons—Every Sunday sisters came to grandfather's to be with brothers—pride only guide of his actions—made him good student." Some of these biographical facts are woven into the scheme for the extant fragmentary first scene.

ROBESPIERRE
An Interpretation
Notes

Scene One—Home at Arras—R[obespierre]. 14 (?)—scene with Sisters— their comment on his growing habit of day-dreaming, solitude—old before [his] time—responsibilities—money worries—(inferiority, world's injustice—great pride—shame)—their worry that he thinks of father—his denial of thoughts— defense imperturbable exterior—(as throughout life)—he is feeding pet pigeons —says meditating on their lives so carefree, happy, innocent as contrasted to ours—and that led him to consider injustice of human life, and to take oath to himself to become defender of justice and liberty—

They leave him, impressed—then his real daydream—imaginary pursuit and confronting father—judging him without mercy, as is his duty—condemning him to death—realization no death penalty for father's crimes—but there should be for such base treachery—

Sister interrupts for meal—frightened by his expression—but he immediately smiles—denies—says sad thoughts—mother—can never think of her without tears—

O'Neill concludes his notes with a short biographical section for the second and third scenes: Robespierre enters the "college Louis-le-Grand at Paris"; he becomes a member of the Academy of Arras in November 1783; and in April 1784 he "delivers speech of acceptance—moral actions, eulogy of predecessor."

Throughout the notes, O'Neill presents a sympathetic, sensitive—but realistic—portrait of Robespierre; he admired the courage and moral integrity of the revolutionary leader, called "the Incorruptible" and other—disputable— names: "savior of democracy" and "protector of the rights of man." Prior to developing the Robespierre idea, the dramatist had described characters in other works as ardent Jacobins: Ramsay Fife in the notes for *Dynamo*, Evan Harford in *A Touch of the Poet*, and Richard Miller, a self-portrait, in *Ah, Wilderness!*.* There are no extant notes for the Robespierre idea dated later than March 1938, although Theresa Helburn's letter of July 5, 1939, to O'Neill suggests he may have continued working on the play but subsequently destroyed this material: "Bennett Cerf told me you were thinking of a new play, having discarded the Robespierre idea." The author did not inform Helburn in his response of July 10 that on the very day she had written her letter to him he had started the "notes and prelims" for *The Iceman Cometh*, obviously finding the early twentieth-century play a more relevant outlet for his political statements than the Robespierre work.

The play that incorporates intact many of the ideas in the first scene of the Robespierre work is "Blind Alley Guy," which O'Neill began in January 1941 but never completed. There are many similarities between its hero, Walter White, and Robespierre. Both seek solitude, daydream, and rebel against the world's injustice. They demonstrate some warmth for their mothers and sisters— as much as their cold natures allow—and hatred for their fathers; but they are incapable of feeling any emotion for others. The two have, however, great affection for their pet pigeons.

While Robespierre sincerely wanted to bring a new era of equality and freedom to the French people, the methods he employed to change the political system, as O'Neill acknowledges, would later be used by Hitler and other twentieth-century dictators: purges both within and without his party to eliminate anyone who posed a threat to him; a repressive secret police to retain present power; a National Education system in which children would be taken from their parents to be trained by the state to achieve the goals of the fatherland: a perfect society in the future. Resembling Brecht's Arturo Ui, Walter White is an

---

*The seventeen-year-old Richard tells his family: "You can celebrate your Fourth of July. I'll celebrate the day the people bring out the guillotine again and I see Pierpont Morgan being driven by in a tumbril!" Richard has read Carlyle's *French Revolution* and maintains it is a "great book"—especially "that part about Mirabeau —and about Marat and Robespierre."

American Hitler-like gangster. The threat of totalitarian dictatorships is one of O'Neill's primary concerns in the early 1940s. He spends much of July 1941 working on "Blind Alley Guy." The following month—on the 24th—he writes to Langner, prescribing, in a humorous manner, a remedy to cure the madness of a Robespierre or Hitler.* He was serious, however, in his efforts to depict oppressive regimes and embarked—perhaps inspired by the research done for the Robespierre idea—on a series of plays, showing the modern equivalent of the Reign of Terror that madmen had unleashed in the world: the presence of Hitler haunts "Blind Alley Guy"; Mussolini's shadow stretches across the Atlantic, terrorizing Malatesta, who had fled Italy seeking safety in America. Finally, in his portrait of the World Dictator in "The Last Conquest," O'Neill presents a composite picture of all historical despots, ever ancient, ever new.

°ASTRONOMER†
(December 21, 1938)

Astronomer—large family—who from studies becomes obsessed with the terrible unimportance of life—so his effect on all interrelationships of family is

---

*O'Neill told Langner that the next time they met they could exchange stories about their current ailments and

> if anyone asks us about the war we'll say, "What war?" There's nothing like having a real good ailment. It's one thing that never bores you, or leaves you at a loss for a word. I'm sure if one of the Knitting Women had called to Louis XVI as he ascended the guillotine, "Well, Capet, how're the old kidneys lately?", he would have waved the headsman aside and begun a serious conversation. . . . At this point the headsman would have interrupted with a little anecdote about his arthritis, and all the Knitting Women would have told of their hot flashes, irregular menstrual periods, varicose veins, flatulence, flat feet and what not. Danton would have muscled in with a long harangue on the horrible hangover he had yesterday morning. Robespierre would have addressed the mob for two hours on the new pills he was taking to get rid of his pimples. The Revolution would have been forgotten. . . . I think the quickest way to stop Hitler is for some Allied agent, disguised as a good listener, to ask him, "Well, Adolph, how are the old hysterics lately?" Hitler will promptly ask for an armistice in which to start the tale properly, and then sue for peace at any price in order to gain leisure to relate all his symptoms. . . . But I better stop or I'll be writing you a brand new farce. You know me, Pal. Always, as I've said, writing about character plus life!

†See 1927 idea: "Play of Astronomer."

one of evil and destruction—symbolically he becomes the dark center around which their lives evolve—

His final megalomania—that all this limitless chaos is a product of his own mind—

The pity—that he feels this chaos taking him away from meaning—from love and all human values—and cannot help himself—like a rival—finally, his horrible loneliness and nostalgia for his old human place and meaning—but at same time, his exultation in facing truth—in identifying himself with a chaos so vast—in choosing for his home, interstellar space—

°PLAY IDEA
[1938]*

Of woman who marries widower with two children—her passionate love—jealousy of past—real affection for children as themselves but hatred for them as mother's children, children of his love for another woman—

Decision [to] murder them—she does this with great skill—only her husband at last suspects—then he becomes embodiment of her guilt to her—a combination of fear he will hate her if he is sure—and her feeling he desires death because he is sure leads her at last to murder him.

Then, at last, her suicide—she realizes something she always wanted to do—the necessity for another life, forced by her fate in this—a life in which the children will be hers, the part of his love for first wife hers, she will be that first wife.

O'Neill did not use a special notebook for his ideas for plays in the 1939–1942 period. He did, however, record new concepts in the Work Diary, later writing scenarios for a number of them and eventually completing several plays (see next chapter). Some ideas were entered in the Work Diary but were never developed beyond the note-taking stage:

5/20/39   Get idea play outside Cycle, one day, Paris, Napoleon's coron[ation].

"Time Grandfather Was Dead"
8/15/40   Interrupt work L.D.J.I.N. to make notes on ideas for two plays (outside Cycle, too)—timely but timeless spiritually—re present world collapse & dictatorships —no titles yet

---

*This is the final idea presented in the notebook; it follows the 1938 "Astronomer" idea.

8/17/40   Notes on the two new ideas for plays—title for one "Time Grandfather Was Dead" [title for other "The Last Conquest"]

8/18/40   "Time Grandfather Was Dead" idea (notes)

1/20/41   "Time Grandfather Was Dead" (some notes on this play idea)

3/15–16/41   "Time Grandfather Was Dead" (notes—again head full this idea)

7/31/41   "Time Grandfather Was Dead" (this idea forces itself on top—notes)

8/2–11&15–17/41   "Time Grandfather Was Dead" (notes—outline)

12/20/41   New idea—transcontinental train—all types U.S. cit[izens].—the old man who is Uncle Sam—his scorn for their selfish attitudes—endeavors inspire them with ideal, etc.—one-act?—notes

3/24/42   Ideas, two plays—golden wedding idea & death grief idea

7/5/42   New Idea propaganda play to awaken people—we all seem asleep—it's too far away yet

4 • The Late Plays
Completed and Contemplated:
1939–1943

THE ICEMAN COMETH
(1939)

After working four and a half years on the Cycle, O'Neill states in June, 1939, that he feels "fed up and stale" on it, adding: "will do me good [to] lay on shelf and forget it for a while—do a play which has nothing to do with it" (W.D.). The following day he writes: "Read over notes on various ideas for single plays—decide do outlines of two that seem [to] appeal most and see—the Jimmy the P[riest's].—H[ell]. H[ole].—Garden idea—and N[ew]. L[ondon]. family one" (W.D.). O'Neill envisions, in this brief notation, his two greatest plays, *The Iceman Cometh* and *Long Day's Journey into Night*, both set in 1912, the most portentous year—personally and artistically—in the author's early life. If Ned Malloy in "Exorcism,"* the precursor of *The Iceman Cometh*, is an accurate self-portrait, O'Neill utters his "Yes" to life after an unsuccessful suicide attempt in 1912 at Jimmy the Priest's. The second view of the dramatist —as Edmund Tyrone in *Long Day's Journey into Night*—shows him at the family home in New London shortly after this experience, trying to give his life a sense of purpose. When an illness is diagnosed as tuberculosis, Edmund-Eugene is sent to a sanatorium where he reads Strindberg and resolves to become a playwright.

Re-creating the people, places, and events of 1912 brought O'Neill "personal satisfaction," as he later remarks. "These two outside plays I've done have been on my mind for years."† In *Long Day's Journey into Night* he attempts to purge the tragic memories of the past and to still the ghosts of his family that forever haunted him, as notes for earlier ideas and plays reveal. In *The Iceman Cometh* he pays tribute to the close friends he made during his "down and out" period at Jimmy the Priest's, a waterfront dive, in 1911–1912; the Hell Hole, a Greenwich Village barroom-hotel, in 1915; and the taproom of the Garden Hotel, located across the street from Madison Square Garden. O'Neill states: "The dump in the play is no one place but a combination of three in which I once hung out. The characters all derive from actual people I have known— more or less closely and remotely."** That first tentative list of characters identifies these "actual people" by name:

> Tom W. —Rep[orted]. that he has never left place since wife's funeral— great sentimental respect for this myth which he has encouraged —grand excuse—has built up myth about her as loving help-

---

*See discussion of this 1919 idea in Chapter 1.
†Letter to Dudley Nichols, October 13, 1940.
**Letter to Kenneth Mcagowan, November 29, 1940.

mate—fact is she nagged him to death and he was relieved when
she died—but he's believed by all, even old timers who knew her
have finally believed it—truth is he was face to face at time with
fact drink has got him and he could go no farther and didn't
want to—

Jimmy B.—Boer war record, stat[istics].—finding wife [in] bed [with]
staff officer, his excuse—but "tomorrow" his proof to himself
she can't do that to him—actor longing to prove he can make
Tomorrow come true—deep sincere longing to give up—

Bull   —Bartender—periodical drunk—who is never going to [drink]
again—who is in love with the whore, Cora—who is determined
to reform and marry her—live in country where he has never
been, except in Boys Club outing as child, and on political club
rackets later—his ideals of this are vague, sentimental, Promised
Land—he gets her to believe in this in spite of herself, just out
of love—she was raised on farm—she doesn't believe he'll never
drink again—nor believe a man can be happy married to [a]
whore or ever really forget and forgive past—the real wish of
her life is to have him for pimp and work for him, give him all
money so he needn't work—It is Bull who encourages Jimmy in
"tomorrow" and Tom to get out of house. At end, he becomes
pimp—goes on his drunk—

Terry   —Who sees and is articulate about real meaning of what is going
on—who regrets they can't leave themselves alone—can't forgive
themselves for not being what they are not—his growing irritation and hostility to Bull—

Bella   —Jovial cynic—

Joe S.   —Jovial cynic—

Bob. M.   —Anarchist—incorruptible fanatic—coldly pure, no women, no
booze—passionate idealist—in hiding—suspicion wanted on
Coast for bombing activities with Wobblies—savagely intolerant
[of] weakness—about 30—

Lefty   —Neopolitan immoralist—gangster—jovial, humorous and yet
hard as nails—

Major A. —same as life—

Viljoen   —

As O'Neill interchanges real and fictitious names in his notes and outline,
the diagram on the following page is included.

Actual personages	Names assigned in notes and first set design for Act One	Final list in 1939 outline	Names in published play
Tom Wallace	Tom—Hope—Harry	Harry Hope, "Old Harry"	Harry Hope
Lefty Louis	Lefty—Rocky	Rocky Morello	Rocky Pioggi
John Bull	Bull—Lyons—Chick	Chick Pioggi	Chuck Morello
Joe Smith	Joe	Joe Mott	Joe Mott
James Byth	"Jimmy Tomorrow"	Jimmy Cameron	James Cameron "Jimmy Tomorrow"
Major Adams	The Major	Captain Lewis	Cecil Lewis "The Captain"
Christian De Wet	Viljoen—the General—Wetjoen	Colonel Wetjoen	Piet Wetjoen "The General"
Terry Carlin	Terry—Larry	Larry Slade (Egan)	Larry Slade
Hippolyte Havel	Hip.—Hipp.	Hugo Kapnar	Hugo Kalmar
Donald Vose	Bob M.—Potter	Don Parritt (Perris)	Don Parritt
Al Adams' son	Adams—Morris A.—Morris	Willie Oban (Yorke)	Willie Oban
Jack Croak	Mosher	Ed Mosher	Ed Mosher
	McGloin	Bill McGloin (Mac)	Pat McGloin
	Buzy Garrity	(not listed)	(not listed)
	Pearl	Pearl	Pearl

Names assigned in notes and first set design of Act One	Final list in 1939 outline	Names in published play
Margie	Margie	Margie
Cora	Cora	Cora
Hicky	(not listed)	Theodore Hickman "Hickey"
	Farrell, dish[washer].	
	Schwartz, cop	Moran
		Lieb

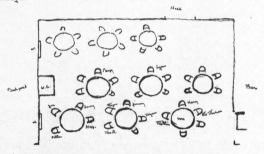

First page of the scenario for *The Iceman Cometh*. Photo provides a sample of O'Neill's minuscule handwriting.

The names of the three women—Pearl, Margie, and Cora*—who are probably composite portraits of prostitutes O'Neill had known, remain the same throughout the various stages of composition. While listed in the 1939 dramatis personae, neither Farrell, the dishwasher, nor Schwartz, the cop, is mentioned in the notes. In the published text Schwartz is an offstage character (both Joe and Rocky allude to him); omitted entirely is Buzy Garrity, a dope addict and pusher, who is originally assigned a place at a table in O'Neill's first drawing of the back room in Act One and a minor role in the early outline. The first three people on the preceding list of actual personages are Tom Wallace, proprietor of the Hell Hole, and his two bartenders, Lefty Louis and John Bull.† Joe Smith is a former roommate at the Hell Hole; the two friends from Jimmy the Priest's are "a press agent for Paine's Fireworks named Jimmy Bieth [Byth] and one Major Adams, a red-nosed inebriate of sixty-odd who had been cashiered years before from the British army."**

The playwright's interest in the Boer War was probably aroused initially by Jimmy Byth's vivid account of it. Byth was, as Sheaffer notes, a publicity agent for a theatrical re-creation of "The Great Boer War Spectacle" presented at the St. Louis World's Fair in 1904 and a year later in New York. As Byth "reminisced about Generals Cronje and Viljoen, about Captain Lewis and the flight of Det Wet, all names and incidents featured in the exhibit, O'Neill drank it all in."†† While the former English soldier is given the name of the historical Captain Lewis in the published text, he retains the characteristics of Major Adams, O'Neill's friend at Jimmy the Priest's, as the early notation beside his name— "same as life"—indicates. The prototype for the Boer general, "Viljoen"— whose name is later changed to General Piet Wetjoen—is the famous General Christian De Wet; he and his brother Piet waged numerous campaigns against the British. Included in O'Neill's two columns of historical names are "Piet" and "Christian"—as well as the surnames De Wet, Kemp, Joubert, Cronje, and De La Ray. The actual General De Wet and the fictitious General Wetjoen have numerous similarities: appearance, physical strength and their pride in it, nobility of character, battles in which they fought. O'Neill did extensive research on

---

*In the "prelims" stage O'Neill considered other possibilities: Ida the Goose, Big Nora, Sophie Lyons, Freda, Cora the Blond. These appear on a list of eighty names the dramatist compiled in his effort to determine ones that would reflect the various ethnic, social, and political backgrounds of his characters.

†Sheaffer's *O'Neill Son and Playwright* (p. 333) provides information about these three men, whose names appear in the dramatist's early notes.

**George Jean Nathan, *The Intimate Notebooks of George Jean Nathan* (New York, 1931), p. 32.

††Sheaffer, *O'Neill Son and Playwright*, p. 130.

the Boer War, recording information on significant dates and battles, to present an accurate continuum of it in the now-friendly conflict between the two former foes, the British Captain Lewis and the Boer General Wetjoen.

The dramatist uses two groups of characters—anarchists and corrupt grafters —to re-create the political atmosphere and the friends he had known at the Hell Hole. Larry Slade is a former anarchist like his prototype Terry Carlin, one of O'Neill's drinking companions in 1915 and a man who remained a close friend for two decades.* The model for Hugo Kalmar is Hippolyte Havel, a colorful Czech friend who had become an anarchist at the age of eighteen. After years of imprisonment, suffering, and persecution, Havel found refuge in London and became Emma Goldman's lover in 1899. The dramatist portrays these two anarchists in his 1915 play, "The Personal Equation," as Hartmann† and the Russian Olga Tarnoff.

The prototype for the Potter-Parritt character is Donald Vose, whose anarchist mother, Gertie Vose, and Emma Goldman became friends in 1897. Goldman's account of Vose's betrayal of his anarchist friends is similar to the fictitious Don Parritt's. Vose came to New York from the West after the *Times* building explosion in Los Angeles, and, though shabbily dressed, he treated his drinking companions nightly—supposedly waiting for money from home to return to California. Later, during the trial, he admitted that he had been employed by Detective William J. Burns to gain the confidence of David Caplan, who informed Vose his anarchist friend, Matthew A. Schmidt, had fled to New York. Acting under instructions, Vose contacted Goldman and other anarchists in New York, seeking and obtaining information about Schmidt who, with Caplan, was arrested and charged with the crime.** While he did not actually betray his mother as does Parritt, Vose behaved treacherously to Goldman, who resembles the fictitious Rosa Parritt.

Characters illustrating the political corruption of the early twentieth century include Pat McGloin, Rocky Morello, Joe Smith, and Harry Hope, who in his

---

*In a postscript to a letter dated February 14, 1934, Carlotta O'Neill tells Kenneth Macgowan: "Gene buried both Terry Carlin and Jack McGrath the early part of January."

†Sadakichi Hartmann is listed among Goldman's friends in New York in the early twentieth century. Identical terms are used to describe Hartmann and Hugo; both have "long black hair," dark/black eyes which "peer near-sightedly from behind thick-lensed spectacles." They dress in black and wear a white shirt and a "flowing Windsor tie." Long, the anticapitalist in *The Hairy Ape*, also wears a "black Windsor tie" when he accompanies Yank to Fifth Avenue, where proletarians are trespassers.

**The Vose story appears in *Living My Life*, Emma Goldman (Garden City, 1931), pp. 550–51, 566.

ward heeler days was a "jitney Tammany politician." The most developed example in the notes, however, is Morris Adams, son of a "policy king," who is later called Willie Oban," "son of the late world-famous Bill Oban, King of the Bucket Shops." According to O'Neill's original plan, the Morris-Willie character, whose model is a son of the notorious "Al" Adams, plays a major, socially significant role. The first page of O'Neill's 1939 notes for *The Iceman Cometh* describes "Al" Adams and his downfall. He was a friend of Deputy Comissioner of Police William* S. Devery, whose brother-in-law Michael J. Brennan was indicted with Adams in 1902. Adams was sent to Sing Sing for his illegal policy activities in 1903; when released the next year, he tried to establish a chain of bucket shops. Alienated from his family, he commited suicide in 1906 in his room at the Hotel Ansonia. Adams had a daughter, Evelyn (O'Neill gives this name to Hickey's wife), and four sons, who called their father "the Governor," a term Hickey uses to address Harry Hope. Two of the sons were lawyers, educated at Harvard and Heidelberg. A third son, Louis, was arrested and sentenced to six months on Blackwell's Island for attempting to shoot his father. His statement, made while boarding the police boat, to Michael J. Burke, the mate of the steamer and a friend of many years, sounds like one of Morris-Willie's lines in the play: "I was drunk; that is the only way I can account for it. I have no kick coming about my sentence. I am surprised, though, at my friends, that they have done nothing to get me out of this scrape."† The personal background and statements attributed to Morris Adams in the notes and Willie Oban in the published text suggest O'Neill had either known "Al" Adams's son Louis or spent considerable time analyzing published articles on the "policy king" and his family.

In his response of December 30, 1940, to a question Macgowan had asked about the salesman in *The Iceman Cometh*, O'Neill writes: "What you wonder about Hickey: No, I never knew him. He's the most imaginary character in the play. Of course, I knew many salesmen in my time who were periodical drunks, but Hickey is not any of them. He is all of them, you might say, and none of them." The fact that O'Neill never knew Hickey—that he was not, like most of the characters, one of his friends at Jimmy the Priest's or the Hell Hole— explains the most significant revelation in the early notes for this play: Hickey was not originally an integral part of it; he was, rather, an afterthought. Hickey's name is not mentioned in the outline until the end of Act One; it is not included in any dramatis personae. Also missing are the names of the two detectives— Moran and Lieb—whose sole purpose in the play is to arrest him at the end. In

---

*When Joe Mott as a young man wanted to open a gambling house, Harry Hope had sent him to his "good friend," a Chief called "Big Bill."
†"Island for 'Al' Adams's Son/Six Months to Serve for Attack on His Father, the Ex-Policy King," *New York Times*, November 5, 1904, p. 7.

the first notes Bull, the bartender, plays the role Hickey later assumes, as the long passage describing him indicates. "It is Bull who encourages Jimmy in 'tomorrow' [to make his tomorrow pipe dream a reality today] and Tom to get out of house." Observing these actions arouses Terry-Larry's "growing irritation & hostility to Bull." The specific purpose of the Bull-Hickey character is to shatter not only the characters' pipe dreams but also their close friendships. When Macgowan urged the dramatist to condense Act One, O'Neill in his response speaks of the necessity of building "up the complete picture of the group as it now is in the first part—the atmosphere of the place, the humour and friendship and human warmth and *deep inner contentment* at the bottom." If he failed to do so, he cautions, "You wouldn't feel the same sympathy and understanding for them, or be so moved by what Hickey does to them."* O'Neill's main theme in the first outline for *The Iceman Cometh* is that man desperately needs friendship; it is *the* link that binds and sustains the characters gathered at Harry Hope's saloon.

June 9, 1939—Outline, Act One

The political atmosphere at Harry Hope's saloon is established at the beginning of the outline with the early introduction of Adams-Oban and Potter-Parritt. Their discourses on anarchism and the corruption of capitalism summarize O'Neill's social statements: neither "ism" is able to provide its followers with sufficient hope for the present; as a consequence, they retreat into a world of "tomorrow" pipe dreams. His portraits of the disillusioned, disenchanted end products of both systems serve to illustrate also man's hopelessly flawed condition. The recent arrival of the newcomer, Potter, motivates Larry Slade's long speech, in which he explains the need of the characters to pretend, at least, to believe in their own pipe dreams and in the "other's hope." Later he says: "The lie of a pipe dream is what gives life to the whole misbegotten mad lot of us, drunk or sober."

The first scene opens with "Adams' song—his conversation [with] Joe & Larry—Potter wakes up—bewildered—asks Larry—then remembers—got back from Coast, drunk, went to Ferrer school† to get Larry's address—suspicious of

---

*Letter to Macgowan, December 30. 1940.

†Goldman states that before going on a tour in January 1911 she participated in the inauguration of the Francisco Ferrer Center, named after the Spanish educator and martyr, who was shot because of his possible involvement in the plot to assassinate Alfonso XIII. The Potter-Parritt character of the first outline is another view of Jamie O'Neill. Like Jamie, Potter "got back from Coast, drunk" and guilt-ridden after betraying his mother. Temporarily "off whores," both men turn to a trusted friend, longing to confess the "sin" against the mother and to be absolved.

suspicious attitude at School—came here." When Potter wonders where he is, Larry asks ironically: "Do you know Blake†—Prophetic books?—Palace of Dipsomania—Wayside Inn for those who fall by the wayside—it's Bedrock Bar—where you can have your hope and still eat it—or drink it." Larry alone has no hope; but, as he says, the others "come here to seek the past finally or they come here in misery, or come hooked here on death, without pain—there is no future, so you can hope a dead hope—you can accept yourself without pain." In this outline Larry has not been one of the former lovers of Potter's mother, eliminating the possibility that he may be the younger man's actual father and not a mere father-figure. Potter senses he can trust Larry and tells him of his involvement in blowing up a court house on the Coast—"The halls of capitalist injustice"; he had carried the dynamite in a suitcase to the site. He says that someone "sold to Burns—all arrested—all but me—I left no trace—questioned me—I said you can kill me but I'll never tell—beat me up."

One by one the men in the back room wake from their drunken sleep. The speeches of the first three to do so reinforce the theme of political graft and corruption. Joe describes his days of grandeur when, as a successful gambler, he paid protection money to McGloin—"a lieutenant then"—who one day got "too hungry" and "forgot to pass it on." McGloin was fired but wants to be reinstated to "make pile, retire country, relive Irish times—keep away from police and booze—above all from whores—marry country girl that hasn't got flat feet from walking a beat on city pavement, hawking her tush." When McGloin says he was "framed—dirty politics," Morris Adams accuses him of lying; he had seen the book registering payments. "I can remember my revered father, who resented police, remarking that McGloin was the damndest buzzard of the lot. You are as guilty as hell." McGloin calls old Adams a buzzard; Morris agrees and asks: "What do I get drunk for? I learnt that at Harvard. I went to Harvard to forget him—and then I went to law school—my father arrested." Morris notices Potter: "You are a stranger. You don't know a Prince addresses you. My father was a policy king, second only to Al Adams." Discovering Potter is an anarchist, Morris threatens him: "One word out of you about Kropotkin or Bakunin or Emma G[oldman]., my poor fellow, and start to sing a song I learned at Harvard." When Hip wakes up and begs for a dollar, Morris says: "My God,

---

†O'Neill drew inspiration from three English Romantic poets: Coleridge, Byron, and Blake. The dramatist gave Carlotta Monterey *The Writings of William Blake* at Christmas 1927, saying: "As a patriotic Irish clan egotist I want to give you all the O'Neill you can endure without fetching a shriek—so what gift more to the point than the immortal beauty (reproduced) of the grandest of all O'Neills, past, present and to come?" Donald Gallup states that the "inscription refers to the tradition that Blake's grandfather was an O'Neil (*Inscriptions: Eugene O'Neill to Carlotta Monterey O'Neill*).

what Saviors have come to—Confucius, Buddha, Zoroaster, Christ & now Hip. Can you give me one good reason, Sir, why you haven't yet been martyred for the cause? I can think of none. It strikes me as a grave oversight, a miscarriage of justice." The characters humor Hope, who wakes up in a vile mood as he remembers his promise to go out to vote the following Tuesday; he tells his bartenders to put a "cash only" sign on the register. Bull, the bartender, is described here as an ex-prize fighter who had survived two bouts with Sam Langford; he has two dreams: to get in shape again for another match and to marry Cora.

In the published text, each character, on awakening, musters the necessary courage to face the day ahead fortified by the thought of Hickey's impending visit; the utterance of his name builds to a crescendo by the end of Act One. In contrast, the salesman is mentioned in the outline only before his entrance at the end of the act. When Hickey comes in, the crowd greets him enthusiastically. He says his reason for coming is to see Cora and Bull get married. Bull is pleasant but resentful: "Thanks, but that's me and Cora's business." Although disturbed by Hickey's "detached sensitive benignity," the group's faith in him is renewed when he orders drinks for all. He refuses to join them but offers a toast: "Here's to Tomorrow that really becomes today—a today where you, Jimmy will, etc." Hickey then "goes over each one's tomorrow." As soon as Hickey goes upstairs to get some sleep, the group, now resentful and anxious, wonders if he is taking dope:

they ask dope peddlar—No—Bull says reassuringly, only a joke—always playing jokes—he'll be soused to the gills before night—Yes, showing photo & drinking and saying she's true to him and the fireman—Larry says "maybe he's called there once too often. That's the hell of it. You have to pretend to be so brave. You call and call your fear and dare it to come and laugh defiantly—and lo the Fireman Cometh." "Ah, you crazy old bastard! Would that make him happy?" "He spoke more of peace. It could mean peace from waiting and waiting—" "Ah, well, what the hell! He left corn for drinks, didn't he?" Bull starts to drink—(?).

June 13, 1939—Outline, Act Two

Although he states on June 7, 1939 that he gets "fine title 'The Iceman Cometh' instead of tentative 'Tomorrow' one I had" (W.D.), O'Neill writes the words "Credit Tomorrow" at the top of the first page for Act Two in the righthand corner, a position reserved for his contemplated titles. In the first act the fireman assumes the role the iceman will later play in the joking allusion to the lover of Hickey's wife. It is highly unlikely O'Neill ever seriously entertained the possibility of the implied title at the end of Act One: "The Fireman Cometh." At the top of the third page of the notes for the second act, the words "The

Iceman Cometh" are written in the right corner. However, the words "Credit Tomorrow" show that the theme of pipe dreams is the central focus of the play as O'Neill begins the outline for this act. He uses this theme now to show the threat Hickey poses to the relationships of the characters assembled at Harry Hope's. By the time O'Neill finished the outline for Act One, Hickey had become the catalyst to force the social outcasts at the saloon to relinquish their pipe dreams; in later drafts of this act Hickey assumes a messianic role.

Act Two opens in the bar two days later. It is evening. Since his arrival, Hickey has managed to disrupt formerly close ties, destroyed the harmonious peaceful atmosphere, and sown the seeds of despair and doubt in the viability of dreams. In describing the setting, O'Neill writes: "Scene shows bar, beginning of backroom—and if memory comes alive." Larry, Joe and Buzy are at the bar; Bull has not appeared to relieve Rocky, who blames "that bastard, Hicky*— what's he want to come here for on wagon?—why don't he let people alone?— like a damned minister, preaching religion—what the hell is he driving at with his bull about finding yourself and making tomorrow be today—I thought maybe he was coked up." Buzy tells them that he "ain't sold him nothing—No, I ain't, not nothing. I'm through, going to take cure myself—no bastard's goin' to tell me I try [to] make addicts because I'm ashamed & want everyone else [to] be like myself." The whores "pipe up—true—Buzy indignant—you're liar, only business—well, you try [to] make addicts just the same, and that makes you a lousy skunk, don't it?—Buzy going to slug—Rocky grabs both—Buzy has gun—Joe makes peace."

Rocky cannot entice anyone in the group to drink. Sober, the Major and Wetjoen antagonize each other. When the former announces he is going back with Payne's Fireworks, the latter remarks: "Ha!—a fit job for British officer— that is nearest to War they should ever come, fireworks! You should have seen them at Modden River." The Major retaliates: "It was you who advised Cronje [to] stop and fight battle when he could have escaped. You were sick of fighting. You wanted [to] surrender the moment the tide turned. They stoned you on streets of Johannesburg. A lion in victory, a jackass in defeat." The whores inter- vene, and both apologize resentfully: "It's that damned Hicky."

Potter enters, visibly shaken by Hickey's words: "Face it, my friend. I don't think you ever wanted [to] save man. You wanted [to] destroy him because you'd failed and hadn't courage [to] blame yourself—you hate man as Judas did." Hip awakes and turns to Morris: "Buy me a gin. All scared of Hicky like little kids. Poor little Hicky! He's dead. Let me put flowers on his grave." Before he passes out again, he calls Potter a "little monkey face stool pigeon." When Potter says Hip is "crazy as hell," Larry defends his friend: "He spent ten years

---

*The "e" is omitted in Hickey's name throughout the outline.

in a political prison in Hungary* for the Cause. I respect that even if I saw long ago that the Cause is sprouting another hungry bastard like you and me dressed up in the fake whiskers of fair words to look like Santa Claus. He had guts and still has if whiskey hasn't eaten 'em. You would never spend ten years in prison, no matter what price you had to pay." Everyone is awed and frightened by Larry's warning that Hickey has brought the cold touch of death with him; "and when it's real to you it's most desirable—Be God, you don't welcome it then—you want to cling to the last shreds and tatters of your long life." Larry then gives his "beloved Christ, let me live" speech that does not appear until the end of Act Three in the published text. He then feels a surge of pity for Hickey; "it's easy to see he can't have reached where he is except by a path through the middle of hell and as a leader preaching the peace of ashes!"

Near the end of the act, Hickey enters. Called a son of a bitch for his meddling, he insists he wants only to bring peace to his friends. When Larry asks "with concerned carelessness" how his wife is, Hickey says: "Evelyn is taking a long, much-needed rest." Margie injects: "A vacation, you mean—with the Iceman?" Hickey responds with a strange smile: "Yes, I think you might say she is in the arms of the Iceman (then darkly) I am sorry to have to tell you my dear wife is dead." At once, everyone—"all except Larry"—is full of contrition. Hickey continues: "Her death was good riddance—I mean, for her, to be rid of me—I feel no grief—I mean for her sake—it was inevitable—she was much too good for this world—too good for me—now she's dead, thank God—I mean, thank God for her sake." Hickey leaves to encourage Hope and Jimmy to face themselves and the world outside. There is general agreement that his efforts will fail. In this early outline, "they tried it once—Hope got half way across street—auto came near him—Jimmy got his job back—fired in three days—said he left just as Hope said suddenly remembered wife last time on his arm going to church."

June 16, 1939—Outline, Act Three, Scene One

In the outline, as in the final draft, the third act opens in the bar the following morning with the two bartenders discussing the problems they had the previous night with their women. In the early notes Margie and Pearl do not have the pipe dream later ascribed to them: that they are "tarts" and not "whores." However, they want Rocky to give up his job; "we ain't goin' be your whores unless you're our pimp—maybe we can each of us hook a nice sucker who'll marry us—a farmer and we'll have flowers adjoining—we've always

---

*O'Neill thought Hippolyte Havel was Hungarian. One page of notes, headed "Hung.", comprises a list of names—some beginning with the letter "H" such as "Heves" and "Havtan."

wanted [to] live in [the] country." Bull and Cora's dream has been shattered. One of them or both—whichever version of the story is accepted—had "gotten soused on the way to Hoboken." Cora had accused Bull of being ashamed to marry a whore; "but you keep hanging around me, having all the shanty loving you can muster from me—when you're drunk you can't think my money's dirty—you grab every nickel I don't hide—if I had a baby's bank you'd rob it sure as hell—you can choose between me and your work, you big overgrown sober bastard!" Bull curbs his desire to drink because it would "give such satisfaction to that bastard Hicky." Rocky encourages him and implies Bull is a pimp. The two men are "about to fight" when Larry and Joe enter; the latter acts as peacemaker, reminding the bartenders: "You boys been pals ever since—we all kids together." The three younger men agree that Hickey is the cause of all their problems and—in a sequence omitted in the published text—make plans to murder him. Larry pleads with them:

"Don't let him bring death in. That's what he wants."—they turn on Larry like gangsters—"Keep out of this and you ain't heard nothing, see! If you dare squeal—" Larry mad "Squeal! If I'd wanted to squeal I've known things I could have sold to Burns that would have made me rich. When I was in Movement, if I wanted sell out the Revolution—" "Ah, to hell with that dope dream! Fuck the Revolution!"—Larry gets wild—they get amused and amazed—contrite—soothe him—"Sure, you'd blow up the world. We know you've got guts. Here, have a drink and cool off."—Larry shamed—lost philosophy—then argues, not kill Hicky—to blame and not to blame—something in him—something he's done—if we knew—he's afraid [to] drink for fear he'll tell—if we could get him drunk and he'd talk, he'd be old Hicky again."—"Maybe try that—Larry get him drunk—trick him in room—etc."

The men can forgive Hickey for many things if only "he'd leave Hope alone—Hope's so happy as is—this place, he's made it like home—and poor Jimmy Tomorrow—hell, he knows he can't get that job back—booze has got him—then they change strangely—hope—might make it, at that—caught up with own hopes—if others of them could, I could."* Larry becomes philosophical: "Yes, that's the trouble with tomorrow. You want it and you don't want it. It's a free dream but could you live in it? Would it kill you or give you a new life? You'd meet yourself face to face then maybe yourself would murder you, or you'd have to murder—."

The other characters—sober and shaky—enter; each is determined to pursue his dream: Wetjoen as a longshoreman; the Major as "superintendent in full

---

*This idea is repeated in *Long Day's Journey into Night* when a drunken Jamie Tyrone discovers his mother had started taking drugs again: "It meant so much. I'd begun to hope, if she'd beaten the game, I could too."

charge" at Payne's Fireworks; Morris in the D.A.'s office; McGloin in the police department. Hickey appears with Hope and Jimmy—"like the preacher goin' with guys to the chair." In the outline "they all, led by Jimmy and Tom—Hicky go out."† A few minutes later Tom comes in, shaken. Hickey follows, saying affectionately, "Now, Tom, you know that wasn't the way—you simply met yourself face to face on other side of street where he's been waiting all these years for you. We'll try again." The others protest: "Let him alone. He's beat you, you son of a bitch!" Hope rallies, determined to "get drunk just to get drunk." He urges everyone to join him in a birthday celebration and threatens Hickey:

"You'll celebrate with us, be Jeez. Drink for drink. If we have to hold you and pour it down your neck. We've had enough of your bull."—Hicky resists for second with fear—as if to run out of place—"Hold him, Bull. You'll be old Hicky again, by God—tell stories—crack jokes—try to make us all laugh again —you'll tell us about your wife and the Iceman."—chorus of revengeful jeers— Hicky sober again—says strangely—"all right—you don't have force me— anything you please—it's all over now—I've done all I can do for all of you. (Raises his glass) Here's to your health and happiness, Harry, and long life to you, if you want it."

In this early version Hickey becomes, like the others, inebriated. At the end of the scene he tells them his wife was murdered. When Rocky asks: "Who done it?" Larry bursts out angrily: "You damned stupid Dago! Can't you leave the man alone in his sorrow and torment? Must you be buttin' in when you've no business? Harry, I'll leave this dump of yours if you can't keep your damned help from spyin' on your guests. (fumes) There's no privacy here." Hope warns Rocky: "Keep your mind on tending bar if you want to keep your job."

June 21, 1939—Outline, Act Three, Scene Two

It is after one the following morning at the opening of Scene Two, which later becomes Act Four. With the exception of Rocky, everyone—including Bull, who has gone on a wild spree—is drunk; but "it is a hopeless, sodden drunkenness which appears more like the detached, passive daze of opium addicts in the stage just preceding a death-like sleep." Alcohol has had no effect on Hickey, who stopped drinking only for a brief period the previous evening to write and mail a letter. Rocky notices the time: "Happy means having drinks every 15 minutes. I'm late on this one." Hickey checks the time and says he has some-

---

† In the final draft Hickey remains inside and tries to get Larry to stop lying to himself. In this passage in the outline, O'Neill gives Harry Hope and Larry Slade the names of their real-life counterparts.

thing to tell them all before he leaves to keep an appointment. His confession here—while not so long as that of the final draft—contains a few surprisingly different twists and responses from his listeners. He compares the peace and freedom he has found to "the heavenly bliss of the Promised Land the preachers speak about." To encourage his friends to take the last step leading to deliverance, he tells the

whole story of my love for my late departed wife, Evelyn.—I suppose Hope and Jimmy having once been married men will understand best—but since all had someone or something and lived with it—if it wasn't a wife, it may have been a mother, or a sister, or a cause—or oneself, eh, Larry?"

He tells the story of himself and Evelyn—and as he tells it, he draws out the stories of the others and they join in with them, descriptions [of] lives, until at end he puts it up to them "Well, you can see, can't you, that the time had to come when something, some very little thing, like her kissing me goodnight or saying 'I know you'll never drink again' would show you you had to do now, at once, what you'd wanted to do for so long"—(pause)—Hope bursts out "I know. Kill the God damn bitch"—(then all, all join in one by one with a fierce revengefulness) Hicky says "Yes, that's exactly what I did. I murdered Evelyn— knife—in her sleep—she felt no pain." McGloin reacts automatically "arrest you"—stares at him—"none of my business. No, by God, help you escape. I know old ropes, etc."—all say "Yes, help you."—Larry says "You don't see the point. He doesn't want escape his peace." "Yes, you must learn my philosophy about physical death."—Cops come in—"better not try escape" (to McGloin) "we'll forget what you said, Pat. You're drunk."

After Hickey is taken away, Potter attempts to explain his guilt feelings to Larry but does not make his later complete confession: "It isn't on her account. I'm glad as far's she's concerned—it's thinking of those other guys—I never thought of them." In this outline Hip, rather than Larry, condemns Potter to death: "Pig of a stool pigeon! Traitor! To the guillotine!" Larry sits in silence while the others conspire to create the ultimate pipe dream that Hickey is insane; they believe he will be sent to the nuthouse and not to the chair.

Then sound of Potter hitting in back yard—pause—"What hell's that?"—Larry "It's Justice falling off the roof. Don't interfere with it." Hip "Death to all spies and traitors! Long live the Revolution! Drink you stupid bourgeois monkey faces!" Hope inclined to have someone investigate but Larry dissuades "You'll find out tomorrow. To hell with it. Here's your health, Harry, and long life to you!"—all drink.

The play closes as each character asserts the validity of his pipe dream and passes out. Rocky, still sober, shakes Hip awake: "Come on, you Anarchist bum. Have a drink." Hip exclaims: "Drink! I tell you it comes soon. I will live to see it, I tell you. 'The days grow hot, O Babylon! 'Tis cool beneath thy willow trees.'

Drink little monkey face!" Rocky drinks with him. "Sure! That's the stuff! Free booze and free lunch beneath the willow trees!"

O'Neill completed the scenario for *The Iceman Cometh* on June 24, 1939, and started the outline for *Long Day's Journey into Night* the following day, finishing it on July 3. He put aside this play, however, and decided to write *The Iceman Cometh* first, recording his progress in the Work Diary. In the set drawings made at this time, the author now assigns the characters their fictitious, rather than their actual, names.

July 6, 1939	—set drawings
7–10	—notes
11–12	—characters
13	—I, start dialogue
August 7	—Finish 1st draft I—over 40 pages!
8–9	—II, notes, prelims
10–11	—II, begin dialogue
25	—Finish 1st draft II—long but grand!
28	—III-1, prelims
29	—III-1, start dialogue
September 20	—Finish 1st draft III-1
21	—III-2, prelims
October 12	—Finish III-2 & 1st Draft of play
13	—Notes for revision
November 26	—Finish 2nd Draft
27	—Start going over typed script of 2nd draft—decide change III-1 to III & III-2 to Act IV
December 14	—Finish 3rd Draft of play
20	—Finish minor corrections, cuts, and will now call "The Iceman Cometh" finished—one of best plays I've ever written!
January 3, 1940	—Finish trimming

As the first idea and early outline suggest, O'Neill originally conceives *The Iceman Cometh* as a memory play. He assembles a group of homeless, hope-forsaken outcasts, who—as he states—"all derive from actual people I have known," in a dump called Hope's, "a combination of three in which I hung out." They are sustained in their more lucid alcoholic moments by a belief in their pipe dreams and each other. Shortly after the première of *The Iceman Cometh* O'Neill explains his aspirations for the American theatre to Langner and adds: "We must live in that pipe dream—or die—(as I believe I've said in this play). Love remains (once in a while); friendship remains (and that is rare, too). The rest is ashes in the wind! We have friendship. so what the hell!"*

---

*Letter to Lawrence Langner, October 9, 1946.

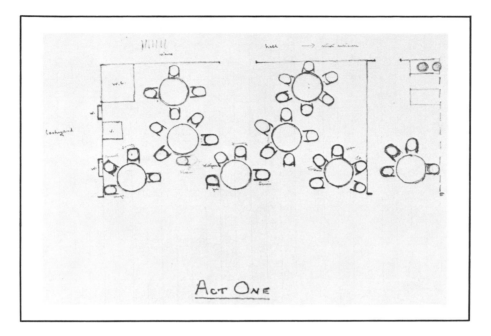

Act One

Friendship—to live in the pipe dream or die: these seem to be the only alternatives in the play. As Larry Slade observes, death comes with Hickey; he *is* the Iceman, for he kills what man needs most for life, according to O'Neill: his pipe dream and his ties to his fellow man, the only visible proof that he belongs. The reluctance of the characters to face the outside world to pursue their pipe dreams stems not only from their awareness of the impossibility of realizing them but also from the fear of losing their only realities—the consolation of friendship, the security of having a "home" at Harry Hope's. The worst punishment Hope can inflict on Willie Oban for singing his ribald song and disturbing the sleep of others is to order him to his room. Willie begs to be allowed to remain with the others who, it should be noted, frequently spend their nights huddled together in the back room. Only when Hickey, the intruder, comes do the men flee in desperation to their rooms upstairs, with some taking the heretofore scorned precaution of locking their doors. Hickey, like Parritt, the other outsider, is the foe. Both are pariahs, friendless, at this man's last refuge, Harry Hope's. Parritt has no pipe dream to provide him with any semblance of hope; he has betrayed not only his mother but his best friends in the movement. The same can be said of Hickey. He has killed his pipe dream, as well as his wife; in his attempt to destroy the illusions of his friends, he betrays them. It is both appropriate and symbolic that Parritt and Hickey die—physically and psychologically—at the end of the play.

As O'Neill develops the outline for *The Iceman Cometh*, writing three

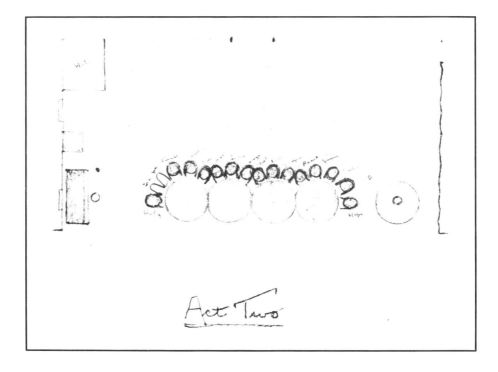

drafts for it, and works out the ultimate fate of Parritt and Hickey, the imagery and theme of death are subtly woven into the whole fabric, necessitating, for the ex-Catholic author, the inclusion of scenes of their confession and absolution. Absent in the early outline is the rich religious symbolism written into later drafts: references to the Day of Judgment; the messianic characterization of Hickey; the Last Supper imagery of Hope's birthday party—that second feast of Belshazzar, as Larry calls it, "with Hickey to do the writing on the wall."

The reference to the feast of the last king of Babylon and Hip-Hugo's final speech in both the outline and completed play—"The days grow hot, O Babylon! 'Tis cool beneath thy willow trees!"—serve to reinforce several themes. Hip-Hugo's pipe dream is to lead a revolutionary anarchist "mob to the sack of Babylon"—modern capitalist society. The weakness in any movement's attempt to achieve political reform or eliminate corruption within a system lies not in the fragility of the dream but in the frailty of men who envision change. Earlier, in speaking of his flawed anarchist friends, Larry says: "The material the ideal free society must be constructed from is men themselves and you can't build a marble temple out of a mixture of mud and manure. When man's soul isn't a sow's ear, it will be time enough to dream of silk purses."* The strident tone advocating change in the early section of the outline is muted. By the time Hip-Hugo utters his final speech, all the characters, after reasserting their pipe dreams,

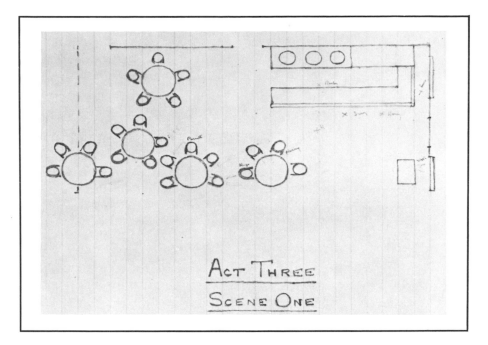

have sunk into careless drunken oblivion. Their tragedy is that they are victims of their own flawed natures as well as of life. Like Daniel, Larry is the only one capable of interpreting Hickey's message as a prophecy of doom: "Be God, I'm the only real convert to death Hickey made here. From the bottom of my coward's heart I mean that now!"

There is an alternative—a middle ground—to the two choices offered: the dream or death. Larry has the ability to see the two sides of death and to desire both the actuality of it and a death-in-life existence. He rejects his pipe dream—the wish to die—and expresses a strong desire to live at any cost, in any state. The character with whom O'Neill identifies most closely in *The Iceman Cometh* is Larry Slade. The one long passage of the early outline that reappears nearly intact in the final draft is Larry's "let me live" speech. In 1944 when O'Neill could no longer hold a pencil to write, Lawrence Langner sent him a Sound Scriber, hoping the dramatist would be able to dictate his plays. In a practice session, O'Neill read his "favorite bit"—Larry's third-act speech. He tells Langner:

---

*Compare this passage and O'Neill's remark to Nichols in a letter on October 13, 1940, expressing his belief that noble-minded statesmen no longer exist: "They all seem to believe any end justifies any means—and the end to that is total ruin for man's spirits. Whether there is social revolution or not, it won't matter a damn. What have you left when you turn over a manure pile—but manure?"

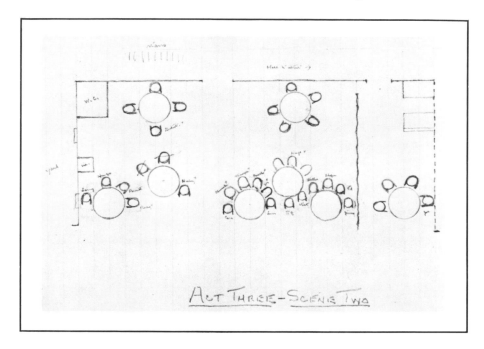

When I played the record back and listened to the voice that was my voice and yet not my voice saying: "I'm afraid to live, am I?—and even more afraid to die! So I sit here, my pride drowned on the bottom of a bottle, keeping drunk so I won't see myself shaking in my britches with fright, or hear myself whining and praying, O Blessed Christ, let me live a little longer at any price! If it's only for a few days more, or a few hours even, let me still clutch greedily to my yellow heart this sweet treasure, this jewel beyond price, the dirty, stinking bit of flesh which is my beautiful little life!"—well, it sure did something to me. It wasn't Larry, it was my ghost talking to me, or I to my ghost.

By the time *The Iceman Cometh* was written in 1939, death had come to Carlin and most of O'Neill's friends from the Jimmy the Priest's-Hell Hole days; but in this play he re-creates them all—their ghosts talking to him and he to them. He exorcises the ghosts of his friends in this play—just as he will those of his family in his next play, *Long Day's Journey into Night*.

LONG DAY'S JOURNEY INTO NIGHT
(1939)

On June 6, 1939, O'Neill writes: "Read over notes on various ideas for single plays—decide outlines of two that seem appeal most, and see—the Jimmy the P[riest's].—H[ell]. H[ole].—Garden idea—and N[ew]. L[ondon]. family one." He completes a scenario for the first idea, *The Iceman Cometh*, on June 24 and begins work the following day on the New London family play. Three extant sets of notes show how he develops this vaguely stated idea into his greatest drama: the autobiographical *Long Day's Journey into Night*: (1) the early preliminary jottings, June 25, 1939; (2) a five-act outline, June 26-July 3, 1939; (3) "prelims," new concepts, set designs, February 22-March 18, 1940.

June 25, 1939—"Long Day's Journey," Notes

The two tentative titles that head the first set of notes—"A Long Day's Journey" and "Diary Of A Day's Journey"—reveal O'Neill's early intention to telescope the series of separate familial events in the progressive time sequence of a single day. The time span for the first act, the only one plotted in this collection of notes, is "from after breakfast to the first trip upstairs." A causal connection is established between Edmund's sickness and the Mother's return to drugs. These two familial concerns emerge here—as in later drafts—as the focal point of the play.

The younger son has appointment p.m. with Doctor to hear results—the others already know because Father has talked with doctor over phone—

The strain of knowing has been too much for Mother—has started her off again.

Only the Father and two sons, as yet unnamed, appear in this first scene; the mother is in the "kitchen giving orders to two servants." When the younger son goes upstairs to get his pipe, the father assures his suspicious elder son that the mother is "absolutely cured" and attacks him for "sponging on poor old father." The son argues: "I'm earning keep here working on grounds, gardener, Fordham grad, gold medal for English." At the end of the scene, the Father urges his son to reform: "still chance for you, summer up here—leave whiskey alone—beer—realize your own fault, make up mind—as long as you don't feel licked in yourself—you've got brains, etc." When he discovers his brother has tuberculosis and is to be sent to a State Farm, the elder son angrily attacks the Father: "You think he'll die & don't want [to] waste money on him." Enraged, the Father replies: "You hope he'll die—always jealous—waiting around for me to die—sponge on mother—especially if she—." At this point, the younger son returns; his father and brother are "very solicitous and affectionate." The last words here are: "M[other] enters."

"New London play" O'Neill's first two pages of notes for *Long Day's Journey into Night*

In the next section, labeled "Gen[eral] notes," O'Neill lists the causes for the Mother's drug addiction and retreat into the past:

Mother's memory guilt love of child that died—blames husband—yet recognition it was love for her, jealousy, made him selfish—and so, bewilderment, bafflement—escape backwards via dope—

Dead son becomes only child she loved—because living sons cause too much pain—

Back to loved—admired father who cannot be admired because of his treatment of mother whom she ought to have admired, loved, but really held in contempt—

Final escape—back beyond marriage to convent—to Mother Elizabeth—to Virgin Mary—

The dramatist works out a systematic series of confrontations to show the love-hate relationships that exist within the family:

Shifting alliances in battle—(direct movements to correspond)

Father, two sons versus Mother
Mother, two sons versus Father
Father, younger son versus Mother, older son
Mother,   "   "   vs. Father, older son
Father & Mother vs. two sons
Brother vs. brother
Father vs. Mother

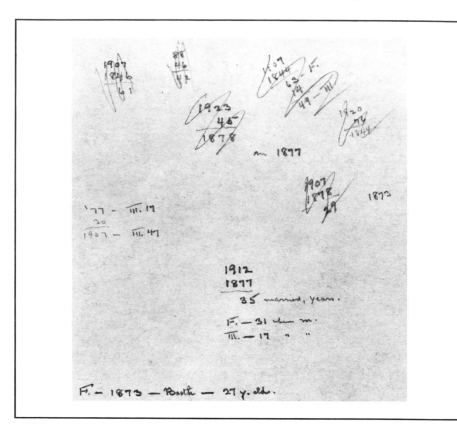

One page of computations indicates O'Neill originally planned to set the play in 1907; it also reveals his deliberate attempt to depict his own family in the play. To determine the ages of his father, mother, and brother in 1907, he subtracts their year of birth from this date. He verifies their date of birth by subtracting the age of family members from the year in which each died. The dramatist writes: "It is 30th Wedding Anniversary?—Father, reproaching Mother, acts hurt and sentimental about it—she reminds him how often he had forgotten—or remembering, pretended to forget, hoping I had forgotten—so there need be no presents." An alternate plan, which he eventually adopts, is worked out at the bottom of the page. After subtracting the year of his parents' marriage, 1877, from 1912, he states: "35 married years. F.—1873—Booth— 27 y[ears]. old."*

---

*O'Neill refers here to his father's early stage success as a Shakespearean actor when James O'Neill alternated the roles of The Moor and Iago in *Othello* with the renowned Edwin Booth.

June 26–July 3, 1939—"The Long Day's Journey," Scenario

June 26—Act One, outline

The title, now changed to "The Long Day's Journey," is still a tentative one as others are listed: "The Long Day's Insurrection," "Retirement," and "Retreat." The four central characters are given tentative names here; they remain nameless, however, throughout the scenario.

Characters

James Luttrell	The Husband and Father (66)	Edmund Tyrone Antrim*
Stella	The Wife and Mother (52)	Mary Cavan "
James Luttrell, Jr.	The Elder Son (34)	Edmund Tyrone, Jr.
	The Younger Son (24)	Hugh

Time, a hot day in August, 1912.

The whole action of the play takes place in the living room (sitting room) of their summer home during one stifling August day in 1912.

    Act One   —   8:30 a.m.
    Act Two   —12:45 p.m. (just before lunch)
    Act Three—after 1
    Act Four —evening
    Act Five —midnight

No humorous narration of the Shaughnessy-pigs-in-the-pond episode appears in this first scene. The mood of the four characters as they enter the sitting room is somber. A strong undercurrent of suspicion pervades the atmosphere. When the Father kindly reproves the younger son for not eating enough at breakfast, the Mother is annoyed and "a bit strained, as if something she pushes away from self—nothing [the] matter with him!" She catches the secret glances of the men and asks: "Anything wrong with my hair?" The Father and elder son quarrel and then go out to work in the garden. The Mother longs to reach out to the younger son, to "appeal to him—which his bitterness and suspicion ignore— keeps pooh-poohing his illness—'I couldn't bear—just now—having you really sick—you are my baby.' " He reacts tenderly: "Of course, I'm not really sick— you mustn't worry about me." She feels "reassured and yet not reassured—goes to window—chagrin at Father working by road—'too stingy to hire gardener.' " The Mother criticizes the Father for his miserliness, speaks bitterly of her sickness, and reminds her son she was in perfect health until he was born. "Well,

*Like Tyrone and Cavan, Antrim is a county in Northern Island.

don't blame me. I couldn't help being born." Exasperated, she says tensely: "It is impossible to talk to anyone in this house without it ending in a quarrel. Go up to my room for a while. Perhaps if I can take a little nap." The son tries to stop her, but she turns on him and asks: "Why do you look at me like that? . . . it isn't fair for you all to be so suspicious without any reason—it makes it so hard."

June 27—Act Two, outline

In this first outline, as in the final draft, the three men are totally obsessed by the fear the Mother is taking drugs again. The elder son comes in and says the Mother should be watched. His brother responds: "You're always thinking the worst! You want everyone to fail and be beaten, because you—." The elder son retaliates: "All right, I'm licked. But you don't show any signs yet of setting any rivers on fire. (Then contritely) Hell, we don't mean this, either of us. We're pals. You know I'd give anything to believe Mama had been cured forever—it's no good to shut your eyes. From that—they never come back—or almost never." The Mother enters, looking "guilty and strange." The elder brother says: "You can see what I was afraid of is true." She defends herself angrily: "You've [a] vile mind—no wonder with the kind of woman you associate with." She then attacks the "Father's tightness." The younger son "at first joins in—then excuses Father—they turn on him."

By the time the Father comes in, the three have "become friendly, intimate," and laugh at him when he examines the whiskey bottle they have watered. The Father "is hurt and pathetic, 'another joke on the Old Man?' " The Mother is solicitous: "You look tired, you mustn't (turns on sons) shouldn't joke at your father—more respect—some fathers would throw you out in street, after way you have both disgraced your parents, etc." Then, seeing his wary glance, she says: "You are as bad as boys and they're as bad as you. It isn't fair—worst thing is you will drive me—." The Father remarks hastily: "Now, now, only joke. I meant when you get affectionate, I ought to look out for squalls, eh, Boys." After the sons go in to lunch, the Mother says: "You know I wouldn't ever again—after you've been so kind—bought me car—even if there is no place for me to go—you know I would never this time." Her husband exclaims: "Don't lie." She begins to sob. "They stare helplessly at each other, the helpless stare of a man and woman who have known each other and never known each other. Then in silence they go in to lunch."

June 28—Act Three, outline

In the first scheme for the third act, the Mother goes upstairs immediately after lunch. Her departure is followed by an "admission by all three—'God damn it!' 'Jesus!' " A brief, non-humorous, reference is made here to the pigs-in-the-pond incident. O'Neill uses the names of the actual New London people involved, who will appear later in *A Moon for the Misbegotten*. The Father announces he will do no more work that day: " 'Just remembered I promised [to] see Dorsey at club about property' (complaint Harkness about Dolan—pigs in his ice pond)." The younger son is derisive: "Maybe wash his dirty Standard Oil money clean to have pigs in pond." The Father starts to chastise him; remembering his son's condition, he is remorseful and gives him ten dollars for the trip uptown to the doctor.

O'Neill alters the "arrangement [of] this first part." The exchanges—particularly those between the parents—provide greater autobiographical insights into the four O'Neills than those in the final draft of Act Three. The Father urges the Mother to go for a drive, but when both he and the elder son refuse to accompany her, she becomes obstinate and declares she will stay home. The Father responds angrily: "Nothing satisfies you, nothing any good, all for nothing now, was assured for something, oaths you've broken." A fierce argument erupts between the couple. She mocks her husband; he has always been "jealous—first of Elder Son, then of Edmund—he was killed by your jealousy*—last, you were jealous of Younger Son." The Father assures her he "loved" her; "his birth made you so sick, never the same. That God damned doctor—if he hadn't started giving you morphine because he didn't know." She argues: "Your fault, parsimony, if I had had expensive doctor—and I did not want another child—Edmund's death made me feel so guilty—." The Father admits they had made a "mistake—if Younger Son had never been born—and with all suffering he has caused what is he—fired from college—ruined his health—has brains and spirit —not like Elder Son—he has brains but lazy and weak." The scene ends "on note of recrimination but with a mutual wish Younger Son had never been born."

In the next scene the younger son brutally attacks the Mother for taking drugs, asking: "Why did you?" She explains that she was worried about him and that all of them were so suspicious: "not believing made me so nervous—(it is really admission without admitting)—never before you were born." He is bitter: "I am sorry I was born. I swear, if I knew giving my life could cure you." Sadly, she replies: "Oh, I know you would do anything—your Father—your brother too—but I swear I will not—I swear I was so nervous, lost now—." As the three men leave the house, she accuses them of deserting her and spitefully taunts them with a statement certain to arouse their concern and guilt: "Think I shall go to town after all—thing I must get at drug store."

---

*Ella O'Neill's second son, Edmund, died as a child after she had left him in her mother's care to accompany her husband on a theatrical tour.

June 29–30, July 1—Act Four, outline

Certain aspects of the physical and psychological condition of the Mother, now totally transformed by morphine, cited here are omitted in the final text. She is described as "very hipped up now, her manner strange—at the moment a vain happy, chattering girlishness—then changing to a hard cynical sneering bitterness with a bitter biting cruelty and with a coarse vulgarity in it—the last as if suddenly poisoned by an alive demon." The dual innocent/cynical nature O'Neill observed as a youth in his mother had a profound psychological effect on him; as a dramatist, he depicts a gallery of characters similarly split. New information about the Mother, revealed here, links her with Christine Mannon in *Mourning Becomes Electra*. The mother, like Christine, has been left independently wealthy by her father; both women use the money for clothes even though their husbands resent this act of independence. In this play, the Mother must have depleted the source of income—perhaps to support her habit—for the maid, who had accompanied her to town, speaks "about hocking ring that p.m." to get money to pay for the "medicine" at the drug store. The Mother reminisces about the early years of her marriage—the "ostracism, solitude, hotels, trains, no home" and blames her "mother and husband [for the] death [of] second child." She is reluctant to discuss her younger son, saying: "Worry, worry, it was a great mistake—I don't want [to] remember—In fact, I don't remember—as much of time since then like a dream." The "long day" is still designated as the parents' anniversary; the Mother tells the maid to appease the cook by bringing her a drink to celebrate the occasion, adding that the Father "doesn't like anniversaries—cost money—and remind him getting old—14 y[ears]. older—was great mistake—more like father—."

The Father, returning with both sons, tries to pacify his resentful wife: "Surely you couldn't think any of us wouldn't be back for dinner on Anniversary." She rebukes the three: "Why didn't you stay where you belong—old story—not in a home but a barroom—and leave me alone." The elder son remarks caustically: "You're making us wish we had." Defensively, she strikes out at the Father: "You let them dare to accuse me. Well, you wanted children and you have them. I hope you're satisfied. It is too bad Edmund could not have lived and we might have had one son we could be proud of. But you murdered him." When the Father questions her condition, she exclaims: "You drive me crazy with your suspicions. I know what you think. You think it's morphine, that I've gone back—But it's a lie." Later, recalling why her husband sent the sons away to school, she admits: "I might have corrected my own wrong then. I could have rejected. Yes, I loved you very much—start of the troubles—I was so happy before I loved—before marriage and children—and it comes to this—we four here together now—all that we are—from love—we are so alone—we are everything to each other—even hate." The scene concludes with the Mother's refusing to listen to the younger son's explanation of his visit to the doctor and going in to dinner with the Father and elder son.

In O'Neill's revision of the scene, just the Father and younger son return home. The Father attacks his elder son "with contemptuous hatred—warns younger son against him." The Mother attacks the Father, blaming him "for what elder son has become—forced him on stage—always hated actors—first easy money—weak—but not born weak—so brilliant at school—You were jealous, you who have no education, ignorant, etc."

July 2–3—Act Five, outline

O'Neill considers two new titles, "Vista" and "Anniversary," as he begins the last act. When the scene opens in this version, the younger son has already returned from his walk—having stopped for a "drink at Dolans"—and is playing "hearts or casino" with the Father, who talks about the Mother's condition, past, and relationship with her parents and husband:

Up in her room—you remember—same old games—gradually farther and farther off—mad—quiet without quieting—like a drunk—only been drunk once—looking for something or someone. God knows what—you know way—And talking, talking of the past, digging up old grievances—you'd think before she married me she'd lived in heaven—her father spoiled her—you'd think he was an angel—a teetotaler till he was forty, then started drink it all up—it killed him—no, no angel—and her mother a nice enough woman but a common little Irish woman. And her piano playing—you'd think she was sure to be concert artist if she hadn't married me and had children—blame, blame, blame! I'm fool [to] notice—not responsible—but I know it! same as whiskey, truth comes out. She doesn't blame herself. She blames me.

The son says his Father is to blame and reviews the "whole history accusingly": his miserliness with the family and generosity to "other spongers," his decision to send a sick son to the State Farm. O'Neill presents a far more compassionate picture of the Father here than in the final draft, where the early softness in his nature and tremendous vulnerability are muted. He is crushed by his son's words: "Go anywhere you like. I don't care what it costs if it makes you well and you'll get hold of yourself and be a man. Don't you know that [is] true when it comes to present? Don't you know you're my son and I love you? Let's not quarrel. I still have high hopes of you in spite of all you've done to kill them, etc."

A long passage included here and later omitted reveals the great fear that haunts the men—that the Mother, either consciously or unwittingly, might take her own life. Forever embedded in their minds is the memory of her earlier suicide attempt when she had run out of morphine. Thinking his wife has "gone to bed at last, thank God," the Father pauses and then exclaims: "God, now I'll have the fear again of an overdose." The younger son shudders:

"For God's sake, don't say that (Then arguing) No, she is too good a Catholic."—"Good God I didn't mean—I meant by accident."—"No, she's had too long an experience (He pauses, then accusingly) Did you say you'd have the fear?" Father rage and horrified "The Irish in you! I don't know what you mean—I don't want to know."—Younger son horrified at [him]self, "I didn't mean anything—I mean I didn't—not seriously—trying to get your goat."

When he hears his other son in the hall, the Father goes out on the porch. The elder son comes in "drunk and nasty—scene between brothers." The elder son reveals his bitter animosity: "Where'd you sneak off?—the good boy, eh?—come and stay home—the bum comes home late, drunk—fine!" Remembering his brother's condition, he apologizes and begins to attack doctors: "all gangsters and crooks—after the dough, keep you sick, pass you from one to another, etc." The younger son exclaims: "Jesus, at the Last Judgment you'll be shouting it's a frame-up." His brother laughs: "Well, be at wake, etc. I'm laying 10 to 1 if you can't slip St. Peter a piece of change—you can go to hell! Put money in thy purse. Honestly, if thou canst, etc.—the only dope—don't be a sucker, be a wise guy!" In a long speech, reminiscent of Hickey's confession in *The Iceman Cometh*, the elder son reveals his bitterness about whores and his mother, his ambiguous feelings about his brother, his self-disgust and reasons for drinking:

"better be too drunk to talk—pass out—like a hophead—one dream when no one can touch you—(Drink) all I mean is, got off [on] the wrong foot—never could find way get back in step—perhaps didn't want to—wouldn't want to—the gutter is the way to peace—doctors said two years ago, keep on drinking couple of years more and it'll kill you—doctors all fakes—hold out hope you're going to be cured—and yet here I am—my damned heart still going marvelous (very drunk) that last drink [was] the K.O.—before I pass out, all I want to say is—good luck, kid—all I've got—don't curse you now—God bless you." (Passes out almost completely)

O'Neill's conception of the Mother in the scenario's last act differs substantially from the view of her in the published text. Her condition, when she enters, reveals she has taken more morphine that evening. However, she is not a completely detached, ghost-like spirit; she converses—at times quite rationally—with her sons and husband. She wears a "wrapper over nightgown—hair down, her eyes like glazed stars—in her manner and movement vague and aimless yet intent and concentrated—she seems to see them and yet not to see them—she murmurs 'glad to see you both came home for dinner—good boys—when you're late nothing left to eat.'" The younger son says bitterly: "You ought to read Heine's poem on morphine, Mother." She replies vaguely: "Morphine! I have enough now to last for while—when that's gone, pawn another piece of jewelry —Doctor said I was taking enough drugs to kill [a] herd of elephants (She smiles with a precocious childish pride—they shudder) First week at cure so horrible— it's so suspicious later on—have to pawn all jewelry—and the times when you can't get—oh, so horrible!" She defends her dependency on morphine: "How did I know—and when I did know it was too late—too late ever more—too late forever! But it doesn't matter—now I am safe—now I really don't care—it's like a dream of something once happened to another woman." She rebukes her son for being suspicious and her husband for being stingy. Many of the accusations and the statements about "one-night stands, children taken away" that she makes here are later transposed to earlier acts in the final text. When the younger son tells her he might possibly die, she stares at him; there is in her response a veiled threat of accidental or deliberate death:

> Well look at me—what you have done—your father and brother, too, but you were [the] last straw—it would serve you right if—No, my baby—I love you the best—I love them, too—you know I don't mean—but you won't leave me alone—you treat me with suspicion and scorn and contempt when I can't help—you would think I liked being in hell—you drive me to hate you. But you might as well give up trying now—you can't touch me now—I'm safe beyond your reach. You can't make me remember, except from [the] outside, like a stranger—audience at a play—the real may make her cry but the events and tears [are] part of [the] play, too—she [is] not really hurt—and anyway I won't remember anything now tonight except what I want to remember—time when I was happy—at convent—before I married—although I was happy for [a] time after I married too—yes, your father has many faults but we adored each other.

Noticing her husband is not present, she calls him in from the porch and "fusses over him, sits him in his chair, pillow behind back, talking all time." She reminisces about her innocent convent schooldays, the romantic period preceding her marriage and her disillusionment after it, the sacrifices she has made for her husband and children. To her own question "Why?" she answers: "because I loved, because I knew he loved—but if I could have foreseen I would have cut my heart out rather than love—love is so horrible—look at us four now—it is true each one loves all the others in spite of hate—it is sad." The Mother's final speech, which concludes the act, contains the only reference to religion in the scenario. When the younger son says that they all love her and asks her to forgive them, she replies: "Oh, no! You cannot touch me now. I have put love behind me—all love except my love for the Blessed Virgin—and some day she will forgive and love me again and I can pray to her again without shame and then she will help me and I will love myself—one day." The final stage directions state that the Mother is now entirely unaware of the three men; she looks at her hands; "two tears roll down her wax-like face from her unthinking eyes." In the margin beside this last passage, O'Neill writes: "Mother (quote at end—quotes strongly) 'Forgive us our trespasses as we forgive those who trespass against us.'"

After finishing the outline for "The Long Day's Journey," O'Neill immedi-

ately begins "notes and prelims" for *The Iceman Cometh*, completing the final
revisions and cuts on January 3, 1940. Two days later he states: "The Long
Day's Journey (read outline—want to do this soon—will have to be written in
blood—but will be a great play, if done right)" (W.D.). He resumed work the
following day on the first two Cycle plays but set them aside on February 22, the
day he got a "better title" for his New London play: "Long Day's Journey into
Night." This new title heads the third set of notes. The first ten pages of the
collection, containing references to Act Five, were written before the first draft
of March 21; the last six pages were made after O'Neill changed the work to a
four-act play on July 9, 1940.

February 22–March 18, 1940—"Long Day's Journey into Night," notes

The opening section, entitled "Weather progression," contains O'Neill's
first reference to the fog; he parallels the worsening condition of the weather and
the deteriorating state of the Mother's mind. A condensed version of this passage
follows:

> I—Fine morning—fog is clearing—Tyrone hearty about this—Mother
> hopes so, depression of fog

> II—Sunshine dims—damp in the air—but Tyrone still optimistic—leftover
> from yesterday

> III—At end, first distant blast of foghorn in sound—Tyrone says it may stay
> out, not come in harbor—Mother refers to drive

> IV—Dense fog—dark early—Mother says ⌊she⌋ minds foghorn because [it]
> makes silence so intense and alive afterward—each drop from trees on
> eaves is like a tear* that drops in your heart—yet she likes fog now—
> no one can see—so easy to remain unrecognized, to step aside and
> avoid meeting—to run back and hide

> V—Dense fog, black night—Mother exults in it—it is in her—cannot see
> an instant of future—it is all dream, nothing is what it is—(She has
> taken walk, coat over nightdress?)

> (After morphine effect, she likes fog, foghorn—finally becomes un-
> conscious of it—while it drives rest of them crazy)

---

*See the description of the Cabot home in *Desire Under the Elms*. The maternal
trees—symbolizing the dead mother of Eben, a self-portrait—brood "like exhausted
women" over the house; "when it rains their tears trickle down monotonously and
rot on the shingles."

Notes—for Revision

Like the "weather progression" scheme, the notes for revision reveal O'Neill's preoccupation with the Mother's condition, which becomes now the focal point of the play.

Act One—O'Neill now plans to instill in the three men a "more hopeful belief—even on Jamie's part, that she is cured." Reflecting the lifelong guilt he felt, the dramatist again suggests that "Edmund's sickness" motivates the Mother to take morphine:

What really happened—she had been frantic—given in—gone to bathroom, spareroom—then, thinking of Edmund, for his sake had conquered craving which was brought on by continued worry about him—at end, she tells Edmund this—he wants [to] believe but can't help suspecting—it is this lack of faith in him, combined with growing fear, which makes her give in.

Act Three—In this early version, the Mother—after the departure of the three men and her prayer—"with help of Virgin Mary"—explains why she needs the "medicine" to Cathleen: "my hands—morphine for nerves, for rheumatism —only thing does any good—such beautiful hands once."

Act Five—To the last act, O'Neill adds Jamie's quote, "Mother O' mine," and his "hophead" reference. The Mother is assigned a new speech, near the end of the play, which perhaps reveals Jamie O'Neill-Tyrone's true attitude to his father. The Mother

snaps into awareness again—the trouble is all love each other—so easy to bear if indifferent, or could just hate—but no, we have to love each other—even you, Jamie—when you say [you] wish father would die—oh, I know you mean that at times—I have meant it, too—but you know very well you love and respect, too—outside you're proud of him and position from nothing—you may make sarcastic remarks but you do it jokingly—etc. good boy at heart, Jamie.

The play closes with the Mother's spiritual lament; part of this passage appears in Act Two in the final version:

very end—Virgin Mary—never came to help—but she will when none of you may believe in me for a second any more—when I am all alone and no one in world believes—then she will believe in me—she will understand pride—sin against Holy Ghost—but she is a woman. Don't know why she shouldn't come to me—I must have sinned in some way—I must seem wicked to her—but I can't remember anything bad I have ever done.

One page of computations is certain to lead to new speculations about O'Neill's plans for *Long Day's Journey into Night*. After completing the play, he allegedly stipulated he did not want it ever produced or even published until twenty-five years after his death. Yet, he makes a concerted effort here to determine the running time for both a five-act and a four-act production. Five numbers—22, 12, 17, 20, 30—appear in one column. The other column contains four numbers; the second, 29, combines the 12- and 17-minute second and third acts. The three minus ten (−10) figures between the four acts indicate a plan either for three intermissions or additional time should the acts run longer than he expected. After determining the drama will take "131 minutes" to stage, O'Neill works out a schedule for its start and conclusion: "8:30–10:41." While he seems to have made a definite decision to call the play "Long Day's Journey into Night," he provides two alternate titles: "Long Forgotten" and "What's Long Forgotten."

March 21, 1940—Act One, start dialogue

O'Neill worked on the first draft of Act One the last nine days of March and seven days in April, finishing it "in bed" on the 30th of that month. Again he put aside the play, stating on June 26: "force myself to read 1st draft, 1st Act and am surprised to find myself deeply held by it" (W.D.). Explaining the apparent neglect of this play to Dudley Nichols, he writes: "Ever since the May debacle started in Europe I have been in a thoroughly demoralized state of the bitterest pessimism, unable to think of anything else, or do any work until this last week when I began to get hold of myself again" (July 7, 1940). He makes a similar statement to Langner on July 17, adding he is working on the play "after a lapse of several months spent with an ear glued to the radio for war news. You can't keep a hophead off his dope for long!"

July 9, 1940—Act Two, Scene One,* start dialogue

July 13, 1940—Notes for whole play

O'Neill continues the third collection of notes, making a list of "recurrent items" he plans to stress in the play: Jamie's effect on Edmund, McGuire, electric light, hands, Mother about doctors, their talk about his "going away," influence [of] books on Edmund, don't start in on Jamie, suspect the worst, matter with hair. O'Neill plans now to "cut out Virgin Mary talk to Edmund at close of II-2" and to add a passage in Act Four—Tyrone to Edmund—"for years I didn't know she was taking it."

---

*On July 9 O'Neill decided to make *Long Day's Journey into Night* a four-act play. The original Act Two is now that act's first scene; Act Three becomes its second scene.

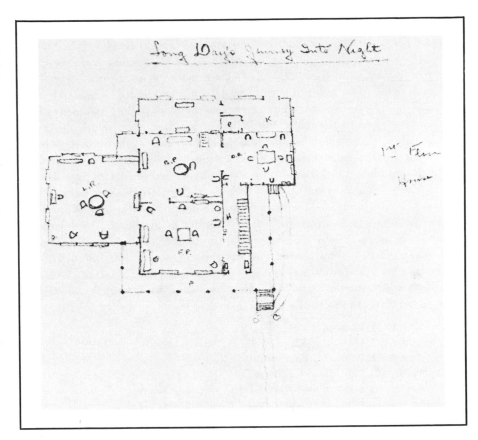

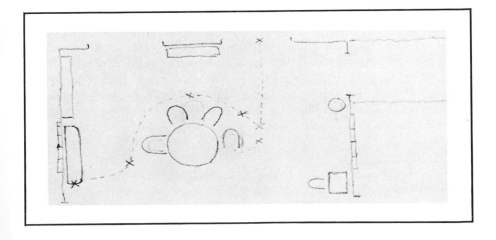

The dramatist draws two set designs for the play. The intricate first floor plan of the Tyrone home is an exact replica of the O'Neill family's New London house before it was renovated and the porch section extending from the living room to the front eliminated. The other sketch is an accurate visual representation of the living room as it is described in the published text. The broken lines in this drawing indicate two characters enter from the front parlor; Jamie goes from the door to a chair at the table; the Mother, according to the stage directions, "moves like a sleepwalker, around the back of Jamie's chair, then forward toward left front, passing behind Edmund" and walks finally "left to the front end of the sofa beneath the windows" where she sits down. A two-page description of Mary Tyrone's wedding dress follows the set designs. The passage is in Carlotta O'Neill's large, legible handwriting, a definite contrast to all the other notes of this study in the dramatist's nearly illegible handwriting. The description is essentially the same as that of the published text, but the word order differs in a few places. Only the last sentence of this early version is later omitted; Mary Tyrone asks her husband: "I wonder did you even notice any of this?"

Work Diary entries, dated after the completion of the third collection of notes, reveal O'Neill's subsequent progress on the play:

>   July 24, 1940—Act Two, Scene Two, prelims
>   August 7, 1940—Act Three, prelims
>   August 31, 1940—Act Four, prelims
>   September 20, 1940—Finish first draft
>   October 16, 1940—Finish second draft°
>   March 17, 1941—Start going over and cutting, revising
>   March 30, 1941—Finish going over typed script—second and I think
>   final draft—like this play better than any I have ever
>   written—does most with the least—a quiet play!—and
>   a great one, I believe.

On June 6, 1939, O'Neill records his first idea for the Jimmy the Priest's and New London family plays. The two dramas that evolve from a simple one-line statement, *The Iceman Cometh* and *Long Day's Journey into Night*, are linked not only autobiographically but also creatively. Just as the significant events presented chronologically in these plays occurred in the dramatist's life in a one-year span, 1911–1912, he re-creates them in the same time frame, 1939–1940. To Nichols, he writes on October 13, 1940: "These two outside [the Cycle] plays I've done have been on my mind for years. Now they are written. Not that it can be of any consequence in the world we will soon have to face, but

---

°In her letter of October 25, 1940, to Theresa Helburn, Carlotta O'Neill writes: "Gene has finished another play that I am typing [*Long Day's Journey into Night*]. As I work, my heart is breaking! That man can write! And he is alive with ideas. That is the main reason he does not want to stop for production now. That and his health."

it's at least a personal satisfaction." The years spent developing the semi-autobiographical Cycle characters, such as Simon Harford, a self-portrait, and his
neurotic mother, Deborah, who closely resembles Ella O'Neill, strengthened his
resolve to tell the story of his own tragic family. He presents a more truthful and
complete portrait of the four O'Neills and their relationships in his early notes
and scenario than in the final draft of the play; the most significant difference is
the emphasis in the former on the dual-natured mother as the betrayer, "the
guilty one."

   In the October 13 letter to Nichols, O'Neill states that he has gotten "over
the worst" of his war jitters: "Just what I'll do next I haven't decided yet. Perhaps take up the cycle again. Perhaps do another of the many outside ideas I have
made notes for." He says that he has no intention of producing either *The
Iceman Cometh* or *Long Day's Journey into Night* "for a long time. The future
for a free writer seems to grow shorter each day and I want to stick at writing
and get all I can finished while I can." By writing *Long Day's Journey into Night*,
he had, as he says, faced his dead at last—and himself; he was free of the ghosts
of the past. The autobiographical account of the past ends here temporarily; his
main concern now is the present and future. The author embarks on a series of
dramas which he, as a "free writer," feels compelled to create—each dealing
with the dangers totalitarianism poses to twentieth-century man.

°THE VISIT OF MALATESTA
(MALATESTA SEEKS SURCEASE)
(1940)

On January 4, 1940, the day after completing the final draft of *The Iceman Cometh*, O'Neill makes "notes on idea for comedy with the tentative title 'The Visit of Malatesta'" (W.D.). The next day he reads over the outline for *Long Day's Journey into Night* and is tempted to "do this soon." He works on these two ideas on alternate days between February 22–26 and March 1–3. It seems incongruous that the dramatist contemplates writing a comedy at a time when he is deeply immersed in plans for the tragic play that would, as he says, be "written in blood." However, there are links between these two family plays set in Connecticut and between them and *The Iceman Cometh*, which he had just completed.

O'Neill first plans to use a 1912 backdrop for "The Visit of Malatesta" and to develop subjects and character types introduced in the two other plays set in that year: the political corruption and anarchism of *The Iceman Cometh* and the moral disintegration—primarily through greed—of a first generation immigrant and his family as depicted in *Long Day's Journey into Night*. When the war in Europe intensifies in 1940, leaving no doubt about the expansionary aspirations of Hitler and Mussolini, O'Neill—determined to show the threat totalitarian regimes posed to modern man's freedom—changes the setting of "The Visit of Malatesta" to 1923, shortly after the Fascist emerged as sole leader in Italy. Unlike the characters of *The Iceman Cometh* and *Long Day's Journey into Night*, who—despairing of their meaningless present and future—sink into alcoholic oblivion, those in the comedy are offered a clear and certain hope by its hero, Cesare Malatesta, an accurate re-creation of Enrico Malatesta, the legendary Italian anarchist insurrectionist.

As Kenneth Macgowan observes, O'Neill is "a kind of chain-stitch playwright . . . his ideas and materials and technique develop through a long chain of links bound inextricably to one another."[*] The dramatist began *The Iceman Cometh*, as his first notes indicate, intending to emphasize two social concerns of the early twentieth century: political graft and anarchism. As the work evolves, the emphasis shifts to the characters themselves—as individuals—to their attempt to retain their pipe dreams and friendships with the advent of Hickey. "The Visit of Malatesta" is an outgrowth of *The Iceman Cometh*. One of the names O'Neill lists for possible use in the latter is Daniello. The second major character in "The Visit of Malatesta" is Tony Daniello, an Italian immigrant, who, with his wife Rosa and friends, Pete Gebardi and Gus Bascone, had fought

---

[*]Kenneth Macgowan, "The O'Neill Soliloquy," in *O'Neill and His Plays*, eds. Oscar Cargill, N. Bryllion Fagin, and William J. Fisher (New York, 1961), p. 449.

for the anarchist cause with Malatesta years before in the old country. Their statements, voicing the sentiments of Kropotkin, Bakunin, and Proudhon, echo those of the three former or present anarchists in *The Iceman Cometh*: Larry Slade, Hugo Kalmar, Don Parritt.

In addition to the anarchist references common to both plays, there are numerous other similarities: the barroom setting with living quarters upstairs; the concept of corruption and graft, with politicians and policemen "on the take"; a large cast of characters who express their opinions on, and argue about, social and economic issues. The two bartenders in *Iceman*, Chuck Morello and Rocky Pioggi, like the barkeeper Tony Daniello in "Malatesta," are Italian-Americans. The anarchist mothers—called Rosa in both plays—are advocates of free love; they may possibly have been the mistresses of former anarchist leaders—Slade and Malatesta—who are now disillusioned with the movement, and may have borne them illegitimate children, who appear in the dramas. Most important, however, is the similar theme of waiting for the expected messianic outsiders—Hickey and Malatesta—in joyful anticipation. Yet, when these men arrive, they bring no affirmation of the status quo but a disturbing message of salvation, a warning to friends that they must change their lives, reform, abandon their pipe dreams.

O'Neill modeled the characters in *The Iceman Cometh* on "actual people" he had known; in his reference of February 11, 1941, to the "Malatesta comedy idea," he writes: "[I] like this—never have written about Italian-Americans although in past have known many of them as close friends" (W.D.). The actual names of these friends do not appear in the notes for "The Visit of Malatesta"— as they do in *The Iceman Cometh*, making it impossible to determine whether they were—like Terry Carlin/Larry Slade and Hippolyte Havel/Hugo Kalmar— anarchists. The author's idealization of the movement in the late works, particularly in his portrait of Malatesta, reveals that he continued to view anarchism, with its utopian goals, as he did in his youth, as a preferable alternative to capitalism with its sundry social effects: loss of individual dignity and human rights, the unequal distribution of wealth, and greed.

Clemenceau once remarked: "I am sorry for anyone who has not been an anarchist at twenty." In the record of the seven-year cycles of his life, O'Neill reveals formative influences in 1907–1908 when he was twenty: "M. O. Grey— his studio—anarchism, Nietzsche." His first exposure to anarchism came at an even earlier age, however. He was probably aware of the Socialist-anarchist group, l'Avvenire, established in New London in 1903, which published *Il Nostro Programma*.* While a student at Betts Academy in Connecticut, he went to New York City on weekends and frequented the Unique Book Shop operated by Benjamin R. Tucker. Louis Sheaffer notes that Tucker was "one of America's

---

*Max Nettlau, *Enrico Malatesta: Vita E Pensieri* (New York, no date), p. 258.

leading radicals, the chief spokesman of 'individualist anarchism' "—a man who, "according to O'Neill, greatly influenced his inner self."* The store featured works by the leading American and European spokesmen for the movement: Emma Goldman, Proudhon, Kropotkin, and the "Christian anarchist" Tolstoi. O'Neill's age at this time approximates that of the seventeen-year-old Richard Miller in *Ah, Wilderness!* (set in 1906) who, like the twenty-three-year-old Edmund Tyrone in *Long Day's Journey into Night* (set in 1912), is a self-portrait. Statements the fathers make to their sons in these plays are particularly relevant. Richard refuses to celebrate the Fourth of July when "the wage slave [is] ground under the heel of the capitalist class." After Richard's long tirade against capitalism, his father says: "Son, if I didn't know it was you talking I'd think we had Emma Goldman with us."[1]† In *Long Day's Journey into Night*, when Edmund tells his family about the Irish tenant Shaughnessy's refusal to humble himself "in the presence of a king of America," his father remarks: "Never mind the social gabble. . . . Keep your damned Socialist anarchist sentiments out of my affairs." The kings of America, as the dramatist implies here are—like Harder, the Standard Oil millionaire—the wealthy capitalist barons. In his 1914 poem "Fratricide," O'Neill attacks these plunderers, pointing out that the poor are told they must fight and die bravely to protect American interests; but the chief beneficiaries, of course, are rich profiteers: "What cause could be more asinine/Than yours, ye slaves of bloody toil?/ . . . to broil/And bleed and groan—for Guggenheim!/And give your lives for Standard Oil!"**

The author has, obviously, absorbed the thoughts of Proudhon, Bakunin, and Kropotkin, but what he preaches is an Americanized version of anarchism. Nowhere is this more evident, or the cry for social change greater, than in his 1921 play *The Hairy Ape*. Yank is the epitome, the symbol of all the exploited workers of the world, the end product of the dehumanization of industrialism. He is Rousseau's Noble Savage, the anarchists' ideal man, born free but enslaved by society's corrupt institutions and eventually imprisoned on Blackwell's Island, as was Emma Goldman. The IWW, an anarchist affiliate, is accused in this play—with great irony—of being a dagger poised to destroy America "where all men are born free and equal, with equal opportunities to all, where the Founding Fathers have guaranteed to each one happiness, where Truth, Honor, Liberty, Justice, and the Brotherhood of Man are a religion" guaranteed by the Constitution.[2]

In his indictment of America, which he viewed as sick spiritually, O'Neill

---

*Sheaffer, *O'Neill Son and Playwright*, p. 102.

†See notes at end of chapter.

**Eugene O'Neill, "Fratricide," *Poems 1912–1942*, edited by Donald Gallup (New Haven, 1979), p. 55.

attacks materialism and greed, the main obstacles to the anarchist dream of social and economic equality, not only in his plays and poems but also in his public statements. His words in a 1946 interview preceding the première of *The Iceman Cometh* reveal his belief that the battle has been lost: "We've squandered our soul by trying to possess something outside it, and we'll end as that game usually does, by losing our soul and the thing outside it, too." During the interview he says that he knew all the characters in *Iceman* who dream of social and economic equality, that the Anarchists, the Wobblies and French Syndicalists are real, but that the dream is an illusion: "It would take man a million years to grow up and obtain a soul." He later adds: "I think I'm aware of comedy more than I ever was before, a big kind of comedy that doesn't stay funny very long."* His 1940 idea, "The Visit of Malatesta" is a "big kind of comedy," which would express O'Neill's concerns and beliefs in its serious moments. In the first notes for the play, Malatesta, speaking of the defeat of anarchism in Italy, says: "that dream was beautiful—but only Utopian dream—not possible until man grows a soul—in a thousand years, perhaps."

The dramatist has often been criticized for not addressing the social problems of America; but in this play he presents one that was and is, unfortunately, common: what it means to be stigmatized as an immigrant or unwanted alien—even in a pluralistic society. The work depicts the Italian Daniello family's struggle to survive in a hostile land. In the author's early concept of him, the father, Tony, nourished by dreams of the idealistic goals of anarchism, clings to his old political beliefs; the second-generation son, Angelo, nurtured by American materialism, seeks to use the violent tactics of anarchism to achieve prosperity. And into the fray to bring a realistic message to both men comes Malatesta, the legendary anarchist hero—respected and honored for his courage, wisdom, and integrity. Conflict and comedy ensue when Malatesta tries to convert not only father and son but also the entire Daniello family and its circle of friends.

Long Day's Journey into Night has rightfully been hailed America's finest tragedy; "The Visit of Malatesta" would have been its richest comedy—conceived as it was in the same last period of great creative maturity. For good reason O'Neill veered from using the Irish, as he had done previously, to depict the plight of immigrants, a change necessitated for characterization as well as plot. The Irish, for all their verbal wit and comic antics, are also subject to moods of deep despair, brooding, and gloomy introspection and are often undemonstrative. In contrast, the Italians, as represented by the Daniellos, are not only humorous, happy, and vibrant but also open in their revelations of self, effusive in their emotions. Unlike the similar setting of the barroom/home of the Irish Melodys in *A Touch of the Poet*, where tragic undercurrents and deep family animosity prevail, the Daniello establishment is noisily exuberant; any

---

*Croswell Bowen, *Curse of the Misbegotten* (New York, 1959), pp. 311, 313.

misunderstandings and problems are resolved in a good-natured, easygoing fashion.

The notes and outline for the play illustrate how thoroughly O'Neill explored the life of Malatesta, the anarchist movement in Italy, and that country's political, social, and economic problems in the late nineteenth and early twentieth century. Unfortunately, only one page of his research escaped destruction— that listing the most significant dates in Italian anarchism—from Mazzini's death in 1872 to the "general strike led by Malatesta and Mussolini" in June 1914.* O'Neill attempts to establish Enrico Malatesta's actual age in 1912 and 1913, the years initially considered for the setting of the play. Believing Malatesta was born in 1858 (the actual date is 1850), he concludes that his hero was fifty-five in 1913. After changing the date of the setting to 1923, the author disregards the age of the historical Malatesta, making his fictitious counterpart fifty in order to portray him as a dashing romantic figure, capable of arousing the passions of three women in the play. The personal and public life, the political background, and the characterization of the imaginary Malatesta approximate those of the legendary hero with one exception. Enrico Malatesta came to the United States in 1899, made a publicized cross-country lecture tour, and became a political force in Paterson, New Jersey, and along the East Coast. He did not, however, make a second visit in 1923, seeking a haven from Fascist tyranny. In reality, he spent the last ten years of his life, 1922–1932, virtually under house arrest and close Fascist surveillance.

January 4, 1940—"The Visit of Malatesta,"
notes on idea for comedy

O'Neill writes one page of notes describing Tony Daniello and his children but omitting any reference to his wife and Malatesta. Tony is fifty, "popular with Italians—political power—fat, prosperous, contented, benevolent husband and father—yet absurdly cherishes romantic past as young man in Italy when he was anarchist and friend of Malatesta." His elder son is twenty-five and "has all his father's practical side—an Italian-American realist—(Tony D. in appearance and nature)—his father's lieutenant in all practical affairs." The younger son is nineteen and has "all his father's idealistic revolutionary side." The elder daughter, thirty, is described as "the contented discontented—her satisfaction is dissatisfaction." No age is given yet for Tony's younger daughter, who is "quite beautiful—the picture of big-eyed Italian female romantic sentimentalism." The setting is a "small city—Tony's saloon and residence (upstairs)—time, around 1913."

---

*To compile this list, O'Neill uses Helen Rex Keller's *The Dictionary of Dates* (New York, 1934), Vol. I, pp. 316–322.

February 23, 26, March 2, 1940—"The Visit of Malatesta" *

The setting is now described as a "small city, Conn[ecticut].†—around 1923—Tony Daniello's saloon (residence upstairs)—and his beach cottage." Three factors prompt O'Neill to change the action of the play from 1913 to 1923. First, he wants to show Malatesta victimized by the Fascists, who came to power in 1922. Second, the notes indicate that both Tony and Rosa Daniello participated in anarchist riots prior to the assassination of King Umberto I in 1900. Because of Rosa's pregnancy at that time when she glowed as the "flame of the revolution," Tony was forced to marry her. Both were imprisoned before managing to escape to the United States. A 1923 setting enables O'Neill to present an older second generation of Italian-Americans who have been formed and contaminated by false materialistic values: the seductive eighteen-year-old May Daniello and her ambitious brother Angelo. Third, Tony Daniello operates a speakeasy in the days of prohibition, a setting that prompts Malatesta to contrast the former self-sacrificing nobility of his old friends and their present lawless corruption and materialism and motivates his crusade to reform them.

Characters * *

Tony Daniello (48)
Rosa, his wife (43)
Francina (40) first cousin Rosa
Angelo   two of seven surviving children out of nine—5 living
May (18)   away, N.Y., Chicago, Boston—Maria, Johnny, Al
Pete Gebardi, a head gardener on estate, old pal of Tony's, fellow immigrant, associate Anarchist days
Gus Bascone, shoemaker, (ditto) bachelor
Big Jim Delehanty, a cop, old friend [of] Tony's, an Irish independence patriot
Pat Connor, boss of city machine
Cesare Malatesta (50)

While the dramatist indicates here that Tony and Rosa have other children, he does not refer to any of them except Julietta, the widowed elder daughter. Her character and role are assumed by Rosa's first cousin Francina, who is described as "thin and temperamental—a lot of ham in her—self-dramatizes and delights in scenes and passionate outbursts." Additional information is provided for

---

*O'Neill gives the work another tentative title on the first page of the notes: "Cesare Seeks Surcease."
†The dramatist again seems to have chosen his hometown New London for the setting. Pete Gebardi is the "head Gardener on millionaire (Standard Oil) estate."
* *A note in the left margin states: "Humbert assass[inated]. 1900."

Tony Daniello; he is "a typical satisfied Italian-American bourgeois" and "a good Catholic because he is but he explains this away on practical grounds." The former elder son now bears the name Angelo and remains as originally conceived. The description of the younger daughter, May, is essentially the same, but to it is added her disdain for small-town beaus; "there is no romance in them—she is a great reader of words—she dreams of marrying a millionaire, or a hero of one sort or another—the beau her parents favor is the son of political boss." Rosa Daniello, as she emerges here and in the 1941 notes, is certainly one of O'Neill's most lovable and loving, good-humored and humorous characters. She is

hugely fat and healthy, mustache, immensely good-natured, affectionate, tolerant, matter-of-fact, realist—adores Tony and children—is amused by his romantic dreams of radical past—she remembers them well as she knows all of group—was ardently for the free love, no sin aspect of liberty—the memory amuses her—she was pretty and lost and stupid as May is now—Tony was her accepted lover and when she got pregnant she made him marry her—but she cheated on side, principally with Malatesta, and she is not sure but thinks Julietta is his child.

The character descriptions are immediately followed by what O'Neill terms the "Story"—essentially an account of Malatesta's life as it relates to his anarchist activities in Europe. Only at the end of it is Malatesta described physically:

He is tall, thin, handsome, romantic-looking, grey mustache, goatee, aristocratic, dressed well always in black—years in prison have left mark—outwardly unbroken, undaunted—inwardly tired, a bit bitter, disillusioned and hopeless about Utopia—lonely, too—longing for rest and a home—food, warmth, serenity, a wife, children, etc. Malatesta speaks English with British accent—very correctly —result years of exile in England (after escape Italian prison) where he made living as tutor—then he had sneaked back to Italy but had been arrested and sent to prison—but again escaped after years—to England—then got into U.S.—lecture—his first visit.

The real Enrico Malatesta arrived in the United States in August, 1899, and spent much of his time in Paterson, New Jersey, when not lecturing. He wanted the periodical published by the anarchist group of that city, *La Questione Sociale*, to reflect the ideology of his Ancona magazine, *l'Agitazione*. A small band disagreed with Malatesta on the issue of organizaton and started a rival publication, *Aurora*, edited by Ciancabilla, who allegedly shot Malatesta in the foot during a heated discussion. "At great risk to his own life, Gaetano Bresci sought to shield Malatesta and disarmed the assailant."[*] Bresci was later selected by

---

[*]Luis Fabbri, *Malatesta* (Buenos Aires, 1945), p. 116.

the Paterson anarchists to return to Italy and avenge the massacre of a group of innocent beggars who were mistaken for revolutionists by the police in Milan* On July 27, 1900 Bresci assassinated King Umberto at Monza. Malatesta left the United States on March 10, 1900, and arrived in London in April. In the play he is viewed as a hero by the Italian-American anarchists—the mastermind who plotted the king's assassination. However, "Malatesta denies he had anything to do [with the death of] Humbert—terrorist group fanatics—true anarchism never justifies bloodshed."

The twenty-three years that have elapsed between Malatesta's first visit to the United States in 1900 and the fictitious second trip have been spent either in exile or prison. The description of him in the play when he is finally freed in 1922 by the Italian government is historically accurate. O'Neill states:

Malatesta, physically exhausted by years in prison, bewildered and a bit frightened by the world when he is released, disillusioned and embittered by his confreres in Anarchist leadership, some of whom abnormally jealously regret his return for fear he will oust them but each scheming to use him to help oust rival, etc. What he particularly hates is their readiness in plans for future to justify all the means of the tyranny [Fascism] they are fighting provided they use them for their ends. They must be brought back. By him. But he is unfit now. He must have rest in entirely new atmosphere, get back health and mental calm, perspective, etc. He thinks of U.S. where Movement can hardly be said to exist—he remembers his old friend Tony and his old mistress [Rosa], and this latter's yearly invitation to visit—from letters he has caught atmosphere of untroubled, contented family home—all he has missed. So he leaves. The Italian government is glad [to] wish him on U.S.—and his comrades are glad to [get] rid of idealist.

The rest of the "story" told in the 1940 notes shows the discovery Malatesta makes of the existence of another kind of tyranny, the enslavement by materialism, in the Daniello circle of family and friends.

---

*Emma Goldman states that Bresci acted on his own and was not selected by his associates to commit this "propaganda by deed," as historians maintain. While attending a meeting in Paterson after the assassination, she discovered that Bresci had asked his friends to return immediately the one hundred and fifty dollars he had loaned them to publish *La Questione Sociale*, providing no explanation. The group raised the money, but "the Italian comrades bitterly resented Bresci's behavior branding him a miser, who loved money above his ideal. Most of his friends even ostracized him." Goldman concludes that news of the assassination shocked these friends, who sought to make amends for the injustice done Bresci by undertaking the support of his daughter (*Living My Life*, p. 289).

The situation in the Daniello family is such that his coming brings out and makes active all the longings for liberty in its members, vague dreams of contented discontent which, but for his coming, would remain that. Prosperity and comparative idleness have made Tony regret the lost anarchist ideals of free love— his eye has roved to a young gal, whom he knows he could get. Angelo is ambitious. Law-abiding (more or less). He has visions of becoming Artichoke King of the state, and if hired assassins and terrorism by bombs is a short cut, why not? Malatesta will approve of assassination and bombs, as matter of principle, and of defiance of law. May is just generally lazily vain and rebellious. She doesn't like high school, the rule of father and mother at home is too strict, she doesn't want to marry and be bored—she has idea of crusading for birth control and woman's rights, because if she knew surely how not to get pregnant she could have a lot of fun—especially with an adventurous lover who had the courage to defy all rules.

What O'Neill presents here is a spirit of latent lawlessness within his characters, who aspire to defy moral, religious, and familial codes. The only Daniello who is free of any desire for power, money, or sexual adventure is Rosa. Yet she, too, will eventually be revealed as flawed; the 1941 notes show her succumbing to materialistic greed. In the early notes, however, whereas all the other Daniellos live with a secret "pipe dream," Rosa is an absolute realist. She states: "I pay fat for wisdom. The more I saw of life the more I was convinced that the desire for food can be gratified without disillusionment." Rosa accepts with tolerant amusement the fact that her husband is a philanderer and understands her daughter's sexual desires. O'Neill points out that "her fear is May will give it away because she sees so much in May like her at same age. Her realistic attitudes highly shock her family."

Throughout the 1940 notes, Malatesta is depicted as the best of men, free of self-interest and vainglory, possessing innate nobility, integrity, and a belief in the goodness of his fellow man. He has been disillusioned by his recent experiences in Italy, where he witnessed man's cruelty, injustice, and greed—all sanctioned, encouraged even, by a totalitarian government. But now in the United States, a democracy—supposedly advocating justice, equality and the brotherhood of man—he expects, but fails to find, these principles practiced. O'Neill's description of Malatesta in the last paragraph of the 1940 notes reveals that he is developing a new concept of his character:

He fights against meanness and disillusionment by bursts of passionate detestation of society, goes to extremes, used to believe there could be transition, almost bloodless, to ideal society because of man's essential goodness, but now he says there must be complete destruction first, past must be wiped out—those who resist must die, etc.—but then he sinks into exhausted depression—he feels he used to love man but now he despises him, and that is wrong, is a fault in him.

February 10–16, 1941—Malatesta Comedy Idea, notes

O'Neill completed the second draft of *Long Day's Journey into Night* and tried again to develop the Cycle plays before continuing work on his comedy. He makes some "General Notes" and gives it a new title: "Malatesta Seeks Surcease." His new concept of Malatesta in 1941 necessitates the change of title. In the final section of the 1940 notes, Malatesta doubts the goals of the movement can be achieved by peaceful means and advocates violence as he did when he was young and a disciple of Bakunin. The 1941 Malatesta emerges as a disciple of Proudhon and seeks surcease, planning to give up the movement to attain personal peace and happiness. Perhaps additional research prompted O'Neill's more historically accurate presentation of his hero. Following his release from prison in 1922, the real Enrico Malatesta abandoned his anarchist activities and lived out the remainder of his life—another decade—quietly in Rome with his mistress Elena Melli and her daughter.

Notes for the new 1941 interpretation of Malatesta state:

Malatesta disillusioned, bitter, sad, sick and weary, seeks surcease and sanctuary within the family—in jail, his broodings in solitary have turned back in nostalgic memory to his own family—with remorse, regret—for he had disregarded them —also regret hadn't married Rosa—brilliant student—then radicalism—Humbert's assassination, conviction, Lipari Island—one brother has become important Fascist—he gets Cesare pardoned (to get rid of disgrace) on pledge he will abstain political activities—then both Fascist police and his Anarchist pals warn him to get out of country [in] 24 hours or be liquidated—both have it all fixed smuggle him into U.S. What he finally demands is money enough to get him to town, Conn[ecticut].

In the notes for Act One, the Daniellos and their Italian friends—their idealism enkindled—joyously anticipate the arrival of Malatesta. Rosa laments: "The nearer he gets, the fatter I feel." Four minor characters, Tony Daniello's friends—two Italians and two Irishmen—are introduced. Although these first generation immigrants are ardent nationalists, professing a belief in the ideals of the revolutionary movements of the old country, they are self-seeking materialists, putting into practice the lessons learned in the new world to obtain wealth by any means.

The shoemaker Gus Bascone,* "a bachelor with bitter scorn for woman's

---

*O'Neill apparently uses Bascone's trade to evoke the memory of Nicola Sacco, a shoemaker. In July 1921 Sacco and Vanzetti were found guilty of murder and sentenced to death. Many within and without the Italian community viewed them as martyrs—condemned because they were anarchists. Protest meetings, worldwide demonstrations, and appeals delayed their execution until 1927. The dramatist would probably include topical references in the 1923 anarchist play—as he does in previous works—mentioning this notorious case.

suffrage and a hatred for feet and factory shoes," and Pete Gebardi, the "head Gardener on millionaire (Standard Oil) estate,"* are constantly arguing. Like the General and the Captain in *The Iceman Cometh*, they are friendly foes. The shoemaker denies, while the gardener affirms, the existence of God. The former asks Gebardi: "how can he be Anarchist if he believes in God." The gardener rejects "the Church's God—a stained glass Pope of the Bourgeoisie" but believes in the "God of Poor, the Supreme Anarchist—when Revolution comes, we will take him away from bourgeoisie—Church, too—call by different names." The two men also quarrel about what should be done with the Standard Oil capitalist, who had tried, at first, to give the gardener directions. Gebardi states: "I told him. You are a fool. Would I tell you how to run your copper mines, etc. The boss, he has brains. He says all right." Basconi insists: "He should be shot." The gardener replies angrily: "He has brains, I tell you. He has millions, great success. He will never give you chance to shoot him. The minute he sees anarchism marching he will join us." The two men agree on one thing, the importance of wealth, and brag about "how much money saved each month —once to go back to Italy—but now to buy house, land."

Big Jim Delehanty, the Irish cop and independence patriot, has a running quarrel with the English. He spends more time enjoying the convivial atmosphere in Tony's saloon than "pounding a beat." His only concern is to avoid detection by the machine boss, Pat Connor. On one occasion when Connor comes in unexpectedly and catches Delehanty drinking, the wily Irishman "has to arrest someone, so picks quiet harmless stranger at the bar for disorderly conduct— followed him in to make sure." Later Delehanty returns. He has been "hiding outside until Connor left. 'Grand man is Pat, but unreasonable at times.' Angelo derisive—'Yes, he thinks a cop ought to be sober sometimes and walk a beat instead of sitting in gin mill and being God's gift to bourgeoisie,' etc.—good-natured banter, kidding."

Pat Connor spends almost as much time as Delehanty at the saloon; he and Tony are "old pals—came up ladder together." The ward-heeler talks about getting out the Italian vote, but he is also concerned about May's rejection of his son, "who is using it as an excuse to get tanked up." Connor warns Tony that May is getting talked about as a flirt, that her virtue is being questioned. Tony

---

*The prototype for this character is possibly Charlie Santoro, an Italian-American, who was eighty years old when I met him in 1969 at the Waterford estate of Edward Harkness—the Standard Oil millionaire O'Neill depicts as Harder in *Long Day's Journey into Night* and Harker in *A Moon for the Misbegotten*. Santoro had worked on the Harkness estate for fifty-five years. As notes for the former play indicate, O'Neill often walked over to the Waterford home of Dolan, the tenant farmer, whose land bordered the Harkness property. In the early notes for the latter drama, Dolan (later Phil Hogan) recruits an Italian friend to serve as a witness in the plot to trap Jim Tyrone in bed with Josie.

says reassuringly that his wife sleeps in the same room with May "witha da door locked. May too lazy climb from window—and second floor, anyway. Too stupid beat mother. My Rosa knows all da tricks." Even the shoemaker and gardener express their concern about May: "Can she be married off before she's seduced?—like her mother once was—so long ago. And we believed in free love." They rave about Rosa's former beauty—"a flame—and now, a truck—2 ton—she would rather have a bowl of spaghetti than Casanova—the way of life." Later, Rosa reminisces about the past: "men used to call me the angel of the barricades, the rose of revolution—they said my spirit was a bright wind, the inner flame of freedom—and I believed them—I know now they meant I gave it away free."

When the machine boss leaves, Bascone and Gebardi argue about "what's to be done with Connor when Revolution comes." The shoemaker, "the extremist says, must be shot." The gardener disagrees: "No, he's good fellow—and controls machine—will become Anarchist—as we'll need his machine—against the counter-revolution—he is good Republican party member because it pays, but when he sees Anarchism pays better—." Tony and his two friends discuss Malatesta's coming visit. Their conversation veers from memories of anarchist triumphs of the old days to their hopes for a resurgence of the movement in their adopted country. O'Neill reveals the dramatic climax he plans for the end of Act One. After his arrival, Malatesta makes the startling announcement that he is giving up the movement. When they are alone, the Daniellos and their friends discuss ways to persuade Malatesta to change his mind. "Finally the main family plot is to get him married to Francina. Shoemaker (bachelor) taunts, 'Yes, that will restore his love of liberty.' "

February 17–18, 1941—"Malatesta Seeks Surcease,"
Act One, outline

As Act One opens, the Daniellos are making preparations for Malatesta's arrival. Tony goes to the train station to meet his friend. Bascone and Gebardi are "full of romantic mystery—stupid of Tony to think he would come openly on train—Italian police will be following, U.S. sent police looking for [him]." The characters are depicted in the scenario as they were originally conceived in the early notes. Realizing a match between Malatesta and the attractive widowed elder daughter lacked comedic potential, O'Neill substitutes Rosa's cousin, the prim, puritanical Francina, dramatically swathed in widow's weeds, professing sorrow for her recently deceased dull husband yet keeping a sly eye open for a dashing, vibrant replacement. She antagonizes the entire family and deserves her nickname, "the Black Death." Even the jolly, high-spirited Rosa is constantly at odds with her cousin. Francina enters now in "deep mourning—sits down casting gloom—everyone irritated, but constrained to pacify—urge drink, food—

blasts one after another—no one is amused but Rosa and May." To her mother, May whispers: "She needs a man, don't she, Mom. You're always telling her that." Francina overhears her remark: "May, your mother thinks love is like a dish of spaghetti. When one is gone, you just help yourself to another." Rosa says: "Well, there is something in that." Francina eagerly awaits Malatesta's visit, for then she will have "someone to talk to who still dreams of freedom, who is not a slave to food and money and hooch and shoes and the dirt of gardens and graft, etc."

At the end of Act One, Malatesta finally arrives, exhausted from his long journey and frightened. Seeing Big Jim Delehanty in his policeman's uniform, he says: "So, my good old friends, you betray me like all the others. You have the police waiting." The family laughs; the policeman is a good friend. Delehanty "shakes hands, warm welcome—'I'm all for you when it comes to Ireland and bloody destruction to tyrants. But mind you, I part with you when it comes to denying God and the Roman Catholic church.'" Malatesta "begins to crumple up—explaining weakly, no money, nothing to eat—faints." Rosa rushes to the kitchen; Angelo looks at Delehanty and laughs: "Imagine his passing out after taking a slant at you. Well, at that, it ain't so surprising."

In his last reference in the Work Diary to "Malatesta Seeks Surcease" on March 2, 1941, O'Neill states: "Outline I—like this idea but have lost grip on it—trouble is too many good ideas—can't settle on one—(the war, perhaps)." Contrary to his usual practice, he does not state in the Work Diary when he outlined the second and third acts. He apparently completed the scenarios for them in the February 23–March 1 period and then jotted down the "many good ideas" for Act One, which appear in the notes after Act Three, on March 2.

Act Two, outline

The act opens with a scene in the Daniello family dining room the morning after Malatesta's arrival. The three women—Rosa, Francina, and May—have just finished serving Malatesta breakfast in bed. A family council is held to discuss his future. "Angelo is worried that Malatesta may be recognized—big story in papers—then everyone begins to think [of] speakeasy and how much money we make—and everyone gets mad they're not making so much—and they write letters to complain, etc.—and next thing there's a padlock on the speak." There is mounting evidence throughout this act of the materialism of the Italian-American characters, motivating Malatesta's later denouncement and his attempt to reform them. Earlier the men thought how pleasant it would be when Malatesta arrived; they would sit and "drink good wine and talk of Revolution." Now they are "uneasy lest Malatesta start anything in this country—worry for their business—rationalize—besides, time is not ripe—everything prosperous—no discontent—time to lie low—make plans for Day—when we are all poor and starving—etc."

The second act closes with Malatesta's startling revelation that he has become a teetotaler; a worse blow is struck when he condemns the use of alcohol by others. His speech, denouncing the demon drink—"capitalist poison to dull the minds of people"—has a disturbing effect on the Daniellos, who are amassing a fortune from their speakeasy. Sensing their antagonism, Malatesta abandons his anarchist rhetoric and "puts it differently—'for the happiness of family. Alcohol corrupts love and respect within family.' They all solemnly agree with him—he goes on, 'one thing we can all do—give up the poison, alcohol.'" When Malatesta goes out, their disgusted response is: "A Probie!"

Act Three, outline

In *The Iceman Cometh* Hickey's successful campaign to get his friends to relinquish their pipe dreams and dependence on alcohol has tragic consequences; in contrast, Malatesta's crusade for reformation and temperance has only comic results. Act Three opens

A month later—Malatesta going strong on the reform of the family—fully recovered in health now, full of energy and immensely talkative—his manner persuasive but firmly dictatorial—Francina has become his ally in this Puritan movement—she has pointed out the failings of members of family which he must reform—and she particularly implants the idea of herself as the poor relation, the humiliated drudge, the defenseless widow—all [the] time she is shrewd and calculating underneath—and firmly blackmails each member of family she discovers disobeying his edicts—He has whole household in subjection but [treats each with] severity [for] disobeying his laws—Rosa's acting—drinking of others—selling of drinks—urges abandonment of everything but innocent growing, close to simple things of earth.

Malatesta's latest suggestion that they sacrifice their "greedy savings to help educate men to see Prohibition is salvation of family" and his "hints that lecturers are needed to go forth [to] spread the gospel of deliverance from alcohol" prompt the Daniellos and their friends to assemble secretly in the backroom. "Rosa (the realist who loves diamond rings and food) becomes the brain behind all the plot to get rid of Malatesta and Francina—When finally men are desperate about what to do with Malatesta, to get rid of him, Rosa talks to each and says she will fix it." The scenes, in which Rosa "talks to each," would certainly provide much humor; for she resorts—clearly and simply—to blackmail. To Gus and Pete "her price is a diamond ring—but she will let them off easy—from both, not from each—she tells husband same—and Angelo and Connor—she holds up Delehanty for promise to buy her each week a two-pound box [of] chocolate creams." There is poetic justice in Rosa's extortion. Years before, as the flame of the revolution, she had—in her innocence and adherence to the anarchist concept of free love—given herself to at least three of the men involved. In more recent years, she has played the role of the loving, forgiving wife, indulgent mother, and accommodating friend. These men had taken advantage of her; they had made her the butt of their thoughtless—and at times obscene—jokes. The play could appropriately be subtitled "Rosa's Revenge."

When Rosa explains that her plan requires their getting Malatesta into Francine's bedroom, Angelo protests: "But he won't go to her room. What would he go for? Christ, even after twenty years in the can, nobody would fall for—." The men discover that the "whole scheme depends on marriage and he is a damned fool but he is not such a fool as to marry her—no one is!" Rosa replies: "That is where I am the brain. I will fix it." Connor says: "Well, it's true anything on earth can be fixed if you know the ropes."

Having considerable experience in love affairs, Rosa easily arouses Francina and Malatesta's interest in each other. She convinces Francina that Malatesta "means what he says about family." Her awareness that Malatesta—like all the other men in the play—is completely captivated by the obvious charms of her daughter prompts Rosa to tell him that Francina has a "figure like May's— she does not dress to show it off—she is modest—but I assure you if you saw her taking a bath, you would be surprised." Rosa plans to use the old "bed trick" here with May as bait. May, however, is not as stupid as the family believes. Before she enters into the conspiracy, she "holds [her] mother up for diamond ring." Rosa admires her cunning but is annoyed. Francina reluctantly agrees to play the role assigned her but protests the involvement of a potential rival. Rosa is unperturbed by the predictions of failure; she knows Malatesta's sense of honor will compel him to marry the substituted Francina. The notes reveal that the plan is successfully executed.

O'Neill concludes his work on the "Malatesta comedy idea" with the words: "To the Day! To the Night!" Possibly, he refers here to familial Janus opposites—the lighthearted comic qualities of the Daniellos in "Malatesta Seeks Surcease" and the darksome tragic traits of the Tyrones in *Long Day's Journey into Night*. He may be suggesting through the day-night antithesis man's dual nature; the characters in both dramas aspire to the good but are hopelessly flawed. At the same time he is working on these two plays—simultaneously for a period—he is also developing ideas for his duality of man play, "The Last Conquest," depicting "Good-Evil—opposites in Man—symbolic spiritual conflict today and in all times." In *Long Day's Journey into Night* the characters embark on a torturous voyage, a regression from day—symbolizing their ephemeral moments of self-awareness and faint hope for future self-realization —to night, representing their despair and retreat into the tragic web of an irreversible past. "Malatesta Seeks Surcease" also uses the concept of a voyage; but it is a hopeful progression, showing the central character's rejection of the enslavement of the past, the nightmare horror of Old World totalitarianism, for the safe refuge in a seemingly bright new land of innocence and promise. The message is the same in both plays: the odyssey of Western man encompasses the search for self, leading to the discovery of his inner flawed condition.

Malatesta leaves a country with a totalitarian Fascist regime, apparently representing Evil, for a democratic society, supposedly symbolizing Good. In the former he is persecuted by the Italian authorities; in the "free" society he is harassed and has to disguise himself with a beard and glasses to avoid detection by the American police. He is a dissenter and suspect. While the individual is blatantly oppressed in a dictatorship, he can suffer a similar fate in a democracy where laws are passed or broken to gain or maintain power or wealth. What, in the best of worlds, should illustrate contrast only serves to reinforce the similarity. O'Neill uses his beleaguered anarchist hero, buffeted by both groups, to make this point. Like Proudhon, the dramatist believes that no government can bring equality and social justice to its people—that each is established and controlled by man and is doomed because man is hopelessly flawed. The one exception, of course, is the legendary anarchist leader, Enrico Malatesta, a man who had spent fifty years of his life attempting to improve the lives of others—suffering exile, imprisonment, deprivation of every kind; a man who was humble, joyous, generous—giving all that he possessed to the poor and working as a common artisan with his hands.[3]

O'Neill originally envisions Malatesta's fictitious counterpart in 1940 as an ardent believer in the innate goodness of his fellow man. When the Axis dictators unleash their madness and fury upon the world, the dramatist despairs "about the future of individual freedom." To him, the war was not merely a conflict between countries but the eternal struggle between the powers of good and evil; the survival of the remnants of Western civilization's moral and spiritual values was at stake. He sends not a warrior into the fray but a mild-mannered reformer with a warning and a message of hope for man. The new Malatesta who emerges in 1941 is a Christ figure. Betrayed by trusted but jealous Judas-like friends in the movement in Italy—his Garden of Gethsemane—he undertakes a Via Dolorosa, his visit to the New World. One definition of the word "visit" is: "to come in order to comfort or bless, said of the Deity." He comes unto his own, his beloved friends the Daniellos, seeking surcease from suffering, from corruption. What he discovers in their household pains and dismays him; each is consumed by greed or a base desire. The central message of the play is summarized in Malatesta's admonition to his materialistic friends: "Utopia is impossible until man outgrows his base greed—his spiritual immaturity—and develops a soul. No Movement can do it—they lead to greed for power—each man and woman strives within himself or herself to conquer own natures." Patiently, he urges change. The word "revolution," which implies radical change, is used frequently in the notes. The characters want to *talk* of revolution but refuse to alter their own lives. Malatesta becomes the living symbol of their repressed noble aspirations, instilling in them feelings of guilt; and they conspire to betray him.

Significantly, O'Neill's work on "Malatesta Seeks Surcease" stops at this point. The "chain-stitch playwright" develops in his next idea the betrayal-crucifixion theme, using the real Christ rather than a messianic figure. His statement in 1946 about his "big kind of comedy that doesn't stay funny long" perhaps explains why he abandons his attempt in 1941 to convey his message in the comic mode. In his last reference to the Malatesta work on March 2, 1941, O'Neill states that he likes this concept but has "lost grip on it—trouble is too many ideas (the war, perhaps)." The next day he outlines "The Last Conquest," which again issues another warning to modern man but without the humor that characterizes "Malatesta Seeks Surcease." There is no mere threat of oppression by a Fascist leader thousands of miles away; man is now enslaved in a World State, persecuted by a brutal dictator. The new work shows the consequences of the failure to heed Malatesta's message—O'Neill's favorite Biblical quotation: "For what shall it profit a man, if he shall gain the whole world and lose his own soul?" In "The Last Conquest" modern man is a tragic, damned Faustian creature, having lost not only his freedom and prized acquisitions but even the awareness that he possesses a soul. "Malatesta Seeks Surcease" is the first in the trilogy of ideas developed between 1940 and 1943, in which man's inner good-evil struggle reflects a similar global conflict of opposites. It is unfortunate that the "Malatesta comedy idea" was never completed, never staged; O'Neill was not to discover whether his fellow Americans, unable to discern themselves and their true flawed, fragmented reflection in a narcissistic pool of tears, could do so through laughter.

Notes

[1]O'Neill's fascination for anarchism and Emma Goldman is partially the result of his close friendships with her family and friends. It seems highly probable that he met the famous anarchist in Provincetown, where he resided in 1916. Teddy Ballantine, who staged the first production of *Bound East for Cardiff* with the Provincetown Players on July 28, 1916, was married to Goldman's niece Stella. When a bomb exploded in the Preparedness Parade in San Francisco on July 22, 1916, Goldman terminated her lecture tour and decided, as she states in her autobiography, "to go to Provincetown for a month to visit with Stella and her baby." Hippolyte Havel, one of O'Neill's close friends and Goldman's former lover, was also in Provincetown that summer. She had met the Czech anarchist in late 1899 in London and traveled to Paris with him in January 1900, remaining in that city until after the assassination of King Umberto on July 27. Havel accompanied her when she returned to the United States.

Goldman hired Mary Eleanor Fitzgerald in 1913 to work on the anarchist publication *Mother Earth*. Five years later Fitzi, as she was called, became secretary of the Provincetown Players at the Macdougal Street theatre and a friend of O'Neill. In 1924, after leaving Russia in disillusionment, Goldman settled in Paris. Harry Weinberger, a New York attorney, obtained an extended French transit visa for her. At that time Weinburger was the Provincetown Players' legal representative; he later became, until his death in 1944, O'Neill's personal attorney.

Another important link between O'Neill and Goldman was the dramatist's lifelong friendship with her nephew Saxe Commins, Stella Ballantine's brother. The two met in 1916 when the Provincetown Players opened their Macdougal Street theatre, and Commins was showing more interest in his playwrighting efforts than his medical studies. Commins, aided by Hippolyte Havel, edited *Mother Earth* when his aunt was on a lecture tour. Commins eventually became O'Neill's editor and adviser. Strangely enough, O'Neill records his first brief idea for the Malatesta comedy on January 4, 1940. A later entry reveals that Commins visited him on January 19—a few weeks before he made his extensive notes for this new play.

It is impossible to ascertain what each of these acquaintances contributed to the development of the Malatesta idea. Commins may have shared with O'Neill his aunt's recollections of the legendary anarchist, whom she had met several times. Havel could have provided valuable information; Goldman called him "a veritable encyclopedia. He knew everybody and everything in the movement of the various European countries" (*Living My Life*, p. 259). Whether O'Neill's source of inspiration came from friends or his own reading of anarchist literature, his portrait of Malatesta—both the public figure and the private man —is historically accurate.

[2]Compare passages in the play and Goldman's statements. Long, O'Neill's anticapitalist spokesman, accompanies Yank to Fifth Avenue. Stopping at a jeweler's window and seeing the "bleedin' prices," Long comments: "One of these 'ere would buy scoff for a starvin' family for a year." Yank, who has been called an ape, wants to strike out at the rich for economic and social inequities. When Long tells him that the votes of the on-marching proletarians will effect a change through peaceful means, Yank says contemptuously: "Votes, hell! Votes is a joke, see." Yank's attempts to communicate with the wealthy churchgoers on Fifth Avenue bring a policeman to the scene; he is sent to Blackwell's Island for inciting a riot. Emma Goldman is similarly charged and given a one-year sentence on the Island for a speech she made at an 1893 rally in Union Square:

> The labour politicians make common cause with your enemies to keep you
> in leash, to prevent your direct action. The State is the pillar of capitalism,
> and it is ridiculous to expect any redress from it. Do you not see the stupidity
> of asking relief from Albany with immense wealth within a stone's throw
> from here? Fifth Avenue is laid in gold, every mansion is a citadel of
> money and power, yet there you stand, a giant, starved and fettered, shorn
> of his strength. . . . They have not only stolen your bread, but they are

sapping your blood. They will go on robbing you, your children, your children's children, unless you wake up, unless you become daring enough to demand your rights (*Living My Life*, pp. 122–23).

[3]There are many similarities between the Malatesta that emerges from O'Neill's notes and the historic figure that Goldman describes. When she first met him in London in 1897, he was living behind his small shop. "The considerable inheritance from his father, consisting of land and houses in Italy, he had deeded without any remuneration to the workers who occupied them, himself continuing to exist most frugally on the earnings of his own hands." Goldman states that while she had no interpreter "his kindly smile mirrored a congenial personality and made me feel as if I had known him all my life."

Goldman lists the impressive delegates at the International Anarchist Congress in Amsterdam in 1907 and remarks: "But the most outstanding personality among them was Enrico Malatesta. Of fine and sensitive nature, Malatesta had already in his youth embraced revolutionary ideals." She discusses his role in the anarchist movement in Italy: "Whether he happened to be in Switzerland, France, England, or the Argentine, an uprising in his native country always brought him to the aid of the people. . . . His entire life was one of storm and stress, his energies and exceptional abilities devoted to the service of the anarchist cause." She personally "fell under the spell of Malatesta" and "loved his capacity to throw off the weight of the world and give himself to play in his leisure. Every moment spent with him was a joy, whether he exulted over the sight of the sea or frolicked in a public garden" (*Living My Life*, pp. 166, 403–04).

°THE LAST CONQUEST
(1940)

On August 30, 1940, O'Neill describes his first concept of "The Last Conquest": "Work on fascinating new idea I get for duality of Man play—Good-Evil, Christ-Devil—begins Temptation on Mount—through to Crucifixion—Devil a modern power realist—symbolical spiritual conflict today and in all times." In this "spiritual propaganda play," as he calls it, "Evil conquers the future world (seemingly)." The idea is the dramatist's creative response to the world events of the previous year. On August 31, 1939, he notes: "up till 3 a.m. to listen [to] Hitler's war speech against Poland"° (W.D.). Throughout the spring of 1940 he cannot shake his "war obsession," which, he admits, "is becoming neurosis—can't save even myself by not working and despairing about the future of individual freedom" (W.D., June 25, 1940). Implicit in this statement is his belief that he can save others, as well as himself, by working. This conviction, coupled with his deep concern for individual liberty, had prompted him to launch a crusade in the canon to free man from the shackles that bind him. In the problem plays of the early 1920s, man's chains are forged by economic exploitation and ethnic discrimination. Man's unbridled greed and sense of racial superiority lead him in the 1930s to the threshold of Auschwitz and spawn the master-monsters of political oppression O'Neill depicts in his antitotalitarian trilogy and in related ideas that he developed in the early 1940s.†

Greed creates and sustains the world of victors and vanquished in "The Last Conquest": the oppressors, who have realized Hitler's dream of European and global conquest, and the enslaved, who—fearing the loss of material possessions—had preached appeasement,°° the doctrine of containment rather than

---

°Hitler's demand that the city of Danzig (now Gdańsk) be returned to Germany led to the invasion of Poland, precipitating World War II. Germany annexed Danzig on September 1, 1939.

†On August 15, 1940, two weeks before recording the first idea for "The Last Conquest," O'Neill makes "notes on ideas for two plays . . . timely but timeless spiritually —re present world collapse and dictatorships." In his end-of-the-month entry he identifies these ideas as "timeless timely, ventriloquist play and Time Grandfather Was Dead."

°°Chamberlain thought he could appease Hitler by sacrificing Czechoslovakia in the infamous Munich Agreement of September 1938. President Roosevelt deplored Chamberlain's "peace at any price" and prophesied the English would abandon the Czechs and then "wash the blood from their Judas Iscariot hands." Yet the United States failed to assume moral responsibility to avoid bloodshed. For example, American officials refused to change the immigration laws to provide a refuge for persecuted Jews, who subsequently—and needlessly—died in Hitler's horror camps.

resistance. In the work that precedes the propaganda play "The Visit of Malatesta" "Malatesta Seeks Surcease"), O'Neill points out the way to avert such a conquest. After escaping the tyranny of Mussolini, Malatesta dreams of "freedom for world." Realizing that the Fascists came to power (as the Nazis would do later) by bending the law, he has "a change of viewpoint about law—as anarchist believed laws made criminal—now he knows laws are necessary"—those that guide man to subdue his base instincts in familial and social relationships.

In advocating this principle, Malatesta reflects the views of Proudhon and O'Neill.* "Proudhon's sense of man's divided nature and of his original sin brings him far nearer to belief in God than most anarchists have been. For him God and man confront each other, and their struggle is the struggle of man with the better part of his own self."† This twofold conflict is, in essence, the theme of "The Last Conquest" and demonstrates once again O'Neill's avowed interest in the relationship between man and God and his belief in the dichotomy of man—with his lower materialistic, physical side engaged in a never-ending battle with his higher idealistic spiritual nature. A passage in the first set of notes for "The Last Conquest," written on August 30, 1940, illustrates the

duality of Man's psyche—opposites—with application [to] present world crisis: renunciation versus possession—he that gaineth his life shall lose it versus greed for power—humility versus pride—the believer in the soul of man versus the condemned materialist and self-styled realist who can see only the cunning animal with intelligence as real—the stultification in latter attitude because it is self-justification which conceals self-loathing.

In the "duality of man" play, the dramatist writes the final coda to the story of the doomed Faustian-split heroes depicted in his work of the 1920s and 1930s. "The Last Conquest" shows the damned in the hell their base nature created; the constant refrain in the play is the Biblical quotation: "What shall it profit a man, if he shall gain the whole world and lose his own soul?" Like *Lazarus Laughed*, "The Last Conquest" is a morality play, a religious pageant. Both are political, as well as spiritual, propaganda plays. The early Biblical work concludes with the crucifixion of Lazarus as the acquiescent crowd shouts: "Hail, Caesar!" The victorious, but accusatory, Caligula utters the last line: "Men forget!" Because men two thousand years later have this same tendency to forget, because they value material possessions rather than freedom and integrity, they fall prey to twentieth-century Caesars. Ever mindful of Hitler, Musso-

---

*In his public statements, as well as in his plays, O'Neill proclaims himself an anarchist. During a rehearsal for *The Iceman Cometh* in 1946, when asked where he stood on the labor movement, he said: "I am a philosophical anarchist." Croswell Bowen, *Curse of the Misbegotten* (New York, 1959), p. 130.
†James Joll, *The Anarchists* (Boston, 1964), p. 68.

lini, and Stalin, O'Neill portrays his World Dictator as the apotheosis and legatee of these modern tyrants:

There is no physical resemblance between him and any of the dictators of totalitarian nations, like Hitler of Germany, who has preceded him and whose realistic wars, although they met temporary material defeat in the end, triumphed in principle and so ravaged and maimed and tortured the already sick and faithless souls of men, that they paved the way for final world-wide, spiritual exhaustion and the acceptance of the new Salvation and the Divine Tyrant Redeemer principle in a Holy and Indivisible World State. The Savior of the World owes much to these men, whose spiritual heir He is, but of course He can never admit He owes His power to anything but His own Divine Genius and He had decreed that no memory of these men must ever be spoken or written.

The plot of the 1940 "World-Dictator fantasy of a possible future," as O'Neill describes it,[*] is "the attempted last campaign of Evil to stamp out even the unconscious memory of God in Man's spirit." Proclaiming himself divine, the dictator believes he has successfully eliminated the remembrance of God from the minds of his subjects. A plan is devised to test this assumption by His Minister of Spiritual Affairs and Superstitions, the thirteenth member of His Supreme Council, composed of the chiefs of His army, navy and air force, and the various Ministers of His cabinet. By first entitling the play "The Thirteenth Apostle," O'Neill shows that as he begins this work he views the Black Magician, as he is called, as the central character. He is, in reality, the Devil, the power behind the throne. The Savior of the World, as well as the other twelve ministers, is only a dummy in the early version, a figurehead manipulated by the Magician. The power struggle, as O'Neill's original idea states, is the Devil's last campaign against his ancient adversary for final, complete possession of men's minds and souls. The Magician plans to re-create the scenes preceding and including the crucifixion, determined to draw from the cynical masses the laughter of ridicule as Christ repeats his doctrines urging humility and renunciation of worldly possessions. Laughter was used in *Lazarus Laughed* to affirm life, the existence of God; now it will be used by the Devil to deny Him.

O'Neill wrote ten sets of notes—from August 30, 1940 to December 13, 1942—for "The 13th Apostle," changing its title frequently before finally deciding on "The Last Conquest."

August 30, 1940—The 13th Apostle, first notes on idea

Two alternate titles heading the notes—"Straw for the Drowning" and "A Straw to More Than Straw"—clearly illustrate O'Neill's altruistic purpose in

---

[*]Letter to Dudley Nichols, December 16, 1942.

writing this work: to offer doomed mankind once again—as he did, for example, in his 1918–1919 play, appropriately called *The Straw*—a faint "hopeless hope." After assuming "many characters in play"—those who betray Christ—the Devil becomes, literally, by the time O'Neill finished his notes for it, "The 13th Apostle," cursing the fate that condemns him throughout time to murder repeatedly the God-Man he secretly loves and worships. Through the Magician, perhaps the most complex character in the canon, O'Neill demonstrates again that even in this base creature the evil he empitomizes is mixed with the desire, at least, for good.° Earlier Christ figures, such as Lazarus and Malatesta, in spite of their many virtues, pale when compared to the all-merciful, all-loving God-Man, the dramatist's most magnificent creation. If O'Neill believed—truly believed—in the concept of the Christ he envisions here, the death wish he expresses throughout his adult life is understandable.

In this first version of the Temptation on the Mount scene, the Devil is compelled—by the script written at the beginning of time—"to force his values on Christ," to make him "sell self, to prove there is no soul, to take possession of it," reminding him that Judas' betrayal is a "natural means to end and symbol of man's soul always for sale." The scenes that follow include: the Last Supper; the Entrance to Jerusalem—a "burlesque of Caesar's triumph," in which the "people jump at chance for fiesta, carnival, drink"; the Devil's denunciation of the High Priest and Pilate, his cry to the crowd "Let us crucify him"; the crucifixion, when the "crowd's revengeful sadism gradually turns to horror and pity." Fearful of losing power over the mob, the Devil sends the secret police to intimidate and beat the multitude gathered around the cross and declares: "I shall build chalet here—for meditation on the nature of man—on his selfishness, his stupidity—his adoration of power—his envy of the courage of [a] crook."

August 31, 1940—Propaganda for "More Than Straw for the Drowning," notes

O'Neill gives a new twist to the "Dialogue in the Night"; the first temptation scene is reversed: "it is the unseen (?) man on the cross who tempts the

---

° As he did when portraying Tiberius and Caligula, who secretly love Lazarus, O'Neill, in delineating the Magician, shows again his great compassion for all creatures. His early days at Jimmy the Priest's and the Hell Hole brought him an awareness of his own and others' flawed nature. When explaining the characters in *The Iceman Cometh* to the actors during a rehearsal, the author told them: "Raw emotion produces the worst in people. Remember, goodness can surmount anything. The people in that saloon were the best friends I've ever known. . . . Their weakness was not an evil. It is a weakness found in all men. . . . In all my plays sin is punished and redemption takes place. Vice and virtue cannot live side by side. It's the humiliation of a loving kiss that destroys evil" (Bowen, *Curse of the Misbegotten*, p. 310).

Devil with all the peace of the spirit of renunciation." When dawn brings light to the scene, the Devil is startled to see that the "figure on Cross is he—and he has on Christ's clothes—Devil stunned—not he—who?—I've seen before many times—who?—It is I!—no, this is another of His fake miracles." Even though he puts on his own clothes, the assembled crowd kneels when the Devil steps forward. He is horrified at himself for feeling pity for the multitude, bowed in adoration: "Listen, my Brethren, do not kneel. I am as the least of you. I am the Son of Man." He is bewildered and begins his "old dictator mob-moving harangue—in asides, his disgust with its lies—his horror that he had begun to believe them himself—Christ's words keep breaking through—his confused remittance—possessed—but joy in it, too—getting rid of self, freedom—finally, his speech becomes Sermon on Mount."

February 5, 7, 1941—"The 13th Disciple," Christ-Satan & duality of Man play

O'Neill changes the title slightly to show the Devil as one of the "Disciples —Christian clergy of all time—each representing a different epoch down to present day."* He gives the play a universal, panoramic dimension, setting it not only in "Jerusalem but also ancient Rome and capitals of today—megalopolitan capitals of all civilizations at similar periods [of] decline of cultures and advent of Savior." The character Loving in *Days Without End* represented the Mephistophelian side of John and was only visible to him; in this early version of "The Last Conquest," Satan, invisible to everyone except Christ, is the "corrupt realist in Judas—is Judas but isn't—just as he is the Peter who denies Christ, thus denying his spiritual self—the flesh denying the spirit, as Judas' flesh was betrayed [when] he sold his spirit for the realistic value of 30 pieces of silver." The last scene of this version shows Satan "in bitter despair, sitting bound at the foot of the cross" yet claiming paradoxically that the "last great victory is won." He asks himself: "Is there never an escape from this eternal cycle of recurrence in which victory is defeat?" As the curtain drops, the marionette ranks raise their hands "in hail salute as He stares at them."

March 3–13, 1941—The 13th Apostle, original scenario

In this scenario "The man, Son of the Spirit" and "Satan, the Great, a Magician," are living; all other characters are "life-size marionettes (or dwarf

---

*In depicting the modern era, O'Neill would probably chastise the Catholic and Protestant heads of churches who failed to denounce Nazism when there was still time to halt its spread. They, like leaders of nations, entered into a conspiracy of silence.

ventriloquist dummies)."* O'Neill outlines eight scenes and states that all
are laid in a secret place deep within the duality of Man's soul—an ancient
battlefield of the Spirit, haunted by memories of murder and birth, of greed and
sacrifice, of loathing and aspirations, which dwell in the Past Everlasting, the
deathless Symbols of Fate and Salvation. The time is the Future which is the
Present, which is the Past.

Scene One—The Mount of Temptation, just before dawn

The Man and the Magician, wearing identical robes, arrive at the summit.
The Magician carries a "big box on [his] shoulders—box of tricks." He complains bitterly about having to reenact the same old drama and asks: "Why can't
you keep on playing dead? The wounds on your hands and feet have hardly
healed since the last time. When will you give up this hopeless salvation dream
of yours?" He pleads to have the chalice removed. The Man's attitude is "one of
gentle, affectionate brotherliness." He says: "Come, my Brother. It is not proper
for a King's victim, a manifestation of Caesar, the power behind all thrones and
behind the altars of all man-made gods to be so depressed." The Magician, "like
an old actor making up for part he has played many times," sheds his robe, takes
from the box the black uniform of the Minister of Foreign Affairs, and puts it
on. He ridicules the Man for always playing his role in old clothes, saying that
the people will distort his words to justify any greed. "They will reduce your
voice to a rising and falling pulpit singsong in abandoned churches on Sunday
mornings—They only believe in Gods who are manifestly tested and pronounced
free from adulteration, mechanized, stream-lined, and economically determined." As the dawn breaks, the Magician's voice grows stronger, "like an old
actor revived by approach of curtain." He sits on the box and "makes up the
conventional Mephisto[phelian] face." He urges the Man to "give it up—let's
get drunk—Baudelaire" and issues one last warning: "This time it is really to
death—without the publicity of resurrection—for even gods can live on earth
only in the soul of man—and I have killed that soul—this time I will the final
victory."

From the box the Magician takes a dummy: "Caesar again—but Tiberius
had a mind and this little man has only the cunning I gave him—dictator

---

*A Book of Puppetry, which Jerome Magon sent to O'Neill in December 1939, may
have inspired him to experiment with marionettes. In his letter thanking Magon, the
dramatist writes: "The book is [the] most interesting I have ever seen on the subject."
He also expresses his gratitude for the photograph of the puppet production of
Marco Millions. "The sets especially catch my eye. They are excellent. And the
drawing of Nicolo Polo is damned amusing. Did you ever think of doing The Hairy
Ape?"

dummy—the God Father of his own divinity—theologians of Alexandria would have had a great time rationalizing that nut." To the Magician, the dummy represents the "final perfect expression of the highest low desire in the heart of every man—the lust for power—the fear of liberty—you had better beware of this little monster—he faces men as they are and uses them accordingly—he sees they are still beasts if you but scratch their surfaces." The Temptation begins when the Magician orders the dummy to prove to the Man that the "soul has no value when you can sell it, that selling it is the only way to prove it exists in the world of realism—make him your best offer." The dummy arrogantly offers the Man the "spiritual leadership of New Order—work under me—but don't tell them you are Son of God—because they think that I—." The dictator's Hitler-like qualities are manifested. As the crowd approaches, the dummy wants not to be seen "consorting with a Jew, even if he is only ghost of a dead Jew. Don't let your being a Jew bother you. I have had a family tree manufactured for you which shows you are, like me, the son of an Aryan emigrant to Palestine." The Man rejects the proposal "with contemptuous pity." There is the sound of marching feet—"goose step up a mountain side." Given a signal, the Man addresses the crowd and delivers the Sermon on the Mount. When he concludes, there is silence; the triumphant dummy orders the crowds back to their barracks, saluting "the New Order! You have nothing to lose but Liberty! Forward in the name of the State! I promise you that never will there be peace on earth! The future must be destroyed! There must be nothing left in the spirit but the desire for death!"

After the people leave, the Magician wearily begs the Man: "Please give it up! I do not like [the] role of judge and executioner. Give them up. There is nothing you can do. And nothing further I need do because now they will destroy themselves." When the Man refuses to comply, the dummy flies into a rage and orders an immediate halt to preaching "What shall it profit [a man, if he shall gain the whole world and lose his own soul?]." He argues that this philosophy is dangerous as men "will believe any lie however incredible if it flatters their vanity—they might begin to believe again they have souls—that is bad—you cannot have a soul." He orders the Magician to "ridicule and make a fool of him—corrupt his disciples—get them [to] betray him." The Magician tells the Man that the dummy is not the actual ruler but the symbol of the "modern world spirit."

Scene Two—Triumphant entry into the Holy City, Reviewing Stand, the Amphi- |
    theatre of Games; the same morning

O'Neill describes the setting for this scene: "Leader's platform—Throne with Dummy—Dummy staff grouped around—lines of dummy troops—painted drop rows of spectators, all in gesture of salute—bands, flags with sickles, hammers, swastikas, etc." The Magician wears the uniform of the chief of secret police on this national holiday, "the New Feast Of All Fools." The parade begins: "tank with dummy driver—with merry-go-round ass on wheels—The Man is seated on the ass—Leader laughs and all laugh." Invited to address the crowd, which has been ordered to laugh, the Man begins a parable but is interrupted by the multitude's mocking jeers.

Scene Three—The Temple of the State—before immense Idol of Moloch—Liberty
          as evil demon under foot—or the soul; that afternoon

The Magician, now the High Priest of the Bureaucratic Priesthood, is dressed in priestly robes. He tells the Leader, who starts to describe the new mythology, that it is not necessary to explain the nature of man: "They are like monkeys with a ball of twine. If they accepted simple truths, they would have to live by them." The Magician asks the Man:

Where is your whip to drive money changers out of [the] Temple—or do you believe with them that these belong in this temple—that now, at last, man has found a faith which is in harmony with his true aspirations? Give unto Caesar, etc.—it works out in the end—as now—that Caesar gets all because he makes himself God—with my help and advice.

Scene Four—The Last Supper, an immense banquet hall in the Leader's palace;
          that evening

The Man and his disciples "are driven in by guards—all are in chains." The Magician in a welcome address to honor the Man speaks of the Leader's "generous broadmindedness and continuing desire for friendly relations and cooperation, in spite of the rebuffs he has received to his kindly advances—The Man and his Disciples are in no sense prisoners but guests." The Man is given a last chance "to join in the new order—the Kingdom of Heaven on earth. The Leader's patience is exhausted." The Magician greets the Apostles with "mocking good fellowship—like old times"; but he is apprehensive about the evening: "Night air is bad for realism—it is better to be drunk when meeting ghosts." After the Man changes water into wine, the Dummy, in an effort to surpass Him, will sacrifice the "lives of a million men—now taste—wine into blood, yet see—after that the second is easy—taste again—blood into water." The Last Supper scene follows and ends with the drunken Magician giving the Man an ultimatum: "give you [the] night to think it over—go into Garden—beautiful night, learn again how sweet it is to be alive—in morning, arrest—you will get fair trial in my court—my Master has appointed me special judge." When alone with the Dummy, the Magician begins drinking heavily; finally, in disgust, he spits in the Dummy's face: "that is what I think of my victory."

Scene Five—Garden of Gethsemene; that night, dawn

The Man is alone, praying. The Magician enters and offers to take him to "a place called the Blessed Isles—no one knows but me—I often go there to recoup my strength when the stupidity of man gnaws like a madness at my brain—no man has ever lived there—there is sky and sea—peace—you would agree [to] stay there until old age puts a natural end to this life of yours on earth." When the Man rejects the offer, the Magician begs to have the chalice taken from his lips; he can no longer bear his eternal punishment: "to see only the ugliness and greed of men, their stupidity and madness—to tempt them to self-destruction—so easy, they are so weak and greedy—You and I are the opposites within men—in eternal conflict—but now, at last, I feel that I have won."

At dawn the Magician has the guards bring Judas to the garden for the betrayal scene. The traitor begs the Man: "Do not forgive me, Master, or I shall have to hang myself." The Magician taunts the Man: "I told you they will all sell their souls. I needed only one and chose the one with the greatest envy and the simplest price, money. The others all have their prices." The Man is then placed under arrest.

Scene Six—The Temple of Justice, Statue of State (Nordic Kali) behind judge's stand, beneath Kali's feet is the blond goddess, crushed figure of Justice; morning of the same day

The Magician, with the Dummy on his knees, now assumes the role of judge, assured by the secret police that the crowd outside will respond to his signal. The Prisoner is brought in, and the scene follows "as in New Testament up to 'What is truth?' " The Magician anticipates the Man's response: "A thing of the spirit. Love one another. All men are brothers. I am afraid you have no place in a realistic world. In fact, my judgment on you is that your very existence is an act of treason against the state." At a signal, the mob shouts: "Crucify him!" The Magician says mockingly: "The voice of your loving brothers. Which is the voice of the people and so of the State, and so of Caesar. It is finished."

Scene Seven—Calvary, sunset, nightfall of the same day

A great crowd has assembled on the slopes of the hill, leaving only a small clearing at the summit, "in the middle of which is the crucified, unseen, facing rear—Magician dressed now in old medieval black costume of executioner with a black mask covering upper part of face—Dummy sits on ground with back propped against foot of cross, facing front." The crowd watches the scene "dispassionately, without pity, without the enjoyment of cruelty, like people to whom torture has become a commonplace incident, disciplined to crush all natural feeling in themselves." To the Magician, the Man "takes longer to die this time." The faces before him reveal he need not worry; "there is not spirit enough in all these millions to furnish a lama with a soul!—he is really participating in this

torture of this Man on the Cross and he prays for the mercy of death to end it."
A Voice from the Cross gently reproaches the multitude: "O Son of Man,
Brothers of Mine in the Spirit, why have you forsaken me?" There is a vague stir
from the ranks, "a dumb puzzled look sweeps over their faces as if their minds
are touched fleetingly by a ghost of long-forgotten memory—the Magician forgets his role for a moment—is exultant—'They heard! They felt!'" He remembers the role he is to play and snatches up the Dummy; the crowd automatically
salutes: "Hail, Caesar!" He sneers at the Dummy: "You fool! In the night the
soul may chance to awake—and turn from watching the fate of things outside to
the truth within." Then the Magician pleads with the Man on the Cross: "Courage! You must live through the night!—terribly important—the future fate of
men depends on it—you must have seen how for a moment your spirit in them
dimly awakened—You cannot desert them now." He says that if the Man is too
weak, he "will speak for him—is a ventriloquist." The Magician questions his
motives for not wanting the Man to die without hope and remarks unconvinc-
ingly: "I have my magician's vanity, I love to deceive fools. (Changes to pleading) But you must not die until—I would not have you die without hope
—(Looks up) he is dead—I must speak for him."

Scene Eight—Calvary, dark, dawn, sunrise of the following morning

In the darkness of the night, the Magician tells the parable of the Siamese
Twins, illustrating "the duality of man—the opposites—nature of the opposites." One twin, the Realist, "was the stranger outwardly—became dominant
physically—but could never make the other admit his value." The other twin is
content to "be powerless, not desiring any possessions except the freedom of his
soul." The dominant twin becomes a "conqueror in wars, a great general, a
dictator—makes the people proclaim him the Emperor of World—plans a great
coronation ceremony." He is so disturbed at the ceremony that he starts to put
the crown on his twin's head. The laughter of the crowd spoils the ceremony.
That night he looks at the twin sleeping peacefully beside him. "He strangles
him—and in the morning the attendants find that a terrible miracle has been
accomplished—in the great royal bed there is only the one figure, that of the
Great Emperor, who during the night had committed suicide."

At the conclusion of the story there is a "rising murmur of vague understanding from the crowd which develops into a cry of joyous freedom which
turns to a hymn of Thanksgiving (Easter music)." The Magician speaks for the
dead Man on the Cross:

O Sons of Man, Brothers on the Cross! Why have you forsaken me? (Silence) I
am the Spirit within each of you, the free spirit, the soul, the secret longing for
self-sacrifice, etc., the divine simple good in you which though it be crushed for a
time is forever unconquerable. I am the Resurrection and the Life in you, and
whosoever, etc.—shall never die.

The multitude responds: "We promise! It shall never die!"

At sunrise, the crowd stares at the figure on the cross, their arms out-stretched to Him, their faces exultant. Putting on his military clothes, the Magician becomes cynical: "The blessed day again after the dreams and confessions of the night. Now we can see again what we really are." He warns the Dummy: "We had better go into exile for a while (Grumbles) I shall have to start my conspiracy all over again—just when I thought the final victory was in my grasp—just when I had dreams of being allowed to retire." Before leaving, he gazes at the figure on the Cross: "A merry trick to play on me to use me and my manhood and my worst pity for my fellow men to win the gain again—to make of me a 13th Apostle! We will play this drama out again and yet again! I still have a trick or two. So don't think this is a final victory." O'Neill inserts a note for the Magician's last comment; he can "go on with battle because he thinks to bring others to see the future, when future will no longer be repetition of past—when men will no longer be bound on the wheel of past stupidities—when you and I can at last be reconciled within the soul of Man."

April 2–7, 1941—Notes made before writing first draft of Prologue

In O'Neill's last creative period, 1940–1943, political and autobiographical material interlock. He abandons the anarchist family play, "The Visit of Malatesta," on March 2 and begins the scenario for "The Last Conquest" the next day. After completing this outline, he works from March 17 to April 1 revising *Long Day's Journey into Night*. In this play, Jamie Tyrone, in his frustration and jealousy of his brother Edmund, resembles the dominant Siamese twin in the Magician's story. Jamie, whose countenance has a "Mephistophelian cast," tells Edmund: "Hell, you're more than my brother." He admits hating Edmund's guts: "The dead part of me hopes you won't get well. . . . He wants company, he doesn't want to be the only corpse around the house." O'Neill's first reference in the April 2–7 notes, whose sole focus is Lucifer, is to "the eternal opposites within the dual nature of Man—twin brothers." The author interrupts work on "The Last Conquest" on April 9 to write the outline for *Hughie*, whose "Wise Guy" hero, Erie Smith, bears a strong resemblance to Jamie O'Neill. By the time he develops these two plays, O'Neill has conceived the idea for "Blind Alley Guy" with its "Wise Guy" gangster hero. Lucifer, in the Prologue notes, says that materialism has led men "into a blind alley."

In the notes preceding the Prologue, Lucifer analyzes fallen man. He feels "a sense of brotherhood for all men" and says they would recognize their "brotherhood of identity" if they possessed "a little reality in what they call Christianity." Although forced by fate to instill in them those vices that caused his own fall, he cannot conceal his great compassion and sympathy; "I can even pity them." This pity demands "their annihilation—give Man death and let the poor mad fool be released from himself and sleep at last in peace." Man has misused science, making it "into the law of a God which was himself—bewildered, longing for the simplicity of meaning again, he found the simplicity of evil—which demands nothing but appetite and greed—he is no Son of God now." Lucifer attributes the enormous number of primitive stonelike monuments in the new World State of man's loss of a sense of humor; they were constructed by people who adore "no God, just adore themselves." The chief symbol of the new mythology, the "apotheosis of man emptied of spirit," is the Dummy Leader with "his blank face, primitive carved eye sockets without eyes, an enormous mouth—crowned with wreath like Caesar—he is I in everyman, the part of him which is mine."

May 27–June 19, 1941—Prologue

After finishing the second draft for *Hughie*, O'Neill starts the Prologue for "The Last Conquest," calling it here a "fantastic pageant dealing with the recurrence of an ancient duality in a possible realistic future." He also conceives at this time the symbolic statue of the Goddess of the State, the Mother of the Savior of the World and incarnation of evil. She is a far more monstrous and destructive figure than the Mother Dynamo, which destroys Reuben Light, who worships this symbol. The Prologue's setting is "The Hall of Black Mirrors in the Savior's Palace on a night in the Future—once upon a time in that spiral of the past we call the future."

The Hall of Black Mirrors has a black marble ceiling and floor. Its side walls are lined with high black mirrors. The shrine of the Divine Dark Mother is at the rear; the idol of the Goddess stands on a high altar. The room has the "semblance of a crypt devoted to an oblique self-worship." The only light falls on the Savior of the World's ebony throne, placed at the middle of a table flanked by twelve chairs, which are occupied by the members of the Council. The chair at the typewriting table is occupied by the Minister of Propaganda. The Council members, the "Super Elite class of the World State, do not appear to be living men. They are too small, for one thing—no larger than a ventriloquist's dummy." Their faces and bodies have "a wooden quality, all the faces carved imitations of each other—emotionless faces, coldly intelligent, insensitive, capable, ruthlessly determined. Every member wears the uniform of his exalted rank." The Dummy Leader is now called the Savior of the World; he "seems to be a living man, although because of the mystic trance He is now in, it is difficult to tell. He appears large and powerful, but in reality He is a small man not over four feet in height." His large pale greenish-blue eyes are "still and glassy." Although middle-aged, he "still possesses a depraved and deprived adolescence, a youthful cruelty, an immature imperviousness to the sight of sorrow and pain. Above all, he has the quality of a medium, a hypnotic subject, a fanatic who is empty and lifeless when not possessed by his fanaticism, an actor who is a starring vehicle for the part he plays."*

The Prologue opens with the entrance of the Magician, a tall man, over six feet, who has an immensely powerful frame:

broad shoulders, great chest, slim waist and hips, muscular long legs and arms. His body is like that of a young athlete in his prime, but his swarthy face is marred by deep lines and his hair is iron grey. It is a face which has the quality of being molded in bronze. A hawk's face with a big aquiline nose, piercing dark eyes which seem always fixed on the peaks of a far-off mountain, a jutting angular jaw, a thin-lipped, flexible orator's mouth, a broad intellectual forehead. A face that is like a symbolic mask of the spirit of evil, implacable pride, and yet has a mocking trace in its expression of the conscious mountebank and charlatan. A tragic face too—or perhaps it is merely bored and weary—bored by victories and wary of times.†

The Magician lowers the six-foot long white coffin-shaped box that he is carrying to the floor and "clicks his heels and raises an arm in the ancient Roman salute"** to the Savior. He explains his new campaign to the Conclave—"the Savior's last conquest which will assure Him final, absolute dominion over the minds of every man, woman and child." As Minister of Spiritual Affairs, he has been monitoring the thoughts, and particularly the dreams, of men. Nothing subversive has been detected yet; the dreams are only "harmless visions of

---

*In his letters and Work Diary, O'Neill frequently refers to Hitler as "a ham actor," "a dictator who is also a fifth rate ham." Some of the attributes the dramatist gives the "Savior" appear in Jung's description of the German dictator: "Hitler belongs in the category of the truly mystic medicine man. His body does not suggest strength. The outstanding characteristic of his physiognomy is its dreamy look." Quoted in *Adolf Hitler*, John Toland (New York, 1976), p. 525. Note also the similarities between the "Savior" and the malformed Caligula in *Lazarus Laughed*, who has "glazed greenish-blue" eyes; "his mouth also is childish." Its boyish cruelty "has long ago become naively insensitive to any human suffering but its own." Like the World Savior, Caligula tells the people: "I am your God."

†Compare the description of the Magician and that of Tiberius in *Lazarus Laughed*, who is "tall, broad and corpulent but of great muscular strength." He has a "long nose, once finely modeled," and a "forehead lowering and grim." Beneath his half mask, his "lips are thin" and his "chin is forceful and severe." He, too, is bored and weary of battles. His complexion "is that of a healthy old campaigner."

**O'Neill uses Hitler's military pageantry in this play. Toland states that Hitler borrowed the Roman-style salute "from Caesar by way of Mussolini" but claimed that the stiff-arm salute was German (p. 147).

requited minor greeds." What is dangerous is that "men can still dream of the future at all. It proves that spirit still exists in them unconsciously now, a certain faint memory lies dormant." Men vaguely remember an old legend of a

Divine Savior God of Ancient Times, who became a son of Man because of his love and pity for mankind, that he might sacrifice himself and suffer and die in order to save them from evil and awaken the good in them that they might live as brothers, loving one another, and so transform our world of greedy hates and lust for possession into the Blessed Kingdom of Peace on earth. It dates back to the age of man's mental infancy when he indulged himself in childish moral fantasies about Evil and Good, flesh and spirit, the eternal opposites in his nature which waged a battle for the final salvation or destruction of a ghostly supposition he called his immortal soul.

According to the Magician, the dangerous element in the legend is that the crucified God rose from the dead on the third day. The safety of the State demands that men believe in the absolute finality of death. The prophecy that this ancient Redeemer is to appear a second time on earth poses a grave threat to the Savior's absolute power "because so long as men can remember no matter how dimly and subconsciously the faintest dream of a return of the spirit, they have not been completely conquered." The Magician wants to launch a daring campaign before "men's unconscious dreams gather strength and become at last a conscious hope." He plans to stage a mock second coming as a "gigantic theatrical pageant, an enormous farce in which he will be compelled to repeat his former salvational career on earth for the amusement of all our loyal subjects." Jeering laughter will purge men's minds of the memory of this Savior. The Master will be forced reluctantly to crucify him not because he is a rival "but simply because under the law of our enlightened realistic State, the mentally disabled are executed."

Actors who specialize in farcical character parts will be recruited from the State Theatre to portray his followers, Apostles, and Disciples. To re-create the old Savior, the Magician will utilize his experience in creating illusion and disillusion, in hypnotism, in ventriloquism. He has made a "living likeness, working entirely from memory." From the box he takes out a life-size man's figure dressed in a white robe and contrived so cunningly "it seems like a living man who had fainted or had just died." The Magician pushes a button, throwing light upon the figure's face. "It is the face of Christ, the man of sorrow's face, gentle, infinitely pitying and sad—a piece of wood carving executed by an artist who has worked with genius."

With attention diverted from him, the World Savior becomes petulant and jealous; passified, he gives the Magician permission to start the last conquest at once. A propaganda campaign is planned; every newspaper in the world will announce that "a man has appeared who claims he is Christ, the Redeemer of ancient folklore." The next day's report will state that the man's claims are valid and that the Master will interview him. On the third day the Divine Master will proclaim "a world-wide holiday, a Festival of All Fools," to allow this Redeemer to reenact the "ridiculous incidents which were once believed to actually have occurred during his former salvationist career on earth."

Before leaving, the Magician presses a button to illuminate the shrine of the Goddess of the State. Her body is a polished blue-black; the face, an enameled glistening white, is "framed by a mop of thick, coarse blond hair. With the exception of her belly, which is obscenely fat, gorged and distorted, she is frightfully emaciated." Her breasts "hang down flatly like deflated rubber bags." Her china-blue eyes "glare with ferocious insatiable hunger; her bloody tongue is thrust out from between big sharp fang-like teeth and pallid thick lips." As the Mother Goddess of Destruction and Death, she wears a "necklace of skulls and is girdled with snakes." Perched on one thigh is a statue of the Savior of the World. "Crushed beneath her big, manly fist is a female figure in a Grecian robe, presumably the old discredited Goddess of Liberty, the torch dropping from her dead hand."

Addressing his creation, the Magician says ironically: "Our Gentle Lady of Cannibalism! A faithful image of man's permanent longing for the security of suicide." He raises his arm in salute to the Savior, bidding Him, His Mother, and his colleagues good night. His eyes then turn to the figure of Christ: "And to you, good night, Image of my conquered Enemy and Opposition within the soul of Man." He goes out and for a moment the picture remains—"of the Goddess of the State, the Savior of the World lost in his glassy-eyed mystic trance, the wooden puppet figures of His Conclave, and the kneeling image of Christ."

June 23, 1941—Prologue revisions

In revising the Prologue, O'Neill makes a significant change: "Keep dummies cut—or any hint by Magician that figures not alive." The Savior of the World is now a "real living character" and "our narrator." He is described as a "small man, not over five feet—mystic egomaniac—a fanatic hysteric—Satan uses him as perfect instrument for a stronger will." While some dictators in the past professed their divinity, they were rational enough not to "believe in it themselves although they longed to and encouraged belief in mob—but this one really believed it, believes in myth of his divine origins." The Magician, who no longer "identifies himself as Satan," describes himself as the "director of the drama, ringmaster of the circus, leader of the orchestra."

June 25–27, 1941—Scene One, notes

Like numerous earlier flawed, doomed characters in the canon, the Magician wants desperately to confess and to be forgiven. He talks to the wooden figure of Christ as though it were alive: "Let's pretend—need someone to talk to—can't understand me any more—no evil when no good life." Having spent thousands of years living in the "soul of man turned into sty," he believes he has worked out his punishment. He longs for a "good life" and asks to be sent to the "Blessed Isles*—I want to be alone for a million years to dream and forget." O'Neill prophesies his own death in an isolated hotel room when he writes a final speech for the Magician here: "The best is to die in a room alone, calumniated, as a token of faith that man has [a] spirit to be saved, proving it by his death—or by his thousands of years of torture as a token of faith man has a spirit which can be damned."

July 3–7, 1941—A few notes

The dramatist makes an important decision at this time: to have the actual spirit of Christ miraculously infuse the wooden figure. While rehearsing the ventriloquist dialogue, the Magician is startled when a voice suddenly comes from the figure; he is triumphant: "Knew you must accept this challenge—satisfaction." Christ says: "I accept this drama as you have planned it, O Son of Modern Man." He will speak only at night when he is alone with the Magician and remain a puppet with words put into his mouth. The Magician accepts the arrangement; he will play fair and use only Christ's own words.

On July 4 and 6 O'Neill draws the set designs for the Prologue and eight scenes. He tries to continue work on the play but states on July 7: "gone dead on it—a few notes—will put aside, try something else." He spends the next four months developing "Blind Alley Guy," whose gangster hero is a small-scale American counterpart of Hitler.

April 9–28, June 11–19, 1942—"The 13th Apostle," notes*

O'Neill develops a new concept of the Savior of the World, whose personality—as well as his appearance—now resembles Caligula's in *Lazarus Laughed*.

---

*Stating that he is "sick of cruelty and lust and human flesh," Caligula confesses to Lazarus: "I would be clean." Assured that he is not "the Enemy of God," Caligula says: "My corpse no longer rots in my heart"; he promised to "make the Empire one great Blessed Isle."

*When he resumes work on the play in 1942, O'Neill continues to call it "The 13th Apostle" but lists here other possible titles: "The Forgotten Had Forsaken," "A Fantasy For the Godforsaking," "A Fantasy of Good and Evil," "The Black Magician," "Fantasy of the Last Campaign," "The Last Challenge," and its ultimate title "The Last Conquest," assigned on June 11, 1942.

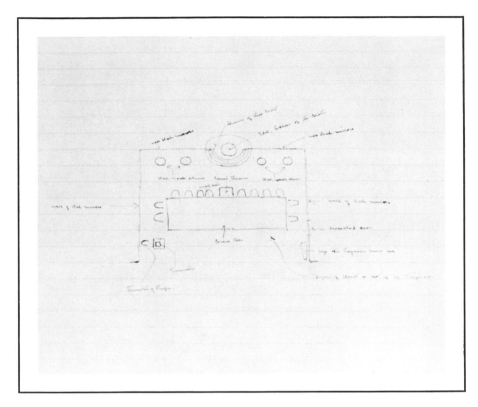

Prologue: "The Hall of Black Mirrors in the Savior's Palace."
The faint pencil sketches for "The Last Conquest" were drawn
by O'Neill in 1941 on white looseleaf paper that has yellowed
with age.

The Savior is "petulant, childish, spiteful, self-indulgent." Because of his small
stature, he feels inferior to the tall Magician and threatens to have his legs
amputated. "The Magician soothes him by reminding him his predecessors
[were] all small men—Alexander, Caesar, Frederick the Great, Robespierre,
Napoleon, Buddha." The Savior "lives in a trance of self-worship." At times he
displays a childlike dependency and calls the Magician "Daddy." Very often,
however, he is "an absolutely immoral, ruthless, primitive savage child with no
taboos but many superstitious terrors."

The focus in this set of notes is the final scene on Calvary. Seeing the awed
reaction of the multitude to the death of Christ, the Savior of the World asks the
Magician to plan a painless and convenient crucifixion for him: "That's what
I've always wanted, Daddy. To be crucified. And naturally, I mustn't die. And
not to save others. That's absurd. To increase my own power and glory." The

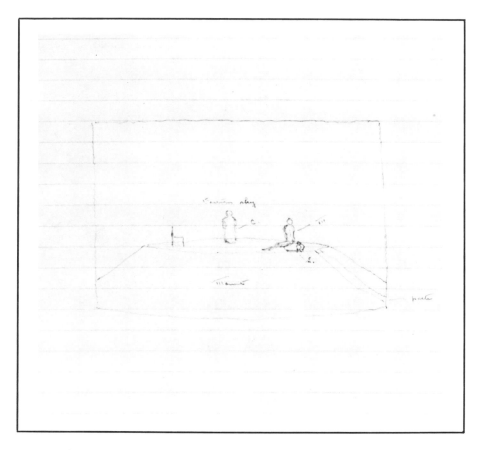

Scene 1, The Mount of Temptation: O'Neill shows the path leading to the mountain summit where the Magician and the Savior of the World confront and tempt Christ.

Magician responds ironically: "I am afraid I have already arranged it, Majesty —or your subjects are arranging it—perhaps not quite as you wish." O'Neill devises two different endings here for the play. In one, after the crucifixion, the Magician says to the Savior of the World: "Well, this is a defeat for me and annihilation for you—sad, isn't it, when we were on the eve of complete triumph —but it has its compensations—look at people—eyes." In the second version, the Magician meditates on the eternal "contest of souls and bellies—tonight we lie awake dreaming of stars instead of counting the loss and gain of petty lust (salutes figure on cross) Hail, Caesar. They are worth dreaming again." Turning to go, he hears the voice of Christ: "Someday thou shalt be at my right-hand in Paradise." The Magician stares at the Cross and asks: "Was he talking to—me?

Scene 2, The Amphitheatre of Games: The Magician stands
before the Savior's reviewing platform, directing the parade.
Christ sits on a life-sized wooden merry-go-round ass, drawn by
a baby tank. In the background are painted rows of spectators.

I see. He means after the mercy of my final defeat. Brother, I will remember that
promise—it shall be my blessed isle."

August 20, 1942—"The Last Conquest," notes for Scene One

In the preliminary notes for the new draft of the Temptation on the Mount
scene, the Savior of the World, in a speech written by the Magician, offers to
share his power with Christ if He will give up His "silly idea of the duality of
Man's nature—that he is composed of the opposites of flesh and spirit—good
and evil." As in the first version, Christ answers: "What would it profit man to
gain the whole world and lose his own soul?" In an aside, the Magician addresses the crowd: "He thinks that Man—that is—each of you has a soul.
(Laughter) He nobly refuses to exchange nothing for everything (Laughter)."

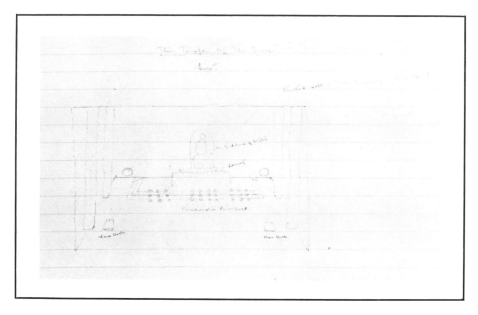

Scene 3, The Temple of the State: The Bureaucratic Priesthood
at a service in the temple. Two slave docks appear in the foreground.

The crowd is now comprised of "living adoring people"; "instances of man's
sympathy with Christ appear." Secretly, the Magician is pleased: "It all goes to
show you cannot kill what is in the innate heart of men—always exceptions to
rule even in collective state." He complains to Christ: "Man is sick, sick from
what I have done to him, but also sick of himself. And I am sick of him, but also
sick of myself, what he has made me, of the image of me he has created." He
then laughs cynically: "The Devil was sick—the Devil a saint would be, etc."

November 19, 1942—"The Last Conquest," notes

O'Neill attempts now to write a second scenario for the play, stating on
November 19: "Give this a try again—want to do [it] because might do lot of
good—real propaganda for the spirit—fine idea, original technique—but develop some inner struggle about it that has held it up." He provides a possible
cause of this struggle the next day: "I think the inner conflict is because it is at
its final curtain a declaration of faith by one who is faithless—like D[ays].
W[ithout]. E[nd].—a hope for faith instead of faith—and also a futile feeling
that no one will see the truth, not even the author." On November 21, he decides
to "concentrate on it as [a] play—try to be the objective dramatist—after all,
many a thief sincerely admires honesty."

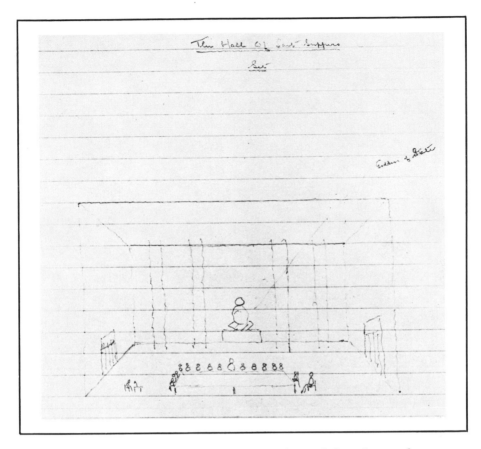

Scene 4, The Hall of Last Suppers: At the mock Last Supper the Magician stands at the center of the table giving a welcome address to honor Christ and his Apostles.

In the new Prologue, O'Neill notes: "change Satan to immense corpulent figure." He now becomes a sadistic Falstaffian character. The Savior of the World, now called the Leader, is described as a "boy-like Hermaphroditus but not fairy, sexless." The figure of Christ does not come to life solely at the bidding of the Magician but whenever the multitude manifests the innate goodness of man.

Scenario, Second Draft

November 20, 1942—Scene One, Temptation on the Mount

Scene 5, The Garden of Sadism: Guards bring Judas to the
Magician in the Garden of Gethsemane. Christ kneels in prayer
beside the tree. At the left a shrine depicts the Goddess of the
State as Our Lady of Torture.

Satan taunts the figure of Christ, which remains silent throughout the scene,
for not daring to come, and speaks wearily of men's decadence.

He mentions [the] death of democracy—men grew tired of the responsibility of
living free with no higher law than the criminal code to define the use of freedom
—their spirits corrupt and fat—the goddess of Liberty fat woman in a circus—
democracy with a paunch and bad heart and impotent. There is no conflict—no
good nor evil—they are all spiritually dead—a fine thing for me to be—a fat
corpse ruling the brains of corpses—I am a pathetic fat man, a gorged physical
cannibal king, who vomits the carrion human flesh, which is all he has left to
eat—Help me restore their pride, to make them live again the conflict of Good
and Evil.

The dramatist lists here the different ways the Goddess of the State is
depicted in the play; he later changes the view of her in Scene Six to Scene Five.

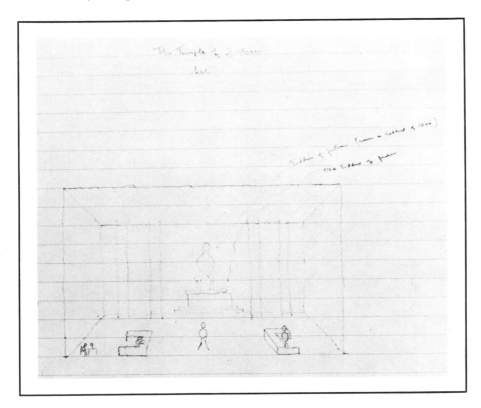

Scene 6, The Temple of Justice: Christ, "The Prisoner," right foreground, standing before the Magician, center. In the background is the massive statue of the Goddess of the State.

Prologue	Our Mother of Destruction and Death
Scene Two	Our Mother of Victory (War and Conquest)
Scene Three	Mother of Bureaucracy and Fertility, Fecundity
Scene Four	Our Mother of Gluttony (Cannibalism)
Scene Six	Mount of Olives, Our Mother of Earth—Nature
Scene Seven	Our Mother of Law (Justice under feet)
Scene Eight	Our Mother of Sacrifice

November 23, 1942—Scene Two, The Amphitheatre of Games

Sitting on a life-size wooden ass, which is drawn by baby tanks, Christ enters the "stadium of the Superior/Chosen Race." Before descending to the arena, Satan gives the Leader a ringmaster's whip—"Your most potent scepter." The Leader addresses the crowd, denouncing the dangerous heresy that the Goddess of the State created him and, therefore, takes precedence over him.

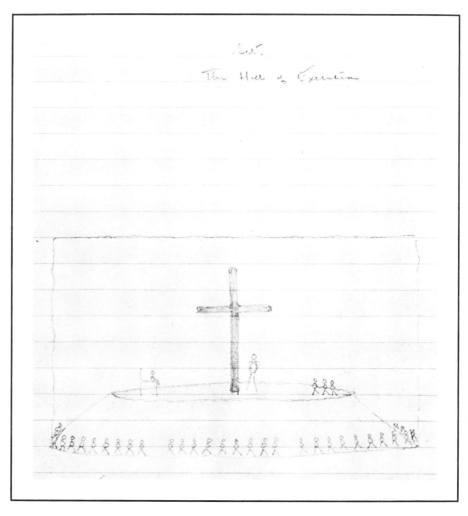

Scene 7, The Hill of Execution: O'Neill draws miniature stick
men to represent the great crowd "assembled on the slope of the
hill." The Magician stands by the cross of the dying Christ.

"Watch how I lash the old bitch (He turns and strikes the statue—a dead
silence)." In an attempt to lessen the shock of this sacrilegious behavior, the
Magician remarks jovially: "Our Master, the Savior of the World, was only
demonstrating to you that even in Divine Families there are misunderstandings
and women must be kept in their places." The crowd laughs in approval. Privately, he chastises the Leader; it is bad "for public morale to wash the family
linen in public. The public still cherishes its memorial Mammy songs. I suggest
you make up and kiss her." Christ delivers the Sermon on the Mount; the Leader

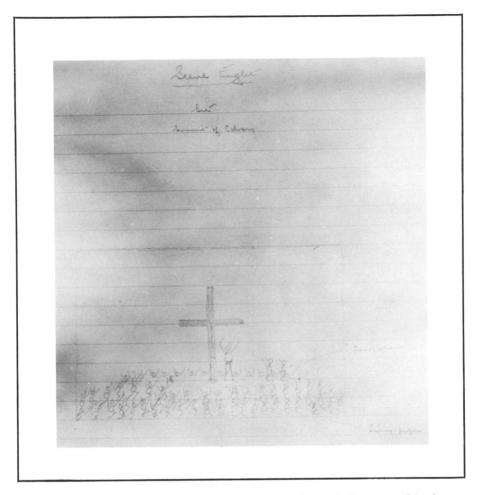

Scene 8, Summit of Calvary: The exultant and now believing multitude and soldiers kneel in adoration. The Magician rejoices in his own defeat.

is jealous and amazed that the people "are really listening of their own free will." After soothing the Leader, Satan leads Christ back to the ass and whispers: "You are a fool to hope they will remember your words and see any meaning to them—listen to their cruel and jeering laughter as you go out. I will meet you in the Temple. It was corrupt enough when you saw it last but you will be amazed at the modern realistic improvement we have made in its symbolism and corruption." Satan dismisses the Leader: "Go now and play a while, and forget him." The Savior romps like an adolescent.

November 25, 1942—Scene Three, The Temple of the State—interior—Goddess
                    of the State as Our Mother of Bureaucracy and Procreation

Satan escorts Christ into the Temple. A service is in progress honoring Our Mother of the Holy Face of Insatiable Famine. The Savior denounces his mother, the Great Whore of Babylon, and begins to beat Christ. Satan chides him and puts the whip in Christ's hand: "Here. Repeat your old legendary whipping act—if this time, you can grow angry. But I think you will understand that these poor vermin would not understand why you whipped them since no knowledge of good and evil remains in them." Christ speaks: "Father, forgive them for they know not what they do." Satan tells Christ that they will now "visit the concentration camp where disobedience and disbelief were segregated and discoverers eliminated." The Savior departs, saying he must prepare a last supper for them. Satan smiles: "He is going to poison us both, the little fool."

| November 27, 1942—Scene Four, The Hall of the Last Supper

Satan leads Christ into the room, supporting him although he appears "progressively more like [a] living man but his movements are still like mechanical figure." He tells Christ that the room was "inspired by many banquet halls in which people were poisoned—Caesars and Borgias, etc." The Apostles, their "legs manacled to chair legs—wrists handcuffed behind their backs," are seated at the table. Satan addresses Peter: "You have not forgotten your instructions?" Peter replies: "No, your Excellency, I shall deny him three times before cockcrow." Satan rebukes him for clinging so desperately to life at his advanced age. In a speech that echoes Larry Slade's in *The Iceman Cometh*, Peter begs: "Oh, even for a moment's more at any cost. I am afraid to die." Satan turns to Judas: "And you?" The traitor answers: "I know my orders—30 pieces of silver justify any means. I shall have no guilty memories this time. I shall not be a damned fool and hang myself." Satan responds: "I had considered that the only decent thing you ever did."

The Last Supper begins; the miracle of water to wine and of wine to blood is performed. The miracle of the State follows; blood becomes water. The Leader commands everyone to drink. The ten Apostles are killed by the poison; warned by Satan not to drink, Peter and Judas pretend to be dead. Satan asks the bewildered frightened Leader: "Can the Prince of Poison be killed by poison? You are a fool! Or my wooden figure here?" The Leader angrily accuses Satan of bungling the Last Conquest spectacle; he is "a poor director." When Christ rises and walks out of the room by his own power, the Savior is terrified. To calm him, Satan says that the figure is still under his control; "he goes to meditate in the Garden—at my suggestion—as you do so often."

| December 3, 1942—Scene Five, the Garden of Gethsemane

When the scene opens, Christ is shown alone, kneeling in prayer. Satan enters with the Savior but immediately puts him to sleep. He starts to place him in the Mother-statue's arms but sees she is embracing someone else: "A very unholy Lady—this manifestation—Our Lady of Modern Nature." He recalls the creation of Adam and Eve and his first great success. The Father had been too hopeful about His new creature. Condemned to live in this creature's spirit, Christ and Satan "knew He had created a thing which possessed a shallow spirit—the clever greedy animal easily trained to perform tricks for food but too stupid even to see a meaning in his life except the greed of his belly." Then Satan, dreading the old agony of the crucifixion, begs Christ to have His Father destroy men and parole him to a "million years in the Isles of Oblivion." Receiving no response, he makes a final request: "Let me take your place—I can stand crucifixion—easy—fake nails—red paint—anyway, what is pain to me but an obvious affliction—or I'll agree to feel it as a man would."

December 5, 1942—Add Living Character, the Perfect Citizen of the World State |

Making a radical change in his concept of the play, O'Neill localizes the Good-Evil conflict by adding a new character, who personifies man immemorial: the Perfect Subject-Citizen of the State, the Tribune of the People. He is a "hulking, low-browed, submissive, cowed" creature, possessing "huge gorilla-like strength but so completely enslaved [he] doesn't need manacles any more." His eyes are "vacant—without a hope or dream or thought—his great strength always exhausted—all he seems to desire is sleep which he does at every possible moment." In outlining the role this representative of The People plays in the Prologue and scenes, O'Neill sketches a tentative third scenario for "The Last Conquest."

In the Prologue, the Citizen sits on the floor in a corner like a Court Fool while Satan interrogates him: "Do you remember Christ?" The Citizen replies: "Never heard about it, or I've forgotten, maybe like to forget." Fearing he has made a mistake, he adds: "Oh, you mean our Savior of the World. Listen, I pray every morning and night, as ordered." Satan sets up the figure of Christ and commands him to "take a look at his face. Do you remember?" The Citizen admits he had seen a picture of the figure in an old book his grandfather had hidden under a mattress.

I knew all books were forbidden, got afraid police would find—so went and told—they let me off with 50 lashes, me and my mother—hung grandfather—made me watch—funny [to] see him laughing—I laughed—the police patted me on back—gave me a glass of beer—cold beer—never forget that—so kind, the police—(suddenly) In picture in book this guy was nailed on cross—or someone who looked like him. Are you going [to] crucify this fellow? I'd like to see that. I don't see many shows any more.

The Citizen has a "dim sure instinct that Satan is his real God and Slave-Master" and at the end of the Prologue kneels before him. "Satan has to tell him to face Goddess."

In the first four scenes the Perfect Citizen plays a peripheral role physically, acting as a cheer leader for the Crowd to incite its laughter. On a second level, he represents its slumbering consciousness slowly, but perceptibly, awakening. In the third scene he talks "as if Christ were alive—obstinate about it until threatened and then laughs at Son of God." He "doubles as Peter and Judas" in the fifth scene; at the end of it he "whispers a warning to Christ not to drink—a frame-up, water poisoned." During the Agony in the Garden, the sixth scene, the Citizen tells Christ: "I'd offer to take your place, used to pain, but too scared of death—long for it but scared." Acting as Pontius Pilate in the seventh scene, the Citizen is intimidated by a warning that Christ is a dangerous conspirator and accedes to the Crowd's demand: "Let him be crucified." Weakly, he announces: "I want to wash my hands—I ain't responsible." O'Neill does not specifically state that the Citizen's devotion to Christ prompts him to take a heroic stand in the eighth scene, the Crucifixion. When the people groan in sympathy with Christ, orders are given "to lash—make laugh." At the end, Satan speaks for Christ: "I am dead but I am alive. Look in your hearts and you will find me alive. I die a million deaths then but still I live, etc."

December 8, 1942—A few notes on the end of "The Last Conquest"

O'Neill includes, for the first time, a scheme for a ninth scene, which would form an epilogue. Satan is shown alone after the Crucifixion, pondering the failure of his Last Conquest. "Ordinary simple men and women come to visit the spot." To ascertain the impact Christ's coming and death has had, Satan, pretending to be "a stranger from the moon just arrived by latest plane," converses with them. The people are ecstatic: "It is good to be free—to have a soul again—to know there is good and evil in our hearts and we can choose." The "stranger" reminds them that "it was Satan who tempted you" and adds: "You will forget. The spirit is intangible, unseen, while greed and power are realistic facts to anchor dreams upon." The people assure him: "We will not forget this time. The God in us is stronger if we choose. Christ is our refuge and our strength and evil cannot prevail." Now that they "have destroyed the World State and its hideous religion" they plan to "build new temples of the real where [they] will worship the spirit of God in man." The stranger warns them: "You had better erect temples to Satan too—just so you won't forget and be caught as always, unprepared, by the evil in you—so you may come to know yourselves at last." In what would probably have been the final speech of the play and an optimistic counterpart to the last line of *Lazarus Laughed*—"Men forget!"—the people say triumphantly: "We have learned our demons. We will never forget God again."

By devising this new scene, in which men proclaim an awareness of their dual nature and a belief in the God living without and within them, O'Neill overcomes the fear expressed the previous month: that he who was faithless could not voice "a final declaration of faith." The Perfect Citizen seems to be a spiritual self-portrait. The old book, representing his grandfather's strong religious faith which the child betrays, symbolizes the dramatist's exposure to, and rejection of, Catholicism in his childhood. Although he comes to believe in Christ and is willing to live and suffer for Him, the Citizen vacillates at times and remains uncommitted, irrevocably. If the play had been completed, perhaps the Citizen would have been shown in the final scene leading the people in their profession of faith in Christ and His doctrines.

O'Neill did not abandon "The Last Conquest" because of a spiritual impasse. After making another attempt to continue the work, he writes on December 13, 1942: "No go—decide will have to quit on this again—or on anything else—one of my old sinking spells is on me—lower than low—mind dead" (W.D.). Three days later in a letter to Dudley Nichols, he states that when he works on "The Last Conquest" he experiences the feeling that his creative impulse is

blocked by the hopeless certainty that it could not be understood now, or its possibilities admitted—more than that, a feeling in myself that, until this war, which must be won, is won, people should concentrate on the grim surface and not admit the still grimmer, soul-disturbing depths. I censor myself, so to speak, and with this shackle added to recurring spells of illness and mental depression —In short, "The Last Conquest" remains for the most part in scenario, although it constantly haunts me.

Nichols maintains that as late as 1948 O'Neill was still deeply absorbed in this "projected work of immense scope."[*] The dramatist had shown the play to him "on different occasions, and it was always growing." Nichols writes: "I even offered, at the last, to write it out for him as he had told it to me and then keep rewriting successive drafts until it would be very near to what he imagined, but of course this was impossible. . . . To me it is tragic that he was never able to complete this magnificent project." The greater tragic irony is that mankind can comprehend, at last, the grim "soul-disturbing depths" of "The Last Conquest," realizing, as never before, that the greed and selfishness of men and nations can destroy freedom and make the futuristic world O'Neill envisions a present reality.

---

[*]Nichols' explanatory note for his collection of letters from O'Neill—dated 1932 to 1948 (Beinecke Library, Yale University).

°BY WAY OF OBIT
HUGHIE
(1940)

O'Neill states on November 29, 1940, that he gets "new idea for series [of] monologue plays—short—'By Way of Obit.'—for book more than stage, perhaps—scene, one character, one marionette° (life-size) The Good Listener —I do brief outlines for five of them" (W.D.). A few days later he makes notes for three other one-acters. The Work Diary identifies the eight† plays in the "By Way of Obit" series as:

11/29/40	Pig H[ell]. H[ole]. play
11/29/40	R.R. man play
11/29/40	J[immy]. the P[riest]. idea of guy who recited Homer
11/29/40	Hughie
11/29/40	Minstrel man idea
12/1/40	Miser one
12/2/40	Rudie (the chambermaid play)
12/2/40	Blemie one.

Unfortunately, O'Neill destroyed the original outlines and notes for all of these plays and provides little information about them. Two early drafts—one handwritten, the other typed—for the only completed drama, *Hughie*, are the sole survivors.

The author wisely discards his original plan to make the Good Listener in the series a marionette. In a letter to George Jean Nathan on June 19, 1942, he describes the character to whom each story is told as "a person," who does "little but listen. Via this monologue you get a complete picture of the person who has died—his or her whole life story—but just as complete a picture of the life and character of the narrator. And you also get by another means—a use of stage directions, mostly—an insight into the whole life of the person who does little but listen." The "stories"—had they been completed—would also have

---

°*A Book of Puppetry*, which Jerome Magon sent to him in December 1939, may have encouraged O'Neill to experiment with marionettes in the series. Three months before recording the notation for "By Way of Obit," he conceived his idea for "The Last Conquest"; only two characters in this play's original scheme are living; all the others are "life-size marionettes."

†On May 23, 1941, when he drew "sets for several of [the] plays," O'Neill states: "will be 8 in all, I think." The next year, however, on February 9, 1942, he refers to what may have been a ninth play for the series: "Thompson—rat idea—outline." He makes notes at this time for all the one-acters—specifically identifying them—with the exception of the "Miser one" and "Blemie one," either of which he may have developed as the Thompson idea.

provided new insights into the early life of the dramatist. Through them, he retreats autobiographically into the past; creatively, he comes full circle. The characters would be modeled primarily on people he knew or befriended at Jimmy the Priest's (1911–1912) and the Hell Hole (1915–1916). His first 1918–1920 notebook shows that he had contemplated twenty years earlier two series containing plays resembling some of the one-actors planned for "By Way of Obit":

Stories—Jimmy the Priest series;
Gunman Series—"The Pig of the Hell Hole," "Exit Baby Doll," "The Dirty Half-Dozen."

The word "gunman" links the early and late series and denotes an auto-biographical central motif in O'Neill's 1939–1943 work. The people O'Neill met at the Hell Hole, as Sheaffer points out, lived on the fringe of society: thugs, "sneak thieves, pimps, an honest gambler or two, and until the law cracked down in 1917 on streetwalkers in bars, some of the fallen sorority. . . . The Hell Hole was the favorite hangout also of the Hudson Dusters," an all-Irish group, which—while it terrorized the inhabitants and police of Greenwich Village—admired and protected the young author. O'Neill's friendship for them was attributable, partially, to his "regard for those outside the pale, for those strong and daring enough to go their free lawless way."[*] He may have intended to depict the Hudson Dusters as "The Dirty Half-Dozen" in the "Gunman series."

Among the Hell Hole habitués in *The Iceman Cometh* is Joe Mott, a former gambler, who becomes violent, "like a gangster," in an early draft for the final act of the play. O'Neill had attempted to present this character, whose prototype was a close friend, in the 1921 idea: "Joe—tragi-comedy negro gambler (Joe Smith)." In "By Way of Obit," the author would again portray early acquaintances and stories either about or related to them. Erie Smith, "the Gambler in 492, the Friend of Arnold Rothstein," in the extant *Hughie* is a "Broadway sport and a Wise Guy—the type of small fry gambler and horse player living hand to mouth on the fringe of the rackets" and infesting "the bars of minor speakeasies." In "The Visit of Malatesta" ("Malatesta Seeks Surcease") Angelo Daniello, who operates a speakeasy with his father, plans to use hired assassins and violence to become Artichoke King of the state. The most striking example of the gunman motif is found in "Blind Alley Guy," which, as originally conceived, told the story of its Mephistophelian gangster hero, Walter White/Black.

Into his late work, O'Neill injects a second idea from the 1918–1920

---

[*]Sheaffer, *O'Neill Son and Playwright*, pp. 333–34. The Dusters may have provided a collective model for the gangster hero of "Blind Alley Guy." The other characters in this play feel an aversion to him but also a "fascination at freedom of the utterly immoral, unscrupulous and ruthless."

notebook—play of "Jim and self—showing influence of elder on younger brother." Sheaffer observes that the author's father was deeply "concerned over his older son's influence on the other." The biographer also notes that Jamie, after his touring experiences as an actor, had "stories for his favorite audience, his brother."* Jamie becomes Erie Smith,† a "teller of tales," in *Hughie* and would probably appear in another guise as the narrator of the story told in the "Rudie—chambermaid play."

O'Neill's brother Jamie—with his stories and gangster-related gambling tendencies—inspires not only *Hughie* and some of the one-acters in "By Way of Obit" but also other late plays or aspects of them. An examination of the 1940–1943 period reveals a "chain-stitch" pattern, linking these dramas and the Obit series. The author finishes the second draft for the autobiographic *Long Day's Journey into Night*—whose last act contains Jamie Tyrone-O'Neill's confession of jealousy and hatred of his brother—in October 1940 and conceives "By Way of Obit" the following month. He continues work on the series in December and the next month records his first idea for "Blind Alley Guy," whose gangster hero has parents who closely resemble Ella and James O'Neill. In February 1941 the dramatist develops the "Christ-Satan idea (Good-Evil—opposites in Man)," "The Last Conquest," containing a "story," Satan's tale of the Siamese Twins, in which the jealous brother—in a burst of hatred and frustration—kills his sensitive poetic brother. After making final revisions for *Long Day's Journey* from March 17 to April 1, 1941, O'Neill then resumes work on *Hughie*, finishing its first draft on April 30 and the second draft on May 19. He again takes up "Blind Alley Guy," working on it almost exclusively from July 15 to October 27 and interrupting it only on October 21 to note: "By Way of Obit (Rudie (the chambermaid play)—awake with mind full of this—notes)." A week later on October 28 he records the original idea of *A Moon for the Misbegotten*: "based on story told by E[dmund]. in 1st act of 'L.D.J.I.N.'—except here Jamie principal character."

The focal point in *A Moon for the Misbegotten* is Jamie's confession that he had, while accompanying his mother's dead body on a train trip from California to New York, spent nights of dissipation with a prostitute, who is called a "blond pig." Jamie himself must have told this sordid true "story" to his brother. After completing the first draft for *A Moon for the Misbegotten* on January 20, 1942, and making general notes for "By Way of Obit" on February 1, O'Neill develops two one-acters in the series on February 3: "Pig of the Hell Hole play" and "R.R. man play." He takes up the "Jimmy the Priest play" three

---

*Sheaffer, *O'Neill Son and Playwright*, p. 99.

†According to Sheaffer, Jamie O'Neill, "who liked to play the horses," as did Erie, "spent hours studying the racing sheets and exchanging tips with other gamblers" in the taproom of the Garden Hotel in New York (*O'Neill Son and Playwright*, p. 319).

days later, the "Thompson—rat idea" on the ninth, and the "Minstrel man idea" on February 10–11. The final reference to the "By Way of Obit" series occurs on June 22–23, 1942, when the author indicates he is "going over" *Hughie*. A year later he makes his last creative effort: finishing *A Moon for the Misbegotten* and attempting to complete "Blind Alley Guy."

All the plays of the late period—and not merely the "By Way of Obit" series—are obituaries, linked by O'Neill's obsession with the dead and the past. In the two acknowledged autobiographies, *Long Day's Journey into Night* and *A Moon for the Misbegotten*, the dramatist faces the ghosts of his own family. He depicts his deceased former friends in *The Iceman Cometh* and people connected to him in some way in seven of the "Obit" one-acters. In the eighth he planned to eulogize his deceased Dalmatian, Blemie. He outlines this play on December 2, 1940, when he is deeply grieved by the failing health of his beloved dog. When the dog died two weeks later, O'Neill writes: "Blemie dies a.m. C[arlotta]. & I completely knocked out—loved him for 11 years—a finer friend than most friends!" (W.D.: December 17, 1940). The next week, while recuperating in bed from the flu, the author writes "The Last Will and Testament of Silverdene Emblem O'Neill" (December 26, 1940). One section of the "will" states: "if I should list all those who have loved me it would force my Master to write a book." The narrator in the Blemie play would probably be a self-portrait, who would in his monologue enumerate those who loved this dog. The death wish, which O'Neill attributes to Blemie in the 1940 "last will and testament," echoes a frequently expressed desire of the dramatist. Blemie would like to believe in a Paradise but is a realist: "I am afraid this is too much for even such a good dog as I am to expect. But peace, at least, is certain. Peace and long rest for weary old heart and head and limbs, an eternal sleep in the earth I have loved so well. Perhaps, after all, this is best."

Hughie

A note, dated May 22, 1952, and written by Carlotta O'Neill, appears at the beginning of the later of the two extant drafts for *Hughie*:

> a one act play
> "Hughie"
> which was to have been the first
> of a series of seven or eight
> one act plays done in the same
> manner. All of them to come
> under the general title
> "By Way of Obit"

Only the significant differences between the early drafts and the final published text will be cited here.

In the dramatis personae of the first versions, the Night Clerk is identified as "the listener." The specific time of the action is given in the stage directions; located above the tiers of mailboxes is a "clock whose hands point at three twenty-five." The Night Clerk is "in his early forties but looks older." Fairly tall, he is "thin, narrow-chested and stoop-shouldered." He has blue, rather than brown, eyes, and "his big uneven teeth are in a bad condition." Words later omitted from Erie's description are in quotation marks: he has "flabby" arms, a "thick" neck, fat cheeks "beginning to sag," a "flesh" nose, "pale" blue eyes, "thin" sandy hair, and a bald "shiny" head. When he enters, "Erie isn't drunk now but he looks bleery and booze-shaken, nursing a bad hangover and tapering down toward his usual cautious daily ration after an all-out bat." More emphasis is placed in the earliest draft on Erie's gangster connections and his subservient role "on the fringe of the rackets." He is "used as the errand boy and contemptuously tolerated as the butt of jokes by the Big Shots, too insignificant for the police"; he "never knew enough to lead them to anyone important to bother about, too timid ever to commit any serious infraction of the law." He and his kind believe they are "oracles of the One True Grapevine," when actually "they are used to pass along and give publicity to the misleading lie, because it is well-known stunt. It is difficult to see anything in him one shouldn't despise."

In the first version Erie is suspicious and aggressive when the Night Clerk says that his name, like that of the deceased, is Hughie: "You wouldn't kid me, would you, Buddy? Because I ain't in no mood, and you might get a smack in the kisser." Erie confesses here that Hughie's funeral started him off on a bat: "First funeral I was ever at. I couldn't take it. Gave me the willies." To him, the hotel has not been the same since Hughie was taken to the hospital: "And now he's dead. God, it's like an undertaker's parlor. To bed! What for, nothing I try I can't sleep." In his long monologue explaining his relationship with the deceased, Erie gives numerous examples of Hughie's gullibility; he "wasn't wise to nothin'. He was a sucker who'd always been a night clerk in bum hotels. We didn't have nothin' in common—not anymore than you and me have." The "gambler" reminisces about the day he took Hughie to Belmont, saying the Night Clerk got so excited "you'd think he was coked up, or something." Here the horse Erie would rather sleep with than "make the whole damn Follies" is Blue Larkspur and not Man o' War.

There is more evidence in the early versions that Erie, in spite of his bravado, is down on his luck. He provides a flimsy excuse for not following the horses South each winter: "getting lazy in my old age, I guess." Then he admits: "It's been tough lately. I'm jinxed. I don't win a single bet since Hughie—." Erie is perceptibly more lonely here; he admits he was glad to go to Hughie's home for dinner: "I get sick of hotels sometimes." Although verbally critical of Hughie's "plain" wife, believing she scared her husband and "had his number," Erie reveals his true feelings—his admiration of her, his desire to be invited to return: "There was something not so bad about her. Well to hell with it, she didn't give me a chance." Throughout the play, the lonely Erie seeks to establish a relationship with the new Night Clerk, trying to detect similarities between him and the deceased. The Night Clerk, however, pays no attention to him, and Erie says in a "bitter and aggrieved air: 'You're not much like Hughie after all." Erie makes a final futile effort and then "gives him up with a dejection that approaches despair and again attempts to pry himself from the desk."

Erie is far more fearful here of the consequences of "welshing" on the loan he negotiated to obtain money for Hughie's funeral wreath. He did not, as in the published text, "put the bite" on "dead wrong" guys. He tells the Night Clerk: "I didn't win that hundred bucks gambling. Why the hell would I be worrying like I am if I'd won it? I had to borrow it, and I couldn't borrow it nowhere but from Arnold Rothstein." The Night Clerk responds "(with tremulous hope) 'I suppose you must know a lot of the Big Gamblers?'" Erie replies distractedly: "But I didn't—until I raised it. I knew just how much I needed, see, because I told the florist what I wanted and asked him what it would set me back." He adds: "I had to do it for him, fix it, but now—I'm superstitious."

As in the final version, the Night Clerk's defensive wall of indifference and silence is penetrated when Erie implies he knows Arnold Rothstein. Although he admits the tales about his gambling exploits are lies, Erie insists the stories he told Hughie about killings "really happened." Erie boasts to the Night Clerk in the earliest extant draft: "I'm a great guy for telling the tales"; yet it is plausible that he did participate in the highjacking robbery he describes. He says: "I didn't say how or when. I left it mysterious."

What O'Neill leaves unanswered is this question: why in the early 1940s was he obsessed with the feats of gangsters and gamblers? Walter White/Black in "Blind Alley Guy" is "associated with a bootlegging gang," driving the truck and serving as guard. The author spends the month of September 1941 on "Blind Alley Guy," interrupting this work from the fifth to the seventh to go over *Hughie*, as he wanted his son Eugene, who was visiting him, to read the play. The dramatist writes on September 4: "Eugene reads 'L.D.J.I.N.'—greatly moved" and on September 6: "E[ugene]. finishes 'T[he]. I[ceman]. C[ometh].'—again much moved" (W.D.). After reading *Long Day's Journey into Night* and discovering the history of his father's family, the son could, no doubt, discern his uncle Jamie in the portrait of Erie Smith in *Hughie*. Had the son been cognizant of his father's days at Jimmy the Priest's and the Hell Hole and of the scheme for "By Way of Obit," he would have viewed the series as a sequel to *The Iceman Cometh*.

BLIND ALLEY GUY
(1940)

O'Neill dates his first notes for "Gag's End—R. H. Play Idea" December 16, 1940. His failure to record this information in the Work Diary can be attributed to the death of his beloved dog Blemie the next morning. He abandons the new work and does not take it up again until January 21, 1941, when he writes: "R. H. play idea (some notes—tentative titles 'Gag's End'—or 'Blind Alley Guy')" (W.D.). As the author enters his final creative period, 1940–1943, world events of the present begin to merge with memories of the past; his ideas in these years make either an autobiographical or an antitotalitarian statement. He presents all four O'Neills in *Long Day's Journey into Night* (1940–1941) and portraits of all but Jamie in the semi-autobiographical *A Touch of the Poet* (1942). His brother appears as Jim Tyrone in *A Moon for the Misbegotten* (1941–1943) and, partially, as Erie Smith in *Hughie* (1940–1941). As originally conceived, "Blind Alley Guy" is another autobiographical vehicle; however, as the drama evolves, it juxtaposes internal familial and external political conflicts.

The play's gangster hero is initially called "Ricky," a nickname for Richard, the name O'Neill gives the self-portrait in *Ah, Wilderness!* He never completes the word beginning with "H." wherever this initial is used to identify the play or its hero. The central character is later called Harvey White, whose alias is Howard Black. The "H." could represent "Howard," his evil side, symbolizing a duality similar to the John-Loving dichotomy in *Days Without End.* Hypothetically, the "H." could signify Hitler; however, the early notes contain no political references.

On November 29, 1940, approximately two weeks before making the first notes for "Blind Alley Guy," O'Neill outlines *Hughie*, whose narrator, Erie Smith, is described as a Broadway "Wise Guy," a "small fry gambler," who lives "on the fringe of the rackets." The word "Guy" has for O'Neill connotations of underworld life, and he uses it in the title of his gangster play. The author seems determined in this period to develop the idea he records in the 1918–1920 notebook for a gunman series, based on the small-time gangsters, the Hudson Dusters, who befriended him at the Hell Hole in 1915–1916. "Blind Alley Guy" in the early notes is set in 1918. Its hero, Ricky, although born in a small town in upper New York, "breaks away to go to New York City."

December 16, 1940—"R. H. Play Idea,"
original conception

The focus of the first set of notes is the "character, upbringing of Ricky." As a boy, he is "quiet, reserved, solitary, but subject at times to fits of a strange, cold formidable fury which frightens everyone." Later, as a youth, he runs away from home frequently and "hops freights—gets to know hoboes—feeling of kinship with them as outcasts who can't belong [to] social structure—through them contact with non-moral attitude about property—theft, etc." He grows fearless and ruthless; "murder becomes meaningless because it seems to him to be of no importance whether he or anyone else dies." He rebels against society but "not from any sociological motive—he has the same scorn for radicals he feels for all politics or parties." Even though "he hates the small town where everyone knows everyone," he keeps returning to it, drawn by the love—which he cannot reciprocate—of his family, "a tie which seeks to keep him bound." In this respect, Ricky resembles his creator. Here and in subsequent notes, traits and attitudes of the dramatist are given to the central figure; those of Ella and James O'Neill are attributed to Ricky's parents.

January 21–30, 1941—"Blind Alley Guy," Notes

O'Neill decides on January 26 to use "Blind Alley Guy" as a "title for R. H. idea until get better one" (W.D.). The characters are introduced and named: Ed (Edgar) White,* his wife Tess, their daughter Cassie, their son Harvey— alias Howard Black, "Blackie"—and his wife Dora. The focal point of the play at this time is the love-hate family relationships; it is set in 1918 in the "small-town type lower middle class sitting room of White family." The Whites do not know that Harvey is a gangster. He explains his five years' absence from home by saying that his job with a large construction company requires him to travel continuously throughout the country. Outwardly, the Whites regret not seeing him, but "inwardly they dread visit and are relieved."

Ed White, now semi-retired, has sold his house in town and bought a small farm. His prosperous hardware business is managed by his daughter and "an assistant whom he has taken into partnership since engaged to Cassie." The father is a good, simple, hard-working man, "uncomplicated, sense of what is right and wrong, religious in a taken-for-granted mild way, an affectionate family man—bewildered by any display of passion." His wife is a "congenial mate on the surface—loves him—but deep underneath this is a disappointment in him— she had dreamed of him as romantic, passionate lover—the reality had been too mild, too much—she had come to love her son more than her husband." The attitude of mother and daughter in this play resembles that of Mary Tyrone and her sons in Long Day's Journey into Night; "both women show resentment father's sentimentality, no real feeling—preoccupation with store, duty, church

---

*The author uses the name "Edmund" for his father in the early dramatis personae for Long Day's Journey into Night. Ed White resembles both James Tyrone/O'Neill and the Reverend Hutchins Light in Dynamo.

(they wonder if he really knows what he believes)—good man—etc.—but at once—contrite and affectionately humorous about father."

After a "gambling stick-up," Harvey decides to go home, convinced that the police will never look for him there. The three Whites are shown at the beginning of the play waiting for Harvey and Dora to arrive. As he did in *The Iceman Cometh* and "The Visit of Malatesta," O'Neill uses the theme of waiting for an outsider who, when he comes, will change the lives of the other characters. The author states his intention: to show the gradual effect on Harvey and Dora "and on the family of their being there—the family soon sees something wrong with marriage—they begin to take sides. The deep affection, sympathy, understanding, compassion between them at start—closeness of family." When Harvey enters, "all past begins to him again." His family recalls "his strange callous lack of feeling from a boy—his complete immorality." He speaks affectionately of his pigeons and mourns the death of his cat; "their hatred of him for this—derisive laughter—until it brings on one of his quiet murderous rages." Dora lives in mortal fear of her husband. When the Whites ask her to tell them about his job, she says: "He'd kill me if I did—like he'd squash a fly." Tess and Cassie both "taunt and sympathize with Dora—she couldn't make him feel either."

O'Neill makes notes now for a new concept of the play. Harvey is not to appear in it; yet it is the "story of his life, revelation of his character, as brought out in their memories, jealousies, resentment, frustrations, conflicts, guilt, all due to their relationship with him." The play opens twelve hours before his execution at San Quentin. The dramatist considers two plans here. In the first, the Whites know that Harvey is a condemned criminal and about to die; they reveal their bitter hatred for him and hope he "will be terrified at last moment—they know he won't—will remain indifferent—so they hope there is a hell." O'Neill abandons this scheme and shows the Whites ignorant of Harvey's ruthless past and imminent execution.

When the play opens, Dora arrives alone, arousing Cassie's suspicions. She is jealous and joyous to see that Dora has lost her looks. In a "general note" in the margin, O'Neill states: "Dora has dyed [her hair] blond as disguise—never did before—because that was like moll."* Dora asks "with too casual casualness" about the newspaper. The expression on her face, as she reads it, startles the Whites. Seeking an explanation for Dora's agitated condition, Cassie says:

---

*O'Neill seems to have had a particular woman in mind when he conceived Dora in this play and Cora in *The Iceman Cometh*. Included in the preliminary list of names for the prostitutes in the latter is "Cora the Blond." Named simply Cora in the final version, she is, like Dora, a "thin peroxide blonde." Her round face shows "the wear and tear of her trade," but there are still "traces of a doll-like prettiness." Cora is a petty thief. When she makes her first entrance, she has just "rolled" a sailor.

"If you've had trouble with Harvey, we'd understand it wasn't your fault—we know he's not easy to live with—not like anyone else—something inhuman." Dora seizes on this acceptable excuse and pretends that she is upset because of a quarrel with Harvey. Tess reminisces about her son, her memories "starting as fond and then betraying bitterness, lack of love." The scene ends with Cassie alone on stage reading an article about the notorious criminal "Blackie," who had been denied a reprieve—"to chair following morning." A final note in this section indicates that Cora, like Hickey and Parritt in *The Iceman Cometh*, would make a dramatic confession at the conclusion of the play: "I was the girl who turned in Blackie."

July 15–19, 23–30, 1941—"Blind Alley Guy"

In July 1941, when O'Neill takes up "Blind Alley Guy" again, he is just emerging from a period marked by obsessive "war jitters," similar to the one he experienced in spring 1940. He expresses his apprehensions in a series of ideas in the early 1940s, each issuing a warning to free men about the dangers of totalitarianism. He begins his creative campaign to alert mankind on August 15, 1940, recording two ideas which would represent "world collapse and dictatorships" and concludes it in June 1943, when, in the last notes he would ever write, he makes a final attempt to complete "Blind Alley Guy." Accordingly, when he resumes work on this play on July 15, O'Neill changes his central character to a Hitler-like gangster.* Undoubtedly, the new political dimension given to the offstage hero owes much to "The Last Conquest," which absorbed the dramatist from May 27 to July 7, one week before he resumes work on "Blind Alley Guy." The same two themes appear in both plays: the threat of totalitarianism and the duality of man's psyche. The World State tyrant of "The Last Conquest," as O'Neill remarks, is a futuristic view of dictators "like Hitler of Germany." While the battle between good and evil is waged in this drama between two characters, Christ and Satan, the conflict is centralized in the later one in the soul of one man: Harvey White/Black. In "The Last Conquest," evil, personified by Satan and his fascist dictator-henchman, wears a public face, visible globally; its private face is unmasked in "Blind Alley Guy," revealing a tyrannical, mentally unstable gangster, who is not only an "enemy of Society" but a foe to his own family.

O'Neill heads the July notes: "new conception without Blackie" and states: "He does not appear in play—but he is dominant character in it as his whole life

---

*By a strange coincidence, Brecht is working in 1941 on *The Resistible Rise of Arturo Ui*, which shows the similarities in the rise to power between a Chicago gangster and Hitler. O'Neill uses newspaper headlines and articles to parallel historical events and their theatrical counterparts; in contrast, Brecht employs placards.

is recorded through his effect on each of the four members of his family, his father, mother, sister and wife." The author portrays Blackie as a familial monster, translating in personal terms and on a small scale the universal horror and destruction his historical counterpart is inflicting on mankind. The dramatist writes:

> Tie-up through interpretation of his character with that of Hitler—aversion and fascination at freedom of the utterly immoral (assertive and prudish), unscrupulous and ruthless who dominates at any cost—at same time, insights by women into emptiness, non-belonging, emotional sterility* behind this—resentment, bitterness, contempt and pity—recognition he makes weapon of inability to feel while at same time his greatest secret longing is to feel—boring, sad appreciation of his loneliness and isolation from his kind—revenge on them as if they had rejected him, etc.

O'Neill obviously investigated Hitler's life thoroughly; the parallels between the historical and fictitious figures are too exact to be coincidental. Blackie, like Hitler, excels in sports in school and becomes a "little ringleader"; neither, however, graduates from high school. Both feel a kinship with nature and are reared in a similar environment. Hitler's father moved from the city to a country village, Leonding, having 3,000 inhabitants; Blackie's leaves town for "a small farm outside a village of 3,000 or so inhabitants." Both fathers inflict harsh beatings on their sons who react in a similar manner. Hitler, after reading that silent endurance was a proof of courage, "resolved never again to cry" when whipped. The next time he was punished, he "counted silently the blows of the stick; from that day on "his father never touched him again."† In "Blind Alley Guy," the father punishes his son with "woodshed lickings but finally gave up in defeat" when Blackie "accepted them without resentment or crying." He also threatens his father: "Either you give up licking stuff or I'll pack up and leave home so I won't run the risk of killing you." The sons find an ally in their overprotective mothers, who attempt to mitigate the anger of their husbands. Klara Hitler obviously loved her son Adolf more than her daughter Paula. In "Blind Alley Guy" Tess has "never been able to mend her way of unequal

---

*Dr. Rudolph Binion maintains that by the time Hitler was nineteen he was "intellectually and emotionally retarded after having lived idly with his widowed mother for some years past at suffocatingly close quarters." Binion notes that the seed of his anti-Semitism was probably planted in 1907 when his mother was undergoing extremely painful iodoform treatments for cancer. Consciously, Hitler loved Dr. Block, her Jewish physician, "like a kind father; unconsciously, he blamed Block for his mother's cancer." Quoted in *Adolf Hitler*, John Toland (New York, 1976), p. 538.
†Toland, p. 12.

love—for R.*—Father and Sister's resentment against Mother because of her greater love for R." Alois Hitler, speaking of his half-brother Adolf, states: "My stepmother always took his part. He would get the craziest notions and get away with it. If he didn't have his way he got very angry. . . . He had no friends, took to no one and could be very heartless. He could fly into a rage over any triviality."† Throughout the notes for "Blind Alley Guy," all the characters mention Blackie's outbursts of fury, his solitary nature, his ruthlessness to others.

O'Neill apparently attempts to parallel Blackie's relationships with his sister Cassie and mistress-wife Dora and those in Hitler's turbulent personal life. Cassie is a combination of Hitler's half-sister, Angela Raubal, and her daughter Geli. Toland observes that Hitler's fondness for Geli "went far beyond that of an uncle. He loved her, but it was a strange affection that did not dare to show itself, for he was too proud to admit to the weaknesses of an infatuation."** In 1931, while living with her uncle, Geli committed suicide—"perhaps in desperation, perhaps in jealousy." There were "innuendoes that the Führer himself had done away with his niece . . . that the bridge of her nose had been broken and there were other signs of maltreatment."†† Cassie feels an incestuous attraction for her brother; she "can't marry man she loves—can't trust or believe —R. had got her to state where [she] consented [to] give herself—then he had slapped her face—'dirty bitch!' " Because of her obsessive love for her brother, Cassie is fiercely jealous and antagonistic towards Dora and makes disparaging remarks about her. Hitler's sister Angela disapproved of his "liaison with Eva Braun, whom she privately referred to as *de blode kuh* (the stupid cow)." According to Toland, Angela "refused to shake hands" with her "and usually saw to it that there was no room at Haus Wachenfeld" when Eva came to visit.*** Blackie's wife, Dora Bond, resembles Eva Braun in some respects; both live an underground existence, loving desperately men who are hated and feared by civilized society and are either unwilling or incapable of reciprocating love. The indifference of these men brings the women psychological, as well as physical,

---

*The July notes show the play in transition; some of the former autobiographical aspects linger. The son is referred to as "R." whenever his relationship with his family is discussed. The heading "R. H. play" appears frequently at the top of the pages in this collection.

†Toland, p. 9.

**Ibid., p. 264.

††Ibid., p. 267.

***Toland, p. 415.

pain.* The parents of both feel disgraced because of their daughters' association with notorious misfits.

The major portion of the July notes is devoted to "Dora's story of final days" with Blackie, narrated to Cassie after she deduces that the criminal condemned to die is her brother. Dora says that her husband "was sick of the game" and wanted to settle down; but he had to find the right place—"said he had exact picture in mind." She describes his desired refuge to Cassie, who exclaims: "But that's this place." Dora agrees: "Yes, I got that right away. He wanted home." As Dora's words suggest, O'Neill is undecided where to locate the place Blackie selects: "Finally in Vermont (or Berkshires)†—'this isn't it but maybe it'll do.'" The couple moves into the house, but Blackie realizes that "he'd failed before he started—didn't mean anything—except pigeons—but I kept hoping—got pregnant." Later, during the "gambling house stick-up," Blackie kills a drunk. He escapes but leaves his fingerprints. Fearful of the future, Dora has an abortion. When she tells Blackie and asks his forgiveness, he is totally indifferent: "Hell. It's only a god damned kid." She broods over this remark and seeks "revenge—feels she will some day murder B[lackie].—finally goes out and phones N[ew]. Y[ork]. police—afterwards remorse—tells B." He scorns her offer to "stay with him—die together"** and also rejects her escape plan, determined to "go to Chair—show them they can't faze me with that little act—make me care a damn about life—or fear death." Reluctantly, Dora follows his orders to get in the car and drive to his parents' home. This outline concludes shortly before the time Blackie is to be executed and shows the parents still unaware of their son's fate but Dora and Cassie "proudly defiant—best hope for fear—'they can't make him afraid—he'll show em.'"

In late July O'Neill transfers the setting of the play from the East Coast to an area he knew equally well: a valley in Northern California. To retain the concept of distance—that a continent separates Blackie from his family—his

---

*Dora is beaten by Blackie; Eva, despondent when Hitler neglected her, shot herself in the neck in 1932, severing an artery. After a second suicide attempt in 1935, Hitler, realizing finally her complete devotion to him, rented an apartment for his mistress near his own Munich home. Dora is given the surname Bond, which approximates the sound of Braun, only after the Blackie-Hitler connection is introduced in July.

†In selecting these locales, which have mountainous areas, O'Neill is perhaps evoking Hitler's retreat Haus Wachenfeld, later called the Berghof, on the Obersalzberg.

**On September 1, 1940, Hitler, in his address to the Reichstag, announced the invasion of Poland. Among those in the audience was Eva Braun, who told her sister: "This means war." While the crowd cheered, Eva wept: "If something happens to him I will die too" (Toland, p. 661).

execution is now scheduled to take place in Sing Sing rather than San Quentin.*
The White home, with its "100 acres of orchards and fields on hills near small
village," resembles the author's ranch house, with its 160 acres of groves, located in the Las Trampas Hills, skirting the town of Danville in Northern California. Tess White has inherited this property—a "remnant of big ranch"—from
her father, who had been a "failure at ranching." Obviously another portrait of
Ella O'Neill, Tess has a "strange, withdrawn, ingrowing quality—dreamy and
detached—sentimental Nature appreciation—lover of sunsets, etc. superiority in
this over husband and daughter." Like Ella, she is considerably younger—ten
years—than her Irish husband, a "big, ruddy muscular man." Tess has had three
children: "first is daughter, a disappointment—next child dies—then at last, a
son—and she stops having children, her purpose accomplished." Whereas Ella
was a Catholic, Tess is a Protestant; she has, however, a similar "religious
nature but has gotten away from narrow Methodist creed in which she was
brought up into a vague God-The-Spirit-Behind-Everything—believes she is psychic."

August 21–25, 1941—"Blind Alley Guy," Notes

The dramatist spent nine days in early August on "Time Grandfather
Was Dead," whose focus is the "world collapse and dictatorships." Resuming
work on "Blind Alley Guy" on August 21, he states: "now this idea is tops
again." Four days later he expresses his belief that it "can be unusual, thrilling
play" (W.D.). He now enters his final period of making notes before beginning
the scenario and reinforces the parallelism between the Nazi dictator and his
offstage hero.† Striving possibly for a Teutonic name that would sound similar to
"Hitler," O'Neill now calls his central figure Walter, which signifies "ruling the
hosts." The name is appropriate as Walter views himself as a demonic, as well as
a mob, leader. In developing the "character of Walter" here, the author lists
attributes and traits found in Hitler:

resemblance in frustration (unconscious), inability to feel, which is driving motive behind criminal, anti-social career—hatred for society in which he feels
alien, longing for death sublimated into desire for destruction—no real belief in
social program—owe it to own mob—hatred for Christ, unconscious ambition
[to] supplant, become victor Anti-Christ—reason he hates Jews—liberty means

---

*Like Blackie, Hitler had been sent to jail. He spent over a year, feeling he had been
betrayed, in Landsberg prison after the failure of the Munich Putsch in 1923.
†Offstage characters play a significant role in several earlier works as, for example,
Simon Harford in A Touch of the Poet and Rosa and Evelyn in The Iceman Cometh.

his liberty alone as supreme master—Walter an anti-Semite—became Communist, then Fascist—admiration not for social theory but for leaders, Lenin, Stalin, Hitler—none for Mussolini—'wop loud-mouth ham'—first attracted to Communism as agent destruction U.S. as is—but always a lone wolf*—never wants to belong—won't be used by party line—use.

New material is added here to Dora's earlier "story about Walter." She quotes "what he used to say about Hitler, Stalin—his strange confidence that he alone understands Hitler—'That guy and I could be pals. I know what makes him tick. Only I guess he'd never stand that from anyone. He wouldn't admit scared to face himself. That's where I've got it over him. I've got more guts. I'm not even scared of myself'." Dora then adds: "Can you believe it, he honestly thought he was greater than Hitler."

The conversation between Walter's parents in the next section indicates his home environment served to nurture his bigotry and fanaticism. The father—who is described as a "typical American," an isolationist, and "great lodge member"—maintains that Hitler is "not responsible" for the current world crisis: "H. has some good ideas, he thinks—re[garding] Unions—and suppression [of] religion." His wife protests: "That's trouble with world. Lost God." When he points out that the Portugese and Italians had not done so, she says: "Better have religion suppressed than Catholic." Ed argues: "The Jews—Orthodox, I mean—they're still religious." Furious, she attacks him: "You can say that to me—them Christ-killers.† I'm ashamed of you. You're [a] no good American. Papists and kikes ruined the country. I don't say there aren't good ones—but all the same, never should have let them in here—bad for country. Look at gangsters—all wops, Jews and Irish and Polacks." He reminds her: "I'm part Irish." She responds: "Well, I meant shanty Irish. You're not shanty descended. Your grandfather had 100 pounds when he landed—if you weren't lying when you told me." "No, that's true. He owned his own land—and shanty —sold out."

---

*Before seizing power and acquiring the title "Führer," Hitler was frequently introduced as "Herr Wolf." His first name, Adolf, derives from the Teutonic word meaning "fortunate wolf" (Toland, p. 102).
†Dorothy Parker attended the 1934 performance of the Passion play in Oberammergau, "which blamed the Jews for the death of Jesus." She notes that when Christ was hoisted on the cross, a spectator remarked: "There he is. That is our Führer, our Hitler!" (Toland, p. 377).

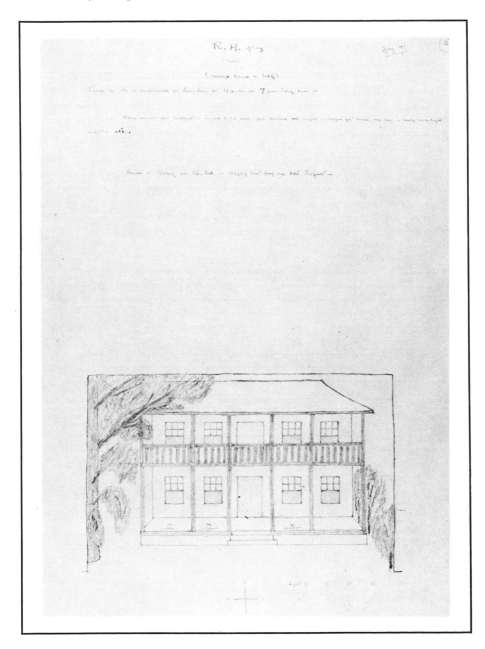

The play is now set in 1941, a date not specifically stated by the author but determined by the ages of the characters in given years. O'Neill provides additional background information about Walter. An athletic hero in high school, he is a "lazy, uninterested student" and "disappears a few weeks before graduation —previous secret association with bootlegging gang." He returns home in the fall, "drawn to Dora's love for him." He seduces her the following spring and has the "episode with Cassie at this time—plays on jealousy of Dora." A few months later when he runs off again, Dora "goes to pieces—gets reputation as wild girl, parties, scrapes, booze, affairs which mean nothing." Eventually she reforms and marries a dull, hard-working man who is "ten years older." She returns "after month's honeymoon to find Walter back—comes there to hide out after bank robbery in which he shot a cop—sated with lawless thrills." Although Walter warns her—"I'm what they call a crook"—she runs away with him. Her husband "divorces her two years later—she waits for Walter [to] suggest marriage—he never does until attempt settle down."

One idea O'Neill records in 1933 is to reverse the situation of *Strange Interlude*, in which Nina Leeds needs three men to fulfill her needs. He does so here; Walter is a male Nina, inspiring "a strange conflict of emotions in the three women, his mother, sister and Dora, who love him in a deep maternal protective tenderness toward the boy who can't mature, who was born crippled in his inability to feel—as if he'd been born blind and deaf and dumb." While something within them always understands and excuses him, they feel an aversion for this "born monster, an ugly and maimed man" and a "scornful antagonism of mystified passionate worm toward an impotent lover." They resent his indifferent and "realistic attitude which dooms them—dooms love, defeats them—leaves them meaningless—yet it inspires them also with desire to be as free as he is—to be ruthless—to use any means to get what they want." Tess, who is closely associated with nature, is O'Neill's eternal earth mother. She has "thick gray hair almost white, dark complexion, high cheekbones, hollow cheeks, big dark eyes, long lashes, heavy brows, trace of mustache, wide full-lipped mouth, angular jaw—still an unusually good-looking woman for her age—personality a contrast." At times she is "insensitive, detached," and relaxes "into a vague, daydreaming quietude." In matters pertaining to "her ranch-housewife activities," she is "relentlessly efficient" and a demanding employer. A "superior distinctive pose among townswomen" isolates Tess, and she becomes a "great reader."

Dora assumes the role of the well-intentioned, self-sacrificing prostitute frequently depicted in O'Neill's plays. Once exceptionally pretty, she now "looks sickly" and "at least ten years older than she is." Her haggard, drawn face is "too old not only in appearance but in the quality of its expression. There is the hardness and sorrow and pain and defiance of years of bitter experience in it, and, at [the] moment, a touch [of] defensive cynicism that gives her the look of a prostitute." She has a "straight thin nose, a sensitive mouth with full lips, big gray eyes. Her hair is obviously peroxided." Her eyes have a "flat, depthless look as if they were merely organs of sight cut off from registering thought or feeling, and this makes them appear repellent and cruel."

Like Sara Melody and other O'Neill daughters, Cassie "resembles both parents." She is thin but has a good figure, chestnut hair, and "hazel eyes, quiet, thoughtful, intelligent dreaming—inwardly there is conflict—a confusion of not knowing what it is or wants to become—source of the conflict goes back to her brother—secret hostility to mother because Walter her pet—extremely prudish attitude about Walter and Dora—immoral conduct." She admits she is unfair to her fiancé to postpone their wedding repeatedly and knows she should release him, but she retains the "vague hope something will happen so one day it will be all right."

Ed White is now forty-nine, a year younger than his wife, and a semi-retired proprietor of a butcher shop. He is broad-shouldered and fat and has "thinning blond hair, bald spot—fat face, double chin, fair skin baked red, sunburn dotted with freckles, blue eyes, round—small, full-lipped mouth, good teeth—attractive grin—general boyish expression of face—likable energetic personality." He was injured in the leg in World War I and walks with a noticeable limp.

August 30–31, 1941—"Blind Alley Guy," Act One, outline

The play opens, as does *Long Day's Journey into Night*, with the family gathered for breakfast. An "argument on Hitler, unions, etc." can be clearly heard through the open windows of the dining room. "It continues as the three come out on porch." The reference to Hitler in the first line of the scenario, like Mary Tyrone's remark about the fog at the beginning of *Long Day's Journey into Night*, suggests a menacing exterior force threatening the family and the progressively worsening condition of one of its members: here, the son. When Cassie goes to the gate for the newspaper, the parents' conversation immediately veers to Walter—"memories, etc.—resentments—maybe it is better [he] never comes home—again talk Hitler ('Walt like H.—no feeling for other's feeling'?)." In this version, Dora arrives unexpectedly. Ed and Tess go to the car and greet her affectionately, but "Cassie waits—bitter apprehension." She "responds stiltedly" when Dora kisses her warmly and apologizes for her ghastly appearance and Walter's absence. When they are alone, the suspicious Cassie demands to know the truth about her brother. Warily, Dora changes the topic of conversation and talks about her recent illness—pneumonia. Suddenly, she sees the newspaper and asks about the war news: "You know, Walt has the craziest hunches. He isn't pro-Nazi, he isn't pro anything, but he really admires Hitler. He thinks he has the right idea about people." Cassie remarks: "He would. He hasn't changed then." Dora responds: "He's tried to. But not in his opinion about people and life. He believes you've got to be realistic and not sentimental and face the truth and not feel anything one way or the other." She scans the newspaper and shudders when she comes to "one headline on an inside page." Anxiously, she asks: "What time is it?" O'Neill states: "motive all through play, of Dora's smashed wrist watch." Frequent references to the time are made in subsequent acts; the sense of impending doom increases as the family goes through this long day; by nightfall even the unaware parents—particularly the psychic mother—realize instinctively some tragedy threatens their son.

September 3–4, 1941—"Blind Alley Guy," Act Two, outline

As in *Long Day's Journey into Night*, the passage through the day and, subtly, the significance of time are suggested by the specific references to meals. Act Two opens "after lunch" with voices raised in an argument in the dining room, as in the first act, and the family coming out to the porch. Ed takes up the paper but does not read it; he questions Dora about Walt. Nervously and imprudently, she says that "she can't talk now—I'll tell you all about it after seven." Cassie asks her: "Why any time after seven" and why is she so interested in eastern time? When the parents go into the house, Dora warns: "Look out, Cassie. I don't like you—because I know you hate me. So cut out the old third degree stuff. If you keep on, I might get sore and let you have it—then you'll wish you'd minded [your] own business." Cassie persists. The act concludes with Dora making another hostile threat: "I'm sick of your questions. I'll shut you up so you won't ask more—reason I left him—I found out he's a crook— you're not surprised, are you? I guess you knew he'd wind up a crook—and now he's in jail—that's the truth and I guess it'll hold you for a while."

September 8, 13–17, 1941—"Blind Alley Guy," Act Three, outline

Carrying the newspaper, Cassie enters Dora's room and finds her repacking her suitcase, determined to leave immediately. Dora remarks that she should "never have come to this house—not when Cassie was there." She pretends that she left Walt because he was unfaithful to her: "He'd make a pass at any skirt around, even his own sister—just to show he was realistic—beyond any laws— and to prove he could—prove his power—he didn't want you—I'm the only woman he ever really wanted." When Cassie "breaks down—denies," Dora taunts her: "That's [the] reason you can't marry—hate me—hanging on to Walt—can't free yourself—well, you'll be free soon." Surmising the truth, Cassie turns to an article in the newspaper about a "criminal named Walter Black,

'Blackie'—opposite to White—sounds like Walt—he always chose the opposite —says he committed many killings—says never would have been caught if it hadn't been his wife informed cops." At first defiant, Dora finally confesses: "That is Walt. That's me. Now how do you like it?" Crushed and broken, Cassie begs her not to tell her parents; bitterly, she castigates Dora for betraying Walt.

September 18–19, 1941—"Blind Alley Guy," Act Four, outline

Like the first two acts, the last act opens showing the exterior of the White home. The family is having dinner: "voices from dining room—Tess and Ed arguing world crisis." Later, on the porch, Ed and Tess, in separate scenes, entreat Dora to forgive Walt and return to him. The parents relive their memories and express their grievances against Walt. When alone with Dora, Cassie persuades her to confess the truth: "recurrent waves of hatred, jealousy, sympathy, identity between [the] two as story progresses." At the conclusion, Dora defends her betrayal of Walt and tells Cassie she would "have done the same. You know damned well you would—thing to do—what he wanted—in love with death now—all he ever loved anyway."* To prevent her parents from discovering the truth, Cassie devises a plan by which they will, at a later time, receive word that Walt was killed instantly in an accident. The two women suddenly remember the time: "nearing seven—they cling together, terrified—stare at Cassie's wrist watch." The play closes with Tess and Ed sitting placidly in their old-fashioned rockers and Cassie and Dora in "straight back armchairs—rigid, clutching arms." When Dora hears the cuckoo clock striking seven, she cries out, feeling "pain like electric shock." She begins to sob: "I loved him, I tell you, Cassie, I loved him no matter what he did. I couldn't help it. I still love him." Ed consoles her: "I'm sure he knows how much you love him, Dora—and appreciates it." She murmurs, "Yes, maybe he does—now!"

September 20–22, 1941—General Notes for "Blind Alley Guy"†

A new plan for the play appears in the notes O'Neill makes before starting the dialogue for Act One. He sharpens the focus of the work and shows the gradual erosion of values within the family structure in America. He alters

---

*Compare this statement and that of Edmund Tyrone, a self portrait, in *Long Day's Journey into Night*: "I will always be a stranger who never feels at home, who does not really want and is not really wanted, who can never belong, who must always be a little in love with death!" Those familiar with O'Neill's biography and philosophy of life will recognize many similarities between the author and his hero.
†Three alternative titles head this section of notes: "Exit an Enemy Alien," "Rocket's End," and the resurrected "Gag's End."

completely his original concept of the three Whites; they are now amoral, selfish agnostics: "Loss of all ethical and moral values by Ed, Tess and Cassie—complete scepticism in which they take pride—(although in private relations each is honorable)—no faith in old religion—government all grafting politicians—sex morality of no meaning, ancient bigotry—don't vote except special local issues which affect selfish interests." Cassie sings in the church choir "for money reason only."

The dramatist makes a notation to "change date to year Hitler's seizing power—approval—what we need over here—purge, 1934."* By portraying the Whites now as godless materialists and having them support the ruthless German dictator, O'Neill delineates the prototypes of the apathetic Americans who will later inhabit the totalitarian World State of "The Last Conquest" and willingly submit to its tyrannical "Hitler-like leader." O'Neill describes the central motif of the play: "Recurrence argument Ed and Tess about Hitler—opening Acts I, II, & IV—follow same pattern—each ends on note of affinity to Walt." The characters are described as drawn to Walt "as if he were an evil freedom which tempts, fascinates and horrifies." According to the dramatist's new scheme, the second act "brings in the gangster mob leader similarity—Ed's old admiration for Capone (and Walt's)—(and anyone's)—justification [of] his killings—kill or be killed."

September 23–29, October 9–13, 20–27, 1941—Act One, start dialogue

The first act opens "around seven-thirty in the morning of a day in July, 1934." As in the scenario, voices, raised in a heated discussion, can be heard coming from the dining room. "News in day's paper adds fuel to argument—[Hitler's] best friend Röhm, murder—new revelations, his refusal to commit suicide."† Röhm was shot at 6:00 P.M. July 1; the specific "day" of the action

---

*On January 30, 1933, President Hindenburg accepted the inevitable and reluctantly made Hitler Chancellor of Germany. Toland entitles the chapter discussing Hitler's seizure of power: "An Unguarded Hour," prefacing the material with a quotation from Karl Marx: "Neither a nation nor a woman is forgiven for an unguarded hour in which the first adventurer who comes along can sweep them off their feet and possess them" (p. 307). O'Neill was provided with a first-hand account of the mood in Germany during this period by his older son, who was a student there in 1932–1933. The dramatist's Work Diary entry on May 4, 1933 reads: "Eugene's Twenty-Third Birthday University of Freiburg, Germany."

†The events cited here and elsewhere in the notes indicate O'Neill had researched the rise of Hitler and Nazism. Ernst Röhm and Hitler became good friends in 1921. Because of Röhm's utter devotion, Hitler made him commander of his paramilitary unit, the *Sturmabteilung* (Storm Detachment), called the SA. When Röhm demanded a

of the play is probably July 2 or 3. Ed and Tess express their opposite opinions about Hitler's role in Röhm's execution.

Ed   Well, I say he's no better than a lousy gangster murderer!

Tess   And I say you can't blame him. He had to. It was self-defense.

Ed   Self-defense, my neck. You know that's damned nonsense, Tess.

Tess   It's the plain truth, from what I've read. They were planning to double-cross him, weren't they? And he found out about it. Well, what would you want him to do? Wait and do nothing? He knew if they got hold of him they'd kill him in the end to get rid of him. The only way out was for him to kill them first. Just try putting yourself in his place, and be fair. I'd do exactly what he did.

In this opening dialogue, O'Neill draws a parallel between Hitler, whose friends plan "to double-cross him," and Walter, whose wife betrays him. Throughout the play, the isolated Ed and Tess receive two kinds of "news"— both unreliable—from the outside world: of Hitler's actions in Germany and their son's activities in this country. O'Neill makes a "general note," stating: "From first their uneasiness—still afraid [to] get news of Walt—overcompensate for this." Brecht parallels the rise of one man, Arturo Ui, a gangster, and Hitler. In O'Neill's play not only does the central character identify with Hitler but members of his family support the Nazi dictator. To O'Neill, the family represents the microcosm that reflects the macrocosm. The new characterizations of the Whites emphasize their loss of moral and ethical values, their bigotry, their indifference to individual freedom and basic human rights. On a day when total power was finally consolidated and within Hitler's grasp, the demonic Walter White, his American counterpart, is scheduled to die; yet those who spawned him survive.

---

military role for the SA and a Second (economic) Revolution, his political rivals in the SS, Himmler, Göring, and Goebbels, convinced Hitler his friend was plotting a coup d'etat to usurp the power of the army. On June 30, Hitler ordered the SS to shoot SA leaders but refrained from including the imprisoned Röhm's name on the list. Toland states that on July 1 Hitler "was going through one of the most traumatic crises of his turbulent career. It reached a climax that afternoon when he was forced to approve the execution of Röhm. Even Hitler's sentence of death was marked by affection. He instructed Brigadeführer Theodor Eicke to give Röhm the chance to commit suicide" (p. 362). Röhm greeted his SS executioners with the words: "All revolutions devour their own children." He was given a pistol with a single bullet. Eicke and his men waited fifteen minutes in a passage and then returned to the cell and shot Röhm, whose dying words were: "My Führer!" (Toland, p. 363).

After breakfast, the Whites come out to the porch and reveal their feelings about the coming visit of Walt and Dora. The three dwell on the pain Walt has inflicted upon them until, in a manner similar to Mary Tyrone's in *Long Day's Journey into Night*, Tess says: "But let's not rake up the past. It isn't fair when we all know from Dora's letters how completely he's changed in the past three years." Ed is skeptical and tells his wife that Walt inherited his free and independent spirit from her: "I'm sure he hasn't changed in that because it was born in him. Got it from you, Tess—stubborn as hell and bound to have his own way or die trying. Me. I've always been a weak submissive guy." Cassie points out he did not sound like one in the breakfast argument.

Ed   You wouldn't have me stand by and listen to your mother admiring
          that rat without a word of protest, would you?

Tess   (roused) It's no question of admiring him. I was just claiming
          that if you face the facts of the position he was forced into, you
          would have to admit in his boots, you'd do just what he did. It's
          you who used to admire him. I've heard you say time and again
          you took your hat off to him, and you wished we had someone with
          his guts at the head of our government to smash the Communists
          like he's smashed them.

Ed   All right. Sure. I said that. I still say it. But these men he's just
          had killed in that purge weren't Communists. They were nearly all
          people who'd started with him and helped him get to the top. One
          of them was his best friend. (Indignantly) That's what finished
          him for me. It shows him up for what he is—a yellow, double-
          crossing, murdering rat! By God, I hope one of them he didn't rub
          out gets him! Someone will, too, wait and see.

The Röhm affair is used in this version to suggest the similarities between Hitler and Walt. The former destroys his friends; the latter inflicts suffering on his family. "Double-crossing" is again mentioned here and foreshadows Dora's confession of betrayal. Just as Tess justifies Hitler's actions, Ed defends Walt's: "You couldn't hold him responsible the way you would any other boy—for all the crazy things he did and said to hurt people." He is suddenly contrite: "Here we are digging up the past again. Let's cut it out. We'll be in a swell mood to welcome him home, if we keep holding old grudges against him."

When Cassie goes to get the mail, Tess reminisces about the past and her son's strange nature. "There were times you couldn't believe he was human. He just couldn't feel anything. He had to go his own way, alone—(This almost desperately) Oh, Ed, can't we keep off the subject of what Walt used to be?" She changes the conversation and speaks of Cassie's refusal to set a definite wedding date. "I told her I'd been watching Tom and I could see how sore and hurt he's getting. He's beginning to suspect she doesn't love him." Cassie returns with the newspaper: "A lot about your old pal in Germany. I'm going to keep the paper away from you two if I have to sit on it—that is, until it's cool tonight. It's going to be no day for heated arguments." The telephone rings; there is a telegram from Dora stating she would arrive that evening alone. Walt had to go to Oklahoma to solve a construction problem. Cassie looks at her parents and remarks: "How relieved we are, all of a sudden! Why haven't we the honesty to admit that we simply can't picture Walt as he's changed and we'd still be afraid to have the old Walt around. Afraid he'd get bored after a day or two—but afraid most of never knowing what he might suddenly say or do to hurt you." Ed speaks bitterly: " 'So what of it.' I remember him saying that all right. It was his pet slogan. He ought to put it in his will to have that engraved on his tombs— (he checks himself and curses angrily) God damn it, can't we quit harping on what Walt used to be like?" Ed expresses his concern for Dora; she would have to "keep rolling to make it" by evening from Los Angeles. The sound of a speeding car is heard. It cuts into the ranch. Ed "springs to his feet—angrily— 'Who the hell—By God, I'll tell him off, whoever he is! Damned maniac!' (The car is heard roaring up the twisting road. They are looking off left. The noise of the car stops.) "

May–June 1943—"Blind Alley Guy"

On September 29, 1941, O'Neill temporarily abandons "Blind Alley Guy," saying: "I can't move it—same old stuff again—too many ideas in head—lose interest not in idea of play but in writing it—a why bother in this world feeling— too much war preoccupation (which doesn't help anything)." He resumes work on it the next month but again experiences difficulties with the play: "it still won't come right—decide put aside till its time comes" (W.D., October 27, 1941). The dramatist then devotes the next year and a half to developing the idea he records on October 28, 1941 for *A Moon for the Misbegotten*, finishing the second draft in May 1943. As he did so often in the past—take up a work started earlier after completing a play—O'Neill returns to "Blind Alley Guy" in "late May." He begins this last set of notes with a plan for his most dramatic use of sound since *The Emperor Jones*. A cuckoo clock now serves—as the tom-tom did in the earlier drama—as a reminder, a device marking time until the death offstage of the play's central character:

Effect—the cuckoo clock which Tess has bought for husband for Christmas present—a joke on his escape into memories of old house and family life—keeps striking at intervals throughout play—its silly sound punctuating the growing tension, becoming a voice of the doom of passing time—and at end the voice of death.

O'Neill includes in these notes specific ideas he wants to emphasize in the play:

Act One—In the first lines of the play the dramatist stresses Cassie's jealousy of Dora and its cause: the incestuous brother-sister relationship. Tess says to her daughter: "You still have [a] grudge against her, don't you." Cassie indignantly denies the accusation, but Tess persists: "All [the] same, always felt you were jealous of her when she and Walt fell in love. You and Walt were always so close." Cassie denies this vehemently: "We were not. I can't imagine anyone feeling close to Walt. He wouldn't let them, even if they accepted—even if he wanted himself. As for love, he couldn't feel love. He thought love was just—." The rest of the act is the same as earlier versions, concluding with Dora's arrival in a distraught condition.

Acts Two/Three—The emphasis here is the effect of anxiety and tension on Dora; she "cannot help showing inner strain—all three watch this—Edgar and Tessie come to conclusion fight with husband—she grasps at this." They console her: "know what he's like in his spells—his complete unawareness of all moral values—examples—Cassie remains suspicious of something more."

Act Four—O'Neill includes in the final scene a reference to the death of Hitler, linking him for the last time to Walt, who is to be electrocuted at 7:00 p.m. The dramatist accurately prophesies in 1943 the way Hitler would die two years later on April 30, 1945. Cassie asks: "Will they get Hitler?—Ed affirmation—Tess negation—ask Dora's opinion—in end he'll get sick of himself and commit suicide. They'll think they killed him but it'll only be because he killed himself— (Dora had suggested to Walt to kill himself—at end)."

Ed puts on the radio, believing that the "7 o'clock comedian program," which is about to begin, would "cheer Dora up." She begs Cassie to stop the striking of the cuckoo clock: "It'd be too horrible [to] hear that silly sound at seven." Cassie disconnects the clock. When she returns, Dora says with hysterical bitterness: "just thinking—maybe wrong—Walt would love that—he'd be amused—give that twisted grin of his—like to hear cuckoo, cuckoo as they turned on the current—he'd say way everybody's life should end—it's all cuckoo." In spite of Dora's attempt to remain oblivious to time, a voice on the radio announces: "It is now 14 seconds before 7." Dora breaks down: "Turn it off, for God's sake."

The notes for "Blind Alley Guy" conclude with a very short section dated "June 1st '43." This is perhaps the last passage O'Neill ever wrote as playwright. Its subject, like that of his first play, A Wife for a Life, is the man-woman relationship. Dora questions Tess about her attitude to Ed and says: "I always felt you had a secret contempt for him because of World War injury—felt he was looking for excuse to be content with what he had—but at same time loved him more because more dependent on you—and now his high blood pressure—more contempt and more love." The scene ends with Tess remarking: "Women are all crazy, I guess, when love gets 'em."

A MOON FOR THE MISBEGOTTEN
(1941)

S[haughnessy]. play idea, based on story told by E[dmund]. in 1st Act of "L[ong]. D[ay's]. J[ourney]. I[nto]. N[ight]."—except here Jamie principal character & story of play otherwise entirely imaginary, except for J[amie].'s revelation of self.

—Work Diary, October 28, 1941

As the first recorded reference and later notes indicate, O'Neill's primary purpose in writing *A Moon for the Misbegotten* is to dramatize his brother Jamie's inner nature and tragic fate. The author's decision to eulogize his brother in the last play of the canon can be viewed as both a personal and a creative retribution. In previously completed and contemplated works, the dramatist develops the idea contained in the early 1918–1920 notebook for "a play of Jim and self—showing influence of elder on younger brother." The struggle for dominance/survival between the brothers is depicted in the symbolic battle waged either by one dual-natured Mephistophelian/ascetic figure or by two characters who represent a similar antithesis. Only by revealing Jamie's destructive attitude to him in the last act of *Long Day's Journey into Night* can the dramatist purge himself of the bitterness, resentment, and hatred he felt for his brother. In the sequel to this play, *A Moon for the Misbegotten*, he manifests his deep pity and affection for Jamie and an awareness of his desperate loneliness.

The two late autobiographical plays are linked thematically by the "S." or Shaughnessy story about an Irish tenant farmer, whose land is owned by James Tyrone, Sr., which Edmund relates in *Long Day's Journey into Night*. Edmund outwardly and his father inwardly gloat that the "wily shanty Mick" wins a "great Irish victory" over Harker, his Standard Oil millionaire neighbor, by defending and exonerating his adventurous pigs in a trespassing dispute. The prototype for Shaughnessy is James O'Neill's tenant, John "Dirty" Dolan, whose name appears in the early notes for *Long Day's Journey into Night*. The pigs-in-the-pond incident mentioned briefly in this work becomes a minor theme in *A Moon for the Misbegotten*, labeled the "Dolan play" in the first 1941–1942 notes. The Dolan farm, however, provides merely the backdrop against which the tragic story of Jamie O'Neill's last days is enacted.

The dramatist is extremely enthusiastic about this "strange combination comic-tragic" work, as he calls it, during the initial period of note-making and outlining from late October to early November of 1941. The attack on the United States on December 7 and this country's subsequent declaration of war, however, have a debilitating psychological effect on his creativity. He remarks on January 20, 1942: " 'A Moon for the Misbegotten'—Finish 1st Draft—but had to drag myself through it since Pearl Harbor and it needs much revision— wanders all over the place" (W.D.). Because of his mental depression and his deteriorating physical condition, he puts aside the first draft of *A Moon for the Misbegotten* and does not resume work on the play until a year later in January 1943.

October 29–November 1, 1941—"Dolan Play," "The Man of Other Days"
Outline Acts I to III

There are a number of differences—in theme and focus—between the 1941–1942 and the 1943 drafts of *A Moon for the Misbegotten*. The first title of the play, "The Man of Other Days," indicates that the focal point is, as the original idea states, Jamie's "revelation of self." Initially, O'Neill takes a subjective approach in dramatizing his brother's true nature and aspirations as, for example, in one scene—found only in this early outline—in which Jamie narrates stories illustrating his opposing dreams. O'Neill writes this scene as brother, in the white-heat of subconscious remembrance when the mind is seared from the burning memory of the past, and then withdraws while the more objective consummate artist steps forward from the shadows in later drafts and modifies the reflections before him.

The major theme of the final published version of *A Moon for the Misbegotten* is Jim* Tyrone's attempt to find, through confession, forgiveness for the desecration of his mother's memory and life of dissipation and to achieve through the absolution of the mother-substitute and priestess, Josie, moral regeneration and redemption. In contrast, the focal point of the first draft is the strange symbionic relationship established between these two characters. Their subsequent explorations of the inner self, which culminate in the confession of opposing dreams and total self-revelation, bring not only self-awareness—normally a life-affirming positive step forward, but also love-awareness—unfortunately, for them, a life-denying dead end. In the published text, Josie's rival for Jamie's affection is the ghost of his mother haunting the moonlight; in the earliest notes her competitor is the most seductive being mortal woman ever faced: the beautiful Cynara; Tyrone is hopelessly, fatally in love with death. This realization does not come, however, until late in Act Three; in the first acts of the 1941 version she is filled with hope yet has misgivings because of her grotesque physical appearance. "As a defense she builds herself up as a slut—bawdy and brazen—she saves herself for a man who will see that inside her is beauty—she falls in love with Jamie—her father guesses this—it is really what is behind his idea of framing Jamie." The father persuades her to seduce and compromise Jamie by telling her Tyrone intends to sell their home and land to the Yankee foe, Harder. In the first draft the crafty old Irishman actually comes

---

*O'Neill calls his brother "J." and "Jamie" in the early notes and outline and "Jim" in subsequent drafts.

home "with two cronies he has brought as witnesses—lured them with promise of drink." Because this scene is dramatized and not merely, as later, discussed, the 1941 draft has two characters, Cassidy and a "wop," who do not appear in the final version.

The most developed section in the first scenario is what O'Neill terms the "extraordinary love scene" between Josie and Jamie in Act Three. Here Jamie is not repelled by sex as in the published text. On the contrary, he reveals a definite physical desire for Josie, making the fulfillment of it a precondition for the Dolans' retaining their farm: "I wouldn't accept if Harder offered a million. Won't sell if—if you don't repulse my advances, so to speak." He knows that "lots of men haven't had" her as she claims. Doubting he could ever truly love her, Josie says: "And is that why you want me, because you think I'm [a] virgin? You're sick of pretty whores and you'd like a virgin for a change to divert you, even if she is a great ugly lump as big as two men. Well, if you won't think I'm [a] virgin, you're [an] imbecile. So come in to bed now." He responds: "All right"; yet she hesitates: "But I'd like to know you better first. A virgin shouldn't sleep with a stranger at any price." Josie urges him to tell her and the moon, the "great keeper of secrets," about himself. His parable apparently reflects Jamie O'Neill's true despairing attitude to life—a painful revelation, which the dramatist eventually eliminates:

Once upon a time a child was born of well-to-do but devout parents—and the first thing he did was look around at the round earth and realize he'd been sent to the wrong planet and God had double-crossed him and so he began to curse and they slapped [him] on the back and he reached for a bottle of whiskey and said to himself: "By God, I'll show you! Try and catch me now." And so he lived on cursing and drinking and being slapped on the back, and no one ever caught him, and at last a lucky day dawned and he died and returned to his real home. That's all. And please don't slap me on the back.

Also excluded later is Jamie's admission that he hated acting, and "so it took revenge on him, and made him a bum—on and off, a ham." He talks of his mother's death, becomes depressed, and starts to leave to go back to the inn where "there will be laughter." The exchange between the two in this version is similar to the one between Eben and Abbie in the seduction scene in *Desire Under the Elms*, in which Eben laments his dead mother. Reminiscent of Abbie, Josie exclaims: "I'll laugh for you, if you like. I know you like laughing at things. You ought to learn to laugh with things. With life and not at it. There's laughter at the heart of life."

With the insight that love provides, Josie begins his story:

There was once a boy who loved goodness and honor and kindness and purity and God with a great quiet passion inside him. Your pride is so hurt, isn't it, when anyone says there's good in you, or ever was good. You feel naked and ashamed. He was still wet behind the ears—a sucker, a sap, a fall-guy, but he soon got wise to himself—all in the bag, etc.—So he thinks he's murdered the boy, does he? The foolish, boastful creature! Sure, it's as plain as the nose on his face, it's only the boy who's alive and the rest is a Broadway ghost—or a ham actor made up as a ghost—who's always out of a job and can't find any life to haunt except its own living death.

Jamie "tries to be derisive" and asks if the "wise dame from Wiseville" knows who she really is. Josie replies: "That's easy. I'm a woman who was born ugly with a heart full of love. I'm the opposite of a whited sepulcher, if I do say it myself. I'm a big, strong, ugly unpainted barn full of golden gifts that I can't give anyone because no one wants to see inside." In this first draft, there is no lust or fear of "the aftermath that poisons" in Jamie's attitude to Josie. He "takes her head—kisses her eyes, nose, lips, throat, breasts, saying with each kiss, 'You're beautiful!' " When she asks him if he wants her in bed, he answers: "Yes! You fool! But I don't want to want that." Then the memories of other nights begin to haunt him—the "many dawns with silver-sandled feet creeping through the shades of hotel rooms with empty blood-shot eyes, sick with the love of death." She now kisses him passionately: "To the devil with your nonsense. You'll take me to bed now, won't you?" Again he replies, "Yes." She is disturbed and does not move: "Since you've kissed me I've lost the feeling I know you. You'll have to tell me more of yourself so I'll know you again." Josie asks him about his dreams; and when he denies he has any about himself, she says: "Two dreams we all have. One or the other creeps in our mind whenever we're off guard. They're deadly enemies. It's a fight to the death to see which will own your life." She then tells him her two: "the triumphant beautiful ruthless harlot who knows men but never loves—makes men her slaves—that's the first—then [the] virtuous married woman whose joy is to be [a] slave to husband, children and house."

Reluctantly, Jamie reveals his first dream—of "the cynic who believes in nothing—as he tells her [he] grows full of disdainful pride." She comments: "Ah, you're proud of that one, aren't you? It's a Lucifer* dream, so afraid of being hurt." Urged to tell his second, "he does contemptuously—kid stuff— dates back to school—catechism—the man who loves God, who gives up self and the world to worship of God and devotes self to good works, service of others, celibacy—as he goes on contempt disappears and a note of hopeless yearning comes—He is ashamed." Josie understands him: "Ah, that's the one you really love, isn't it?—a poor holy dream, don't be ashamed—Well I've been

---

*Jamie's opposing dreams are similar to Satan's in "The Last Conquest," whose Promethean pride led to his downfall. Secretly Satan loves God and man and is weary of his isolation and dissipation; he longs, like Jamie, to be forgiven past transgressions.

trying to seduce a Saint. Or to tempt a Lucifer so proud and frightened he couldn't believe in joy if his heart was full of it."

If, as the original idea states, the focus of the play is Jamie's "revelation of self," the confession of opposing dreams constitutes the most important passage in the first draft. Jamie is described in this play, as in *Long Day's Journey into Night*, as having a "certain Mephistophelian quality." Yet Josie emphatically states that Jamie is a "boy who loved goodness . . . there's good in you." O'Neill in *A Moon for the Misbegotten*, his last completed play, repeats the same message of earlier dramas: that man is ever the victim of an eternal duality, his good and evil natures. Through the confession of opposing dreams, O'Neill clearly identifies his brother as a split Lucifer/Saint figure. The recurring demonic/ascetic hero depicted in the works of the 1920s and 1930s is, therefore, a carefully disguised portrait of Jamie. He is Dion Anthony in *The Great God Brown*, Reuben Light in *Dynamo*, John-Loving in *Days Without End*.* By excising the words "Jim and self" in the idea for a play about his brother and himself in the 1918–1920 notebook and by eliminating the opposing dream passage from *A Moon for the Misbegotten*, O'Neill attempts to conceal the psychological effect Jamie had on him. However, the last act of *Long Day's Journey into Night* reveals the "influence of elder brother on younger" in his personal life and the formation of his character; the collective notes for works having dual-natured heroes show the effect Jamie O'Neill had on his brother as a creative artist.

At the conclusion of Jamie's story, Josie says: "Ah, to hell with dreams! What are they but thoughts that are sick and weak and crying for comfort, thoughts that hide under the bed far from life which steal into the room. But I don't hide under the bed. I'm I, whatever I am, and I'm glad of it. And I love you, whatever you are. And tonight's tonight, and we'll take it, and to hell with past and future!" O'Neill indicates that Act Three would conclude with Josie's line: "And now come on to bed."

November 2–3, 1941—"Dolan Play," "The Moon Bore Twins"
Outline Act IV

When commencing Act Four on November 2, 1941, O'Neill changes the play's title from "The Man of Other Days" to "The Moon Bore Twins." The former title is appropriate for the original theme: Jamie's revelation of self. As Act Three evolves, this concept becomes part of a larger, more comprehensive plan. The extraordinary love scene demonstrates that Jamie and Josie are kindred souls; the new title, "The Moon Bore Twins," indicates a shift in focus to

---

*What also links these three characters to Jamie, in dramatic representations of him as in real life, is their obsessive love for their mothers.

their relationship. At the beginning of Act Four their love is not hopeless; both are lonely but are not, as yet, doomed or misbegotten. There is no hint here of the central theme of the final 1943 draft: Jamie's guilt-ridden confession of sins against the mother to Josie or any awareness on her part that he is a damned soul coming to her in the moonlight to "be forgiven and find peace for a night."

The early notes for Act Four provide additional insights into Jamie's character and an intimation of the future O'Neill contemplated for Josie. The act opens as the "moon is setting as dawn comes." Josie, holding the sleeping Jamie in her arms, remarks: "This is the night when the moon bore twins, me and my brother here. And it's the night when I, a virgin, bore a child who died at birth." When Jamie awakens and finds his head on a woman's breast, he "reacts with automatic sad cynicism and quotes Cynara." Josie asks: "Who's Cynara? It sounds [like] Latin in the Mass. Is it the name for death?" Unlike the published text, he immediately remembers what transpired the previous evening, takes her in his arms, and kisses her: "You're the one really beautiful woman I've ever known—and thank God I did sleep with you!—and didn't." They profess their deep love for each other. Only now does Josie realize the hopelessness of this love: "in the long years to come, we can remember the other's loneliness and not be so lonely." In this early version, Jamie proposes to her: "I—I'd like to marry you—but I've nothing to offer." Realizing a future together is an impossibility, Josie tries to conceal her sorrow with a humorous remark:

It's not marriage should be between us. Sure in a month I'd lose patience with your coming home drunk and take the broom handle to you. No, it's nothing like that between us. It's a better thing. It's the two of us in the world alone, two that do be dreaming, two born of the sadness of beauty, two in the dark night, two waiting in the dawn homesick for the land of heart's desire where only dreams come true.

Frightened by her emotional response, Josie accuses Jamie of making a poet of her. She mentions the chores that must be done and urges him to go before the arrival of her father, who will certainly create a scene. In the published text, Josie's statements suggest she will devote her life to caring for her father. Here another future is indicated. When Jamie tells her he will come back before leaving for New York, she says:

Keep away. I'll have you know I'm an engaged woman from now on—[I will] accept Mulroy today—he's been begging me to marry him since he tried to seduce me. I let him have a box on the ears that rattled his brains—he's a good enough lad, a bit free with the girls but I'll soon knock that out of him. He has two cows and two farm horses and 20 pigs and a fine bit of land I can boss— he'll give me children I can love—the first will be a son and I'll call him Jamie.

In her next statement, Josie mournfully resigns herself to her fate: "Well when you're next reciting poems about death to a whore by the light of an electric sign, remember me. Take pity on her. There's no rival a woman is more jealous of than death. Don't I know." They say goodbye to each other. Josie tells him not to look back but is joyous when he does: "God bless you, Jamie. I'll never love another." She sees her father coming, laughs at the joke played on him, and hurries off to the barn.

By early November, when the scenario is nearly finished, O'Neill has changed the focal point of the play several times; its tentatve titles indicate the stages of evolution. Once he decides to portray Jamie and Josie as doomed lovers, destined to be parted, the dramatist assigns the play a new title on November 3: "Moon of the Misbegotten," refining it on November 12 to "Moon for the Misbegotten" ("much more to the point," as he notes in the Work Diary).

After determining the nature of Jamie and Josie's relationship and writing the scene of their parting, O'Neill faces the final creative problem of the scenario: how to conclude the play. The 1941–1942 collection of notes contains three different versions of the last scene of the play. One section in the first of these—written on November 3—implies that Jamie Tyrone's father is still living. Dolan brings home his drunken witnesses and asks an amused Josie: "Where is he? You slut, you! Are you after giving it away?" When Josie tells him she has changed her mind about marrying Jamie, the old man threatens her: "Well, you will. I'll go to his father, I'll sue, etc." There is no indication in the early scenario that O'Neill intends to make this autobiographical play an epitaph for his brother; the work becomes one later in the 1943 draft when the author sets it in September 1923, shortly before Jamie's death. From its inception to the completion of the first draft, the drama provides a reminiscent view of the brother, a vehicle designed, as the author states, for "Jamie's revelation of self." It could, therefore, have been set prior to the death of James O'Neill Sr. on August 10, 1920.

In the first draft of the conclusion of the play, Dolan calls his daughter "a fine whore" if she slept with Jamie without receiving any money. Josie says: "He promised to send me twenty dollars." Outraged, Dolan exclaims: "When there's two Sundays in a week. God pity you! I'll make him marry you!" When Josie informs him that she will marry Mulroy and name her first son Jamie, the father's hopes are raised: "Then he did! You think you'll be in family way? Then we've got him!" Finally, Josie informs him Jamie did propose but that she refused his offer: "I'm a great ugly hulk in the bright day and you can't live in a dream of the moon when only the mind of you shows. And even if I was beautiful, he's in love with one more beautiful—her name is Latin for Death, and he's loved her all his life." The deep bond of love and understanding between father and daughter is more apparent in this and other early versions of the play than in the published text. At the close of the scene Josie remarks: "You're a good man, Father, and a kind man, and you see a lot no one would think a man like you would see, who'd skin a lion for the tallow." He boasts: "I would! And sell his hide to a Yankee for a Persian rug!" The play ends humorously. The father shouts a taunt to the Standard Oil man passing in his car. Deeply satisfied, he exclaims: "To hell with England, down with bloody tyrants, and God damn Standard Oil!" Josie says: "Amen!"

Finishing the scenario for *A Moon for the Misbegotten* on November 3, 1941, O'Neill begins Act One four days later, writing scene and character descriptions, making "scene plans," and starting the dialogue. He completes the first draft of this act on November 26 and states: "getting great satisfaction [from] this play—flows." The following day he makes additional notes for Act Four and writes a second version of the play's final scene. In the new ending, Josie reveals her true feelings for Jamie to her father. He justifies his lie to her—that Jamie planned to sell the farm—as part of a scheme to get him to marry her. Josie tells her father that she could have gotten Jamie without this trick. Then, sadly, she admits her love could not save Jamie: "He's bound to die because he longs to. He's in love with a beautiful cold lady named Cynara, and that's the Latin name for Death. Sure, he's always been faithful to her and her alone." It is her father who suggests she marry Mulroy: "What if he's a fool, he might give you sane children." Although heartbroken, Josie bravely begins to tease him: "Sure, living with you has spoiled me for any other man." He takes up her tone and demands his breakfast. Calling him a "bad-tempered old tick," she turns and looks wistfully down the road and then goes into the house. Alone, the father reveals his mixed feelings of sadness and rage. In the closing speech of the play, he asks: "Who are you cursing, you old bum? Is it Jim? No, whatever happened, he meant no harm to her. Is it meself? No, for I had the best intentions. Is it life you're cursing, then? Be God, that's a waste of breath, if it does deserve it."

The dramatist works on the first draft of Act Two from November 28 to December 11, on Act Three from December 12 to January 3, 1942, and on Act Four from January 4 to 20. Part of O'Neill's single-spaced typescript of this first draft is extant: the last two pages of Act Three (pp. 101–102) and all of Act Four (pp. 104–115), which provides a third concept of the last scene of the play. Comparing the handwritten notes and scenario and the typed dialogue of the first draft is an excellent means of studying O'Neill's method of composition. In the latter the characters are finely delineated; their emotions and mannerisms are revealed in the stage directions; the dialogue "flows."

The typescript shows that the author has a clearer concept for the ending of the play. The father, who is now called Hogan, tells Josie that he lied "to make you go and get him [Jim] from the Inn." He admits it was part of a scheme to get Tyrone to marry her. Again Josie explains Jamie's love for the beautiful Cynara and then describes her strange relationship with him—that she provides him with the kind of "love no other woman would give him." Seeing that the explanation is beyond her father's comprehension, Josie forces a teasing tone:

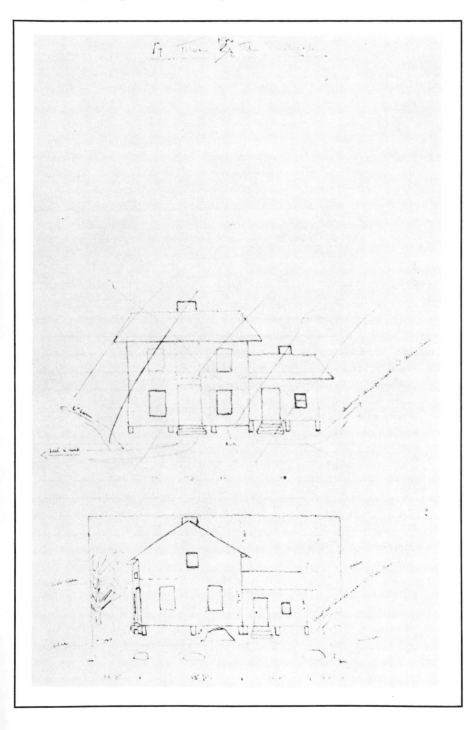

"Promise me this, you little, funny, ginger-haired old scheming goat, you. Promise me you'll never play Cupid again. And I promise you I won't disgrace you anymore with my proud lying and boasting I'm the slut of the world." Her father is relieved and encouraged by her next statement: "After I've lived down my bad reputation, I'll marry some decent man who's a hard worker and will be a help on the farm—and who'll give me children. For I know I've a great love for children and I'll make a good mother. I mean, some day after Jim Tyrone is—(Her voice falters) I never want to talk about this again, Father." He tries to cheer her, saying they should "go and make sure Harder's fence is still down, so the pigs won't miss their bath. (He sighs with comic regret) When I think of that jackass in his jockey's pants, it's a terrible sorrow to me we don't own a herd of elephants." She fails to respond and stands looking down the road to the Inn, her face full of tragic sadness and pity. Gently, he says: "Don't Josie. Don't be hurting yourself, Darlin'." This version ends with Josie rallying and going into the house to make breakfast. After the father's final speech, which is identical to that of the second version, the curtain falls.

There are a number of contrasts between the 1942 first draft of Act Four and the final version O'Neill writes a year later. In the former, Josie's scene with her father is just as long as the section depicting Tyrone's awakening at dawn and his departure; in the latter, Hogan appears only briefly at the end of Act Four. The differences between the last speeches and speakers in the two drafts are indicative of the changes O'Neill makes in the focal point of the play. In the early version, Hogan's words close the play as he curses life, the tragic flaw in Tyrone's character, the hidden powers that prohibit the marriage of two people who love each other. In the final draft, Josie utters the last speech as, watching Tyrone's figure receding down the road, she pronounces a final absolution and benediction: "May you rest forever in forgiveness and peace."

Several causes can be cited for O'Neill's decision to change the theme of *A Moon for the Misbegotten*, to add a new spiritual dimension to it and to the characterizations of Jim Tyrone and Josie Hogan when he writes the final version of the play in 1943. First, as Work Diary entries indicate, his physical condition had deteriorated; the tremor of his hand is more pronounced. To the man who could express his thoughts only by writing them—as though his arm were the channel, his hand the extension, of his creative mind—this debilitating condition signaled his demise as an artist. *A Moon for the Misbegotten* was important to the dramatist for two reasons. On the personal level, he would never in some future play be able to express his own forgiveness, his love, and spiritual wish-fulfillment for his brother. On the creative plane, the ghost of the doomed Mephisthophelian/ascetic Jamie O'Neill, which had haunted him and his plays for so many years, would finally be laid to rest.

With the rise of nazism, which he perceived as the release of evil upon the world, threatening to extinguish good, O'Neill in his work of the early 1940s manifests an obsession with spiritual concerns. During the year prior to writing the final draft of *A Moon for the Misbegotten* in 1943, he makes extensive notes for his "spiritual propaganda play," "The Last Conquest," which depicts "Good-Evil—opposites in Man" and has, as he states, a "final curtain declaration of faith." If completed, the work would have been the most religious play he or any other American dramatist ever wrote. The parable of the Siamese Twins in "The Last Conquest,"—in which one physically dominant, jealous brother kills his poetic, idealistic twin—has obvious autobiographic overtones. O'Neill's early title for *A Moon for the Misbegotten*, "The Moon Bore Twins," may be his subconscious admission that Josie is his alter ego. Jamie's confession to Josie that he had desecrated the memory of his recently deceased mother must have had a real-life counterpart with Jamie the teller of this sordid tale, his brother the good listener.

The dramatist himself provides an explanation for the contrast between the 1941–1942 and the 1943 drafts in his letter of December 16, 1942 to Dudley Nichols:

> As for work, Pearl Harbor caught me enthusiastically writing a new non-cycle play, "A Moon For The Misbegotten." After that, I couldn't concentrate. Managed to finish the first draft but the heart was out of it. Haven't looked at it since. There is a fine unusual tragic comedy in "A Moon For The Misbegotten" but it will have to wait until I can rewrite the lifeless post-Pearl Harbor part of it.

The time for rewriting comes several weeks later. O'Neill states on January 3, 1943: "Read 1st draft, A Moon For The Misbegotten—want to get this really written—real affection for it" (Work Diary). Three days later he starts the new version of the first act, working on it until January 31 when he notes: "Finish I, 2nd draft (what I am up against now—fade out physically each day after about 3 hours—page a day because [I] work slowly even when as eager about play as I am about this—Park[inson's]. main cause—constant strain to write)" (Work Diary). The only extant notes for the second draft of *A Moon for the Misbegotten* are dated February 1, 1943. As in the first draft, the author concentrates on the relationship between Jamie and Josie. The notes for "rewriting I" state: "Show more explicitly that while she knows marriage is impossible idea, and won't admit that she even dreams of affair with him—hopes he might want her to—but immediately feels he can't want her physically because 'great cow like me.'" The dramatist devises a new conclusion for Act One: "End—Jim alone on steps—his pain after others gone—disgust with self—'Nuts! Cut it out, you bastard. Leave her alone.'"

The notes for Act Two focus on Hogan's scheme to persuade his daughter to seduce Jamie: "Phil emphasizes that T[yrone]. doesn't know how long he may have to wait for estate—house, great temptation of Harder's offer." The dramatist works on the second draft of Act Two from February 4 to March 6, when he finishes "an entirely rewritten II." Starting the third act the next day, he realizes "this will have to be entirely rewritten, too." It is at this time that the author makes his major thematic change, weaving into the third act Jim Tyrone's attempt to find forgiveness, through his confession to Josie, and redemption. O'Neill's statement on March 26 reveals that he is encountering problems with this new approach: "slow—go back rewrite—difficult points [to] get right." On April 10 he notes: "Finish completely rewritten 2nd d[raft]. III—only complaint is takes so long—work so slowly now, no matter how interested" (Work Diary). He makes the following entry two days later: "read over old IV—will probably have to be entirely rewritten in light of what precedes in 2nd d[raft]." O'Neill devotes the remainder of April to Act Four and is still reshaping it on May 3,* 1943, when he records the last entry on his creative efforts in the Work Diary.

In making substantive changes in *A Moon for the Misbegotten* in 1943, O'Neill is motivated by personal, as well as artistic, considerations. He desires not merely to rewrite the first 1941–1942 draft, which, as he says, lacked heart, but also to retell Jamie's story. In spite of his disparaging remarks about Jamie in *Long Day's Journey into Night*, the dramatist sincerely loved his brother and was deeply distraught by the humiliation and pain he endured in his last illness. Jamie O'Neill began to court his beloved Cynara long before the actual date stated in *A Moon for the Misbegotten*: September 1923. In her letter of July 18, 1923, to the playwright, Frances Cadenas, a friend, describes the critical condition at that time of Jamie, who, because of the pain in his hands, is unable to write.† Similarly afflicted later as he is creating *A Moon for the Misbegotten*,

---

*O'Neill apparently completed *A Moon for the Misbegotten* that month as he resumed work on "Blind Alley Guy" in "late May," 1943.

†Mrs. Cadenas tells O'Neill that after receiving his letter that morning (July 18, 1923) she went to see his brother at Riverlong in Paterson, New Jersey:

I first talked with the Doctor in charge and he told me there was quite some improvement in Jim since he first went there. He says that the Condition is an alcoholic neuritis and that is what is causing the intense pain and possibly affecting his eyes. The Doctor also states that he is physically in a critical condition and with time and care, he thinks we'll cure him.

Jim's story is that he does not feel any better, and that the pain is not only in his limbs but in his hands this week. He does not like the place, the food is wretched, and that he cannot sleep during the night or day. The method of treating this neuritis is giving him ten drinks of whiskey during the day and some other kind of a drink before the whiskey which burns like fire and acts as a purgative. He says he has the best room in the house but does not know what he is paying for it.

I will now tell you my opinion. I think Jim looks better and his conversation is more connected than when I saw him last Thursday. He is very

O'Neill could not fail to identify with his brother. Probably the remembrance that he himself lacked heart and did not visit Jamie when he was ill and in need of comfort prompts the dramatist to provide his brother, in an artistic endeavor, with the personal and spiritual consolation he lacked in real life. O'Neill maintains that he wrote *Long Day's Journey into Night* "with deep pity and understanding and forgiveness for all the four haunted Tyrones." What he seeks, personally and reciprocally, as he concludes *A Moon for the Misbegotten*, is the forgiveness he extends to his brother Jamie, through Josie, in the last line of the play: "May you rest forever in forgiveness and peace."

SUMMING UP

O'Neill tried in "late May" of 1943 to resume work on "Blind Alley Guy," but his physical condition made the effort almost impossible. The final notes for this play are dated "June 1st '43." After that date the prolific hand is stilled, the voice silenced.

In the nearly three decades since the dramatist's death, scholars here and abroad have attempted a definitive assessment of his work and his place in modern drama. In these efforts they lacked the crucial clues to his development contained in the O'Neill collection at Yale. With the release of this long suppressed material, it is now possible to achieve a comprehensive evaluation of O'Neill the man and creative artist. All of the material presented must, of course, be analyzed, synthesized, and interpreted. This work may now begin.

Perhaps the single most significant revelation gleaned from the newly released O'Neill material—one that will aid scholars immeasurably in their interpretation of the writer—is its pervasive autobiographical nature: the repeated depiction of the four O'Neills in various guises, from the early 1918 scenario for "The Reckoning" to the last unfinished 1943 play. There are distinct differences between the vividly revealed autobiographical figures in the early drafts for plays and the muted portraits in the final texts. Collectively the ideas and notes chron-

---

thin, pale, trembled a great deal and of course weak. I read him a little part of your letter and he was very happy to hear a message from you. He cannot read or write so he asked me to write for him and to tell you about his condition. He also expresses a great desire to see you.

I am sorry to have to write this unpleasant letter, but I don't think you need worry at present.

I shall keep in touch with the Sanatorium and go over to see him as often as I am able to, and if there is any change I shall telegraph you at once. I'm sure a letter from you would be very bracing. He has a male attendant who reads to him.

icle O'Neill's actual life experiences and allow us valuable insight into his complex personality.

Eugene O'Neill had his detractors during his lifetime and after his death, but no one can dispute his immense contribution to the American theatre. At the time of his death in 1953 he was, unhappily, much neglected by critics and theatre alike. He died doubting the worth of his work; he never doubted his own artistic integrity or his utter dedication to his craft. With the release of the posthumous plays and the long restricted Yale material, O'Neill's stature as a dramatist is now secure.

The information in the following appendices appears exactly as O'Neill recorded it in his private files, which are part of the O'Neill collection at Yale University.

Appendix A

CYCLES*

Oct. 16, 1888–'89 — Road—N[ew]. L[ondon].
(2) '89–'90 —   "   "
(3) '90–'91 —   "   "
(4) '91–'92 —   "   "
(5) '92–'93 —   "   "
(6) '93–'94 —   "   "
(7) '94–'95 —   "   "

(8) '95–'96 — M[ount]. S[t]. V[incent]. (Sept. 1)
(9) '96–'97 — M.S.V.
(10) '97–'98 —   "
(11) '98–'99 —   "   —De La Salle
(12) '99–'00 —   "   —De La Salle
(13) '00–'01 — De L.S. —Asbury Park
(14) '01–'02 —   "   —Betts Acad[emy]. leave Cath[olic]. schools—brush with Cath[olicism].

(15) '02–'03 — B. Ac.   —N.L.
(16) '03–'04 —   "   —N.L.
(17) '04–'05 —   "   —N.L. start "reporting life"
(18) '05–'06 —   "   —N.L. (Darrows) —Princeton
(19) '06–'07 — Princeton—N.L.
(20) '07–'08 — M.O. Grey—his studio—anarchism, Nietzsche
(21) '08–'09 — 1st marriage—N.J. farm Bellows—loafing, write sonnets, leave for Honduras

*O'Neill arranges significant events in his creative and personal life in a pattern of seven-year cycles. He uses a similar plan in the notes for a number of plays whose heroes are self-portraits.

(22) '09-'10 — Honduras—"White S[ister]."—Buenos A[ires]. (Eugene born)
(23) '10-'11 — Buenos A. etc. —Jimmy the P[riest's]. —Am[erican]. Lines
(24) '11-'12 — Jimmy the P. —Vaudeville—N.L. Teleg[raph].—(Begin writing) (Divorced)
(25) '12-'13 — N.L. Teleg. —San[atorium].—Begin plays "Wife for Life" "Web" "Thirst"—Rippins
(26) '13-'14 — Rippins—"B[read]. & Butter" etc.—Harvard
(27) '14-'15 — Harvard—G[reenwich]. Village (Write "The Sniper" "Belshazzar" "Personal Equation")
(28) '15-'16 — G. Village—Provincetown—P[rovincetown]. P[layers]. at P.—"B[ound]. E[ast]. F[or]. C[ardiff]." (write "Before B[reakfast]." "The Movie Man"—"Now I Ask You")

P'town—G.V.   (29) 1916-'17 — P.P. in N.Y. "Bef. B." "Fog" "The Sniper" (write "Ile" "The Moon [of the Caribbees]" etc.)
last of N.L. home

P'town—G.V.   (30) '17-'18 — "In The Zone" (W.S.) "Long V[oyage Home]." "Ile" "The Rope (Marriage) (write "B[eyond]. t[he]. H[orizon]." "Where [the] C[ross]. Is M[ade]." "Dreamy K[id].")

P'town—W.P.P.   (31) '18-'19 — "Where C.I.M." "The Moon" etc. (write "The Straw" "Chris [Christopherson]" "Exorcism")

P'town—Prince   (32) '19-'20 — "Dreamy Kid" "B.T.H." "Chris" (Shane Born, Father dies—write "Gold" "Anna C[hristie]." "Emp[eror]. J[ones].")

P'town—G.V.   (33) '20-'21 — "Emp. J." "Diff'rent" "Gold" (write "Diff'rent" "The First Man")

P'town—N.Y. apart.   (34) '21-'22 — "Anna C." "The Straw" "First Man" "Hairy A[pe]." (write "Hairy Ape," "The Fountain") (Mother dies, meet C[arlotta].)

P'town—R'field   (35) '22-'23 — No Prod. (write "Welded" "All God's C[hillun]. Got W[ings]." "The Fountain") new P. P. starts

R'field—last of P'town   (36) '23-'24 — "Welded" "All God's C." (write "Ancient Mariner" "Desire Under Elms" "Marco M[illions].") (Jamie dies)

Last of R'field   (37) '24-'25 — "Desire Under E." "Glencairn" (write "Great G[od]. B[rown]." Rewrite "M. M.") (Oona born)

Bermuda—Belgrade   (38) '25-'26 — "The Fountain" "Brown" (write "Lazarus Laughed" "Strange Interlude") (stop drinking) Yale d[egree]., met C. again

Bermuda	(39)	'26–'27 — B.T.H. revival (write "Strange Interlude") (fell in love C.)
Last of Berm.—France	(40)	'27–'28 — "M.M." "S.I." (write "Dynamo") (elope C.) (sell R'field)
China—France	(41)	'28–'29 — "Dynamo" (start "M[ourning]. B[ecomes]. E[lectra].") (Divorced—married to C.)
France	(42)	'29–'30 — No Prod. (write "M.B.E.") Blemie
France—N'port	(43)	'30–'31 — No Prod. (Finish "M.B.E.") return U.S.
N.Y.—Sea I.	(44)	'31–'32 — "Mourning Bec. El." (Start "Days W[ithout]. E[nd].")—write "Ah, Wilderness") (build home S[ea]. I[sland].)
Sea Island	(45)	'32–'33 — "Ah, W." (writing "D.W.E.") (return toward Cath[olicism].) away from tragic sense of life
Sea Island—N.Y.	(46)	'33–'34 — "Days W.E." (Finish "D.W.E.") (return toward Cath[olicism].)
Sea Island	(47)	'34–'35 — No Prod. (N.Y.) (write prelims, scenarios, etc. of Cycle) back to tragic sense of life
Sea Island	(48)	'35–'36 — No Prod. write 1st draft 1st play 7 cycle (1829) & added 1st play 8 cycle (1806) 7 d.
Seattle—Cal.	(49)	'36–'37 — No Prod. Nobel Prize—breakdown health—sale Sea Island—write draft new 1st play, cycle of Nine (1775) Hospital—Woods House
Lafayette—Tao House	(50)	'37–'38 — No Prod.—1st draft 4th play (9 cycle)
	(51)	'38–'39 — No Prod.—2nd " start "The Iceman Cometh"—War starts
	(52)	'39–'40 — No Prod.—Finish "The Iceman Cometh".—"Long Day's Journey Into Night"—France falls
	(53)	'40–'41 — No Prod.—Blemie dies—scenarios, outlines new ideas—start "A Moon for the Misbegotten"
	(54)	'41–'42 — No Prod.—Pearl Harbor—finish 1st d. "A Moon for the M." (n[o]. g[ood].)
	(55)	'42–'43 — No Prod.—"A Touch of the Poet"—"A Moon for the Misbegotten" (2nd d.)—start "Blind Alley Guy"
	(56)	'43–'44 — No Prod.—revision "M.F.T.M." "A. T[ouch]. O[f]. T[he]. P[oet]."—Tao House sold Feb.—S[an]. F[rancisco]. apartment
	(57)	'44–'45 — No Prod.—S. F. Apart. in Jan.
	(58)	'45–'46 — To N.Y.

Appendix B

List of all plays ever written by me, including those I later destroyed, giving where and when they were written.

E. O'N.

1913

Title	*Where Written*
"A Wife For A Life" (Vaudeville Sketch)	Our house—New London, Conn.
"The Web" (One Act Play)	" " " " "
"Thirst" (One Act Play)	" " " " "

Total

Three one-act plays

1914

"Recklessness"—(One Act Play)	Rippins', New London
"Warnings"— " " "	" " "
"Bread And Butter"—(Four Act Play)	" " "
"Solitude"*—(Three Act Play)	" " "
"Fog"—(One Act Play)	" " "
"Bound East For Cardiff"—(One Act Play)	" " "
"Abortion"—(One Act Play)	Our house, " "
"(Title Forgotten [Dear Doctor])"—(One Act Adaption of Short Story)	Harvard—English 47 (Room on Mass. Ave., Cambridge)

Total

6 one-acters—two long plays

---

*O'Neill apparently forgot that he had entitled this play *Servitude*.

1915

Title	Where Written
"The Sniper"—(One Act Play)	Harvard—English 47
"The Knock On The Door" (One Act Play)	Cambridge (not for Baker)
"Belshazzar" (Long Play—Six Scenes)	" "
"The Personal Equation" (Four Act Play)	Harvard, English 47

("Belshazzar" written in ostensible collaboration
with Colin Ford but I did most of it)

Total
2 one-acters—two long plays

1916

"The Movie Man" (One Act Comedy) Satire	Fisherman's Shack, Provincetown
"Before Breakfast" (One Act Play)	" " "
"Now I Ask You" (Three Act Farce-Comedy)	" " "
"Tomorrow" (Short Story)	" " "
"The Movie Man" (Short Story made from play)	House, New London

Total
2 one-acters, one long play, 2 short stories

1917

"Ile" (One Act Play)	Atlantic Hotel, Provincetown
"The Long Voyage Home" (One Act Play)	" " "
"The Moon Of The Caribbees" (One Act Play)	" " "
"In The Zone" (One Act Play)	" " "
"The G.A.N." (One Act Comedy)	Francis' Flats "
"S.O.S." (Novelette—sea theme)	" " "
"The Hairy Ape" (Short Story)	" " "

Total
5 one-acters, 1 novelette, 1 short story

1918

"At Jesus' Feet"*—(One Act Play)	Studio, Provincetown

---

*O'Neill refers here to *Shell Shock*, written shortly after he moved into the Studio in Provincetown following the death of his friend Louis Holladay on January 22, 1918.

Title	*Where Written*	
"The Rope"—(One Act Play)	"	"
"Beyond The Horizon" (Three Act Play)	"	"
"The Dreamy Kid" (One Act Play)	Francis' Flats	"
"Where The Cross Is Made" (One Act Play)	" "	"
"The Straw" (Three Act Play)	Rented House	"

Total
4 one-acters—2 long plays

1919

"Honor Among The Bradleys" (One Act Play)	West Point Pleasant, N. J.
"Chris" (Long Play—Six Scenes)	" " " "
"The Straw" (Revised Version)	" " " "
"Exorcism" (One Act Play)	Rented House, Provincetown

Total
2 one-acters—1 long play—and rewrote "The Straw"

1920

"Gold" (Four Act Play)	Rented House, Provincetown
"Anna Christie" (Four Act Play)	Peaked Hill, "
"The Emperor Jones" (Long Play—Eight Scenes)	" " "
"Diff'rent" (Two Act Play)	" " "

Total
4 long plays

1921

"The First Man" (Four Act Play)	Rented House, Provincetown
"The Fountain" (Play in Eleven Scenes)	Peaked Hill, "
"The Hairy Ape" (Play in Eight Scenes)	" " "

Total
3 long plays

1922

"The Fountain" (Revised Version)	Peaked Hill, Provincetown
"Welded" (Act One & Scene One of Act Two)	Brook Farm, Ridgefield, Conn.

Total
½ new long play & rewrote "The Fountain"

Title   *Where Written*

1923

"Welded" (Act Two, Scene Two & Act Three)   Brook Farm, Ridgefield
"Marco Millions" (Preliminary Work & last   Peaked Hill, Provincetown
    scene)
"All God's Chillun Got Wings" (Play in Two   "   "   "
    Acts)

Total

1½ long plays—preliminary work "Marco Millions"

1924

"Desire Under The Elms" (Three Act Play)   Brook Farm, Ridgefield
"Marco Millions" (Two Part Version—each   Peaked Hill, Provincetown
    part full length play)

Total

3 full length plays

1925

"Marco Millions" (Condensed into one three   "Campsea," Bermuda
    act play)
"The Great God Brown" (Four Act play)   "   "
"Lazarus Laughed" (Acts One & Two)   Brook Farm, Ridgefield

Total

1½ long plays & rewrote "Marco Millions"

1926

"Lazarus Laughed" (Four Act Play)   "Bellevue," Bermuda
"Strange Interlude" (1st Five Acts)   Camp, Belgrade Lakes, Me.

Total

2 long plays (1st acts of "Lazarus Laughed"
written in '25 were destroyed
and rewritten in toto)

Title	*Where Written*

1927

| "Lazarus Laughed" (Revised) | "Bellevue," Bermuda |
| "Strange Interlude" (Nine Act Play) | "Spithead," Bermuda |

Total

2 long plays (1st Part of "Strange Interlude" written
in '26 was entirely revised) & "Lazarus Laughed" revised

1928

| "Dynamo" (Three Act Play) | Villa Marguerite, Guéthary, France |

Total

One long play

1929

"Dynamo" (Revised for book)	"Les Mimosas," Cap d'Ail, France
"On To Betelgeuse" (Act One)	" " " "
"Mourning Becomes Electra" (Trilogy)—	"Le Plessis," Saint Antoine-du-
(½ of 1st draft)	Rocher, Indre et Loire, France

Total

Two long plays (approx.)

1930

| "Mourning Becomes Electra" (½ first | "Le Plessis," Saint Antoine-du- |
| draft, 2nd, 3rd, 4th & ½ 5th draft) | Rocher, Indre et Loire, France |

Total

3 full plays (approx.)

1931

"Mourning Becomes Electra"	"Le Plessis," St. Antoine-du-R.,
(½ 5th & full 6th drafts)	France &
	Hotel Atlantico, Las Palmas,
	Canary Islands

Total

One full play (approx.)

Title	*Where Written*

1932

"Days Without End" (1st, 2nd & 3rd   "Casa Genotta," Sea Island
    drafts—4 Acts)
"Ah, Wilderness" (Four Act Play)   "   "   "   "

1933

"Days Without End" (4th, 5th, 6th & 7th d.)   "Casa Genotta," Sea Island
"Ah, Wilderness" (Revised)   "   "   "   "

Grand Total (counting "S.I." as two plays—"M.B.E." as 3)

29 long
24 One-acters

1934

Near breakdown from overwork following production "Days Without End"—six months compulsory rest—work in fall on "Career Of Bessie Bolan" & other ideas [for] new plays

1935

Begin work on Cycle of Seven Plays (spiritual, material, psychological history of American family 1828–1932)
Write scenarios first three plays and outlines of remaining four
Later decide [to] extend Cycle to eight plays, taking it back to 1806 by new first play

1936

Write 1st draft of "Hair Of The Dog" (2nd play in series) & 1st draft (all but last act) of 1st Play, "Greed of the Meek"—get stuck on last part of this play and cannot figure out method of ending it
Add (in outline & notes) still another 1st Play (including 9 in all)
Breakdown of health at end of summer—resolve sell Sea Island house & move to Coast
Seattle, November—Nobel Prize
End of year in hospital, Oakland

1937

Hospital, 1st months—not fit at all till June
Write $\frac{2}{3}$ of new first play of 9 Cycle—but again get stuck on last part of this one—psychologically too complicated
End of year sick again, neuritis—move into new home

Bibliography

Atkinson, Jennifer McCabe, ed. *Children of the Sea*. Washington, D. C.: NCR/Micro-card Editions, 1972.

Blanco, Antonio de Fierro. *The Journey of the Flame.*° Boston: Houghton Mifflin Co., 1933.

Boulton, Agnes. *Part of a Long Story*. Garden City: Doubleday & Company, 1958.

Bowen, Croswell. *Curse of the Misbegotten*. New York: McGraw-Hill Book Company, Inc., 1959.

Brooks, Van Wyck. *The Flowering of New England 1815–1865.*° New York: E. P. Dutton Co., Inc., 1936.

Clark, Arthur H. *The Clipper Ship Era.*° Riverside, Connecticut: 7 C's Press, Inc., 1910.

Clark, Barrett. *Eugene O'Neill*. New York: Robert M. McBride & Company, 1926.

———, ed. *European Theories of the Drama*. New York: Crown Publishers, 1947.

Fabbri, Luis. *Malatesta*. Buenos Aires: Editorial Americalee, 1945.

Goldman, Emma. *Living My Life*. New York: Alfred A. Knopf, 1931.

Grantham, A. E. *Hills of Blue.*° London: Methuen & Co., Ltd., 1927.

Joll, James. *The Anarchists*. Boston: Little, Brown & Company, 1964.

Josephson, Matthew. *The Robber Barons—The Great American Capitalist 1861–1901.*° New York: Harcourt, Brace & Co., 1934.

Keller, Helen Rex. *The Dictionary of Dates.*° New York: Macmillan, 1934.

Macgowan, Kenneth. "The O'Neill Soliloquy" in *O'Neill and His Plays*, Oscar Cargill, N. Bryllion Fagin, and William J. Fisher, eds. New York: New York University Press, 1961.

McKay, Richard. *Some Famous Sailing Ships and Their Builder Donald McKay.*° New York: G. P. Putnam's Sons, 1928.

Nathan, George Jean. *The Intimate Notebooks of George Jean Nathan*. New York: Alfred A. Knopf, 1932.

Nettlau, Max. *Enrico Malatesta: Vita E Pensieri*. New York: Casa Editrice "Il Martello," no date.

O'Neill, Eugene. "Fractricide" in *Poems 1912–1942*, Donald Gallup, ed. New York: Ticknor & Fields, 1980.

°Books cited by O'Neill in his notes and notebooks.

————. *Inscriptions: Eugene O'Neill to Carlotta Monterey O'Neill*. Privately printed. New Haven, 1960.

————. *More Stately Mansions*, Donald Gallup, ed. New Haven: Yale University Press, 1964.

Sepharial. *The Kabala of Numbers—A Handbook of Interpretation.** London: William Rider and Son, Limited, 1911.

Sheaffer, Louis. *O'Neill Son and Artist*. Boston: Little, Brown & Company, 1973.

————. *O'Neill Son and Playwright*. Boston: Little, Brown & Company, 1968.

Sophocles. *Oedipus Rex* in *Drama*, Otto Reinert, ed. Boston: Little, Brown & Company, 1966.

Spengler, Oswald. *The Decline of the West*, Volume I.* New York: Alfred A. Knopf, 1926; Volume II,* 1928.

Stirling-Maxwell, William. *Don John of Austria or Passages from the History of the Sixteenth Century 1547–1578.** London: Longmans, Green, & Co., 1883.

Thoreau, Henry. *The Heart of Thoreau's Journals.** Boston: Houghton Mifflin Company, 1927.

Toland, John. *Adolf Hitler*. New York: Doubleday & Company, 1976.

Index

Page numbers in italics refer to illustrations